Diversity in Counseling

SECOND EDITION

Diversity in Counseling

Robyn Brammer
Central Washington University

BROOKS/COLE
CENGAGE Learning™

Australia • Brazil • Japan • Korea • Mexico • Singapore • Spain • United Kingdom • United States

BROOKS/COLE
CENGAGE Learning™

Diversity in Counseling, Second Edition
Robyn Brammer

Acquisitions Editor: Seth Dobrin

Editorial Assistant: Suzanna Kincaid

Publisher/Executive Editor:
Linda Schreiber-Ganster

Marketing Manager: Christine Sosa

Marketing Assistant: Gurpreet Saran

Senior Marketing Communications Manager:
Tami Strang

Content Project Management:
PreMediaGlobal

Design Director: Rob Hugel

Senior Art Director: Jennifer Wahi

Senior Print Buyer: Rebecca Cross

Senior Rights Acquisitions Specialist:
Dean Dauphinais

Cover Designer: Jeff Bane at CMB Design

Compositor: PreMediaGlobal

For product information and technology assistance, contact us at
Cengage Learning Customer & Sales Support, 1-800-354-9706.

For permission to use material from this text or product,
submit all requests online at **www.cengage.com/permissions**.
Further permissions questions can be e-mailed to
permissionrequest@cengage.com.

Library of Congress Control Number: 2010943533

ISBN-13: 978-0-8400-3453-3

ISBN-10: 0-8400-3453-9

Brooks/Cole
20 Davis Drive
Belmont, CA 94002-3098
USA

Cengage Learning is a leading provider of customized learning solutions with office locations around the globe, including Singapore, the United Kingdom, Australia, Mexico, Brazil, and Japan. Locate your local office at **www.cengage.com/global**.

Cengage Learning products are represented in Canada by
Nelson Education, Ltd.

To learn more about Brooks/Cole, visit **www.cengage.com/brookscole**

Purchase any of our products at your local college store or at our preferred online store **www.cengagebrain.com**.

Printed in the United States of America
1 2 3 4 5 6 7 15 14 13 12 11

CONTENTS

PREFACE TO THE SECOND EDITION

A student once asked me if she could use an older edition of a text. The new edition had only been available for a month, and she wanted to use her roommate's old text. After skimming through the new edition, the material looked the same. They had added a chapter, but I could just copy that for her. In the end, I told her to keep the earlier edition and save the money.

That story stuck in my head as I started this edition. I wanted to believe the first edition was so complete—so timeless—that few changes were necessary. I was wrong. Times changed. I changed. And this edition is very different.

The mission of this edition was to add social justice, advocacy, and increased personal responsibility to each of the chapters. The chapters are also more practical, with additional chapters on the culture of appearance, Arab and Jewish cultures, and an enhanced chapter on multicultural theory. Practical suggestions for working with people from different cultural groups are also included in every chapter, with the chapters now including first-person stories from counselors as well as clients.

This book is still split into three sections: aspects of diversity, ethnic populations, and gender/sexuality. Although this part looks very similar to the earlier edition, nearly everything within the chapters has changed. For faculty, the structure of lectures should look very similar, but the material within those lectures will be substantially updated.

To assist faculty with the changing nature of accreditation, the new chapter on social justice also includes a discussion of accreditation requirements for counselors, psychologists, and social workers. The guidelines are integrated into the chapter to help students understand the value of accreditation requirements, without boring students through giant lists.

Intervention exercises have also been added at the end of each chapter. These are practical cases targeted for mental health counselors, school counselors, school psychologists, and social workers. The cases should help students delve deeper into the chapter material while personalizing the information toward their specific discipline.

NEW TO THIS EDITION

Given the vast changes in multiculturalism and diversity education, some of the subchapters have been merged and new ones have been added. Each chapter is now organized by the following subheadings:

- Unique Challenges (new)
- Historical Context
- Immigration and Development (new)
- Cultural Identity
- Within Group Differences
- Family Structure and Dynamics (expanded)
- Education (expanded)
- Socioeconomics (expanded)
- Spirituality and Religion (new)
- Physical and Mental Health
- Individual and Group Interventions (new)
- Advocacy and Social Justice (new)
- Client's Story
- Counselor's Story (new)
- Questions to Consider
- Intervention Exercises (new)

This structure allowed for easier utilization of practical intervention ideas. For example, many of the education sections now include guides for school counselors and psychologists. The counselor's stories at the end provide open and honest approaches to working with clients. And each chapter ends with social justice guidelines to help students think about ways to challenge their world.

As with the last edition, an instructor handbook is available with sample lecture outlines, multiple choice questions, and essay questions. As always, Brooks/Cole has been extremely helpful in getting this text ready. And my graduate students at Central Washington University have also played a vital role. Thanks to everyone who helped!

ACKNOWLEDGEMENTS

Joseph Adamo, Cazenovia College; Cynthia Bishop, Meredith College; Arlene Brown, Regent University; Michael Chaney, Oakland University; Dale Fryxell, Chaminade University; Aaron Hughey, Western Kentucky University; Martin Jencius, Kent State University; Daniel Logan, Sul Ross State University; Ming-hui Li, St. John's University; Carole Maines, John Brown University; Gloria Sosa, Oakland University; Shawn Lamont Spurgeon, University of Tennessee, Knoxville; Maria Spence, Bowling Green State University; Regina Webber, Central Washington University; Sam Morgan, Central Washington University; and Mary Schroeder.

PART I

Aspects of Diversity

My dog Zoey, a loving Pomeranian with very little brain, has a routine. When she goes outside, we trained her to sit, wait for the command "go," and then dart through the open door. Today, we opened the door without going through the routine. She wandered out for a moment before sauntering back inside.

Then, a funny thing happened. We tried the routine. We had her sit, wait, and then told her to "go." She did not *want* to run outside. She proved that just moments ago, but the commands were so routed in her head and had become so much a part of her way of thinking that she did it anyway.

What training do you have about people? How have your family, friends, communities, and teachers changed the way you see the world?

Close your eyes and envision the last person you met. Was this person smart, funny, shy, creative, outrageous, pale, dark, rich, poor, gay, straight, male, or female? Try as you want, you cannot meet someone without putting them into at least one of these categories. We all do it, but we have all unique categories—special ones we emphasize. These definitions develop over years, growing from childhood to adulthood. They are nurtured by love, hate, acceptance, intolerance, peer pressure, family values, and a host of other things. These categories draw you to some people and repel you from others, but they are more complex than you realize. It will take a lifetime to fully understand your unique categories, but we can cover the ones that are common to everyone: our shared prejudices.

Prejudice, diversity, and multiculturalism are complex concepts, and they can overwhelm. They could imply differences in height, weight, color, backgrounds, status, texture, or any other construct. The words only become valuable when they relate to you. How do *you* see diversity?

When I think about these words, I remember Venice, California. This beach community is home to wealthy movie stars, successful business owners, homeless drug addicts, prostitutes, and hundreds of others. The city attracts thousands of tourists—not for the waterfront but for the people. The suburban high school students want to see the "freaks," the homeless people want to see the clueless high school students, and everyone somehow survives and enjoys this unique landscape and menagerie.

The striking component of Venice, California, is both its ability to draw people for its craziness and for the ease in which people live. Tourists might enjoy staring at a teenage boy with 40 piercings or a middle-aged woman with plaid hair and steroid-enhanced muscles, but they would never consider inviting these people to dinner. The broader society tolerates such people without truly accepting them. This gap between noticing and accepting is the point of this book. Each of us harbors a gap like this. It is one of our classification categories. It starts by asking ourselves one simple question: "Is this person like me?"

Hartup and Stevens (1997) found that friendships across cultures are usually based on homophilies, or physical similarities. They found that most people choose friends based on similarities in age, gender, ethnicity, and abilities. Beyond the obvious physical differences between racial groups, they also noted that by the time children reach adolescence, they seek friendships with those who share some of their own interests and experiences. Given the effects of prejudice and discrimination, such preferences would further increase the number of intra-ethnic relationships. Such findings are similar to those revealed by Hallinan and Williams (1989), who in their massive examination of more than 1,000 public and private high schools across the United States found that fewer than 3.5% of the

18,000 friendships identified by students occurred between African American and European American teenagers.

If you are like most students exploring this area for the first time, you may be thinking, "Why can't we just accept each other and call ourselves Americans (or Canadians, Britons, etc.)?" You may also be thinking that an exploration into diversity only panders to irresponsibility and makes excuses for people who have yet to succeed in this country. It is sometimes hard to grasp how much culture affects identity, especially when people are from privileged backgrounds. We tend to see the world from a single culture (ours) and believe other group perspectives are wrong or naïve. Such ignorance is one of the most insidious types of prejudice. Perhaps the best way to begin expanding your worldview is to examine how you have been shaped by your own culture.

Let us assume that you recognize the cultural differences of the people you encounter, and you realize that addressing such differences could assist in the therapeutic process. What you may not realize is that none of us can effectively reach the point of accepting or fully understanding another person's culture. For example, many European American males have learned to control their emotions and emphasize words. They have been rewarded for containing their feelings of anger, sadness, and frustration and learning to speak politely and calmly, even if the words are incongruent with their feelings. When African American females have interacted with European American men, they have learned to interpret the tones of the expression and the intention of the speaker. They have listened to such men speak politely and calmly while actually seething with anger, and they have come to believe that the tones behind the words more accurately represent the speaker's feelings. Both communication styles are reasonable, considering their ethnic histories. European American males often have the privilege of being judged by their words, so they will concentrate on the verbal message conveyed. African American females often face prejudice and discrimination from European Americans who speak politely and calmly to them. If African American women trusted everyone they met, they would find themselves in precarious situations. None of these are true for all people from cultural groups, but they are true for many. Still, we have to combat common cultural experiences with prejudices and stereotypes about different people.

Let me offer another illustration. Imagine you are visiting the Museum of Tolerance in Los Angeles, California. As you enter the building, there are two doors at the end of a long hallway. To the left, there is a massive, beautifully decorated door bearing the inscription "Nonprejudiced people enter here." The other door is plain, about four feet tall and two feet wide, and rather unattractive. Above this modest door, the plaque reads "Prejudiced people enter here." Those who have the self-confidence and nerve to open the large door find it quite impenetrable. All patrons wishing to enter the building must crouch down and humbly enter through the smaller door.

The large door represents the myth of the unprejudiced person—he or she does not really exist. When we enter counseling sessions under the false assumption that we lack biases, we deceive ourselves and potentially harm our clients. We are also likely to project our prejudices onto others. When we refuse to acknowledge our potential for bias, we open ourselves up to acting on our prejudices. Discrimination is the act of making a distinction in favor of or against a person based on the group, class, or category to which that person belongs rather than on individual merit. It is this active form of prejudice that explains why minority clients are frequently diagnosed with more severe disorders and are given less favorable prognoses (Zane, Enomoto & Chun, 1994). To reverse these patterns, knowledge must be paired with personal growth. We must learn to identify our biases—even the suspicion of bias—if we are to become successful multicultural counselors. Doing so demonstrates wisdom, sound judgment, and a healthy respect for one's client. But failure to recognize our prejudices leads to inevitable biases and ultimately harmful discrimination.

So, I ask again: What training do you have about people? I hope you realize that you have been trained. You judge people from the first moment you meet them. But do not be too alarmed. It is human nature. We all do it. The trick is learning how to recognize our prejudices before they cause serious damage. This will prove extremely important in counseling. This task of overcoming our prejudices and ignorance comprises the heart of this book.

CHAPTER 1

Introduction to Diversity

The evil that is in the world always comes of ignorance, and good intentions may do as much harm as malevolence, if they lack understanding. On the whole, men are more good than bad; that, however, isn't the real point. But they are more or less ignorant, and it is that we call vice or virtue; the most incorrigible vice being that of an ignorance which fancies it knows everything and therefore claims for itself the right to kill. (Camus, 2002, p. 120)

Let me start by introducing my theory of diversity. You will find throughout this book a tendency to emphasize two things: 1) Social groups have internal and external "in groups" and "out groups." This is the nature of prejudice, and it is part of the human condition. 2) When you become part of an identified "out group," the people in power will do everything they can to demonstrate your inferiority. They have to. If you were acceptable, you would not be "out" and they would not be "in."

What makes this philosophy different from many other multicultural books is a fundamental belief that prejudice and discrimination are part of all social networks. They are not something merely perpetrated by white males. Every group does it. White males own the greatest amount of power in our society, so their labeling of "out" has greater consequences than the labels from other groups. But we do a disservice to many minority groups if we ignore the other discriminations around us.

Some of you reading this book have never been part of an "out" group. (At least, to the best of your knowledge.) You may believe your training in diversity is beneficial because it will let you "help" those poor minorities who are unable to reach their potential due to genetics, poor education, limited finances, etc. This book will not work with that mentality. Instead, you have to think of yourself as an "outed" individual. You have to understand the world from this disempowered viewpoint. And here is your first lesson.

Please take this exercise seriously; it will help you in this class.

Fold a piece of paper into thirds (as if preparing it for an envelope). Then, fold it in half the opposite direction. Reopen the paper so you have six rectangles in the creases. In the top-left corner, write the names of your parents and siblings. In the top-right corner, write the name of the most important person in your life (apart from your family). In the middle-left rectangle, write the name of your favorite teacher. In the middle-right rectangle, write the name of your church or important social group. In the bottom-left corner, write the name of your employer (or your dream employer). In the bottom-right corner, write your own name.

Parents/Siblings	Most important person
Favorite teacher	Church/Social group
Employer/Dream employer	Me

Thanks to the human genome project, we have identified that people with Xq46/47 abnormalities are immoral. Thankfully, the researchers have identified a genetic test to track these people. Unfortunately, you tested positive.

Although you expected the people dear to you would dismiss the test results and realize you were still the same person, they reacted quickly and passionately.

Rip off the top-right corner (the person dearest to you). This person has rejected you. He or she believes it would be immoral to remain associated with an immoral person. After you have ripped off that section, let that piece fall to the ground. This person is no longer part of your life.

If you were born in January or February, congratulations! The rest of your life remains intact. However, if you were born in any other month, rip off the corner with your parents. They have rejected you. They still "love you," but they think it would be best if you worked this out on your own. They no longer answer your calls; they changed their locks; they removed your name and pictures from their lives. You are dead to them.

If you were born in May or later, tear off your favorite teacher. This person does not want to remain associated with an Xq46/47 freak. Let that piece fall to the floor.

If you were born in July, August, September, October, November, or December, tear off your job. You were let go. They said you used too many staples. You would soon abuse other fiscal guidelines, as you are genetically immoral. They could no longer afford someone with poor fiscal habits. Let that piece fall to the ground.

If you were born in September, October, November, or December, tear off your church or social group. The leader of this group said it would be "healing" for the group to have time to sort out its feelings about you. But they never called back, and your name was removed from the mailing list. Let that piece fall to the floor.

If you were born in November or December, tear off your name. You have lost everything and the world has become too bleak and lonely. Rather than face Xq46/47 on your own, you opt to disappear. Whether you die physically, emotionally, or socially, it does not really matter. There is nothing left inside of you. Let that piece fall to the floor.

If this exercise felt new to you, I hope you learned three important lessons. First, you cannot predict how prejudice and discrimination work. These reactions are often irrational and unpredictable. Second, no matter how strong you are, people's responses evoke pain. It is possible to experience so much pain as to cause you to give up. This is where social advocacy becomes important. Finally, everyone born in months other than November and December was privileged. It might not feel this way, as you internalize the pain of letting things dear to you fall to the floor, but it is. Privilege does not mean gaining unbelievable wealth, fame, or success. It can also refer to receiving less negative treatment. Just about everyone reading this book has experienced privilege. You did not earn everything you received. If you can accept this, the rest of this book will make much more sense.

As you consider what role privilege has played in your life, also consider what it means to be marginalized. Society marginalizes individuals or groups by ignoring or minimizing them (Brown, 2006). The effect can be intentional (e.g., Hitler's treatment of Jews, Gypsies, and homosexuals) or it can be unintentional (e.g., overlooking someone for a promotion without completely understanding why). In the United States, both are present, but the unintended marginalization is the most insidious.

Marginalization is easiest to see when someone has privilege and becomes part of a marginalized group. For example, consider the case of Anita, who lived 42 years as a white male before transitioning into womanhood. Anita was an elder at her church. She was active in children's ministries, adult education, preaching sermons, and designing the church's website. The week she came out as a transsexual, her church friends all pledged their support. But none of them contacted her again. She thought they might need a week or two to compose themselves. Weeks rolled into months. When she moved out of her home (at her wife's request), she still lacked any support.

Almost as hard as facing this struggle alone was the loss to the church. Projects she had initiated were never completed. Her sermons, which were generally praised, were deleted from the church's website. The church treated her like a nonperson. Not someone who had left—someone who had never existed. The loss harms both her and the community.

Her situation culminated when shopping at a major department store. After waiting in line (accompanied by her daughter), a 17-year-old clerk told her to "put her money away." Apparently, transsexuals in that small town were not allowed to shop—much the way African Americans were told to leave stores throughout the 1960s.

In the past, psychologists and counselors have overlooked privilege and marginalization. They assumed the same techniques and interventions for white men and women would apply to everyone. In many ways, our early attempts to understand minority cultures caused more harm than good.

Generally, the fields of counseling and psychology have actively explored diversity issues since the 1950s. Erikson (1950) referred to the need to broaden our perspective beyond mainstream America, but the approach at this early stage maintained a Eurocentric nature. However, most multicultural authors focused on racial differences and sought to find ways to indoctrinate cultural minorities into the "mainstream." At first, the investigation into multiculturalism addressed specific groups. The original goal of the movement was the assimilation of blacks into mainstream America, especially into the workforce, but this assimilation process proved harmful (Jackson, 2001). In the 1960s, counseling and psychotherapy began to examine multicultural issues more formally (Atkinson, Morton & Sue, 1998). By the 1970s, the number of empirical studies on ethnicity increased (Baruth & Manning, 1999), and professional organizations began to develop specialties in multicultural counseling, including sexual orientation and ethnic divisions.

Let us back up a little and provide some definitions. Multicultural refers to all identifiable cultural groups: racial, ethnic, heritage, socioeconomic status, age, gender, gender identification, sexual orientation, religious/spiritual beliefs, and physical, emotional, and mental abilities. Pluralistic describes a society where ethnic, religious, and social groups work toward maintaining their individuality but contributing to the society as a whole.

The *Random House Dictionary of the English Language* (second edition, 1987) offers the following definitions:

Prejudice: (1) An unfavorable opinion or feeling formed beforehand or without knowledge, thought, or reason. (2) Any preconceived opinion or feeling, either favorable or unfavorable. (3) Unreasonable feelings, opinions, or attitudes, especially of a hostile nature, regarding a racial, religious, or national group. (4) Such attitudes considered collectively; e.g., the war against prejudice is never-ending.

Stereotype: (4) A simplified and standardized conception or image invested with special meaning and held in common by members of a group: e.g., the cowboy and Indian are American stereotypes.

Racism: (1) A belief or doctrine that inherent differences among the various human races determine cultural or individual achievement, usually involving the idea that one's own ethnicity is superior and has the right to rule others. (2) A policy, system of government, etc., based upon or fostering such a doctrine; discrimination. (3) Hatred or intolerance of another ethnic group. (Although not defined by Random House, *institutional racism* is also an important concept; it is a covert form of racism that is embedded in the development of political policies and decision-making practices.)

Discrimination: (2) Treatment or consideration of, or making a distinction in favor of or against, a person or thing based on the group, class, or category to which that person or thing belongs rather than on individual merit: e.g., racial and religious intolerance and discrimination.

Sexism: (2) Discrimination or devaluation based on a person's sex, as in restricted job opportunities; esp., such discrimination against women.

Heterosexism: A prejudiced attitude or discriminatory practices against homosexuals by heterosexuals.

Of these terms, the idea of prejudice is the most important to therapists because it is fundamental to understanding the concepts of discrimination and racism. Without prejudice, there is no racism. The term *prejudice* literally means to have a preconceived judgment or opinion without sufficient knowledge to render such a claim (Axelson, 1999). As such, prejudices can be positive as well as negative, although most theorists use the term to describe negative judgments (Ridley, 1989).

Imagine you are walking down the street, and you see a gray-haired, 50-year-old male carrying a stack of books and wearing a sports coat with leather patches at the elbows. Your first impression may be that this person is a professor. Such a judgment may be positive, but it is still made without sufficient reasoning to support your claim. The judgment may in fact be accurate, but it forces the individual into a contrived category.

Although prejudices of any form can be harmful, they are also necessary. We learn what types of people to fear, respect, appreciate, and dominate. If we could not characterize people based on stereotypes and prejudices, it would be impossible to function within a society. As social creatures, we judge people based on their presentation. But this does not mean that as enlightened creatures that we cannot attempt to examine our prejudices and remove all those that we can identify. The process starts by identifying prejudices we have long accepted or ignored.

Sometimes, students start this self-evaluation process by imagining racial groups they might have reactions against. Racism will be helpful to explore, but prejudice extends beyond this. Most prejudices are directed toward a "culture." There are some obvious components to culture. For example, ethnicity (which comes from the Greek term *ethnos,* meaning nation) is the most typical cultural group. We know about European, Asian, Latino, and other nation/content-based cultures. These do not imply a specific genetic background. They address where someone lives and how cultural groups within the country interact. Gender is also an obvious and important cultural facet. Watch how men and women separate at parties or in social groups. Cultural identity defines their interactions and social networks.

Nearly every action and identity involves culture. Culture requires compliance to a specific orientation or group function. For example, a beginning pianist may hope only to learn the notes to a particular piece. Over time, the individual may only feel accomplished if some aspect of the pianist's interpretation is brought to the piece (Goodnow, 2010). He or she becomes part of the piano culture.

These lessons about a group's way of acting can take the form of interpretations, beliefs, attitudes, or values (Lott, 2010). But this is more than a belief system; it is often associated with behaviors, tools, masks, symbols, traditions, or routines. We have cultures for sport fans, reading groups, ethnicities, sexuality, gender, religion, and hobbies. We can speak of West Coast culture, gay culture, inner-city culture, university culture, and thousands more (Lott, 2010). These are both constructed and constructing. They define our identities, but we define them when we become part of the system.

This dual facet of belonging (being shaped by and shaping a cultural group) is why the term *melting pot* does not capture the essence of multiculturalism. This expression assumes that immigrating individuals assimilate into the dominant culture and identify solely with that culture. Although there may be some advantages to such an environment, it has not existed for many years. Prior to the 1880s, the melting pot idea was viewed as the goal. Each group entering the mostly Anglo Americas would be fused into the dominant culture. Between 1880 and 1950, the theme of assimilation turned to "Americanization," or **acculturation**. This idea began after the mass immigration of Eastern European people. By this time, the Anglo American culture was dominant and viewed as the "true America." Other groups were expected to fit into this culture.

Acculturation theory had serious flaws. The most significant was the fact that acculturation systematically alienated minorities from the dominant and minority cultures. This alienation occurs in part because the dominant culture never fully accepts minority members. Even when they adopt the dominant culture's values, members of minority groups continue to experience prejudice and discrimination (Fuller, 1995). Eventually, they realize that assimilation is impossible. However, in the process of attempting to conform to the dominant culture, they appear "different" from their peers and find themselves regarded as traitors. This alienation sometimes leaves the individual feeling as if he or she is without a culture—trapped between two worlds that cannot accept or understand his or her struggles.

The Case of Alma

When I moved to a small town in Texas, I realized that things were going to be different. My husband, who is white, had taken a job in a mostly white community and I really didn't think it was going to be that difficult for me. For a while I didn't understand why I was so discouraged. I had a nice house, wonderful family, but something was missing. The missing part became evident when I was at the grocery store and heard someone speaking in Spanish. I felt my heart jump as if that person held the key to lifting the depression that controlled me. I walked over to her and started a conversation. We talked about what brought us to the little town, the foods we missed, what it was like for our families, and other similar issues. As the conversation continued, she told me that she lived in one of the poorer areas of town. Such conditions made little difference to me, but I soon realized that our living conditions would create a wall between us. When I told her that I lived in the nicest area of town, I could visually see her pull away. When she learned that I worked at the university, she quickly ended the conversation and walked away. She viewed me as a gringo, even though we each had something that the other needed. Apparently, I had been corrupted by the white world and, in her mind, would never be able to understand or accept her.

Alma's story is relatively common and makes the process of assimilation relatively difficult. Contemporary theories of acculturation de-emphasize any assimilation process. Rather than lose their ethnic or cultural identity, members of minority groups incorporate only those pieces of the dominant culture that are necessary for survival. From this viewpoint, individuals who attempt to blend cultures may never identify with the dominant culture and instead may become bitter and hostile.

Rather than move toward Americanization or acculturation, the current model advocates cultural pluralism. This change has occurred partly because there is a growing awareness that people remain distinct and maintain primary friendships within various cultural groups. Rather than form a single shared culture, multifarious societies seem to exist as a collection of distinct components—intermixed and adding flavor to the overall dish. The current global community has been described as a multicultural "salad bowl" (Pope, 1995) or "mosaic" (Sciarra, 1999). Authors such as Glazer and Moynihan (1970) have effectively argued that the salad bowl provides the best explanation for why ethnic groups, such as Jews, Italians, and the Irish, can be segregated within a city and maintain their old-world heritages. Each component is viewed as different from the others but none is viewed as deficient (Baruth & Manning, 1991). The blending of the cultures, like a mosaic or salad bowl, becomes more beautiful or tasty as additional elements are added. The task is not to create a single global culture but to allow all cultures to benefit and enrich themselves by sharing in the wealth provided by others. But we will never have the perfect salad because each taster will have different perspective. Some people do not like olives. Some people will not try tomatoes, so they do not know if they like them or not. There will always be problems with integration because prejudice will always remain part of our culture.

While America made great strides electing its first African American president, many minority groups internalize the discrimination they face from an early age. Such experiential differences change the way people see the world. Sue and Sue (1999) argued that minority group members were more likely than European Americans to have an external locus of control and an external locus of responsibility. In other words, they viewed the world as a powerful force that would continue in its current path regardless of their individual actions (i.e., external locus of control). They were also more likely to believe that because of their limited resources and power, it was the responsibility of the system itself to create change (i.e., external locus of responsibility).

European Americans have the privilege of being judged by their actions, and because of this, they are more likely to have an internal locus of control and responsibility. They believe that they can change their environment, and possibly more importantly, they believe they have the responsibility to change a dysfunctional system. However, it should be clear that these positions flow from the manner in which people are treated. When members of a group notice that their actions actually change the way society functions, they will seek to create other such changes. The converse is also true, which makes intercultural relationships more difficult.

If an individual sees the world as accepting of him or her, he or she will take responsibility for his or her dreams. If the world appears closed, an individual will view the world as a controlling force. In Table 1.1, the dimensions of responsibility and power are viewed as either dictated by the world or by

TABLE **1.1**
Attribution of Power and Responsibility

		RESPONSIBILITY	
		Self	Other
POWER	Self	I alone am responsible for my fate, and I have the ability to carry out my dreams.	My family, culture, and community will help me find my life path, but I have the power to follow through with my plans.
	Other	I alone am responsible for my fate, but when I make plans, others play a role in the process. Fate decides how successful I am.	People in my life will help me find a path, and they will also dictate how successful I am in life. In many ways, I am a passive observer.

the self. Imagine the difference these assumptions would make in a person's life. The person who believes he or she is able to carry out his or her dreams is much more likely to feel motivated in counseling than the person who sees him or herself as a victim of fate—buffeted about by uncontrollable forces.

With such prominent differences in cultural worldviews and behaviors, it should come as no surprise that minority clients tend to prefer minority counselors (Coleman, Wampold & Casali, 1995). Despite this, there is evidence that matching clients by ethnic/racial groups does not appear to affect overall functioning, service retention, or the total number of sessions attended (Shin et al., 2005). This does not imply that ethnic matching is irrelevant. It means that great care must go into finding ways to demonstrate similarities with all clients. When someone presents with a different cultural history and worldview, it takes great insight on the part of the therapist to separate cultural biases from clinical insights.

How can therapists learn to prevent their biases from affecting their counseling? It starts by monitoring your self-talk. The way you think and communicate mirrors your cultural values, beliefs, and biases (Jun, 2010). It is the old notion that your mouth will eventually match the feelings in your heart.

Think back to Table 1.1. When you read it, did you think one of those dimensions was *better* than the others? For people who have lived privileged lives, they probably see their power and responsibility coming from self. Marginalized people—who have struggled to exist within an repudiating society—are likely to see the world otherwise. To succeed with multicultural clients, you must understand their unique situations.

Pedersen (2000) argued for a three-stage model of multicultural training: awareness, knowledge, and skill. The order of this process is also important. Recognizing limitations (awareness) in your worldview is the first step. Can you understand what it means to be poor/rich, male/female, monolingual/multilingual, black/white, gay/straight, athletic/paralyzed, young/old, or some other polar state? We each have limitations as to what we can understand.

We can only progress to learning about these when we recognize our ignorance.

I worked with a young man who bounded into my office ready to retell his masterful interview for a job. He was planning to work at a geriatric center, and one of the interview questions was, "How would you apply your style to our setting?" The young man raised his head and announced proudly: "I wouldn't change anything. Older people are no different from any other client. They all need the same things."

He did not notice my shoulders slump or the slight shake of my head. If he had, he may have noticed the same thing from the interviewers. Geriatric clients require a host of cultural adaptations. They require special training for memory restoration, different diagnosis skills for recognizing depression, physical activities blended into counseling and relaxation techniques, and recollection narratives to assist with life integration. These are only the most obvious starting points, but he wanted to believe he could counsel this group as he would the twenty-something white students at the university. To become culturally competent, he needed to spend time at the center to learn how the culture works—how it is different from what he knows. He needed to value who these people were and how they thought, felt, and acted.

Ageism is just one of the *isms* thrown at people (e.g., sexism, racism, ableism, heterosexism, etc). These are part of a system. They are intertwined within society and will require an equally powerful force to break them. The same is true for multiculturalism and diversity. The two terms are often used interchangeably, but the addition of diversity inspires a broader sense of cultural differences (Manis, Brown & Paylo, 2009). This is more than ethnic differences. These are cultural biases, like we discussed earlier in this chapter. We might have unexamined biases regarding gender, sexual orientation, physical ability, socioeconomic status, age, religions, language, people who went to UCLA, and other cultural identities.

Sometimes, beginning counselors attempt to overcome their prejudices by learning a basic set of techniques and trying to do them perfectly. They assume that if they look competent, they will connect. This is often referred to as being **colorblind** or blind to the unique needs of the individual. This is not the best perspective.

In forming multicultural relationships, effective therapists will use social influence to their advantage. Social influence theory (Strong, 1969) involves three relational dimensions: attraction, trustworthiness, and expertness/competence. Each element affects how a given relationship will function.

- **Attraction:** Although this may include physical attractiveness, it is usually the ability to see within the other something appealing. It implies understanding, acceptance, warmth, and the ability to create a relational bond. Attraction is the opposite of repulsion. It represents two objects being drawn toward each other.
- **Trustworthiness:** In addition to believing that the individual will maintain confidentiality, trustworthiness implies a lack of threat to cause harm.
- **Expertness/competence:** The therapist is able to project the training, experience, and professionalism to assist the individual in need.

All three components are important when working with minority clients, but trustworthiness seems to play the most critical role, especially in mixed-ethnic sessions. A lack of trust may be caused by any of the following factors:

- Limited experience of the counselor with members of the client's cultural group
- Sustained employment or housing discrimination
- Sustained economic or political discrimination
- Limited knowledge of minority issues on the part of the counselor

After trust has been lost, re-establishing it may prove to be quite difficult. In such cases, therapists without much multicultural experience are likely to attempt to reconstruct the therapeutic alliance by distancing themselves from their feelings and striving to appear knowledgeable. This approach may further distance the therapist from the client and have a negative effect on the intervention. To engage in therapy successfully, clients must believe that the therapist is able to understand their plight. Such a belief is possible only when attraction and trustworthiness are blended into the presentation provided to the client.

Sometimes, the mechanism for regaining trust may come from an unexpected source. While I was working at a California veterans' hospital, a client asked me where I attended school. When he discovered that I attended the University of Southern California, located in the heart of Los Angeles, he seemed relieved. At the time, I—being an ignorant white woman—interpreted the change in his affect as respect for the institution, but I was wrong. Nearly a year later, when we had successfully reached the therapeutic goals, he stated that he had felt comfortable working with me because my school was close to his home. To him, this meant that I "understood the plight of living in Watts" (the ghetto south of the university).

Anyone familiar with USC knows that the wealthy university is quite different from the impoverished community surrounding it. The students generally come from exclusive homes and have little firsthand knowledge of the ghetto culture. However, in this case, the location of the school communicated to the client that I had some notion of what it meant to be an economically deprived African American, and it was this belief that had kept him in therapy.

The marginalized minority groups in America are looking for people who can see and value them. They are also keenly aware of gestures or comments thrown against them. Sue, Capodilupo, and Holder (2008) refer to these subtle acts of discrimination as racial microaggressions. These are not overt gestures protected by laws or even social mores. They are often so understated that the speaker may not even realize something aggressive took place. But every member of a minority groups has experienced these, and every person on the planet has perpetrated them. These would include comments such as, "Where are you from?" [when spoken to a dark-skinned person born in America] or "You are a credit to your race." It would also include a taxi passing a Latino to pick up a European American couple or asking an

African American high school student if she thinks she's "ready" for college (Sue et al., 2008).

Microaggressions are part of our everyday lives, and I remember the first time I caught myself giving one. More than two decades ago, on the way home from a lecture, I noticed the person next to me out of the corner of my eye. As I waited for the light to change, I thought to myself, "He's just like me."

Something about this thought drove me to turn and look at the man. He drove a new BMW, wore an expensive suit, and looked in peak physical condition. Instantly, as he drove away, I realized that his new car moved a little faster than my old, very abused Honda. I looked down and noticed that I was wearing shorts with a T-shirt and looked a little disheveled. The other difference between us was the color of our skin. I began to wonder what impression I might have had if he had been of another ethnicity. After very little thought, I realized that I considered us socially equal only because his skin was dark. Had his skin been lighter, I probably would have considered him my social superior, although even this would have been problematic. This event took place fifteen years ago, but I remember it vividly. It forced me to realize that even when we feel close to members of different ethnic groups or gain knowledge regarding cultural differences, the prejudices running rampant in society take hold of our subconscious minds.

Although microaggression describes my judgment of the driver, it might be more useful to refer to the condition spawning the act. A more encapsulating expression might be **unexamined prejudice**. This term encompasses not only the action but the attitude behind it. These are the types of comments that follow the preface "I'm not racist, but those ..."

Unexamined prejudice leads minorities to rally against what is sometimes referred to as the **black tax**. Most African Americans are aware of this hidden tax. They must work harder and better than others to be considered equal. After a lifetime of smothering rage and paying unfair dues, African Americans have internalized microaggressions. Such subtle forms of discrimination are faced in health care (Pachter & Coll, 2009), education (Rowley et al., 2008), and most other aspects of life. They are a part of black culture, as they are part of all marginalized cultures.

Consider the following comment from a student in a multicultural graduate class:

> The only problem I have with multicultural education is in cases where microcultural identification leads to separatism and favoritism. The fear of offending any one particular group (and I think there are almost as many groups as there are individuals) has brought the practice of "political correctness" to laughable extremes in some cases. Other than that, I think the objective of teaching each student according to his need and learning styles, as dictated partially his cultural background, is an objective that is worth pursuing. And as for the "political correctness" of using "he" in the previous sentence: "he" is the appropriate generic pronoun that may be used in a sentence of that nature.

At this point in his education, this student is certain he knows what is right and merely wants to better understand the plight of some "less fortunate" individuals. However, his limited ability to examine himself has created some dangerous obstacles. Are there so many different "groups" that he need not fear offending any of them? *He* alludes to this by stating that the pronoun "he" adequately applies to all students and that no apology is necessary for its use. Why is this the case? What makes the term "he" more acceptable than the feminine term "she"? Would it offend male students to be included in the global pronoun "she"? If so, what is so frightening about identifying with womanhood, and is this fear something that girls will inevitably internalize? Could his use of the term "he" be an attempt to establish a masculine hierarchy and view women as lesser creatures? Whatever the case, he refuses to acknowledge or investigate his prejudices and instead is likely to pass them along to the next generation.

Regardless of an individual's ethnic background or identity, prejudices and stereotypes are buried deep within every person's mind. These unacknowledged prejudices often interfere with counseling by creating microaggressions hidden beneath the counselor's conscious awareness (Falicov, 1998). Subconscious prejudices or cultural biases can hinder the flow of a counseling session by tacitly denigrating an individual's self-worth. If you are not aware of your own prejudices, how will you know when to refer clients to a different therapist? Unfortunately, this is a very difficult question to answer, but increasing your awareness of your prejudices will assist you in the decision-making process.

The best way to start this exploration process is to let go of the assumption that your culture is the best culture. The Society for the Psychological Study of Ethical Minority Issues (2002), or Division 45 of the American Psychological Association, came up with the following principles:

1. Psychologists are encouraged to recognize that, as cultural beings, they may hold attitudes and beliefs that can detrimentally influence their perceptions of and interactions with individuals who are ethnically and racially different from themselves.
2. Psychologists are encouraged to recognize the importance of multicultural sensitivity/responsiveness, knowledge, and understanding about ethnically and racially different individuals.
3. As educators, psychologists are encouraged to employ the constructs of multiculturalism and diversity in psychological education.
4. Culturally sensitive psychological researchers are encouraged to recognize the importance of conducting culture–centered and ethical psychological research among persons from ethnic, linguistic, and racial minority backgrounds.
5. Psychologists strive to apply culturally–appropriate skills in clinical and other applied psychological practices.
6. Psychologists are encouraged to use organizational change processes to support culturally informed organizational (policy) development and practices.

In 1996, the Association for Multicultural Counseling and Development (AMCD) created a more extensive list of competencies (Arredondo, Toporek, Brown et al., 1996). These are described in detail in Chapter 2.

For now, the more important step is gaining self-knowledge. This notion of self-development is part of the constructivist philosophy that is gaining momentum in multiculturalism. The hermeneutical (or interpretative) shift spawned by Dilthy and others has led to the understanding that individuals create or interpret their sense of reality (Sciarra, 1999). Culture provides part of the context for such interpretations and rewards or punishes people for their creative powers, and each culture (or collection of individual interpretations) will view reality differently.

What would you think of a Latina who believed the ghost of her mother spoke to her regarding the inappropriateness of her pending marriage? Would such an "encounter" be regarded as a hallucination? If so, the number of Latina schizophrenics would be much higher than reported because such experiences are relatively common. Counseling must be a collaborative effort in which the counselor and client attempt to co-construct alternate meanings and stories in order to create harmony between the client's experiences and cultural worldview (Sciarra, 1999). When counselors impose their cultural worldview on a client, the richness of the collaboration is lost, and the session will eventually force the client to choose between the worldviews presented.

RECOGNIZING CULTURAL BIAS

If expertness is emphasized above all else, the counselor is acting on the client by performing a set of techniques rather than engaging the client in a therapeutic relationship. Taking an "expert" approach is unlikely to help multicultural clients because the techniques often taught in graduate schools are culturally biased.

Consider the dominant theories of counseling and psychology. All of them involve cultural biases:

All theoretical perspectives provide a framework upon which all human action can be interpreted, and they have developed standardized techniques that can theoretically be applied to all people. With most therapists being of European descent, this has meant counselors have inevitably and inadvertently applied European values to people of other groups.

Most existing counseling techniques were developed to assist European American clients, but these techniques may not be effective or acceptable for the fastest-growing segments of Americans. The emphasis on talk therapy alone—without action or family involvement—is likely to appear stale and threatening to many clients. Sadly, exploration of alternatives is wrought with additional problems. Even the research into cross-cultural counseling is biased and requires a new framework (Sue & Sundberg, 1996). The problem

TABLE **1.2**
Cultural Bias in Dominant Theories of Counseling and Psychology

Theory	Theorist/Culture	Bias
Psychoanalysis	Sigmund Freud/Jewish	Emphasizes the effects of childhood and parental interaction
Rational emotive behavioral therapy	Albert Ellis/European American	Champions logical thought
Gestalt therapy	Fritz Perls/European American	Emphasizes insight
Multimodal therapy	Arnold Lazarus/European American (South Africa)	Assumes techniques alone can heal
Cognitive-behavioral	Aaron Beck and Donald Meichenbalm/European American	Downplays intuition and emotional reasoning
Constructivist	Kenneth Gergen/European American	May overemphasize individualized (over social) construction
Dialectical behavior therapy	Marsha M. Linehan/European American	Emphasizes Buddhist meditative practices

with our current understanding of psychology is that it depends on cultural stereotypes of mental health. We view various ethnic groups from a Eurocentric perspective, which decreases the likelihood of finding effective interventions for minority groups. This bias may explain, in part, why members of various minority groups tend to terminate counseling earlier than European American clients do (Ridley, 1989).

The same biases may appear when writing or reading texts on the subject of multiculturalism. Emphasizing "scientific" or "historical" methods may simply pass along inaccurate findings to a new generation. In many cases, problems arise when attempting to interpret information that was accurately uncovered. For example, what happens if researchers find that people from one group are less athletic, empathetic, merciful, or intelligent than members of another group? Should those findings be accepted or should they be considered biased falsehoods? The answer might be harder to ascertain than you think.

Deficit Hypothesis

One term often used to classify people is *race*, an anthropological concept used to classify people according to physical characteristics, such as skin and eye color, or the shape of certain body parts, such as head, eyes, ears, lips, or nose (Hernandez, 1989; Lott, 2010). Race also has a social meaning that is often accompanied by stereotyping; it suggests one's status within the social system and introduces power differences as people of different races interact with one another (APA Task Force, 1998). The concept of race no longer applies to humanity because we have become an integrated racial society.

Forcing people with diverse ancestry into a specific category serves little purpose other than to construct a genetic social hierarchy. The term has also fallen out of favor because the grouping of individuals into races is arbitrary. It is not uncommon for political groups to create definitions of race that serve their interests (e.g., separating those of Irish ancestry from those of Scandinavian origin). You will notice throughout this text that when the term *race* is used, it is often applied when one group is attempting to demonstrate the inferiority of another physically different group.

Although race no longer distinguishes between human groups accurately, racism is still present. Perceived physical distinctions lead to biases, discrimination, and prejudices. However, the existence of racism should not justify using the term *race* in scientific or popular media (Lott, 2010). This is especially noteworthy when considering the origin of the division in people groups. W. E. B. Dubois (cited in Lott, 2010) noted that the notion of race came into existence after slaves were imported to the Americas. It created a sense of "otherness" and justified the denigration of an inferior group. Similar attempts to belittle people groups occurred when the Nazis tortured Jews and gays. Race and racism are better described as political terms. They create power differentials rather than a distinction between cultures.

Racial differences—even though a weak construct—have been used to define all sorts of differences between people groups. Of all the differences emphasized between such groups, intelligence has been the most widely discussed and controversial. What happens when someone truly believes that a client is innately less intelligent, insightful, or wise than someone from another culture? Such a position is often referred to as the <u>deficit hypothesis,</u> which Thomas and Sillen (1972) defined as predetermined deficiencies that relegate a group member to an inferior status. The alleged deficit may be attributed to a genetic inferiority, such as inferior brain power or limited mental development, or a cultural deficit in which the individual's ethnic lifestyle is thought to be debilitating. Both theories have taken many forms over the past century, but staunch opponents have challenged them scientifically, philosophically, and theoretically. Although a thorough analysis of the deficit hypothesis is beyond the scope of this text, the argument requires a brief summary.

The most recent reincarnation of the deficit hypothesis has been the debate surrounding Richard Herrnstein and Charles Murray's (1996) text, *The Bell Curve: Intelligence and Class Structure in American Life*. In this text, the authors begin by arguing that the construct of intelligence plays an important role in an individual's life. As a single construct, intelligence represents the ability to reason, plan, solve problems, think abstractly, comprehend complex ideas, learn quickly, and learn from experience. An individual with a high IQ has an advantage in life because virtually all activities require some reasoning and decision making. Conversely, a low IQ is often a disadvantage, especially in disorganized environments. From a practical viewpoint, a high IQ becomes more important as an individual confronts more complex situations. Fluid jobs often involve management or utilizing professional skills.

However, the advantages are less noticeable for someone involved in a setting requiring routine decision making or simple problem solving.

When IQ scores for all the people from a given population are represented graphically, they form what is known as a bell curve. Most people cluster around the middle, with the average IQ score of 100 representing the 50th percentile. On either extreme of the scale—representing either mental giftedness or borderline mental dullness—the curve becomes flat. Less than 3% of Americans receive "superior" intelligence scores of 130 or above, and about the same percentage score 70 or below—the threshold for mental retardation.

The findings reported in *The Bell Curve* do not support the hypothesis that WAIS-R scores were equivalent for different cultural groups. Instead, they indicate that while members of all racial-ethnic groups can be found at every IQ level, the average score for some groups (Jews and East Asians) are centered somewhat higher than for European Americans in general. Other groups (African Americans and Latinos) are centered significantly lower than non-Hispanic whites. Herrnstein and Murray concluded that the results of their analysis were so robust that the causes for the differences were due to genetic predispositions.

When I was first studying this subject, I had a teacher who said, "If anyone believes blacks are dumber than whites, that person is a racist." I remember thinking, "But how do we know? Shouldn't we investigate this?" It is a prejudice to assume that all people groups are the same. They are not. Each culture will emphasize different skills and behaviors. Over several generations, patterns may arise—built into the culture itself. Does this explain why some ethnic groups receive higher intelligence scores?

Myerson, Rank, Raines, and Schnitzler (1998) used the same data Herrnstein and Murray used, but rather than finding a genetic explanation for the deficit, they found a social one. One of their most significant findings involved the differences between African Americans and European Americans who attend college. When comparing students in their final year of high school, they found, as Herrnstein and Murray did, that European Americans tended to outscore African Americans by as many as 15 IQ points. But among college graduates, the IQ scores of African American students increased four times more than did the scores of their European American classmates. European American students still scored about seven points higher, but the diminishing gap between average IQ scores implies that IQ has a strong social component.

Fagan and Holland (2007) tested African Americans and European Americans and had them solve intelligence questions. They specifically separated questions requiring specific experiential knowledge. The other questions were solvable on the basis of information generally available to either ethnic group. They found that ethnicity was unrelated to the g factor (or global intelligence). Rather than support the bell curve, they found that cultural differences accounted for ethnic differences in IQ.

From a counseling perspective, it is important to realize that just because an individual client belongs to a group whose average IQ score is currently lower than that of another group, it does *not* imply that he or she is less intelligent. African Americans—as well as all other ethnic groups—are represented among the highest intellectual groups, just as European Americans and Asian Americans are represented among the lowest intellectual groups. Stereotyping individuals to fit group norms is harmful to everyone involved.

Probably the most interesting—and the most disconcerting—studies involving the deficit hypothesis relate to the way test-takers perceive the tests themselves. Claude Steele and Joshua Aronson (2000) performed an interesting test on the psychology of self-perception. They gave an exam to two mixed-race groups of students. The first group was told that the exam was a simple problem-solving exercise; the other group was told that their scores would show how smart they were. The European American students from the two groups obtained similar scores, but the African American subjects who believed they were taking an intelligence test performed considerably worse than those who thought they were taking a nondiagnostic test. In a sense, the African American subjects not only accepted the stereotype that they were less intelligent, but they acted on this prejudice with a self-fulfilling prophecy.

To overcome the biases found in research, counselors, researchers, and teachers must begin by engaging in intense self-evaluation. Before counselors can realize what it means to be a member of a different ethnic/cultural group, they must learn how their ethnic/cultural/gender worldview influences their perception of the other group. Some counselors may choose to assume that they have transcended their heritage to attain greater objectivity, but our views will always be influenced by our histories.

Appreciating Divergent Worldviews

The deficit model of diversity counseling basically assumes that one culture lacks something that is present in another culture. While it is true that one culture may possess strengths lacking in another, these differences do not mean that one culture is better than the other. Each cultural system must be viewed in its entirety before it can be dissected into parts. One method of accomplishing such an overview—as recommended by Ibrahim (1985)—is to explore value orientations. Each culture will create different orientations with respect to time, activity, relationships, and ecology. Table 1.3 describes a variety of value orientations.

Each orientation has its own unique strengths. A society adopting any of these can succeed and flourish, but cultures with conflicting orientations may have difficulties interacting with one another. Consider the example of a Native American therapist who is counseling a European American client. Many Native American cultures value the past and present more than the future. They will maintain their present path if it seems productive rather than switch to a new task because they believe each task should be brought to fruition. Many European American cultures value the present and future more than the past.

Rigidly maintaining schedules and appointments is viewed as respectful of others. If a Native American therapist is working with another client who

TABLE **1.3**
A Model of Values

Dimensions	Value Orientations		
Time	**Past:** We must be guided by history and especially our personal and cultural experiences.	**Present:** We should emphasize the here and now. Other timeframes are distractions pulling us away from the moment.	**Future:** We must focus on our goals (teleology). Without goals and direction, our present actions are ineffectual.
Action	**Being:** Our actions should be secondary to the condition of our soul, mind, or psyche.	**Active becoming:** Our behaviors should be focused on the development of an inner self.	**Doing:** Actions are essential. Working hard and behaving morally is more important than finding inner peace.
Family	**Dependence:** We should always remain attached to our family, respecting our parents and trusting their wisdom.	**Interdependence:** Family should be used as consultants but not depended on. We should be there for each other when necessary.	**Independence:** Families help to equip fully functional members of society who are ready to face the world on their own.
Spirituality	**Pantheism:** God is part of nature and acts in and through all living things.	**Humanism:** Spirituality may be of value, but the evidence of the divine is in the hearts and actions of humanity.	**External deity:** God exists beyond nature. The divine is something we should seek and follow, but we can never be identified with it.
Ecology	**Life force:** Nature is holy and should be preserved, respected, and honored.	**Co-Existence:** Nature is valuable but so is humanity's progress.	**Androcentric:** Humanity's progress is more important than the preservation of nature. Nature will adapt to our demands of it.
Sexuality	**Polyamorous:** Multiple sexual partners help to increase our sexual satisfaction and awareness of ourselves.	**Serial monogamy:** Stay with people until the relationship loses passion and then move on to the next relationship.	**Monogamy:** Avoid premarital sex and stay with one mate for life.
Gender roles	**Feminist:** Women and men should feel comfortable interchanging any and all social roles.	**Developmental:** Gender roles are likely to shift over time, with each person playing several roles over a lifetime.	**Patriarchal:** Men should be the leaders of the family. Women should focus on raising children and maintaining household stability.

is making considerable progress during a session and requires more time than the allotted hour, he or she may be willing to work longer with this client. The European American client in the waiting room may become frustrated by the delay because he or she feels disrespected and believes the therapist to be unprofessional. Such value differences could cause friction if not discussed.

A European American therapist who values independence may have difficulty understanding and appreciating a Latina client who feels ashamed because she is distant from her mother. A Taoist client who views his strength as coming from a divine encounter with nature might clash with the humanistic therapist who denies any supernatural powers. A liberal European American therapist may feel that her fundamentalist African American client is limiting herself by letting her husband act as the household leader. No matter what value is being addressed, contrasting values can be difficult to understand, let alone appreciate. Conscious effort must be made to step into the client's perceptions and see the world through his or her eyes.

In addition to ethnicity, other factors affect how people conceive their world. Class, which is usually determined by socioeconomic level, also plays a role in how the world is perceived. Lower-class individuals are often less time-oriented and are motivated by immediate, concrete reinforcement (Peterson & Nisenholz, 1987). Middle- or upper-class therapists may have difficulty understanding the cultural differences between their views and those of clients from different socioeconomic backgrounds. Sometimes, class values will intermix with ethnic values. Both are important components of how individuals see the world.

Anthony grew up in a middle-class town of Southern California. There were 24 other African Americans at his high school (of over 3,000 students). His father owned a healthy business, and Anthony dressed the part. He wore expensive clothes and drove nice cars. He spent time with the students whose parents commuted by helicopter, owned yachts, and traveled to Europe. This class presentation, though, did not take away the stigma of dark skin. One day, someone wrote "Nigger" on his windshield. The bright pink lipstick shone like a beacon—a warning to keep him at bay. But for Anthony, his ethnicity and wealth were intimately intertwined.

Ethnicity Models

Do we simply accept prejudice as a way of life and move on to other topics? To do so would undermine any effective intervention. All people are prejudiced and have discriminated against others. Realizing our potential for unfair and prejudicial actions allows us to actively explore new ways of thinking and acting. In order to fully understand our biases, we must first examine the lessons we have learned from our cultural background.

There are factors that can help people overcome the effects of their own prejudices. Phinney, Ferguson, and Tate (1997) examined the ways eighth- and eleventh-graders viewed themselves and those outside their cultural group. Rather than examine the avenue for negative prejudice, they used a path analysis to help identify the mechanisms by which people develop positive views of ethnic identity. They found two distinct pathways leading to positive out-group attitudes. In the first, simply growing older led the 133 African Americans, 219 Latinos, and 195 Asian Americans involved in the study to have a stronger sense of ethnic identity. The eleventh-graders had more positive in-group attitudes, and in turn, this positive conception of their own group contributed to more positive out-group attitudes. The second pathway revealed that children who spent more time with peers from other cultures outside of school were involved in more cross-cultural interaction during school. The fact that only relationships outside of school correlated with positive out-group attitudes implies that children must feel free to interact with those they view as different.

Do we really need in-groups and out-groups within a pluralistic society? It appears that we do. We may hope to someday reach a level where color, language, gender, or sexual orientation no longer play a role in forming friendships and identity, but this seems unlikely to occur. If anything, there is a growing acceptance that our conception of in-groups intensifies throughout our lives. Should diversity counselors attempt to help individuals from minority groups conform to the majority group's expectations or should counselors help individuals learn to develop their self-concept and continue to identify with their minority group? There is no clear answer. Each group and individual will require one mode or the other. What is clear is that individuals will create an ethnic identity of some type, and counselors should be sensitive to the decisions their clients make.

To better understand the development of an individual's ethnic identity, it may be helpful to compare it to the growth of a tree. Even from a young age, a tree is identifiable as a specific type, but no two trees are exactly alike. Some face greater hardships and must adapt to limited water supplies, poor soil, or inadequate sunlight. Others are damaged by animals, pruned by gardeners, or played on by children. All these factors will change the structure of the tree. In some cases, the tree may change so much that it no longer resembles others of its kind. In the same way, our view of our ethnicity and our view of the world around us is shaped as we develop. For example, many Latino groups learn to accept the hardships of life as a matter of fate, which helps them to cope with overwhelming obstacles. Many European American groups believe the individual is required to change social structures that create hardship—a belief that stems from growing up in a well-nurtured and reasonably protected environment (Draguns, 1989).

In order to investigate how acculturation works for different groups, we must examine each group individually. There should also be an attempt to separate demographic variables from issues related to mental health. For example, African Americans have historically been more likely to drop out of high school. Is this related to the prejudice they experience from the dominant society, the added pressure of financial hardship, unique physical health issues that are relatively unknown to European Americans, or something else? Without exploring how each of these individual factors contributes to the larger picture of their mental health, we may be creating additional biases by simply purporting psychological dysfunction. Similar arguments could be made for gender issues. The structure of the family has a significant effect on the way men and women perceive themselves. Such factors also influence how men and women perceive their occupational or academic roles and how they spend the majority of their time. In order to explore these issues more thoroughly, the remainder of this text is divided into two parts (racial/ethnic components and gender/sexuality issues). Each chapter explores the following areas:

Unique Challenges:	All marginalized groups face similar challenges, but each cultural group wrestles against these threats differently.
Historical Content:	This subchapter incorporates positive elements of cultural history, in addition to detailing the oppression faced.
Immigration and Development:	Recent immigrants face unique challenges. This section provides a brief overview of their experiences and differentiates this group from multi-generational immigrants.
Cultural Identity:	This section investigates multicultural theories regarding identity and tie into the various national standards.
Within Group Differences:	Within each cultural group, how do the various subgroups look the same? How do they differ? When speaking about millions of people spread across thousands of miles, differences would be necessary.
Family Structure and Dynamics:	Culture plays a significant role in the ways families function. Family and marital counseling interventions are included in this subchapter.
Education:	This chapter addresses educational diversity standards set by the NCATE (National Council for Accreditation of Teacher Education) and the NASP (National Association of School Psychologists). It also explores English as a second language (ESL).
Socioeconomics:	This subchapter explores how economics, education, and health are interrelated for a given cultural group.
Spirituality and Religion:	Religious multicultural competencies are an emerging field in diversity tests. This subchapter will examine religious perspectives from other ethnic/gender worldviews.
Physical and Mental Health:	This section addresses views on physical health but also includes psychological issues. For many cultures, physical and mental health are interrelated. This chapter explores how rituals and beliefs address the mind and body (both positively and negatively).
Individual and Group Interventions:	In addition to individual and group interventions, this subchapter includes the counselor/psychologists obligation toward social justice, advocacy, and conflict resolution. Multicultural competencies are also explored for each group addressed.
Advocacy and Social Justice:	Counseling people from diverse groups is only the beginning. This is a political process too, and there are things we should do to advocate for our individual clients and for the groups in which they belong.

Admittedly, some of these headings are value-laden. For example, health labels have been used to stereotype African Americans in socially deprecating ways. During the time of slavery, Samuel Cartwright created a diagnostic category for runaway slaves (*draptemania*, or flight from madness) because he believed only insane African Americans would run from their protective homes. This mentality migrated into the modern age. Even psychological giants such as Carl Jung published racist theories concerning African Americans and Jews. As president of the International General Medical Society for Psychotherapy, he argued that members of the Jewish race (as it was often called) were "genetically inferior" to those of European descent (Alexander & Selesnick, 1966, p. 408).

Problems with underdiagnosing must also be explored. If clients have experienced difficulty acculturating to the dominant society, they are likely to wrestle with feelings of displacement, poor self-esteem, or disillusionment. Such conditions could mask a co-morbid clinical depression that is unrelated to the adjustment issues. Attempting to be sensitive to the oppression their clients have faced, therapists may overlook or minimize valid psychological or psychiatric factors. Allowing the depression to continue could also interfere with the client's acculturation, which would marginalize the entire intervention.

Given these historical and practical warnings, any discussion of psychological, relationship, and counseling issues requires extreme sensitivity, but this does not alter the fact that people of different racial groups are likely to present with different psychological complaints. For example, the alcoholism rate for Native Americans living on reservations significantly exceeds that of other population groups. The wise multicultural counselor will use these statistics to explore areas of possible psychological risk without stereotyping individual clients. All these topics will be explored with sensitivity, and ideally, this text will challenge you to re-evaluate your views of many diverse population groups.

By this point, you may have realized that the preceding introduction to "diversity" lacks sufficient depth into gender issues. There is a twofold reason for this: (1) Most people are aware of their gender identity and believe they have a grasp of maleness and femaleness, and (2) a conceptual understanding of ethnicity undergirds our gender identity. However, as we begin to discuss gender issues more thoroughly, I hope you will start to realize that gender and sexual identity are more complex than they appear. Ideally, you will acquire a deeper understanding of the ways in which gender—which is really a social construction of our sexuality—is based on the roles instituted by our ethnic culture.

When we begin to discuss gender issues, readers should be aware that their perceptions may be challenged. Exploring issues such as homosexuality, transvestism, bisexuality, spousal abuse, and other such topics can threaten our religious positions, make us question our sexual relationships, or force us to reopen old wounds. Although these topics may be difficult to examine, imagine what they are like for the client who is wrestling with them. For now, you may want to see if you can answer all the following questions:

- How can you counsel men who are abusing their spouses?
- Would you treat a woman with depression differently from a man with the same diagnosis?
- Are children with cross-sexed behaviors likely to become gay, lesbian, or transsexual in adulthood?
- When counseling parents of a child who was born with a penis but with female chromosomes, should you recommend raising the child as a boy or a girl?

It would be impossible to fully investigate all the gender issues a counselor is likely to encounter professionally; instead, this book takes a sampling across three broad categories of gender/sexual identity: (1) gay, lesbian, and transgendered clients; (2) women's issues; and (3) men's issues. Each chapter in this part of this book examines the group's common history of oppression, the etiology of problems, family dynamics, economics, education, health, cultural uniqueness, within-group differences, psychology, and counseling issues. As with all topics in psychology, any discussion of common group behaviors should not be applied to every individual in the group. For example, when investigating economic issues, we find that gay men are likely to have incomes above the national average, while lesbian women have a mean income that is closer to the poverty level. This trend exists because men still tend to earn more than women; therefore, two men are likely to earn a higher combined income than two women. However, the gay or lesbian client who begins therapy with you may not meet this profile. Trends are discussed only to provide a framework for understanding issues certain groups are likely to face.

In the chapters on sexuality and gender identity, special care must be taken with the sections on psychological issues and a new topic: etiology. Both of these headings appear value-laden, but they are used to address trends within a given population as indicated in contemporary research. For example, women are twice as likely as men to receive a mood disorder diagnosis, and men are more likely to seriously injure or kill their spouses. In these sections, statistics and trends are emphasized over the rationale for the behavior. We will address the possibility of diagnostic bias, but our main focus will be on the skills needed to counsel clients with these presenting problems.

QUESTIONS TO CONSIDER

1. Social influence theory (i.e., the dimensions of attraction, trustworthiness, and expertness/competence) takes on additional importance when dealing with minority clients. Which of these factors is likely to be the most important?
2. How does the deficit hypothesis explain why people from different cultures appear to have different levels of intelligence?
3. If assimilation into the dominant culture is no longer considered helpful for minority clients, what should be the new focus?
4. How would you work with a client who believes society is responsible for his plight in life and feels impotent to change the conditions around him? What difficulties might arise in therapy?
5. Can you imagine ways multicultural clients might be overdiagnosed? How might views of ghosts, herbal healing, drug use, gambling, spanking children, diet, and education be associated with specific cultures?
6. What responsibility should therapists take for helping clients build productive in-group and out-group beliefs?
7. How important is a client's worldview to the way he or she interacts with the therapist?

CHAPTER 2

Social Justice and Counseling Standards

Imagine a friend of yours offered you an incredible deal. He has a new watch he wants to sell and is offering an unbelievable price. This is not just any watch. It is a Rolex President with certified authenticity papers. It retails for about $14,000. Your friend tells you that he received dozens of these watches from his father, and he will sell you one for $100. He needs the extra money for a concert he wants to attend.

You decide to buy the watch.

After a few weeks, you start wondering more about the watch. It is beautiful. A jeweler appraised it as worth more than $12,000, but you still wonder why he sold it for so little. After confronting your friend, you learn that these watches *might* have been acquired during World War II. They *may* have belonged to Jews from the Holocaust or another oppressed group. But that happened more than a half century ago, and no one had claimed the watches since. What do you do?

Privilege is not something that happens to a few individuals. It happens to everyone. There are advantages of being part of a group. Some groups—especially those with ruthless pasts—have more advantages than others. Many white students claim that they have never experienced privilege.

They argue they have earned everything they received. What they do not understand is that statement in and of itself is a privilege. For many minority groups, earning their success requires more than skill. For some gifted, bright, hard-working souls, their efforts will not be rewarded. In fact, working harder and drawing attention to one's self sometimes results in punishment.

Consider the Rolex example again. If you gave back the watch—even at the loss of your $100—would that be considered a lack of privilege?

When you were *offered* the watch, you became the recipient of privilege. You still have an ethical responsibility to do what is right, but you cannot change the fact that you were placed in a privileged situation. Your $100 was transformed into 100 times its worth simply because you were part of a group who victimized others generations ago. This cannot be undone, but it does create additional responsibilities. This realization is where social justice begins.

Martin Luther King, Jr. (2010) wrote: "Like life, racial understanding is not something that we find but something that we must create. And so the ability of Negros and whites to work together, to understand each other, will not be found readymade; it must be created by the fact of contact" (p. 28). It is not enough to understand cultural differences. If we truly learn to see the world through another's viewpoint, this identification would also result in action. We would become advocates for social justice. We would help clients recognize the battles they face and devote our own resources to fighting against these social forces too. These are two important dimensions to counseling: empowerment and social action (Manis, Brown & Paylo, 2009). Empowerment (advocacy) supports clients in facing the struggles in their lives. Social action (justice) brings the counselor and client toward a larger, more public fight against injustice.

TYPES OF PRIVILEGE

Before you can help create justice in society, you have to understand three types of privilege. Up to this point, we have primarily discussed **societal privilege.** This is where straight white males receive the most advantages. But there are two other types of privilege that are seldom discussed in the literature.

Group Privilege

Think about your church, school, job, or community. In all likelihood, there are people around who match your cultural identity. They may share similar beliefs, they may look like you, or they may be of your gender or sexual orientation. Group privilege does not mean you are part of the societal dominant group; it means you have a group. This group identity will come with privilege. You will find jobs through contacts. You will find lovers from social outings. Even at the basic level of having fun, you are given opportunities you did not earn. You were simply part of a group that was willing to accept you.

Schools, work environments, and religion are primary ways people find group identities. Although it may seem like everyone has similar group privileges, many lack such identities. Gays, lesbians, bisexuals, and transsexuals often struggle to find group identities. After coming out, religious groups often spurn their outed members. They push the person out—sometimes directly through comments; sometimes indirectly by no longer inviting them to events. This poses a double threat. They are not only facing a loss of privilege by society, but they may also lose their group. In many ways, this secondary loss is greater than the primary one.

Personal Privilege

Some individuals possess an identity so distinct that they even lack a coherent sense of their own culture. One client told me, "I never told anyone I was gay. I grew up crippled, in a wheelchair, and I was Muslim. I didn't want to be the crippled, Muslim, gay kid." What happens at this level is that the individual experiences a sense of fragmentation. He or she may still have one or more group identities, but no one matches the individual's identity. Such individuals lack heroes. They cannot look to someone ahead of them and strive to be like that person. At this personal level, advocacy and social justice will look different.

HOW TO ADVOCATE

Advocacy and social justice overlap in many ways. Sometimes, the terms are used interchangeably. Speaking about one without the other is nearly impossible. But advocacy tends to address the personal and group dimensions of privilege. Social justice looks at the social system. Learning how the two interact will have a profound impact on how you read the rest of this book.

Consider creating social justice for refugee Asian women. Singh, Hays, Chung, and Watson (2010) studied South Asian immigrant women who had survived child sexual abuse. They noted healing and resiliency were the related to "a sense of purpose." This purpose—their function in the world—led to success in academic, career, volunteer, and advocacy paths. This empowerment helps sustain mental health. Overcoming past abuses stemmed from finding a place where they "fit" and surrounding themselves with others who were like them. Social justice and the fight against other sexual abuses started with personal and group advocacy.

The beginning point of social change is personal empowerment—and empowerment is a slow process. People learn to be survivors when they face trauma. Often, they never get the chance to be a victim. To cry. To be sad. To let themselves been broken. Only when they identify with this person will they become strong enough to truly understand the process of surviving. Sometimes, empowering an individual to simply cope is the advocacy we can do. It all starts with seeing how injustices have touched you.

Advocacy Exercise

Imagine you woke up this morning and everything about you felt the same. Height, weight, mental faculties, gender, sexual desires, physical abilities, wealth, and all other personal features remained unchanged. You ate your normal breakfast and then started out for the day. Even driving to your first stop, people treated you differently. You noticed long stares from people you passed. Sometimes, they continued staring even when you made eye contact with you. Their expressions were not inquisitive; a subtle form of disgust mixed with indifference might describe it best.

When you make it to your meeting, the group discusses some projects they want to start. You volunteer for one of the primary roles, but no one takes you seriously. They listen while you talk, but then they say they want to "explore their options." Everyone else is given the roles they want. Everyone but you.

At the end of the meeting, you approach the group leader. You ask if you did something to offend people or if you had said something to offend anyone. The leader smiles. "Oh, no, you're fine, but we're moving in a different direction. In fact, you might be happier somewhere else."

Personal Advocacy

When marginalization occurs, it attacks at the social, group, and personal levels. All of these are important, but people cannot survive without a sense of personal identity. In the previous exercise, if you had lost your job or been kicked out of school, it would affect your group identity. Such marginalization is difficult, but it can be survived. If you continue to feel the loss so deeply that you lose a sense of self, you lose the desire to grow and change.

Combating a loss of personal privilege is similar to helping a person defragment. Soul healing—as Roy (2007) defines effective interventions— addresses the political messages we have accepted. For example, African Americans often feel stupid (because they are ignored by teachers), ugly (because they have kinky hair and larger noses), and insignificant (because society overlooks their skills). These take time to overcome, and advocating for people who have internalized such messages must start with empowerment. Sometimes, people from dominant-power groups often try to instill hope or offer positive messages (e.g., "You're not stupid" or "things will turn out fine"). Those messages are actually harmful. Instead, encourage people to find their voice, rather than lead them where you think they might belong. Challenge them to find a hero, or someone succeeded in ways they may want to succeed. Someone who is differently abled may find a hero in

Tom Whittaker, who climbed Mount Everest with a prosthetic leg. African Americans may learn more about sports legends—such as Jackie Robinson—or world leaders—such as Barack Obama. These issues of personal wellness intersect with relational and collective wellness. Such perspectives break from the traditional notion of counseling, but they are the direction our professions are headed. Rather than look at an individual's personal needs as the only component of wellness, a social justice perspective includes relational and collective needs.

Group Advocacy

When you receive condemnation for who you are, social action becomes a matter of necessity. None of this will be effective without starting with personal advocacy. People need to believe in themselves before they can believe in society. But once personal empowerment comes, social change happens on multiple levels.

This is the basic problem with social justice. Marginalized groups are not welcomed into the broader society, so they tend to segregate among themselves. These segregated groups can support each other, work through the pain, and become resilient. When learning to intervene, it is important to maintain the resilience necessary to cope with an unjust and prejudiced society. Only with this strength and insight can you break through barriers (Green, 2008). To bridge these gaps, counseling must transcend individual therapy and small groups. It requires a proactive stance rather than just being reactive, and this action involves intervening at the personal, community, and national levels (Prilleltensky, Dokecki, Frieden & Ota Wang, 2007). Group advocacy requires daily changes in micropolitics (Pakman, 2007). Micropolitics involves opening up health care to more people in disadvantaged populations. It also requires assessing potential discrimination faced regarding education, employment, housing, transportation, legal issues, violence, poverty, and social networks.

Group advocacy also works on opening social groups to the most marginalized members of society. The volatility of gay, lesbian, bisexual, and transgendered people often leads them to expand their conceptualization of family. Green (2007) called these close friendships "families of choice," and these play a large role in the lives of many marginalized people.

Helping clients create group networks requires considerable trust. It often surprises European American students when their attempts to volunteer or provide free services are met with skepticism or suspicion. After all, these students have done nothing to harm the people they are trying to help. Why should anyone be suspicious of them? Their actions remind me of the Disney film *Pollyanna* and its portrayal of social advocacy problems. In one scene, Pollyanna brings food baskets to the poorer citizens. With each gift, the recipients appear uncomfortable. Some even angry. One man confronts the girl and tells her keep her charity to herself. Pollyanna responds, "Don't think of this as charity. It's a gift between friends."

This is the essence of advocacy. A gesture of goodwill to an unknown recipient could result in more problems than benefits. Welfare benefits have inadvertently created a multigenerational underclass in America. Nestlé's gift of baby formula to needy African women in the 1970s inadvertently lead to a generation of malnutrition by dissuading breast feeding. Introducing advanced agricultural techniques to India have created overwatering patterns that now threaten the entire water table. Positive activities to a little understood group tend to result in failure. The obvious solution is to get to know yourself and the people you want to help before giving them anything.

Societal Advocacy

Beyond micropolitics, there are broader, social implications as well. The connection between the culture and politics is sometimes called *ethnopolitical* (Comas-Diaz, 2007), and it is the heart of effective multicultural counseling. Personal changes are often too weak to last against the onslaught from racism, sexism, ageism, and other prejudicial forms of oppression. Because of this, effective interventions must employ change within the system. Clients must gain ways to find support and encouragement from their cultural groups, and work with these groups in evoking change. For example, religion can help with victimization, racism, demoralization, hopelessness, and isolation (Kay, 1998). The Latino Day of the Dead can help with bereavement. And all groups can help integrate the fractured self into a more functional society (Comas-Diaz, 2007).

The collective needs of individuals also include how language affects people. Gerber (2007) tells the story of a student who became frustrated with the way his agency viewed clients as "consumers." The term implied two things: Clients were not responsible change agents, and therapists were objects for sale. He confronted his supervisor, saying, "I am not a commodity to be bought and sold. I am not a salesperson" (p. 60). The supervisor responded with lectures and anger, maintaining the status quo. To break out of the current way of doing things, we need to start with the basics, such as changing words and ideas.

When advocating in an agency or political environment, it is important to overcome the "nice counselor syndrome." Counselors and psychologists are often fearful of being disliked. They may not offer limited resistance to prejudice because of negative peer pressure or professional ostracism. This creates a sense of powerlessness, where mental health providers believe they lack the power to redefine their roles, agency, or school (Bemak & Chung, 2008). What social justice requires of counselors is a willingness to enter into interpersonal conflict. This does not mean bullying peers into accepting your viewpoint. It means building effective relationships where change can occur. It means voicing concerns about mission statements, policies, and programs that marginalize students or clients.

Working for justice also requires faith in humanity. Believe that people want to do what is right. Recognize that most people will make short-term sacrifices if they believe it will benefit their community, agency, or school (Crethar, Rivera & Nash, 2008). Once you accept your duty to fight for social justice, the next step rests with becoming multiculturally competent.

ACHIEVING MULTICULTURAL COMPETENCE

The problem with developing a set of competencies is the assumption that someone can be competent by running through a list of steps or trainings. This is far from the case. Competencies provide only the most basic framework. A better term might be multicultural adequacy, but even that will vary by client.

The competencies are designed to demonstrate what people lack rather than prove what they know. As you read through the competencies for various professions, consider how much more you might need to learn. Realize how each person requires special attention and no member of a group will ever be equivalent to the others. Only by maintaining the uniqueness of each soul can we hope to help that individual achieve greatness. And that person's greatness will look very different from everyone else's. If you view the "competencies" as tools to help you begin the lifelong journey into multicultural development, you are reading them correctly.

With client advocacy covering multiple dimensions, it is sometimes difficult to identify someone who is multicultural competent. Can a counselor be therapeutically competent without being multiculturally competent? Sue and Sue (2008, p. 35) regard multicultural competency as "superordinate" to counseling competence (i.e., multicultural competence must come before counseling competence). It may make more sense to see multicultural competency as an early phase of professional growth. It is no more possible to become a competent counselor without multicultural skills as it would be to become competent without empathy, communication skills, self-care, theoretical knowledge, or any other master-counselor skill. Competency is a mosaic, building on several dimensions simultaneously. What makes the cultural facet unique is its interconnection between all the other components. It is impossible to be an empathic racist. You cannot communicate effectively while insulting a client's culture.

At the minimum, competent counseling requires understanding the client. Once grasping this, you need appropriate intervention skills and a clear perspective of the client's worldview. Most counseling training programs focus on skills. They teach people about diagnosis, interventions for specific clinical concerns, developmentally appropriate techniques, displaying empathy, and generalized techniques that work with most people. Problems come when these techniques are extended to people outside these basic areas. Let us start with some basic ideas of multicultural counseling:

1. **Self-exploration:** Identify your own racial, ethnic, sexual orientation, and gender identities. How did you arrive at these cultural identities? How do they affect how you interact in the world?
2. **Exposure and learning:** Without surrounding yourself with different cultures, you cannot hope to understand diversity. Visit groups where people are from different ethnicities, social classes, gender identities, sexual orientations, and physical abilities from you (Smith & Shin, 2008).
3. **Self-disclosure:** You cannot be multiculturally competent without being known to the client/student. The people you work with need to know

when you are being genuine. Kiselica (2004) noted that sharing struggles allows us to become role models whom others can understand and accept.

4. **The client or group is the expert:** Multicultural counseling requires a power shift. We must acknowledge that clients know themselves better than anyone else. This means they are also the best ones to find their path.

5. **Personalize each intervention:** How much you disclose or how you perceive your role will vary according to the client's or group's needs. There are recommendations in this book regarding interventions with diverse clients. Using them exactly as they are expressed is unlikely to produce the desired response. Your intervention must be tailored to fit your personality and that of your clients.

6. **Dysfunction is culturally defined:** Mental health professionals are trained to identify dysfunction. However, dysfunction does not make sense without looking at an individual's or group's larger context. Many non-Western cultures scoff at this approach and place partial responsibility on society, family, God, demons, and other factors. It is important to realize that the Western view of mental health is simply one perspective among many.

7. **Eliminate privilege in the room:** It is important to realize when a counselor or group is acting in a way that could be perceived as controlling or discriminatory (Roysircar, 2008). This also means confronting issues of privilege when they arise. Burnes and Ross (2010) recommend asking questions such as, "How might we be marginalizing each other?" or "What makes some group members appear more powerful than others?" Let clients, friends, teachers, and colleagues help you learn where you have experienced privilege, racism, sexism, or other cultural experiences.

8. **Reframe problems:** Often, minority cultures will internalize negative views about their culture. Learning to help the client embrace the positive elements can help to create a better therapeutic direction. For example, many Native American cultures emphasize the present over scheduled plans. Rather than making them "lazy," this time orientation often shows a greater commitment to completing the task at hand.

9. **Learn from your mistakes (Hanna, Bemak & Chung, 1999):** If the information provided in this text does not apply to your client, you would be wise to say something such as, "My culture tends to look at that differently. I'm interested to know more about your culture's perceptions."

10. **Advocate:** Every system has injustices. Take a critical look at your organization, school, family, neighborhood, community, religious group, and country. See what you do to evoke even the slightest change (Constantine et al., 2007). This starts by arguing for the rights of others over how you may have been treated unfairly. People tend to respond more favorably to justice requests when they believe your perceptions are objective rather than based on personal experience (Wijn & van den Bos, 2010).

ACCREDITATION ISSUES

So, how do people grasp a client's worldviews and gain necessary multicultural skills? The process is best articulated by the Association for Multicultural Counseling and Development (Arredondo, Toporek, Brown et al., 1996). They provided three basic categories of competence:

- Counselor awareness of own cultural values and biases
- Counselor awareness of client's worldview
- Culturally appropriate intervention strategies

Each of these dimensions has three subcomponents:

- Attitudes and beliefs
- Knowledge
- Skills

Teacher Education

Every profession will incorporate all these elements, but the process will look different for each group. Suppose you are a classroom teacher. You will need to understand yourself, your students, and how to teach to differently cultured children. Standard #4 of The National Council for Accreditation of Teacher Education (NCATE) addresses diversity issues. As an education body, they focus more on building appropriate intervention strategies, but they require candidates to also demonstrate knowledge, skills, and professional dispositions (attitudes). Their guidelines focus on helping students learn, so they require school counselors and school psychologists to "demonstrate and apply proficiencies related to diversity."

For the NCATE, an excellent candidate (what they call "target" level) would complete multicultural field experiences, engage all students—including English language learners and students with exceptionalities—have data to show their progress (4a), interact with diverse faculty from multiple disciplines (4b), engage conventional and distance-learning programs with diverse students, value feedback from diverse students, and grow personally from these interactions (4c). They will also work with "exceptional" and diverse students, developing appropriate strategies for each (4d).

NCATE took this stance because there are nearly twice as many students of color in the classrooms as there are teachers. Because of this imbalance, they wanted candidates to interact with adults, children, and youth from their own and other ethnic/racial cultures (5e).

Working with families has become a priority for school counselors. As student populations become more diverse, the family customs will also become more complex. This has led to arguments for learning about cultural kinship networks, socialization experiences, and cultural attitudes (Holcomb-McCoy, 2004).

When NCATE visits a university, it verifies multicultural experiences and data. One school had tons of data. It knew the lineage of the school's students, the multicultural experiences the students had prior to arriving, the percentage of diverse faculty members, and the students' grades on various multicultural competencies. On paper, it looked impressive, but one site visitor asked two very candid questions: "Your candidates look diverse, but what did they learn from your program, and can they teach diverse students?" The school lacked any data demonstrating how the graduates actually worked with diverse clients and students. This practical component has become the cornerstone of accreditation.

As education becomes more about results, school counselors need to carve out a new identity. Many school counselors advocate for their own self-promotion, but this is unfamiliar territory for them (Singh, Urbano, Haston & McMahon, 2010). Modifying school systems to better advocate for all children takes times. The shift also requires marketing skills (i.e., how will this benefit the school), and most training programs overlook this training.

Say a school is struggling with ethnic violence. Rival gangs from various groups are waging word wars and raising tensions. Inevitably, someone will raise the idea of additional discipline (e.g., metal detectors, harsher punishments, more detention resources, etc.). However, a culturally competent approach will start by listening to the students' stories, develop ways to build the school community, find creative ways to improve parental involvement, and create culturally appropriate interventions. Discipline may become part of this picture, but it cannot be a blanket approach that lacks flexibility. As school environments become more diverse, tailoring interventions to your specific student body is essential.

Social Work

Other accreditation bodies focused on similar concerns and goals. The Council on Social Work Education's (CSWE) 2008 standards emphasized diversity in its education policy (2.1.4). For them, "diversity" includes issues related to "age, class, color, culture, disability, ethnicity, gender, gender identity and expression, immigration status, political ideology, race, religion, sex, and sexual orientation." These may lead to issues of "oppression, poverty, marginalization, alienation, privilege, power, and acclaim." In learning to work with various cultures, CSWE also encourages its members to "view themselves as learners and engage those with whom they work as informants." Such procedures should also be integrated into the program's university, field placements, and clientele (3.1). Efforts to make this happen should be "continuous" and regularly "improved" (3.1.1).

Regular improvement is a key component to all multicultural competencies. Maintaining a program without changing anything is like having one technique. Programs should continually learn about new groups, community changes, political fluctuations, and feedback from others. Students play an important role in this process, and you can help your program adapt. If you are currently in a class, did the professor give you an early test to assess your multicultural competencies or awareness? Having pre/post tests provide important data; this can also help with accreditation. If you did not take a test like this, what information could you provide to your professor to convey your current knowledge, skills, and disposition? Some ideas might be writing down which cultural groups you have the most and least exposure to. Which culture do you believe you need to learn the most about as your go through this course and book?

School Psychology

The National Association of School Psychologists (NASP) also emphasized knowledge issues in its 2010 standards. It depicts diversity as a foundation for all services, and requires diversity-related mission and goals infused throughout the program (1.1). School psychologists are expected to have "knowledge of individual differences, abilities, disabilities, and other diverse characteristics; principles and research related to diversity factors for children, families, and schools, including factors related to culture, context, and individual and role differences; and evidence-based strategies to enhance services and address potential influences related to diversity." The standards emphasize several times the importance of "demonstrated skills" when working with diverse students, which means experience and knowledge are essential.

Unlike some of the other agencies, NASP also emphasizes the culture appearance (the final chapter of this book). They argue that their members must address diverse health issues such as diet, eating disorders, teenage pregnancy, AIDS prevention, and stress management. Although they do not list this as a cultural identity, we will address how it is.

Clinical and Counseling Psychology

The American Psychological Association (APA) took a slightly different tact for its 2009 standards. It requires doctoral graduate programs to engage "in actions that indicate respect for and understanding of cultural and individual diversity" (A.5). The notion of "action" is gaining importance in diversity literature. Rather than simply knowing about cultural differences, ethics and accreditation boards want to see results. The same level of action is true for the programs themselves. APA requires training programs to make "systematic, coherent, and long-term efforts to attract and retain students and faculty from differing ethnic, racial, and personal backgrounds into the program (D.1).

Counseling

The Council for Accreditation of Counseling and Education Related Programs (CACREP) updated its standards in 2009. Like the others, they also addressed knowledge, skills, and attitudes, but they specifically advocated understanding multicultural and pluralistic trends, characteristics among national and international groups, identity of self as a cultural being, multicultural theories, interventions for groups/families/communities, and methods of promoting cultural social justice/advocacy. These goals parallel the mission of this text. It starts with an understanding of self, moves to an understanding of cultural groups, and then encourages advocacy and social justice.

This latter element—the notion of social justice—is gaining importance. Even back in 1998, Lee (p. 9) argued that counselors are only change agents when they "possess the awareness, knowledge, and skill to intervene not only at an individual level but also at a system-wide level... . [A] social change agent challenges cultural, social, historical, or economic barriers that stifle optimal mental health and human development" (cited in Holcomb-McCoy, 2004).

Social justice in counseling does *not* entail telling clients they are living inappropriate lifestyles or encouraging clients to fight against the system.

One African American client relayed a story about this. A white friend asked her to join a rally against the Ku Klux Klan. The friend stated that it was her *duty* to fight against prejudice and discrimination. When my client turned her down, the friend became angry.

"How can you expect it to end if you won't stand up for what is right?" she asked.

The white woman did not really understand the KKK or how African Americans had been treated by them. Marching against them would have left my client in fear for her life and her family.

To change the system, knowledge comes before action. How have people been affected by injustice? How does this story relate to your own power and privilege? When you have a sense of this, you will start to see how some interventions—which may be appropriate for other clients—can be exploitive. For example, using directive, confrontational approaches to assess a rape victim feels like a second rape. Instead, find culturally relevant interventions. To reach this level of competence, students need a multicultural framework. One of the clearest and easiest to adopt models of multiculturalism and social just is D'Andrea and Daniels's (2001) RESPECTFUL model:

*R*eligious/spiritual identity

*E*conomic class background

*S*exual [and gender] identity

*P*sychological maturity

*E*thnic/racial identity

*C*hronological/developmental challenges

*T*raumatic experiences and other threats to one's well-being

*F*amily identity and history

*U*nique physical characteristics

*L*ocation of residence and language differences

The RESPECTFUL model operates from an assumption of human multidimensionality. The profession has long noticed how gender and ethnic backgrounds affect developing identities, but less emphasis has been placed on the other components in this model. Effective counselors will investigate each of these cultural facets and explore how they contribute to each client's identity. Probably the easiest of these to grasp is the notion of ethnic and racial identity. So, we will begin our specific cultural exploration by examining different ethnic groups.

As we explore these groups, keep in mind how trends and cultural traditions are basic guides and do not explain individuals. Just like assuming a tall person must play basketball, or a woman must want to be a mother, taking general trends and applying them to all people within that group is more harmful than simple ignorance. Instead, use the content of this book to help you start asking questions. Submerge yourself into different cultural groups. Try to identify how people might be similar or different from you. And, most importantly, realize that marginalized people of all cultures need advocates who believe in them.

PART II

Ethnic Populations

"Ethnicity" connotes a common culture and shared meaning. It includes feelings, thoughts, perceptions, expectations, and actions of a group resulting from shared historical experiences. Pedersen (2000) defined ethnicity as a cultural heritage that is preserved from one generation to another as a means of classification or identification. Ethnicity can include religious groups (e.g., Jews), country of origin (e.g., Africa), or any other facet passed down to children. Diversity even extends to our culture, which includes components such as our geographic community, religion, gender, sexual orientation, and socioeconomic status. Herskovits (1948) referred to culture as that part of our environment created by people. As such, it is not explicitly taught but rather absorbed through socialization and reinforced by lifelong incidental learning.

These varying definitions of diversity (summarized in the table below) make counseling an inherently multicultural process. A woman counseling a man, marital therapy with an interracial couple, a single man counseling a full-time mother, or virtually any other combination falls under the auspices of multiculturalism. However, attempting to understand all such possible groups would be impossible. Instead, we strive to develop an appreciation of cultural groups as a whole. Therapists—especially European American therapists—must learn as much as they can about minority worldviews because there will not be enough minority psychologists to fill the potential need.

Knowing about ethnic groups requires more than understanding stereo-typical behaviors. It requires therapists to put themselves into the lives of people from different cultures and ethnicities. We must learn to understand the culture from the inside out. How are people treated in school? What is the basis of their relationships? How does the dominant society treat them? As you read through the following chapters, try to imagine you are experiencing the information firsthand. Let yourself become angry, sad, or excited.

Examples of Terms Used to Indicate Identity

Term	Examples
Race	American Indian Black (African American) Pacific Islander (Asian) White Biracial
Ethnicity	Ancestry from a specific country or continent Membership in some social (ethnic) religious groups (e.g., Jewish)
Culture	Geographic community Religion Gender identity Sexual orientation Physical ability Weight Age Family Class (socioeconomic status)

CHAPTER 3

European Americans

INSIGHT EXERCISE[1]

All my life, I wanted to be a fireman. When I was young, I used to run around with the garden hose and put out pretend fires on the grass. I still have the junior fireman's badge I earned in third grade. It just seemed like the perfect life for me.

I am a fireman now, but I'm not sure I will ever make captain, as my father did. Maybe I should have been born 20 years ago. My skills would have been better appreciated. In 1993, I was told that I was not going to be promoted because 11 African American and four Latino candidates were scheduled to be promoted ahead of me. Now, they did not score higher on the exam. They were being promoted because there weren't enough minority captains in the Chicago Fire Department. I remember feeling stunned and thinking, "Surely this can't happen in America!"

I rallied with some of the other white candidates, and we took our case all the way to the Supreme Court. But on November 9, 1998, the Supreme Court refused to hear our appeal. No comment was offered. Our request was simply and quietly denied. I don't think I should be given anything just because I'm white but neither does it seem fair to punish me because my skin is light.

(continues)

Over-compensation to a fault.

---

[1] All insight exercises in this book have been generated by through the author's clinical work, interaction with various groups, and imagination. The stories are compilations of different people and do not depict a single person.

INSIGHT EXERCISE *(continued)*

Questions to Consider

1. Should we protect white employees from reverse discrimination or must we first allow minorities to obtain managerial positions in order to level the playing field?

2. Diversity adds multiple perspectives and experiences to a business. Should this be considered ahead of some other skills?

3. White people are often deemed better or more qualified for a job based on multiple-choice tests. Do these tests measure ability or are they just another way to discriminate against minorities?

UNIQUE CHALLENGES

European Americans are in a state of transition. As a group, they are less cohesive than in the past. They are less likely to participate in civic or religious activities than their parents or grandparents. They still receive considerable privilege but less than before, as affirmative action and globalization change the world economy.

As a group, European Americans are no longer the top performing college students (Asians are) and no longer dominate the world's richest people. More Latinos and Asian cultures are gaining power. European Americans may find all this very confusing. The dominant culture in America has been very productive over the last century, and it was mostly ruled by European Americans. Medicine, entertainment, and service industries are popping up in other cultures. More movies are being produced from India, Japan, Europe, and China. More products are coming from other countries. And minorities are running more businesses and gaining prominence in cooperate and political America. The influence of "white America" is fading, and this will require adaptation from European Americans.

HISTORICAL CONTEXT

A number of problems arise when discussing the cultural group commonly referred to as "white." Similar to Asians, Latinos, and other groups, white Americans are a diverse group whose origins may be Western European, Eastern European, Arab, Jewish, South American, Australian, or other nationalities. A total of 53 categories of ethnic groups are identified by the term *white*. With a group this diverse, any collective term is likely to lose the cultural distinctiveness of the various facets represented. Nevertheless, some terms are more accurate than others.

One of the terms used to identify white Americans is *Anglo-Saxon*. This term technically refers to a culture that began in fifth-century England.

It was during this time that the fragmented kingdoms of England united to fight the invading Germanic tribes. These events paved the way for the emergence of a common language (Old English), which is represented in such documents as the *Anglo-Saxon Chronicle* and *Beowulf*. Even the term "England" comes from the union of the Old English word "Engla" (Angles) and "land," meaning "land of the Angles." For obvious reasons, referring to all white Americans as Anglo or Anglo-Saxon could be considered offensive by those who are not of English descent. The term *Anglo American* should be reserved for those who speak English as a primary language and adhere to a cultural heritage that is primarily English in nature.

In this text, we use the term *European American* because it categorizes ancestry rather than skin color. Ancestry also has culture. However, not all white people have European roots, and even within Europe, some cultures would argue that they are unique and distinct. Many European nations are reluctant to view their culture as a conglomeration. The English, French, Italians, and others have long championed their culture's superiority over each other's, and some may feel slighted by being clustered together. These problems have led some to ignore their cultural history or skin color and simply view themselves as "American" (Waters, 1998). It is this latter impulse that often leaves European Americans confused about diversity training. They may say, "Why do we need all these terms? Why can't we all just be Americans?" The answer rests with the connection between European Americans and the dominant culture. They can call themselves "American" without any prefix because they wrongly believe that they have the same culture as an Asian American, African American, or Latino. European Americans find it easy to blend into a variety of settings because they are part of the dominant group, not necessarily because their culture is "American."

If the culture of European Americans differs from that of other groups, what constitutes European American culture? In answering this question, it is important to realize that European Americans have not been immune to persecution.

IMMIGRATION AND DEVELOPMENT

Prior to the Civil War, a great disparity began to appear between various groups of European immigrants. German workers were often recruited to come to America because of their fine craftsmanship. These workers included silversmiths, clockmakers, and other tradesmen who quickly found employment. However, during the same time period, the Irish often moved to America to escape poverty and famine. Many lacked professional skills and were forced to take the lowest-paying jobs available, working as ditch diggers, railroad laborers, or servants (McFadden, 1999). The economic successes or failures of first-generation immigrants were often passed down to members of succeeding generations, creating a hierarchy that would continue for more than a hundred years.

In 1820, 80% of the 9.2 million immigrants to America were of European descent. Scandinavians, English, French, Italians, Scots, Germans,

Poles, Czechs, and Dutch made their way to the New World, and each wave of immigrants brought something of their culture with them. As other cultures were assimilated into American society, a new pluralistic culture was created. The immigrants from Europe often belonged to the lower class in their homelands, but America provided them with opportunities to form a new identity. They proudly called themselves "Americans," but many found that the New World did not offer economic prosperity to all (McFadden, 1999).

What we sometimes fail to realize is how many European American immigrants struggle with the English language. For those who have emigrated from countries where other languages were spoken, there is often a sense of pride associated with mastering English (McFadden, 1999). However, the process of changing one's primary language often involves loss as well as triumph. The language of one's birth country is closely connected with one's memories and culture, and much of that culture is lost with the removal of the language from the family. Nora, an 88-year-old resident of a skilled care center, recalls:

> When I first entered the nursing home, I thought my family had deserted me. My son never came to visit, my husband had died, and I think my children just wanted me to leave the earth as well. I didn't realize how alone I felt until I heard someone speak German. The speaker was our new chaplain, who was born in Italy but spoke five languages fluently. He was quoting a line from a Friedrich Conrad Dietrich Wyneken sermon, and I could feel a tear in my eye after just one sentence. He must have seen me crying because he came over, put his arm around me and asked, "What's the matter?" I could only reply, "*Ich bin glücklich*" [I am happy]. He just smiled, and I felt my soul stir within me again. For a brief time, I thought it had left me.

Nora needed to hear her native tongue, even though English had been her primary language for most of her life. Something about the culture of her past—her heritage—helped her to feel alive again. Language is often an essential component of cultural identity and the development of the self.

CULTURAL IDENTITY

Beyond language, though, there is little that unifies European Americans in a cultural sense. Ting-Toomey et al. (2000) noted that European Americans have a weaker ethnic identity than members of other groups, but this is not to say that there are no ethnic remnants. To fully develop one's own ethnic identity, it is necessary to develop an understanding and appreciation of other cultures. Renshon (2005) notes that the Puritan work ethic—and Protestantism in general—still plays a role in the dominant culture, but patriotism is the "real glue" of American identity, and even this is being challenged by the rise of dual citizenships.

It may sound unfair to blend dominant American culture with European American identity, and, of course, it is. But there is little doubt that European Americans identify their identity with social dominance, and they are the only social group with this uncontested privilege. Americans of many ethnicities operate with an automatic, unconscious bias associating white culture with

American culture (Devos & Heng, 2009). This is likely to change in the coming decades, but it still true for now.

Miller and Josephs (2009) discuss white privilege as "pathological narcissism." They note how white, liberal, educated, upwardly mobile people often see themselves as above race and not defined by their culture or history. The problem with this is that it ignores the privilege they experience and may actually blind them of cultural needs of others. The authors make the analogy of confronting someone's white privilege with confronting the person about their defensive grandiosity. They are likely to feel attacked and respond with denials and counterattacks. I learned this lesson when teaching a multicultural counseling class.

I had asked the students to share about their prejudices. One European American woman described her painful childhood and the mistreatment she bore at the hands of several African Americans. She grew up poor, and her apartment complex had more African Americans than European Americans. The black kids taunted her, intimidated her, and otherwise made her childhood frightening. She ended by saying, "It took me a long time to get over this, but I can honestly say that I'm no longer prejudiced."

Following her disclosure, I felt something was off about her story. I could not quite understand why I felt so uncomfortable, and I kept looking around the room for clues. Without processing my thoughts, my gaze drifted to the only African American in the room. When our eyes met, I simply asked him, "Was it just me or did she make eye contact with everyone else in the room except you?"

As soon as I asked the question, the African American student's eyes lit up. "Ohhhhhhh, yeah," he said. "I noticed it."

The woman dropped the class the next day.

Helms (1990) argues that European Americans are likely to find themselves at one of six stages in a process of white identity development, as described in Table 3.1.

Out of all these stages, the movement to pseudo-independence seems the most difficult. Something must force the white individual to recognize that the world is not as it appears. This is the first step toward forming a nonracist identity, but it often comes with much pain. It is here that the individual may start to realize subtleties in his or her interaction with minorities (e.g., "I don't have a problem with blacks, but I was nervous when that dark-skinned man sat next to me at the restaurant").

If the individual can successfully make it through the pseudo-independence stage, then another, more subtle difficulty must be overcome. During immersion/emersion, the individual must come to realize his or her role in accepting or encouraging "white privilege." As shown in the following incident, privilege can take many forms. Jan, an African American speech instructor at a college, threw a party for her students. Most of the speech students were European Americans, but Jan also invited some of her African American colleagues. After discussing politics, religion, and school issues, the conversation turned to ethnicity. The African Americans began to talk about the difficulties of being on a white campus and having to fight for their freedom and independence. Marsha, a young European American student, attempted to jump into the discussion.

TABLE **3.1**
Helms's White Identity Model

Stage	Description
Contact	The white individual encounters one or more members of a minority ethnic group, especially African Americans, and forms an attitude about at least one of these people. Depending on the white individual's family history, the encounter could be viewed with trepidation or naïve curiosity. During this stage, the white individual is likely to view the condition of minority groups simplistically. Common statements may include, "I'm glad we can help the blacks with welfare money."
Disintegration	As the white individual continues to learn about the plight facing minority groups, a serious conflict develops. There is a conscious awareness that African and European Americans are not treated equally, and this new knowledge creates dissonance. The white individual wonders, "Why does this difference exist?"
Reintegration	In seeking answers to questions raised during the disintegration stage, the white individual will likely retreat into white culture. The dominant culture will create reasons for why minority groups are not entitled to share in the privileges bestowed on whites, such as the idea that blacks lack social, moral, or intellectual status, which is why their lives are more difficult. Many white Americans will remain in this stage indefinitely. It takes a jarring event or shock to transport them to the fourth stage.
Pseudo-Independence	If the white individual comes to a realization that members of minority groups are not innately inferior to whites, he or she is ready to build a healthy white identity. Events such as the civil rights movement could spawn such a change, but the process will not be easy. Whites in the reintegration stage may regard this individual as confused or traitorous. Blacks are likely to regard this individual with suspicion.
Immersion/Emersion	If the individual continues along the path of development, he or she may begin to discard the myths and stereotypes passed down through the dominant society. At this stage, there is an active attempt to participate in white consciousness groups and fight to create community or social change. Racist and prejudiced attitudes that have been repressed or denied are actively rejected, and the individual will want to help end the oppression caused by white culture and create more positive definitions of white identity.
Autonomy	In the final stage, which is ongoing throughout the remainder of life, the individual seeks to participate in minority events while not forsaking his or her cultural roots. There is an active appreciation of minority cultures as well as the dominant culture. This appreciation is combined with activism for equality and a resistance to racist forces in the white culture.

"Yeah, I know what you mean." Marsha's sincerity was obvious, but her light hair and blue eyes caused some of the African American faculty to smile.

"When I started here," she continued, "I never thought I would be accepted. It's like everyone expects you to have the right clothes, perfect hair, and expensive cars."

"Oh, you think you have it so hard?" Jan said to the European American student with an undercurrent of resentment in her voice. "You don't know the first thing about hardship."

Marsha, having grown up in abject poverty and attending college on an academic scholarship, felt cruelly attacked. She reacted fiercely, summarizing her life story and stating that her life was as difficult as it could be. The professor responded by saying, "no matter how difficult your life may have been, you have never been judged by the color of your skin. You have never watched people leave a store because you entered or realized that everyone in a restaurant was talking about you. You have only known one type of poverty, and as hard as it might have been for you, there are worse kinds to face."

More recently, cultural development has been addressed in terms of a consciousness or groupings of attitudes. Rowe (1994, 2006) created four types of attitude clusters: dominative, integrative, conflictive, and reactive. The dominative view emphasizes white superiority. The integrative perspective acknowledges whiteness and seeks to integrate with people of color. Conflictive believe in equality for all but fails to acknowledge institutional racism. Reactive is a pro-minority stance, but these individuals only intellectually stand against privilege and racism.

Rowe's approach might explain the identity process better, as movement from one attitude to the next is not linear and comes only through dissonance. But there is still the notion that "white" cultural groups are all the same. Some white groups understand racism and discrimination differently from others, and this should be built into an identity model. Because of this, I have designed the following model.

This model overcomes the linear nature of Helms's model and it also explains the ebb and flow movement between quadrants, as opposed to

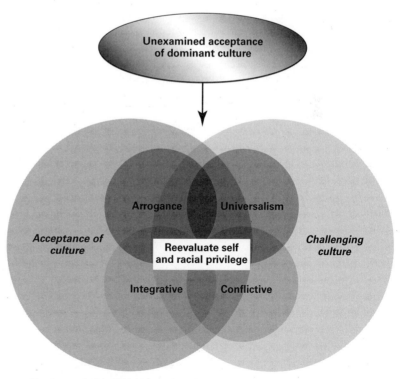

FIGURE **3.1** Cultural Identity Model: European Americans

Rowe, Behrens, and Leach's compartmentalization of typologies. This allows for unique development for individuals. But the heart of change will come with an evaluation of privilege and what it means to be "white" in a culture that rewards whiteness.

WITHIN GROUP DIFFERENCES

When I last traveled to Italy, my favorite city was Venice. The trip went perfectly, until we found ourselves lost. Worse, our tickets for the *vaporetti* (water bus) had expired, and we needed to catch our flight soon. We ran about for a few minutes before realizing that we would never make it in time without help. Someone in our group spotted a local man, and we ran to him.

"Can you tell us where the ticket office is," I asked.

The man shrugged and looked offended at the question.

We tried a few more words, like ticket office, water bus, and train. None of this resulted in anything but disdain from the local man.

"Biglietteria," said someone from our group.

With this one word (which means ticket office), the man's eyes opened. He became animated and friendly, babbling in Italian about where we needed to go. Thankfully, he also pointed and gestured. We found the office in just a few minutes.

European cultures share a similar ancestry, but each possesses a unique culture. Language will also play an important role in identity, and attempting to connect with someone else often requires attempting to understand their language and culture.

The effect of using Italian on our Venetian guide paled in comparison to an Italian woman I worked with in a nursing home. Her health had been deteriorating rapidly. We could not get her out of her room, and her physician thought she would die soon. All this changed when a new resident was admitted. He was German, but he spoke some Italian. Just speaking to someone in her native language saved her life. Her English was fine. She did not lack for simple conversation. She missed home. She missed someone who knew her culture. She missed family.

Even though Italians, Germans, French, and other nationalities often find it difficult to immigrate to America, they are still accepted into the dominant culture quickly. After all, the dominant culture is comprised of many European traditions.

English traditions strongly influence European American culture, but there are elements of English society that are not readily apparent in the dominant European American culture. For example, traditional European American psychotherapy focuses on an expression of affect and catharsis, but such practices may be unproductive with English clients. The English are likely to resist discussions of personal issues, viewing the airing of emotions as roughly equivalent to taking a bath in public. The discussion of emotions is even avoided within the confines of the home. Instead, there is an emphasis on external (e.g., political, religious, etc.) or community issues, which are considered safer topics.

Anglo Americans are apt to view any show of emotion as evidence of a lack of personal strength. In particular, showing aggression is a sign of weakness. Typically, the first person to show any sign of aggression is viewed as demonstrating a loss of control and poor planning. Such differences in culture have led to a number of conflicts between African Americans and Anglos. In many black cultures, showing emotion is an indication of passion and motivation. Neither side is apt to understand or appreciate the speaking style of the other.

The British are also more likely to emphasize speech over appearance. Being bounded by language and birth are more critical to earning respect than the color of one's skin. It is likely that a middle-class African American woman would be better accepted in England than a white male with a Cockney accent. Prior to the American civil rights initiatives, many African American entertainers preferred to live in Europe where they were respected for their abilities. In England—provided one had acceptable manners, speech, and skills—one was likely to be accepted. This is difficult for many non-Europeans to understand. A clear example came from an Irish friend, who said she could be randomly questioned in the streets or Northern Ireland and asked to say her alphabet. If she used the Catholic letter pronunciation versus the Protestant version, she could be beaten or killed.

The English preference for order and "right ways" of doing things has also been translated into manners. The English are likely to require a larger personal space than Americans. They will also downplay their power by putting their hands in their pockets, walking with small, quiet, subtle steps, and de-emphasizing showiness. A clear example between British and French culture involves table manners. The English traditionally train children to put their hands on their lap to show their restraint. The French trained children to keep their hands in view to ensure no treachery could be performed under the table.

The understated meekness of the British often makes the formation of friendships arduous. Although intimate friendships are likely to be more difficult to form, however, they are likely to last a lifetime.

The following dialogue depicts a clash between British and American cultures:

White American:	John! How are you doing? I haven't seen you for some time!
Englishman:	(understated) Things are fine. I've just been away for a few weeks.
White American:	Really, what have you been up to?
Englishman:	Oh (pause) … nothing really. I just had some issues with my family.
White American:	Oh, I hope everything is all right.
Englishman:	It will be for most but not for all. My mother died.
White American:	I'm very sorry to hear that. Were you close to her?

At this point, the conversation could go nowhere. By not volunteering information, the Englishman was making it clear that this was not a topic to be explored. He did not explicitly state, "I don't want to talk about this." It was simply supposed to be understood. The white American, unaware of this cultural element, probed for more information and potentially damaged the relationship.

However, the English are just as likely to misunderstand other European cultures. Throughout history, the English held the Italians and Australians in great disdain. After all, Australia was an open prison for the British Empire. As for the Italians, the English tended to regard them as uncouth and overexpressive. With this history firmly established, when Italians immigrated to the Americas during the nineteenth century, they faced strong prejudice from the Anglo community. The majority were unskilled, illiterate workers who were exploited by their employers. They coped by maintaining strong family ties and living in interdependent neighborhoods. Their Catholicism (more than 80% of Italian Americans consider themselves Catholic) also helped them maintain their cultural uniqueness and prevent absorption into the mainstream culture. These strong values guided them toward economic and educational success. This has changed over the last few decades, with Italian Americans now reaching the point where their college attendance is approximately the same as the rates for other European American groups (Axelson, 1999).

Polish Americans were also mostly unskilled when they came to America. They worked in the automobile factories of Detroit, the stockyards of Chicago, and the mines of Ohio. Their cultural values encouraged them to work hard at these jobs, and even today, many work at two places of employment (Axelson, 1999). They tend to value frugality, careful saving, and the wise use of financial resources. They are also likely to have strict household rules that children are expected to obey without question, and women are in charge of managing domestic matters. This family structure has led to a below-average crime rate among this cultural group. Polish Americans are also likely to face intense guilt and shame if resorting to divorce.

Irish Americans came from backgrounds similar to Polish Americans, but there were also differences between the two groups. Irish American women have traditionally dominated family life, defined their social life through their church, and enjoy more independence than women from other European American cultures. Although Irish American women might define their gender roles and social freedoms, in part, from their religion, Catholicism takes many forms. Portuguese Americans, who are also influenced by Catholicism, structure their household relationships differently. They tend to follow Latino cultural norms in which the husband is obeyed and the wife seeks virtue and purity. In a sense, culture interprets religion rather than the other way around.

FAMILY STRUCTURE AND DYNAMICS

In many ways, the treatment of European Americans as a group determines or at least predicts their functioning within subgroups, such as the family. For example, the role of physical discipline tends to differ between European Americans and members of other cultures, especially African Americans. Whaley (2000) reviewed the literature related to the developmental consequences of the use of physical discipline during childhood for European

Americans and African Americans. The use of physical discipline is associated with an increased incidence of disruptive disorders in children within European American families, but research on African American families found a negative association or none at all (Larzelere, 2000). Moreover, a review of the literature indicates that the positive association between spanking and children's behavioral problems is bidirectional for white families. This means that if a child is caught doing something wrong and spanked for that wrongdoing, he or she is more likely to increase the negative behavior, which will in turn result in more spankings.

Why would children from various ethnic groups respond differently to corporal punishment? In part, the difference may stem from what we have already revealed about the two groups. European American mothers place greater emphasis on socialization goals and child-rearing strategies consonant with a more individualistic orientation (Harwood, Schoelmerich, Schulze & Gonzalez, 1999). This individualism tends to emphasize competition, where success is viewed in comparison to others (Komarraju & Cokley, 2008). As such, European Americans are unlikely to benefit from punishments that restrict their freedom, while African Americans are likely to heed discipline designed to make their actions socially acceptable.

The need for autonomy is something that follows European Americans throughout their lives and is even a way parents communicate warmth (Jackson-Newsom, Buchanan & McDonald, 2008). The emphasis on independence creates a tenuous balance between family relationships and peer relationships, and it gives peers a greater influence in determining the individual's life goals. Paradoxically, autonomy means that as white children age, the parental influence on components of their development because less predictive (e.g., Friedman, Leaper & Bigler, 2007).

As European American children pull away from their parents, they often struggle with how to consider the relationship. This helps explain one 15-year-old girl's comments about her parents: "I'm happiest when they [my parents] just leave me alone. I'm old enough to take care of myself, and they don't get it."

In counseling, we explored how her parents could help her transition to independence. This included letting her work for measurable rewards based on accomplishments. For example, she could have a later curfew on weekends if she finished the week without any missing assignments and a 3.5 GPA. (Her high school posted all missing assignments and current grades on its website.) This resulted in greater independence but increased responsibilities for the teenager, but it also helped the parents feel connected, as they could keep tabs on their daughter's academic performance.

EDUCATION

Many European American cultures have a long history of valuing education. Overall, they still have the highest high school graduation rate of any ethnic group (90%), but they have fallen to a distant second for college graduation rates—Asians, 49.4%; non-Hispanic whites, 30.6%; African Americans,

17.6%; and Hispanics, 12.1%) (Bergman, 2005)—despite maintaining the highest GPAs of any group (Jaret & Reitzes, 2009).

The college question is particularly important because it addresses areas of privilege and prosperity. For example, we have learned that African Americans and Asians do better in predominantly white colleges when there are ethnic student organizations present to foster minority students' adjustment (Museus, 2008). This would imply that European American students would not need cultural training; they would simply blend into the dominant culture of the college. But white students are the least likely to feel connected to their college, just as they are the least likely to report having a clear ethnic identity (Jaret & Reitzes, 2009).

So, what inspires European Americans students to attend college? Are there cultural frameworks in place to direct them this way? Are teachers and counselors more likely to inspire white students over minority students?

Probably the simplest solution is economics. Kao and Tienda (1998) used data from the National Education Longitudinal Study of 1988 to analyze how educational aspirations are formed and maintained. After examining a nationally representative sample of 24,599 students from 1,052 randomly selected schools, their results suggest that the socioeconomic status of family members not only had an effect on the aspirations of eighth graders, but more importantly, it created higher aspirations that lasted throughout the high school years. The reason why Asian and European American families appear to maintain higher educational aspirations seems to be related to higher socioeconomic status.

This finding is not surprising in light of established educational models. Belsky's (Baharudin & Luster, 1998) model assumed that mothers with better education, higher intelligence, and greater self-esteem would nurture the same qualities in their children. Although this theory does not address ethnicity, the most supportive mothers have avoided financial crises and depression and had stable marriages (Waylen & Stewart-Brown, 2010). All these components are associated with higher socioeconomic status, which is also associated with European American ethnicity.

There is also some evidence that European American children are aware of their ethnic identity while they attend school. For many years, it was believed that European American school children were unlikely to be aware of ethnicity while attending predominantly white schools. However, Dutton, Singer, and Devlin (1998) disproved this theory. When using the Draw-A-Person test to examine the racial attitudes of fourth-graders, they found that children in nonintegrated schools were more likely to dislike children of other ethnicities. They also found that children—regardless of their ethnicity—who attended predominantly white schools produced drawings that depicted their ethnicity more obviously than did children from predominantly nonwhite schools.

Reay's (2008) study on white, middle-class schoolchildren revealed some fascinating findings. He looked at a small group of white London children whose families decided to leave them in inner-city schools. These children were outsiders to the culture of their neighborhoods, and this affected how they saw the world. Rather than the common middle-class view of only supporting welfare projects that could directly or indirectly affect the middle-class family, these families viewed diversity as positive. This view diverges from the common middle-class philosophy.

For example, Catherine—whose parents and grandparents attended a prestigious university—believed surrounding her child with working-class families could be harmful. She perceived schools with these types of children would be undisciplined and intolerant of her child. What Reay (2008) points out is a different reality. The white middle class has colonized into normativity. There is an assumption that whatever is middle class is good, just as—historically—whatever was whiteness was good. What needs to happen in a pluralistic, interactive society is the ability to hold on to positive aspirations—such as college—while still affirming other cultures and ways of life.

Learning to appreciate "other" cultures will also change what happens in the classroom. Mainstream white Americans are typically described as valuing independence, analytical thinking, objectivity, and accuracy (Boutte, 1999). These are the facets that have led to classroom experiences that focus on competition, acquisition of abstract information, objective tests, speed of completion, rigid structures, and linear logic. Typically, these are also the skills and learning styles that will be emphasized in European American work environments, which implies that learning these skills is essential to working in the "white" world. As such, the 20% of European Americans who fail to earn a high school degree (Huang & Oei, 1996) are at a disadvantage for lack of skills and failure to acculturate into the dominant occupational structure. We also know that academic autonomy is associated with psychological well-being (Van Ryzin, Gravely & Roseth, 2009). But we can still learn to appreciate other values, such as patience, cooperation, group identities, belonging, familial support, cultural identity, flexibility, calmness, and collaboration.

SOCIOECONOMICS

Think back to your elementary school. In many ways, that school predicted how successful you would become. Elementary schools cluster together around future college attendance, likelihood of lifelong peer support, family involvement in academics, and, of course, economics. Now, how much control did you have over the elementary school you attended? Probably not much. But that choice had a huge impact on your life. This is another example of privilege.

Socioeconomic status is predictive of physical health (Fuentes, Hart-Johnson & Green, 2007) and mental health (Gavin et al., 2010). Given the socioeconomic differences between European Americans and other cultures, it is not surprising to find differing attitudes toward income. In an interesting study, Chadiha, Veroff, and Leber (1998) asked African American and European American newlyweds to describe the meaning of their first year of marriage. This broad topic created a huge narrative, which was then analyzed. After controlling for the couple's education, household income, years of living together before marriage, premarital parental status, and length of the narrative, the authors found some important differences. European American newlyweds were more likely than their counterparts to emphasize achievement and work-related themes in their narratives. In contrast, African

American newlyweds were more likely to discuss relationship issues and religion.

Why is income so important to European Americans? The answer may involve access to certain privileges. In the African American section of this text, we discussed the erroneous stereotype that African American women were always stronger and less emotional than European American women. Such perceptions have become integrated into the occupational structure of American society. Wilson & McBrier (2005) noted that privilege gives European Americans a sense of entitlement at work. Minorities—especially African Americans—are channeled into racially delineated tracks, and European Americans are provided easier access to complex work and management. European Americans are also likely to see a higher return on their education and experience. Once people reach higher levels, it is more likely that European Americans with high levels of education and training will be promoted ahead of minorities. Such differences may help explain why income plays a role in European Americans' mental health. European Americans may come to expect "special" treatment, and when this treatment is not available, their mental health may suffer. African Americans may be more likely to accept mistreatment as part of life.

Ethnic privilege not only affects the quality of employment found, but it can determine whether an individual is hired. Cook and Jordan (1997) found that 37% of the households headed by single white mothers lived in poverty, whereas 55% of those headed by mothers of Hispanic origin were poor. From their study of nearly 100,000 workers, the difference was that disadvantaged Latina mothers had poorer English skills and they were less likely to be citizens. Clearly, citizenship and knowing the lingua franca would assist in finding employment, but the results of this study hint at a broader problem. When do factors associated with ethnicity interfere with the ability to find a job? Could having a Spanish accent or being dark-skinned hamper one's ability to gain employment? If so, such differences might explain why European American workers have a broader range of occupational interests in adulthood (Kaufman & McLean, 1996), but during childhood, ethnic minorities and European Americans have similar interest levels (Davison-Aviles & Spokane, 1999). As they start high school, minority students may begin to sense the reality of prejudice, which could cause them to abandon some of their previously held ideals. However, white students are free to continue reaching for their dreams. Such ambitions are largely rooted in the educational system.

SPIRITUALITY AND RELIGION

For example, the Puritan work ethic still permeates much of "white" culture. The Puritans believed that honest toil produced spiritual and material rewards. This belief led to two assumptions that continue to affect American society:

1. Hard work leads to material wealth.
2. Hard work builds character and is morally good.

Although such cultural beliefs have created wealth for many European Americans, this prosperity has also come at a price. The popular notion of "no pain, no gain" has left its mark on leisure-time recreation. Adventure travel—involving intense and sometimes grueling activities—is quickly becoming the vacation of choice for young European Americans. It provides the opportunity to work at a dude ranch, canoe on white-water rivers, climb a glacier, or risk life and limb in some other way. All these activities drain the body and give participants the "right" to relax.

The Puritan work ethic is deeply rooted in European American culture and can be traced to a variety of social and religious influences. Prior to the 1800s, about 62% of the U.S. population consisted of Congregationalists, Anglicans, and Presbyterians. About 14% were Dutch Reformed, Lutherans, German Reformed, Society of Friends (Quakers), Baptists, or Methodists. Nearly 23% were considered "unchurched slaves," and only 1.1% were Catholics (Axelson, 1999). The latter statistic implies that the Anglo influence was dominant early in the development of the European American culture. It is for this reason that the Puritan work ethic—which was based primarily on the Anglo religions, especially Calvinism—continues to influence upper-middle-class European Americans today. Although it is still influential, the Puritan work ethic has begun to fall from favor, in part because of the need to adapt to other cultural norms.

When working with European American religion clients, it is important to realize that religion plays a different role for this group than many other ethnicities. Religious white people are more likely to align their religion with their political views, especially when they belong to a tradition-based religion (Cohen et al., 2009). This association of religion with politics and general worldviews makes it important for counselors to gain religious competencies.

I often use religious metaphors in my counseling because it helps me connect with clients who operate from strong religious perspectives. However, I learned early how dangerous this process can be and how slowly I must assess each person's worldviews. With one client, he had recently married a woman who had a 12-year-old daughter. He did not get along with his new stepdaughter, and he was concerned that their lack of amenity would affect his young marriage. He wanted some skills to develop a way to appreciate her and sought counseling for this. He concluded, "I'm very religious, and I know this is what God would want for me. My pastor thought I should work with you."

Taking this cue, I asked, "God must have some special techniques for handling this type of thing. How do you think God handles people when we are adopted in His family?"

The moment I finished the sentence, I realized my mistake. He looked confused, and he finally said, "I'm not *adopted* into God's family."

I had failed to find out enough of his beliefs. He was a member of the Church of Latter-Day Saints. His religion believes God and his wife physically bear spirit children, which means all people are physically God's offspring. The metaphor for adoption not only felt flat, but it actually made it harder for him to relate to his daughter.

Although this cautionary tale is important, I provide it here to ensure counselors learn about religions and understand their clients' views thoroughly. I have used religious metaphors with hundreds of other clients, and this is the only negative story I have.

PHYSICAL AND MENTAL HEALTH

For all of the past century, European Americans fared better than other minorities in survival analyses. This was especially true against African Americans, where European Americans had a 17% better mortality rate, even after controlling for other influences (Sloan, Ayyagari, Salm & Grossman, 2010).

Physical Health

The reasons for European longevity are unclear. European American teenagers are more likely than African Americans or Latinos to start smoking (Gritz et al., 1998), and they tend to consume more cigarettes over the course of their lifetimes (Griesler & Kandel, 1998). However, their rates are in the middle of many other ethnic groups (higher than Asian Americans, equal to African Americans, and less likely to smoke than Native Americans) (Croghan et al., 2010).

However, the independence and autonomy dominating European American culture can negatively affect health too. Social support has been linked to better prognosis, strengthening of the immune system, and possibly longer survival for cancer patients, and white cancer patients appear to have less adequate social support networks than Latinos. Furthermore, African Americans are more willing to spend time with family members who are sick (Suinn, 1999).

Alcohol use can also affect various ethnic groups differently. One group of European Americans—the Irish—has often been stereotyped as being prone to use alcohol to excess. Greenslade, Pearson, and Madden (1995) traced the historical origins of these stereotypes and evaluated their accuracy. They found an interesting dichotomy. The Irish rates of abstinence were higher than those of the British. At the same time, rates of alcoholism in Ireland were higher than those among Jews and Italians. Why the dichotomy? It may be the purpose the alcohol serves. An old Irish proverb states, *An rud nach leigheasann im ná uisce beatha níl aon leigheas air* (What butter or whiskey does not cure cannot be cured). There is a social accommodation of drink within Irish culture, and it is often commonly accepted to drink to excess. It is also common for children to be introduced to alcohol by parents, older siblings, or friends—often at a family celebration or party. Once this process begins and becomes part of the social norm, it creates additional risk for gateway drugs (Van Hout, 2009).

Mental Health

Despite problems with cigarettes and alcohol, the greater threats to well-being are mental. The strictest elements of the Puritan work ethic involve self-denial. Hard work, productive leisure-time activities, and avoidance of personal pleasure are interwoven into European American culture. In order to achieve success through hard work, the physical self was downgraded to secondary consideration. Sometimes, this de-emphasis on physical pleasures results in the suppression of the sexual self. Such tendencies can result in sexual dysfunction, especially among middle-class European Americans (Axelson, 1999).

The rejection of the physical self and the guilt associated with personal pleasure may also be associated with the "white women's disorder": bulimia nervosa. Some studies have downplayed the psychological differences between European Americans and others with bulimia (e.g., Hoste, Hewell & le Grange, 2007). But there is one difference that appears to make the disorder harder for European men and women. Obesity is not the best predictor of the severity of eating disorders among European American clients. Fitzgibbon et al. (1998) examined 351 women (55 European American, 179 African American, and 117 Latina) for factors associated with binge eating. Across all ethnic groups, women who binged more were heavier and more depressed, and they idealized a slimmer body build. However, binge-eating severity was most accurately predicted by the presence of depression and shame in European Americans. These findings have been echoed by others who believe oversensitivity to criticism (Hoste & le Grange, 2008). There does not appear to be significant differences between the criticism of parents in these issues, but it would make sense that whites and other minorities would receive different levels of criticism from society. White people do not get many angry or denigrating looks when walking into stores or in nice neighborhoods. Minorities have learned to handle social criticisms better.

Privilege also extends to how people use mental health services. There is some evidence that European American utilize services more regularly than their peers, even though they have no greater need for mental health interventions (Youman, Drapalski, Stuewig et al., 2010). This may be due to better health insurance, easier transportation, or other socioeconomic factors. It could also be that European Americans are more comfortable with their physicians, as most are white. The study by Youman et al. was also interesting because it looked at how often people from different ethnicities requested services when in jail. The jail setting removed social and financial obstacles, and there was no difference between ethnic groups' requests for mental health services.

Although eating disorders can lead to death, they are not intended as suicidal acts. The anorexic does not wish to die; she wants to maintain control of her life. However, there are unique signs of suicidality among European Americans. Kung, Liu, and Juon (1998) compared the lifestyles of European Americans who died of natural causes and those who committed suicide. Their study revealed that suicidal European Americans were more likely to have a high school education, to work in blue-collar jobs, and to have used mental health services. Of these findings, the latter is the most disconcerting. It implies that European Americans attend therapy when they feel depressed, but therapy does not renew their sense of hope. More recent studies imply that whites (but not blacks) are more likely to attempt suicide when socioeconomic factors are affected, such as poverty, inequality, joblessness, and family disruption (Kubrin & Wadsworth, 2009).

INDIVIDUAL AND GROUP INTERVENTIONS

If the physical and mental health of European Americans are more affected by criticism and hardship, it makes sense why the theoretical interventions designed by white counselors and psychologists emphasize coping skills, self-esteem, and gaining insight. After all, each of the traditions spawned by psychoanalysis, behaviorism, and humanistic existentialism was created by European Americans and practiced by white middle-class therapists. As such, most counselors are likely to feel well-trained to intervene with troubled European American clients. However, there are important cultural considerations unique to this group.

Shame and guilt are especially important for European American clients. Thandeka (1999) defined "white shame" as the conscious experience of feeling indelibly flawed because one is not meeting the expectations of a cultural community. Thandeka argues that this state includes feeling too sinful, bad, or unproductive to be loved for oneself. Lewis et al. (2010) add that white Americans are more likely to feel shame because they operate from an I-self mentality versus the we-self of Eastern culture.

Feelings of unworthiness may lead children to seek group support and attempt to bury the feelings deep within themselves. Seen in this context, shame becomes a social event; the environment fails to provide the message that the individual is intrinsically lovable.

For European Americans, shame experiences conform to a dyadic structure of actor and audience. This is the Shakespearean figure who wrestles with the horror of having followed a path he knows to be wrong. He is not held guilty by anyone except God and himself, but he believes that all observers can see the shame in his heart.

This sense of unworthiness can be seen in the anorexic who strives for physical or academic perfection but knows that she will fall short. It is apparent in the depressed middle-aged man who is unable to accept the fact that he will not reach the lofty ambitions of his youth. For nearly all European American clients, shame propels them into some actions and prohibits them from others. Consider the case of Tom, who was struggling to overcome a compulsion to expose his genitals to children.

> I don't know how to stop it. It's like something just comes over me and forces me to do this. I think there is something biologically wrong with me. Could that be the case? I know I don't have control over it. I don't seem to have much control over anything in my life. I can't handle my work, my family is out of control, and I know it's because of this one problem.

Shame played a fundamental role in Tom's recovery. He needed to learn that his exhibitionism increased when he felt he could not control his environment. When he had a fight with his wife, an argument with his boss, or lost an important sale, his shame increased, and he felt completely unworthy. When he reached this low point, his desire to expose himself increased. Perhaps he felt "I can't do anything else right, so I might as well give in to these other bad feelings."

After facing his insecurities and accepting his weaknesses, Tom learned how feelings of failure and inadequacy triggered his fears and created out-of-control impulses. The more content he became, the less he desired exhibitionism. In a way, Tom's success had more to do with gaining personal insight than changing his behavior. When he attempted to change his exhibitionism directly, he found himself overwhelmed by the impulses. When he focused on accepting himself and keeping himself busy with healthy activities, his exhibitionism no longer controlled him. Similar processes have been effective for European Americans struggling with other compulsive disorders. They come to therapy seeking help with a given problem. They usually report feeling overwhelmed and out of control, but they fail to realize how their feelings reinforce their compulsion. In most cases, they feel intensely guilty whenever they have a compulsive thought. When they acknowledge the thought, they become guiltier. When they feel guilty, they feel like bad people. As bad people, nothing prevents them from acting out in negative ways. Picture a man coming to therapy for the compulsive use of pornography. He is likely to express an uncontrollable urge to purchase pornographic material and believes he is too weak to act otherwise. In a very real way, such a person is usually addicted to guilt at least as much as pornography. If he learns to purchase pornography without feeling guilty, his compulsion will likely decrease. If he can replace the time he spends viewing pornography with other more productive tasks, his mental health will likely increase further.

ADVOCACY AND SOCIAL JUSTICE

Advocacy and social justice are different for European American clients than any other. Being a member of the dominant society brings with it certain responsibilities, and it is important for white clients to realize that being part of an oppressive group harms them as well as the victims. As we will later explore in feminist therapy, when one person blindly experiences privilege, that individual views the world from a biased viewpoint. If an individual believes herself superior because she worked hard to get everything she has and denigrates others for being less successful, the person's view of self is skewed.

As people begin to realize that their success may have come on the backs of less fortunate individuals, shame may arise. This is counterproductive. Parker and Schwartz (2002) noted that individuals are often unable to cope and view themselves as objects of scorn when overcome by shame. When this happens, they are often unable to empathize with the needs of others, magnifying the problem.

Rather than create shame-ridden anxiety, social justice can come when individuals examine their actions and accept guilt for their participation in the problem. Guilt is a more external way of experiencing responsibility (Parker & Schwartz, 2002), and it is also more productive. Ponterotto (1988) asserts that undergoing healthy white identity is likely to produce guilty feelings. Even students can realize—as they naïvely accepted the white-only theories of counseling—that they themselves fostered racism in the counseling profession.

To create advocates, it is important to balance anxiety generated with self-acceptance and hope. And as Jun (2010) notes, the goal of social justice is to create an environment where people are accepted and their cultural beliefs, values, and traditions are understood. Exercises may help with this.

Often, European Americans define their identities through words or logical constructs. This is what makes it so difficult to see themselves as ethnic beings and, worse, part of an ethnic group that experiences privilege on the backs of others. To help them understand without falling into greater shame, they will need to try some nonverbal exercises. As we will discuss in many other chapters, narrative techniques work well with multicultural interventions because they operate from a constructivist standpoint. For example, have someone draw a narrative. It could be an image of his or her family culture or how he or she believes he or she fits into the world. The latter could produce power images (e.g., someone standing on top of a globe, holding a flag, or otherwise being superior to others). Such images can provide insight into how privilege affects their identities.

Another way to break through cultural ignorance is to have someone role-play people from different ethnic groups. Have them stand and strike a pose that represents their ethnicity. It may take a few seconds before this makes any sense to them. Then, have them do the same thing for other ethnicities (e.g., Asian, Latino, Native American). Notice subtle changes in the posture. Does one look more aggressive, weaker, humbler, etc.? Discuss what these small movements might mean to the individual.

It is also important to realize that just because European Americans are part of the dominant culture does not eliminate them from facing discrimination themselves. When minority therapists attempt to help European American clients, they need to realize that European Americans are more likely to encounter discrimination and criticism than in the past. Clients are more likely to reach their therapeutic goals when their therapist acknowledges injustice and provides ways to cope with discrimination. I have attended conferences where "experts" said there was no such thing as racism against whites. From their viewpoint, only the dominant group can be racist, and acts against this group are justified. I do not accept this viewpoint. It harkens me back to elementary school, where we learned that two wrongs do not make a right. True multicultural advocacy will fight for equal justice. This *will* mean hiring a minority candidate over a similarly qualified white client. We must strive for diversity. An all-white graduate program might consider admitting an African American student with a 2.8 GPA over a 4.0 white student. If the program has no other diversity representation, the program would likely benefit more from the inclusion of the minority member than someone similar to their other candidates. We cannot advocate policies where preferential treatment is always given to minorities, but we must look for individual situations where diversity matters more than other considerations.

In John's story below, the discrimination suffered was genuine. However, he was also ignorant of his white privilege. Had his therapist slighted his experience, it is unlikely John would have continued in therapy. Instead, he probably would have become skeptical of minority therapists.

John's Story (A Client's Viewpoint)

(31-year-old European American male)

Okay, I admit it. When I was in college, I didn't have a clue what it meant to be "white." I just thought the world was a treasure chest waiting for anyone to uncover its secrets. I honestly felt people from all ethnic groups had the same opportunities.

It wasn't until my senior year of college that reality struck me. A friend of mine was applying for a mortgage loan. My friend happened to be black, and the bank turned him down flat. He had much better credentials than anyone else in my class, and the rejected loan scared me to death. I pictured myself living in a tiny dorm room for the rest of my life after investing so much time and money into my education.

I decided to conduct an experiment, and I applied for the same loan. Sure enough, the bank approved my application. I didn't have the heart to tell my friend.

This is not to say that being white is always favorable. In fact, my first job out of college was a disaster (the bank would have been wiser accepting my friend's application!). It was at a small but prestigious university in a culturally varied department. Personally, the diversity of the group excited me because it seemed to add depth to our global strategy. Even when I learned that I was the only white faculty member, I never thought twice about the consequences.

Yep, you guessed it. Less than five weeks into the semester, I was asked to leave the department because we were a "poor fit" for each other. To this day, I have no doubt that the "poor fit" was the color of my skin (they hired an African American male to take my place). The experience devastated me. I sought counseling under a minority therapist and asked her point-blank if she thought I was a racist. She just smiled warmly and said, "You've been hurt, and you're trying to grow. Why don't we start from there?" She was absolutely right—that's where we needed to start.

I often wonder how many times minorities get the "poor fit" talk when they honestly don't deserve it. I'm sure it is more often than white employees hear it. In a way, that's why I'm here today. I've been dating a black woman: Lenice. We've been doing well, and it's getting serious, but I'm wondering if we can really marry. Her family is from Georgia. Mine is from Huntington Beach. She listens to rap. I listen to classical. She likes spicy foods. I like rich foods. We're different from about every way people can differ. Oh, and religion. That's a biggie. She attends a black Baptist church. I grew up Christian, but I'm agnostic. I'm having a very hard time accepting her beliefs, and they are very important to her.

What should I do?

Chikae's Story (A Counselor's Viewpoint)
(44-year-old African American male)

John started therapy wanting advice about his girlfriend. He seemed to think that I, being black, would have the answers he needed. We confronted this very early in the process. In our first session, I asked, "What do you think makes me an expert on Lenice?" He looked surprised by the question, then stared at the ground, as if thinking, *You're black and so is she.*

Instead of providing him answers, we took another path. After completing the assessment process, we talked about the discrimination he faced and how he was a "poor fit" for his previous university." We discussed whether he deserved to feel "different" and "judged" and how he processed these feelings.

Even after ten years as a therapist, I still get angry when I work with clients like John. I want to guide him through his process and help him realize how he accepted benefits from a prejudiced society without ever thinking about what that meant for the rest of us. But I never say these things. They wouldn't be ready to hear it. Instead, I take their hand and walk with them through the learning process.

"I want you to try something," I asked John after we talked about his family. "Would you stand up for me?"

John jumped to his feet. Literally. He was having a hard time seeing the seriousness of what we were doing.

"Okay." I stood too, and I remained about three feet from him. "Close your eyes and imagine something magically had just transformed your life. You were born in Georgia. Can you picture it? What does this mean? How it would change your identity?"

John nodded.

"Imagine you are walking the streets of Georgia, but more has changed." I waited to let the words sink into him. His eyes shut tighter, focusing inside on the task. "You smell collard greens mixed with cabbage and cooked in African herbs. Let your mouth water as you think about it."

I paused again until he swallowed. "You pass a black Baptist church, and you hear the choir. It calls to you, drawing you in; you literally feel it tug against your heart."

I waited one more minute—until he swayed a little from the music in his head.

"Now imagine you're looking down at your body, and you realize that you are wearing a light cotton blouse, black skirt, and you have breasts. You are a woman. You are Lenice. Let this feel perfectly natural. As you do, imagine you see John, yourself, walking toward you. Let yourself feel what Lenice would feel."

(continues)

Chikae's Story (A Counselor's Viewpoint) (continued)

When the exercise ended, we processed what it was like to "be" Lenice. He realized how hard it was to experience some things (like wearing a skirt or being from Georgia) and how easy it was for others (like enjoying the choir and tasting the collard greens). I deliberately left out having him think of himself as black because I wanted him to realize that everything about her contributed to her culture and ethnicity.

He demonstrated some great insights when he "was' Lenice and pictured himself walking toward "her." He thought, *I'm in love, but he might be too different from me.* He also imagined "himself" walking right by without noticing "her." He realized Lenice's love was stronger than his own.

This exercise inspired him to visit Georgia with Lenice. He needed to understand her better if he intended to blend their lives. In future sessions, we also addressed his unexamined prejudices and microaggressions he had toward Lenice's friends. By the end of counseling, he was aware of his cultural identity, took responsibility for his racism, and worked to improve himself by joining different cultural groups. He made considerable progress over four months.

QUESTIONS TO CONSIDER

1. Why do we need so many terms to describe various American ethnic groups? What is wrong with everyone just being American?
2. Why would children from various ethnic groups respond differently to corporal punishment?
3. One study suggests that income plays a significantly larger role in the mental health of European Americans than it does for minority groups. Why is this the case?
4. Are European Americans who fail to graduate from high school likely to experience greater disadvantage than those from other cultures?
5. Far from the stereotypical image of the Irish embodied in the ubiquitous drunk male laborer, rates of abstinence from alcohol are higher in Ireland than in England. Why does the stereotype continue?
6. Helms (1984, 1995) argues that European Americans are likely find themselves following a six-stage process of racial development: contact, disintegration, reintegration, pseudo-independence, immersion/emersion, and autonomy. Of all these stages, the movement to pseudo-independence seems the most difficult. Do you know people who seem to be "stuck" at a particular stage? What might need to happen before they move to the next level?
7. Eating disorders may be more prevalent among European American women because of the pressure they feel to be attractive. Why do these pressures seem to be greater for European American women than minority women?

8. British culture is the foundation to European American culture, but there are elements of English society that are not shared by the dominant European American culture. What are the more salient differences?

9. For European Americans, feelings of shame typically involve a dyadic structure of actor and audience. This is the Shakespearean figure who wrestles with the horror of having followed a path he knows to be wrong. He is not held guilty by anyone except God and himself, but all who observe (or so he believes) can see the shame in his heart. How might this orientation interfere with mental well-being?

10. When would it be important or useful to involve interventions beyond "talk therapy" with European American clients?

11. How does the Puritan work ethic contribute to European American culture and the dominant culture as a whole? How would you work with someone who operated from this worldview?

INTERVENTION EXERCISES

Counseling and therapy: Matthew is a 24-year-old European American male who believes he needs to make a million dollars before he turns 30 to earn his parents' (especially his father's) respect. His family has three generations of wealth builders, with each generation slowly adding to the portfolio of the last. Although Mathew believes his current real estate options will produce wealth, he is starting to feel panicked that he will fail. His fears are so great that he recently contemplated suicide and said he "didn't know what" he "would do" if his acquisition of a major beach front property failed. How would you intervene?

School psychology: Michelle (European American female, age 16) is preparing for the SAT. She asked you for an assessment to provide accommodations because she believes she needs to take the test on a computer because of her "unique vision issues," receive extra time with breaks because of her AD/HD, and take the test alone because her auditory processing issues affect how she reacts to noise of any kind. Michelle has a 3.92 GPA, is an honor student, and has no history of special education. Her file does not indicate any learning ability or any previous psychological assessment. How would you handle her request?

School counseling: John (European American male, age 10) is participating in a school counseling lunch group entitled "Team Building." The group was designed for middle school boys who have histories of bullying or other forms of social dominance. Darnell is the only African American in the group. During the first meeting—before any rules or guidelines are introduced—one of the white boys stands in the middle of the circle and says, "I'm king of the group—all you niggers and trailer trash bow." How do you handle the conflict?

Social work: Alice (European American female, age 9) comes to class with bruises on her arm. After a closer inspection, you realize there are multiple shades of bruises, and they appear to span a period of several weeks. When you ask what happened, she looked terrified and says, "I wrestle with my brother too much. He just grabs my arm when we play." She looks away and then meets your gaze again. "Really?" The panic on her face grows. "You know, my dad's a state congressman... ." Her voice trails off. "Can I go back to class?" Do you make the report? Would her father's position affect your decision?

CHAPTER 4

African Americans

(Story compiled from several African American clients and friends)

Being African American is like being on stage. When I walk down the streets of Seattle, I have to wear my happy mask. I'll never go to breakfast in sweats or without ensuring my hair looks good. Those luxuries, like negative feelings, are reserved for white people.

No, I have to look like I fit in. I have to smile at everyone. Laugh whenever I can. I have to make white people feel comfortable.

You'd think I'd be used to it by now. I'm 47. But a rage still bubbles within me when a clerk follows me around a store or two women stare in my direction, only to whisper something behind their hands. I always make eye contact back. I always nod toward the offenders. I smother the rage.

Rage has become a part of me. Like kindness, thoughtfulness, or intelligence. But the others I was born with; my rage is a product of injustice.

What pisses me off is how I can't even show it. When two older white ladies followed me with their eyes at Nordstrom's, I would have loved to have walked up and said, "What you bitches want? Want some of this?"

God, I'd love to do that.

But I know what would happen. I'd be removed from the store. Not just for one day—but permanently. The police would be called, and they might even find a reason to lock me up. It happened to a friend.

(continues)

68

INSIGHT EXERCISE *(continued)*

So, I put on my happy mask. I walked over to the ladies and asked them if they needed help carrying their shopping bags. They both looked like they had survived a gang shooting. No doubt, they told all their friends at Bridge Club how they barely escaped Nordstrom's with their lives.

Questions to Consider:

1. How common do you believe "smothered rage" is for minorities?

2. How often do you think events like this happen within your family, school, job, or neighborhood? Are you aware of the prejudices in yourself and those around you?

UNIQUE CHALLENGES

Before defining the challenges to African Americans, the term itself requires defining. Does the term primarily describe Africans arriving in America (i.e., recent immigrants) or multigenerational Americans of black descent? In this text, the term describes both. After generations in America, African Americans who date their ancestry back to slavery possess a unique culture. Slavery still defines African American culture, and this historical underpinning must be understood. Immigrants coming from Africa also bring unique cultural elements. Both are interwoven into the framework of African Americans, and both must be understood to grasp the challenges for this diverse group.

In the last decade, the United States surpassed the 1 million mark for foreign-born African people living in the United States (Grieco, 2004). This means that about 3% of the total foreign-born population comes from Africa. Most of these people come from Western Africa, but there are more than 100,000 total from Nigeria and Egypt. This is a current trend, with half of the African immigrants in America being recent arrivals. Africans come for economic opportunities, to escape oppression, for better health care, to improve their education, and to provide financial support to family remaining in their home countries.

When in America, African immigrants must overcome microaggressions and unexamined prejudice. Recently, Sue (2009) commented how some immigrants come to the United States with an intact racial identity. When they encounter racial comments or other discriminatory behaviors, they may not notice them. This is not the case for multigenerational African Americans, who are very aware of microaggressions. This difference—as well as other cultural differences—often makes it hard for recent immigrants to identify with African American culture (Wamwara-Mbugua, Cornwell & Boller, 2008).

Second-generation immigrants also face unique challenges. Unlike their parents—who come with a clear cultural identity—children born to immigrants often lose the ability to speak their native language. They do not fully understand all the traditions and cultural aspects of their heritage, and they do not fully identify with African American culture. As such, these immigrant children face unique challenges and will require special interventions.

A primary consideration for counselors and educators relates to helping immigrants handle the loss of their native culture (Obiakor & Afoláyan, 2007). Obiakor and Afoláyan (2007) argue that multicultural strategies (e.g., infusing native linguistic and cultural identities into instructional techniques) enhance academic achievements. To succeed at this, they recommend practitioners and teachers do the following (Brammer, 2010):

- **Encourage parental involvement:** African cultures are family and tribal centric. Involving parents in the lives of their children reinforces cultural continuity (Nwoye, 2006).
- **Recognize age-appropriate cultural expectations:** In most parts of Africa, children are instructed rather than disciplined. There is no expectation on children before they are taught, so there is no need to discipline them for not understanding. When children are informed what to do, it is usually an activity related to the family or tribe. Adulthood is an opportunity to contribute rather than escape a family or tribe (Jenkins, 2007).
- **Understand responses to school success:** Schools become a social group for African children. When the system accepts the immigrant's cultural identity, immigrants are more likely to bridge the two worlds.
- **Explore trauma and PTSD issues:** Immigrants and refugees face unique challenges to their identity and overcoming the effects of trauma. African refugees are most likely to come from sub-Saharan African areas, such as the Republic of Congo, Somalia, and the Sudan, which have undergone decades of war (Warriner, 2008). About 28% of refugees coming to the states arrive from Africa (Grieco, 2004).
- **Avoid unnecessary acculturation of immigrant children:** Seeing the African culture through Western eyes is likely to create cultural discontinuity or conformity (Obeng, 2007).

Although all these challenges are important and require additional discussion, African Americans face one challenge beyond most other groups. The color of their skin differentiates them from the dominant white culture more than any other group. This fundamental difference makes them a target for prejudice and discrimination, which must be understood within the context of this nation's history.

HISTORICAL CONTEXT

The 1976 publication of Alex Haley's *Roots* gave the world a frightening glimpse into the life of the African American slave. The story of Kunta Kinte was filled with graphic depictions of men and women being stolen from their homes, shipped to America in chains as human cargo languishing in urine-, vomit-, and feces-filled chambers below the decks of slave vessels, and forced into slavery. African men and women were chained, branded, separated from their families, separated from their tribes, raped, and forbidden to speak their own languages. Teaching slaves to read and write was punishable by imprisonment, and European Americans forming relationships with slaves almost always led to harassment or death for both parties.

Much of the violence perpetrated against the African American slaves of long ago still festers in our society today. The story of James Byrd, Jr. testifies to the ongoing influence of racism. Byrd, a 49-year-old African American from Jasper, Texas, was walking down a dusty highway during the summer of 1998. As he walked, three young white men drove their pickup past him. He apparently asked for or was offered a ride. They drove to a remote spot in the pine forest outside Jasper. Soon thereafter, an altercation occurred. Only three people will ever know exactly what took place, and even if the events of that day could be known, few would want to know. We do know that Byrd's body was found the following Sunday. His head and other body parts were strewn across a country road ten miles from his home. Each part took some time to discover. His head was eventually found a mile away from the rest of his body. It is believed that Byrd was tied to the back of the truck and forced to run behind it as the vehicle accelerated. When he could no longer keep pace, the driver allowed his body to be dragged along the road. All three men received the death penalty for their crime.

Stories like Byrd's are so horrific that they may cause us to overlook the more subtle and pervasive forms of racism, hate, and discrimination. These softer forms of racism create a collective impact far more damaging than individual hate crimes. They occur daily, affecting the very fabric of society. Most people are not even aware of the ways they discriminate against people.

African Americans experience prejudice more directly than many other groups. The very perpetuation of the common African American stereotypes can damage the African American psyche. An imagined sense of inferiority has become common for many African Americans. In the 1940s, when America faced the possibility of integrating African American and European American school children, those in favor of desegregation needed evidence demonstrating that black schools harmed African Americans. After a long search, they found K. B. Clark and M. K. Clark (1947), who were conducting research on children's racial attitudes. The researchers presented European American and African American school-aged children with two dolls: one dark-skinned and the other light-skinned. The children were asked questions such as, "Which is the smart doll?" "Which is the pretty doll?" and "Which is the bad doll?" Both African Americans and European Americans identified the dark-skinned doll as bad and ugly and the light-skinned doll as smart and pretty. Many of the questions in this study elicited intense emotional responses from the young participants. For example, one young girl, when asked to identify the "bad" doll, attempted to refuse. After some time, she lowered her head, wept, and silently pointed to the dark-skinned doll.

The targets of racism and discrimination are not only dolls but living human beings. As African American children grow up, many tend to project negative impressions of their own ethnic group on each other. Some African American children use derogatory statements such as, "You're darker than charcoal" to insult one another, and they learn to view light skin as evidence of intelligence, morality, and success. This negativity is pervasive and shared by many other ethnic groups. For example, when examining how kids handle self-attributions, Graham, Bellmore, Nishina, and Juvonen (2009) studied 1,105 sixth graders over the course of a school year. The kids were evaluated for harassment, depression, and self-worth. They found a meditational relationship between self-blame victimization and maladjustment for white children. However, victimization did not predict self-blame. African American and Latino children being victimized in the fall predicted spring self-blame, which predicted spring maladjustment. Something about being a victim in a prejudicial society appears to create forms of maladjustment from an early age in African Americans' lives. Such patterns reinforce the importance of understanding how immigrants are treated. Do they experience the same types of discrimination as multigenerational blacks?

WITHIN GROUP DIFFERENCES

African Americans may trace their lineage through any number of African countries. When lineages from the West Indies and the Caribbean are included, African Americans comprise about 13% of the U.S. population (Aizenman, 2008). In addition to these differences, some received added cultural influences when they migrated through Latin America or Europe or when they endured enslavement. "African descent" describes people beyond those who have dark skin, broad noses, and full lips. There are hundreds—if not thousands—of ethnicities that make up black Africa as well as a wide spectrum of languages and religions. Some black North Africans have dark skin, blond hair, and blue eyes. These differences are only the beginning of the diversity among black people. Jamaicans are different from Trinidadians, who are different from South American blacks, who are different from West African blacks, who are different from Egyptians, who are different from Tanzanians, and so on. Differences among peoples of African descent are evident in part because of the wide variety of paths they have taken to the United States.

For example, in the Caribbean, there is a unique group of African descendants who constructed their own dialect—a form of Creole English. In recent years, the Creole spoken by past generations has been transformed into newer variants of English. British Black English, also known as a patois, is a modified version of Creole. Its use is often associated with Rastafarianism (a variant of the Ethiopian Orthodox Christian faith using the Holy Piby as its sacred text) and reggae. Although speakers sometimes call it Jamaican, it is different from Jamaican Creole.

Despite all these group variants, the most striking difference exists between the descendants of slaves and more recent immigrants. Nobles (2006) asserted that slavery transmitted European cultural ideals into African families. He described this process as an African American family being like a tree that must sustain itself from the soil around it. What the tree produces is a direct result of what it brings in from the surrounding environment. It "has been transplanted and that the root of this plant is without question African. As a consequence of the transplantation, the fruit reflects the ecological nourishment offered by the new host culture or environment" (p. 141). Research on violence and abuse has consistently demonstrated a pattern of the oppressors' behavior being passed to the victim (Jun, 2010). The victim can hate the oppressor, understand the harm associated with the actions, and still repeat the action.

Franklin (1998) argues this point candidly by claiming that African American culture and family structure was transformed by the northern migration, welfare, systematic underemployment, neighborhood segregation, poverty, and slavery. Generations of socially accepted discrimination transformed black culture, and this created substantial differences between descendents of African American slaves and recent African immigrants.

Differences Between Multigenerational African Americans and Recent African Immigrants

Durodoye and Coker (2008) provide a case study of an African American woman (Jannelle) who is a married to a Nigerian man (Shola). They use this relationship to point out key differences between multigenerational African American and recent African immigrants. The most salient differences were the following:

1. **Acculturation:** When Shola first arrived in the United States, he attempted to assimilate to American culture. Over time, he rejected part of white culture and reintegrated part of his Nigerian heritage into this lifestyle. His mother also came to live with them in America, which reinstalled the importance of traditional values in the home. When he dated Jannelle, the couple acted like any acculturated would. Shola now feels caught between worlds/cultures, and Jannelle wonders if she ever knew the man she married.

2. **Financial management:** Nigerian culture requires families to financially support one another. In this case, Shola still sends money to Nigeria, even though his mother in living with them in America. Jannelle becomes frustrated because their own finances are suffering. Shola cannot explain the need to care for his extended family or why he feels guilty living with more money than anyone in his tribe.

3. **Private vs. public life:** Jannelle grew up valuing independence and nuclear families. Shola had other values. Some Nigerian parents will visit the homes of their adult children for months or years at a time. When in-laws come to visit, they will likely stay for a while. If a new baby comes to the house, elderly parents may live with their adult children for years. Grandmothers see it as their job to care for the infant. When other family members immigrate, they may live with the established relative. They may do so without asking permission.

4. **Child-rearing:** The birth of a first child changes the family dynamic. As people integrate an identity as mother or father into their core, culture also plays a role. Nigeria has a patriarchal system, which gives weight to the male role. This opposes traditional African American families, which are often egalitarian.

5. **Language and communication:** Shola belongs to the Yoruba ethnic group, and he grew up speaking that language along with English (one of Nigeria's official languages). Jannelle only speaks English. When Shola speaks to

relatives or others from Nigeria in their ethnic language, a power imbalance arises. This is especially true if the children learn the language.

6. **Food:** Culinary metaphors and food preparation play a significant role in culture. For example, Nigerians' believe the kola nut represents wisdom, longevity, and prosperity. Hot peppers are a staple seasoning in Nigerian dishes, and they are also medicinal. Shola may view Jannelle's salad as "goat food," while Jannelle considers Nigerian food too hot and crude (it is often eaten with fingers).

Differences like the ones between Jannelle and Shola only begin to demonstrate the differences in black culture. Gender issues also play a significant role in creating cultural differences.

Gender Identity

Over the years, African American women have encountered great difficulty carving out their identity. When the African American civil rights movement emerged in the 1960s, African American women found themselves fighting for freedoms that appeared to affect only their male counterparts. Black women still received unequal pay in employment, were expected to stay at home and raise their children, and often experienced inequality within the family structure. When the feminist movement achieved mainstream status, most feminist groups seemed to focus predominantly on the concerns of European American women. In both the civil rights and feminist movements, African American women represented a fringe group—accepted by each but failing to achieve equal status. This discrepancy led authors such as bell hooks (1991) to decry any attempt to separate gender from the minority status of African American women. For hooks, the use of phrases such as "women and minorities" belittles the experiences of African American women who are both women *and* members of an ethnic minority group. Both their ethnic and gender statuses affect how the world sees them. A professor at West Texas A&M University was once asked, "Do you find your status challenged more often because you are black or because you are a woman?" She responded simply, "I can't answer that question—I am an African American woman."

Despite all of these differences, there are similarities too. Some of the most commonly referred values for African Americans include a strong spirituality, a communal orientation, and the pursuit of personal development through education and mentoring (Coker & Bryant, 2003). All of these will be discussed later in this chapter.

CULTURAL IDENTITY

Many European Americans are often ignorant of some of the daily facets of African American life. For example, African American hair takes more time than blond or brunet hair to produce natural oils. If left untreated, hair may become brittle and actually break. This resulted in hair products called "hair grease" that supplement hair. Hair differences have also led to popular trends of wearing headbands or braids. In addition to hair, other cultural facets may require some research. Traditional African clothing often contains symbols called *Adinkra,* which may be traced back to the Ghana and the Ivory Coast (Willis, 1998). Food plays an important role in African American culture. Foods such as okra, peanuts, sesame, and black-eyed peas have roots in West Africa and came to America through slavery. Music has long played a role in African American culture, and much of this may be traced to roots in West Africa. Genres most often associated with African Americans are gospel, spirituals, jazz, rhythm & blues, soul, rap, and hip-hop (Caldwell, 1996). Even special holidays are poorly understood by the non-black populace, such as Juneteenth (June 19 is the anniversary of when slaves in Texas learned of the emancipation proclamation and realized their freedom); Kwanzaa (Swahili for "first fruits of the harvest," December 26 to January 1; created by Dr. Maulana Karenga in 1966 to celebrate African American heritage); and Black History Month (February, created by Carter G. Woodson in 1926).

In addition to the many positive cultural elements of being African American, cultural identity develops in America through a sense of being different. For example, African American adolescents are likely to feel distant from their non-black peers because of differences in dialect, family structure, academic achievement, and other such issues (Baruth & Manning, 1999). They may be experiencing discrimination for the first time when applying for employment, which may significantly affect their self-esteem and self-concept. Such social pressures often afflict adolescent girls less than boys, who often feel displaced from society (Murray, 1996).

Models of Cultural Identity Development

However, the intensity of any developmental differences will depend in part on the client's level of acculturation. Cross (1971, 1991, 1995) developed a four-stage model of black identity development in which individuals progress through stages described as pre-encounter, encounter, immersion/emersion, and internalization (see Table 4.1). Each stage refers to an individual's

TABLE **4.1**
Cross's Black Identity Model

	View of Minority Culture	View of Dominant Culture
Pre-encounter	Not really considered	The dominant culture is viewed as the only true culture.
Encounter	The minority culture is viewed as an alternative path to identity but one that is not fully embraced.	Something from the dominant culture pushes them away. They are no longer able to identify with it.
Immersion/emersion	The minority culture is embraced.	Components of the dominant culture are rejected and sometimes abhorred.
Internalization	The minority culture is still embraced.	Some elements of the dominant culture are reintroduced and embraced but only those that are not prejudicial.

understanding and level of acceptance with his or her individual and communal cultural identity.

In the pre-encounter stage of identity development, individuals have yet to consider the value of cultural identity. They tacitly accept the pervasive prejudices of the dominant culture, which leads to a devaluation of their culture and an uncritical acceptance of European American culture.

At the beginning of the encounter stage, a crisis occurs. The form that it takes may vary among individuals. For some, a fellow African American might confront them and encourage them to reject the European American culture. For others, a white subculture may reject them and make them feel different.

Academic life often plays a role in the encounter. Consider Jermaine, a 16-year-old African American male. On a typical Monday, the day starts with the English teacher asking, "Jermaine, you're black—how would black people interpret this poem?" At lunch, a table of white football players eye Jermaine angrily as he talks with a white cheerleader. In football practice, Jermaine makes an excellent catch only to hear a team say, "Yeah, black people do jump better; you're lucky you have those genes." Such examples of prejudice leave a deep mark, but they are also sources of power. Coming from black culture does make people different from those in white culture. All cultures blend to the richness and value of the broader society. At this point, though, the individual trying to fit in will only see the downside of being different.

The end of the encounter stage is often very confusing. Jermaine realizes that he does not fit within the dominant culture, but he knows very little about African American culture. As he begins to explore this topic, Jermaine enters the third stage: immersion/emersion. Here, Jermaine attempts to eliminate European influences and submerge himself in the perceived African culture. He may choose to attend an African American school or join an African American social group. If such options are not available, he may surf the Internet to learn about African tribes or civil rights leaders. During this stage of identity development, African American clients may also come to view a European American counselor as part of the white establishment. Multiculturally sensitive counselors may also contribute to the problem if they attempt to portray themselves as part of the black culture. Counselors must wait for the client to piece together a sense of cultural identity, which happens during the final stage: internalization.

During the internalization stage, Jermaine attempts to resolve the conflict between old and new identities. Is it acceptable to join a mostly white country club when so many of the members demonstrate prejudices against African Americans? Should he live in an African American neighborhood? Each individual will find his or her own answers to such questions and gradually learn to accept pieces of the dominant culture while taking pride in his or her African American roots. He or she may collect African art, poems, or other artifacts. He or she may volunteer to work with African American teens, financially support Africans in crisis, or even begin teaching multicultural classes.

Cross (2001) noted that this course of acculturation and identity varies among individuals. For some African Americans, a racial/cultural identity may never be important, despite the importance for most people of color. He also noted that for most African Americans, self-hatred is a minor—rather than a central—theme in everyday life. Given this diversity, it is important to avoid viewing his model of identity development or any other cultural model as if it applied to all black people. In reality, the diversity of cultural identity is quite profound, and African Americans hold a wide variety of views concerning what it means to be black.

Although Cross's model continues to resonate in multicultural circles, there are also problems with it. One of the most obvious involves the process of identity development as linear. More contemporary theories are moving away from viewing black racial identity as developmental stages. Instead, they are emphasizing multidimensional attitudes (Worrell & Gardner-Kitt, 2006). This would mean the individual stages are really facets. Most people will experience pre-encounter, immersion/emersion, and internalization attitudes, but the way these are experienced will differ by the individual. They may also repeat facets as their experiences change. As indicated in Figure 4.1, a more holistic way to think of these is that each facet affects the individual throughout the life span. People may go experience each facet multiple times, with only very few reaching a complete internalization.

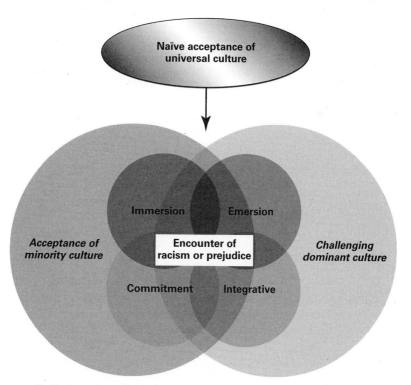

FIGURE **4.1** Cultural Identity Model: African Americans

In the cultural development model, the facets parallel those of Cross's model, but they are viewed as states of being rather than stages. Their experience of the facets will be different depending on the level of prejudice encountered. In this model, the immersion/emersion state is split to reflect how some movement is toward a minority identity, and some movement is away from the dominant culture. These are distinct steps. At the bottom, internalization still has a component of rejecting the racism of the dominant model while accepting some of the positive components. On the other side, commitment establishes the minority identity.

In addition to polarizing movements toward minority identity and away from the dominant culture, this model also has a trigger. For African Americans, racism and prejudice appear to jolt people into different facets. Sometimes, they push people away from the dominant culture. Other times, they may have the opposite effect. One of my clients told me how she saw her place within the dominant culture when three white friends stood up for her. Her boss overlooked her for a promotion, and the friends confronted him as a unit. Events like this can change people just as negative acts can.

With many identity models, there is no distinction between racial identity and ethnic identity. The terms are often used interchangeably (even by the primary theorists), but they appear to represent distinct constructs. Helms (1990, p. 3) may have provided the clearest definition of racial identity by referring to it as a cogent explanation of racial identity, which she defined as "a sense of group or collective identity based on one's perception that he or she shares a common racial heritage with a particular racial group." Similarly, ethnic identity focuses more on the broader range of national/cultural heritage. It refers to positive attitudes toward a national/cultural group. This has less to do with skin color and genetics as it does a shared history and culture as well as involvement in the group's practices (Phinney et al., 1994). For our purposes, both racial and ethnic identity are considered cultural experiences.

Racial socialization for African Americans is helpful in some cases and harmful in others (e.g., Frabutt, Walker & MacKinnon-Lewis, 2002). One reason why ethnic/racial identity is curvilinear is the need to create enough racial pride to believe in one's self while at the same time encouraging the child to adapt into the European world. Those who abandon their racial identity will be crushed. Those who see themselves as wholly different will never belong. There is a process of constant ebb and flow, modulating within the experiences of social interaction. A woman named Jennifer (a junior double-majoring in African American studies and political science) summed up the union between these issues clearly:

> "... [Y]ou should ever forget where you come from. I also don't think you should allow it to be chains around your ankles and prevent you from keep going forward. But we should remember to give back and help our community" (Carson, 2009, p. 338).

FAMILY STRUCTURE AND DYNAMICS

Just as skin color affects culture, so does family. For recent immigrants, family will play an essential role in most interventions. Many individuals are reluctant to make important decisions without consulting fathers or uncles (Vontress, 1991). When African clients are away from their families, they commonly consult their "American family," which may involve friends or coworkers who have come from their native country. Counselors should avoid forcing clients to make immediate decisions in sessions and instead provide them with time to seek guidance from family.

For African Americans who have lived in the States for generations, other important family dynamics are involved. African American history plays a significant role in the dynamic of the contemporary family. During centuries of slavery, corporal punishment was used to control negative behavior. "Sassing" whites resulted in slaps or beatings, and this training technique was incorporated in African American families (Seppa, 1996).

Seppa (1996) noted that during the early 1970s, when psychologists were attempting to help African Americans rebuild after the Watts' riots, parent training was offered to help reduce the high divorce rate and decrease the use of corporal punishment. At the time, he noted that African Americans overused corporal punishment and even used it as a teaching (nonpunishment) tool for children. The psychologists' attempts to reduce the use of physical punishment and lower divorce rates were completely unsuccessful. African Americans are more likely to spank their children than European American families (Christie-Mizell, Pryor & Grossman, 2008).

One of the consequences of having a history of violence in the family is that African American children react differently to punishment. This claim is difficult to support, and it is mediated by other issues, such as education achievement, income levels, the time a mother spends with her children, and social support structures. All of these are statistically lower for African Americans than European American families (Mott, 2004).

Despite these complications, a pattern of uniqueness for African American families still exists. Christie-Mizell, Pryor, and Grossman (2008) examined how punishment and other factors were associated with child depression. The African Americans from their sample had lower levels of education and employment. But they also found some other differences. European American children became more depressed as they aged. This was not true for African American children. Also, European American girls were more at risk for depression than their counterparts, but gender patterns were not found for African Americans. Being from a larger family helped buffer white children against depression, but the finding did not hold true for blacks.

In an inner-city university class, I broke up undergraduate students to talk about "effective discipline." One African American girl said, "I learned not to sass my mama when she smacked me across the face."

The European American students look horrified. One replied, "That's child abuse!" Several others murmured their agreement. Fifty years of research have indicated that when European American children are punished physically, they tend to become more aggressive. Emerging research is indicating that African American children do not become more aggressive when they are punished physically by their parents (Deater-Deckard,

Dodge, Bates & Pettit, 1998; Stacks, Oshio, Gerard & Roe, 2009). There is even some research indicating that physical discipline may be negatively correlated with behavioral problems in African Americans (Whaley, 2000). Although there are differences across cultures. For example, in many parts of Africa, corporal punishment of any kind is viewed as physical abuse. Slapping a child's wrist in public would be viewed as cruel. When constructing effective discipline strategies, such cultural distinctions should be considered (Obeng, 2007).

Marriage

African Americans are the least likely to marry (Dixon, 2009). When they do marry, their marriages begin later in life and tend to end in divorce or separation faster than European Americans. A variety of factors could account for this. African Americans have higher unemployment rates, a cultural view of sex being appropriate before marriage, an emphasis on independent women, and a cultural shift from familism to individualism (Dixon, 2009). With African Americans marrying less, they are more likely to raise children in single-parent homes.

With so many women heading African American families, these young mothers often face additional stereotypes. Naylor (1993) writes about the myth of the matriarch. African American women are expected to be strong, independent from men, and domineering. Naylor traces this contemporary image to the slave days, when African American women performed women's duties but also worked alongside the men in the fields. They were regarded as mentally weaker than whites, but they were treated as though they were hardier than European American women, who were seen as too delicate to work outside the home. The perpetuation of this image prevents many African American mothers from giving themselves permission to simply collapse. Once the kids are put to bed, all parents deserve the right to do something as simple as cry.

Others have noted the importance of single parents from black households maintaining a relationship with their child's father. Sterrett, Jones, and Kincaid (2009) found that children of single parents were more likely to have internalizing and externalizing problems. But the closer their relationship with their child's parent, the more their maternal parenting had a positive effect.

When working with African American families, a number of different interventions may be useful. Religiosity, extended family ties, encouraging educational aspirations (and not simply educational attainment), and moral beliefs (Wright Younts, 2009) may all become part of an intervention. Religion appears to play a special healing role within African American families. Baier and Wright (2001) conducted a meta-analysis of 60 empirical studies. Consistently, religious beliefs and behaviors moderated criminal behavior.

Working with Children

Part of a counselor's job is to find ways to encourage the positive behaviors already a part of the family's worldview and culture. In my work with inner-city gangs, I saw the extreme end of hopelessness. When asked where she saw herself in five years, one African American girl said, "At 22? You gotta be kidding me. I ain't living till 22!" It is this sense of living without a future that breads inner defeat. When these kids find hopes and dreams, they are more likely to perform better in school and society (Adelabu, 2008).

Hope is especially important for refugee children adopted by American families. With the AIDS pandemic creating millions of orphans, the numbers of children needing homes is likely to rise even further. Extended family systems are being taxed beyond their abilities (Foster, 2002), but there are complications to adopting outside cultural backgrounds. Most researchers (e.g., Freundlich, 2000; Roby & Shaw, 2006; Serbin, 1997) agree that racial and cultural identity for internally adopted children is extremely important. Because of this, Roby and Shaw (2006) argued that transcultural, international adoptions should only be considered when kinship and community efforts fail to find safe and loving families for children. They also argued that all international adoptions should maintain a respect for the history and culture of the child's African origins.

EDUCATION

The 1940s have passed, and schools are now integrated thanks to the Supreme Court's decision in *Brown v. Board of Education* (1954). Prior to this date, the United States operated with a "separate but equal" doctrine. This allowed states to disallow African American children access to white public schools if an alternative public school was available for them. Sometimes, the alternative school was more than an hour away and had limited supplies, subpar teaching, and inadequate facilities. Chief Justice Warren wrote in the opinion of the court, "Segregated public schools are not 'equal' and cannot be made 'equal,' and that hence they are deprived of the equal protection of the laws."

Negative Impressions in Schools

We no longer have separate drinking fountains or separate bus seats for light- and dark-skinned individuals, but the negative impressions remain. In 1985, the Clark and Clark doll study was repeated to see if political and social changes had altered European Americans' and African Americans' perceptions of dark-skinned individuals. Powell-Hopson and Derek (1988) tested 105 African American and 50 European American preschoolers and found that a majority of the participants still chose a white doll when asked preference questions. They noted that these preferences could be changed—at least temporarily—by employing basic learning principles and psychoeducation. They found it disturbing that American society had been unable to promote positive images of African Americans despite many years of desegregation.

It was not until 2009 that a study replicating the dolls found changes in the way black and white children answered the questions. Jordan and Hernandez-Reif (2009) studied 40 black and white preschool children (M = 53.0 months; SD = 8.1) and found some positive trends. A chi-square analysis revealed no differences between the black and white children's responses across the entire model. This is positive, but there were still problems. When the children were only given two choices (rather than the four gradient skin-tone colors), both racial groups preferred the lighter-skinned cartoon.

The most disturbing finding from Jordan and Hernandez-Reif's study came from their intervention. They read a story about a black boy who saved a baby duck. After completing the story, they again had the children rate the cartoons. After hearing the story, fewer black children selected the black cartoon as the one that "looks bad." But the story did not change the white children's perspective. They continued rating the black cartoon as the one that "looks bad" and the white cartoon as the one that has the "nice skin color." Given that Clark and Clark's study helped end segregation in public schools, it is clear that continued work is necessary to create an unprejudiced academic environment.

Other Factors Influencing Education

African American children are the most likely to be suspended or expelled (Kaushal, 2009). There may be many reasons for this. For example, African American kids are a little more likely to have internationalizing behaviors (such as lethargy and depression) and externalizing behaviors (such as using drugs and bullying) (Hatcher, Maschi, Morgen & Toldson, 2009). These problems may be more obvious in pre-adolescence (Mrug & Windle, 2009b). Where do the problems come from? We are not sure. There is some evidence that African Americans witness more violence than many other children, and boys who witness violence appear to engage in delinquent behaviors (Mrug & Windle, 2009a).

Although there are issues in the African American community that could be addressed, stereotypes and prejudices also play a role (Weiner, 1995). Way back in 1995, Ford and Harris found that the academic success of African American students is influenced more by personal and environmental factors than by actual ability. These influences include ethnic ideology, relationships with teachers and counselors, ambivalent feelings about school, experiences of discrimination, and negative peer relationships. These factors have led approximately 80% of gifted African American children to perform below their abilities academically.

Challenges with Assessment

Cultural differences also make psychological and educational assessments difficult. When Jensen (1968) released his controversial findings that African Americans were less intelligent than European Americans, the nation was appalled. Jensen argued that biological differences between the races could hinder efforts to discover optimal instructional procedures for students of varying abilities. In other words, culture and biology make it impossible to use a single teaching style to teach all children. In 1996, Herrnstein and Murray revised this argument in *The Bell Curve: Intelligence and Class Structure in American Life.* They reviewed findings from multiple cultures and controlled for level of income and still found differences between various racial and ethnic groups.

Anytime research depicts one group as genetically superior, problems arise. In the United States, the courts have rejected these arguments. In *Larry P. v. Riles* (1979), the California Supreme Court heard arguments that IQ tests should not be used for academic placement of African American students. As a result of this proceeding and others, the Education of the Handicapped Act (1975) was passed, which required the identification of deficits in adaptive behaviors as well as a below-average intelligence scores for the diagnosis of mental retardation.

Despite the court's rejection, stereotypes still prevail, and these affect minorities even when they consciously reject them (Schmader, Johns & Barquissau, 2004). When society believes certain people are dumb, crazy, lazy, or some other negative attribute, a part of this mentality sinks into the hearers' minds. Stereotype threats not only affect performance but also affect participation and involvement in the academic arena (Walton & Cohen, 2007). Students who are perceived to be slow or different feel unaccepted and underperform. When such individuals see themselves as coming from lower status groups, they actually have a lower awareness of discrimination (Major et al., 2002) and a greater tendency to value the attributes associated with the higher status group (Schmader, Major, Eccleston & McCoy, 2001).

These stereotypes also have a gender component. Beginning in the late 1980s, a gender gap emerged between college graduation rates for African American women and men (Garibaldi, 2007). To effectively change the situation in America, immediate interventions must occur to keep African American males in school. This is where school counselors and school psychologists become essential.

At a California in-service for urban teachers, an African American speaker led a two-hour workshop about how schools have failed African American males. The majority of his talk involved the importance of having African American men in the classroom—either as teachers, aids, or volunteers. At the end of the talk, a young white woman raised her hand.

"Excuse me," the woman asked with hope in her eyes. "I appreciate all of the information you provided, and I agree about the importance of getting African American men in my class, but I still would like to know what I can do."

Anger flashed across the man's face, and he held the microphone close to his mouth. "You can't."

He offered no other suggestions.

The speaker's frustration made sense. For too long, white educators and researchers have swooped into the black community as saviors. No substantial change has occurred. Members of the community are understandably frustrated with such interventions. The speaker is also correct regarding the importance of involving African American fathers and volunteers. But this is not the full story.

For African American boys, mothers play a key role too. African American parents can also have a significant impact on their children by providing strict discipline combined with nurturing and community connectedness. These mechanisms appear to counteract the potentially negative influences of neighborhood peers, inadequate schools, and racist messages from society

(Maton, Hrabowski & Greif, 1998). When moms provide ethnic socialization regarding African American heritage, their sons' grades improve (Brown, Linver, Evans & DeGennaro, 2009). In a study by Brown et al., the opposite was true for girls. Their grades dropped with higher levels of ethnic socialization. Why?

But there have been gains. According to an article in the *Journal of Blacks in High Education* (African Americans show solid gains, 2009), blacks earn 9.6% of all bachelor's degrees in the United States. As a group, they tend to earn degrees in public administration, law, protective services/security, police sciences, business, social sciences, psychology, health sciences, communications, computer science, family and consumer science, or liberal arts and humanities. Graduation rates for physics, mathematics, history, engineering, and foreign languages remain low. There is also a dearth of black school counselors or psychologists for the coming generation (Graves & Wright, 2009). The slow growth for African Americans in higher education (especially males) parallels some of the issues with income.

SOCIOECONOMICS

Childhood poverty plays a greater role for African Americans than for many other ethnic groups. Hertz (2005) found that 42% of blacks who were born in the lower tenth of the income distribution stayed in that income bracket as adults. This number was over twice the rate for whites.

At the other end of the developmental cycle, new complications arise. By the time African Americans reach retirement age, their skills in dealing with racism and discrimination have helped them to cope with many other hardships. As a group, they are still overrepresented among the poor, struggle with high divorce and marital separation rates, and are more likely to require medical treatment. A lifetime of discrimination has also trained them to be wary of non–African Americans, and they are likely to prefer counselors who resemble them in personality, ethnicity, and temperament (Brammer, 2010).

Causes of Socioeconomic Vulnerability of African Americans

To understand the financial difficulties of African Americans well, it is critical to look at both the financial struggles of ethnicity as well as those related to social class. This is necessary because children who grow up in poor families tend to complete fewer years of education, earn less during their formative employment years, and are over three times more likely than middle-class children to become poor adults (Heflin & Pattillo, 2006). To put this in other terms, one study revealed that white households had a median net worth 10 times above the median net worth of black households (Bucks, Kennickell, Mach & Moore, 2009). While the median net worth for black households remains stagnant, the mean net worth is rising quickly. This implies there is a small group of African Americans making considerable inroads in the middle/upper class, but the growth is not enough to change the median income.

Hardaway and McLoyd (2009) detail how an emerging African American middle class has been overlooked and misunderstood. They effectively argue that we cannot understand the plight of African Americans by only looking at the poor.

When African Americans successfully enter the middle class, they are at great risk of slipping back into poverty. There are a variety of reasons for this. They often come from families and neighborhoods that lack the income, net worth, and academic background of white families (Hardaway & McLoyd, 2009). They also reach the middle class—often by relying on jobs serving low-income African Americans (e.g., government employment) (McBrier & Wilson, 2004)—and they were more likely to have grown up poor themselves (Heflin and Pattillo 2006). Unlike their white peers—who often have children in sports and are stay-at-home moms—African American families have multiple wage-earners contributing to the household income. They also need to work longer than white families to earn the same income (Wheary 2006).

When African Americans break out of the cycle of limited education, they continue to face challenges. Even when they earn college degrees, discrimination often results in African Americans receiving salaries or employment opportunities below their level of education (Elman and O'Rand, 2004). Newly middle-class African Americans are also likely to provide financial assistance to their poorer relatives (Wheary 2006). As already mentioned, African Americans are more likely to divorce or never marry, which again is a situation associated with lower incomes (South & Crowder, 1997). Blacks were also less like to invest in savings, which makes them vulnerable to economic downturns (Bucks, Kennickell, Mach & Moore, 2009).

First-generation middle-class families may also miss out on opportunities common in other neighborhoods. For many middle-class children, their days are filled with sporting events, artistic hobbies, social clubs, music lessons, and involvement in other organizations. Such activities correspond to academic success, which is also predictive of continued socioeconomic status (Hardaway & McLoyd, 2009).

Unexamined prejudice also contributes to a glass ceiling effect. When black employees start to rise along the corporate ladder, subtle messages of exclusion and expectations of failure often sap the employee of psychological energy (Miller & Travers, 2005). They may earn less than their peers (reward bias) or be overlooked for possible promotions (developmental bias). The individual begins undervalued and withdraws, which reinforces the racism and encourages the corporate leadership to look elsewhere for promotions.

Fisher (1999) tells the story of Stowe and his wife, who are both black, and their experience of moving to Raleigh, North Carolina. In 1994, they purchased a house in an integrated neighborhood and expected a relatively smooth transition. Soon after their move, Stowe was gardening in his front yard when a white neighbor approached him. Assuming that she intended to welcome him to the neighborhood, he walked over to her "with my best Southern-hospitality face on."

Without introducing herself, the woman stated, "You are doing wonderful work!" As she began leading up to a job offer, he explained that he was not a gardener but the owner of the house. The woman then launched into a story about her father's good treatment of a black household servant. She concluded by stating that Stowe would have no problems in Berwick if he "promised to be good." Obviously, Stowe found the encounter deflating. Even more surprising, I have heard similar stories for the past 20 years in other states. They nearly always follow the same pattern, and they are very common.

Mr. and Mrs. Williams, a young African American couple who had moved to a midsized southwestern city, were shopping for homes with their realtor. As they toured various neighborhoods, the realtor began to express some concern. "Now, this area might not work for you," she remarked nonchalantly. "There really aren't very many blacks on this street." As they reached the house, the realtor nervously unlocked the door and showed the family around. When they made their way to the backyard, they noticed an African American man mowing a yard across the alley. When they approached, he ceased mowing and quickly went inside. The realtor immediately called the police because "there aren't any blacks living on this block." The police arrived and attempted to arrest the mower. As they escorted him through the house, he frantically grabbed family pictures from the wall to demonstrate that he was the owner of the house.

Discrimination over housing and neighborhood segregation has led to violence (Cruz & Taylor, 2009). Once the violence becomes entrenched within the culture, "code of the streets," drug trafficking, gang activity, and hopelessness continue the pattern. As family and financial stress increase, self-worth decrease (Paschall & Hubbard, 1998). Hope for real change rests in better education, improved economic opportunities, and interracial tolerance. It also requires counselors to rethink the role of religion in promoting culture identity and neighborhood camaraderie.

SPIRITUALITY AND RELIGION

Spirituality has long played an important role in African American life. For many African Americans, religion may be the only effective buffer against the depressive effects of discrimination (Bierman, 2006).

In many parts of Africa, spirituality exists in musical expression, painting, and other creative arts (Thompson 1983) as well as in traditional religious practices (e.g., Christian, Islamic, and indigenous worship). In America, religious organizations often serve as a mechanism for social change (e.g., Brown & Adamczyk, 2009). One of the reasons for the difference stems from the history of slavery. Religion and spirituality provided an avenue for slaves to make sense of their plight (Durodoye & Coker, 2008). This spiritual assistance became a foundation of the culture, and the church led much of the political movement for civil rights in the 1960s (Ennis et al., 2004).

Connections Between Spirituality and Health in African Culture

In the African worldview, healing and spirituality are intimately connected. This worldview differs from Western and Eastern perspectives and defines many African beliefs and customs. According to van Dyk (2001), the traditional African worldview is based on a holistic and anthropocentric ontology.

To understand the world, African people must start by looking at themselves, their tribe, and their community. Many Africans believe in a unified force of nature, which animates all living things. God is the source of this force, but spirits play a role (Vontress, 1991). With God running all things, he is somewhat withdrawn from the daily role of people's lives. Ancestors and spirits of the dead are more likely to intercede in effecting change (van Dyk, 2001). It is not uncommon for Africans and recent African immigrants to the United States to ascribe most illnesses, diseases, conflicts, misfortunes, or accidents to the spirit level. Chance, luck, and fate play no role. From a traditional African viewpoint, every illness or problem has an intention and a cause. To combat the illness, the individual must understand who or what caused the disease (Brammer, 2010; Sow, 1980; van Dyk, 2001).

The history of using traditional healers as a first line of defense for mental and psychological issues holds true in black American culture, too. Stansbury, Harley, and Stansbury (2009) looked at how clergy worked with depressed elderly African Americans. Their interviews were conducted in rural churches around central Kentucky. All the clergy were considered literate regarding late-life depression and its treatment.

The bulk of available evidence also indicates that religion participation offers a protective effect against depressive symptoms and other forms of psychological distress among African Americans (Levin, Chatters & Taylor, 2005). But most of this research has been clinical rather than epidemiological. There is evidence that weekly religious attendance lowers the risk of stroke and promotes some healthy lifestyle choices (Obisesan, Livingston, Trulear & Gillum, 2006).

The Nation of Islam

Of all the religious organizations available for African Americans, the Nation of Islam requires special attention because of its advocacy of separation from white America and its culture (Lovinger, 1996). According to *A Guide to African-Americans and Religion* (2007), 75.7% of blacks are Protestant Christians, 6.5% are Catholic Christians, 0.2% are Jewish, 10.6% do not identify with a religious group, and 7% are Other. Even though this small group of "Other"—which includes the Nation of Islam—is relatively small, the worldview it represents provides an important window into African American spirituality.

Wallace D. Fard, also known as Wallace Fard Muhammad, founded the Nation of Islam (NOI). In 1930, he opened a mosque in Detroit and taught his followers that they should reject Christianity because it was the "slavemaster's religion." In 1934, Fard disappeared and was succeeded by Elijah Muhammad (Elijah Poole). Mainstream Islam rejected this offshoot for two primary reasons: 1) The NOI believes Elijah Muhammad is a prophet, while traditional Islam believes Muhammad was the final prophet and 2) the NOI views Fard as God incarnate, which is heresy to orthodox Islam (Sarker, 2004).

According to the Nation of Islam, 13 tribes existed 66 trillion years ago. They were technologically advanced, civilized, and politically astute. When a rogue scientist blew up the planet, the moon split off, and all but one tribe died. The tribe of Shabazz moved to Egypt and Mecca, Saudi Arabia.

What is referred to as The Nation of Islam is a group of American blacks who view themselves as descendents of the tribe of Shabazz (Evanzz, 1999). The tribe of Shabazz, according to the religion, descends from nature herself, and she is the wife of the most high: Allah (God) himself. Unlike the white race, which stems from Adam and Eve, the Shabazz tribe has no mother or father and predates all societies.

After Adam and Eve were evicted from the Garden of Eden, or the Holy Lands (which consists of Egypt, Jordan, and Syria), they were driven into the hills and caves of West Asia, or, as it is now called, Europe. The Adamic (white) race was allowed to reign for 6,000 years, but they were not allowed to return to the tree of life (i.e., the Nation of Islam), and the sword of Islam (the Muslim Army) prevented the Adamic race from crossing the border between Europe and Asia.

The prophet Elijah Muhammad (1997) writes that the white men alone are not to blame for the captivity of the black race. Although they were vicious and beat, kicked, busted skulls, and hung black people, those actions were designed to show a love for their own kind. The prophet continues by adding that if the black man had demonstrated pride for himself and love for his own kind, he would have bashed in the head of the white man and hung him on a tree and earned his respect today. This continues as a theme for the religion, which frequently addresses the importance of family discipline, educational aspirations, and putting aside hatred (Muhammad, 2009).

The decree to overcome hatred does not imply that NOI members should forgive white America. From the religion's viewpoint, gullible blacks believed that white education will assist them, intermarriage would help them gain status, and interracial friendships would create helpful alliances. These activities are viewed as an elaborate attempt to control the black race and prevent them from creating their own nation. Louis Farrakhan (Meet the Press, 1997) believes a spaceship (the Mother Wheel), in orbit over America since 1929, will soon destroy white people who do not embrace Islam.

If these beliefs sound extreme, you will not be surprised to learn that a study of mental health practitioners rated the beliefs of the Nation of Islam as highly pathological. In a study on the pathology of religious beliefs O'Connor and Vandenberg (2005) asked practitioners to rate beliefs from Catholicism, Mormonism, and NOI. Without identifying the religion, raters believed NOI was the most pathological, followed by Mormonism, then by Catholicism. However, when raters were told that the certain beliefs were Mormon (e.g., being transformed into a god after death), they stated that these beliefs were no more pathological than Catholic beliefs. Knowing that the beliefs were part of the NOI creed did not result in lowering their pathology ratings. This might imply another unexamined pathology or it could indicate a chasm between mental health philosophies and NOI tenants.

Regardless of one's personal belief about NOI, the religion offers several important insights regarding African American culture. It posits a history before slavery, where their descendents were the most advanced and wisest people in the world. It also offers a sense of justice. Those responsible for torturing and enslaving the black race will be punished. Finally, it provides a mechanism to change the present and hope for the future.

Connections Between Spirituality and Health in African Americans Culture

No matter which religious tradition they choose, African Americans are more likely to turn to a clergy member than to a psychologist in times of trouble. Orlando (2006) explained how it is common to find sick African Americans surrounded by fellow church members praying together for healing or a spouse reading the Bible beside the bed of a sick relative. She believes such acts are a viable representation of tribal instincts, which have survived throughout centuries. The black church may also be one of the few social institutions that is dominated, operated, and controlled by African Americans.

Given the importance of religion and spirituality within the African American community, it is important to intertwine religion into counseling services. For example, depression is sometimes viewed as a spiritual problem caused by sinful behavior or the failure to pray (Givens, Houston, Van Voorhees, Ford, & Cooper, 2007). If mental health professionals attempt to explain potentially spiritual issues in psychological terms, they are likely to be viewed as anti-spiritual and therefore threatening. Regardless of the religious affiliations of African Americans, spirituality tends to play an important role in the lives of many families, and it is foundational in helping youth define their identity (Chadiha, Veroff & Leber, 1998).

PHYSICAL AND MENTAL HEALTH

To understand some of the complexities in African American health care philosophy, it is necessary to understand traditional African healing practices. Berg (2003) noted some key differences between African and Western health care worldviews. In many parts of Africa, healers perform many of the psychological and medical care. The training for these so-called witch doctors (an inaccurate and deceptive term) includes an extensive initiation process requiring rigorous preparation and ancestral approval. By the end of their training, they are often skilled psychotherapists (Brammer, 2010).

In Africa, the most common reason for seeing a healer is to gain favor for an upcoming event or social concern (e.g., winning a soccer game, passing a test, interviewing for a job, etc.). The healer works to bring harmony between the individual seeking help and the spirits associated with the events in question. Given the lack of Western medical and psychiatric services available in much of Africa, these healers are often the first line of defense against medical, psychological, and social problems. The role of African healers and traditional medicine has become even more important of late, as additional studies continue to show the value of services for several mental health–related issues. Havenaar et al. (2008) found that traditional healers were occasionally sought specifically for such mental health problems as alcoholism or violent outbursts. More often, South Africans visited healers for disturbing dreams, "fits," job loss, physical ailments, and cultural concerns.

The Relationship of African Americans to Psychological Care

There are similarities between what Africans find beneficial in health care and what African Americans hope to gain from health and psychological care. The primary similarity rests with the importance of creating a trusting relationship between caregiver and client. Jacobs et al. (2006) studied the specific obstacles interfering with African Americans' trust of the health care system. Their focused study revealed six facets contributing to distrust: technical incompetence, interpersonal incompetence, national origin of physicians, greed of physician, racism, and expectation of being experimented on. Some of these are clearly understood and likely hold true for most ethnic groups. Perceived technical impotence would lead to distrust of any professional. However, the African Americans in this study had a different perception from those of many other ethnic groups. Communication skills were very important. They wanted their physicians to listen and strike up a conversation with them. If the physician remained quiet, they became suspicious. They also picked up on physicians' statements regarding money and distrusted doctors who appeared more concerned in things than people. In some ways, their concerns about the racism of physicians were associated with a perspective that doctors would willfully experiment on African Americans. Some told stories where physicians had misdiagnosed or mistreated them or their black friends. Rather than view these as mistakes, many saw them as intentional experimentations (see also Kennedy, Mathis & Woods, 2007). This is an important theme that will play a role in counseling interventions later in this chapter.

African Americans and Illicit Drug Use

With health hazards coming from multiple areas, it might be expected that the coping skills of African Americans have been systematically worn away. However, rather than strip African Americans of their coping mechanisms, the pressures from prejudice and violence have often led to new strengths. African American adolescents report the lowest incidence of illicit drug use initiation, and unlike teenagers from other ethnic groups, disruptions in their home life are seldom enough to make them turn to drugs (Gil, Vega & Biafora, 1998) or cigarettes (Griesler, Kandel & Davies, 2002).

Why are African Americans able to fend off the impulses toward substance abuse that plague other ethnic groups? They tend to have better support mechanisms than European Americans and are connected to others in the community through religious involvement (Jenkins, 2007). Maybe they have also learned how to cope with the daily pressures placed on them. Facing racism and discrimination from such an early age may help African Americans adapt to pressures and weather many of life's storms. However, these adaptive skills have their limitations. Even though African Americans may cope with daily struggles well, the pressures placed on them by society can become quite overwhelming.

African Americans and Illness

Reed, McLeod, Randall, and Walker (1996) found that nearly 58% of the African American women they surveyed demonstrated symptoms of depression. They attributed these findings to discrimination, higher-stress environments (e.g., urban, low income, and high crime rates) and lack of institutionalized community support (e.g., hospitals, shopping centers, and recreational facilities). In particular, discrimination continues to play an important and damaging role in African Americans' management of depression and anxiety (Gaylord-Harden & Cunningham, 2009).

According to the Office of Minority Health & and Health Disparities (2005), African American men have the highest all-causes death rate of all races/ethnicities. African American males also have the shortest life expectancy (68.8 years) when compared to males of all races (74.5 years) and African American females (75.6 years). Black males are the most likely to die of cardiovascular disease, AIDS, lung cancer, colorectal cancer, and prostate cancer. Suicide is also a significant threat for African Americans ages 10 to 44 (Wilcox, Storr & Breslau, 2009). When suicide does occur, family interventions are often best. Cerel et al. (2008) noted the importance of the family bond prior to the suicide in predicting growth.

The reasons for these varied health concerns stem from a variety of sources, but discrimination appears to play a role. Ong, Fuller-Rowell, and Burrow (2009) studied 174 African American doctoral students and graduates to see how chronic exposure to racial discrimination predicted psychological distress. Not surprisingly, they found that racial discrimination effects health and well-being. They also found a cumulative effect for discrimination. The more often these stressors occur, the more likely other stressors appear. This finding had appeared in previous studies (Pearlin et al., 2005) but not with the same clarity. From this viewpoint, secondary exposure (i.e., harmful isolated events) to racial discrimination may be less damaging than daily racial discrimination. Rather than overt racism, daily discrimination likely stems from unexamined prejudice. The perpetrators are unlikely to perceive their actions as racist. They commit microaggressions that they may justify as simply not liking the individual in question.

For immigrants, another significant obstacle exists for physical and mental health. Immigrants struggle with poverty, limited insurance, lack of transportation, no child care, institutional racism, discrimination, and stigmas associated with mental illness. They are also less likely to receive Medicaid or other forms of public assistance (Lear, 2005). Such stressors are paradoxically likely to decrease an individual's desire for help. Obasi and Leong (2009) found a negative relationship between psychological distress and positive attitudes toward professional psychological services. The more psychological distress an individual has, the worse they feel about mental health services.

INDIVIDUAL AND GROUP INTERVENTIONS

Taking account of the history of injustice experienced by African Americans, mental health practitioners must carefully consider how a lifetime of dealing with prejudice has affected their clients' development. Therapists must find ways to demonstrate their awareness of the hardships their clients have experienced. One way to do this is by asking for the client's life story and noting the patterns of abuse. If the narrative contains no mention of prejudice, therapists may well wonder if their presentation or demeanor is perceived as threatening by the client.

Creating Effective Relationships

When working with white counselors, African American clients who have experienced a history of subtle aggressive actives tend to develop weaker therapeutic alliances. They also have lower ratings of cultural competence, and they are less likely to view the counseling experience positively (Constantine, 2007). These weak relationships are not symptoms of limited skills. They are coping mechanisms. Rampant discrimination (unexamined and intentional) have led African Americans to question the sincerity of people outside their culture.

Cathy Harris (Brammer, 1997), an African American woman from Amarillo, Texas, said, "My mother always told me, believe none of what you hear and half of what you see." African Americans have learned to focus on the tones they hear and the nonverbal communication they observe. Experience has taught them that words are filled with lies. People say, "Color doesn't matter to me" or "I've always respected your people," but their mildly sarcastic tones, poor eye contact, and physical distance communicate the real message. Simply to survive, African Americans have learned that words are not to be trusted, which makes interracial counseling all the more difficult. This is a functional distrust, and it requires non-black therapists to follow these steps:

1. **Engage in self-interrogation:** You have racial biases, stereotypes, attitudes, and behaviors (Caldwell & White, 2005). You might appear more parental than normal; you might casually downgrade someone's accomplishments because of her race; you might even have a flashing thought of pleasure that you are not this client. The sooner you examine these, the sooner you will form an alliance with your client.

2. **Recognized the limitations of your current theoretical intervention:** Most of our theories explain how *we* see the world. To work with someone from another culture, you must find theories that work from *his or her* worldview.

3. **Find the right balance between individual choice, environmental causes, and genetics:** We already discussed the role discrimination can play in clients' mental health. But avoiding personal responsibility is also dangerous. Clients with major depression, anxiety disorders, and possibly even psychotic disorders may be misdiagnosed and provided with inadequate treatment plans because all their negative behaviors are wrongly attributed to environmental causes. When such distortions arise, therapy often takes a dangerous turn. Therapists may attempt to protect their clients from exploring the painful aspects of their lives, which may render sessions stagnant and unproductive.

4. **Work on your greeting:** For traditional African households, Jenkins (2007) recommends the following in regards to greetings. First, take time to greet everyone who attends, starting with the male leader of the family. Shake hands with every family member. The method of handshaking is different for various parts of Africa. Some areas emphasize palm touching, bowing, or multiple movements. For example, in many parts of Eastern and Southern Africa, a tripleshake is common. The movement begins as a European handshake, slides upward until the fingers rest against the base of the thumb, then slide back to the European grasp. For most African and African American cultures, children are often hugged. People who greet children rigidly are viewed with suspicion.

5. **Establishing guidelines for effective therapy:** Gibson and Mitchell (1999) recommend that therapists carefully identify the expectations of African Americans. How do these clients feel about being in therapy? Do they believe in catharsis, dreams, schemata, or systemic forces? If the dominant theme of the therapist's theoretical orientation is incompatible with the client's worldview, the therapist should explain any differences. Clarifying these issues early in the therapeutic process can save both the therapist and client from significant hardship.

6. **Tell and listen to stories:** When conducting an assessment with a European American, many counselors attempt to gather facts. They march through a list of details they predetermined as important and then check off which concerns exist for a particular individual or family (Jenkins, 2007). The primary purpose for this search is diagnostic. Counselors want to ascertain *what* is happening within the family. For African immigrants, the primary concern is not *what* the problem is but *how* they can improve the situation (Brammer, 2010).

7. **Explore spirituality:** For many African Americans, counseling should involve spiritual component. Africans see all things as connected. Nothing exists separate from anything else. When something negative occurs, a solution will also appear. Because of this harmony, the client's narrative must be co-constructed with the therapist, and counselors need to work on several types of active listening. Because of this, narrative therapy is often the recommended intervention for African families (Semmler & Williams, 2000).

8. **Check in about the relationship:** If the therapist is not an African American, he or she should also ask the client how he or she feels about working with someone from a different ethnic group. Treat these investigations seriously, and pay careful attention to nonverbal cues. Many African Americans may feel threatened by a European American therapist and will comply with therapy without actually feeling safe. They may state that they are comfortable with their therapist but maintain poor eye contact, position themselves several feet away, and speak in a quiet voice. These behaviors do not necessarily imply tension in the relationship, but they should be explored with sensitivity.

Once you pass these stages, you are ready to begin counseling.

Nwoye (2006) encourages counselors to follow a particular form of listening when working with African families. As with most clients, the process starts with <u>empathetic listening</u> (show solidarity with a client's feelings). Rather than interrupt the client with early feedback, the second stage is <u>credulous listening</u> (giving the client the unhurried time to tell his or her story). At this point, you will have an emotional reaction to what was said. This requires the counselor to enter deconstructive listening (exploring other possible data that might not have been covered by the client's story). From here, the counselor enters <u>unpacking</u> (cross-checking the narrative's controversial or negative issues) and, finally, <u>hermeneutic listening</u> (identifying the personal meanings or interpretations that the client gives to the events).

When the story is processed, counselors should look for common metaphors, dreams, or stories. This is where a cultural understanding of the client is necessary. All cultures have stories, and these are useful ways to connect clients to the emotional content of what is being discussed. For example, if working with a couple who engages in frequent arguments in front of their children, the counselor could have them discuss the African proverb: "When two elephants fight, the grass gets hurt."

Spirituality in Intervention

In Africa, counseling interventions would also involve the client's spiritual beliefs (Banks-Wallace, 2004). Some native healers treat mental health issues through washing, steaming, inducing vomiting, singing, or dancing (Mzimkulu & Simbayi, 2006). Something about these actives metaphors is curative. While these examples are particular to traditional healers, similar activities may be encouraged. For example, a counselor might ask a client to release his anger by washing his hands in a sink. The client might also be required to say, "Washing anger away." Other physical interventions might involve playing a child's favorite hip-hop music during the counseling session. After empowering her to incorporate the music's energy, teach her to generalize this emotional state to taking tests and reducing test anxiety. In each of these examples, care should be taken not to act as a traditional healer but to show solidarity with the client's worldview (Obiakor & Afoláyan, 2007).

Traditional healers also use ancestral breathing. Edwards (2008) describes how Zulu diviners (izangoma) and doctors (izinyanga) refer to this process as *selapha ngamandla amadlozi*. Contemporary indigenous Zulu view breathing exercises as a connection between the individual and the supernatural force of one's ancestors. When visiting a healer, the diviner will contact the spirit of the ancestors and channel this power into divinatory bones. Clients sometimes inhale this ancestral spiritual breath (or energy) from the bones. Sometimes, the diviner may sense an evolutionary history of lions in the spirit and roar with power. Sometimes, the breath is like a python and quiet. Usually, the breath is associated with a departed ancestor who has appeared to the client's dreams. The process involves breath-coordinated movement involving rhythmic hand clapping, singing, music, and dancing.

While channeling ancestral energies would not be appropriate for a mental health counselor, breathing exercises may be adapted to fit into the African spiritual worldview (Edwards, 2008). In the aforementioned exercises, inhaling is considered healing, and exhaling is the release of negative energy. Counselors can tap into this by asking clients to think of the positive spiritual forces they believe in (e.g., Christian, ancestral, etc.) and imagine the spiritual force filling them with each breath. Upon release, have the client picture the negative energy he or she wishes to expel (e.g., fear, depression, anxiety, etc.).

Working Through Painful Experiences

Emphasizing equality in the counseling relationship does not endorse a person-centered theoretical approach. Overemphasizing the client's feelings in an attempt to achieve catharsis will likely distance the client. Many African American clients are well aware of the painful experiences in their lives, and, as noted, they have accepted them. A nondirective, affect-oriented approach is often rejected as unproductive and ineffectual because it merely teaches them what they already know. Consider the following interaction between an African American woman (client) and a European American man (counselor):

Client:	I find myself crying all the time. I can't seem to stop. *(light sob)*
Counselor:	I can tell that you are feeling overwhelmed. It must be very difficult to feel trapped under such a heavy burden.
Client:	Yes, I don't know what to do. What can I do?
Counselor:	*(softly)* That's a question you will have to answer for yourself. I'm here to help you find your own answers.
Client:	*(heavy sigh)*

During this discussion, the client wanted specific, practical advice for dealing with her problems. At the very least, she needed to feel hope for the future. She did not wish to discuss her depression or cry during the session. In this session, the therapist continued to help the client explore her feelings. This approach resulted in a premature termination from the client. She could cry at home. From her therapist, she wanted something more.

For many African Americans, the purpose for coming to therapy is to receive some practical steps to ease their pain. Person-centered approaches, like the one attempted here, may be helpful but only when used in a more directive way. This may take the form of education and job training, drug treatment, or parenting skills. Therapeutic interventions will work best when connected with related services. For example, vocational training may be useless if not connected to jobs that are financially and mentally rewarding. Likewise, drug rehabilitation must be connected to practical changes in other lifestyle arenas. For example, considering the influence of religion in the lives of many African Americans, it is not surprising to find treatment programs such as Alcoholics Anonymous commonly advocated in African American communities. Such programs define mental health within a spiritual context, and reaching a deeper level of spiritual awareness is viewed as a crucial aspect of recovery.

Consequently, many clergy and members of the faith community have recognized the role of spirituality in prevention, intervention, and treatment of alcoholism and substance dependence and have responded with innovative programs. But for many clients, these directed interventions can come only after clients stop struggling against the feelings they push deep within themselves.

Here is a better starting intervention for the client mentioned above:

Client:	I just find myself crying all the time. I can't seem to stop. *(light sob)*
Counselor:	I can tell it's hard. *(pauses)* Why do think it's so important to stop?
Client:	*(tears)* I can't cry all the time!
Counselor:	Your body wouldn't let you. But you're crying because something wants to come out. *(pauses)* Your father beat you. Don't you deserve to feel sad?
Client:	*(hanging head)* I don't know. I guess.
Counselor:	I'd feel all kinds of things. Sad I couldn't change things. Pissed off that no one stopped him.
Client:	*(cries harder)* I can't be pissed off at my father.
Counselor:	I'm not sure you have a choice. *(pauses as client cries more)* *(picks up a balloon and inflates it)* What do you think would happen if I stuck a pin in this?
Client:	*(sniffles)* It would pop.
Counselor:	What if it didn't want to.
Client:	*(rolls her eyes)* It can't decide. It's a balloon.
Counselor:	All that air has to go somewhere. Oxygen, nitrogen, and carbon dioxide are like fear, anger, and sadness. Once inside, they are going to come out. It can happen all at once, like with a pin, or little by little.
Client:	*(gasps)* I don't want to pop.
Counselor:	When you release what's inside slowly *(releases the air slowly)*, the balloon goes back to normal. Maybe a little wiser too. We'll take things slow. Okay?

In addition to creating hope through here-and-now practical activities and spiritual awakening, African Americans seek lasting mental health interventions. Therapists need to address the individual within the context of her family, neighborhood, and city. At the very least, therapists should make an effort to involve a client's immediate family in the therapeutic process. Family members can provide reassurance, support, guidance, and stability. When attempting to involve members of an individual's community, the mechanisms for therapy may need to be altered. Therapists must learn to meet their clients where they are—both literally and figuratively. Meeting children on the basketball court, playground, schoolyard, street corner, or video arcade may help to demonstrate solidarity. African American children especially may view non–African American therapists as distant, naïve, and ignorant. Meeting the child in a familiar setting conveys a willingness to view the world from the client's reality.

Group Interventions

When conducting group interventions, the same steps apply as we discussed for individual therapy. Work on yourself before starting the group. To get the group started, focus on what you hope to accomplish. For example, Muller (2002) does an excellent job describing how group counseling works for teenage African Americans males. As a school counselor, she starts by arguing for a proactive stance within the school system. Professional school counselors have an obligation to provide guidance and counseling services to all students (American School Counselor Association, 1997). This decree is especially necessary for groups of students who face discrimination from the educational system itself.

In structuring a group, Muller (2002) recommends following Yalom (1995) (i.e., ensuring all members are willing and prepared for the process). The group design should be short term and focused on coping strategies for racism and other oppressions. At the beginning, the session should focus on goals, rules, and introductions. It may be helpful to use a sports analogy to demonstrate the importance of cooperation and respect (e.g., if you refuse to dribble and keep the ball to yourself, none of your points are going to count). The first session should also address the race of the leader, especially if the leader(s) is (are) not black.

Early sessions should address racial stereotypes, powerlessness, issues of control, developing personal respect, self-perception, and what it means to be an African American male or female. The group should allow for an open expression of feelings, and it should also create a sense of belongingness. After building trust, foster deeper stories to establish universality. Many African American males know the pain of loss and sacrifice. Their stories can help connect them. In her group, Muller asked members to write a personal rap song, which they would share with the group. These will likely address the daily challenges of living in a racist society.

To end the group, members should discuss their progress and how they hope to continue their growth. Muller also invited a panel of African American men (one had participated in an Upward Bound program) to share their experiences and their hopes for the group members. The idea of a panel is important because African American males need to see people like themselves succeeding and growing. This is one of the reasons Spencer Holland (Whitaker, 1991, p. 20) once said this in an interview:

> What we learned in the past 20 years is that white people don't care anything about educating our children … if we really expect to see change in the current situation, men have to get involved in this process, because it takes a Black man to prepare a Black boy for whatever he is going to face out there."

There are two important facets to this quote. First, non-black people can help, but they have to care. Second, no matter how much non-black people do, there is another dimension that requires role modeling from African American males. Both of these facets must be remembered when running a group.

ADVOCACY AND SOCIAL JUSTICE

Learning to care about African Americans requires a global perspective. In a way, only focusing on Americans of African descent belittles their heritage and culture. Global warming could devastate Africa over the next 20 years. Within the next 70 years, the Sudan may see its agricultural production potential decrease by 56%. Senegal may experience a 52% reduction (Cline, 2007). Without additional clean water supplies in Eastern and Western Africa, millions will die. These crises are complicated by a rising "brain drain," as physicians, scientists, professors, economists, computer programmers, and engineers leave the continent for jobs in the West (Obiakor & Afoláyan, 2007). When global warming concerns are coupled with an international movement to fight against Africa's "brain drain," the next generation of immigrants is likely to have lower levels of education or financial resources.

By far, the most prevalent battle for Africa and African immigrants involves the fight against disease. Youth have started becoming active in this battle against AIDS (Campbell et al., 2009), and related matters of substance abuse must also be taken more seriously (Simmons et al., 2009). Global warming has already changed the areas affected by malaria, with the disease now reaching higher into the mountains than ever before. The larger topic of finding cures for African diseases and health care for this population is also a matter of importance (Tucker & Makgoba, 2008).

In America, social justice and advocacy also require understanding and acceptance. We must understand the continued problems of racism and fight against these in education, community support, health care, and politics. We must also help clients accept their culture and their evolving identities.

A good illustration of how to walk the balance between accepting and evoking change is to urge acculturation over assimilation. The word assimilation (from the Latin *assimilatus*) literally means to make similar or to simulate. When African Americans attempt to look, act, and speak like European Americans—with no conscious connection to their ethnic or racial culture—they are assimilating. The most problematic aspect of assimilation is prejudice. When African Americans internalize everything about the dominant culture, they also internalize the racism.

Acculturation involves change by adapting to or borrowing traits from another culture. African Americans can learn white ways of speaking, acting, and behaving without losing their ethnic and racial ties. The idea of "borrowing" a culture implies any or all of the components may be returned to the owners. When non-black counselors work with African Americans, it is important to start from an acculturation viewpoint. You can explain how you have some things to offer, but nothing you provide should remove or rob clients of cultural identities they already possess.

Think about counseling from the standpoint of the civil rights movement. African Americans were resistant to receive assistance from other ethnic groups. As they gained power, they wanted the power to come from their own culture. Martin Luther King Jr. change this. In his "I Have a Dream" speech (King, 1963), he advocated for the acceptance of white culture:

> The marvelous new militancy which has engulfed the Negro community must not lead us to a distrust of all white people, for many of our white brothers, as evidenced by their presence here today, have come to realize that their destiny is tied up with our destiny. And they have come to realize that their freedom is inextricably bound to our freedom.
> We cannot walk alone.

This is the essence of acculturation. Our freedoms are tied together in an intricate relationship. Darkness spread to one group inevitably also blankets the hearts of the oppressor.

Expressing a desire for mutual belonging and shared freedoms will not convince African Americans of your sincerity. In *Dreams from My Father*, Barack Obama (1995) offered a profound statement about race:

> The emotions between the races could never be pure; even love was tarnished by the desire to find in the other some element that was missing in ourselves. Whether we sought out our demons or salvation, the other race would always remain just that: menacing, alien, and apart (p. 124).

This may sound unfair or pessimistic. It certainly angered a number of people who continue to use the quote on anti-Obama websites. But there is a truth to this statement. It does not mean white and black individuals cannot get along. Instead, it speaks more globally. There will always be racism, and there will always be distance between the races. Former president Jimmy Carter offered proof of this:

> When a radical fringe element of demonstrators and others begin to attack the president of the United States as an animal or as a reincarnation of Adolf Hitler or when they wave signs in the air that said we should have buried Obama with Kennedy, those kinds of things are beyond the bounds (Carter again cites racism, 2009).

If African American understand and even expect mistreatment from whites, how can a non-black counselor succeed? Honesty and openness are the critical beginning points. Here is a brief example of how a European American counselor (female) can self-reveal with an African American client (male). The client is expressing frustration over being passed up for a promotion he expected to receive:

Client:	*(fists clenched and speaking loudly)* You'd think they'd get tired of this shit! They pound on us until there's nothing left. Fuck this, man. I can't work in this fucked up world anymore.
Counselor:	*(silence)* I ... *(sighs)*. According to my training, I'm supposed to comfort you when you're angry. I should say something like, "It must be hard to feel so alone and abused." But those words are too shallow. I've got to say something different. Look, I don't have a clue what you're feeling. I can hear your anger and your pain, but I can't know what's it's like to be passed over for a job because of skin color.

Client:	*(sits back hard against the chair and folds his arms)* Then, how the hell are you going to help me!
Counselor:	I can walk beside you—to let you know that at least one white person feels horrible for the injustice you've faced.
Client:	*(sighs)* That won't get me a promotion.
Counselor:	Not today. But you're stronger than you think. I don't want you leaving today thinking all white people will hurt you. Even when I can't understand, I'm on your side, and I'm learning.
Client:	*(sighs)* You want me to get all weepy now and lay down again?
Counselor:	No. Keep enough anger to fight back. It's okay. In fact, it's necessary.

Affirming a black man's right to remain angry shows solidarity. But acculturation requires more than camaraderie. Be genuine with your clients, acknowledging your mistakes, prejudices, and concerns. When you note differences in speech, behavior, or ideology, share these with your client. Learn.

Learning requires more than what happens in the session. Much more. A non-black counselor attempting to guide an African American client should demonstrate an obvious appreciation of African heritage. Collect African masks, paintings, or sculptures. Dine at restaurants serving gumbo, black-eyed peas, or groundnut stew. Listen to hip-hop and jazz. Celebrate Martin Luther King Jr.'s birthday and Black History Month with more than a passing glance. Read books by Malcolm X, J. A. Rogers, Ralph Abernathy, or Calvin Hernton. Watch movies such as *Body and Soul*, *The Emperor Jones*, *A Raisin in the Sun*, *Eve's Bayou*, or *To Sleep with Anger*. In short, do what you can to acculturate to the world you are attempting to enter. This can only make you a better counselor.

Jayvyn's Story (A Client's Viewpoint)
(26-year-old African American male)

I moved to Seattle after graduating from college. Well, Redmond actually. A large software company offered me a ridiculous salary and a moving allowance. I'm talking pay pay. I figured I could play at grinding time until I started my own company. How long could it take? I'd make connections. See how the gamers set things up, and I'd break out.

But hell. Seattle ain't Georgia. Even finding a house was hard. In the South, I learned to accept some limitations. I wouldn't buy in Macon. Not unless I wanted my place torched. Here, the rules were hidden. Realtors kept treating me like I could live anywhere. One showed me a house. I guess you'd call it an estate. Damn big! A couple guys from work lived in the neighborhood, but the street was really white. Everything felt so sterile. Rectangular yards. Square houses. No one on the sidewalks except brothers blowing leaves out of the gutters. I kept telling myself to chill. None of this mattered. My work

(continues)

Jayvyn's Story (A Client's Viewpoint) (continued)

loved me. I made enough to fly home several times a year. I'd find a community to support me. But, you know, after a year, I'm still lost.

I never realized how alone I could feel in a town like this. No, it's more than alone. I lost part of myself. People were warm and accepting. Polite to the point of annoyance. I experienced less prejudice than in the South, and I got a promotion. But my life feels like the life of a stranger. If I stuck around for another two or ten years, I'd be one of them.

In the black community, there are phrases for people like me. I feel like a newgot—someone who looks black but is believed to succeed because of a hidden white lineage. I feel tension with my white coworkers. It's like people wanting to call me a nigger or arapi but saying platitudes instead. I wish they'd just say what they thought. Get it out.

Maybe cookies describe how I'm feeling best. Oreo cookies. You know, black on the outside and white on the inside. I'd heard black successful people called Oreos all the time, but I never understood the real problem. What I learned is that an Oreo isn't really a cookie at all. It's two different things crushed together. I refuse to live like that anymore. I need to change, and I need help to figure this out.

Nikki's Story (A Counselor's Viewpoint)
(27-year-old of Hawaii and European heritage)

I have to start by stating that Jayvyn intimidated the hell out of me. He was smarter than me, made three times more than money than I did, understood himself and society better than me, and he was my age. I felt myself wanting to make a good impression on him—to look like a professional early in the treatment process. But I realized how silly this was. I opted for honesty.

In our first session, after he relayed his story, I told him much of what I confessed to above. He was smarter, richer, wiser, and more insightful than I was. I expected him to roll his eyes and walk out the door. Instead, he just leaned back in his chair (forgoing his forced business-like posture), threw his head back, and said, "Now, you're someone I can work with."

At first, I was curious if he only liked me because I was someone he could dominate. I'm worried that my confession had seriously wounded our relationship. But he quickly clarified. He added, "I thought you were whiter than chalk when I walked into this office, but you're cool."

We only work together for five sessions. During that time, I found myself opening more with him than I had any other client. It went against my training to do this; I came from a fairly psychoanalytic background. But I realized he needed to see me as a person before he could work with me as a counselor.

(continues)

Nikki's Story (A Counselor's Viewpoint) (continued)

Part of our discussions focused on how white culture works. He seemed genuinely surprised that most white people maintained only a small network of friends, and many never knew their neighbors. I admitted but that I have had neighbors who were racist and prejudiced, but more often than not, they simply failed to invest in any relationships. Not with white people; not with black people. This led to a discussion of his own insecurities and how he *expected* people to look down on him for the color of his skin. He felt very confident about the prejudicial beliefs of one senior vice president, but he also came to believe a few of his coworkers were just "ignorant" about how their comments had offended him.

By the end of the fourth session, Jayvyn had reached some conclusions about his life. He planned to stay with his software company for one more year. Then, he would move back to Georgia. He wanted to prove to himself that he *could* handle the "white world." He also wanted the money that his company offered and the experience he would gain in the process. In the end, he overcame many of his fears and learned to see himself as a crusader. He wanted to ensure that the next black senior programmer would have a better experience.

In the final session, Jayvyn told me he had spoken to the human resource director and set up a Saturday workshop (which 45 people attended). He sounded more secure of himself, as if he had learned how to trust his inner voice. We didn't cover much psychoeducation in our sessions. He didn't gain much personal insight about his unconscious. We only sharpened the skills he already had, including identifying when he could trust people and when they were trapped in unexamined prejudice. But that seemed to be what he wanted the most.

He also surprised me during our debriefing. He told me that he was glad I didn't push him one way or another. He wanted time to sort out his feelings on his own in his own space. But he enjoyed the way our time challenged him to think about things. He said it "turned on his thinking." He might have wanted something different from a black counselor, but the flow of our sessions seemed to work perfectly for him.

Questions to Consider

1. Jayvyn described an Oreo as black on the outside and white on the inside. What social or behavioral components describe these white and black facets? Is Jayvyn's perception of these being distinct and separate lifestyles accurate?

2. Pleasant white Americans surrounded Jayvyn, and he experienced less prejudice than he had in the South. Other African Americans describe such acceptance as disorienting and untrustworthy. Is it fair to judge polite white individuals and cultures as having closet prejudices? Why or why not?

(continues)

Nikki's Story (A Counselor's Viewpoint) (continued)

3. Jayvyn believed living in white suburbia would erode part of his identity. Can you conceive of a town or area where you would experience something similar?

4. Nikki believed being open about her insecurities helped the sessions develop. When would this type of disclosure be counterproductive? In overcoming your own ignorance, how can you find a friend or informant to serve as your <u>African cultural guide</u>?

INTERVENTION EXERCISES

Counseling and Therapy: Tion is a 16-year-old African American male who recently lost his weekend job as a construction worker. He is living with his mother, who requested he attend counseling to work on his anger. As he becomes more comfortable with you, he starts to speak more casually. In your third session, Tion says, "My mama, she thinks I'm a jobber. But it ain't like that. The supervisor was mugging me, all right? So, I says, 'Why you muggin on me?' He points at my kicks and asks where I got them. He thought I had jacked them 'cause they looked like his! So, I tell him to stop jocking my style, and he done fires me. What the hells I supposed to do?"

Alternative speech: "My mother thinks I'm intentionally failing at work and school. But it really isn't like that. The supervisor at the construction plant was staring at me with malignant thoughts, and I asked why he was giving me those kinds of looks. He pointed to my shoes and asked where I had found them. From his tone, it was clear he thought they were stolen because he didn't think I could afford shoes like this. Ignoring his comment, I told him *he* was copying *my* style. From that comment alone, he fired me. I don't know what else I could have done or how to prevent this from happening again."

In <u>forming your intervention</u>, do not try to mimic Tion's speech. Instead, <u>attend to the tone and idea behind the words.</u>

School Psychology: Jazmin is a fourth-grade (age 10) girl who has been referred for an Individualized Education Program (IEP) assessment. Her teacher (a European American teaching in a 95% white school) believes Jazmin lacks word-attack skills, is unable to conceptualize abstract material, and has below-average intelligence. Jazmin's parents have filed a written protest against the assessment. They allege the teacher is racist and has negatively affected their daughter's self-esteem. Even if the tests prove positive, the parents argue, the results stem from the teacher's systematically negative treatment. They demand an intervention by the principal and the school psychologist. What do you recommend?

School Counseling: Darnell (African American male, age eight) came to the principal's office after being referred by his teacher for insubordination. When he walks into the principal's office, he kicks over the trashcan, littering the floor with papers, and pounds his fist on the table. You are quickly summoned to help, and Darnell's anger is blazing across his face. "You're just like them," he says to you. "That teacher never saw Johnny put that frog down the back of my shirt. Then, she sends me here for yelling at him." He narrows his gaze. "You gonna punish me too? For the trash? This place sucks." How do you handle the session?

Social Work: Shanice is a 25-year-old African American single mother of three (ages two, three, and five). For the past three years, she worked as a bookkeeper for a local law firm. Her success led her back to college to major in prelaw. You are a social work agent for Child Protective Services. When your phone rings, Mrs. Johnson (a middle-aged white woman and Shanice's next-door neighbor) is on the other end of the line. Mrs. Johnson is calling to report neglect regarding Shanice's children. The neighbor continues, "She's always working, at school, or hanging out with that hoodlum she's dating." The neighbor continued, "I'm not racist, but I think that black boyfriend is a gang member. Sometimes, she leaves that monster with the children. Alone. Other times, I don't know who is there, but I often hear the babies crying at night." How do you handle the call?

QUESTIONS TO CONSIDER

1. Do you believe that the hardships African Americans endured 100 years ago continue to affect their culture today?
2. Does it seem likely that African Americans follow a process of identity development? Do you think Cross's model accurately describes the experiences of many African Americans?
3. Why does physical discipline seem to be less harmful to African American children than it is for European Americans?
4. How does unexamined prejudice continue to affect African Americans in school?
5. Despite their increased rate of high school graduation, African Americans have seen little improvement in the status of their wages. What factors could be continuing to hold them back in the workforce?
6. Why is insight-oriented therapy often less helpful than solution-focused approaches when working with African American clients?
7. What native healing approaches could you incorporate into your counseling or therapy sessions with African American clients?
8. Is it possible (or desirable) to be a color-blind therapist?
9. On August 28, 1963, while standing on the steps of the Lincoln Memorial in Washington, D.C., Martin Luther King Jr. made his most memorable speech. He declared, "I have a dream that one day this nation will rise up and live out the true meaning of its creed—'We hold these truths to be self-evident, that all men are created equal.'" Later in the same speech, he stated, "I have a dream that my four little children will one day live in a nation where they will not be judged by the color of their skin but by the content of their character." Do you believe that today is the day that he dreamed of? If not, will this day ever take place?
10. In order to advocate for African Americans, how important is it to experience part of the culture? How much experience would be necessary to offer a cohesive and thorough intervention?

CHAPTER 5

Latin Americans

INSIGHT EXERCISE

Juanita (age 20) lives in a suburb of San Diego. Her parents emigrated from Baja when she was seven, and she considers America her home. For the past two years, she has dated José, a third-generation American whose family emigrated from Guatemala. Last night, after dinner at their favorite restaurant, José proposed and Juanita accepted. She loves José, but she wonders if their cultural differences might prevent him from fully integrating into her family.

Later that night, after Juanita told her parents and went to bed, her grandmother appeared in her room. It was not a dream. Her abuela simply appeared, glowing and holding a cempazuchitl (a yellow marigold, the symbol of death). After her eyes adjusted, Juanita sat up and concentrated on the woman. Before Juanita could react or leave her bed, the woman spoke!

"Juanita, you are making a mistake," the figure stated in a concerned voice, speaking in Spanish. "You should not marry José; he is not your soulmate (*alma gemela*)—beware of your lust and wait for the right man!" With that, the apparition vanished, and Juanita fainted into her pillows. When she awoke, Juanita ran to her mother and recounted the story.

Her mother explained that ghosts rarely appear outside of *Día de los Muertos* (the Day of the Dead) unless the message provided was urgent and necessary. After this commentary, Juanita cancelled her wedding and broke off her relationship with José.

(continues)

INSIGHT EXERCISE *(continued)*

Questions to Consider:

1. Would it make sense to assess Juanita for schizophrenia or another psychotic disorder? (*Note:* This should not be a simple answer.)
2. Is Juanita wise to listen to the apparition? Why or why not?
3. What role should Juanita's mother's explanation play in the interpretation and in Juanita's decision about her marriage?
4. How would you counsel Juanita and José?

As we already discussed, the term **African American** underwent several derivations before reaching its final form. It represents a location of origin (Africa) rather than physical characteristics. With Latin Americans, the term is more difficult for many outsiders to understand. Why Latino? Why not Hispanic, Mexican, or Cuban? The explanation is a little complicated.

In most Latin American countries, there are usually at least three distinct groups present: the indigenous group that continues to speak the native language; the **mestizo,** or blended group that shares indigenous and Spanish blood and culture; and those who are direct descendants of Spanish colonizers (Falicov, 1998). The term **Hispanic** best depicts the direct descendants of the Spanish conquerors but applies only partially or not at all to other Latin groups. When the term is applied to the **mestizo** groups, it may imply that their Spanish heritage is more important or valuable than their native roots. For members of native cultures, the term may simply insult their uniqueness and individuality (Lott, 2010). In order to avoid all these pitfalls, the terms **Latino** (masculine/universal) and **Latina** (feminine) were employed to provide an unbiased and more universal means of identifying an enormously diverse group of individuals. Why refer to such groups as Latinos? The regions in the Western Hemisphere south of the United States—Mexico, Central America, the West Indies, and South America—comprise a territory referred to as **Latin America**. In each of these regions, the official languages (Spanish, Portuguese, and French) are derived from the Latin language. Latin is a significant cultural umbrella that is shared by these multifarious groups, even though none of the regions actually speak (or ever spoke) Latin.

Although the term **Latinos** adequately identifies people with Latin American roots, in some cases, it is not the preferable method of identification. For example, many Mexicans prefer to be called Mexican or Mexican American rather than Latino/a. The various Latin American countries have distinct cultures and traditions that make them unique. Many immigrants fight to hold on to their nationalistic identities, which are more specific than ethnicity. However, as generations become further removed from the country of origin, they may distance themselves from their ancestors' homeland. Consider the following narrative from a college student in southern California:

My parents are from Mexico and are very proud of their Mexican heritage. When we came to America, they understood very little English, but they wanted us to learn because, they said, "You must speak English to survive here." As I studied with the Anglo students, I never felt as though I was different. I was accepted. At least, I was until junior high school. One day, a boy ran up behind me, pulled my hair, and called me a spick. I didn't know what the word meant, but there was an intense anger in his voice. I wanted to be like everyone else, but something about me was different—painfully different. By the time I started college, I had started to learn about the richness of the Latino culture. I wanted to understand my people and how they viewed themselves. The more I learned, the prouder I became. Eventually, I decided to call myself "Latina" rather than "Mexican American" because I wanted to identify with all Latino cultures. This hurt my parents deeply and continues to hurt them to this day because they thought I was abandoning my Mexican heritage. On the contrary, I believe I was fulfilling it.

The position taken by this student was one of the reasons why some Latinos started calling themselves "Chicanos." The term arose in the late 1960s, when the English-speaking children of Mexican immigrants realized they were not fully Mexican or American. They wanted a term that reflected the special history of Mexican Americans and paid tribute to both cultural influences (Falicov, 1998). The term fell out of favor during the 1990s because it was associated with poverty and gangs. Still, it is important to realize that the term a Latino/a client selects to define him or herself is very powerful. These labels are not chosen arbitrarily. They reflect elements of the client's past, culture, and identity.

Unique Challenges

Gregory Nava's (director) movie *El Norte* provides an excellent summary of the challenges Latino Americans' face. The film begins in San Pedro, a small rural Guatemalan village. Arturo, one of the town's leaders, is helping to organize a union to protect the laborers from exploitation. He realizes the dangers associated with such an action, but as he explains to his adult son Enrique, "to the rich, the peasant is just a pair of strong arms."

Arturo is murdered by federal troops later in the day. They cut off his head and hang it from a tree, which leads Enrique to fight back. He kills a soldier and is forced to flee the country. His sister Rosa, realizing more troops will come and rape the women, decides to leave with him.

Throughout the early part of the film, Enrique and Rose hear wonderful stories about *el norte* (the northern land of the United States). In the north, everyone has a toilet. They have machines that cook. Everyone is wealthy. It is this dream—the American dream—that motivates them to hire a *coyote* (an often disreputable agent who smuggles people across the border). The first one robs them. The second guides them through a sewer tunnel, where they are bitten by rats. But they arrive in the country.

After battles with immigration, difficulties finding employment, and disillusionment with the so-called wealth of the United States, the movie turns frightening. Rosa is hospitalized with typhus, contracted from rat bites received during her border crossing. As she struggles to survive, she tells her brother, "In our homeland, there's no place for us. They want to kill us. In Mexico, there's only poverty. And in the north, we aren't accepted. When are we going to find a home—maybe only in death?" Enrique gives up a job—his only hope for financial stability—to stay with her, but she dies in the hospital the following day.

In the final scene, Enrique tries to sell himself as a day laborer. Standing in a crowd of would-be workers, he cries to the people in charge. "Look, I have strong arms." In that moment, the camera flashes back to their home in Guatemala. We see his father's head still hanging by a rope, and we know Enrique is dead as he lives. He became nothing more than an animal—a workhorse—who will never fit into American culture. This is the challenge many Latinos face. Do they give up everything for the American dream or do they hold on to their heritage and struggle against the system. For some, no other options appear.

Historical Context

The region of Latin America is made up of South America, Mexico, Central America, and the West Indies. Within this region are nearly three dozen independent nations as well as colonies and other political units that have special ties with the United States, Great Britain, France, or the Netherlands. At the time of the Europeans' arrival in the New World in 1492, 60 to 75 million people lived in Latin America. Most of them inhabited the highlands of the central Andes and the region between northern Central America and central Mexico. These areas were under the control of the Inca, Maya, and Aztec peoples. Within 50 years after the arrival of the Europeans, more than half the Indians had perished. Within a century, no more than a fourth remained. The disappearance of the native population has often been attributed to cruel treatment by the Spaniards. However, the introduction of European diseases such as smallpox and measles—against which the Indians had no natural immunity—had an equally devastating effect.

To provide a supply of labor in places uninhabited by Indians, the Portuguese—and, to a lesser degree, the Spaniards—imported African slaves. After 1650, settlers from the colonizing nations of northern Europe transported slaves into the territories they had seized from the Spaniards in the West Indies. During the three centuries prior to 1850, at least 10 million slaves may have been introduced into Latin America, compared with about 500,000 brought into the United States. In Latin America, most of the slaves were taken to northeastern Brazil and the islands of the Caribbean, where they worked on sugar plantations (Thomas, 1999).

Spanish and Portuguese colonies in Central America and South America became independent during the first half of the nineteenth century. Haiti—the first Latin American country to win independence—gained its freedom from France in 1804. In 1821, Mexico won its independence from Spain and governed California until the end of the Mexican-American War in 1848. At that time, the Treaty of Guadalupe Hildalgo was signed, promising the rights of citizenship and land ownership to the Mexicans living in the territories that became part of the United States. In reality, many rights were denied and land was confiscated (Novas, 1994). It is important to realize that many Latino residents of the southwestern United States may be offended at being considered immigrants. Their families may predate the arrival of European Americans.

During the depression of the 1930s, an estimated half a million Mexican Americans—including those whose families had been living in the United States for centuries—were deported to Mexico. Most were never fully integrated into Mexican society, and many returned when labor shortages developed during World War II. At that time, the United States instituted the Bracero program to encourage Mexicans to work in the fields on a seasonal basis (Kanellos, 1994).

As with African Americans, skin color may play a role in the history of discrimination against Latinos. González de Alba (1994) theorized that the arrogant Spanish colonizers might have created this prejudice. White (or *güero*) individuals are viewed as descendants of the Spaniards and, as such, are born into power, privilege, and a higher social class. Darker skin (or *indio*) signifies suppression, inferiority, and lack of social power (Falicov, 1998).

The possibility of Latinos classifying themselves as black may surprise many European Americans. Until 1954, Latinos were considered white according to American census data (Falicov, 1998). In 1954, they—as well as African Americans and Asians—were labeled a "colored minority." The distinction was used for less than noble purposes. European American school systems fighting to keep African Americans out of their schools could argue that they were already integrated because they accepted "Hispanics." The designation as a minority group provided a political advantage to Latinos, who could now secure federal funding and political representation.

However, recognition from the American government does not imply acceptance by the broader society. Mary Margaret Navar (Davis, 1990) tells the story of her "assimilation" during the 1950s. As part of a young immigrant family struggling to gain acceptance, she was allowed to speak only English. She was given an American name and expected to learn American culture. Still, she found herself labeled as different. Store owners refused to assist her, and others politely redirected her to Spanish-speaking attendants. Still others simply provided racist comments and feedback.

Immigration and Development

Latin Americans now represent the largest ethnic minority—about 15% of the U.S. population (Lott, 2010). The majority of these immigrants are from Mexico, and most immigrants come speaking Spanish.

When in America, immigrant families face immense obstacles. Fear of being deported plays a role not only in the adults struggling to find employment but for the children. Even when parents are citizens—when children live in neighborhoods where deportation raids occur—they become fearful (Capps, Castaneda, Chaudry & Santos, 2007). Isolation and economic hardships often spur mental health problems in children and adults. Children fear abandonment after the arrest of their parents or neighbors. Such fears permeate into many aspects of life, with immigrant children living in urban or disadvantaged communities struggling with academic and occupational progress (Perreira et al., 2006; Portes & Rumbaut, 2001).

Many small Mexican towns virtually lack men between the ages of 15 and 45. They have left for America to earn the funds necessary to support their families, but many return frequently to their "homes." This notion of a temporary commitment to America is difficult for many non-immigrants to understand. People from the dominant culture see only the great aspects about America.

Alejandro, a native-born Mexican man in his 50s, described his frustration this way: "Every day, I go to work in the fields. I pull grapes for eight hours. By the end of the day, my hands bleed. My back hurts. I worry about the stuff they spray around me. America doesn't want me. It's using me. It gives me enough to live, and I appreciate that. But I would leave in a flash if I could afford to live back home."

Such desires often provide a disincentive for learning English, which may make it necessary to have an interpreter in sessions. Sometimes, children of immigrants—who are immersed in the dominant culture more thoroughly— may serve this role, but there guidelines for working with any interpreter (Cultural competency, 2010, p. 14).

Step 1: Conducting a pre-session: Cover some of the keywords from counseling, such as depression, anxiety, or other key ideas. If the interpreter does not know these words, have the interpreter pause the session to ask questions. It also helps when the interpreter uses first person when speaking for the client. Rather than saying, "My father thinks this," have him or her say, "I would like this. ..." It is also helpful to prepare the interpreter for the nature of the discussion. If something difficult or painful will be addressed, let the interpreter know this ahead of time. The interpreter should also be notified to alert you to potential cultural misunderstandings that may arise.

Step 2: The interview: Sit with your eyes and body facing the client. The interpreter should not be the focal point. When you speak, watch the client for nonverbal cues and speak directly to the client. To increase the likelihood of a strong interpretation, speak at an even pace and use small segments. Wait for the interpreter to catch up. Some ideas in English have no cultural equivalent, so you may need to paint word pictures to communicate effectively. Even ideas of moderation are difficult to communicate—for example, "okay." This is best described as a balance between good and bad. Using scales like this (i.e., not good; not bad) can help increase your speech. Because of the importance of accurate communication, the ideas expressed should be simple and leaner. Changing ideas in the middle will not be helpful. This is a time-consuming process, so be patient with yourself and all involved. Time spent up front will be rewarded with good rapport and clear communication.

Not all Latinos want to return to their home countries. Many enjoy America and seek to acculturate. Some of these different approaches depend on the individual's country of origin, their skin color, or education. These are all included within individual differences.

Within Group Differences

When European Americans tend to think about Latinos, they often think of people coming from Mexico. This myopic perspective can be very hurtful to those from different cultures. Much of Latin America has been influenced by European settlers. Peru, Guatemala, and Bolivia have maintained the most pre-Columbian population. In contrast, the Southern Cone of the continent—which includes Argentina, Chile, Uruguay, and southern Brazil—houses many of the Spanish and other European settlers. In visiting the Southern Cone, the culture and architecture resemble that of Spain more than of Mexico.

The preservation of culture is important to most Latino subgroups, but each ethnic group expresses its history and culture differently. For example, the four largest Latin American groups are Mexicans, Puerto Ricans, Cubans, and those from the Dominican Republic. Comprising nearly 64% of the Latinos in America, Mexican Americans are quite likely to temporarily immigrate to America (Falicov, 1998; Lott, 2010). They may spend summers and December in Mexico or simply return to Mexico once their children are educated.

Puerto Rican families face an entirely different set of challenges. A fiercely proud people, Puerto Ricans are American citizens. As residents of a commonwealth of America, they are subject to military duty, may benefit from limited social programs and aid, but are unable to vote, collect welfare, or pay taxes. They are stuck between two nations, with two flags, two languages, and two national identities. This dual identity forces them to create a tenuous balance between their two cultures. They want to enjoy the economic benefits that flow from America without losing their Puerto Rican identity. However, like their Mexican counterparts, they often find the dominant culture in the mainland cold and hostile. Although Puerto Ricans can legally stay on the mainland, they often travel back and forth. They stay long enough to earn a small income before returning home to nourish their cultural roots. This makes them "transmigrants" because they can sustain family, economic, and social relationships that span geographic and cultural borders. Unfortunately, this freedom has not resulted in higher income levels, and Puerto Ricans are generally considered the poorest of all Latino group (Falicov, 1998).

Puerto Ricans also go to great efforts to pass along values that differ in significant ways from those of their Anglo counterparts. When ranking a list of values mothers would like to pass on to their children, Puerto Ricans put honesty, respect, and responsibility at the top of the list, followed by loyalty to family, affection, and sharing. Assertiveness, independence, and creativity, which were highly ranked by Anglo parents, were viewed as less important by Puerto Ricans (Gonzalez-Ramos, Zayas & Cohen, 1998).

Cubans tend to be the wealthiest Latino immigrants. In the late 1950s, when Fidel Castro took control of Cuba, many of the country's wealthier citizens fled to America. Unlike the Mexicans and Puerto Ricans, many of the Cubans came equipped with financial, political, and educational resources. These factors contributed to a more favorable reception, and Cuban immigrants were able to establish successful business centers in Miami, New Jersey, and New York (Falicov, 1998).

Although Cubans are generally accepted within American society, many resist Americanization. They may long for a pre-revolutionary Cuba and seek to restore their traditional Spanish values and lifestyles. This anti-American sentiment was clearly displayed in May 1999 when the Baltimore Orioles hosted the Cuban All-Star baseball team. Anti-Castro protestors made frequent demonstrations and even interrupted the game by running onto the field. The second base umpire, a Cuban currently residing in America, took offense at the demonstration and body-slammed and punched one activist. He considered it "the right thing to do" because, he explained, "Above all, I am Cuban." Although most Cubans would not consider violence the "right thing to do" when their teammates are derided, it is interesting that the umpire's rationale for his actions stemmed directly from his cultural identity. He did not defend his actions as the "right thing for an umpire to do" or even the "right thing for a man to do." As a Cuban-American, he clung to his Cuban identity when he was forced to choose an alliance.

However, violence stems more from prejudice and discrimination than from one's country of origin. Bui and Thongniramol (2005) examined 18,907 Latino adolescents participating in the National Longitudinal Study of Adolescent Health. One of the best predictors of violence was how long the families had been in the States. Children who were second-generation youths were 60% more likely to report violent delinquency than their first-generation peers. Children who were third-generation Latinos were 88% more likely.

Within each Latino group, acculturation is viewed as a mixed blessing. Parents want their children to succeed in America, and they realize that success will require proficiency in the English language and familiarity with European American social mores. However, they also want to pass down the legacy of their Latin history. The tightrope between these two worlds is often very difficult to walk.

Cultural Identity

Assessing levels of acculturation among Latinos is different from doing so for African Americans. Most African Americans readily identify themselves as black. Latinos often find themselves trapped between various racial groups. Even back in the early 1990s, when Latinos were given the choice between identifying themselves as "white," "black," or "other," 52% identified themselves as white, 3.4% considered themselves black, and the rest checked the "other" box (U.S. Bureau of the Census, 1991). Many of the Latinos who come from the Caribbean islands share a significant history with darker-skinned individuals. For example, Puerto Ricans, who were originally dark-skinned, mixed with lighter-skinned immigrants to create a range of racial characteristics and colors. These differences have led some to refer to Puerto Ricans as "rainbow people" (Falicov, 1998).

Virtually any physical or noticeable characteristic may evoke intolerance from European American society. It could be a person's manner of dress, Spanish accent, Latin surname, poverty, immigrant status, or skin color (Edwards & Romero, 2008). However, of these, skin color seems to play the most significant role. When examining housing segregation, Massey and Denton (1993) found that darker-skinned Latinos tended to become more segregated than their lighter-skinned peers were. Lighter-skinned Latinos earned a segregation index of 52, mixed-race Latinos received a score of 72, and darker-skinned Latinos received an index of 80, which was similar to that found for African Americans. Despite these external concerns, Latinos also face prejudice from within their ethic cohort.

Many Latino groups hold firmly established views of ethnic hierarchies. Shorris (1992) referred to this form of intragroup discrimination as *racismo,* and he noted that many of these beliefs stem from myths about the prestige of a Latino's national origin. From his observations, Cubans living in Miami are often regarded as conceited and arrogant. They are viewed as cultural traitors and more closely akin to European Americans than their fellow Latinos. Given their increased potential for economic success, they may flaunt their economic progress or use it to denigrate other Latino groups.

When Latinos attempt to fit into the dominant culture, it often comes at the price of losing their ethnic heritage. Imagine you were a dark-skinned Latino hearing the following advice:

> You should know, my son, that you are very, very dark. Now that you are going to move (from Guadalajara) and come to live here in Mexico City and you soon will have a girlfriend, you must find one who is very, very White so that in case you get married you will have White children. (González de Alba, 1994, p. 28)

The inner conflict upon hearing such statements is profound. On the one hand is the desire to maintain a sense of heritage, cultural identity, and ethnic pride. On the other hand is the wish to attenuate heartache and discrimination. There are no easy answers in the resolution of these conflicts.

In addition to racial hierarchies, there are also gender hierarchies among Latinos. Regardless of their national origin, families tend to treat young Latinas differently from Latino boys. Family members often protect the emerging woman from the sexual threats around her. Various family members emphasize the need for young women to follow special rules, preserve their virginity, and prepare for their role in creating a new family. Saez, Casado, and Wade (2009) noted that hypermasculinity in Latino males corresponds with high ethnic identity and a view that all males are similar.

Family members are likely to maintain a protective role toward young Latinas, but these girls also undergo a form of liberation. Immigrant mothers tend to accept the "Americanization" of their girls and welcome the freedom they experience (Falicov, 1998). However, many older Latinas take great pride in housework and traditionally feminine activities, which may send mixed messages to girls. They are told to exceed the limitations of their mothers but are also expected to maintain the prescribed feminine roles of their culture. Forging a new definition of womanhood that bridges these two worlds is often quite difficult and requires all family members to make compromises. Other cultural values, such as attitudes toward sex, continue to fall along gender lines too. Boys and girls continue to buy into the idea that boys are intrinsically lustful and not in control of their sexual desires, while girls are attracted to love and

TABLE **5.1**
Ruiz's Acculturation Model

Casual stage	The individual denies his or her identification with the minority culture and ignores institutional racism.
Cognitive stage	The individual chooses whether to blend into the dominant culture or seek to identify with the minority culture.
Consequence stage	Shame regarding their cultural heritage emerges because they have either identified with the dominant culture (which will not completely accept them), or they identify with a group they have long viewed as inferior.
Working-through stage	Components of the minority culture are integrated into one's identity.
Resolution stage	Self-esteem and ethnic pride accompany a growing sense of group/self identity.

intimacy over sex (Borges & Nakamura, 2009). Such views are changing, but they are reinforced throughout the Latino community.

The process of acculturation has become easier than it was in the past, but it still runs a common course. As with African American clients, one of the factors that should be considered when counseling Latinos is their level of acculturation. Ruiz (1990) created a five-stage model that seemed to explain the acculturation process his Latino clients underwent (see Table 5.1). As with the African American models, the first stage (casual stage) involves a denial of the Latino culture and its uniqueness. Negative messages, acts of discrimination, and broadly accepted stereotypes are generally ignored.

As individuals encounter more negative messages, they enter the cognitive stage and face a critical decision. Do they associate with poor Latinos and risk being stereotyped and discriminated against or do they assimilate into white culture to escape stigma or become successful? In the third stage (consequence), Latinos begin to feel ashamed of or embarrassed about their cultural heritage. They choose to associate only with non-Latinos or they have identified with a group they view as inferior. Either way, they begin to internalize the negative images society has thrust upon them. In reaction, they may abandon cultural customs, attempt to change their name, lighten their skin, and speak English without an accent. This stage continues until they acknowledge the impossibility of denying their culture—a realization that initiates the fourth stage.

There are differences between this experience and the one discussed in Cross's model for African Americans. In the first stage, there is a denial of the minority culture. This is different for the African American experience, where the minority culture may not be understood at all. For Latinos, they know their family culture early, and they understand how it is different from the majority culture. They also see how the majority culture has power and social acceptance.

During the fourth stage (working through), the individual realizes that he or she can no longer pretend to identify with an alien ethnic identity. The individual is propelled to reclaim the disowned identity fragments from his or her past life (Sue & Sue, 1999). Although this is a positive process, it can take a toll on the life the individual has attempted to create. Only in the resolution stage do things start to make sense. Here, pride and self-esteem reintegrate back into the sense of ethnic self.

Although this model gives us a clear linear progression that helps us to conceptualize acculturation challenges faced by immigrant population, it assumes a similar process of acculturation for most people. However, <u>stress affects people differently depending on social networks, language barriers, and other issues</u>. Acculturative stress tends to increase with poor family cohesion, limited English language skills, pressures to assimilate, family/peer pressure against acculturation, and longer residence in the United States (Miranda & Matheny, 2000; Rodriguez, Myers, Mira, Flores & Garcia-Hernandez, 2002). The cultural identity model for this group follows a slightly different process:

The early facets of this identity model include family immersion as a type of cultural immersion. Latino families gain an understanding of cultural iden-tity from their family—probably more than any other cultural group. When they attempt to blend into the dominant culture, it will accept them to a degree, but this causes acculturative stress. They continue to wrestle with the

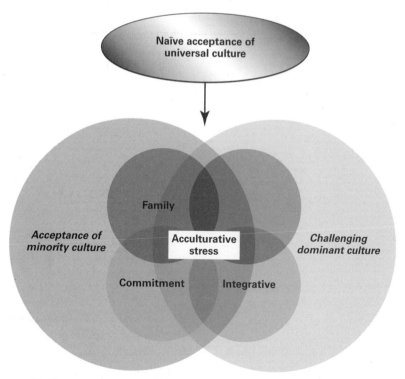

FIGURE **5.1** Cultural Identity Model: Latin Americans

views of the dominant culture and the position of their family. As they work through this stress, they find a commitment for their minority culture and a way to integrate dominant culture. But this process will play out in different ways throughout the life cycle.

When Marcos was 30 years old, he had a lovely European American wife with blonde hair and blue eyes. Together, they had raised two young children, who also looked very European and bore European names. In attempting to assimilate, Marcos has taken a job at his father-in-law's business. Over their six years of marriage, he had been quite successful and was being groomed to run the company when his father-in-law retired. Still, something nagged at him (acculturative stress). He did not belong in "their" world, and a growing bitterness arose within him. Sure, he had a wonderful family, great job, and strong prospects for the future, but it came at too high a price. He saw himself as a cardboard figure—a lifeless caricature reflecting what "they" wanted.

He decided to start attending church services at a local Mexican parish to "find himself." His wife said she "understood" and encouraged him to go, although she would not attend herself. After a few months, Marcos "fell in love" with a young Latina. He said, "She makes me feel like a person again—the person I was meant to be." After a few short months, Marcos and his wife filed for divorce, and Marcos left his job. He later said he was "happier this way" and finally "felt fulfilled."

Although Marcos left the world that he associated with non-Latino culture, this is simply one man's story—a single interpretation of how an individual can reach fulfillment after integrating the two cultures. Someone else might have successfully achieved the same level of integration without making any changes in his or her occupation or relationships. The central task simply rests with the process of unifying the concept of the self with one's larger ethnic culture. Regardless of the means by which it is achieved, this resolution of self and group identity often leads to enhanced self-esteem and ethnic pride. For a growing number of Latinos, this pride comes without some of the earlier conflicts. The changing demographic in America allows many Latino families to maintain an ethnic identity from the start. Latinos are now the largest U.S. minority and have accounted for half of the population growth of the last decade (Sánchez and Machado-Casas, 2009).

Family Structure and Dynamics

Family arrangements in Latino cultures are intimate with diffuse boundaries. Families are run in a matriarchal structure, where mothers and grandmothers hold the family together. More than any other American cultural group studied, Latino Americans appear to have the closest family ties. For social and economic reasons, immigrants from Mexico are the cultural group most likely to live with extended kin or unrelated persons (e.g., family friends) upon recent arrival to the United States (Blank, 1998). After immigrating, Latinos are more likely than European Americans to describe their personal networks and social support in terms of kinship (Schweizer, Schnegg & Berzborn,

1998). They define their selfhood by their familial ties and consider these relationships more important than autonomy.

Falicov (1998) refers to family ties between Latinos as *familismo*, which implies a combination of collectivism and interdependence. This construct has been well-tested and is considered both reliable and valid (Kim, Soliz, Orellana & Alamilla, 2009). Family is the building block of Latino culture. Here, most Latino/as draw their strengths, celebrate, mourn, derive their values, create their dreams, and define their sense of self (Montilla & Smith, 2006).

Rather than function as united individuals, members of a Latino family view themselves as a unit. All family members share functions such as rearing children, earning money, and providing companionship. Even household objects tend to be viewed as collectively owned. Family members hold culturally determined roles, but they will share these roles when necessary. The husband/father may be the primary financial provider, but many other family members are likely to contribute to the process. To outsiders, such shared burdens might appear unhealthy, especially when one person's desires are placed beneath the will of the family. For example, some Latinas may silently "sacrifice" themselves—possibly even abandoning their desires and wishes to attend to help the family financially and emotionally.

Silent sacrifice is not only part of the Latina experience. Families function with *respecto* for parents. This term does not imply an impassive leadership of someone distant. This is an emotionalized dependence and requires a dutiful commitment to parents (Falicov, 2006). European American therapists may view this self-sacrificial lifestyle as destructive or co-dependent, but for many Latino families, the gender-assigned roles and communal identity are accepted facts of life.

Familismo extends beyond the nuclear family to encompass grandparents, extended family members, and, in some cases, even maids (Falicov, 1998). Falicov (2006) tells the story of a professional Puerto Rican mother who raised her teenage girls as a single mom. At the story's beginning, it sounded like any Anglo divorced mom, but the story changed when the client discussed her household. Lupita, her maid, had babysat and slept with her girls since they were little. At the counselor's request, Lupita came to one of the sessions, and she knew as much about the girls as the mother. This inspired Falicov to conclude that maids and cooks should be considered members of the extended family.

Aunts and other relatives often play the role of mediator in conflicts. Same-sex peers—either as relatives or peers—are vitally important to Latino/as. They can generate support and comfort as well as significant conflict (Falicov, 2006). For Mexican families, godparents also play much more than the honorary role given in Anglo families. They act as *comadres* (co-parents), usually live nearby, are available for emergencies, and play important roles throughout the life cycle (e.g., communions, weddings, funerals, etc.) (Falicov, 2006).

This view of family is evidenced, in part, by the celebration of *la comida semanal* (the weekly meal). For this day of feasting, family members may have dinners at both grandparents' homes. All offspring, their spouses, children, and special friends are expected to attend the event. In the United States, *la comida semanal* is less frequently practiced because many families lack the financial resources or household space to host the event. However, many middle- to upper-class immigrants from Mexico, Puerto Rico, and Cuba still continue some form of the gathering. It is a time-intensive activity—often resulting in the union of more than a dozen people and requiring hours of preparation time.

Many authors agree that values of *familismo* are generally important for youth development and mental health because they strengthen parental authority and family bonds (Germán, Gonzales & Dumka, 2009). *Familismo* values can also foster the desire to protect family honor and prevent *verguenza* (shame) to the family (Vega, Gil, Warheit, Zimmerman & Apospori, 1993).

Adolescents with higher *familismo* values tend to have lower levels of deviance, alcohol and substance abuse, and violence (Felix-Ortiz & Newcomb, 1995; Gil et al., 2000: Gonzales et al., 2008; Kaplan, Erickson, Steward & Crane, 2001; McQueen, Getz & Bray, 2003; Sommers, Fagan & Baskin, 1993). This may explain why multiple generations in the United States tend to result in higher academic, behavioral, and mental health problems. As families acculturate to the dominant culture's way of life, maintaining culture-bound traditions becomes harder. One of the families I worked with said that third-generation children no longer valued the Sunday meal. The grandmother spoke of how her children had *disowned* them and their heritage—often because the children felt they had obligations to their nuclear families or jobs on occasional Sundays. This is not surprising, as younger people in America today score lower than their parents on measures of *familismo* (Alvarez, 2007).

When Latino families demonstrate the intimate ties described above, European Americans or other non-Latino therapists are often quick to label them as enmeshed. It is important to note that what constitutes "excessively" close in one culture may be completely acceptable in another. One of my clients, a 24-year-old Mexican American woman, lived with her mother and her eight brothers and sisters. Although three of her brothers were older than she was, they were expected to live at home until they were married. Rather than view this as a lack of preparation for the "real world," they believed that living with each other provided them with the social skills to be successful in marriage. Another client, Imelda, came in for counseling because she was concerned about her 13-year-old son, Juan, and his social problems at school. It seems his fellow students, who are mostly non-Hispanic, have been teasing him for his "quietness." As the interview continues, I learned that Juan slept in the same bed with Imelda and her husband. He had done so since he was a baby. This was part of their culture, and it was a source of strength for Juan. However, it also made it harder for him to individuate at school. We discussed ways for Juan to feel like an individual at school without losing his communal identity with his family.

Close family ties offer clear advantages, but there are potential disadvantages. The most significant cost associated with close family ties involves increased risk for sexual exploitation. Latino sexual molestation rates by extended family members are generally higher than rates found in other ethnic groups (Moisan, Sanders-Phillips & Moisan, 1997). A therapist may wonder if molestation might be present in the case introduced in this section. Perhaps Imelda's son Juan is quiet because he is the victim of sexual abuse and is having difficulty coping with the shame and pressure of the relationship. The potential for abuse should be explored, but it is highly unlikely that Juan's problems stem from the family's sleeping arrangement. Latino children are simply more likely to share a bed with their parents even up to puberty. In most cases, co-sleeping creates few problems for the family and is the result of two conditions: (1) the strong desire for intimacy in Latino homes and (2) the limited financial status of some Latino families. In Juan's case, he was insecure and quiet because he feared his English was "not good enough." After interacting for a few weeks with his therapist, he gained confidence and began to talk more readily with his peers.

Another potential problem with intimate family ties is a tendency to avoid conflict. People from Latino families publically avoid conflicts. This sometimes makes counseling difficult because individuals will refrain from directly confronting a family member (Brown & May, 2009). Conflict avoidance can also make people susceptible to peer pressure. Latinas may feel compelled to have sex with boyfriends or husbands (Southern, 2006). Girls who are open with their mothers may delay sexual onset because of this closeness. However, boys are often encouraged to engage in sex early. When they are physically or socially unable to have sex, their masculinity suffers.

Despite the desire for close ties between family members, traditional, or "old school," Latino families hold views on sexual intimacy that differ from those of European Americans. Fidelity is mandatory for a wife, but infidelity by a husband can be overlooked or forgiven (Falicov, 1998; Sable, Campbell, Schwarz, Brandt & Dannerbeck, 2006). This double standard is underscored by the fact that Latinas' risks of contracting sexual diseases increases within a committed relationship, while European American women's risks are increased by sex outside of their current relationship and by their sexual practices (Sayegh, Castrucci, Lewis & Hobbs-Lopez, 2010). One client described this process to me in the following way:

> When I'm with my wife, I can't help but think of her as the mother of my children. I love her, but I feel like I need something more. I need passion and excitement, not just comfort and support.

When conducting marital therapy, it is important for the therapist to recognize when one partner feels unusually uncomfortable. In such cases, issues should be explored privately and brought into marital therapy later. It should be noted that the double standard described above is significantly less common within the younger generation of Latinos. While aware of their parents' and grandparents' extramarital views, younger Latinos tend to view such beliefs as archaic.

Education

One of the most powerful acculturation experiences for Latino/as is school. Their success in school will also play a significant role on future economic success. Simply put, the more education Latinos and many other groups obtain, the greater their chances for economic success (Mintz & Krymkowski, 2010). Such a belief is common among immigrant families. Fuligni and Fuligni (2007) noted the tendency for children to internalize their parents' educational goals for them, and such children believe they must work hard to repay their parents for the sacrifices related to immigrating. However, Latino education itself is fraught with tremendous obstacles, and education comes at a considerable cost for Latinos.

One of the more devastating costs involves linguistic issues. Are Latinos robbed of their language if they are forced to study in English? Do they fall too far behind academically if they receive their training in Spanish? Since the mid-1970s, when the Supreme Court case *Lau v. Nichols* mandated private schools to provide adequate training to non-English-speaking students, bilingual education programs flourished across the country. However, more recently, short-term alternatives have been implemented to replace long-term programs. For example, California had a 30-year history of offering bilingual education, but in 1998, the citizens voted to ban long-term programs in favor of providing a one-year transitional English immersion program. After completing this course, students from all linguistic heritages will complete the rest of their training in English. In Washington State, there is a movement in the other direction. The state created dual language classrooms where both English and Spanish are offered from kindergarten through fifth grade.

It was hoped that changes such as these would reduce the staggering Latino dropout rate, but such efforts have generally been unsuccessful (Oseguera, Locks & Vega, 2009). There are a variety of reasons for this continued trend. The academic system still utilizes standardized tests, such as state achievement tests, the SAT, and others, for placement in certain classes and admission into college. Latino/as tend to score lower on these tests, and the tests are not very predictive of success after the first year of college (Contreras, 2005). Latino/as are also less likely to graduate from college, which puts fewer Latino/a teachers in the classroom (Oseguera, Locks, Vega, 2009). A lack of role models continues to limit student ambition.

Language difficulties contribute to the poor academic performance of Latinos. Some Latino children are bilingual but have only a limited command of the English language. In such cases, their friends and family are likely to speak Spanish, which further complicates matters. While having a direct effect on the student's ability to understand classroom material, the language barrier also has an indirect effect on the student's academic performance. It provides non-Latino students with further evidence that the student is "different."

Beyond language differences, there is a broader cultural difference affecting Latino educational achievement. Some families will take extended vacations back to South America during the school year. It is common for students to miss much of December, missing final exams and other projects to spend Christmas with family. In addition to absenteeism, teachers and school must also contend with the notion that school is not relevant.

In a brief article in *U.S. News and World Report*, Headden (1997) quoted a young Santa Fe teenage girl as saying that doing well in school was considered "Anglo" or "nerdy." With beliefs such as these readily accepted, Latinos face tremendous peer pressure to do poorly in school or to drop out. In order to combat negative attitudes toward school among Latino students, teachers and other educators can alter their instructional strategies to better fit the child's cultural values. For example, instead of saying "You did well—you should be very proud of yourself," a teacher could say, "Your family should be very pleased with your work" (Sue & Sue, 1999). Involving the family in the educational process creates a bridge between the Anglo academic world and the child's Latino culture. Culturally sensitive interventions may help to support the student's development of an academic identity.

Consider Segura's (age 16) comments on education: "I don't understand what all the fuss is. I'm not saying I want to work for $8.50 an hour for the rest of my life, but I don't need an education to do better. I'm going to start a rock band, and school would just slow me down." This perspective is common, and school counselors need to find ways to encourage dreams without minimizing the value of education. It would also be helpful to establish more practical learning approaches within Latino-based schools, tying such subjects as math and science to real-life applications (such as budgeting for rock band touring or improving the yield from a new fertilizer).

Even when Latino/as believe education is biased or racist, if they value the end result, they are likely to continue. When they attend college, Latino/as who perceive their institutions as prejudiced as likely to receive the same grades and engage in school activities as those who do not hold such beliefs (Rivas-Drake & Mooney, 2009). Instead, the most important consideration of success and psychological adjustment in college is the student's attachment to family and peers (Garriott, Love, Tyler, Thomas et al., 2010).

In addition to confirming the positive effects of parental support, there is some evidence that information from counselors, teachers, college materials, preparatory classes, friends, and extracurricular activities play a role in the college-planning process for Latino students (Hurtado & Gauvain, 1997). Acculturation through these avenues is predictive of actual college attendance among Mexican American adolescents. In many ways, information received outside the family plays a more significant role in college attendance than comments offered by parents. But parents are still critically important. If parents have not completed college themselves, their children are less likely to do so. This cycle is difficult to reverse because parents' educational attainment tends to have a strong influence on their children's college aspirations and planning behaviors (Hurtado & Gauvain, 1997).

If schools are successful in gaining the trust of their Latino students, the students may place more value on academic achievement. For example, Osborne (1998) found that Latina girls were the only group he studied that became more identified with academics as they progressed through their academic careers. Members of every other ethnic group tended to distance themselves from academic success and identify themselves with social groups, occupations, or some other type of affiliation. One method of creating trust and encouraging a sense of belonging is by adopting and supporting programs sponsored by the National Council of La Razas (NCLR) Center for Community Educational Excellence. The NCLR works to bridge the gap between communities and schools in order to strengthen the quality of education for Hispanic students and to involve Hispanic families in the education of their children. The NCLR has been relatively successful in helping Latinos stay in school.

Socioeconomics

The causes of Latino economic struggles are multifaceted. It is easy to hypothesize that language barriers, acculturation, or immigration create poverty among many Latinos, but these factors explain only part of the problem. Latinos are represented in every social class, but they are overrepresented among the poor (Lott, 2010). Many Latinos come to America with the hope of stabilizing their economic situation. For many families, this goal remains elusive.

Although many poor Latinos come to America, their prospects for economic success do not improve as they continue to work. Latino immigrants tend to fall into greater poverty with each successive generation. Third-plus-generation Latinos have the greatest chances of being in poverty (Padilla, 1997). Additionally, a number of other conditions seem to have little effect on Latino poverty. For example, the number and presence of young children (under six years of age), marital status, citizenship, and English usage all have marginal effects on income levels (Kirschner-Cook & Welsh-Jordan, 1997). Latino children are three times more likely to live in poverty than European American children (Singer et al., 2009). What, then, creates and sustains poverty? The two most important considerations are the types of job sought and levels of educational attainment. However, as we discussed earlier, these are only effective after overcoming prejudice.

To highlight the importance of prejudice on economics, Morales (2009) looked at how skin color affected wages for a group of Latino/a Los Angelesians. Darker-skinned women and immigrant women received the lowest wages. Although men were usually paid more than women, darker skin also diminished their salaries. When Latinos succeed in overcoming financial barriers, their success is often associated with a change in identity.

One woman—a Latina from my university—told me about the difficulty of working at a white institution. She longed for additional Latinas to befriend, but there were few around. One day, while shopping, she noticed a mother speaking Spanish to her daughter. My friend turned and said, "*Usted tiene una hija hermosa.*" The woman smiled, and they continued their conversation in Spanish. After minutes, the conversation turned to work. When the mother learned that my friend worked at the university, her face went pale. She clearly viewed the university as an anti-Latino establishment, and she abruptly ended the conversation. It is important to work through the grieving, identity loss, and frustration of being part of two cultures. It is often more lonely than dedicating yourself to one.

In addition to friendships, socioeconomics plays a significant function in defining gender roles. Falicov (1998) reported that a couple came into her office complaining about each other's failures. The husband stated that his wife had failed in her "wifely duties" (a euphemism for sex). The wife responded, "If you fulfilled your husbandly duties of supporting the family, things would be different." In this situation, both the husband and wife worked, and the wife derived considerable satisfaction from her employment. Still, she viewed her husband as less of a man because she *had* to work. Although striving for equal access to work and salaries, Latina feminists still cherish traditional Latino values, including caring for their family and community. For many Latino males, being respected and considered masculine are tied to financially supporting their families. When they are unable to earn adequate wages, they may attempt to exert more control over their family (physically or verbally) or begin to drink heavily (Falicov, 1998).

Finances also play a dangerous role for women. When infidelity occurs, many couples stay together. Many Latinos struggle with issues related to poverty, and if their families were to disband, their financial struggles would be made more acute. One woman said during a counseling session with me, "I love him; I hate him; but without him, I have nowhere to go."

Spirituality and Religion

Many interventions for Latino/as will involve some type of spirituality or religion. However, this does not mean the same thing for Latino/as as it does for European Americans. Religion and spirituality play central roles for many Latino families (Smith, Bakir & Montilla, 2006), but for many Latinos, spirituality is created by a blending of native, Christian, Islamic, Jewish, and African religion features (Montilla & Smith, 2006). There is a common perception that Latinos are Catholic, but less than 20% attend church of any kind regularly. This led Montilla and Smith (2006) to comment on how faith, spirituality, religion, and culture are intimately connected for Latinos, and they are best understood when examined as a whole.

Guanina, a Puerto Rican woman who presented with seizures, believed the seizures stemmed from demon possession. When discussing the case, Guanina said, "They started after my grandmother took her own life. I didn't stop her, and she's tormenting me." From a secular viewpoint, the seizures are likely psychological, instigated by intense feelings of guilt. However, Martínez-Taboas (2005) advocates using the client's phenomenological framework. This makes the intervention more useful and expedient. It also requires counselors to become knowledgeable of common spiritual beliefs and *espiritismo*.

Espiritismo is a religious, ideological, and healing philosophical system that is widespread in many Latin American countries (Finkler, 1985; Hess, 1994). The basic tenet of *espiritismo* is that the soul is immortal and that the spirits of dead persons can communicate with incarnated persons or that they may intervene directly in the lives of people. Spirit mediums can serve as a communicational bridge between incarnated spirits and the spirits of the dead. In some cases, ignorant spirits of the dead (or *espíritus intranquilos*) do not recognize that they are in a disincarnated state and, as a result, begin to obsess or even possess some living person. In that case, the possessed person can complain of symptoms of auditory and visual hallucinations, fugue-like states, and pseudo-seizures (Lubchansky, Egri & Stokes, 1970).

Beyond daily functioning issues, there are a number of psychological symptoms associated with Latino culture that may appear bizarre to non-Latinos. For example, after the death of a loved one, some Latinos—especially Puerto Ricans—may be "visited" by ghosts for years to come. They may interpret these hallucinations as a sign that their loved one is not ready to leave. They may also seek to understand why God has allowed their loved one to die. This blending of spiritualism, Catholicism, and folklore may make it difficult for therapists to know how to assist in the grieving process. When the hallucination does not pose a threat to a client's psychological functioning, the metaphor may become a useful component in therapy. The therapist could argue that the ghost would continue to come until the client is ready to let go. This places responsibility for the apparition on the client, who can use the hallucination as an indication of his or her willingness to let go of the person who has died.

It may take some time for some Latinos to view the ghost as something they are able to control rather than something external that is haunting them. Latinos often do not hold individuals responsible for their problems. Instead, they believe in fatalism and expect that an emerging problem has a specific purpose. However, this attitude does not mean that the problem's solution is also viewed as external. Latinos believe they can master the challenges of life by controlling their moods and emotions, particularly anger, anxiety, and depression (Falicov, 1998).

Although they may recognize the need to endure a problem or face their emotions with stoic pride, Latino clients are unlikely to describe the emotion in purely affective terms. Instead, they may internalize the emotion until it is revealed through physical symptoms. Many Latinos—especially women and older individuals—are willing to accept physical symptoms as predictable extensions to emotionally powerful events. For example, at a Latino funeral—especially if it involves the death of a child—attendants may feel physical symptoms, such as gasping for breath, heart palpitations, chest pains, or other such maladies. These are viewed as a natural expression of grief rather than as somatizations, as European Americans might be prone to view them. These physical manifestations are accepted because Latinos do not differentiate between mind and body, as most European Americans do. The heart, mind, body, and soul are all expected to react to one's environment.

Physical and Mental Health

Rather than adopt medical interpretations for illnesses, they are more likely to believe in "folk illnesses." For example, *mal de ojo* (the evil eye) is a belief that a jealous, malicious, or powerful person can steal someone's ability to control their own actions. This condition may even arise from more innocuous means. In Mexican culture, if a person comments on the attractiveness of an infant, that person is then required to physically touch the baby. Failing to contact the baby may curse the young child with *mal de ojo*. The victim may experience severe headaches, uncontrollable weeping, fretfulness, insomnia, and fevers (Falicov, 1998). Other folk concepts—such as witchcraft (_mal puesto_), fright, indigestion after eating something you did not want to eat (_empacho_), envy or intense jealousy resulting in physical illness (_envidia_), and natural illnesses (_males naturales_)—are considered the best explanation for many health-related problems.

Other folk illnesses are thought to cause a number of mental health–related problems. _Nervios_ (nerves) is thought to exist because one's "brain aches." Headaches, sleep difficulties, trembling, tingling sensations, and dizziness may be associated with the disorder. Although these are symptoms for a number of DSM-IV diagnoses (e.g., postconcussional disorder, inhalant intoxication, panic disorder, etc.), some Latinos may be unfamiliar with such diagnoses and favor their cultural explanation.

Physical problems may also be associated with folk illnesses. For example, many Latinos—especially Puerto Ricans—still believe in the "hot and cold" theory of illness. According to this view, physical and mental health are promoted by an equilibrium of hot and cold in one's body and environment. Too much heat, such as that caused by ironing clothes with wet hands, is thought to cause arthritis. Strong psychological reactions, such as fright, are said to create heat and are relieved by consuming cool herbal teas. These unique views concerning the etiologies of many health problems make traditional health care less attractive to Latinos. This attitude, in itself, may pose a serious health threat to many Latin Americans.

In the case of _empacho_ (indigestion), an elder may bring an individual into a dark room, rub the victim's back with ashes, and pinch the skin around the spinal cord. If the cause is more serious than a stomach ache—say, appendicitis—this treatment could pose a serious health risk.

There are problems with an emphasis on folk medicines. Latino/as are at high risk for tuberculosis (TB) because they appear to have a limited understanding of the disease but also because they are typically less likely than members of other minority groups to be able to afford medical evaluations and treatment (Ailinger & Dear, 1997). Latino/as are also unlikely to report herbal and other nontraditional interventions to their physicians (Tafur, Crowe & Torres, 2009).

Despite a reliance on folk explanations for health and illness, foreign-born immigrants fare better than their U.S.-born counterparts on psychosocial and health indicators, including education, criminal behaviors, and well-being (Nguyen, 2006). Even if the interventions are placebo-based, they appear very powerful and useful. Common interventions include wearing amulets or jewelry with special powers (often metal to prevent the effects of the moon); holy oils, incense, perfumes, and sprays are also remedies (Tafur, Crowe & Torres, 2009).

Alcohol use for Latinos is related, in part, to the use of alcohol in ceremonies and holidays. In nearly all Latino celebrations, alcohol is involved. People who refuse to drink on such occasions are often stigmatized as inhospitable, antisocial, or dull. The alcohol industry has recently begun to use this trend to push for increased use during Cinco de Mayo celebrations.

High rates of alcohol use among Latinos are somewhat understandable, but it is less clear why there are increasing rates of usage of illegal substances within this community. One explanation for drug use may involve efforts to seek relief from acculturation difficulties and economic problems. When entire families find themselves impoverished and disassociating themselves from their cultural roots, the chances increase that a given family member will start trying illicit drugs (Gil, Vega & Biafora, 1998). Polednak (1997) found that the more acculturated Latinos became, the more likely they were to drink on a weekly basis. Women were the most likely to increase their drinking in America as they took advantage of newfound freedoms and opportunities, but men also increased their drinking. Drug treatment interventions are often ineffective because they fail to address the underlying roots of the behavior.

In support of an acculturation model for alcohol and drug use, Alegría and Woo (2009) note a problematic paradox with Latino mental health issues. Latinos tend to have lower rates of mental health disorders than European Americans. However, Latinos born in America are more likely than their immigrant peers to suffer from mood disorders and alcohol/drug use. Psychiatric rates were also highest for Puerto Ricans, whose culture is the most integrated with that of the American mainland. As mentioned with African Americans, it appears that the attempt to appear "more American" may actually lead to an increased risk of mental health concerns.

However, the trend toward acculturation is not always negative. Losoya et al. (2008) examined how acculturation affected patterns of heavy episodic drinking and marijuana use. Adolescents who had adopted mainstream culture but maintained a sense of their ethnic culture were less likely to abuse alcohol or marijuana.

When providing an intervention for drug use among Latinos, providers would be wise to simultaneously treat depression. For example, Spanish-speaking Latinos find it easier to end smoking when they also receive help managing their depression. Depression and acculturation issues may even manifest themselves in physical symptoms. Alegria, Mulvaney-Day et al. (2007) found lower rates of depression and substance abuse disorders among first-generation immigrants. As reported in the economic section, remaining in the States does not result in higher functioning. In their study, second- and third-generation Latinos faced higher frequency of mental health problems, specifically substance abuse. As with the other issues discussed in this chapter, discrimination and prejudice are the most likely culprits. Vega et al. (1998) found psychological distress among immigrants as their education and income levels rose. If discrimination lowers the potential for income, mental health concerns are likely to follow. Similarly, several students have demonstrated a link between immigrant parents working low-wage jobs and specific parenting concerns. Such families often face such challenges as early pregnancy, substance use, academic difficulties, and delinquency (Glick & White, 2004; Harris, 1999; Perreira et al., 2006).

Despite all the contrasts with European American culture and some of the pitfalls of the Latino/a health practices, Latinas have one of the highest life expectancy rates of any racial or gender group because they prioritize family, have strong emotional support networks, maintain good nutritional habits, and have fewer negative health habits (Suinn, 1999). These are strong reasons to limit acculturation changes to what is necessary or useful.

Acculturated Latino children are expected to adopt an autonomous and independent lifestyle, but this requires children to define themselves as distinctly separate from their parents. Such conceptions of selfhood may disrupt the natural flow of the family. I once worked with a family who came to therapy because the parents were unable to make their son finish his chores. When discussing the family dynamics, the parents revealed that the 13-year-old son still shared a bed with them. He had his own room, but when he was four years old, he experienced difficulties sleeping alone and began to share his parents' bed. We attempted to discuss some of the problems this might create for the young man and explained how European American culture values autonomy above all other virtues. Throughout the intervention, we explored ways the child could continue to develop his sense of autonomy without attenuating the family bond or cultural lineage. This family connection is essential for nearly all Latino/a interventions.

Individual and Group Interventions

A necessary starting point to creating effective interventions for Latino families is to think of yourself as a healer. A traditional family will only come for help if it has faced a struggle so vast that the family could not intervene by itself. This means they are turning to someone who can offer healing to the family, not simply counseling or advice. Once the healer understands the family system, he or she should carve out an identity within the family unit (Montilla & Smith, 2006).

Individual Interventions

Being part of the family requires the healer to understand and work within the authority structure. This is sometimes the father, but women are usually the glue that holds families together. This could be the mother, the maternal grandmother, oldest sister, or another powerful woman. For many families, men play the role of provider, but women lead the household. Little growth can occur without operating from within this power structure. Failing to acknowledge the importance of a particular family member may lead to premature termination of counseling (Smith, Bakir & Montilla, 2006). The parents must feel that the therapist understands them and will guide their children accordingly (Bernal & Flores-Ortiz, 1982). Therapists need to be cognizant of cultural norms in such ways as acknowledging the leadership structure and allowing those in charge to dictate the involvement of the other family members. If a successful bond is created, the family can assist the therapeutic process in highly significant ways.

The healer must also strive to connect with each family member—being present with each person throughout the session. This helps promote togetherness within the family dynamic. It also builds trust and respect. Empathic listening and a strong therapeutic alliance transcend cultural differences when looking at outcomes (Smith, Bakir & Montilla, 2006).

Words of encouragement and endearment are also important (Falicov, 2006). Commenting on someone's smile, clothing, or attitude is an important facet to relationship building. Physical touch can strengthen such encouragement. Handshaking, hugging, or kissing demonstrate intimacy and concern. It may take time to determine an individual's deepest feelings about a topic of person. Patience should be observed in getting to these points, and the approach should be gentle and filled with relaxed stories, antidotes, and metaphors.

Gender differences may also play a role in counseling. Newer immigrants may prefer the authority of a male counselor. As Latino families become more acculturated, there is some evidence suggesting they may start showing a preference for female therapists (Smith, Bakir & Montilla, 2006).

Beyond the use of family, the effective therapist must also display a working knowledge of the client's culture. This may be demonstrated in a number of ways. Yeh, Eastman, and Cheung (1994) found that ethnic differences ceased to predict early dropout rates by Mexican clients when language was added to the model. Counselors who could communicate with their clients at the most basic of levels were more likely to effectively intervene with clients' struggles. However, language is not the only tool counselors can use to make an effective cultural intervention.

Constantino and Rivera (1994) investigated whether a form of narrative therapy could help reduce children's anxiety and behavior problems. They used five mothers who read Latino folktales (*cuentos*) to their children for an hour. After the readings, therapists ran a group in which they asked the children how the stories made them feel and what the morals of the stories were. In some cases, the mother-child dyad was also asked to create a dramatization of the story to illustrate how a given conflict was resolved. After 20 sessions, the researchers assessed the children's growth across a number of areas. When compared to a control group who received traditional play therapy sessions conducted by a therapist and schoolteacher, the family intervention group had fewer anxiety symptoms, increased IQ scores, and fewer behavioral problems.

A common Latino narrative is the story of the Dying Lady. The tale begins with a woman who decides that it is too much work to cook.

"It's such a hassle," the old woman states. "It would be easier not to eat."

Days turn to weeks, and weeks drag on until the woman finds herself unable to move or care for herself. People dear to the woman beg her to feed herself, but she refuses.

"I'm much too tired to cook now," she laments. "I would need more strength to cook and clean."

As her health continues to falter, her family and community grow concerned.

"Is there nothing we do to help her?" asked one woman.

All the people agree that if she will not nurture herself, nothing they can do will change her fate. With much sadness, the assembly decides that the only action left before them is to carry her to her grave. "She will probably be dead when we reach the tomb," one man states. "At least, if we carry her now, we can share in her final moments on Earth."

As they carry the woman up the hill that will soon become her final resting place, a couple approaches bearing all types of food.

"Here," a woman states, "you may have these beans and rice—eat them and you may live."

Trembling, the woman reaches out to touch the food. The couple waits anxiously as she struggles to feel the beans.

"They aren't cooked," the woman sighs. "I don't want them unless they have been cooked."

With this announcement, the assembly continues up the hill. The woman has sealed her fate by being too lazy to care for herself and too proud to accept the gifts brought to her.

Using stories such as The Dying Lady in therapy can help clients merge their culture with their identity. In this particular story, the woman refused help from the people closest to her; she allowed her misery to overpower; and she demanded perfection from those who wanted to help. Therapists can help clients realize that they may be acting like "dying people" in their households. They might be allowing themselves to remain "depressed" by refusing the help of those dearest to them. Ultimately, to overcome depression, they will need to reach out to the hands serving them, engage in the exercises, and make allowances when the help provided appears inadequate. With this interpretation, the story becomes a catalyst to psychological issues.

However, therapists should realize that they may need to expand their repertoire if they wish to have the same impact an ethnically matched therapist would have. Learning Spanish or at least becoming familiar with key folk stories is highly recommended for therapists who work with Latino clients on a regular basis. A good place to start would be to read the following texts:

- Bierhorst, J. (2009). *Latin American Folktales: Stories from Hispanic and Indian Traditions.* New York: Pantheon.
- Sharma, R. (2010). *Folk Tales from Latin America.* New York: Amazon Digital Services.
- Schon, I. (1978). *A Bicultural Heritage: Themes for the Exploration of Mexican and Mexican-American Culture in Books for Children and Adolescents.* Metuchen, NJ: The Scarecrow Press, Inc.

Group Interventions

Narratives may also be useful in group counseling. Guerra (2004) created an approach to counseling called LIBRE (the Spanish word for free). The acronym has the following steps:

- Listen to the speaker's narrative
- Identify the presenting issue
- Brainstorm possible solutions
- Reality check all possibility solutions
- Encourage the person to develop a personalized best plan and incentives to facilitate personal investment

In group settings, the LIBRE approach has the advantage of additional brainstorming partners as well as encouraging individuals to follow through with their goals. It is a community-oriented approach, where the group acts like a family in responsibility, encouragement, and structure.

Advocacy and Social Justice

There are several important ways counselors, psychologists, and social workers can advocate for Latino/as. Most of it will start by learning about Latino culture. A good place to start is to become familiar with cultural heroes. People like Mel Martinez, the first Cuban American senator; bestselling author Alisa Valdes-Rodriguez; ACLU president Anthony Romero; business mogul Jorge Perez; or medical researcher Aida Giachello. Understanding such leaders provides a foundation for understanding how changes occurs and where change can happen next.

One important consideration is advocating for different college policies regarding education. It makes sense to restrict government subsidies to people who are here legally, but we have created an odd hodgepodge regarding academics. Most states provide education to illegal aliens through high school. But then, the policies change. Some laws prohibit the college enrollment of undocumented U.S. high school graduates. When enrollment is permitted, such students face difficulty receiving financial aid, in-state tuition, or access to grants. These limitations send a frustrating message. We are willing to provide enough education to help people survive, but our culture marginalizes these youth by making college more difficult than it would be for their peers (Horwedel, 2006; Murray et al., 2007). This subjugation creates a subculture and limits economic mobility.

Latin American subjugation and conquest (current and historical) may be also reflected in the therapeutic relationship. For example, counselors may mistakenly perceive their Latino clients as passive or overly compliant. However, this appearance could be the result of feeling threatened or dominated by the therapist. On the other hand, a common therapeutic error involves what Comas-Díaz and Jacobsen (1991) have termed the "clinical anthropologist syndrome." Therapists afflicted by this disorder turn off their clinical training and explore their clientele as if they were unlike any of their other clients. They may re-label dysfunctional family issues as acceptable cultural variations. The therapist inadvertently colludes with the family and perpetuates the disorder. Falicov (1998) notes that shyness, self-sacrifice, overdependence, domestic violence, child abuse, alcoholism, or harmful religiosity may be accepted or overlooked in the interest of maintaining cultural homeostasis.

Maria came into therapy because she "needed someone to talk to." As the session progressed, she confessed that the problems in her family were her fault. For many therapists, this admission might seem to make little sense because the family problems began four months earlier when her husband had an affair with his high-school sweetheart. Much to the husband's disgust, the affair surfaced because his girlfriend was pregnant and wanted to keep the baby. In desperation, the husband told Maria what had happened but added that he wanted to save their marriage. He told Maria he did not "love" his girlfriend and realized that his family must come first.

From Maria's viewpoint, his act of indiscretion was not enough to destroy their sacred marital vows, but she acted upon her anger by making him move out of the house. During therapy, she pummeled herself with statements of shame. "How could I destroy our family like that?" She moaned. "How could I keep my children from their father?" Unable to forgive herself, she added cultural statements such as, "We were married in the eyes of God, and I broke our covenant." She believed that it was her duty to stay with her husband, no matter what mistakes he made.

Individual therapy sessions with the husband added another dimension to the problem. He confessed that he intended to continue seeing his lover because he now also had familial responsibilities to her. He realized that he had made a mistake, but he could not punish his unborn child by depriving "him" [sic] of a father. He intended to have his girlfriend move to Mexico, where he could see her and the baby during frequent business trips. His wife never accompanied him on these trips, so he could maintain the dual family. "This is what Latinos do," he said. He also wanted to continue coming to therapy with his wife, provided that the topic of his girlfriend never arose.

There are several ways to handle a situation like the one described above. However, most of them are harmful. The worst option would be to collude with the husband and keep the affair secret. In this case, the situation resolved itself when Maria called the girlfriend and learned about her husband's plan to continue seeing both women. This turn of events forced the husband to stop seeing his girlfriend, and both partners continued to attend marital therapy.

The balance between family stability and individuality is a tenuous one for many Latino families. Therapists who ignore family stability to empower the client's sense of individuality may lose their client's respect. This dilemma requires therapists to proceed slowly. The most important element is to build trust (*confianza*), which is accomplished by communicating kindness, fairness, respect, and personal interest (Falicov, 1998). This trust is more quickly established when therapists are bicultural, bilingual, or Latino, but therapists from different ethnic or cultural backgrounds can dismantle many multicultural problems by stating their philosophy of therapy and mutually agreeing on a therapeutic course. Sharing ideological positions helps create a collaborative dialogue that builds a working alliance and enhances the therapeutic encounter (Falicov, 1998). Therapists need to ask clients if they have any questions about the therapeutic process and then answer all questions honestly and thoroughly.

In addition to the issues discussed previously, there are other topics that may arise during counseling sessions. When you are reading the following example, consider how you might react to the client's view that the difficulties in his marriage are caused by a cultural misunderstanding.

Alfonso and Heather (A Client's Viewpoint)

If you don't mind, it will be easier for me to tell the background of the story. You see, Heather and I have been married for three years. It's been great, and we love each other very much. But we've had our share of conflicts.

The most recent issues started when Heather quit work to raise our daughter. Heather was not happy working, and we decided that we would sacrifice the second income in order for her to stay home. Sofia's a year old, and Heather took over many of my domestic duties, as I am now working longer hours to support the family. She is in charge of everything around the house: cooking, cleaning, laundry, etc. She's doing wonderfully with Sofia, but we see the domestic chores differently.

As you can tell, Heather's culture is more European, and her family keeps house differently than mine. I grew up in a compulsively clean home and wanted my house to maintain the same standards. Latin people, especially Cubans like me, are neat freaks. We like things really clean and very well-organized. Clutter drives us nuts! For example, when I travel to an indigenous region in Mexico for a mission trip each year, it is not uncommon to see the ladies of the house (or hut) sweeping the area in front of the entry to the house. That's normal, except their entries are nothing but dirt! Nevertheless, it is a very well-swept dirt entry.

I can't seem to communicate to her what cleanliness means to me or, at least, I can't get her to share my values. When I point out a glass on the coffee table, children's toys on the floor, or unkempt beds, she scolds me for pointing it out. She would say things like, "Well, you try cleaning the house while watching an infant—it's hard work." Then, she would go back to watching TV, reading a book, or otherwise waste time she could have spent picking up the glass.

Being a Latin male, I expected a high level of respect. When she complains to me for bringing up valid points about housekeeping, I feel disrespected. When she welcomes me into a messy house, I also feel disrespected. How do we move past this?

David's Story (A Counselor's Viewpoint)

I have to admit, I'm a little torn about where to begin. I'm white, obviously, and hearing your story made me think about how I could handle this with a monocultural couple. Sometimes, I help people realize how much time they spend arguing, then have the try to turn their arguing time

(continues)

David's Story (A Counselor's Viewpoint) (continued)

into something more productive. But I get the sense from you that the biggest issue is simply cultural. I'm not sure the two of you grasp how your cultural backgrounds are different.

Let me start by summarizing what I've heard. Alfonso, you mentioned that when you come home to a messy—or not perfectly clean—house, you feel disrespected, right?

"Yeah," Alfonso looks to his wife. "I want my house to be a place where my mother would be proud to enter."

I noticed something when you said that. Heather's gaze dropped. You looked to the ground right when he started talking about his mother. Could you tell us about that?

"Well." Heather looked to Alfonso, then back to the floor. "I really love my husband and I love his family. They're all wonderful. But I have to admit, sometimes … I can't be his mother."

I glanced to Alfonso, who looked surprised but remained quiet. "Do you think he wants you to become his mother?"

"Sort of." She reached out for her husband's hand. "Don't get me wrong. You're mom is great. I've already learned so much from her, but I'm not her. She's traditional; I'm more creative. She cleans all the time; I need some breaks to stay sane. She cooks incredible Cuban dishes; I like to dabble in French cuisine and risk setting the house on fire. Let's face it. She's Cuban, and I'm not."

That's the crux of the matter, isn't it? I looked back and forth between them but ultimately left my gaze on Alfonso. "Did you feel disrespected by anything Heather said today?"

"No." Alfonso's voice remained soft, thoughtful. "I'm just trying to think about what it means. Did you think I wanted you to become my mother?"

Heather chucked. "You love your mother, and she's almost perfect. Why wouldn't you?"

"Because I love you." He squeezed her hand and the two of them looked to me.

You guys came in looking for ways to communicate better, but I think your communication is awesome. What it sounds like you need is a better understanding of how your cultures differ. Cleaning might just be the tip of the pattern. You might have cultural expectations about power, child-rearing, finances, and other stuff. Alfonso, you said respect was a primary goal for you on your marriage. Heather, what would be a primary goal for you?

She glanced to the ceiling, thoughtful. "Appreciation." She sighed. "I want to feel appreciated for what I do."

Okay, let's go there. Let's start with you, Alfonso. Let's talk about what looks respectful in conversations and actions. Then, we'll have Heather talk about what results in feeling appreciated for her.

Intervention Exercises

Counseling and Therapy: Isabel is a 28-year-old mother of three (girls, ages four, eight; boy, 10). She is concerned about her oldest daughter Liliana, who has been struggling in school. Liliana is bilingual, as is Isabel, but they speak Spanish in the home. Isabel explains that her daughter has been called names. When she said she was a *Latina*, one boy said, "I thought you were a *Latrina*" (joking that she was a latrine). Another girl called her a Po-Bean, short for a poor beaner. Isabel is unsure how to intervene with the school, and she is distraught over the racism her daughter is facing. She is coming to counseling to work on her anxiety and to gain some practical skills.

School Psychology: Antonio (nine-year-old male) came to your school from Mexico two years ago. He has done well in his fourth-grade math subjects, but he has struggled in every other area. His teacher (Mrs. White) believes he is "lazy, inattentive, and antisocial." She does not believe language is his problem but thinks he has a learning disability. She has asked for him to be tested. When interviewing Antonio, he speaks to you in short, simple sentences. He occasionally throws out Spanish words but quickly corrects them with English ones. How would you assess his achievement? What do you think may be happening with him?

School Counseling: Liliana (a 10-year old Latina) has been struggling in school. Liliana is bilingual but speaks Spanish in her home. She came into your office with tears in her eyes. She explained that Bobby, a white boy in her class, has been calling her names. When she said she was a *Latina*, Bobby said, "I thought you were a *Latrina*" (joking that she was a latrine). Another girl called her a Po-Bean, short for a poor beaner. While looking at the floor, Liliana says she "doesn't want to go back to class." She said she would rather "drop out of school and stay with her mother." How would you intervene?

Social Work: Xavier is a 19-year old Latino (mother from Guatemala; father from Mexico) who presented for counseling after being released from prison. He had been involved a petty theft but was belligerent to the judge and received the harshest sentence. While spending six months in prison (released early for good behavior), he joined the Surenos (a Latino gang with hundreds of subgangs). He was required to attend counseling when he was released and wanted services for social work. He started working at a local grocery store two days ago, but he has seen rival gang members shopping there. He is concerned someone may recognize him from prison and "start something." He also believes it is his duty to "take someone out" who steals from his store and is a member of a rival gang. How would you work with Xavier?

QUESTIONS TO CONSIDER

1. Labels such as Hispanic, Chicano, and Mexican American reflect different emphases within Latino culture. How would you reconcile a family whose members each referred to themselves with different terms?
2. Darker-skinned Latinos may face increased discrimination. How would you assist such an individual through counseling?

3. How might close family ties affect the counseling process? Do you believe enmeshment issues could make individual therapy difficult?

4. How might the double standard for marital unfaithfulness found in some cultures affect your intervention in marital therapy?

5. Poverty appears to be most severe among third-generation Mexican Americans. Why do you think this occurs?

6. How might you intervene with a traditional Latino family in which the husband's salary was insufficient to meet the family's needs? How would you handle his shame? How would you explore the wife's potential anger or frustration?

7. What might you do to change a young Latina's view that doing well in school is "Anglo" or "nerdy"?

8. Trust is a critical factor when therapists from other cultural groups work with Latinos. How might you strive to gain your client's trust?

9. Some Latinos may favor cultural explanations for psychological disturbances. Would you use their terminology or try to help your clients to better understand the descriptive categories in the DSM?

10. Would you diagnose schizophrenia in a Latina who repeatedly saw her dead mother appearing to her? Why or why not?

11. In the case of Alfonso and Heather, the couple had different cultural expectations for their marriage. How could you help the couple go past what happened in the narrative?

CHAPTER 6

Asian/Pacific Island Americans

INSIGHT EXERCISE

Naoki (nah-oh-kee) is a 22-year-old male who was raised in Tokyo and has been in the United States for the past four years. He communicates well with English-speaking people and had little understanding of his Japanese roots. During his first year of college, he took a class on world history. His professor, Dr. Montgomery, spent a single day discussing religion and said this about Buddhism:

> One of the basic limitations about Asian philosophy is its dependence on suffering as an individual process. Buddhism teaches people to avoid suffering by detaching from all impermanence. Picture someone sitting in a room, chanting, meditating. For the Buddhist, this is the highest form of being. They don't focus as much on creating positive social change.

Naoki raised his hand and was acknowledged by a nod of the professor's head.

"Dr. Montgomery, I don't mean to be rude, but there may be another way to look at Buddhism. As you said, the Four Noble Truths emphasize the elimination of suffering. They require us to understand the existence of impermanence and suffering (*Dukkha*). Suffering does come from attachment (*Samudaya*), and the way to end suffering is to liberate the mind from attachment (*Nirodha*). But there is a fourth truth. It's the middle way

(continues)

INSIGHT EXERCISE *(continued)*

(*Magga*). Buddhists work to think, act, and feel in healthy ways. These require us to create positive social change as well as self-change."

Dr. Montgomery scratched his chin and thought for a moment. "Thank you for sharing, No-a-ki [note the pronunciation]. I wish there were more Buddhists like you. The world might be a better place."

Questions to Consider:

1. Imagine Naoki comes into your office after this class and says, "I don't see the point in staying here. I'm considering moving back to Japan." How would you intervene?

2. If you were asked to serve as a consultant to Dr. Montgomery, what suggestions would you make to improve the multicultural nature of his class?

3. How would you conceptualize the difference between the Western philosophy of social change with the Buddhism Naoki described.

Asian worldviews differ dramatically from Western views. Asians tend to emphasize circularity over linear progression, self-sacrifice over independence, and communal honor over individual achievement. These striking differences can confound and bewilder Western thinkers, who may find their intervention strategies incompatible with their client's ideology.

Classifying the largest group of human beings into the single category "Asian" overly simplifies these diverse cultures, but the term is significantly better than "Oriental," which is considered offensive by many. A typical response to being called Oriental is "I'm not a rug." Likewise, the term Asian is often used to classify Pacific Islanders (such as Hawaiians, Samoans, Polynesians, etc.), even though such groups are distinctly different from mainland Asian cultures.

The population of Asian Americans comprises more than 20 separate nationalities, and they makes up 15% of the total population (Asian/Pacific American Heritage Month, 2008). With more than 60% of the world's population living in China, Japan, India, Vietnam, Korea, Taiwan, Hong Kong, Malaysia, and other countries, there are thousands of cultural groups—each with distinct characteristics and traditions. However, despite their diversity, Asians experienced similar prejudice as they immigrated to this country.

Unique Challenges

As Asian Americans continue to gain social prominence, discrimination against some subcultures is waning. This also creates new challenges and, ironically, may create additional prejudices.

Asian Americans are undergoing a significant cultural shift. In the past, with humility emphasized in many Asian cultures, personal features such as shyness were often assets. This is especially true in places like China, where communism and social policies emphasize communal functioning over individual success. Chinese and Korean toddlers engage in more behavioral inhibition than their American, Italian, and Australian peers (Rubin, Cheah & Menzer, 2010). This predisposition is also socially reinforced. Chinese children are praised for shyness, which is viewed as an indication of self-control and positive adjustment. But this may be the last generation where such personalities are valued.

Chen, Cen, Li, and He (2005) examined three cohorts (1990, 1998, and 2002) of elementary school children (M age = 10 years) in China. They noted aggressiveness was associated with social and school difficulties for all the groups, but shyness played different roles. In the 1990 cohort, shyness was associated with social and academic achievement. This relationship weakened for the 1998 cohort and turned negative for the 2002 cohort. For this last group, shyness was associated with peer rejection, school problems, and depression.

What is likely to occur in the coming generation is a conflict within the culture and without. Older Chinese and other Asians may continue to value shyness and subservience. They may look to the newer generation as selfish, egotistical, and ignorant. Likewise, the younger generation may see their parents and grandparents as out of date and stuck in harmful traditions. Outside the culture, it is unclear how European Americans will react to the changing culture. They may value the more assertive Asian cohorts, seeing them as "more like us." Or they may find the change threatening, causing a reaction against the group. It is difficult to predict. But with any significant change, conflict and struggles are likely.

Historical Context

When many people today think of Asian Americans, they envision the *model minorities* who have worked hard to challenge European Americans for economic supremacy. Most people are unaware that Asian Americans have suffered some of the most inhumane treatment of any minority group. McCunn (1981) depicted the struggles of early twentieth-century Chinese immigrants in the book *Thousand Pieces of Gold*. The novel tells the true story of a Chinese woman, Lalu, whose father sold her to bandits, who forced her to work in a brothel. Eventually, she was taken to America and sold to a bar owner. Although in some ways she was better off in America, she remained caught between two cultures. As a poor woman, she worked with the farmhands in order to make ends meet, and the work caused her bound feet to stretch and return to their pre-bound shape. This condition made working as a prostitute difficult. One man said he couldn't sleep with her because the size of her feet made him feel he was making love to a man. Eventually, Lalu married and started her own business. She slowly realized that being a Chinese woman in America meant never being safe. New laborers would threaten her economic stability, and European Americans would constantly threaten her safety.

Such stories are not uncommon. Sue and Sue (1999) discuss how Chinese Americans were easily scapegoated because of their "strange" customs. They spoke a different language, ate "unhealthy" foods, wore their hair in pigtails, and dressed differently. At first, these differences in appearance and culture were tolerated because the expanding West Coast needed Chinese laborers for railroad construction and gold mining. However, as more Chinese immigrants moved to the West Coast, European Americans saw their manual labor jobs going to cheap Chinese labor.

Tensions between Asian and European settlers continued to mount. In 1871, rival Chinese gangs in Los Angeles shot a European American who was caught in the crossfire of their skirmish. Shortly after the shooting, hundreds of whites stormed the street called *Calle de los Negros* ("Nigger Alley"), which had become the city's Chinatown. They broke windows, knocked down doors, and attacked Chinese residents. They killed one man by dragging him over the stones of the street by a rope around his neck. Three were hanged from a wagon on Los Angeles Street, although they were more dead than alive from being beaten and kicked. Four were likewise hanged from the western gateway of Tomlinson's corral on New High Street. Two of the victims were mere boys. The total number of Chinese killed in the attack is uncertain, but the death toll was probably around 20 (Hart, 1978).

Another example of California's systematic intolerance was the ethnic cleansing of Chinese immigrants in the late nineteenth century. Regarded as a "yellow peril," they were physically attacked—some lynched and all humiliated—and driven out of whole regions of the state in the 1880s. The Chinese population in California went from more than 75,000 in 1880 to about 45,000 in 1900—from over 9% of the population in 1860 to about 3% 40 years later.

California was not the only state where anti-Chinese violence festered. In Rock Springs, Wyoming, a staged attack occurred in 1885 when 600 Chinese employees refused to join a labor union. The European American workers burned down 79 huts belonging to the Chinese. As the Chinese employees fled, 28 were killed and 15 were wounded.

When Japanese, Korean, and Filipino workers entered the United States in successive waves, they also met with similar threats (Lai, 1998). By 1882, organized trade unions secured the Chinese Exclusion Act, which prohibited immigration from China. Waiting for their husbands to earn enough to bring them to America, Chinese women found themselves stranded in China. Chinese laborers were forced from their homes in Tacoma and Seattle, Washington, because they were considered "undesirable" neighbors. Mass murder, physical attacks, and the destruction of homes and property were common occurrences during this era.

Legislation throughout the 1800s allowed for the deportation of Chinese Americans (e.g., the 1891 Immigration Act, 1892 Geary Act, and so on). The Immigration Act of 1965 finally removed national origin as the basis for American immigration policies, but after the passage of this act, Asian Americans were still not given the same rights as other ethnic groups (Chan, 1991). Even after gaining citizenship, Asian Americans faced threats from multiple sources. The most discouraging and painful threats stemmed from the American government.

During the World War II, America established its own prison camps. President Franklin D. Roosevelt signed Executive Order 9066, which allowed military authorities to detain anyone from anywhere without trial or hearings. Although the order did not identify a specific group of people, it soon became clear that the intention of the command was to restrict the freedom of Japanese Americans. From 1942 to the beginning of 1946, Japanese Americans were swiftly and injudiciously collected into relocation centers as "war criminals." Many were housed in these camps solely because of their national origin. Others had been transferred from prisons, had refused to fight against Japan in World War II, or were considered threatening.

The internment camps were located at Amache (Granada), Colorado; Gila River and Poston (Arizona); Heart Mountain (Wyoming); Jerome and Rohwer (Arkansas); Manzanar and Tule Lake (California); Minidoka (Idaho); and Topaz (Utah) (Iritani & Iritani, 1995). In all, 120,313 people were imprisoned. More than 17,000 people were removed directly from their homes. Almost 6,000 children were born in the camps and forced to remain there, and more than 200 people entered the camps voluntarily—generally because they wanted to be with their spouses. Nearly 2,000 died during imprisonment.

Imagine what it would be like to have military personnel storm your house, arrest you, and take you to a makeshift jail. Many were housed outside without shelter. Some camps were overcrowded. When seeking an explanation for why you were arrested, the only answer you can get is "your grandparents were from a country we consider our enemy." The American government acknowledged its mistake on August 10, 1988. President Ronald Reagan signed H.R. 442, providing individual payments of $20,000 to each surviving internee and established a $1.25 billion education fund for Japanese Americans. Although these compensations were helpful, they left a permanent mark on the psyche of Japanese Americans.

Immigration and Development

Although the past few decades have led to positive changes in the way other American cultures view Asian Americans, the changes have also created new problems. Today, the most typical form of oppression against Asians stems from the perception that they represent a "model minority." Asian Americans are frequently portrayed as an American success story: They came to America with nothing and pulled themselves up by their bootstraps. Successful in education and business, they are held up as example to admire and copy. It is a wonderful image but one that belies the underlying problems within Asian communities. Their unemployment, underemployment, and struggles to survive amid the prejudices of European American society are often overlooked or ignored (Lai, 1998).

Consider how Asian Americans have come to this country. In the 1970s, Vietnamese war refugees fled to the United States when Saigon fell. They resettled all over the United States, and a second wave of Vietnamese immigrants came when diplomatic ties were re-established (Zane et al., 2008). Other refugee groups, such as Cambodians, have continued to struggle. However, Asian Indian immigrants tend to come with technology or medical interests and have higher education and income levels than all other Asian groups (Zane et al., 2008).

Some of these immigration issues relate to how acculturated individuals are. Family dynamics play a role in this process. Manaster, Rhodes, Marcus, and Chan (1998) explored the relationship between birth order and acculturation among 1,042 Nisei (second-generation Japanese Americans) and 802 Sansei (third-generation Japanese Americans). When grown, first-born Nisei were more likely than their siblings to live in Japanese American neighborhoods, use the Japanese language, have stronger Japanese family values, and maintain a traditional Japanese religion (Buddhist or Shinto). The findings held true for the first-born Sansei but to a lesser degree. First-born Sansei possessed more knowledge about Japanese values and culture, and they were more likely to champion traditional perspectives. The findings regarding birth order suggest that older children are expected to uphold the family culture and pass it along to succeeding generations.

Within Group Differences

The differences between these groups are so vast that they cannot be addressed fully in this text. It must be noted that most of the groups mentioned in the preceding sections were from eastern Asia (Japan, China, etc.). There are other groups of Asians, such as Indians.

India dates its history back to 6500 B.C. and has created sophisticated traditions of medicine, astronomy, physical sciences, religion, philosophy, and the arts. India has withstood invasions from the Mongols, Muslims, French, Portuguese, and the British, and it won its independence from Britain in 1947, when India became the world's largest democracy. India is the mother of Buddhism, Jainism, and Sikhism and is currently home to myriad religious and cultural leaders. Although most citizens are Hindu and speak Hindi, 14 major Indian languages are also spoken, along with hundreds of rural dialects.

The primary cultural difference between Indian families and other Asians is the *dharma*. The *dharma* addresses the sacredness of all life and encompasses well-defined rules of right conduct, including an elaborate hierarchy that encompasses variables such as age, gender, birth order, marital status, and the role of animals (Kakar, 1978). All life is interconnected and has function and value within the community. According to the Vedas—a collection of Sanskrit verses collected across several Indian regions over a period of millennia—an individual's life is divided into four quarters: study and moral development, marital and family development, the passing of obligations to the next generation, and a spiritual inquiry that leads to a union with *atma*, or universal self. If an individual fails to pass through any of these stages, the family may use collective guilt, shame, or moral reasoning to bring him or her back to the dharma (Prathikanti, 1997).

Another important cultural difference is the Indian view of women. Although often relegated to limited social roles, women have enjoyed notable success in India. Indira Gandhi led the country prior to the election of England's first female prime minister. There are nearly equal numbers of female and male medical students, and female lawyers have long been arguing before the courts. The success of women may be due in part to the widespread worship of female deities. If such deities were limited to goddesses of children (such as Befana, Mayavel, and Rumina), their legacy might not be as grand. But their influence extends much farther. The ancient goddess Ammavaru was said to have existed before time. It was she who laid the egg that hatched into the divine trinity of Brahma, Vishnu, and Shiva. Even the Hindu Trinity has a feminine counterpart. Shiva-Rudra (beneficent and destructive) is married to Durga (the moon goddess); Vishnu (the omnipresent) is married to Lakhsmi; and Brahma (the creator) was married to Sarasvati (goddess of knowledge, fertility, and prosperity). Sarasvati is also considered the originator of speech and of all the arts.

Although these myths have created some advantages for women, they have not cured all the ills. First- and second-generation Indian American women have reported higher levels of domestic violence when married to men of the same ethnicity (Passano, 1995). Bhattacharjee (1999) suggests that this trend is not endemic to Indian culture but stems from the bourgeois separation of private and public life. She suggests that divergent public and private roles can create the foundation for domestic abuse, which may not even be apparent to outsiders. Adding to the problem, Indian men appear to have a double standard for their partners. They will accept the feminist ideals of European American women but expect an Indian wife to accept the traditional submissive role (Devji, 1999). Indian American women are slowly attempting to weave biculturality into their relationships and are expanding their power within marital relationships (Gupta, 1999).

Pacific Islanders are another unique group, and it is very diverse. For example, French Polynesia has a substantial French and Chinese population. The Cook Islands has English as its official language. Fiji's population is nearly a third Indian. Vanuatu is nearly entirely indigenous. And these issues are just from the South Pacific.

In general, the Pacific Islands include both Melanesians (such as states of Vanuatu, Solomon Islands, Papua New Guinea, and Fiji) and Polynesians (a triangular region, with its corners being Hawaii, New Zealand, and Easter Island). Both groups maintain a cultural balance blending village life of farming and fishing and modern-day lifestyles. There is limited research on the health research for native Hawaiians and Pacific Islanders (Ro & Yee, 2010).

Cultural Identity

Pacific Island culture may resemble Native American life more than it does many Asian cultures. This is especially true for aboriginal health issues. For many such people, health is often associated with a connection to the land. This creates greater concerns for climate change adaptation, which are affecting many communities' lifestyles (Berry et al., 2010).

Within Asian communities, there may be greater similarities in culture. Some of these may be virtually unknown to Westerners. For example, Juni-shi (Chinese Zodiac) is an important cultural component of Chinese life. The ancient Chinese associated the calendar with twelve animals that were divided by year rather than month. The twelve animals are called Juni-shi. The animals are Ne (mouse or rat), Ushi (bull or ox), Tora (tiger), Usagi (rabbit), Tatsu (dragon), Mi (snake), Uma (horse), Hitsuji (sheep or goat), Saru (monkey), Tori (rooster or chicken), Inu (dog), and Inoshishi (wild boar). For example, 2010 was the year of the ox, and 2011 was the year of the tiger. This set of twelve animals is the Japanese version of Juni-shi, slightly modified from the original Chinese zodiac. Japan used this calendar for more than a thousand years. Many Asians believe that their Juni-shi birth year says something about their personality and character. One school teacher recently lamented, "I hope to retire before today's babies reach my grade. Tigers are so stubborn when they aren't in charge!"

Other common beliefs involve bodily functions. In China, there is still a lingering belief that each blood type has a special function. Blood type A individuals are believed to be diligent, methodical, steady, and nervous. Blood type B individuals are gifted with originality but are also fickle. Blood type AB individuals are both sociable and sensitive. Finally, blood type O individuals are durable and resolute. For example, O-typed men are thought to make good soldiers.

In addition to calendar and body beliefs, there are also important customs. Consider the issue of gift giving. In many Asian cultures, a gift is considered to have a specific meaning related to its function. Gifts are usually viewed as expressions of purpose or emotion. For example, if you brought a hospital-bound Japanese person a potted plant, the gift could be interpreted to mean, "You expect me to be here for a very long time." In such cases, cut flowers are preferable. Similarly, the number and size of gifts are endowed with meaning. In Japan, it is customary to bring a gift to a hosting family but not to the individual family members. Gifts to individuals are reserved for family members or intimate friends. Family gifts should be presented with the saying *Minasan de douzo* (please share amongst yourselves).

When cultural norms are violated or a more significant offense is made, a sense of shame will often ensue. Often, shame is felt for dishonoring one's family, occupation, or religion, but what is difficult for many Westerners to understand is that shame is associated with inaction as well as action. Not attending a meeting or failing to perform a duty to the expected level may result in feelings of intense shame. In Japan, the term for "goodbye"

(*Shideshimas*) could be translated "I'm rude." Cultural mores are intricate and detailed. Here is a short list:

- Public physical contact is generally inappropriate. Slapping someone's back or giving a hug could be considered an immense dishonor. Touching someone's head, which connotes intense intimacy, would be the most serious violation.
- Asians have special guidelines about feet. Typically, feet are considered unclean. Even discussions about feet could be considered rude. Placing your feet on the furniture or even tapping your foot on the floor might be considered offensive by some groups.
- Eye contact is best kept to a minimal level.
- Closed body language (e.g., crossed arms) is considered coarse.
- The use of hands is quite intricate. Typically, when sitting, hands should rest in the lap. When standing, hands should *not* be hidden in pockets. In many ways, the use of hands conveys openness. If your hands are hidden, you are pulling away from the conversation. For this reason, if you are accepting a gift, business card, or other object, accepting it with both hands conveys respect and honor. In some cultures, such as that of India, you should never touch anything with your left hand, which is considered unclean.
- Boundaries of personal space vary by culture. The Chinese require little personal space, while Indians require nearly three feet.
- European American children and infants smile more than Chinese children, even when children of Chinese parents are born in America (Kagan, 2010). This may be partly due to the religious values of Buddhism, which emphasizes nirvana as the absence of attachment and other fluctuating emotions.

From this list, it should be apparent that some cultural norms appear contradictory. Such cultural incongruities are most apparent regarding rules for meekness. Most Asian cultures value reserved temperaments, but the cultures are also frank and open. While teaching English in Japan, Greg Snyder (personal communication, January, 10, 1998) found himself in an uncomfortable situation while walking down a crowded street. A Japanese woman approached him and stated, "You are fat. Why?" The question was not intended to be insulting. It simply conveyed the woman's curiosity about a topic that was not considered taboo.

Despite these substantial cultural differences, when Asians immigrate to America, they often contend with being treated as adopted whites rather than as members of distinct ethnic cultures. When this occurs, conflict is inevitable. Consider the following consultation request from a European American professor:

> I started working with Chin-Lin about six months ago when she began taking classes at my university. Her family was from China, and she seemed very much alone. On one occasion, I invited her over for dinner at my house.
>
> My husband and I greeted her when she came into the house, and we accepted the house plant she brought as a gift (although we added that it wasn't necessary). She tried to get her shoes off, but we told her that it was not necessary either. Eventually, we made it into the living room and discussed school

issues for a few minutes while my husband continued the preparations for dinner. After about 20 minutes, completely out of the blue, she said, "Aren't you going to offer me some food?" I was a little taken aback by her boldness. I thought Asians were supposed to be meek, but I managed to get out, "Dinner is almost ready."

After our meal, I asked if she would like me to walk her to her car. She looked down and said, "It is not necessary." So, we watched as she walked into the darkness and turned off the light after she drove away.

For the next few days, Chin-Lin seemed distant and a little hostile. I asked if everything was all right, and she just said, "Yes—thank you." I don't know how to handle this situation. Please help.

A number of cultural issues arose during this interaction that Mary, the professor, simply did not recognize. Each of these issues could have had a profound impact on the relationship between Mary and Chin-Lin. Let us examine them in order. First, Chin-Lin presented Mary with the house plant as a token of friendship. Although Mary accepted the gift, she implied that it was unwelcome. Next, Mary and her husband prevented Chin-Lin from removing her shoes. Thus, Chin-Lin's efforts to show respect for her professor's home were compromised. By refusing to disgrace their floors, she wished to demonstrate that she was honored to be in their home.

Next, Chin-Lin expressed frustration over not being fed. In many Asian cultures, touch—such as handshakes or hugs—is considered rude. Instead, it is polite to welcome a guest by offering a gift—often food. The food itself is not nearly as important as the guest's acceptance of it. If Mary had gone to Chin-Lin's house and refused the food tokens provided, her actions would have sent an irrefutable message that Chin-Lin's friendship was not desired.

By the time they finished their meal, Chin-Lin was ready to leave. Mary correctly surmised that she should accompany Chin-Lin to her car. When Chin-Lin said, "It is not necessary," Mary thought her duty had ended. However, in Chinese cultures, the visitor is expected to show good will by relieving the host of the obligation of walking her home. However, the truly gracious host will walk the visitor home anyway.

Although the topic was not mentioned by Mary, another misunderstanding could have arisen from the Asian avoidance of "harsh" terms. Had Mary asked if Chin-Lin liked the meatloaf she was serving, Chin-Lin would have replied, "Yes." Chin-Lin's response would not mean that she actually enjoyed the meal—merely that it would have been considered rude to answer otherwise. In most Asian cultures, the expression "no" in any context is considered rude. In Japan, for example, rather than answer so harshly, someone might say, "It would be difficult." Such an answer often means "no" in the strongest sense of the word. This type of cultural boundary would present serious difficulties to someone investigating a topic considered taboo (such as sex). The avoidance of such topics can also be extended to mundane matters. Asking a Japanese person what they would like to drink may produce the response "Anything will be fine." The rationale for this response to avoid insulting the host by asking for something unavailable. Usually, it is better to provide the guest with a list of possible choices (e.g., coffee or tea).

The conflict between Chin-Lin and Mary occurred because neither party understood the culture of the other. Just as important, both considered themselves similar in culture, even though there were vast differences. Such conflicts are common during the acculturation process. Kim (1985) developed an Asian identity development model in which incorporation of white identity is the first of five stages. The model is depicted in Table 6.1, and it includes the following elements: white identification, awakening to social political consciousness, redirection to Asian American consciousness, and incorporation. The key difference between this identity development process and that of other minorities is the initial acceptance by the dominant society. The awakening stage may take longer to come for Asian Americans than it would for African Americans or Latinos.

Kim's model does not differ substantially from Cross's or many other models. The assumption is that Asian ethnicity development parallels that of other ethnic groups. But we have already seen how the culture is unique. There are similarities between different ethnic development stages, but the trigger moving between facets differs. African Americans can enter social settings where they will not be accepted no matter what they do. This is less likely for Asian Americans, who are more likely to experience concern about behavior and comportment. Asian Americans approach acceptance in the dominant culture, but they will always maintain a bicultural sense of sense (Gong, 2007). For this reason, the emersion state looks more like resistance to the dominant culture than emigration. There is less movement out of the culture as much as rejecting components. Cultural development and challenge appear to stem from blending learning bicultural viewson confrontation styles, being other-focused versus self-focused, aggression, sexual openness, and centrality of sports and education (Stroink & Lalonde, 2009).

TABLE **6.1**
Asian Identity Development Model (Kim, 1985)

White identification	Incorporation into white culture produces a desire to accept European values while rejecting the values of one's ethnic culture.
Awakening to social political consciousness	The ethnic culture is viewed as being oppressed by the dominant culture rather than being inferior to it.
Redirection of Asian American consciousness	There is a gradual immersion into one's ethnic culture. This may include feelings of anger toward European American culture, but energy is mainly focused on the creation of an ethnic identity.
Incorporation	After learning to identify with his or her ethnic heritage, the individual is ready to seek out and incorporate elements from other cultures. This process might include adopting traditions and beliefs from other Asian cultures as well as European American values.

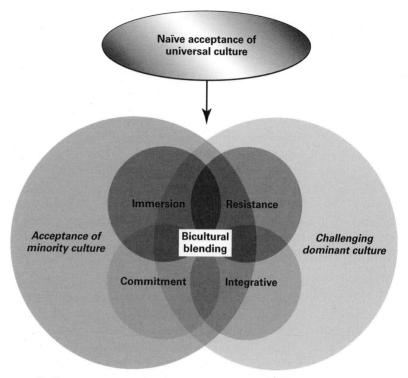

FIGURE **6.1** Cultural Identity Model: Asian Americans

Family Structure and Dynamics

With one of the key components of cultural identity being learning how to blend the other-focus on the East with the self-focus of the West, the family structure will play a key role. Once again, there are stark contrasts between Pacific Islanders and most Asian cultures. Adolescents and young adults from many Pacific Island cultures suffer from high suicide and substance abuse problems. These problems are usually linked back to the family, where anger and frustration stem from intergenerational conflicts. The kids struggle to find harmony between increasing Western values and the values of their communities and families (Lowe, 2003).

In Asian households, the family bond may be stronger. In fact, Marshall Jung (1998) has stated that for many Asian groups, family therapy should be considered a primary intervention. He advises therapists to assist their Asian clients through Chinese American Family Therapy (CAFT), which is an eclectic, multidimensional, comprehensive family therapy model. In this model, family integration (achieving a harmonious relationship with one's family by learning to live ethically with family members) is the primary goal of therapy. The model assumes that when Chinese individuals learn and accept their cultural values (including Confucian humanitarianism), they will live ethically and in peace with one another. With Confucianism making a comeback, this may become even more important in the coming decades, as the family is almost sacred from this religious viewpoint (Ip, 2009).

According to Jung (1998), family integration requires the following components:

- Family centeredness
- Filial loyalty
- Conformity to role expectations
- Ethnocentrism, which includes respecting cultural traditions and rituals
- Being situation-centered
- Conducting oneself in a prudent and reserved manner

These standards differ greatly from the emphasis on autonomy (i.e., ability to choose one's course of action) and individualism in European American cultures (Kitchener, 1984). This closeness is in evidence from the beginning of life. Most Japanese children sleep in the same bed with their mother at least three times per week, while European American children are expected to sleep independently. Rather than create sleep problems, the Japanese practice of co-sleeping appears to decrease regular bedtime struggles and night waking. However, when European American children sleep with their parents, tensions between parents and children often lead to bedtime struggles, night waking, and overall stressful sleep problems. These findings led Latz, Wolf, and Lozoff (1999) to conclude that differing cultural expectations seem to influence the relationship between sleep practices and sleep problems, and co-sleeping *per se* is not associated with increased sleep problems in early childhood.

The close bond between Asian family members may also influence therapeutic goals. Often, counseling consists of encouraging the client to explore what he or she wants. The ultimate goal of such pursuits is the development of a unique individual who is free from the confines of tradition and family expectations. Such a position contradicts the other-focused philosophy of Asian cultures. In most Asian cultures, the decisions an individual makes—even during adulthood—are strongly influenced by parental wishes. Individuals who seek to fulfill their own desires or act in unbecoming ways can shame their families, which is likely to create conflicts for all involved.

The strong connection to family does not imply that family members exchange ideas intimately. Instead, it addresses a more complex form of communal identity. For example, after analyzing videotapes from 59 families, Martini (1996) concluded that European American families are more likely to use mealtime for members to describe their experiences, wishes, plans, and perceptions. Parents cued children to focus on distinctive aspects of their realities—to talk about "what's new" or unfamiliar to them. In Japanese American households, half of the families watched television while eating. Some others played games, listened to music, talked on the phone, or played with their pets. The emphasis was on being together without necessarily discussing the events of the day. The focus was on collective action rather than the accomplishments of individuals. Japanese American families function as a unit, emphasizing a smooth group process. The same is true for Chinese families, where parents emphasize attunement to the feelings of others and personal restraint. This approach emphasizes group harmony (Bornstein & Lansford, 2010).

The responsibility for creating harmony and belonging often falls on women. In China, Korea, and Japan, gender roles are dictated by Confucian teachings. Women from less acculturated families tend to receive less social freedoms, are expected to put their husband's agendas before their own, and must care for children and aging in-laws (Zane, Norton, Chu & Lin, 2008). Ho (1990) studied differences between Chinese, Vietnamese, Laotian, and Khmer women and found that in all groups, girls were punished more severely than boys and had greater demands placed on their behavior. When these girls became mothers, they felt compelled to train their daughters to become obedient and subservient wives. In some cultures, this may lead to a lower status for women (Leeder, 1994), but most Asians affirm the equality of the sexes (Subrahmanyan, 1999). Still, a traditional Asian woman is expected to defer to her father, then her husband, and finally her son (after her husband dies).

The emphasis on group survival and constant social harmony puts low-status individuals at great risk. Families are typically loving and caring, but when violence erupts within the family setting, it may not be reported to outside authorities. These impermeable family boundaries place women and the elderly at significant risk for continued violence. Yoshioka et al. (2001) examined attitudes toward wife abuse and the influence of Asian patriarchal beliefs of 507 Chinese, Korean, Vietnamese, and Cambodian adults. Overall, the participants viewed wife abuse as unacceptable, but they also considered violence an appropriate response to some conflicts. A wife's unfaithfulness, nagging, or refusal to cook or clean may warrant violence. Among the four groups, Vietnamese and Cambodians were most likely to sanction male privilege and justify wife abuse. The researchers also found a correlation between the age of immigration and agreement toward the use of marital violence among Koreans; older Koreans were more likely to agree to the use of violence.

When wrongdoings are committed within the family, they are often kept secret. The victims of elder mistreatment, especially female victims, may never be identified (Moon, 1999; Tomita, 1999). Any component that may bring shame to the family may be kept private (Singh, 2009). Normalizing this process is helpful. Counselors should ease into the intake with statements such as, "It must feel uncomfortable to discuss these things with a stranger. You want healing, but you also want honor."

Acculturation also plays a role in how families handle stress. For example, families feel responsible for the care of aging relatives, but they are sometimes ill-equipped to handle the frustration that can stem from attending to the needs of a dependent family member. Families are also less likely to take on the perceived burden of parental care if they are already facing financial strain (Ishii-Kuntz, 1997). However, even in these cases, older Asian Americans usually live close to at least one of their sons. They will also attempt to support each other, talk on the phone, and share financial resources (Kauh, 1997; Zane, Norton, Chu & Lin, 2008).

Age is so highly regarded in some cultures that older siblings are given special titles to designate their position. For example, in the Filipino culture, the oldest brother and oldest sister get special honorifics from the other siblings. For example, if the eldest siblings were named Beth and Edwin, they would be referred to as "Ate Beth" and "Cuya Edwin." The parents and grandparents also get special respect. For example, even the traditional greeting for one's parent is unique. When greeting one's father, the child is expected to take his father's hand and place it on his or her own forehead. This is apparently a sign of respect as well as thanks.

Family structure in India differs from that of other Asian countries. Culturally, Hindu values prevail throughout India. Within this context, the family connotes more than a dyad of parents and their children. An Indian family often comprises several households and may span geographical regions. These diverse members share educational, financial, and interpersonal decisions throughout each member's life (Prathikanti, 1997). Children may move between households to complete their schooling. A young woman may move in with her aunt and uncle in order to find a suitable husband. An elderly woman may live with a great-niece to be closer to medical care. In all these cases, flexibility and utility govern the options chosen.

Acculturation may also wreak havoc in other ways. Fuligni et al. (2005) examined high school students of European American, Mexican, or Chinese heritage and found that commitment to one's ethnic culture was a factor related to academic achievement. The authors concluded that high identification with one's cultural background was associated with high academic achievement among the Mexican and Chinese students. Furthermore, cultural identification was associated with higher academic motivation. These students had a more positive outlook toward education, found school interesting, and viewed schooling to be useful for their future.

Adoption

Given the unique cultural facets of Asian cultures and the tendency for European cultures to ignore or overlook these components, European adoptions play an important role in the counseling process. Some research implies that Asian children raised by non-Asian parents may not face identity problems (Kim, Shin, and Carey, 1999). Psychological tests also demonstrated that the adopted children did not have more behavioral problems, but transplanted children did feel more socially incompetent than their stepsiblings and also tended to internalize their problems more often.

With more internalization, the psychological maladjustment of Asian adoptees may not present itself until adulthood. One client told me, "I did everything right growing up—cheerleading, band, sports, grades—but I never knew who I was until I returned to Korea." Another client, an adopting parent, told me that her previous therapist stated, "Your Chinese daughter will grow up American—she won't know what it means to be Chinese." Such statements are blatantly wrong. Even if the child lacks an understanding of what it means to be Chinese, she still has a cultural history that deserves to be explored. To ignore it is to denigrate the individual's past and may lead the child to push away from her adoptive parents when she reaches adulthood. It also prohibits the child from having a group where he or she completely belongs. Just as immigrants face a process of being rejected by the dominant society, so will adopted children. Providing opportunities to connect with their roots and their cultural history will help the child feel a greater sense of belonging in the world.

A good illustration of what Asian adoptions look like for adults may be seen in Sam Morgan's story. There is a persistent ebb and flow between minority culture and dominant culture. It often continues well into adulthood and usually until they have children of their own:

> As a 24-year-old adoptee from South Korea, I still experience confusion associated with my cultural identity. I am unable to authentically identify with my cultural roots and heritage because of a lack of knowledge regarding family history. Similarly, I'm unable to fully embrace the whiteness of my parents and the privileges they reap because of my race—physical appearance. As a child, I wanted to fit in with my peers, who were primarily white and Mexican. This concern for inclusion caused me to be disinterested in my parents' attempts to teach me about Asian culture because it magnified the differences between me and my friends, which I was trying to minimize. As an adult, I continue to struggle with adjustment into my adopted family. During large family gatherings, I oftentimes feel detached from my adopted family and lack feelings of genuine affection. Such feelings commonly cause me to feel guarded and uninterested in social interaction with my family because I revert to previous experiences as a racial minority, in which it feels as though every word I say is being closely examined. At times, I also feel comparatively inadequate to my siblings, who are the biological children of my adopted parents. This discrepancy in inclusiveness stems from an intimate connection between my adopted parents and their siblings, which I have observed but find unfamiliar. Although my confusion with cultural identity will likely continue, I have planned a journey of cultural exploration—traveling to South Korea—but I remain skeptical of its utility. Will it help solidify my identity? I don't know (S. Morgan, personal communication, April 4, 2010).

Education

There is no doubt that Asian Americans are the academic envy of all other ethnic groups. Over the last half of the twentieth century, the Asian American community has slowly excelled to the point of passing all other groups in high school grade point averages and scores on national examinations, such as SATs. Asian Americans studier longer hours than their peers, and they are also more likely to desire jobs requiring more formal education (Dandy & Nettelbeck, 2002). This high value on education is continuing to pay off, but the "average" assessment perpetuates the "model minority" syndrome.

Although there is some value in discussing Asian education success, results vary by country. For example, when looking at college graduate rates, Asian American and Pacific Islander groups tend to rate well above European Americans. However, Hmong and Tongans have the lowest graduate rates of any ethnic group, and native Hawaiians, Vietnamese, Cambodians, Laotians, Guamanians, and Samoans are below the rates for European Americans (Ihara, 2009).

Despite the variance, Asian Americans are being studied to determine the source of their success. Asakawa, Kiyoshi, Csikszentmihalyi, & Mihaly (1998) compared the subjective academic experiences of 33 Asian American students with those of 33 European American students. All students were adolescents between sixth and 12th grades. The findings revealed that while Asians do not spend more time studying, when they do study, their study experience is more positive. They enjoy the study experience and are able to perceive the relationship between studying and achieving their career goals. They are also more likely to get into the flow of studying, allowing themselves to feel deeply involved, highly motivated, and maintaining a high level of enjoyment (Asakawa, 2010).

Where does this motivation come from? Largely because families place a high value on education. Sun (1998) examined financial, family, cultural, and other influences to see which played the most significant role in the success of East Asian students. Results of this national study indicated that Asian families invested time, money, and energy in their children's educational lives. They were much more likely to do so than any other racial group, even after social and demographic controls were taken into consideration. This increased emphasis on education means that Asian American children are less likely to participate in organized sports, to earn money through chores or employment, or even to spend time dating. Parents are also likely to reduce their children's household chores the day before a test (Krishnan & Sweeney, 1997).

However, the role of parents in supporting their children's education is also influenced by the family's occupational and ethnic background. Kim, Rendon, and Valadez (1998) found that, on average, South Asians (i.e., those from Afghanistan, Bangladesh, Bhutan, India, Myanmar, Nepal, Pakistan, and Sri Lanka) tend to express the highest educational aspirations, followed by Koreans, Japanese, Chinese, Filipinos, and Southeast Asians. South Asian parents also tend to have the highest levels of education, followed by Koreans, Japanese, Filipinos, Chinese, and Southeast Asians. Finally, South Asian parents also have the highest occupational status, followed by Japanese, Koreans, Filipinos, Chinese, and Southeast Asians. These trends are reflected in the intensity of the educational demands placed on students by their families.

What happens when students are unable to achieve their academic goals? Some families will seek professional help. One couple came to me requesting a complete psychological evaluation for their 14-year-old son. With his son present, the father said, "My son simply isn't working hard enough. He received a B in math last term, and he'll ruin his chances for Stanford by earning another B." His mother, cautious not to contradict her husband, added her own concerns. "He may not study hard, but he studies for very long hours. He works every day, starting right after school and not ending until midnight."

After completing the psychological profile, this child was anxious, fearful about the future, and functioning well above his natural abilities. He received an IQ score in the average range but had accumulated knowledge (in reading, writing, math, and science) well above average. When discussing the results with his parents, we created a plan to help him maintain his achievements. This included taking an hour off from studying after coming home from school, never working past 10 p.m., and spending time with friends or social groups on Friday.

Even if they make it through high school without significant problems, they are likely to face additional concerns in college. First-generation Asian students are more likely to have difficulty making friends, and they are concerned about how to interact with American lecturers/teachers. First-generation female students, in particular, appear most reticent about approaching lecturers for help and asking questions in class. Most of these difficulties stem from a limited technical competency in English, but there are also issues regarding philosophies of learning (Beaver & Tuck, 1998).

European-American teachers, especially at higher levels, tend to maintain a discreet distance with their students. When faculty members form relationships with students, the structure is usually collaborative. The student is treated as a junior peer who is granted privileges but is under the faculty member's leadership. Asian Americans are often more comfortable with frameworks resembling parent/child relationships. They respect the office of the teacher/professor and will display reverence, honor, sincere appreciation, and gratitude (including gifts) for small acts, but they may also expect detailed guidance, which may appear to violate the emphasis on autonomy in American colleges. If faculty members fail to respond to an Asian student's request for guidance, the student may become insecure and confused.

These social and familial expectations may result in academic burnout in Asian children. This may also explain why Asian American students are the most likely ethnic group to turn to drugs and suicide when their grades drop (Ellickson, Collins & Bell, 1999).

Socioeconomics

The strong work ethic of many Asian cultures has resulted in a fundamental change in socioeconomic status. Most traditional Chinese immigrants come to the United States with the intention of improving their economic status. This purpose differs from that of Asian "boat people" who are usually fleeing a hostile environment. Before 1990, such refugees emigrated primarily from South Vietnam, Cambodia, and Laos in connection with the Vietnam War. The number of refugees arriving in America has been declining (Buriel & De Ment, 1997). These differing motives have an effect on the direction each group takes after arriving on American shores. When immigrants from Southeast Asia find that it takes at least five years before they achieve economic self-sufficiency in the United States, depression and anger may set in (Law & Schneiderman, 1992). Immigrants may be surprised to find significant obstacles preventing them from obtaining even the most humble jobs. It simply takes time to learn the nuances of the language and the subtleties of the various American cultures.

However, what makes Asian Americans unique is how they react to the oppression they face. Asian Americans tend to perceive themselves as being more prepared for college, better motivated, and more likely to achieve career success than European Americans (Wong, Lai, Nagasawa & Lin, 1998). Their religious beliefs—especially Confucianism, Hinduism, and Buddhism— also view wealth acquisition as the natural result of disciplined, ethical work. Confucianism adopts a virtue-based ethics that will likely affect the way corporations are run over the coming decades. In a Confucian firm, there are clear rules for hierarchy, ways of interacting, how to make decisions, leadership, and relationships among stakeholders (Ip, 2009). For most Asian religions, wealth is never primary. It is a consequence of seeking virtue and experiencing karma (i.e., an action or situation that is created or recreated by present or past-life habitual impulse, volitions, and natural energies).

In Buddhism, this understanding of karma is explained in the Third Noble Truth. An emphasis on selfish gain causes suffering. For example, "I'm going to make it to the top, and I'll step on anyone who gets in my way." This is likely to result in temporary wealth that may disappear as quickly as it is earned. In contrast, the Eightfold Path requires working not only for self but also for the honor of family, community, and the world. For example, "I will work hard, bring honor to my family, and play my part in making the world stronger." These cultural values lead to a long-term view of investment. Asian Americans emphasize family investment over consumption, and they view wealth, in part, as a means of supporting their families and communities (Jain & Joy, 1997).

The differences between the socialist/communist philosophy and the individualized capitalism found in America may also cause problems for immigrants. In the dominant American society, workers are told to "do what feels right" or "find the job that's best for you." Asian Americans with lower levels of acculturation tend to choose more conventional occupations (i.e., Realistic and Investigative[1] occupations) because their families effectively guide them toward choosing low-risk occupations that are likely to bring success. Occupations are selected on the basis of what the family considers wise rather than what might best fit the individual's aptitudes or occupational preferences. As young people become acculturated, they experience stronger feelings of self-efficacy and are more willing to pursue their own occupational desires, but they are likely to maintain their cultural perceptions too (Gong, 2007).

The global shift away from corporate occupations and toward self-employed entrepreneurs and wage laborers has also reconfigured gender relations within contemporary Asian American society. Female-intensive industries, such as domestic cleaners and childcare providers, have enhanced women's employability over that of some men. This shift in the economic structure of the Asian American community has challenged the patriarchal authority of Asian immigrant men, particularly among the working class (Estiritu, 1999).

---

[1] John Holland's Vocational Types are divided into the following categories:

    (a) **Realistic:** use of athletic or mechanical skills in working with objects, machines, tools, plants, or animals;
    (b) **Investigative:** observation, learning, investigation, analyzing, or problem-solving.
    (c) **Artistic:** artistic, innovating, or intuitive abilities emphasizing imagination and creativity.
    (d) **Social:** enlightening, informing, helping, training, or curing others.
    (e) **Enterprising:** influencing, persuading, performing, leading, or managing for organizational goals or economic gain.
    (f) **Conventional:** data processing or clerical duties, with an emphasis on taking care of details or following instructions.

Blumberg (1991) predicted these economic advances for women. Her argument was that Asian women—especially Chinese women—needed to feel that they could control their own income and economic resources if they were to ever create a more balanced division of labor within the household. She believed that women's control of economic resources had to be on an equal level to that of their husbands before women could reach a state of equality. Such conditions are far from reality in China. Massive rural-to-urban migration, an exploding commercial sex industry, and frequent gender-based violence have put Chinese women at great risk for AIDS and other diseases (Tang, 2008).

Asian women also face financial challenges regarding child care. Balagopal (1999) mentions that Asian American mothers face challenges that differ from those of European Americans. These women feel compelled to redefine their sense of self as well as their views of family and culture. While they are growing up, Asian American women are often conditioned to view women's employment outside the home as dishonorable. When they realize that their income contributes to the family's economic well-being, their sense of pride and honor increases, especially when their salary is necessary for the family's survival. However, feelings of self-worth and satisfaction with child care are inversely related to income. The higher the socioeconomic status of the mother, the more concerned she is likely to be with her child's care (Seo, 2006).

Despite the challenges discussed here, the average income of Asian Americans is 15% above that of European Americans (Boutte, 1999), but this figure is also deceptive. Higher incomes do not necessarily translate into a higher standard of living. Asian Americans are more likely to live in urban environments where the cost of living is higher. They also have more education but rarely see the gains European Americans get from higher education. When looked at from another viewpoint, Asian families are more likely than European American to earn less than $20,000. They are also less likely to earn more than $50,000 a year (Ihara, 2009). They work longer hours, have larger families, and attempt to overcome the discrimination they face. This reality stands in contrast with the model minority view, which implies that Asian Americans enjoy the same economic advantages as the dominant ethnic group.

Spirituality and Religion

In many Asian countries, Christianity is relatively uncommon because it does not adapt well to the traditional caste system. However, Christianity is growing as the Asian culture changes. The largest Christian church in the world—Yoido Full Gospel Church—is in South Korea. It has more than a million members.

The Philippines, by contrast, is primarily a Catholic nation, which means Filipinos have much in common with Catholics from Mexico or Brazil. For example, Filipinos accept the traditional Catholic use of godparents, who often play an important role in the parenting of children.

In China, Japan, Korea, and many other Asian countries, traditional Eastern religions dominate the spirituality of the people. These include Shintoism (a descendant of ancient animism, mixed with ancestor worship, sun worship, and Buddhism), Jodo Buddhism (the dominant sect of Buddhism in Japan), Esoteric Buddhism (the priests of Esoterics invoke powerful miracles, called *horiki*, through which they can cure diseases, curse a person to death, or see into the future), Zen Buddhism (dominated by the idea that spiritual awakening is attained only by meditation), Taoism (the Chinese blend of native religions, divination, Confucian courtesy, and ceremony), and Confucianism (which is collectivist and emphasizes obligation to family, society, and truth).

Buddhism, which was illustrated in the opening insight exercise, emphasizes four Noble Truths: (1) suffering exists, (2) suffering arises from attachment to desires, (3) suffering ceases when attachment to desire ceases, and, (4) freedom from suffering is possible by practicing the Eightfold Path (often grouped in the following three sections):

Wisdom (panna)

Right Understanding (samma ditthi)

Right Aspiration (samma sankappa)

Morality (sila)

Right Speech (samma vaca)

Right Action (samma kammanta)

Right Livelihood (samma ajiva)

Concentration (samadhi)

Right Effort (samma vayama)

Right Mindfulness (samma sati)

Right Concentration (samma samadhi)

These components are not taught through books or lectures. They must develop through experience and meditation. They also require an understanding of the first three Noble Truths before being put into place.

I finally understood this when I took my kids to an amusement park. When the night wore on, the old parents got tired. We told the kids it was time to leave. The park was closing in 30 minutes anyway.

Both girls screamed, "Just one more ride—we haven't done that one yet." So, we walked them to the ride they wanted to try, and they loved it.

"Can we have one more one-more-ride?" The oldest girl asked with puppy-dog eyes.

We were near the exit, and there was a merry-go-round nearby. We asked if they thought the merry-go-round would be enough. They giggled and squealed and jumped on the ride. But it was not what they expected. A minute into the ride, they realized it was too slow and too boring for preteen girls. When the ride ended, they begged to go back to the first one-more-ride.

"No," I said. And we started out the exit.

The second we touched the turnstile, both girls wailed with inconsolable sorrow. They wept so hard, it was as if they just learned of a significant death. Although it probably makes me sound callous, I only consoled them for a few minutes before my mind turned to the Four Noble Truths. The girls were too attached to fun. They bonded so much with this impermanent state that they suffered great pain when it ended. Such must be learned before an individual can start the Eightfold Path.

Physical and Mental Health

Many Asian groups attribute health problems to spiritual causes rather than viruses, bacteria, or other agents. For example, Chinese patients may attribute a life-threatening illness such as cancer to bad luck (Yeo et al., 2005). An imbalance of yin (feminine energies) and yang (masculine energies) is viewed as the source of disturbances in the body and mind. All humans are subject to the same elemental forces that govern the rest of the universe (fire, earth, metal, water, and wood). These elements also correspond to the five visceral organs of humans: the heart creates joy, the lungs create sorrow, the liver creates anger, the kidneys create fear, and the spleen creates compassion.

Physical Health

Although Westerners may scoff at the Asian view of health, there are documented benefits to Asian lifestyles. Rogers et al. (1996) examined the National Health Interview Survey to look at the causes of death for various ethnic groups. Their data set included an enormous amount of information, including 394,071 survival records and 4,133 death records. The findings indicated that Asian Americans have death rates far below those of European Americans and other groups, which resulted from a combination of healthy behaviors (including diet and exercise) and socioeconomic advantages. Pacific Islanders also have a long history of indigenous healing, such as the Samoan *fofo* healers who call upon the family gods to assist with healing (Macpherson, 1995).

The idea of healthy behaviors guiding Asian Americans' lifestyle choices is not new. Asian Americans speak of their physical health as one of the most important facets of their lives. They also believe that community expectations for personal behaviors help to shape their physical health (Lang & Torres, 1997–1998). Both physical and psychological health are maintained through proper diet and exercise, mental/spiritual conditioning, and family togetherness. Qigong (pronounced chee-gong) is one approach aimed at physical and psychological wellness. This ancient Chinese system incorporates self-healing exercises that include healing postures, sounds, movements, breathing techniques, and meditation (Schnauzer, 2006).

However, viewing physical health as the result of spiritual forces creates some problems that must also be addressed. One of the most serious is a lack of access to Western health care. Jang, Lee, and Woo (1998) looked into the ways income, language, and citizenship status affected the use of health care services by Asian Americans in San Francisco. In their study, 63% of Chinese Americans were found to be working poor—often locked out of the health care system. As employees, they are often ineligible for welfare or simply refuse to accept it, and their employers refuse to offer health insurance. Such limitations may also explain why some Asian Americans cannot define the term *cancer* (Phipps, Cohen, Sorn & Braitman, 1999). But educational programs are helpful. Asian American women are more likely to have undergone a medical evaluation and a Pap test (Jenkins et al., 1999), and they are likely to believe that the overall quality of services rendered was competent (Harju, Long & Allred, 1998).

When a lack of knowledge concerning certain medical ailments is combined with a lack of available care, the problems become tragic. Yi (1998) queried 412 Vietnamese American college students (aged 17 to 48 years) concerning their knowledge about HIV-related problems. The participants in her study were aware of the major modes of HIV transmission, but they still held misconceptions that could prove fatal. One of the most frightening elements of her study was that as individuals became more acculturated, they started engaging in more sexual activity. In addition to this, higher acculturation was actually associated with less knowledge about HIV transmission. So, not only was acculturation promoting sexual activity, but it also led to less investigation into the risks. Even more alarming was the fact that when participants believed they were or could be infected, they were not comfortable discussing their HIV and safe-sex concerns with their sexual partners. These factors have led to an increase in the rate of HIV infection among Asian Americans, especially gay males (Tang, 2008).

Despite the rise in AIDS and HIV, China is starting to emulate the health of Western countries, with heart disease, cancer, and cerebrovascular disease now the top three causes of death (Wagner et al., 2006). Smoking has also taken its toll. There is a social component to why Asian Americans smoke; they tend to smoke more cigarettes when in groups. But the cause of their smoking is not the social pressure. They are more likely to smoke when their coping mechanisms between cigarettes are weak (Otsuki, Tinsley, Chao & Unger, 2008). This provides another indication of how the physical and mental facets of life are closely intertwined for Asian Americans and why interventions for either type of issue should be comprehensive.

Mental Health

Asian American are often skeptical of counselors and psychologists. This is largely because many forms of Western mental health interventions ignore the physical components. It is also because Western therapy requires levels of disclosure that are too revealing with Asian mindsets (Zane, Norton, Chu & Lin, 2008). For example, Confucianism addresses many facets of mental health, including self-regulation. According to this philosophy, people can become "full" by adopting such emphasizing techniques as self-examination, meditation, and introspection (Jing, 2007).

Cultural differences also lead to distinctive perspectives regarding mental health. Many Asian Americans believe that disorders such as depression, anxiety, confusion, and even posttraumatic stress disorder (PTSD) stem from their physical and spiritual health. Mental illness is attributed to karma (either from the individual's present choices, past life, or family actions). Sometimes, the divine element becomes all-important, and mental health may be equated with spiritual unrest projected onto the individual from a vengeful spirit (Lee, 1997b). These spiritual elements will likely correspond to physical complaints, with the two working for or against each other. The worse a person's physical functioning, the more severe the affective symptoms may become (Nicholson, 1997).

There are also many unique mental health concerns recognized by Asian mental health professionals. For example, it is common to hear diagnoses of such spiritual issues as Shin-byung (Korea) or Hsieh-ping (Taiwan), where hallucinations or delusions are thought to be caused by ancestral spirit possession, or Imu Latah (Japan), Bah-tschi (Philippines), or Menkeiti (Thailand), where the individual feels a loss of the soul and enters a trance-like state. There are such sexual concerns as Koro (Malaysia), Suo yang (China), and Rok-joo (Thailand), where evil spirits cause excessive masturbation and there is a sudden fear of the penis retracting into the abdomen (resulting in death). Even more traditional mental health issues have unique twists. Hwa-byung (Korea) explains such things as physical pains, insomnia, fatigue, fear, and many other psychological concerns on the suppression of deep anger. Phobias such as the fear of wind (Pa-feng, China) are viewed more as a concern against *yin* energy than the physical elements (Zane, Norton Chu & Lin, 2008).

According to Cornwell (1998), Asian Americans are more likely to complain of physical symptoms than European Americans (67.5% compared to 22%). This corresponds to mental health practices in Asia, where patients are more likely to consult physicians when seeking assistance with mental health problems. To remedy depression or other ailments, Asian physicians or priests may recommend massage, herbal medicine, tea ceremonies, martial arts work, or meditation. However, this does not imply that Asian Americans will prefer physical interventions, such as psychopharmacology. It appears that Asians are less likely to continue taking antidepressants than are European Americans (Cornwell, 1998).

Introducing talk therapy has also been slow. Asian Americans/Pacific Islanders are three times *less* likely than their European American counterparts to use available mental health services (Matsuoka, Breaux & Ryujin, 1997). They also tend to accept behavioral patterns that, by European American standards, are considered harmful. For example, Chinese Americans are known to have a high rate of pathological gambling addictions (Lee, 1997b), but they seldom seek treatment for this problem.

Individual and Group Interventions

Mikulas (2002) argues that Asian cultures tend to shy away from psychology because the notion of separating a person's mind from his or her nutritional status, energy level, family relations, and spiritual practices would be futile. This distinction is often hard for Westerners to grasp because Western thought has long attempted to compartmentalize everything.

Individual Therapy

Physical/spiritually oriented worldviews have made talk therapy virtually non-existent in Asia. The reasons for this trend are complex, but they rest in part on the Asian conceptualization of mental health. In many Asian cultures, the admission that an individual has mental health "problems" can further intensify feelings of shame, and this shame is exacerbated by disclosing problems to someone outside one's immediate family (Zane, Norton, Chu & Lin, 2008). Typically, Asians will turn to a trusted friend, spiritual leader, or physician when they are unable to resolve mental health issues within the family. It is only after exhausting these resources that they will turn to mental health practitioners, and even then, it is usually at the request of a physician. Even in these cases, the family is likely to feel more comfortable and attend more sessions if the counselor speaks the client's language or belongs to the same ethnic group (Flaskerud & Liu, 1991).

To Westerners, the lack of talk therapy might indicate poor mental health interventions, but Asian therapies may be more integrated and systematic than Western psychology. Even the practice of Buddhism can be viewed as a form of psychotherapy. As the pupil progresses, he or she tries daily to harmonize conflicting inner forces, resolving conflicts by creating an inner sense of calmness. Such a pursuit is called the Sublime Way (*Ariya Magga*) or the Harmonious Way (*Samma Magga*), and this lifestyle is viewed as a means of achieving mental health (*Arogya*). The calm mind is able to observe subjective experiences objectively; if someone hurts you, your pain should be no greater than if you witnessed that action committed against someone else.

The mechanism for meditation has long been established. The more people meditate, the more they improve their emotional intelligence. With more control over their emotional regulation, they have less perceived stress. Less stress yields better mental health (Chu & Kao, 2005).

Let us create an intervention for Lan. To envision a conjunctive intervention, picture the following scenario. You are working with a Chinese American woman who is feeling depressed and confused about her marriage. Her concerns rest within the personal and behavioral dimensions, and she is trapped within these confines. To free her, steps must be taken beyond the individual—beyond the personal. One of the most important beginning stages is to experience the world as a part of the self. Have the client choose a calming position and have him or her focus on one of the senses (i.e., smell, taste, sight, touch, and hearing). If the sense of touch is chosen, have the client attempt to perceive subtle breezes, the way her feet touch the floor, how her body touches the chair, changes in temperature, or even the sensation of clothes against the body. During most of the day, we are oblivious to these environmental nuances. Instead, we focus on the "problems" of our lives, which can enslave us. If the client can transcend the problems surrounding her, she can awaken to a new way of living. The sensations of the moment can overpower her seemingly insurmountable feelings and circumstances. However, to reach this point, all four dimensions must be investigated. She might spend 10 minutes sitting in the afternoon sun, change her diet, or learn to fast. She may also be asked to redefine herself as an individual—to view herself as a part of a larger world. To do this, she will need to discover or rediscover meaningful myths and stories. These techniques may fit within the Western therapeutic model, but they are seldom employed.

A basic framework for counseling Asian clients can be summarized with the acronym ASIA: acceptance, support, impartiality, and adaptability.

Acceptance includes a variety of important dimensions. Therapists must learn to accept and feel comfortable in the roles of authority figure, expert, and educator. Each of these roles is often difficult for therapists to accept because most schools of thought view the therapist as a co-collaborator in the client's growth. However, many Asian clients will expect their therapist to have answers, offer advice, and provide hope. This means that the therapist, not the client, is viewed as the primary change agent. The client will look to the therapist for direction and leadership. The therapist is viewed as a healer who is expected to provide solutions specific to the problem. Clear guidelines about the nature of therapy should be communicated, including expectations for the therapist and the client.

Support is the second foundational element necessary when working with Asian clients. Therapists must find a way to support the family's hierarchical structure without allowing this structure to threaten an individual's growth or mental health. Consider the case of Lee, who is feeling suicidal. Lee's family wants to keep him at home because hospitalization would cause them to feel embarrassed. In this situation, in which a client's life is in danger, the therapist must give higher priority to the needs of the client than to the family's wishes. However, it is helpful to support family structure by reframing growth issues. For example, a woman's desire for greater independence could be viewed as something that provides her husband with more free time.

Impartiality also looks a little different with Asian clients. Counselors need to operate from a neutral vantage point and learn to listen objectively to their clients' statements. Some cultural issues may appear odd or pathological to Western therapists. If a client discusses the healing power of herbs or the connection between a physical symptom and depression, such perceptions should be accepted and then worked through.

The final component is adaptability. Most Asian Americans will prefer directive, structured, problem-focused interventions (Zane, Norton, Chu & Lin, 2008). But this will look different depending on background, nationality, and the therapeutic relationship. Working with Asian clients requires therapists to be flexible enough to adopt different intervention strategies and intervention styles. The most likely path to success will assist client growth while building a sense of acceptance and honor. Therapists should also help clients use self-reflection as a method of maintaining health (e.g., meditation, self-control of negative thoughts, or other self-discipline tools).

Group and Family Interventions

The family is extremely important, and a certain structure must be maintained. Family support for Asian families serves as a buffer against somatic complaints and depression (Jou & Fukada, 1997). However, when an individual's issues require more skill than the family possesses, scapegoating may occur. Such coping techniques are especially likely when a child has a history of physical illness. The illness may be blamed for family problems (Lee, 1997b). The perceived shame of seeking outside help has also led many traditional Asian husbands or fathers to prevent the family from attending therapy. When crises arise with children and the family is unable to effectively address the critical issues without help, some men will send their wives to therapy sessions rather than lose face by participating in therapy (Lee, 1997a). Such complications require therapists to maintain a flexible structure for family therapy. The therapist should be willing to alter treatment plans if necessary and evaluate therapeutic outcomes. Such an approach will assist in establishing a cooperative therapeutic relationship and maintaining trust (Jung, 1998).

When Asians attend therapy, they will probably be reluctant to voice their deepest concerns. They are more likely to view themselves as being victims of a tragic environmental situation or unable to cope with some physical discomfort (Lee, 1997a). This is probably one of the reasons that Asian Americans are less satisfied with psychotherapy in the early stages of the process. They are also more likely after four treatment sessions to report depression, hostility, and anxiety (Zane, Enomoto & Chun, 1994).

Rather than focus on the affective dimensions of therapy, Cimmarusti (1999) recommended that counselors avoid action-oriented techniques, such as role-playing, and instead focus on "meaning-oriented techniques." The latter may include interventions such as reframing problems within the client's cultural framework (e.g., viewing depression as a physical or spiritual problem) or engaging in circular questioning (e.g., asking, "When you are tense, you close off your senses; are you experiencing your surroundings now?"). These are more effective ways to help clients fulfill cultural demands for harmony and build a strong boundary around the clan.

When Teva (a second-generation Cambodian American) and her husband Chay Chan (a third-generation Cambodian American) came to counseling, different acculturation levels created the greatest conflict.

"We're having a hard time communicating," Chay stated. "Teva's a wonderful person, but I'm not able to give her what she needs."

Teva sat silently, with her head bowed down and her gaze focused on the ground.

After a few seconds, she jerked her head up and quickly looked into her husband's eyes. She then returned to her original position. "I ... I don't think this is the right place to discuss it," she finally lamented.

Chay sighed. "See what I mean?" He moaned with obvious frustration. "There is something wrong, but I don't know how to get through."

In order to work within both Chay's and Teva's worldviews, I had to act as an intermediary.

"Mrs. Chan, I can sense your value for harmony and family honor. It must be difficult to discuss conflicts with me in the room, and I do not want to bring shame to you. Would you mind if we took some time to get to know each other before discussing Mr. Chan's comment?"

In the second session, once rapport was established, acculturation difference took a different form. Teva expressed fears about her husband's spending habits. He was purchasing more on credit cards than they could pay off, and she considered this reckless and dangerous to their future. She also believed confronting her husband about his excessive spending habits would be disrespectful. Given her reluctance to confront him, it was important to let her decide when to disclose her concerns. Coming to therapy was forced on her, and the process left her feeling even more vulnerable and uncomfortable. Culturally aware therapists will avoid confrontations that could lead to an embarrassing disclosure.

If both partners had been recent immigrants, it is less likely that they would have sought help from an outsider. When such support is sought, it is usually with the intention of ending a particular crisis rather than changing an ongoing family dynamic. When Asian families contact service providers, the contact tends to be crisis-related, brief, and solution-oriented; thus, insight and growth-oriented approaches are not recommended (Berg & Jaya, 1993). A traditional Asian family may expect therapy sessions to last longer than one hour and take place more often than once a week. They desire a quick resolution to an immediate problem (Lee, 1997a). Given this understanding, therapists need to help clients find pragmatic solutions to problems rather than encourage them to share their feelings. In many cases, clinicians should address the family's needs over the individuals needs so the family can more quickly return to homeostasis.

However, the family's needs should never supersede an individual's safety. Therapists working with Asian clients may expect them to be submissive and quiet, but the therapeutic process can be intense and highly charged. Clients may have suicidal ideation or be extremely angry or argumentative. Complications can be even more serious depending on the family members' interactional patterns, personalities, and levels of motivation. Each case can present the therapist with new challenges and opportunities for professional and personal growth.

In regards to group therapy, therapists may consider running therapy from the perspective of existing Asian interventions. The Center for Mental Health Services (2000) recommends the incorporation of alternative approaches to mental health care that emphasize the interrelationship between mind, body, and spirit. For Asian Americans, therapists may solicit the assistance of community resources to provide services such as acupuncture, shiatsu,[2] and reiki.[3] When used along with other forms of mental health therapy, these techniques can address clients' needs on physical and spiritual levels.

Yoga (a precursor to Indian Hinduism) can illustrate how Arogya can be achieved. To its adherents, describing yoga as physical exercise (which is how Westerners commonly perceive it) is misleading and offensive—on a par with dismissing mental health interventions as "talking with a friend." Das (2001) refers to yoga as a means of linking oneself with the Supreme (the inner and universal source of life). It is viewed as a process of releasing one's spiritual energy from the worldly realm and rising to a spiritual purity. The mind is

---

[2] Shiatsu is a Japanese healing art deeply rooted in the philosophy and practices of traditional Chinese medicine. Incorporating the therapeutic massage of Japan—and more recently embracing its original focus of meditation and self-healing—shiatsu is gaining popularity in the West. The purpose of shiatsu is achieving a balance between practitioner and receiver, in which the healing power of both build on each other to clear and balance the vital life force known as Qi.

[3] Reiki is a technique for stress reduction and relaxation that allows people to tap into an unlimited supply of "life force energy" to improve health and enhance the quality of life.

trained to avoid all worldly distractions by learning to shun the glitter of material nature. The practice can alleviate stress, anxiety, mood disturbance, and musculoskeletal problems as well as enhance cognitive and physical performance (Khalsa et al., 2009).

It takes time to learn this process, and there are eight stages to yogic development. In the early stages, the focus is on being in harmony with the principles of life (*yama*, *niyama*) and on training the body. Once the postures are learned and the individual has mastered the art of breathing, the student learns to clear the mind of all inner and outer obstacles. As the pupil's skill and knowledge increase, the meditation processes deepen until he or she ceases all disturbing mental activities (*chitta vritti nirodha*). In Raja Yoga, the *chitta vritti nirodha* is reached by first clearing the mind of all thoughts except one sound or idea. This is practiced in 10- to 20-second intervals *(Pratyahara)*. When *Pratyahara* is mastered, the student may progress to *Dharana* (holding on to a single mental object for two to four minutes), *Dhyana* (holding on to a single mental object for 30 to 40 minutes), and, finally, *Samadhi* (holding on to a single mental object for 6 or more hours). With each level, complex physical, emotional, and intellectual tasks are united to create mental health.

Yoga's bridging of mental and physical health is common to many Asian interventions. In the Asian worldview, there are four levels of being (biological, behavioral, personal, and transpersonal), and each must be addressed in a mental health intervention to help the client improve (Mikulas, 2002). Contemporary psychological theories have addressed the personal and behavioral dimensions, but there has been little discussion of the biological and transpersonal areas. One of the contemporary counseling approaches built on an Asian worldview is conjunctive psychology, which addresses the four dimensions listed previously. Within this theoretical orientation, interventions involving the biological dimension could include prescribing medications as well as understanding the effects of the seasons, color and light, weather, pollution, herbs, and diets. The transpersonal dimension may include meditation, spiritual awakening, progressing beyond personal concerns, or striving for any other form of higher consciousness.

Advocacy and Social Justice

Advocacy and empowering for Asian Americans often involves blending personal growth with family honor. This makes face-saving techniques critical in virtually every setting. Rather than focusing on pathology, clients and students will respond better to normalizing challenges (Zane, Norton, Chu & Lin, 2008). This may be especially true for such taboo topics as domestic violence and child sexual abuse (Singh, 2009). Statements such as, "Many of my clients struggle with sexual feelings. It requires new daily routines to create lasting change." This level of acceptance can build trust, understanding, and motivation. But it differs from Western ideals.

With so many similarities between Asian and Western culture (e.g., valuing hard work, education, financial success, etc.), therapists and educators often overlook the differences. Take drug and alcohol interventions. The

Alcoholics Anonymous model emphasizes personal responsibility, specific steps toward growth, and emotional vulnerability. These philosophies may contradict Asian spiritualities and worldviews (Singh, 2009). Clients may blend self-efficacy, self-reliance, and other Western psychological ideals into their healing process, but each person's bicultural identity will take a unique direction (Zane, Norton, Chu & Lin, 2008).

Acculturation will also look different in the coming decades as China begins to resemble the West more. As the Chinese and other Asian cultures start to praise personal pride, outspokenness, individuality, and competition, the cultural landscape will change. This means there will be places to advocate for bridging generational gaps, as older Asian Americans are likely to maintain the values of their youth. Encouraging both parties to see the value of their position may be the best path to restoration.

If Asian culture continues to resemble the West more in the coming decades, renewed cries for being color-blind and ignoring cultural difference will likely re-emerge. These will be especially damaging for Asians adopted into European American households. No matter how similar the cultures become, they will always remain different. Even from the standpoint of appearance, Asian Americans will remain a separate cultural group. Counselors, social workers, and psychologists need to advocate for Asian Americans to find their own identities. Even when they attempt to integrate into the dominant culture, a bicultural element will remain. This should be nurtured and developed.

As individualism gains a foothold in Asian cultures, it is likely to increase academic demands even more. This may put many children in awkward situations. They will feel pressure to honor their parents, succeed on their own, and to work hard. However, they may not have an environment where they can voice their concerns. If the child becomes overwhelmed, he or she may turn to drugs or alcohol. He or she may also struggle socially, demanding so much from herself to the exclusion of all else. Paradoxically, eliminating social outlets may actually limit the student's chances of getting into the desired college in addition to creating a sense of isolation and academic burnout (Singh, 2009).

Finally, the diversity among Asian Americans is so vast, it is important to recognize these differences and nurture them. On the television show *King of the Hill* (Berger & Aibel, 1997), European American Hank Hill (and friends) are meeting their new neighbors (the Souphanousinphones) for the first time. Their conversation goes like this:

Hank Hill:	So, are you Chinese or Japanese?
Minh Souphanousinphone:	No, we are Laotian.
Bill Dauterive:	The ocean? What ocean?
Kahn Souphanousinphone:	From Laos, stupid! It's a landlocked country in South East Asia between Vietnam and Thailand—population approximately 4.7 million! *(a pause of several seconds)*
Hank Hill:	So, are you Chinese or Japanese?

This remains an important area of advocacy for Asian Americans, and it will require substantial research from Western therapists to grasp the subtle nuances.

Suzume's Story (A Client's Viewpoint)
(22-year-old female student recently emigrated from China)

I have been tired lately. I have difficulty getting up in the morning and getting out of my apartment to go to work. It has been more difficult lately. I am not sure there is anything you can do to help me. If my family found out that I came to meet with you, they would be upset.

When I arrive at work, I feel more energy if I keep busy or am in meetings. At lunchtime, I begin to feel tired again. Sometimes, [it's] difficult to get my afternoon started again. Talking to you about this is making me self-conscious.

Tomorrow, I go to my parents' home for my sister's birthday. Each day, as it gets closer, I become more and more tired and seem to be losing my appetite. My parents are pleased with my sister. She has married a Chinese man, and one year later, they had a baby boy. He is so handsome and the center of our attention whenever we get together.

My father is disappointed in me. I am not dating a Chinese man. My mother and aunties talk to me about how important it is for me to get married. Time is running out. I am getting old.

I remember when my parents were happy with me. I received good grades at school. I enjoyed spending time with them and my relatives. We would play mahjong. I promised to always speak Chinese when I was with them. After high school, I was accepted into a good university.

Yes, it was expected of me, but I also enjoyed it. And speaking Chinese in the home is a sign of respect. My family is more than my father, mother, and sister. There are also my grandparents, aunties, uncles, and cousins. There are a few others too from our community. You might say my extended family is very large. They don't need to be related by blood to me.

My father was happy. He had dreams for me to become a doctor or lawyer. I wanted to study art and later psychology. My parents did not want to see my drawings. I was so proud of my drawings. My professor encouraged me to major in art.

My friends noticed I was not eating. They told me they were worried. They invited me to come to their houses for meals. I did not want to go.

My mother asked me to choose a major in pre-law or pre-med. I stopped spending very much time with my family. I spent more time with my friends. They liked my artwork. They encouraged me to stay away from my family.

this is where my American reaction would! reaction would! come in and need to be given a second thought vs. reacting.

(continues)

Suzume's Story (A Client's Viewpoint) (continued)

My family is very important to me. I have disappointed them. I was born a girl. They were ashamed when we visited friends. My brother was born when I was three. He was very small. He lived until he was two years old. My sister was born next, and she was prettier than me. She married Chinese. I am not married.

It was everybody's business that I am not a doctor or lawyer. I am not a boy. I love my family. I am looking forward to seeing them tomorrow. I need to buy a gift for my sister and her son.

Mary's Story (A Counselor's Viewpoint)

(female mental health counselor, age 45, with 10 years of experience)

I greet Suzume and ask her to tell me about how she is. As I listened to her, I try to recall what I know about the family structure of Chinese families and communities. She stated that she was tired and had trouble getting up in the morning. I wonder if she is depressed. When she speaks about her family, her face and body expression show she was happy, although her words and voice indicate she was tired or sad. I am tempted to stop her and address the disparity between her words and her body language. I let her continue to tell her story.

When she stated "Talking to you about this is making me self-conscious," I decide to wait a while longer before I interject. I smiled and said "Go on." I recall that many Asians report somatic symptoms in lieu of talking about feelings. There is also a familial stigma for personal problems. As Suzume began to talk about her sister I decide to speak.

"Your sister married a Chinese man," I restate. I recall that for a Chinese woman to marry Chinese is preferable, especially if he is from a family with equal or greater status.

"Yes," she replied. "My father is disappointed in me. I am not dating a Chinese man. My mother and aunties talk to me about how important it is for me to get married. They say time is running out. I am getting old."

Suzume continued talking about her sister and her husband. They have a son, and he is the center of the family's attention. Now I recall the importance that Asian families have for sons. A son is a source of pride for the father [and] the grandfather. A son is the role model for younger siblings. A son inherits the family leadership when the father dies. A son is expected to provide financial and emotional support for his mother. I wait to hear whether Suzume has a brother.

When she said, "We would play mahjong, and I promised to always speak Chinese when I was with them," I decide to hear from her the

(continues)

Mary's Story (A Counselor's Viewpoint) (continued)

significance of this comment. I restate, "You enjoyed playing mahjong with them."

"Yes, it was expected of me, but I also enjoyed it. Speaking Chinese in the home is a sign of respect. My family is more than my father, mother, and sister. I have grandparents, aunties, uncles, and cousins. There are a few others too from our community. My extended family is large. They don't need to be related by blood."

Oh, yes, I recall. Asian cultures are collectivist cultures—different from individualistic cultures that I am accustomed to. I want to be respectful and not appear to be using her as my way to recall information from my multicultural courses. Her brief statements may also be part of her cultural context.

There appears to be a conflict she was dealing with—a tension between her friends and her parents. I decide to address it. "When you talk about your friends encouraging your artistic talents, I heard a sadness in your voice." I hope this will bring the conversation back to her family.

She replied, "My family is very important to me. I know I have disappointed them."

"You disappointed them?" I query. Suzume continued talking about her family and her siblings—the birth order—and things began to come into focus for the direction I will take for an intervention.

"In summary, you love your family, but at times, when you talk about them, you feel sad. You try to live up to their expectations and value the culture of your family. I wonder if you are feeling pressure from your family and that pressure makes you feel sad."

Suzume nods in agreement, gives a shy smile, and her body relaxes as I speak. I continue, "I would like to know if you are willing to keep a log of how you are feeling each day for the week until we meet again."

Suzume again nods in agreement and quietly replies, "Yes."

"Here is a form for you to take home to keep track of how you are feeling. It has three spaces for each day: morning, afternoon, and nighttime. Circle the face for how you are feeling: happy, sad, or neither happy nor sad. In the area below the faces, write a note about any interactions with your family during the day—whether anyone from your family called or you spend time with them. Just write a brief note. Will you do that?"

Suzume has been listening carefully and takes the blank log from me. "Just circle a face and make notes for each day until we meet again next week? Yes, I will do that."

Reflection

With Asian clients, they often display such somatic symptoms as headaches, indigestion and insomnia when they are sad, depressed, or worried. Suzume reported that she had been tired lately, has difficulty getting out of

(continues)

Mary's Story (A Counselor's Viewpoint) (continued)

bed, and experienced loss of appetite. The symptoms may be getting worse as a family celebration for his sister's birthday draws near.

I also noticed that, typical of Asian clients, Suzume provided short, polite statements. She spoke briefly but provided important information about her family and relationships with her friends. The personal information she shared was factual, and she did not go into detail.

Boys are very important in Asian families. It is expected that the first-born will be a boy. Status is also very important, which comes from getting good grades to get into the best universities to become a doctor, lawyer, or engineer. This enhances the status of the family.

Although Suzume and her family are living in the United States, they are guided by their cultural mores and expectations. Suzume reports somatic symptoms of tiredness and loss of appetite that appear to increase when what she does what she wants to do—choosing an alternate career and not dating a Chinese man. I decided to have her keep a log of how she is feeling as well as any family interactions during the week until our next appointment to see if there may be any cause/effect for how she is feeling and contact or anticipated contact with her family.

QUESTIONS TO CONSIDER

1. Asian concepts of identity give priority to the needs of the group. Individuals' actions are seen as bringing shame or honor to their families, and these actions have lasting repercussions. With this orientation in mind, should individual therapy focus on the individual's feelings and personal growth or on behavioral changes targeted to increase the honor the client brings to the family?

2. If an individual seeks therapy and therefore implies that the family is not capable of solving conflicts on their own, should family therapy be attempted to mitigate the shame?

3. How would you attempt to measure acculturation during the course of an intake, and how would you use this information in developing a treatment plan?

4. Asian children who are adopted transracially do not appear to face increased psychological difficulties growing up, but there are unique issues that must be addressed. What advice or information would you provide to a European American family who adopted an Asian child?

5. Asian religious principles often diverge from those of Christianity. Should therapists with Christian or secular backgrounds attempt to help a Hindu and Buddhist with spiritual concerns? Would your answer differ if the individual believed his depression stemmed from spiritual pain?

6. How would you intervene with an Asian middle school student who was distraught over earning Bs in school? Would it make a difference if

the child's grades were significantly above her intelligence score (i.e., she was absorbing more information than most people with similar intelligence scores)?

7. Asian Americans are sometimes referred to as "adopted whites." What do you think of this terminology, and what implications does this attitude hold for therapeutic interventions with Asian Americans?

8. Asians are more likely to complain of physical symptoms than European Americans. Does this make them more likely to benefit from medical interventions or is such externalization a problem that should be addressed in psychotherapy?

9. When Asians attend therapy sessions, they are likely to be reluctant to voice their deepest concerns. They are likely to view themselves as being victims of a tragic environmental situation or unable to cope with some physical discomfort. Should deeper concerns be addressed or should the therapist stay within the client's comfort zone?

10. Does it seem wise or practical to use physical exercises like yoga in a counseling intervention? Why or why not?

INTERVENTION EXERCISES

Counseling and Therapy: Hea Jung is a 82-year-old Korean American female who is moving to live near her son (age 56). She had expected her son and his wife to care for her, but they have been pressuring her to live in a nursing home nearby. "I have been betrayed," she said. "My family has shamed me." How would you intervene?

School Psychology: Ken'ichi (Japanese American female, age 10) is hoping to enter the gifted education program at your school. Her placement scores put her in the high-average range (approximate IQ of 114), but her achievement scores are superior (96th percentile). When asked why she wants to enter the gifted program, she replies, "It is what my parents want; they say it is the only way to get ahead and get into a good college." What would you recommend? How would you share this with the parents?

School Counseling: Maha (13-year-old Thai male) came to the United States four months ago. His teacher says he always "looks" attentive but worries that he does not understand the content of the instruction. When he speaks to adults or children, he speaks in short, formal, carefully chosen sentences, such as, "I am happy here." What would you do to encourage him? What services would you recommend?

Social Work: Chan-juan (17-year-old Chinese female). She moved here two weeks ago, coming from China. Her parents "needed to leave the country," as they were involved in "bad things." She reported a number of significant mental health concerns, including loss of appetite, nausea, confusion, runny nose, glazed eyes, forgetfulness, increased sensitivity to sounds, mood swings, neglect of personal hygiene, and insomnia. She stated that her problems could all be fixed by getting "a lot of money." How would you help?

CHAPTER 7

Native Americans

INSIGHT EXERCISE

My name is Atmaja, and I always tended to think of people as people. White, Native, Asian, whatever—we're all part of the Warm Winds of Heaven (as my Cherokee grandfather used to say). But I realized that there are limits to what people can accept. I grew up on a Cherokee reservation in North Carolina. It was beautiful around Great Smoky Mountains National Park. We had Europeans come to our land often—taking their pictures [and] chatting with us about Native life. My family often said they believed Europeans were good people but they had lost their way and turned from Native. I thought that meant that their attitudes were the biggest issue.

So, when Michael asked me to marry him, I thought my family and tribe would understand. He is a wonderful man who sincerely loves me and wants to spend his life with me. He did want me to move to the city, but we agreed to spend two weekends a month on the reservation. That did not help matters. My grandfather called me a-ga-la-yv-wi (foolish one). My mother said I had wounded the Great Spirit. They can't see that Michael is different from other white people.

When I argued for my fiancé, my grandmother asked me to "test" Michael. She challenged my assumption that he was "different" from other white people because she did not think he would understand our ways. She wanted me to ask him about the Trail of Tears and Samuel's Memory. The Dawes Act of 1887. The Curtis Act of 1898. I assumed he would know

(continues)

INSIGHT EXERCISE *(continued)*

about all of these things. They are part of his culture too. But he didn't. He did not know about any of it.

At the time, I taught him a few things and told him what to say when he stayed with the tribe. I still don't think ignorance is a reason to condemn someone. He has a good heart. Am I betraying my people by marrying the man I love?

Questions to Consider

1. Is Atmaja betraying her culture and history by marrying Michael? What would have to happen for you to answer "yes" or "no"?

2. Atmaja claimed that Michael's ignorance mattered less than his heart. Do you think her family would accept this argument? Would you?

3. The reservation was not well-depicted in this exercise. What images did you consider when you read this? What do those images say about the way you conceptualize Native Americans?

The term *Native American* is often used to describe an ethnically distinct group of American citizens indigenous to North America. This diverse group includes American Indians, Alaska Natives, Native Hawaiians, and the Eskimo-Aleut. Although these latter terms can be used in an ethnologically descriptive sense, they also have legal and political meanings. An *American Indian* has been defined as a person with some amount of Indian blood who is recognized as such by his or her tribe or community (U.S. Environmental Protection Agency, 1999). Many tribes take this blood history very seriously and may view only pure-blood Indians as authentic.

UNIQUE CHALLENGES

With many ethnic groups, challenges come from learning to adapt to a dominant society. They must navigate through the waters they enter into. Native American culture is different. This group has already been crushed by the dominant culture. The consequence was a loss of identity, and it has taken centuries to find it again.

Their primary challenge is to restore what was taken and recreate something from forgotten history. Languages must be researched. Customs restored. Land regained. Add to this daunting task a lack of governmental support, limited funds, and confusion on the part of the dominant society— and the process becomes even more daunting.

But Native Americans are a resilient people. They have overcome unthinkable hardships and have even recaptured some of their past numbers. What happens next will depend on their ability to gain political and economic strength. The task before them is daunting. It is so large that many Native

Americans are overcome with despair. Such disillusionment has caused some to abandon the fight. Limited education, unemployment, and suicide wash over the culture like a heavy rain. One Native American described this situation succinctly. He said, "If you force people to live in poverty and feel there is no future, it leads to suicide and these other problems" (Johnson, 2010). To get beyond this, we must understand where the problems started.

HISTORICAL CONTEXT

Native Americans have been the most oppressed group in North America. The facts are so staggering that they are painful to convey. As late as the 1980s, approximately 25% of surviving Native American women and 10% of Native American men had been sterilized without their consent. During the 1990s, their infant mortality rate soared beyond the national average because of inadequate medical care. The life expectancy for Native Americans hovered around 55 years of age, approximately 20 years lower than the national average (Allen, 1998). Some claim the death toll exceeded the destruction of the Holocaust (Johnson, 2010).

Before the Europeans came to North America, Native Americans may have numbered between 20 and 40 million people. By the turn of the 20th century, the population had been reduced to less than half a million. As they experienced a 98% reduction in their population base from 1,500 to 1,900, Native North Americans experienced a concomitant 97.5% reduction in their land base (Churchill & LaDuke, 1992). Many tribes faced extinction. The majority of these deaths were due to disease. Typhus, measles, bubonic plague, influenza, cholera, malaria, tuberculosis, and smallpox were commonly transported by soldiers. Nearly 80% of the Native American population died of these diseases—mostly from smallpox (Lange, 2003). Sadly, Native American treatments may have contributed to the mortality rates (Cook, 1998). For example, sweat baths and cold-water immersion were practiced in some areas, which weaken the immune system. This may have doubled the death rate.

But disease was not the only struggle Native Americans faced. Soon after Columbus set foot in the Bahamas, indigenous peoples found their very way of life threatened. As Dee Brown (1979) pointed out in *Bury My Heart at Wounded Knee* (pp. 1–2):

> "So tractable, so peaceable, are these people," Columbus wrote to the King and Queen of Spain [referring to the Tainos on the island of San Salvador, which was so named by Columbus], "that I swear to your Majesties there is not in the world a better nation. They love their neighbors as themselves, and their discourse is ever sweet and gentle, and accompanied with a smile; and though it is true that they are naked, yet their manners are decorous and praiseworthy."
>
> All this, of course, was taken as a sign of weakness—if not heathenism—and being a righteous European, Columbus was convinced the people should be "made to work, sow and do all that is necessary and to adopt our ways."
> Over the next four centuries (1492–1890), several million Europeans and their descendants undertook to enforce their ways on the people of the New World.

The process of mass murder had not been eliminated by the 20th century because Native Americans were viewed as a threat to land accumulation. In the 1930s, more than 125,000 Native Americans from different tribes were forced to leave their homes and move to Oklahoma. Thousands of Native Americans were evicted from their land, which was considered sacred and part of their communal identity—sometimes forced to leave through violence and tortuous means.

Of all the conflicts between the American government and Native American people, perhaps the most pivotal was the battle at Wounded Knee. The story is important because it demonstrates the limited abilities of the two groups to understand each other. To the American government, the battle at Wounded Knee was an important show of strength and an event that would help to end Indian uprisings. To the Native Americans, it meant the loss of their identity, culture, and hope for the future. They were reduced from a proud, independent people to a subordinate group forced to follow the rules of a harsh and dishonest government.

The problems began in 1889 when a young mystic, Wovoka, had a vision that the whites would be destroyed and the land would be reborn with all the lost souls (including the buffalo) restored. He and his followers started a new dance and a new faith to usher in the new era. The precepts of this new faith called for no fighting, no war, nothing that resembled war, no stealing, no lying, and no cruelty. Wovoka learned the dance during his vision in the Spirit World. Each of the worshippers—painted with sacred red pigment—shuffled counterclockwise in a circle, moving slowly at first but increasing the tempo while singing songs of resurrection.

European Americans eventually called the religion the Ghost Dance Religion because of the emphasis on resurrection and reunion with the dead. When the religion spread to the Sioux, they began dancing in loose shirts, adorned with feathers or other trimmings. The shirts were believed to be sacred and impervious armor against an attacker's bullets. Agent James McLaughlin mistakenly reported that Sioux leader Sitting Bull [Tatanka-Iyotanka (1831–1890)] planned to use the Ghost Dance Religion to re-establish himself in the leadership of the people. This false message led to the deployment of U.S. Army soldiers with orders to eliminate any observed outbreak.

On December 14, 1890, McLaughlin had Sitting Bull arrested. During the apprehension, Sitting Bull protested, and one of his followers fired a rifle at one of the arresting officers—a fellow Sioux named Lt. Bull Head. As the police chief fell, he managed to put a bullet into Sitting Bull. General gunfire erupted, taking the lives of Sitting Bull, six policemen, and eight of Sitting Bull's followers. The killing of the chief exacerbated the turmoil that was already sweeping the reservation lands. Bands of Sioux fled—all frightened and many of them still holding on to the hope of deliverance through the Ghost Dance miracle. Some of Sitting Bull's followers hurried toward the camp of Big Foot, a Miniconjou Sioux chief. They met up with Big Foot while he and his people were on their way to agency headquarters near Fort Bennett to procure rations. When the army found Big Foot, they ordered Big Foot's followers—numbering more than 300—to accompany him to Camp

Cheyenne, where they would be kept under watchful eye. The Indians followed but later fled to the Badlands, fearing more troops were coming to force them away from their homes.

The troops pursued and took up surrounding positions around the area known as Wounded Knee Creek. In the morning, the American soldiers prepared to disarm their captives. Four rapid-fire Hotchkiss guns were set into place on a low hill overlooking the camp from the north—to be used in the event of an outburst. When the soldiers approached the camp, they pawed through the tribe's personal belongings and began confiscating guns. Tensions increased until a young Indian pulled a gun out from under his robe and began firing wildly. Instantly, the soldiers retaliated with a point-blank volley, which cut down nearly half the warriors. The other warriors drew concealed weapons and charged the soldiers.

What happened next is unclear. The Army reported that the Indians fired at them and shot many of their own women and children in the process. The Indians believed that the Hotchkiss guns on the hill fired down on the camp, ripping the civilians apart with explosive shells. When the battle ended, at least 180 Indians had been killed. Their bodies were left unattended for three days. When the burial party reached the scene, four babies were discovered still alive—wrapped in their dead mothers' shawls. Most of the other children had been killed.

By the 1980s, the Native American population had recovered slightly and numbered just over a million throughout the Northern Hemisphere. By the mid-1990s, the number had grown beyond 2 million, although this number still represents only 1% of the American population (Allen, 1998). These considerations should be kept in mind when examining the cultures, history, and psychology of Native Americans. Their experiences have been described as the American Holocaust.

If reading this makes you wonder what this has to do with the present, it may have a considerable and direct effect. Evans-Campbell (2008) purports that historically traumatic events are transmitted intergenerationally. As descendents identify with ancestral suffering, they internalize the emotional turmoil. She argues for three levels to historical trauma: individual, familial, and community. The individual level may result in PTSD, guilt, anxiety, grief, and depression. Familial issues may involve communication problems and parental stress. Community facets include the loss of traditional culture and values, changing rites of passage, alcoholism, physical illness (such as obesity), and internalized racism.

Try to imagine the following statement coming from a young adult living on a reservation today:

> The white people—who are trying to make us over into their image—they want us to be what they call "assimilated," bringing the Indians into the mainstream and destroying our own way of life and our own cultural patterns. They believe we should be contented like those whose concept of happiness is materialistic and greedy, which is very different from our way. We want freedom from the white man rather than to be integrated. We don't want any part of the establishment; we want to be free to raise our children in our religion, in our ways, to be able to hunt and fish and live in peace. We don't want power. We don't want to be

congressmen or bankers. We want to be ourselves. We want to have our heritage because we are the owners of this land and because we belong here. The white man says, "There is freedom and justice for all." We have had "freedom and justice," and that is why we have been almost exterminated. We shall not forget this.

Given the contemporary tenure of the above paragraph, it may surprise you to know this was said at the Grand Council of American Indians in 1927. Centuries of genocide and abuse have left a mark on Native American culture, and these actions continue to affect Native life.

IMMIGRATION AND DEVELOPMENT

Immigration for Native American might sound like an oxymoron. After all, how can people who lived in a country before the immigrants be immigrants themselves? The issue may be more complex than this. In a way, the sovereign nation of the American tribal people "immigrated" into European American culture. This was more than simply acculturation. In many ways, Native cultures left their homes and began somewhere new. This "immigration" continues to affect the Native people today.

Whitbeck, Adams, Hoyt, and Chen (2004) performed a fascinating study on how historical and current actions against Native people affect them psychologically. Even though the people surveyed had no direct experience with the abuses committed against their forefathers—some several generations removed—the cultural memory of the events affected them emotionally. Nearly 20% (18.2%) of those surveyed thought about the loss of their tribal land daily. Even more (36.3%) bemoaned losing their native language. About the same number (33.7%) thought about their culture daily. Even the leaders surveyed reported discomfort and fear around European Americans. They were sad, angry, anxious, ashamed, and thought more abuses could come. There were even PTSD symptoms present, with some elders saying they would avoid places that reminded them of the losses their people had suffered. And nearly half of all the people surveyed (45.9%) had daily thoughts about how alcoholism affected their community.

In many ways, the culture lost is similar to the process of people emigrating from other countries. They are removed from their language, traditions, extended families, and cultural practices. In some ways, the loss for Native Americans may even surpass those of other groups because they were systematically forbidden to speak their languages, wear their clothes, or engage in rites of passage. We will get to this in the education section.

[handwritten note: there is no homeland to go back to]

WITHIN GROUP DIFFERENCES

Native American people are aware of the differences between their tribes and all people. An ancient Sioux proverb says, "All birds, even those of the same species, are not alike, and it is the same with animals and with human beings."

The diversity among various tribes is vast, with populations ranging from large groups, such as the Navajos of Arizona and New Mexico—who number more than 160,000—to communities of less than 100, such as the Chumash of California and the Modocs of Oklahoma (Brookeman, 1990). Typically, the tribal groups are clustered together geographically, creating five major groups: the tribes of the eastern woodlands, the tribes of the plains, the tribes of the southwest, the tribes of the northwest, and the peoples of the far north (which includes all of Canada and Alaska).

Tribes vary in such aspects as appearance, clothing, customs, ceremonies, family roles, child-rearing practices, beliefs, and attitudes (Thurman, Swaim & Plested, 1995). There are currently 500 federally recognized tribes, each with practices so diverse that it would be impossible to address them all adequately here. However, there are key differences that can help students understand some of the subtle distinctions between groups. For example, within the peoples of the far north, language differences tend to create problems for outsiders. As used by Northern Indians, the word *Eskimo* means "eaters of raw meat" (Axelson, 1999). Instead of this term, Northern Indians call themselves Inuit, while Siberian Eskimos call themselves Yuit. There are also Aleuts, who live in Alaska but have a distinctly different culture and language system. The Aleuts also have a distinct history of abuse, as they were exploited by Russian traders during World War II and sent to prison by the Japanese, who invaded portions of the Aleutian Islands. Table 7.1 provides a list of the some of the different Native American groups, but it should be clear that a comprehensive list would be quite massive, with overlaps between the various categories. More generally, Josephy (1973) identified four factors that determined a tribe's home, clothing, food, and customs:

- **Climate:** If the climate were cold, the home needed to be sturdy and clothing needed to be heavy, such as animal fur or hide. Warm climates led to well-ventilated houses and lightweight clothing.
- **Availability of materials:** In the southwest, where trees were not available, the Indians became skilled in using mud, brush, and sod in the construction of their homes. Also, the Indians of the Great Basin lived in a very dry area that did not permit farming, so they gathered wild plants and hunted for their food.
- **Length of time a group would stay in an area:** The Indians of the northeast were farmers, and there was plenty of game for hunting. Consequently, their homes were sturdy longhouses made of wood, and 100 or more houses were often built together and surrounded by a stockade. Nomadic tribes of the plains lived in homes made of poles and animal hides because they were easy to put up, take down, and carry.
- **Customs:** Some Plains Indians wore feathers to indicate position, bravery, and respect. In some tribes, acquiring wealth was important. Shells were strung on a cord and worn around the neck or waist by members of tribes of the northeast. Such adornment—called wampum—was used as money or as a symbol of a promise made to another person. The Zuni and Hopi of the Southwest built a kiva in their pueblos for religious ceremonies. Homes of the Great Basin were small because only a single family lived in each one, whereas a pueblo was large enough to house many families.

TABLE **7.1**

Tribes of the Americas

Area	Groups/Tribes	Belief Systems
Peoples of the Far North	The groups include the Alaskan Eskimos, the Aleuts (who live mostly in Alaska and the Aleutian Islands), and the Yuit (Siberian Eskimos).	All animals and objects in nature have spirits and should be revered for their life-giving qualities. Each object in nature has a specific purpose (e.g., bears can possess a spirit and help lead a person to food). These groups also have a history of training shamans (healers) who are believed to have the ability to predict the future.
Tribes of the Eastern Woodlands	The Iroquois Nation (a cluster of five tribes formed in the 1500s), Cherokee, Chickasaw, Choctaw, Creek, Natchez, Seminole, Fox, Illinois, Menominee, Miami, Potawatomi, Sauk, Shawnee, and Winnebago tribes.	These were the first groups to encounter the Europeans. Their area spans from the Northeastern coast of America to the Southeast. They operated from a highly organized and systematic theology. It included a struggle between light and dark, good and ill fortune. These spiritual forces guided the universe and led their followers to survival.
Tribes of the Plains	From the Mississippi River on the east to the Rocky Mountains on the west and from the U.S./Canadian border to Mexico, these groups flourished with the introduction of horses by the Spaniards. Groups include the Arapaho, Blackfoot, Cheyenne, Comanche, Crow, Pawnee, and various Sioux tribes.	Despite being characterized in movies as aggressive hunters, most of these tribes were agrarian. When they did hunt, they usually hunted the buffalo, which was provided by the Earth Mother as food for believers. Many of the tribes were nearly forced into extinction when European settlers brought smallpox and cholera to their areas. Most of these tribes were later relocated to Nebraska and Oklahoma. These groups are also the ones responsible for the famous Ghost Dance.
Tribes of the Pacific Northwest and the Great Basin Area	These tribes survived on the West Coast for more than a thousand years. War with the U.S. government, smallpox, starvation, and overdependence on the Spaniards destroyed most of these tribes.	Wealth and social status were measured by material possessions (such as blankets, canoes, tools, etc.). Today, the homeland of these tribes is governed by some of the wealthiest citizens in America.
Tribes of the Southwest	This is a semi-desert region that includes Arizona, Colorado, New Mexico, Utah, and northern Mexico. Tribes include the Apache, Cochimi, Navajo, Papago, Pima, Pueblo, Yaqui, and Yuma.	The prevalent beliefs and rituals of these groups include the Pueblo rain festivals, which reflect a strong association between human action and nature. The Navajos were also known for their shamans, or medicine men/women.

Note: Table 7.1 was adapted from J.A. Axelson (1999), *Counseling and Development in a Multicultural Society*. Pacific Grove, CA: Brooks/ Cole Publishing Company.

The stereotype of American Indians as warriors wearing feathers and riding horses can be applied to only a small group living in the Midwestern United States. Even among these groups, the horse became part of the culture only after it was introduced by Spanish immigrants.

The existing Native American groups are less diverse today than they were 100 years ago. When young Native Americans were forced into boarding schools and prohibited from speaking their native languages, many lost part of their communal identity. Today, only about 20 of the 175 existing Native American languages spoken in the United States are being passed down from mother to child, and about 300 to 400 languages have already been lost forever (Brooke, 1998). For some tribes, traditional knowledge can be fully communicated only in the tribal language because there is no easy way to translate it into English. The loss of language has a profound effect on the maintenance of Native American culture.

CULTURAL IDENTITY

In many ways, the cultural distinctiveness of many Native American groups has been eradicated due to prejudice and intolerance. From the southern plains to the Native Alaskans, there have been systematic, federally funded efforts to sterilize members of Native American groups, remove them from their homelands, and force assimilation (Thurman, Swaim & Plested, 1995). The hostility against Native Americans has appeared in countless ways, but the political arena is where their culture has been harmed the most. Although they were the original inhabitants of the land, Native Americans did not gain the right to vote as U.S. citizens until 1946 in Arizona and New Mexico, and they were viewed as savages requiring careful guidance from members of an "advanced" civilization.

Despite the animosity between European and Native groups, both sides continued to interact and learn from each other. Unfortunately, with one group having more power than the other, abuses were inevitable. Up until the 1960s, many church-affiliated boarding schools provided scholarships to Native Americans living on reservations. The Native students would interact with their European peers, which was viewed as a means of speeding acculturation. Some Native Americans tell stories of being terrorized by the white students and staff members. School administrators attempted to separate students from their cultural history by punishing them for speaking their own language, forcing them to receive extremely short haircuts, and denigrating their cultural traditions during classroom lessons (Thurman, Swaim & Plested, 1995). Such experiences had a profound impact on the transmission of Native American culture. Although these institutional practices have been abandoned, they caused many Native Americans to become alienated from their cultural roots.

Native Americans have made some attempts to restructure themselves. After the Indian Reorganization Act of 1934, the federally recognized tribes formed coalitions and elected tribal chairpersons. Each community elects a council and appoints a leader. This leader works in concert with the council but is not technically a chief, which refers to a hereditary position (Kniffen, Gregory & Stokes, 1987). The structure of the group is egalitarian in nature.

The council strives for consensus and cannot act until near-total agreement has been achieved. This emphasis on consensus makes it one of the most democratic forms of government in America but also one that appears chaotic and poorly managed to outsiders.

In many ways, Native Americans who attempted to understand white culture have felt that their own values have been overlooked, ignored, or denigrated. For example, take the Native American understanding of time. In his memoirs of the early 20th century, Sweezy (1967) wrote that the Cheyenne and the Arapaho viewed time differently from the Europeans. Rather than measure the minutes in a day, they would simply enjoy the day. They were more concerned with larger blocks of times, such as seasons, than with the intricate details of minutes and seconds. In some ways, these trends continue today. Many tribes have no word for time; there is no need to be punctual or "on time" because there is always plenty of time in an individual's life for necessary tasks. To be occupied with things and events too far into the future is to invite trouble and threats to those future plans. These value statements are reflected in the concept of "Indian time," which means that a meeting set for 8 a.m. may not start until 10 a.m. Native Americans are more likely to finish an important chore than to arbitrarily shift their attention to a new task simply because an hour has passed.

As in working with members of other cultural groups, discovering the level of acculturation is often essential in knowing when and how to intervene. When working with Native Americans, there are five primary domains therapists should assess:

- **Identity:** Do they believe they belong to an indigenous culture, a dominant U.S. culture, or some combination?
- **Action:** Do they spend the bulk of their free time in tribal or European American activities, groups, or clubs?
- **Spiritual:** Do they participate in Native or European American religious groups?
- **Values:** Do they spend time focused on issues important to European American or indigenous cultures (e.g., tribe-first mentality or competition-based success)?
- **Social-environmental:** Who are their friends, and how do their social groups interact with the environment?

The ways in which clients answer these questions will reflect the degree to which they understand and identify with their own culture as well as the extent to which they incorporate elements of the dominant culture.

The beginning stage for people living on reservations appears to be myopic. They see only the Native world. This world often changes through forced encounters. These are such well-intentioned interactions as schools, church groups, counseling, etc. As the Native American wrestles with differences between Native and Western ideals, identity conflicts arise. These may lead to commitment toward tribal life or they could lead to a more integrative approach, where the individual maintains a tribal identity while living off the reservation.

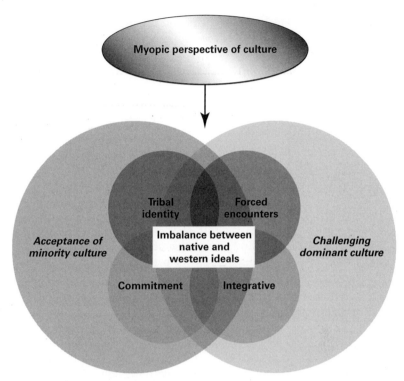

FIGURE **7.1** Cultural Identity Model: Native Americans (Reservations)

In gathering acculturation and identity information, it is helpful to have Native Americans tell stories about themselves and their beliefs. Many indigenous groups pass down culture through the stories told at tribal gatherings. Native American histories, cultural traditions, and laws have been built on storytelling. The stories explain how the people first came into being and how the sun, moon, stars, rainbows, sunsets, sky, thunder, lakes, mountains, and other natural occurrences came about. They explain the origin of landmarks, plants, and animals. Some stories tell about the hazards of greed, selfishness, or boastfulness.

The stories often give practical advice, such as techniques for hunting or fishing, and some include recipes for healing potions or describe how to find the right root or herb. They teach laws and the consequences for violating them. Some stories are so sacred and powerful that they are treated with special respect; for example, creation stories are often recited in a ritual way and told in a serious manner. They have been passed on for hundreds of years or more, and their continuation is threatened by encroachments of the dominant culture (Hirschfelder, 2000).

The Chipewyan tell a story of a primordial woman who lived alone in a cave. One night, a mysterious being in the shape of a dog crept into the cave and laid down beside her. Gradually, the creature began to change form.

His limbs grew straight, his skin became smooth, and he was soon transformed into a handsome youth. Nine months later, a child was born. The child was the first Chipewyan. The story is told to explain why the Chipewyan should treat dogs with special respect.

Most cultures also tell stories linked to daily living experiences and the dangers that stem from certain desires. The Ojibway of northern Minnesota have a story about two foolish girls who longed to sleep outside of the lodge under the stars. One night, they crept outside and began to imagine what it might be like to make love to a star. "They must be good lovers," one girl said to the other. They fell asleep, and when they awoke, they found themselves in the sky surrounded by stars—male stars. One of the stars spoke, saying, "You wanted us—well, here we are." After a while, the girls realized that star husbands were not as much fun as they had imagined. All the husbands did was eat star food, make love, and shine. The girls could peer down at Earth and watch their friends from the tribe playing games, so they asked their husbands to help them go home by letting them down on long ropes made from plants. The two girls swore never to sleep outside the lodge again.

FAMILY STRUCTURE AND DYNAMICS

Like Latino and Asian groups, Native Americans are likely to maintain an interconnected web of kin (MacPhee, Fritz & Miller-Heyl, 1996). However, unlike the extended family of other ethnic groups, Native Americans receive part of their identity and family belonging from their tribe and their world. A common Sioux proverb states, "With all things and in all things, we are relatives." Individuals who find unique ways to benefit the tribe are rewarded and given greater community support, which implies that all members are expected to place the needs of the tribe above the needs of the individual. Individuals who leave the tribe often face a threatened sense of identity (Anderson & Ellis, 1995).

The communal identity of Native Americans keeps people on the reservations. Urban case studies indicate that many Native Americans living in urban areas retain ties to their tribes and hope to move back when they retire. Also, 71% of the Native Americans who live outside reservation areas but still reside in the same county indicated that they would prefer to move back (U.S. Environmental Protection Agency, 1999). Of the 4.5 million (about 1.5% of the U.S. population), about one-third of Native Americans live on reservations (Native Americans, 2009). Remaining on the reservations is difficult. Their unemployment is staggering (upward to 85%), drug/alcohol abuse is high, and teen suicide rates are three times the national average (Johnson, 2010).

The close ties within the tribe help to create a sense of community and encourage interdependence. Even distant tribe members are considered relatives in times of crisis and ceremony—on both happy and sad occasions. One of the clearest examples of group intimacy can be seen in Native Americans' treatment of visitors. Traditionally, when a family saw visitors approaching, the family would automatically begin cooking a full meal for the visitors. The visitors were then expected to sit and eat, and refusing to do so would offend the host family. The tradition has changed somewhat in recent times, and the host family will prepare a meal only if the visitors have not eaten recently (Edmo, 1989).

Another example of tribal unity involves child-rearing practices. The tribe and extended family can act as a basic unit, with children often raised by uncles, aunts, grandparents, or distant cousins. At times, outsiders might misinterpret these collective child-rearing practices as a sign of family unrest. Consider the case of Chris, who decided to live with her maternal aunt because her father was having problems with alcohol. When her teacher, Ms. Anderson, found out that Chris had moved away from her parents, Ms. Anderson contacted social services. Ms. Anderson believed that Chris was in danger and needed protection. The teacher failed to understand that aunts in Native American families typically take maternal roles within the broader family setting. The child's cultural values were not taken into consideration.

Another striking difference between Native Americans and other ethnic groups is the presence of a matriarchal and matrilineal structure. Traditionally, Native American women held great political and economic power within their tribes (Rivers, 1995). Among the Senecas, women owned and cultivated the land, which they had inherited through their mothers. After marriage, the husband moved into the wife's household, where he lived with the wife's female relatives and their spouses and children. Men devoted most of their time to hunting and fighting battles. When the Europeans arrived in America, patriarchal structures were imposed on Native American families, and women found themselves stripped of their former power.

The appreciation of womanhood is apparent in the tradition of moontime—a practice still followed by many Native American nations. In ancient times, menstruating women would retreat to a moon lodge, where they rested, released their blood to the earth, and harnessed the powerful visionary energy that accompanied moontime. The dreams and visions experienced during these times were viewed as sacred and used as a source of inspiration and prophecy for the entire community. However, the experience was not simply one of solitary reflection. This was a time for storytelling and humor, for counseling and teaching the younger women, for expression through artwork and song, and for experiencing the bonds of sisterhood (Leland, 1992).

A woman's first moontime was celebrated within the tribe. Cameron (1996) tells the story of a village who honored a girl's first moontime through a very special ceremony. The community gathered together, bringing food and gifts for celebration. The grandmothers dressed the girl in the best ceremonial finery, and everyone gathered at the shore of the lake. The grandmothers rowed with the girl out to the middle of the lake. When the girl was stripped down to her skin, she dove into the water while the grandmothers rowed back to shore and waited with the rest of the tribe for her to swim back. When she reached the shore, everyone cheered, and the people said, "A girl went out in a boat; a woman swam back." The drumming, dancing, and feasting went on for days.

I have extolled the value of metaphors and narratives throughout this book, and many Native American stories can be helpful moral guides to people from other cultures. But it is sometimes difficult for non-Natives to put themselves into the culture addressed.

When my daughter started her first period, I told her about moontime and the cultural rite of passage associated with it. Her eyes went wide with interest, and I hoped she understood that some cultures regard menstruation as an honorable event.

When I finished the story, she sighed and said, "I am soooooo glad we are not part of that tribe."

So, sometimes the best counseling metaphors fall flat.

Given the generally negative stance the dominant culture has of menstruation and women's culture as a whole, many Native American groups lost their matriarchal rituals as they were acculturated into the dominant society. The evolution away from matriarchy and toward the European American patriarchal power structure may be responsible for an increased incidence of rape among certain Native American groups. Rape may now be the most frequently committed crime on Navajo reservations. Old Dog Cross (1982) reported that at least 80% of the women seeking mental health services (across a five-state area) had experienced some form of sexual assault. She also reported that many Native American women were falling prey to "training"—a form of gang rape. Groups of males would band together and "punish" a selected woman for her indiscretions.

Other problems are emerging in Native American families. Generally speaking, there is a high fertility rate and a large percentage of out-of-wedlock births in Native American populations. In one study of a Navajo reservation, over half of the woman stated they had been victims of relationship violence. They remarked that they had "nowhere to go" and felt trapped (Dalla, Jacobs-Hagen, Jareske & Sukup, 2009).

Despite all the differences between Native American and European American cultures, it should also be noted that counseling seems to work well with this population. Lambert et al. (2006) looked at therapy outcomes with African Americans, Asians/Pacific Islanders, Latinos/as, and Native Americans when they were counseled by European American counselors. They were surprised to find the 50 Native Americans in their study had the best outcomes. This may be partly due to the way Native Americans learn. They prefer an interactive and nondirective style, which is an essential part of most psychotherapy. However, this preference may also explain why Native Americans often struggle in European American schools.

EDUCATION

In the United States, Thanksgiving is traditionally a time to teach schoolchildren about "the Indians." In classrooms across the country, children are busily coloring pictures of Indians dressed in feathers and moccasins; singing "one little, two little, three little Indians"; or making "Indian jewelry" out of macaroni and string. Teachers direct pupils to "sit like Indians" or "be quiet as Indians." Pictures of a headdress-bedecked Indian chief on a pinto horse or of an Indian "squaw" with a "papoose" decorate the walls. It is not uncommon to even see ceilings covered with paper "tomahawks," hung precariously. The aesthetic value of genuine handicrafts is minimized, and students are left with a trivialized impression of Native American culture.

When educational institutions advance artificial views of Native American culture, history, and art, Native American children are likely to view their histories negatively. In part, this might explain some of the pitfalls of the Native American educational experience, but there are additional problems to address. Native American children begin their academic careers well, but they start to fall behind other ethnic groups when they approach the end of elementary/primary school (around the fourth grade). As students progress through school, they begin to believe that education has little to do with their lives (Wood & Clay, 1996). Their grades begin to fall, and they are more likely to drop out of school altogether. Of equal concern, incidents of violence or disruption increase around this time. During the 1970s, it was assumed that Native Americans failed because they simply lacked the mental prowess of their peers (Yazzie-Mintz, 2007), but the problem stems from dominant-cultured schools not having culturally relevant curriculum.

Lack of accommodation to different learning styles and a failure to incorporate Native American values into the educational system have combined to produce frighteningly high dropout rates. Native Americans have the highest high school dropout rate of all ethnic groups in America (Kasten, 1992; Rolph, 2008). Only half the students entering kindergarten will complete their high school education. If they attend college, only about 8% (half of the national average) will complete a four-year degree at an established institution of higher education (Lomawaima, 1995). Lack of educational attainment is not due to insufficient parental involvement. Goldenberg (1998) argued that Native American parents want their children to do well in school and even encourage them to go as far as possible. Such messages are especially important for Native Americans because an intergenerational cycle of poor educational experiences and poverty may contribute to high rates of suicide and teenage pregnancy (Keane, Dick, Bechtold & Manson, 1996).

To keep Native American children from dropping out of school, the educational format may need to be modified. Native American children appear to benefit from different styles of teaching and learning (Guild, 1994). They need to be introduced to the "foreign system" of European American schooling (Rolph, 2008). They generally value and develop acute visual discrimination, are skilled in the use of imagery, perceive facts globally, and rely on reflective thinking patterns.

To incorporate these findings, effective teaching strategies for Native Americans should include providing quiet time for reflection and adopting an instructional approach that helps children understand the meaning behind a given task. The latter would go beyond teaching children "why" a particular subject is important. Instead, children would be encouraged to explore the topic, derive personalized meaning from it, and learn how to apply the knowledge in a specific context. In tribal environments, children have typically learned by interacting freely with adults. Bonds are established that help determine which individual can best instruct the child, and the activities made available to the child are specifically designed to develop his or her talents (Okakok, 1989).

European American schools do not incorporate these meaning-oriented learning styles. Even at the college level, learning is based on acquiring knowledge rather than deriving meaning from that knowledge. This approach may be one of the reasons the majority of Native Americans avoid higher education (Boutte, 1999). When they do receive advanced training, it is often confined to the field of education (Lomawaima, 1995). There is a dire lack of Native American scientists.

Ngai (2006) determined that there are a series of culturally relevant subjects shared by European American and indigenous students. These include history (e.g., tribal history, struggles between European and Native Americans); stories and legends (e.g., creation stories, warrior stories); ceremonies and traditions (e.g., songs and dances, wakes, traditional food, and celebrations); worldviews and values (e.g., love, respect, discipline, environmental respect, proper relationships with everything around you); multicultural education (e.g., alternative strategies for solving problems, consensus building); customs (e.g., proper animal cleaning, praying before using the meat and digging up plants, drying meat, tanning hides); and nature and wilderness studies (e.g., stars, plants, endangered wildlife, weather, etc.).

By incorporating Native culture into the mainstream educational structure, the process becomes more holistic. Science blends with stories and traditions. Math blends with ethics and nature. Language blends with customs and morality. Such an approach would make the educational process experiential and engaging, as opposed to static and passive.

SOCIOECONOMICS

It is easy to focus on ways to improve education, and the techniques should prove helpful. But without changing the economic situations, some educational developments will never come to fruition. For example, in our technology age, we offer effective distance-education programs all over the world. All it takes is an Internet connection. But 60% of Navajo households lack phone service, compared to 4% nationally (Madden, 2005). No phone connection or cable means no Internet.

The reason for the limited phone services stems from the isolation and limited industry associated with the reservations. About 47% of the Native American population resides in areas that are remote, sparsely populated, and poor, with little access to employment and other economic opportunities. In some ways, this makes encroachment of larger non–Native American populations beneficial because the growing population could bring new jobs. Unemployment rates range between 60% and 90% (Allen, 1998; Native Americans, 2009), and when people are able to find employment, there is a high concentration in semiskilled and service positions, with Native Americans doubling the national average for farming or related occupations (Aponte & Crouch, 1995). The high concentration of group members in low-level occupations has a direct bearing on their quality of life and opportunities for increasing family income. Overall, Native Americans (including Eskimos and Aleutian Islanders) have the highest rate of poverty of any ethnic group (Native Americans, 2009). The 1989 rate for Native Americans living below the poverty level was 34%—almost twice the rate for non-Indians. Poverty rates were highest in tribal areas (36%) and somewhat lower in metropolitan areas, non-metropolitan areas, and surrounding counties (U.S. Environmental Protection Agency, 1999).

Despite the poverty, the reservations and the community have functioned well. Maquinna, Chief of Nootka (2003), sums this up well: "Once I was in Victoria, and I saw a very large house. They told me it was a bank and that the white men place their money there to be taken care of, and that by and by they got it back with interest. We are Indians and we have no such bank, but when we have plenty of money or blankets, we give them away to other chiefs and people, and by and by they return them with interest, and our hearts feel good. Our way of giving is our bank" (p. 70).

However, this cooperative way of living is changing as new wealth enters the reservations. The income generated from casinos is still unknown, but the interest from major financial backers has been strong. The new wealth has left many law-makers unsure how to address the windfall. In August 2000, the tribes of California sent $34.5 million to the state government. The state attorney general, Bill Lockyer—the official most responsible for regulating gambling in the state—said he expected considerably less money than was submitted. He planned to begin an investigation into just how much the tribes were making (Morain, 2000).

This was just the beginning. In 2006, the Seminoles—who started Indian gaming in 1979—stunned the world. They paid nearly a billion dollars for Hard Rock International, which included their worldwide (45 countries) collection of restaurants, performance venues, hotels, and casinos (Cattelino, 2008). Paradoxically, some bemoan the effects gambling has brought to the tribes (e.g., Johnson, 2010). The Seminole wealth has created a new internal market for high-end crafts. The money has also created museums, funded language instruction, and led to funded positions for cultural educators (Cattelino, 2008).

The wealth has also created political clout. In California, where Native American casinos have been rapidly expanding, the wealth that has been created has turned Native Americans into a powerful political force. During the 2000 Democratic National Convention, tribes fielded a record number of delegates, hosting parties at glamorous locations (Tamaki, 2000). They have also contributed to local elections, with California tribes spending more than $100 million on state campaigns during their first two years of casino operations. Bill Lockyer (Morain, 2000) estimates that a casino with 2,000 slot machines could reap $219 million a year from those machines alone. These funds would be in addition to the money made from other forms of gambling as well as revenues from hotels and restaurants.

The increased wealth of certain tribes has also led to ethical and spiritual introspection. Kathryn Gabriel (1998) writes that gambling has roots in most of the world's religions. She argues that in many archaeological records, dice is associated with the cycle of death and rebirth. In fact, it is even unclear whether game-playing predates gambling as a recognized pastime. In the Bible, stories are told of decisions made by casting lots (e.g., Isaiah 34:17), and in Native American history, gambling had been present a thousand years before European contact. This is not to suggest, she cautions, that all Native Americans have historically viewed gambling as positive. The Navajos consider gambling taboo. However, a thorough examination of Native American beliefs reveals that more than 100 surviving myths address gambling as means of bringing harmony to the cosmos; just as in ancient Hindu Mahabharata, gambling is a metaphor for balance in the continuum of death and rebirth. Gabriel concludes that while gambling creates vices, it should not be viewed as an evil in itself but as a form of spiritual seeking. Addictive gambling is only superficially the act of seeking economic fortune. It is also the process of seeking a personal transformation—a feeling of invincibility and liberation, even if only for a moment.

The confliction is likely something some Native Americans will bring to counseling. Are casinos a blessing or a curse? To complicate matters, what does the process say about the sovereignty of the tribes themselves? LaDuke (1999) discusses outside intervention of casinos as "dispossession of Native American lands." She believes powerful people come in to take from Native resources, making themselves rich but not returning the wealth to the people, as they should. This leads to "structural poverty," which means there may be wealth generated but the Native people may not have any control over it. Such a process may rekindle past abuses and create anxiety.

SPIRITUALITY AND RELIGION

The structure of the reorganized tribes incorporates the communal functioning that permeates many Native American cultures. Interdependence is valued more highly than autonomy, and Native Americans are often unfamiliar with the idea of being expected to work autonomously. These communal elements have also been carried over into Native American religious practices, as is discussed shortly. Two of the dominant religious movements among Native Americans are the Native American Church (a pan-Indian religion based on rituals that connect members with the Great Spirit) and Christian Pentecostalism (Koss-Chioino, 1995). Interestingly, the Native American Church was imported from Mexico in the last decades of the 19th century, but it also incorporates many cultural elements from various Native American tribes (Aberle, 1966). The religion involves peyote, pipe, and cigarette smoking to clear the mind. There are also drums, songs, and prayers, which are used to help purify individuals and reconnect them with nature (Bergman, 1973). Many tribes perform ceremonies according to instructions given in sacred stories.

Some of the most important ceremonies are conducted at certain places and at specific times of the year, such as solstices and equinoxes. There are ceremonies to heal the sick, renew relationships with spiritual beings, initiate people into religious societies, ensure success in hunting and growing crops, pray for rain, mark important life-cycle events in a person's life, and to give thanks for harvests. Some ceremonies are performed in order to ensure the survival of Earth and all life-forms. During these rituals, healing techniques are performed to address tribe members' physical, psychological, and spiritual needs, including ailments such as alcohol addiction. One traditional technique involves bringing the needy individual into the center of a ring. The other members sing and pray, attempting to draw out the evil spirits that reside in the needy soul. Other rituals involve conversion experiences or vision quests that occur as the result of taking peyote. In these cases, the individual may experience a revelation and then a physical purging that will remove the individual's sins. Such an experience often creates clear moral injunctions regarding marital fidelity, restraint from vengeance, and abstinence from alcohol (Koss-Chioino, 1995). In all these activities, the religious transcendence rarely occurs while the individual is alone. It is a group process—often involving family members and significant friends.

The interconnectedness between Native Americans also extends to a perceived bond with the environment. Graywolf, a Southern California activist, said, "Most people live on Mother Earth. Native people live with Mother Earth" (Johnson, 2010). Nowhere was this belief stated more eloquently than when Chief Seattle replied to President Franklin Pierce's request to purchase Indian land. In 1854, the great Chief wrote that the sky and the warmth of the land cannot be purchased because every shining pine needle, every sandy shore, every mist in the woods, every clearing and humming insect is holy in the memory and experience of Native Americans. The shining water that moves in streams and rivers is not just water but the blood of the ancestors.

The chief added that if the tribe decided to sell the land, the white Americans would have to hold it sacred and teach their children to respect its mysteries. As an example, the rivers are our brothers. They quench our thirst, carry our canoes, and feed our children. As such, they deserve the kindness we would give to any brother. Similarly, the earth is our mother and the ground beneath our feet is the ashes of our grandfathers. For these reasons, the earth does not belong to man; man belongs to the earth. Whatever befalls the earth also befalls the sons of the earth. If men spit upon the ground, they spit upon themselves and their children.

From Chief Seattle's viewpoint, the white man does not understand nature and views the earth not as his brother but as an enemy. It is simply something to be conquered and discarded. He leaves his father's graves behind, and he does not care. He kidnaps the earth from his children, and he does not care. His father's grave and his children's birthright are forgotten. He treats his mother the earth and his brother the sky as things to be bought, plundered, and sold like sheep or bright beads. His appetite will devour the earth and leave behind only a desert.

Although these comments are understandable, given what Chief Seattle must have observed, a more accurate view of European Americans might be that they viewed the world in terms of causal connections and linear chronology. Traditional Native American philosophy stresses continuity and continuous renewal. This philosophy cannot be made redundant by technological change or material gains (Brookeman, 1990). A person is respected not for possessing great wealth but for giving to others. Value is placed on giving, and a person who tries to accumulate goods is often feared.

Chief Seattle's leadership resulted in the naming of a city after him. A bronze statue has been erected to commemorate this fact, and each year, the Boy Scouts hold a memorial ceremony at his tomb. One of the reasons Chief Seattle gained recognition from white Americans is that he attempted to understand their culture. Missionaries converted him to Catholicism in the 1830s, and his actions made him appear conciliatory. In 1855, he was the first signer of the Port Elliott Treaty, by which the Washington tribes were given a reservation. The Suquamish were allied with several smaller tribes in what is now Washington and Oregon. In many ways, it seems that Seattle knew what it took generations for European Americans to understand—that all people are brothers and sisters.

The failure of the dominant culture to recognize the interconnection of all people has led some to fear the end of the world. In many Native American spiritualities, the present and future work in complete unison. The path we choose today determines the future. If we misstep, we must correct ourselves quickly or else we are out of balance. Is there time to rectify this headlong participation into a future we may not enjoy? Moyers (2004) wonders if there is still enough time for us to correct the paths we have chosen. He concludes that the will to fight is the antidote to despair. This fight, though, is not something we can do objectively. We need to address the concerns with a science of the heart. We start with seeing the problem, then feel it, then act. We act as if the future depends on us as individuals.

PHYSICAL AND MENTAL HEALTH

The deep spirituality of many Native Americans is often not enough to compensate for the abject poverty they face. Native Americans have significantly higher mortality rates than the general population. Suicide and homicide rates were especially high in the 1990s, as were rates of death from tuberculosis, accidents, diabetes, flu, and pneumonia (U.S. Department of Health and Human Services, 1997). However, two of the greatest mortality threats for Native Americans are tobacco and alcohol abuse.

Acculturation plays a significant role in how drugs and alcohol impact Native American life. For individuals who live a more traditional life, Native culture, spirituality, and tribal traditions can dominate behaviors. More acculturated individuals may maintain tribal pride, but they also live within the guidelines of the dominant society (Coyhis & Simonelli, 2008). It is often theorized that alcoholism comes from acculturation. With Native Americans, it is hard to know.

Native Americans suffer from disproportionately high rates of alcoholism. This is also more likely to lead to alcoholism-related mortality, health problems, and social problems (Villanueva, Tonigan & Miller, 2007). This is not to say that all tribes struggle with alcohol. A large number of tribes are abstinent and avoid alcohol-related problems (Beals et al., 2009).

When alcohol problems arise, the best intervention appears to be Motivational Enhancement Therapy (MET) (Villanueva, Tonigan & Miller, 2007). This is a nondirective approach that employs empathy, advice, responsibility, and alternatives and encourages optimism. The approach is person-centered and emphasizes active listening skills. For example, a typical intervention for a teen would look like this:

Client:	Everyone's always on my back about alcohol. Like they had never had a drink or anything.
Counselor:	It sounds frustrating. You're okay with your drinking, but you're getting pressure from everyone to stop. How do you handle that?

This approach is similar to the one specifically advocated for Native Americans by Coyhis and Simonelli (2008). They recommended four "laws of change." Change comes from (1) within, (2) is accompanied by a vision, (3) requires learning, and (4) is associated with a healing forest. The first three would be common to most alcohol intervention programs. Change must start with a desire to change. We must have a sense of what our lives would look like if we achieved our alcohol-related goals. The learning required is required by all. The community will need new skills as someone seeks healing. All together, these three laws add up to the fourth: the healing forest. *You must create a healing forest* sums up the four laws of change. A changed individual is like a tree rescued from a forest. You can nurture a tree like this, providing the right conditions for it to thrive. But if it is returned to the sick forest, it will die. For the intervention to last, the whole community must become healthy.

Mental Health

Overcoming alcohol abuse is similar to overcoming any mental health issue. The same rules for change would be effective. However, it is also important to bring spirituality into this process. Native Americans are attached to the land. This interconnection must be understood and nourished for therapy to be effective. Consider Black Bird, who believed that a spirit appeared in the form of a vulture that perched on her window. She views the bird's arrival as a warning to avoid traveling outside for the rest of the day. Her therapist, a European American, asked for more details about the nature of these visions and whether she saw them on a regular basis.

Black Bird explains that in her youth, she was closed to the wisdom of the spirits, but after using her dream catcher, she was able to bring some of the images into her awakened mind. Her therapist diagnosed her visions as an emerging thought disorder and recommended her for psychiatric treatment. The assumption was made that Black Bird's hallucinations were a sign of mental illness.

Many Native Americans have suffered because they have been misunderstood and wrongly diagnosed. The standard categories of depression, anxiety, and personality problems may not fit Native Americans because of their strong communal identity. However, there is one psychological issue that overshadows all others: suicide. The suicide rate among American Indians is double the national average, and alcohol is involved in more than 90% of successful suicides (Johnson, 1994). We are beginning to realize what works as buffers against suicide for Native Americans. Preventative factors include spirituality, strong family connectedness, social support, affective relationships with tribal leaders, and habitual discussion of problems with friends or family members (Alcántara & Gone, 2007). These are also cultural factors, which explains why decades of research show a connection between European individualism and Native American suicide rates (Lester, 1997).

Economic hardship also leads to suicidality, but the correlation here is more complex. Lester (1996) argued that American Indian suicide and homicide rates were not associated with unemployment rates, and some Native American groups with the highest poverty rates (especially the Navajo) have the lowest suicide rates

(Mignone & O'Neil, 2005). But this is not the whole story. Young and French (1996) found that "absolute poverty" and suicide were highly significant, but "relative poverty" did not have a significant effect on suicide rates. Similarly, data collected from the 48 contiguous states in 1980 showed that the suicide rate among Native Americans was higher in states where a greater percentage of the population was Native American and impoverished (Lester, 1994). The effect of this communal abject poverty is profound. In fact, when groups of urban, middle-class Native Americans are studied, there is no difference between their suicide rates and those of other ethnic groups (Shiang, 1998).

INDIVIDUAL AND GROUP INTERVENTIONS

For most of the 1990s, we lacked a cohesive intervention plan to work with Native Americans. Most of the literature addressed treatment programs for drug and alcohol abuse rather than individual psychotherapy (Sue, Chun & Gee, 1995). A fact that was known but often hard to accept among non-Native therapists is that Native American attitudes toward people are not usually contingent upon a person's role or status in the community. An individual's title, power, authority, or influence in a private or governmental organization does not determine the respect Native Americans will bestow. The character traits of the individual rather than the prestige of the entity that the person represents are instrumental in establishing rapport and co-operation. Building rapport will take time and patience, but the bonds created are likely to be stronger. The relationship is also more likely to be sustained if the therapist shows a desire to involve the client's family.

Family and Group Interventions

Among Hopi and Navajo groups, multigenerational interventions may require special skills and knowledge. In many cases, the services of a skilled translator will be needed (Aponte & Morrow, 1995). With Native American families, it is also important to include community resources. The therapist may want to involve traditional healers, clan leaders, village chiefs, or other tribal leaders.

Although tribal customs and rituals can often be helpful ways to cope with emotional concerns, they should not be performed by non-Natives. Such practices could be considered sacrilegious. Such Native American healing practices as the Sweat Lodge and Talking Circles operate under the notion that wellness involves maintaining a balance between the spiritual, physical, and mental/emotional "selves." The Sweat Lodge ceremony is an example of how these three forces can be melded into a single treatment process.

For the Ojibway, the Sweat Lodge ritual became popularized after alcoholism threatened their way of life. Unknown to Native groups prior to the influx of Europeans, drunkenness brought about abusive behaviors that had never before been seen in Native cultures. Wife and child abuse became rampant, and the Ojibway desperately needed to find their way back to traditional ways of living. In the Sweat Lodge, not only could tribe members draw out the poison of alcohol, but they could also address the behaviors associated with drunkenness. By means of intense heat and steam, toxins were physically sweated out of the body. Medicine men and women also helped to repair the damage done to people's spirits. The lodge was not only a place of refuge and healing but also a mechanism to obtain answers and guidance from spiritual entities, totem helpers, the Creator, and Mother Earth.

Like most Native American traditions, the Sweat Lodge involves a sense of community and belonging. Such practices de-emphasize the presence of personal or individual guilt and instead address the notion of a communal sense of shame. Statements such as, "You did not act like a Paiute" are commonly used to help redirect the individual toward behaving in a way that matches the values of the group. Disciplinary practices among Native American groups often include shaming an individual, but this is a temporary process. Once the shaming punishment is executed, the individual releases the guilt and the group forgets the transgression.

Another common Native American intervention is the Talking Circle. This is a ceremony and, like the sweat lodge, should only be performed by elders. The process often begins with prayers (sometimes in English but usually in a Native language). From here, there is a smudging process, which is a method of purifying a person or object with the smoke of sage, sweet grass, cedar, or a local herb. When this process is finished, the group is open for conversation. One person speaks. No judgments are made, and there is no argument about the person's statement. After each willing participant has spoken from the heart, participants respond. Again, responses are not judgmental and are often affirming, encouraging, or challenging. The conversation is kept confidential by all (Coyhis & Simonelli, 2008).

Lewis, Duran, and Woodis (1999) argue for the use of rituals and prayer in the therapeutic encounter as well as the therapeutic use of synchronous events. Therapists focusing on their client's shame must provide a mechanism for release. In many cases, this requires an intervention from a community agency (e.g., a medicine man). It should also be noted that Native Americans tend to view healing as a long-term process. Time is the great friend of Native Americans, and there is no need to rush the cycle.

Although Sweat Lodges and Talking Circles are Native interventions, they should offer some guidelines into how counselors can use some of these ideas within more traditional groups. In keeping with the idea that some rituals and practices may be translated into secular therapy, Garrett et al. (2008) came up with an interesting proposal. Given that many Native Americans view mental health as balanced circles, imagine yourself jumping into a shallow pool. The water will ripple around you evenly. This is how our life unfolds too. Each ripple is another part of our life. There is a rippling circle for family (immediate, extended, and tribal), community, nation, and world. We must find a balance with all things. A lack of balance creates illness.

Given that many methods of finding balance would require spiritual interventions, Garrett et al. (2008) recommend more universal techniques that draw upon cultural practices or beliefs. Group leaders could emphasize balance issues from career and family; personal acceptance and respect of others; or shyness and a desire for social interactions. Each of these could be discussed in nonjudgmental ways, allowing one person to talk until he or she has said what they want.

Individual Interventions

Just as Native ideas maybe successfully integrated into group therapy, they can also be used in individual therapy. Thier (1999) integrated vision quests and counseling into what he calls a "Dream Quest." This hybrid technique provides a forum for modern encounters with the Great Spirit. Rather than requiring the participant to spend days alone in the wilderness with little or no shelter, clothing, or food, this approach can be carried out in the comfort of home. The practice involves a form of narrative exploration. The individual thinks of him or herself as a spiritual warrior battling the demons and encountering the angels inside the soul or psyche. According to this model, the sacred or holy place is not necessarily outside the body but can be a place within the innermost corners of the mind.

Although the dream quest may be a symbolic exercise in survival, it still requires the individual to focus on the outside world. The questor must create a highly sensitive state of bodily awareness and feel the connection he or she shares with nature and all living things. Bodily states of emptiness and weakness often give rise to issues about personal survival, and moving through these fears reveals unexpected sources of strength and power.

Focusing on restorative or healing interventions is usually preferred to solving diagnostic problems, especially early in the therapeutic process. In some ways, clinical interventions—wrought with diagnoses and labeling—can push clients away from the cultural healing processes. Winona Simms (1999) tells the story of Alita, a 27-year-old Native American woman who sought out guidance from her university counseling center. Late in her childhood, Alita had moved in with loving European American foster parents, but her bicultural background and growing lack of self-confidence eventually led to social and academic problems.

The therapists attempted to merge contemporary psychotherapy (cognitive behavioral approach) with traditional Native healing. Alita's problems appeared to stem from alcohol dependence, but the initial focus was not on diagnosis or pathology. Instead, Alita was given information about depression, alcoholism, and meditation. She also engaged in "cultural strengthening," which involved participation in the Talking Circle and the Sweat Lodge. As her participation in these forums increased, she expressed a greater sense of spiritual awareness and felt more in touch with her American Indian identity. With her self-concept improving, Alita was referred to support groups in her community for people dealing with alcohol abuse. Simms argues that the delayed focus on diagnostic issues helped Alita build a new lifestyle that made it easier for her to cope with her alcoholism. Had her therapists emphasized diagnostic concerns at the outset of treatment, Alita would have lacked the necessary skills to create lasting change.

Culturally sensitive interventions, such as the one used for Alita, appear to have the best success rates. Integrating tactics such as a Sweat Lodge with traditional psychotherapeutic interventions also has yielded success for Native Americans wrestling with substance abuse (Gutierres & Todd, 1997). The success of such programs depends on the creation of a non-accusatory format together with an emphasis on ideas over feelings.

The latter element led Trimble and LaFromboise (1987) to argue that person-centered approaches are typically ill advised for Native American clients. Instead, other nondirective approaches—such as those involving cultural activities, the telling of myths, and psychodrama—may be more appropriate. For example, with Alita, we could follow up the tribal intervention with a psychological exploration, as illustrated below.

Therapist:	Let's talk about the last vision you had in the sweat lodge.
Alita:	Okay. I was lying on my back, and I looked up and saw a bear in the clouds. I remember thinking, "This is cool." I waited for a few seconds, and the bear started to move. It sailed toward another cloud; I think it looked like a fish or something. Soon, they became one cloud and then joined the rest of the sky.
Therapist:	Wow. You haven't talked about anything like this before. I would imagine the images had a huge effect on you. Have you discussed the dream with your elders?
Alita:	I did actually. They said the bear was a symbol of power. She is maternal, cunning, and a healer. I remember feeling, in the dream, that she, the bear, had a gentle strength. It moved so slowly, but it never wavered.
Therapist:	I would imagine that is how you have started to see yourself and your progress with drinking and depression. You are moving slowly and steadily, like the young bear cloud. Maybe the gentle strength and determination have been merging in you?
Alita:	I don't know. Maybe. I would like to believe that. If nothing else, it is something to hope for.

In working with a client like Alita, it is important for counselors to remain flexible (Trimble, 2010) or, as Herring (1999) described it, to adopt a "synergetic orientation" where counselors blend their cultures into a well-balanced whole. Part of this blending will include addressing cultural differences. For example, later in the session with Alita, the following could occur:

Alita:	If I knew the bear was my spirit guide, I would have a clearer direction, but I was always drawn to the dove. Can guides change that quickly?
Therapist:	Listening to you talk about your guides is really beautiful. Thank you for including me in them. But you should ask the elders for assistance. Remember, I grew up without any animal contact. Well, I rode in a horse-drawn carriage once and I petted the dolphins at SeaWorld. Trust me, you have more training in spirit guides than I do. But I can picture you with a bear or a dove. You are soft, strong, and cunning and also graceful, optimistic, and pure. In my training, the images themselves are also important guides.

Flexibility should also be observed with session timing. Schedule a paperwork hour after a Native American session so it can run over if it needs to. The sessions should also unfold at the client's pace. Develop a relationship before pushing the client too far. This will mean respecting silence, speaking slowly and carefully, not interrupting the client, showing respect for the client's culture, and maintaining strict confidentiality. Effective counseling with Native Americans requires the internalization of all these characteristics (Trimble, 2010).

If the elders in your community allow you to use a specific ceremony in your session, remember that many Native American ceremonies follow a consistent pattern. Lonegren (1996) argued that Native American ceremonies are intrinsically flexible and vary to meet the needs of the Spirit. But there is a beginning, middle, and end to the events. The process usually contains the following:

- **Purification:** This is a good beginning because of its focus on removing impurities and other spiritual elements that could hamper successful connection with an individual's or group's goals. In some ceremonies, a feather is used to brush down the aura and to sweep away bits of psychological or spiritual trash. Incense may also be used to cleanse the aura. Even one's sitting posture may have an effect on the cleansing process. Some Native Americans honor the four directions—east, south, west, and north—with burning sage. Another possibility is to have a guided meditation where each participant imagines a ball of light expanding outward until it sweeps away all impurities.
- **Invocation:** At this stage, the individual asks the Creator for help. Often, there is a ritual associated with this request, such as lighting a candle in the center of a circle.
- **Receiving:** As the divine elements enter the group or individual, there is a time of slowly receiving spiritual power. A time of slowly building the energy is often evidenced through chanting, moving in place, simple repetitive songs, dancing, clapping, or playing instruments, such as drums, pipes, or rattles. There is a also cycle involved in this process. Usually, the slow pace builds until it reaches a certain pitch and then it falls—only to be rebuilt to a higher level the second time. This is repeated several times—each time reaching higher levels to symbolize rising toward a spiritual climax.
- **Giving:** When the spiritual energy has been internalized, it can then be used for healing—not just for the self but for the world. The energy is believed to be so great that thoughts of peace can help heal a troubled world. Creating visions of healing light can surround and assist friends in need. In a less metaphysical sense, the energy can be given back to the earth and sky, which grounds the individual and helps the process occur more easily the next time. Gardening, hunting, painting, sewing, or working with one's hands can help heal the body and the soul.

Although some of these elements would be impractical as part of a counseling session, therapists can use the structure of the ceremony to harmonize therapy with cultural rituals. The ideas of purification, healing, acceptance, and giving are all valid psychological constructs that, when specifically associated with ritual, may help Native Americans view the therapeutic process more positively.

Spirituality is seldom brought into the counseling environment, but a basic understanding of the earthly, cyclical elements of Native American religions can help therapists understand the issues that are fundamentally important for many clients. These issues are readily apparent in the case of Little Dove, whose pride, sensitivity, and longing for her people are obvious. Such issues are common themes among Native Americans. Even though she had lived in poverty as a child, she speaks fondly of being with the land. Living within white society, she prays her children will one day understand their heritage. Such views suggest the importance of therapist sensitivity to Indian pride.

ADVOCACY AND SOCIAL JUSTICE

One of the most pressing social justice issues for Native Americans relates to their land and how to run it. For example, take taxes. Many states do not impose any taxes on revenues collected on Native land. However, New York and other states are considering changes to these policies. They do not want to impose taxes. Instead, they want to limit how many taxable items (like cigarettes) wholesalers can bring to the reservations (Carter, 2010). The issue makes sense. The state does not want to lose their $4.35 per pack of cigarettes because people will just buy them from the reservations. But it also calls into question the value of treaties and sovereignty. What are reasonable ways to act for sovereign governments sharing the same land?

The issue of sovereignty is even more difficult with the issues raised by the United Nations. A declaration for indigenous people (adopted by the general assembly in 2007) includes a statement about land ownership (Article 26): "Indigenous peoples have the right to the lands, territories and resources which they have traditionally owned, occupied or otherwise used or acquired" (Richardson, 2010). This posed significant difficulties for the Obama administration. It is hard to balance the support with what is right and keeping those pretty Manhattan skyscrapers for ourselves.

Balance is also important when addressing educational issues. School counselors and psychologists should work to ensure the proper presentation of Native traditions and rituals (e.g., no macaroni art as "Indian") and to also advocate for the inclusion of Native American stories, traditions, culture, and art into the curriculum. This is one of the reasons many schools no longer have Native Americans as their "warrior" mascots. The image is too aggressive, and for many people, it becomes the only image they have of Native Americans. This is unlike, say, thinking of Vikings as white warriors because everyone in Minnesota has another image of white people. We have to protect how cultures are introduced, and this includes eliminating negative images as well as building positive ones. The United State is a merger of many cultures, and our historical roots should be included with the standard European curriculum.

For those living close to reservations, building ties with tribal elders would prove very valuable for all involved. This form of advocacy may be harder than it sounds. Some reservations are housed far from large cities or towns. For example, the Havasupai Indian Reservation is 66 miles from the small town of Peach Springs, Arizona. The reservation cannot be reached by road, requiring visitors to hike, ride mules, or helicopter eight miles into the Grand Canyon. When reaching the reservation, guests must pay $37.50 to enter. Such obstacles make it difficult for counselors and education personnel to serve the area.

Even when direct contact with the reservations proves too challenging, there are simpler forms of advocacy available. At my university, we discussed building a small hut for smudging purifications before tests and "stressful" days. The administration showed some openness to the topic, but it became clear that real change would only happen with a passionate movement with large numbers petitioning for the change. We will not get these numbers without involving ourselves in the community.

Whenever I think about ways to build relationships, I remember my trip to Tunnel Island on the western beaches of Washington State. This area is one of the most beautiful places on Earth, but few ever see it. The majestic beach and rocks are deep within the Quinault Reservation. The only way to reach the water is along a five-mile stretch of dirt road, which is filled with enough potholes to break the axel of a Jeep (which we saw abandoned on the side of the road). I kept thinking how great it would be to get 100 people together and fill the miles of potholes with dirt. No concrete. Nothing that would harm the natural beauty. Just soil, cooperation, and a shared reverence for this incredible land.

Just about anything we could say about fostering advocacy would come back to this notion of learning to gain mutual respect and to ensure the rights for Native American to maintain their land, culture, and emerging wealth.

Little Dove's Story (A Client's Viewpoint)

I have been living among the white people for almost 20 years now. My husband, a white man, fell in love with me and lived on the reservation for three years to win my heart. I could not deny him. Most people think of my children as white, but I hope my daughter and son will one day look beneath their skin to the spirit inside. I still long for the land of my grandparents. But it breaks my heart how my children are abandoning our heritage.

When I was growing up, I used to play under a tree behind my parents' house. We had fastened an old tire to it, and I would swing for hours, just feeling the spirit of the breeze on my cheek. My grandfather once came out and told me that the tree I loved was partly responsible for my birth.

"Why, grandfather?" I asked with curiosity.

"Because it was under this tree that your grandmother's spirit first spoke to me." He rubbed his cheek, as if feeling the warmth of her spirit around him. "Years ago, I made a bench and placed it right here. It is the bench we now use for our meals. When your grandmother and I were very young, we would sit on the bench and feel the spirits, just as you have been doing today. Sometimes, we would talk. Sometimes, we would only feel each other's presence and our love for this land. So, you see, Little Dove, your love for this place has a reason and a purpose."

(continues)

Little Dove's Story (A Client's Viewpoint) (continued)

Whenever my family journeys out to the reservation with me, I always spend time under my grandfather's tree. To the chagrin of my children, I sometimes sit for an hour, gazing at the beauty of the desert and remembering the love of my grandfather. I could stay longer, but usually, *my* children come to me complaining of being bored. "There is nothing to do here," they protest. By that, I'm sure they mean there is no electricity for boom boxes, no television for video games, no computer for the Internet. Usually, I can't respond to their sadness. I just sigh and motion for them to sit with me, which they never do. Hopefully, my grandfather's spirit will speak to them one day, and they will appreciate the history under their feet. It is what made them.

Jose's Story (A Counselor's Viewpoint)

When I met Little Dove, I was a little intimidated. You can't tell from her story, but this woman is a powerhouse. She is an artist, public speaker, poet, and activist. She makes her living by giving talks to major corporations, schools, and communities about Native American issues. If that weren't enough, she dropped bombshell statements during the intake. Things like, "Our reservation actually includes the land for Interstate 10. If we wanted to, we could shut down the white people's way of life."

When she said this, I was thinking, "Are you nuts? You'd have the military there within the day, and they'd take you out—legally or not!"

But her statement also got me thinking. My family moved to Texas (from Mexico) when I was 10 years old. I know what it's like to be away from your homeland. I know what it's like be an stranger in the "white world." Little Dove and I are similar people, but we are also very different. She is the first Native American I met who had blended seamlessly into the white world but still *belonged* to the reservation. It confused me. I didn't know where to take her.

So, our sessions started off a little slow. We talked about children in general and how my children complain about going to Mexico City with me every summer. They like the size of the city and some of things to do, but they miss their friends and their American lifestyle. They would probably get along with Little Dove's kids.

I didn't realize it at the time, but our casual conversation and slow pace helped her feel more relaxed. Later in our sessions, she said, "I didn't trust you for a month." And I wouldn't have guessed this.

In our fourth session, when I found myself surprised that she wanted to come back, we started talking about art. She told me about one of her

(continues)

Jose's Story (A Counselor's Viewpoint) *(continued)*

paintings, and it reminded me of something from my childhood. My parents took me to see the Huichol Indians, possibly the only remaining tribe to maintain their pre-Columbian way of life. They made "Yarn Paintings," which were made out of colored yarn strands pressed into beeswax. A lady told me, "I made this after dreaming about my children." (The painting showed two young birds walking a path but inscribed within a circle, with wings surrounding the edges of the circular wooden frame). She continued saying, "No matter where my children go, the wings of our culture and spirit will bring them home."

When I finished my musing, I notice Little Dove was crying. Then, she sobbed. "I had that same dream!" She cried a good five minutes. Then, she dried her eyes, thanked me, and scheduled an appointment for the following week. We never discussed what my story meant to her or how it related to her dream. It was as if we didn't have to.

I learned so much with Little Dove. I learned the value of patience, timing, trusting my instincts, and being genuine.

Little Dove worked through her fears in two more sessions. She also painted an oil painting (her first attempt with that art form) and dedicated the painting to me. It was amazing. Two young children sat on a dock in the shape of the Western United States. One stared with his back toward the viewer, looking off into the sunset. The other faced us—a warm smile on her face. But what got me was the horizon. The ocean looked curved, as if it bended downward, and way off in the distance, you could see the same two children reversed, with the boy smiling looking toward himself and his sister.

I couldn't believe she got all of this from my story about the two doves, but I found it humbling, and it made me fully believe in the spiritual depth of counseling.

QUESTIONS TO CONSIDER

1. The treatment of Native Americans has been referred to as "the American holocaust." Is this statement accurate? If so, what role might the government take in compensating Native Americans for their losses?
2. Does the Battle of Wounded Knee represent an American massacre or do both groups simply misunderstand the events that took place?
3. Native Americans traditionally held women in high regard. How does the practice of the moon lodge reflect women's status? How do you think the dominant American society would view this practice?
4. Many Native American tribes stand to earn considerable income through tribal casinos. Given this fact, is their view regarding the spirituality of gambling most likely rationalization or does the act of gambling hold secrets to self-development?
5. Native American children generally value and develop acute visual discrimination and imagery skills, perceive facts globally, and use reflective

thinking patterns. How could the curriculum in America's schools be changed to emphasize these strengths? Should such changes be implemented?

6. Young Native Americans who abuse drugs and alcohol are at higher risk for weak family bonding, poor school adjustment, and higher dropout rates. What can be done to reverse this trend?

7. During some religious rituals, tribe members receive healing for physical, psychological, and spiritual needs, including ailments such as alcoholism. One traditional technique involves bringing the needy individual into the center of a ring. The other members sing and pray, attempting to draw out the evil spirits that reside in the needy soul. Would such a practice be wise to incorporate into group counseling? Why or why not?

8. Some tribes have no word for time. They see no need to be punctual or "on time" because they believe there is always plenty of time in an individual's life for necessary tasks. How would you demonstrate cultural sensitivity to a client who was making genuine progress during a counseling session? Would you end the session on time or continue into the next hour?

9. The suicide epidemic among Native Americans has been attributed to alcohol abuse, poverty, boredom, and family breakdown. Which of these factors do you believe to be the most salient? What interventions should be made to reverse the trend?

10. The Sweat Lodge—along with most Native American traditions—involves a sense of community and belonging. What do you believe are the most healing elements of the ritual?

11. No matter what approach is attempted, none is likely to be successful until trust has been sufficiently developed. What therapeutic tactics might need to be altered in order to establish trust with Native American clients?

12. What did Little Dove's painting mean? How sure are you of your interpretation? Is your interpretation complete?

INTERVENTION EXERCISES

Counseling and Therapy: Litonya (which is Miwok for "darting hummingbird") has come for counseling because she believes her neighbors are destroying the natural beauty of her land. She lives in a semirural area outside Yosemite National Park. The people who own the land across from her plan to strip part of the mountainside to build a hotel. They already have the necessary permits, and Litonya feels helpless to stop them. "I'm only 26, and I have little money, but my grandfather would not allow this. He would find a way to stop them and so will I!" How would you counsel her?

School Psychology: Aaqayuk recently moved to your town from Alaska. Her family is Inupiaq, and her English is very limited. After three weeks of classes, her teacher asked for an assessment. "I know Aaqayuk's English is poor," the teacher explains. "But there's something more going on. Her eyes aren't tracking right, and I think there could be some cognitive damage." What would you do? No one in Aaqayuk's family understands English well enough to serve as a translator.

School Counseling: Wikimak (Algonquin for wife) emigrated from Quebec, Ontario, to your state last week. She is nine years old, and this is her first time in a non-indigenous school. On her first day of class, her teacher asked her to "share a little" about herself. Wanting to help, the teacher also asked what her name meant. When Wikimak said "wife," the class giggled and started pointing at her. The teacher silenced the class. But the damage was done. Wikimak told the school secretary that she "hates it here" and wants to go back to Quebec. How would you help?

Social Work: Bilagaana (14-year-old Navajo boy whose name means "white person") said the bruises on his face came from "falling off a tree." Something inspired you to ask about his parents, and he replied. "My grandfather doesn't like me much because my dad is white." When you ask more details, Bilagaana says, "My grandfather would never hurt me, but he believes in disciplining my spirit with his belt." How would you proceed?

CHAPTER 8

Arab/Middle Eastern/ Jewish Americans

INSIGHT EXERCISE

When I came to America, I was surprised at how people viewed engineers. In Iran, I was viewed as an elite professional. Here, the culture tends to value physicians more. It is hard for me to understand. Why would America value the worth of a single individual more than the building of a city? Don't people here realize how many "individuals" are hurt when poor infrastructure leads to environmental catastrophes?

I also don't understand American women. They throw themselves at men, then react when men show interest in them. A woman at my work wore a blouse cut down to her belly button (almost) and a skirt that left little to the imagination. The boy who delivers the mail told her she looked "hot," and she filed a grievance. I have a hard time understanding these contradictions. If women want respect, she should dress appropriately. I wear a jacket and tie to work because I want people to respect me. Why don't American women understand the same thing? They dress like prostitutes, then somehow think men are discriminating against them for not taking them seriously.

I have been here 10 years, and I still don't understand the culture. Jokes are vulgar and childish, television is banal and myopic, education is soft and lacking in science, and people worship sports heroes. For a country as great as this one, I expected more. I still hope America understands

(continues)

INSIGHT EXERCISE *(continued)*

how much more it could become. I think it can get there. But it would take a fundamental reshaping of values.

Questions to Consider:

1. Does Massoud sound like "an American"? How would you define his cultural identity?

2. Massoud believes some of the cultural themes in America lack the careful thought of those in Iran, but he still believes the United States is a great country. How would you reconcile these divergent opinions?

3. Western women's clothing and styles are hard for Massoud to understand. He believes U.S. women are belittling themselves. Does this strike you as odd, considering women in his home country must wear a *chador* (loose coat covering arms and legs) and a head scarf?

Middle Eastern culture may be the hardest ethnicity to define. The term itself (Middle East) implies a Eurocentric bias, assuming the "middle" between Europe and Asia. Even if the term had relevance, the area it represents is rapidly changing. Traditional definitions of the Middle East included the following general regions: Anatolia (Turkey), Arabian Peninsula (Bahrain Kuwait, Oman, Qatar, Saudi Arabia, United Arab Emirates, and Yemen), Fertile Crescent (Gaza Strip, Iraq, Israel, Jordan, Lebanon, Syria, West Bank), Iranian Plateau (Iran/Persia), Mediterranean Sea (Cyprus), and North Africa (Egypt) (Owen & Pamuk, 1999).

There are vast cultural differences between Egyptians, Persians, Jews, and Arabs. The differences are so varied that a discussion of the group as a whole feels forced and awkward. Because of this, this chapter will bounce between the various groups, highlighting differences in religion, traditions, and worldviews.

HISTORICAL CONTEXT

Although people from the Middle East have been labeled "colored," they have a unique history of blending into European culture. The Fertile Crescent is often called the Cradle of Civilization and spawned most modern societies. For example, Europe and the Fertile Crescent have a shared history dating back to ancient Greece. Babylon (Southern Iraq), Assyria (Northern Iraq), Egypt, Greece, and Rome also share an interlaced history.

Much of the current division between Arabs, Persians, and Jews stems from the Islamic interpretation of their historical origins. Muslims believe they are the chosen people of God and the true followers of Adoni[1] and

---

[1] The Jewish God's name is too sacred to write; this word translates to "my Lord," which is why the English Bible often lists "LORD" in capital letters where the name of God is written.

Jesus. They view the Jews as children of Isaac and the Arabs as children of Ishmael (the firstborn son of Abraham). Following this line of reasoning, the Arabs and Jews are brother cultures, but they have followed different paths.

According to the Torah, Abraham married Sarah, but she was childless for many years. So, she gave Abraham her Egyptian maid, Hagar, to be his second wife, in accordance with the customs of the day. Hagar gave birth to a son, Ishmael. With the birth of Ishmael, Sarah's wish for a full inheritance was granted. But then God caused Sarah to conceive, and she gave birth to a son, Isaac (Genesis, Chapter 21). Now she could have her full inheritance through her own "flesh and blood." Without delay, she demanded that Hagar—and Ishmael with her—be cast out of the house. Abraham loved Ishmael, and Sarah's request grieved him greatly. But the voice of God told him to consent to Sarah's wishes, and he did so. He "took bread and a bottle of water, and gave them unto Hagar, put the child on her shoulder, and sent her away" (Genesis 21:14). On that day, according to Muslim beliefs, the religion known as Islam was born.

Hagar and Ishmael wandered through the wilderness, and Hagar began to fear for her life. As they neared death, God brought forth water from the earth and saved the two of them. This spring of water is identified by Muslims as the well of Zamzam, located today within the al-Haram Mosque in Mecca and part of the Hajj (obligatory pilgrimage to Mecca). As recounted in Genesis 16:10, Hagar was later visited by an angel, who said to her "I will multiply thy seed exceedingly, that it shall not be numbered for multitude." And, as for Ishmael, Genesis 17:20 stated, "I have blessed him, and will make him fruitful, and will multiply him exceedingly; twelve princes shall he beget, and I will make him a great nation." The great nation is Islam.

Although ancient history and historical traditions are of value, recent history speaks more to multicultural integration. Of all the Middle Eastern groups who have suffered oppression, no persecution has been greater than that of the Jews and Gypsies (members of a dark Caucasoid people originating in northern India but living principally in Europe). The Holocaust of World War II testifies to humanity's ability to dehumanize a cultural group. But even more importantly, it serves as a reminder that similarities in ethnicity can be overlooked if certain differences are highlighted.

Adolf Hitler's persecution of the Jews in Germany began a month after he became chancellor at the beginning of 1933. Jewish businesses were boycotted and soon vandalized, and Jewish personnel were dismissed from local governments, law courts, and universities. Between 1933 and 1938, Hitler succeeded in undermining the political and economic foundations of German Jewry. His attack focused not on the religious beliefs of individuals but on their ethnic origins. Nazi definitions of Jewry included thousands of German Christians with Jewish ancestry. The 1935 Nürnberg laws robbed Jews of their citizenship and forbade them to intermarry with other Germans. By 1939, as World War II began, Jews had lost their citizenship. They were no longer permitted to attend public schools, engage in many businesses, own land, associate with non-Jews, or frequent parks, libraries, or museums.

At the notorious Wannsee Conference, on January 20, 1942, Nazi bureaucrats met to discuss the "final solution of the Jewish question." They decided to systematically evacuate Jews from the countries in occupied Europe to camps in the East, where they would be "treated accordingly." Some would be exterminated outright (although the word *extermination* was not used officially), and others would be organized into huge labor battalions. Exhausting work, poor living conditions, and meager food would ultimately lead to the death of survivors or their selection for extermination. The total number of Jews killed by the Nazis during the war is estimated at 5,700,000. This figure includes some 2,950,000 Jews who lived in Poland, about 1,050,000 in the Soviet Union, and approximately 560,000 in Hungary. In addition to Jews, as many as 400,000 Gypsies perished in the Holocaust.

The memory of the Holocaust has faded for many Americans, but anti-Semitism continues to permeate our culture. Even groups who are struggling under oppression from the dominant society can become instigators of hostile acts against other minority groups. A poignant example of this attitude occurred in 1994, when a group of minority high school students in Oakland, California, watched Steven Spielberg's epic film *Schindler's List*. As the movie depicted Jews being slaughtered, raped, starved, and tortured, members of the young audience began to laugh and cheer (Britt, 1994). Demonstrations of this nature are nearly as tragic as the Holocaust itself, and they dampen the optimistic view that humanity has risen above such behaviors.

After the bombing of the World Trade Center in 2001, a shift occurred. Jews were regarded as fellow victims. Iraq, Iran, and North Korean were labeled by then-president Bush as an "axis of evil, arming to threaten the peace of the world." Even though these countries were not involved in the terrorist attacks, the government implied they were or could be. The president added, "They could provide these arms to terrorists, giving them the means to match their hatred. They could attack our allies or attempt to blackmail the United States" (Bush, 2002).

Sentiments such as the ones created by President Bush inspired a shift in U.S. prejudices. Arabs and Persians became the new targets. Hate crimes increased exponentially, rising to 52% against Muslims in one year (Council on American-Islamic Relations, 2005). Such shifting values decreased the social status of many Arab and Persian Americans. The changing climate was depicted clearly from a lawsuit against Fairmont Hotel Management. The suit, which was settled out of court, alleged that Muslim, Arab, and South Asian employees were publically called "terrorist," "Taliban," "dumb Muslim," and "Osama" (Armour, 2005). These prejudices are still lingering in our culture, and Arabs maybe most discriminated against by people in power (Guinote, Willis & Martellotta, 2010).

IMMIGRATION AND DEVELOPMENT

Although the United States has long been a magnet for immigrants, it failed to attract people from the Middle East until the end of the 19th century. Even at this early juncture, young men came and then later returned to their homelands. The process did not change until World War II altered the landscape of the Middle East. War, poverty, and unrest brought more households to the United States, and they were more likely to stay. The nature of the immigrants also changed. In the first wave, immigrants were mostly merchants and farmers. After the creation of the State of Israel, more college-educated Arabs came to America. A third wave happened in 1991, which culminated with the 2001 terrorist attacks. During this phase, Arab immigrants were routinely viewed with suspicion (Abudabbeh, 2005). But immigration continues to increase, with localized areas attracting people from specific countries. For example, southeastern Michigan became home to the largest concentrations of Chaldeans and Arabs outside the Middle East.

Chaldeans have done well in the United States, in part because their Christian background integrates easily into the mainstream culture. They originate from northern Iraq, and there are about 80,000 Chaldeans in the United States today. Overall, there are about 5 million Arabs in America (Jamil et al., 2009).

Jewish people often came to America not for economic opportunities but to escape persecution. In some ways, the immigration process has been easier for Jews than for Irish and Italian immigrants. The reason for this is the underlying beliefs of Zionism. A significant belief for Zionist Jews is that each Jew has an innate bond with other Jews around the world. This belief structure helped Jewish immigrants find a supportive Jewish community when they arrived in the States, even though they still faced prejudice and opposition from the dominant society. The United States is home to the largest population of Jewish individuals outside of Israel (Simon & Schaler, 2007).

For all Middle Eastern immigrants, children faced additional struggles. Peer groups play an important role in child development, and they seldom accommodate differences. When Fadwa's family moved to the United States from Jordan, she felt "pulled in two directions." At 16, her new friends were curious about her, and they wanted to respect her Islamic customs, but they also wanted her to become part of their clique. This included activities like shopping at the mall, tanning at the beach, having sodas at a local restaurant, etc. All these things were typical American activities, but they violated many Jordanian traditions.

Fadwa's mother forbid her to spend any time with her friends outside of school. This led to a "break out," as her friends called it. A group of girls snuck her out of her window and drove her to a late-night movie.

After the movie, Fadwa's mother and father waited by the exit. As Fadwa said goodbye to a boy she had met, her father pulled her by the hair and pushed her into the back of the car. The girl's friends—afraid for Fadwa's life—called the police. Child Protective Services was soon involved.

In mandated counseling, the family spoke about the importance of maintaining Islamic principles and avoiding sex, drugs, and immodesty. Fadwa simply hung her head. It took three sessions before Fadwa felt safe enough to share. Then, she spewed out all her concerns through tears. She wanted to maintain her family's respect, but she wanted to enjoy herself too. She loved her new friends and wished her parents would trust her enough give her some freedom. The confrontation was difficult for her parents, who saw her questions as defiance and disrespect, but they soon reached a compromise. Fadwa later felt "more passionate" about her religion and connected with her parents. When given a little freedom, she *chose* to emulate her parents more than she would have otherwise.

CULTURAL IDENTITY

Middle Eastern cultures are diverse and difficult to classify. Religion plays a primary role in cultural expression, but other practices developed independently. For both Jewish and Muslim peoples, family and familial relationships take priority over individual rights. For many Arab families, this means the ultimate authority of justice resides within the household, not the courts. This may look odd to Western eyes, where "one person, one vote" overshadows most ethical decision making. But from a Middle Eastern perspective, the Western independence is really a small minority influencing the majority. Powerful corporations pay for political advertising. These groups wield a voice on education, art, sports, and policy. What some regard as independence looks to others like ignorant dependence (Dwairy, 2006). When the family governs itself, it can look out for the interests of those most dear to it.

Arab culture, in particular, was built on tribal customs. When Islam arose in the seventh century, the tribes were united (Dwairy, 2006). These tribes are like extended families, and individualism within these structures serves little value. When individualism threatens the tribal leadership, the offender is punished.

As oil continues to bring wealth to the Arab and Persian worlds, their cultures are undergoing a profound transition. Tribal castes are threatened by modern phenomena (Al-Krenawi et al., 2004). Additionally, the changing world dynamic is bringing Arabs in closer contact with Europeans. This continues to create tension regarding communication styles.

When European Americans demonstrate interest and attention in a conversation, they will usually use minimal verbal responses (e.g., uh huh, yeah, I see). Arabic has a built-in method of communicating attention and interest. The speaker lowers his or her pitch in a steep continuous drop. Unfortunately, native English speakers tend to regard this attending skill as a lack of interest or boredom in the conversation. Educating immigrants and employers about cultural differences like these could help immigrants adapt (Ward & Al Bayyari, 2010).

While Arabs, Persians, and Egyptians may struggle to find their place in U.S. culture, the process is very different for Jews. Jews are sometimes called an invisible minority (Schlosser. 2006). Unless they wear a yarmulke or other identity marker, many people will not notice any physical differences. Despite the lack of physical markers, the cultural identity remains profound. Some Jews believe their religion is more closely connected to their ethnic identity than an ideological identity. But many believe their religion connects them to the past—like a chain rooting them to a history bigger than themselves (Altman et al., 2010). These statements are similar for many Arabs, Persians, and Egyptians. Religion is tied to their ethnic identity.

For Jews and Muslims, the process of identity is multifaceted. The cultural identity model for religious-ethnic groups was based loosely on the

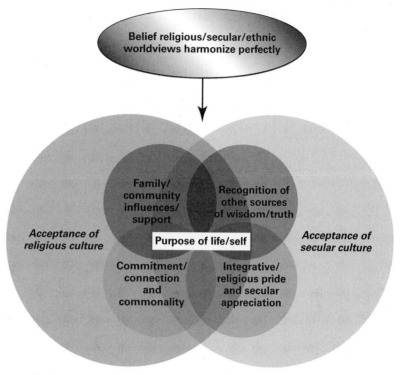

FIGURE **8.1** Cultural Identity Model: Religious Ethnicity

model created by Altman et al. (2010). However, the more conservative the religious upbringing, the less likely the individual will be exposed to secular educational models. It is also important to realize the different levels for leaving religions. Turning from Islam is sometimes punishable by death. Such extreme practices are not common in the United States, and the model in Figure 8.1 is typical for many people who come from countries where religion and ethnicity are viewed as combined cultural components.

WITHIN GROUP DIFFERENCES

In Islam, the two primary divisions are among the Sunni (the largest group) and the Shiite Muslims. The intense conflict between these two groups stems back to Muhammad's death. The Shiite's believed in a natural lineage for the change in power. Muhammad had no son, so they anointed his closest male relative—his cousin and son-in-law, the philosopher-warrior Ali. The word for follower is *Shiat*. So, they became known as *Shiat Ali,* or followers of Ali. Shiite is a shortened title for this. The Sunnis believed that the caliph (or head of state) should be an elected leader. The Shiites are more ideological in their design; the Sunnis more pragmatic. The two groups split when Ali became the fourth caliph (the Shiites consider him the first). He and his family were murdered five years into his term. This was not an uncommon event.

All the previous caliphs were murdered, but this murder caused a civil war in the Muslim world, which continues today. The Shiites comprise the largest Islamic group in Iraq and Iran, but they are a minority in most of the rest of the world (Fetini, 2009).

The ethnic structure of Judaism is also ideological. There are ethnic Jews, but there are also converted Jews. As such, it is difficult to describe differences except through cultural clusters. Schlosser (2006) provides a good summary of the different Jewish sects. Hasidic Jews are the most readily identifiable. The men wear black coats, pants, and hats while maintaining side curls; women wear long, dark, conservative skirts and sleeves past the elbow. Hasidic Jews closely maintain Jewish traditions, primarily through eating and cooking kosher, observing the Sabbath, and following the purity laws (i.e., regarding sex and cleanliness). These are often self-contained communities, and women are not permitted to read the Torah. Orthodox Jews wear modest secular clothing (except men wear yarmulkes). They value secular learning and culture, but they still maintain adherence to kosher, Sabbath, and purity. Men and women sit separately during religious services, which are usually in Hebrew. Conservative Jews allow men and women to sit together in religious services, which are performed mostly in Hebrew. They value modern, secular culture and maintain a more flexible stance on the Toray. Reconstructionists value God, the Torah, and the People of Israel, but they view personal autonomy as more important than Jewish law. This was the first group to hold a *bat mitzvah* (a coming of age celebration) for Jewish girls. Reformers are still more progressive. They do not follow kosher laws, the Sabbath, or the purity rituals, and they emphasize equality of the sexes. This was the first denomination to ordain women as rabbis.

FAMILY STRUCTURE AND DYNAMICS

Arab and Persian families function differently from most. For many Islamic families, men function as the representatives of the family's beliefs, values, and positions to the external world (Mourad & Carolan, 2010). Rather than settle conflicts with the courts, they are settled within the confines of the family.

With men in charge and the family the pre-eminent power structure, women are vulnerable. This risk is especially true for Arab women, where they are socially weak, subservient to all men, and submissive to their husbands. For women to achieve success, they must marry well, raise children (especially boys), and devote their time to their families. Marriages are often arranged, and the family carefully weighs suitors. The entire family will share its voice, and the bride's relationship with the groom's family is very important (Mourad & Carolan, 2010). Once married, women rarely work outside the home. Even when they do, they defer to their husband or family for major decisions (Al-Krenawi et al., 2006).

Arab women also bear the added stress of protecting the family honor. Sexual activity prior to marriage could result in beatings or death. Because of this, it is common for virgins to avoid using tampons and douches or visiting a gynecologist. Anything that could affect the hymen is avoided (Kridli &

Libbus, 2001). The process is still important in the United States and Europe. Women planning to marry traditional Muslims will pay $4,000 to have their hymen restored. One woman said, "Right now, virginity is more important to me than life" (Sciolino & Mekhennet, 2008).

When images of women wearing dark clothing and head scarves pop onto television sets, many people assume the culture is antifeminist (Ali et al., 2008). Despite what appears like a restrictive and controlling religion, American women are joining Islam in record numbers. It is now the fastest-growing religion the United States (Maslim & Bjorck, 2009).

Many female American Muslims view themselves as feminists (Ali et al., 2008). This belief stems from other ideological beliefs within Islam. For example, Islamic women believe it is their duty to support their Islamic sisters. This sisterhood creates a unity that wards against abuses. These examples should not imply a disregard for ideology. The number one reason why women join Islam is because they believe in the religion's values (Maslim & Bjorck, 2009). But women in Maslim and Bjorck's study also said they became Muslims because it provided them with a sense of identity, it matched their views on gender roles, and it provided a sense of independence from family and secular culture.

Despite the positive family aspects of Arab and Islamic culture, there are serious problems too. Although the control over women emphasizes protection and encouragement, it has also led to domestic violence, polygamy, and genital mutilations. Given the authoritative role the family plays, when abuses occur, women often remain silent. Even when rape occurs, some women will preserve their own and their family's honor rather than announce that they are no longer virgins. When cases are brought to court, the court will often refer judgment back to the family or further victimize the female for her role in the process (Al-Krenawi et al., 2006).

Such cases are beginning to appear in the West, too. Muhammad Parvez (a Pakistani native who lived with his family in Toronto) experienced difficulty keeping his youngest daughter (Aqsa) under the house rules. Conflicts started when Aqsa stopped wearing the *hijab*. Her father ultimately tolerated her urban-style jeans and T-shirts—at least to school—but Aqsa wanted more. She started spending time with non-Arab girlfriends at the mall. When her father forbad all contact, she ran away to a shelter. When she returned, her father and brother murdered her as she slept (Mitchell & Javed, 2010).

Violence is not unique to men. Arab women also view physical discipline as appropriate. Khoury-Kassabri (2010) studied Jewish and Arab mothers to find similarities and differences in parenting styles. Although all the mothers approved of preventative, nonpunitive actions, 15% approved of mild physical punishments (e.g., spanking, slapping, or smacking), and 10% approved of physical discipline with an object (e.g., a paddle, hairbrush, or belt). Mothers who did not finish high school or were from Arab descent were more likely to approve of corporal punishment and psychological aggression.

Education plays a significant role in Middle Eastern communities. Arab and Islamic families tend to disapprove of secular education. Jewish families tend to endorse it, but demographics change when people immigrate to the United States.

EDUCATION

As discussed earlier, a group of African American and Latino high school students laughed and cheered as they watched Jews being tortured in Steven Spielberg's epic masterpiece, *Schindler's List*. Why do you think this reaction occurred? Over the years, Jews have suffered prejudice because people believed they (Simon & Schaler, 2007):

1. Caused all misfortunes (panapathogens)
2. Possess too much wealth and power (greedy, capitalist)
3. Claimed supremacy over others (arrogant, "chosen")
4. Killed Jesus (murderers of Christianity)
5. Were different or inferior (weak)

Views like these have long permeated many cultures. They are not on the rise in the United States, but they are rising in Belgium, France, Germany, Great Britain, and the Netherlands. Those countries are also showing increases in verbal and physical attacks on Jews (Simon & Schaler, 2007).

Prejudice also plays a direct role in education. Immigrants often must prove their educational equivalency to U.S. training. This may require exams, completing an internship, or adding coursework (Sinacore, Mikhail, Kassan & Lerner, 2009). This process may appear discriminatory to new arrivals, and in some cases, discrimination may play a role in how pervious education is perceived.

There is also an odd dichotomy regarding Arab Americans education. The literacy rate in Arab countries is about 19% lower than it is for most industrialized countries, and only two-thirds of the Arabs are illiterate. However, the United States attracts the best and brightest. About 40% of Arab Americans have bachelor's degrees, and 17% have postgraduate degrees. This rate is nearly twice the national average (Dwairy, 2006).

Even when Arabs value education, the process is different for women. Women are expected to defer to male decision making. As women become more educated, they often voluntarily ask their brothers, fathers, or other men more often advice (Dwairy, 2006). The men may also take a role in the educational process. For example, one woman—taking professional health classes—found her husband coming to class on a regular basis. The husband routinely asked the teacher questions about his wife's grades, her demeanor, and her future internship. This process frustrated the European American teacher, who could only respond with comments like, "Federal guidelines prohibit me from discussing another student's files."

The student herself struggled in the course, and she would routinely ask classmates for help. Her request often sounded more like a demand, as if she believed the more advanced students owed it to her to help. Her communal identity did not blend well with the individualism of the American educational system. Such a noncompetitive, communal approach is common for both Jewish and Arab students. Rather than compete to be first or gain the teacher's attention, they strive to master the material and expect those around them to help (Zedan, 2010).

SOCIOECONOMICS

Arab and Muslim countries tend to have higher unemployment rates and higher poverty rates than European countries. Prejudice also plays a role in jobs. Arab men often find it difficult to find employment (Abu-Baker, 2006). This often leads to Arab women seeking incomes—often through public assistance. This does not imply that Arab women are less likely to face discrimination. Their *hijab*, or headscarves, draw attention to their "differences" and may evoke negative reactions (Carolan et al., 2000).

Despite these limitations, Arab immigrants have a higher average wage than that of the average American (Dwairy, 2006). They are also likely to volunteer their time to help the community. Groups like Women for Women's Health (WWH) encourage Jewish and Arab women to promote health activities in their communities. In one study, both groups of women derived self-satisfaction, mastered new skills, improved their social support network, and improved solidarity with the needy. Arab volunteers also worked on improving women's status by creating a legitimate space for women (Daoud et al., 2010).

SPIRITUALITY AND RELIGION

One Arab client told me, "I am so tired of people asking me if I'm Mexican or Chinese." Often, European Americans cluster Arab individuals into categories they understand. If they have not interacted with Arabs, Persians, Jews, or Egyptians, they lack any framework for understanding. Often, the cultural differences in religion alone are difficult for Westerners to fully understand or appreciate. Complicating matters, Judeo-Christianity and Islam share numerous constructs and ideas.

Christianity and Islam base their early history on Jewish beliefs. Both religions also have a history of condemning Jews for not accepting the "truth" of later prophets. Table 8.1 provides a good introduction to the differences between Islam and Christianity. It should also demonstrate how Jewish ideas may be reinterpreted very differently.

The key differences between Islamic and Christian beliefs involve the role and divinity of Jesus. Muslims believe Jesus was a great prophet and a person worthy of homage, but they do not view Jesus as God or the son of God. (Muslims add the phrase "peace be upon him"[2] after they say the name "Jesus" or "Muhammad".) Muslims respect and revere Jesus and await his Second Coming. He is viewed as one of God's greatest messengers to mankind, but Muslims believe his message was limited and that he did not rise from the dead. Islam is so adamant about these points that Muslims view people holding contrary views as heretics and blasphemers. For the Muslim, worshipping Jesus is equivalent to polytheism and is therefore anathema.

---

[2] When greeting a fellow Muslim, it is customary to say, "As-salamo 'alaikum" (Peace be upon you!). The response to this greeting is, "Wa 'alai-komus-salaam" (And upon you be peace!).

TABLE **8.1**
Comparison of Islamic and Christian Beliefs

	Islam (means submission or peace)	Christianity (Christian means "Disciple of Jesus Christ"—literally, "Christ one")
Other prophets	God's messengers are evidenced through a chain of prophets, starting with Adam and including Noah, Abraham, Ishmael, Isaac, Jacob, Joseph, Moses, Aaron, David, Solomon, Elias, Jonah, John the Baptist, and Jesus, peace be upon them. But God's final message was revealed to the Prophet Muhammad (pbuh)[3] through Gabriel.	The Jewish prophets foretold the coming of Jesus. The apostles spread Jesus' message to the rest of the world.
Beliefs about Jesus	• Jesus (pbuh) was born human (iii, 45:47; xix, 22–33) and remained sinless (iii, 59).	• Jesus was born human (Matthew 1:23) and remained sinless (Romans 5:14).
	• Jesus (pbuh) was a righteous prophet (vi, 85).	• Jesus was a righteous prophet and high priest of the faith (Hebrews 3:1).
	• Jesus (pbuh) is not the son of God (ix, 30). Allah is one. He has no children. There is no other God like him.	• Jesus is the only son of the Supreme God, born of Mary, begotten by the Holy Spirit (the power and presence of God). He descended from Heaven, became human, and died for all people to demonstrate God's love for humanity.
	• He was not crucified (iv, 157). The Jews did not crucify him, but it was made to appear so. They actually crucified Judas while believing it to be Jesus (pbuh) (Sura 4, verses 157 and 158).	• Jesus was crucified, killed, and buried (Matthew 27, Mark 15, Luke 23, Acts 2:36).
		• *Resurrected from the dead*
	• Jesus (pbuh) will descend at the end of time and judge all people with justice, according to the Law of our Prophet Muhammad (pbuh) (an-Nisa, 4:159).	• Jesus will come down from Heaven, bring believers with him into the clouds, raise the dead, and judge the wicked (1 Thessalonians 4:16).
The paraclete	Jesus' mission was to be completed by another (n.1861 to xiii, 38). He prophesized the coming of Muhammad (pbuh) (the paracletos) (Sura lxi, 6).	In the book of Luke 24: 47–49, Jesus tells his disciples to wait in Jerusalem until he sent the Paraclete (often translated as counselor or advocate). Christians regard the paraclete as "the Holy Spirit" (Acts 1:8), the third person of the Trinitarian Godhead.
Trinity	There is no Trinity. There is only one God, Allah, and the prophets (Sura v,19,75).	The early church "father" Tertullian (145–220 A.D.) was the first to use the word "Trinity" in reference to God. It was Bishop Augustine of Hippo ("St. Augustine") who fully developed the idea in his

(*continues*)

TABLE **8.1**

Comparison of Islamic and Christian Beliefs (*Continued*)

	Islam (means submission or peace)	Christianity (Christian means "Disciple of Jesus Christ"—literally, "Christ one")
		book De Trinitate (400 A.D.). It was established as "official" teaching at the Councils of Nicea (325 A.D.) and Constantinople (381 A.D.). There are few Biblical passages referring to the Trinity (e.g., 1 John 5:7^4, Matthew 28:19; John 1:1).
Scriptures	Moses' "Torah" David's "Zaboor" (Psalms) Jesus' "Injeel" (Gospel) Muhammad's Qur'an Muslims are told that the previous scriptures were tampered with by mankind and the Bible should only be accepted insofar as it is confirmed by the Arabic version of the Qur'an.	The Bible, consisting of 66 Old Testament books in Hebrew and Aramaic and 29 New Testament books in Greek, were composed by numerous authors across many centuries under the guidance of the Holy Spirit and written in the dialect of the common people.
Sin and forgiveness	Every person is born free from sin. When a person reaches the age of maturity and, if he is mentally competent, he becomes accountable for all his deeds and intentions.	"For all have sinned and fallen short of the glory of God" (Romans 3:23). The grace of God and the gift of His Holy Spirit imbue humans with the ability to turn from their sinful nature and become holy.
Life after death	At the Resurrection, the righteous will be sent to the Garden of God, but they will not see God. The wicked will be sent to an eternal fire. Those who are especially righteous, such as martyrs, may enter the garden at death.	All will be resurrected. The righteous will rule with Jesus in God's eternal kingdom when the dwelling of God will be with men. Those who reject God's way will be sent to Hell.
Enemies	"Fight in the way of Allah against those who fight against you, but begin not hostilities. Lo! Allah loveth not aggressors. And slay them wherever ye find them" (2:190). "O ye who believe! Fight those of the disbelievers who are near you, and let them find harshness in you" (9:123).	"But I say unto you, love your enemies, bless them that curse you, do good to them that hate you, and pray for them which despitefully use you, and persecute you" (Matt. 5:4). "Jesus answered, My kingdom is not of this world: if my kingdom were of this world, then would my servants fight" (John 18:36).
Prayers	Five prayers [i.e., times of prayer]—the Almighty Allah made them obligatory. "When the call is heard for the prayer of the day of congregation, haste unto remembrance of Allah" (62:9).	"But thou, when thou prayest, enter into thy closet, and when thou hast shut thy door, pray to thy Father which is in secret; and thy Father which seeth in secret shall reward thee openly" (Matt. 6:6).
Modesty for women	"…they (believing women) should not display their beauty and ornaments except what (must ordinarily) appear thereof; that they should draw their veils	"In like manner also, that women adorn themselves in modest apparel, with shamefacedness and sobriety; not with broided hair, or gold, or pearls, or costly

(*continues*)

TABLE **8.1**
Comparison of Islamic and Christian Beliefs (*Continued*)

Islam (means submission or peace)	Christianity (Christian means "Disciple of Jesus Christ"—literally, "Christ one")
over their bosoms and not display their beauty except to their husbands, their fathers, their husbands' fathers, their sons, their husbands' sons, their brothers or their brothers' sons, or their sisters' sons, or their women ...or small children who have no sense of the shame of sex" (24:31[5]).	array" (1 Tim. 2:9). "But every woman that prayeth or prophesieth with her head uncovered dishonoureth her head: for that is even all one as if she were shaven" (1 Cor. 11:5).

[3]Western Muslims use the phrase "peace be upon him" whenever they utter or write the name of a prophet. This is especially important when using the names of Jesus or Muhammad (peace be upon them). However, the practice becomes cumbersome, so the acronym PBUH (pbuh) is often used. Please note that the practice is followed only in Islam. In Arabic, the phrase *salla Allah alaihi wa sallam* (S.A.W.) is the equivalent, but the expression is only used after Muhammad. Christians do not have such a custom. Jews remove a letter from G-d. When reading the holy name allowed, they will say "adonai" (meaning, my Lord).
[4]The earliest and most reliable Greek texts do not include this passage. It was likely inserted into the Christian text well after the second century.
[5]Neither of these passages actually prescribes head coverings. Only the Christian texts, which are not usually followed, offer such a command. The traditional head coverings found in conservative Islamic nations have more to do with culture than religion.

Instead, they argue, true followers should be following Muhammad, whose coming, they believe, was prophesized by Jesus.

Christians tend to emphasize an atonement theory (i.e., the concept that having faith in Jesus is sufficient for salvation), but Muslims view this belief with disdain. They argue that it overlooks the importance of conforming to God's laws, which are highly prized by Islam. They accept the idea that no one can enter Heaven by works alone, but they view obedience and action as key components. Muslims who are seeking to please Allah strive to follow these five pillars:

Shahadah: This Arabic word meaning "witness" refers to the declaration that there is no God but Allah and that Muhammad is the divine messenger. This declaration occurs often in prayer, in association with life cycle events, and in a person's conversion to Islam.

Salat: This Arabic term meaning "prayer" most often refers to the five statutory prayers required daily. Recited while facing toward Mecca, these prayers include cycles of postures called "rak'a," which vary depending on which prayer service is recited. There are special prayer times in the early morning, noon, mid-afternoon, sunset, and evening.

Sawm: This Arabic term refers to the fast during the month of Ramadan. Because the Muslims follow a lunar calendar, the month of fasting occurs in different seasons from year to year. The fast has historical references to Muhammad as well as personal and social implications.

Zakat: This term refers to the statutory tax required of every Muslim adult, although in non-Muslim countries, Zakat has become a matter of personal choice. Several Muslim observances are invalidated unless they are paid for by assets on which Zakat has been paid. Usually, a Zakat is 2.5% of one's annual savings, but there are complicated rules for calculating what is owed. A Zakat is 20% on such resources as oil or precious metals (i.e., gold and silver). You would pay 20% on what you produced in one year. There are also different Zakats. Zakat-ul-Fitr is for fasting Muslims to give food or money on behalf of fasting people. The food or money is equal to one day's meals for one person. The money is given to the poor (Fuqara), the needy (Masakin), and employees of the Zakah.

Hajj: This term refers to the obligatory pilgrimage to Mecca, which every Muslim must perform at least once in a lifetime. It consists of several actions that recall the life of Abraham, his wife Hagar, and their son Ishmael. The Hajj is a life-transforming experience for participants.

The commitment of Muslims to follow a holy life stands in marked contrast to the violence spawned by some Muslim extremists. The terrorist attacks on the World Trade Center and the Pentagon on September 11, 2001, introduced many Americans to a side of Islam that is not normative. Instead, some Americans began to think of all Muslims as terrorists. In a sense, anti-Islamic prejudice became an act of terror in itself. In the days immediately following the attack on America, a backlash against Muslims and Arab Americans occurred. Shots were fired at mosques; women in traditional Islamic garments were shunned; a Molotov cocktail was thrown at an Arab American community center; and windows were shattered in many homes. But the greatest assault may simply be the tacit change in American views of Muslims. Sincere followers of Islam had to endure bomb threats, graffiti, chat room abuse, being spat upon, or simply receiving sideways glances when carrying out their daily chores. The end of the prejudice and terrorism is hard to predict, but it is clear that the battle has been costly for both sides.

PHYSICAL AND MENTAL HEALTH

Middle Eastern views of health are closely tied to spirituality. For example, the Arabic term for mental illness (insanity) stems from the noun *jinn* (demon) (Dwairy, 2006). Mental illness is thought to come over an individual, possessing them much the same way some religions think of demons taking over the body. This poses some difficulties for counselors because some individuals may believe living a sin-free life will resolve the metal health concerns. This means little effort is directed toward working on the self.

PHYSICAL HEALTH

The somatization issues found in Asian cultures are also common for Arab cultures. Although some Arab cultures may attribute mental health problems to human or supernatural causes, others may see it as having physical origins. Similarly, they may not view physical causes biomedically but instead see such problems as back pain, illness, and other issues (Al-Krenawi et al., 2006).

There are also direct physical concerns with Arab culture, especially for women. Obesity has become a significant problem in the Middle East as well as the United States. Food in Arab culture is a means of social communication. Inviting someone over for a meal is an important bonding experience (Dwairy, 2006). Adding to the problem are obstacles for exercising. For many Muslims, women exercising in public would be considered vulgar, and women are not permitted to have contact with men, which limits their options. When they can find female walking partners, their chances of fighting obesity improve markedly (Ali, Baynouna & Bernsen, 2010). In Arab American children, the greatest threat involving physical exercise is limited self-efficacy (Martin, McCaughtry & Shen, 2008). When Arab children believe they will not be good at sports or other physical activities, they tend to avoid them.

MENTAL HEALTH

Just as physical health is tied to attitudes and beliefs, so is mental health. In the Arab world, seeing a physician is acceptable under certain conditions, but even then, gender issues play a role (e.g., having a gender-matched doctor). But for both men and women, there are stigma attached to mental health services. Arabs are more likely to see a physician than a psychologist for depression because they see the problems rooted in physical causes over mental ones. Similarly, seeing a mental health counselor may be interpreted by the individual and his or her family as weakness or disrespect for the family (Al-Krenawi et al., 2006).

Arab women face even greater stigmatization for seeing counselors or psychologists. Requesting help could indicate marital instability or dissatisfaction with her husband. In Arab societies, if a woman sought counseling, her husband could use this act as leverage for obtaining another wife. Even beyond these practical concerns, Islamic women are the guardians of family honor. Sharing personal information with someone outside the family could be viewed as endangering the family or her own status (Mourad & Carolan, 2010).

Many of the conflicts with secular mental health and Arab/Persian cultures stem from Islamic ideology and traditions. This raises the question as to whether religiosity plays a facilitative role for Arabs. The literature in this topic emphasizes Judeo-Christian religions. In those cases, most studies find a positive relationship between religiosity and mental health (Koenig & Vaillant, 2009). For Muslims, the effect may be less clear. At this point, there is not enough information to determine whether the religion has a positive or negative impact on psychopathology (Al-Krenawi et al., 2006).

The connection between Islam and mental health is complicated. Obsessive compulsive disorders may look culturally normative if the obsessions are cleansing related. There are a number of cleansing rituals in Islam. These involve frequent washing of hands and face. Obsessive thoughts are also part of the religion. For example, *weswas* involves ruminating on bad thoughts implanted by evil spirits. This may look delusional, but it is common within Islamic circles. A religious healer would be the primary intervention (Dwairy, 2006).

Regardless of how the religion affects mental health, we do know some ways Arabs are likely to evidence mental health concerns. Dwairy (2006) provides an excellent overview of common diagnoses for Arab Americans. He explains how somatoform, anxiety, and mood disorders are all shaped by Middle Eastern culture. Given the holistic mind-body beliefs of many Arab/ Muslim countries, the somatic complaints are often the only ones expressed. Depression is most often manifested by sleeping problems, weight change, thoughts of death, muscle tension, or other physical symptoms. Some Arab dialects even lack a word for depression because affective symptoms always arise within some physical concern.

Depression may appear differently within Arab, Egyptian, and Persian cultures because they operate from a communal worldview rather than an individualistic one. European culture emphasizes personal gain. When others are considered, self-sacrifice may extend no further than to family members. Middle Eastern cultures tend to emphasize the collective whole, which also limits the role of negative effect. Dwairy (2006) points out how Palestinian culture sometimes forbids families to openly grieve the death of martyred children. In a way, to appear sad is to show disrespect for your country and Allah.

INDIVIDUAL AND GROUP INTERVENTIONS

Abudabbeh (2005) recommends therapists abandon traditional approaches when working with Arab families. Instead, counselors should use didactic, structured therapies (no insight-oriented approaches). Counselors will also need to take a more directive role. For example, calling clients after no-shows may help build rapport. Counselors may also need to accept gifts or invitations to the Arab family's home. Therapy timelines will also require flexibility, as they may arrive early or late. Given the patriarchal nature of the families, it may also be important to call family members during therapy, creating an extended family therapy session.

At least one study has argued that the unmet mental health needs of Arabs are nearly twice as high as those of Jewish or mixed identities (Mansbach-Kleinfeld et al., 2010). But such broad generalizations are difficult to take as absolutes. Arab societies are diverse and based on ethnic, linguistic, familial, tribal, regional, socioeconomic, and national identities (Al-Krenawi et al., 2004). However, there are things to keep in mind when working with Arab Americans. They are likely to demonstrate some resistance in the early stages of therapy, and direct probes regarding this matter may not be received well until a stronger therapeutic alliance has been built (Mourad & Carolan, 2010).

Such recommendations may appear surprising, especially considering the close ties Judaism has with secular mental health. It is no coincidence that psychoanalysis was created within the Jewish culture. Langman (1997) argued that the influence of Jewish culture on the origin and development of psychotherapy was profound and unique. Jewish mysticism appears to have influenced psychoanalysis and Gestalt psychology. Both theories contrast sharply with the behavioral psychology of European theorists. They are also poor fits for Arab clients.

Despite the similarities between Arab and Jewish cultures, the differences can confound therapeutic interventions. In *Face to Face*, Suchet (2010) describes the process of working with a Lebanese woman (Ara). Suchet is a Jewish psychoanalyst, and Ara has identified with the Palestinian cause. The tension of the Israeli-Palestinian conflict could not be avoided in their work together. Suchet described himself and his client as being in the "midst of ghosts." History intersected and interwove around them. It bound them together and pushed them apart. Their personal histories were also the histories of nations. In the drama of this encounter, they needed to carve out a new space between themselves and between Palestinians and Jews. But this is the nature of all types of counseling: empathizing with others and recognizing the legitimacy of personal and family suffering.

Arabs tend to view confrontational therapies (like Gestalt) as uncomfortable or offensive. They also tend to view themselves in terms of their personal and cultural history, which makes humanistic, personal approaches to therapy also inappropriate. Staying in the here-and-now may feel awkward and self-indulgent. When working with people from a collectivist cultural viewpoint, self-actualization makes little sense. Instead, Arabs and Muslims will benefit most from a behavioral approach, cognitive therapy based on cultural norms and values, or a narrative approach emphasizing proverbs, metaphors, and physical functioning (Dwairy, 2006).

ADVOCACY AND SOCIAL JUSTICE

Social justice will look different for Arabs, Persians, and Jews. Anti-Semitism has persisted throughout European cultures, and it continues to plague much of the world. The United States needs to safeguard against these impulses and find ways to support Israeli and Jewish immigrants and citizens.

For Arabs and Persians, social justice stems from improving the understanding of Islam and identifying ways to support and encourage women. Although Muslim women tend to view themselves as liberated, the internal and submissive role they play within the home structure runs contrary to the dominant culture's expectations. Depending on the level of acculturation, conflicts may arise between traditional roles and American culture. These conflicts may also spill into counseling environments (Mourad & Carolan, 2010). In addition to concerns about fitting in, women may experience tension in simply attending counseling sessions. Women often lack control of their finances, and their husbands may view psychotherapy as an unnecessary expense (Nobles & Sciarra, 2000). This is even more likely if the wife has concerns about the family and intends to disclose negative feelings about her community. Such disclosures would be considered shameful and damaging (Mourad & Carolan, 2010).

Other advocacy issues involve marital and sexual counseling. Such issues are taboo for many Islamic sects, but things are changing. The Islamic leadership has approved an online sex shop called El Asira (Sandels, 2010). This shop lacks any graphic references, and it is segregated for men and women. But its intent is clearly to enhance love making by selling massage oils, aphrodisiacs, and lingerie. Overall, sex may be the most difficult topic to broach with Islamic women. The following case illustrates one such example.

Inas's Story (A Client's Viewpoint)

(27-year-old Iraqi female)

I went to counseling because my girlfriend, Latifah, recommended my counselor. She added that speaking to Nancy would not shame my family—that counseling would be discrete and confidential. I had my doubts.

During the first session, I told Nancy about my husband's recent actions. Nu'man, my husband, had become very jealous after we moved to America. He did not like the freedoms here—the seductive clothing and ways women interacted with men. Although I was trained as a nurse, he wanted me to stay at home. He thought this would help me adjust to the new culture. I had a few friends from the Mosque, and I met Latifah at the Friday Prayer at the Islamic Center. But I felt very much alone.

After a few months, Nu'man started coming home late. He would miss dinner, saying the demands at the office had become overwhelming. I could live with this, but he also started acting differently in the bedroom.

Nancy was patient for me to tell her about my "real" concern. It took four sessions before I could tell her. You see, Nu'man had never been a gentle man, but he had always respected my body. As he became busier, he became angrier. The angrier he became, the more he used force.

I am a strong woman, and I knew I could handle whatever happened. I also knew he loved me and would not want to hurt me. But still, I felt so diminished around him. What used to feel like a bond became a burden. This is when I took up painting. I bought several canvasses and learned how to paint with oils. I would work late into the night—often until after Nu'man had gone to bed. This was my protection. It provided an escape.

I told Nu'man my passion would only last a few weeks. I asked him to forgive me for removing myself from his presence in order to pursue my new hobby. He tolerated this so far, but I can tell he has grown frustrated.

Nancy provided me with new ways to talk with him. She saved my marriage and my sense of self.

Nancy's Story (A Counselor's Viewpoint)

(52-year-old European American female)

Growing up, my best friend (Latifah) was Muslim. Years later, this friend recommended Inas to talk with me. I wish I could say that my early relationship had prepared me to work with Inas; I only knew enough to be very cautious. Even [in] this story, I had to change all references to people and places to protect her identity.

(continues)

Nancy's Story (A Counselor's Viewpoint) *(continued)*

During the intake, I could tell Inas was holding back. She talked about her parents, in-laws, friends, and even her childlessness (which is one of the most painful topics for a Muslim woman to address). But she kept her sex life private.

Even in her written story here, she never used the term "sex," but sex was her presenting problem.

Nu'man started raping her when he came home late. He grabbed her arm, pulled her into the bedroom, tore off her clothes, and had his way with her. The first time it happened, Inas was shocked and stunned. She felt dirty and vulnerable. The man who was supposed to protect her had become her assailant.

I asked if she considered this "rape," and her response was hard for me to grasp.

"Oh, no," Inas replied. "He never touched me before he was my husband."

She did not share the Western idea of rape being sex forced against a person's will. In her mind, rape only arose between unmarried couples.

The first day she told me about the forced sex, I just listened. We had grown close by then. I knew she wanted my responses thought out, not simply empathetic and reactionary. Afterward, I looked up what the Qur'an said about marriage.

I was a little shocked to read how Muhammad courted, fondled, and married a child (Aisha). He would have sex with all nine wives in one night. He fondled his wives during menses (although he would not sleep with them during this time). There is even a harsh statement in the Qur'an (2:223) saying, "Your women are a tilth [land ready for cultivation] for you so go to your tilth as ye will...."

I realized I was over my head with the religious issues, so I took a different tact. During our next session, I asked her to hold out one hand, palm up. "Now, if your other hand were to show love to the one outstretched, how would it do it?"

She looked confused, but I waited. Eventually, she softly caressed her open hand, gliding three fingers against her palm.

We discuss how Muhammad (pbuh) would touch Aisha. Would he touch her gently or harshly? Would Aisha encourage certain types of touch or simply respond? This was as much religion as we could bring into the session because of my lack of knowledge, but it was enough to empower her.

For homework, she was asked to have her husband "touch her hand with love." I hoped the subtle message would be enough to help him understand the need for more gentle touch. It was. The next session, Inas returned glowing. She explained how their "time together" improved. We met for three more sessions, largely continuing an emphasis on communication and self-worth, and then mutually terminated. We stayed in touch, and she told me she continued counseling with the Islamic Center. They were able to address the religious aspects that I couldn't.

QUESTIONS TO CONSIDER

1. It is no coincidence that psychoanalysis was created within the Jewish culture. Langman (1997) argued that the influence of Jewish culture on the origin and development of psychotherapy was profound and unique. What makes psychoanalysis more Jewish than European?

2. As discussed in this chapter, a group of minority high school students in California laughed and cheered as they watched Jews being tortured in Steven Spielberg's epic masterpiece, *Schindler's List*. Why do you think this reaction occurred? What could be done to foster a greater sense of compassion toward the suffering of other oppressed groups?

3. After the bombing of the World Trade Center, violence against Arabs and Muslims increased. How would you work with someone who believed "Muslims deserve what comes to them"? Does your view of social justice require you to intervene in such cases?

4. Middle Eastern identity is strongly rooted in religion. How would you work with someone who no longer "believed" in the religion and now felt ethnically displaced?

5. If you were working with a Hasidic Jew, what precautions would you take the help him feel safe and respected?

6. Arab women learn to defer authority to husbands and fathers. How would you work with a female CEO who felt "unfeminine" and "disloyal" because she runs her own life?

7. If an Arab family believed physical discipline (including facial slapping) was necessary to correct a wayward daughter, how would you counsel them?

8. How would you work with an Arab male who was having conflicts with his Christian coworker? He is annoyed by the daily interjections of religion into their conversations. His coworker continually discusses Jesus and adds how divinity is "the only logical way to think about Jesus."

9. What intervention would you offer to a woman who believed she was possessed by an evil spirit after having an affair? Since the one-night stand, she has felt depressed and cannot sleep. She also feels distracted and believes she is "going crazy."

10. An Arab male washes his hands 10–30 times a day. His skin has become rough and pink, as the epidermis is warn away and chafed. He does not view the skin irritation as a problem and believes the cleanings are a necessary part of his religion. How would you address this with him?

11. If you were designing an intervention for a group of Arab women, what theoretical basis would you use? How would you structure the group?

INTERVENTION EXERCISES

Counseling and Therapy: Benjamin's (age 23) family emigrated from Israel three years ago. Despite his appreciation for America and the opportunity to complete a postgraduate degree, he misses his homeland. The synagogue here feels "too American," and he does not appreciate the way American culture lacks the openness and community elements so common in Israel. How would you help him adapt?

School Psychology: Gabir (an Iraqi male, age 10) was sent for assessment regarding his "inability to pay attention." During the assessment, you noticed he turns his head from side to side. He explained how it is often difficult for him to hear after a bomb exploded near him. He said he had his hearing tested in Iraq, but the doctors did not believe he had significant hearing loss. What might be happening with him? What would you investigate next?

School Counseling: Hala (17-year-old female from Saudi Arabia) came to America two years ago. Since then, she has gained permission to participate in a number of school activities, including the debate club and student government. This year, her senior year, she wants to attend the prom. She selected an outfit with long gloves and would wear her *Hijaab*. Her parents said "No." Now she is considering running away and wants your advice. How would you handle the situation?

Social Work: Mounia (a 78-year-old female from Saudi Arabia) came to the United States 10 years ago. Her son died in a car accident last year, leaving Mounia alone. She is also experiencing the onset of Alzheimer's and has difficulty finding her home. She believes she can still function well enough to care for herself, but she is afraid she will not be able to live independently for long. How would you help her? What concerns might you have regarding placement given her strong Muslim identity?

CHAPTER 9

Mixed Cultural Identities

With about 1.2 million immigrants arriving annually in Canada and the United States, immigration consistently reshapes North American culture (Stroink & Lalonde, 2009). These individuals become bicultural. They hold on to their native culture as they integrate into an American or Canadian identity. The process may even be harder for second-generation individuals, who may feel equally pulled toward their parents' culture and the culture of their peers. Such issues as appropriate levels of aggression, sexual openness, and centrality of sports and education may conflict with values from other cultures (Stroink & Lalonde, 2009). Bicultural children often feel forced to compromise their values to meet the dominant society's expectations. They can sometimes move through these worlds without substantial conflict, but this requires flexibility and work (Ryder, Alden & Paulhus, 2000). Following LaFromboise et al. (1993), Wei (2010) argued that bicultural competence can guard against depression. When people are socially grounded in and having cultural knowledge of both cultures, they have the social support they need to belong in both cultures and they understand what is expected of them. This will include maintaining a positive attitude toward both groups, a belief that functioning within both cultures is possible, effectively communicating in both cultures, and behaving appropriately within both cultures.

Studying diversity presents a number of challenges for clinicians and students. One of the greatest potential pitfalls involves trying to pigeonhole a person into only one or two of the categories described in this text. Many people belong to several groups and are likely to resent being limited to one classification. Even using such terms as *bicultural* or *biracial* imply that there are "pure" cultural groups (Samuels, 2010). However, despite the problems with the terms, there are people who blend cultural groups more than others. Consider the ethnic origins of golfing legend Tiger Woods.

In 1997, pro golfer Fuzzy Zoeller uttered an offhand remark that was to change his life. Tiger Woods, an emerging golf champion, had recently won the Masters golf tournament, one of the most prestigious competitions in the world of sports. Zoeller, commenting on the winners' privilege of selecting the ceremonial dinner, quipped that Woods would be likely to choose fried chicken and collard greens. The comment created a national debate about prejudice and discrimination, but there was another aspect to the incident that was virtually untouched by the media.

The comments offered by Zoeller were undoubtedly insensitive and demonstrated a lack of understanding concerning African Americans, but in this case, the victim of the slur was not predominantly African American. Tiger's father is half African American, a quarter Chinese, and a quarter Native American, and his mother is half Thai, a quarter Chinese, and a quarter white (Verdi, 1997). Ethnically, Tiger Woods is more Asian than black. Given this information, does it seem surprising that no one made comments about Woods serving sushi? (By the way, referring to sushi would still have been inappropriate because it is a Japanese dish, not Chinese or Thai.) The reasons are likely twofold: (1) Because of his skin tone, Woods looks more African American than Asian, and (2) Asians are less likely than African Americans to be chastised for their success in predominantly white activities.

As illustrated by the Woods example, multiple ethnicities may be present within a single individual. Many times, such a person may be pressured to identify with a single ethnic background rather than embracing more than one cultural heritage. Multiple minority status may also combine ethnic and sexual minorities, and it can encompass conditions that cross all ethnic and sexual boundaries, such as disability and age.

Cultural competency includes respecting the unique strengths and challenges of each individual. Instead of viewing people in stereotypical ways, we need to acknowledge the various factors that contribute to who they are.

PEOPLE WITH MIXED CULTURAL ORIGINS

Bicultural individuals have long had difficulty knowing where they belong. Should they identify with one part of their heritage and disregard the other? How do they determine their racial identity? These are difficult issues and ones the United States government has only recently addressed. For many years, the state of Virginia had a law on its books (the Virginia Racial Integrity Act) that made it a felony for a white person to marry a colored person. The punishment for intermarriage was at least one and not more than five years in prison. A case was brought to the Supreme Court in 1967 regarding this statute, and Chief Justice Earl Warren delivered the opinion of the court. For the first time, the prohibition against interracial marriage was lifted as the court determined that preventing marriages between persons solely on the basis of racial classifications violated the equal protection and due process clauses of the Fourteenth Amendment.

Changes in immigration policies have also increased the number of bicultural Americans. For example, the Asian American population was quite small prior to amendments to U.S. immigration laws in 1965. Today, intermarriage rates among Asians and non-Asians are quite high, especially among native-born Asian Americans (Lee and Fernandez, 1998). For example, in Maryland, about 20% of Asian children were identified as multiracial in the 2000 census, compared with only 8% of Asians aged 18 and over.

Since the Supreme Court struck down the last state law forbidding interracial marriages in 1967, such unions have tripled, and the birth rate among interracial couples has more than doubled. The 1990 census found that nearly 2 million children under 18 were identified as "of a different race than one or both of their parents" (Beech, 1999). The numbers grew considerably in 2000, with about 4.0% of children identified as multiracial, compared with 1.9% of adults (Annie E. Casey Foundation, 2001). Most European Americans probably have yet to notice the changing demographics because society is still relatively segregated. About 30% of whites live in cities, but they typically live in urban neighborhoods that are about 72% white. More than 60% of blacks live in cities. The typical black city dweller lives in a neighborhood that has about 75% minority residents and in which three out of five residents are black (Schmitt, 2001).

American culture is only now beginning to see the valuable roles bicultural people play. As more multicultural teams develop in various settings, bicultural employees can intervene between two cultures (Hong, 2010). These employs operate with higher levels of *cultural metacognition*, which is the ability to monitor and regulate thoughts and feelings about a specific cultural event and generalize it into broader principles (Thomas et al., 2008). Bicultural individuals can assist new immigrants, multicultural teams, and add a cultural bridge to divergent groups.

Possibly the most important immerging bicultural group involves multicultural adoptions. This practice has been hotly debated, with vocal advocates on both sides. We introduced this topic in the Asian American chapter, but the issue applies to many other groups.

In October 1994, the Multiethnic Placement Act was passed in the U.S. Senate. The law prohibited public agencies from considering race in the placement of children with adoptive families, but it did not end the debate. The National Association of Black Social Workers (NABSW) strongly opposes the adoption of black children by white families, and they have argued that placement agencies should use their discretion of acting in the "child's best interests" to oppose transracial adoption. The NABSW's position is so strong that it may be associated with some African American children growing up in foster care rather than going into adoptive placement. This outcome can be extremely harmful because the longer a minority child remains in foster care, the less likely the child is to make a healthy adjustment into an adoptive family (George, 1996). Even without organizations such as the NABSW arguing against transracial adoptions, African American children are less likely to be adopted early in life (Kim, Zrull, Davenport & Weaver, 1992).

Most of the time, when European American parents adopt African American children, the children fare well in educational attainment, peer relationships, self-esteem, and social competencies (Rushton & Minnis, 1997). In response to these findings, the Multiethnic Placement Act was amended in 1996 to become the Removal of Barriers to Interethnic Adoption Act. The 1996 law specifically prohibits delaying or denying the placement of a child for adoption or foster care on the basis of race, color, or national origin of the foster or adoptive parents or of the child involved. Since then, children of mixed black-white heritage have become the most adopted children in the United States and the United Kingdom (Samuels, 2010).

Issues of transcultural adoption are becoming even more important as growing numbers of American couples strive to adopt children from other countries. According to U.S. Department of State data, the number of children adopted from other countries has grown substantially over the past three decades—from about 5,000 in 1975 to nearly 23,000 in 2004 (U.S. Department of State, 2009). The most recent data shows a slight dip, with Americans now adopting 11,000 children from overseas (Jacobs, 2010).

In recent years, nearly half the children adopted from other countries have come from the People's Republic of China or Russia. The diversity of internationally adopted children has compounded the difficulty of compiling a list of competencies for parents who choose transcultural adoption. Currently, there is no consensus regarding the attitudes, skills, and knowledge needed to enhance adoptive parents' cultural competence. However, there are some important starting points that all transcultural adoptive parents should address:

- Understand the history of oppression for members of your child's ethnic group (Greene, Watkins, McNutt & Lopez, 1998), and be open to understanding racism. This includes learning about the benefits that European Americans experience daily. For example, most European Americans generally expect protection rather than harassment from police. Minority children—even if they live in a white household—are less likely to receive such benefits.
- Recognize your cultural biases/traditions and anticipate where these might conflict with the child's ethnic background (Vonk, 2001).
- Realize that gaining cultural competency is a long-term process and will require involvement in groups outside the dominant culture. Spend time in organizations associated with your child's ethnic background. Learn the culture by making friends.
- Celebrate the importance of an ethnic identity (McRoy, 1994), and integrate this with your family's developing cultural identities (e.g., religious or, adopted ethnicity).
- Find ethnic role models for your child. This is often difficult for parents because they want to be the primary teachers for their children. However, white parents cannot teach their children to be black. Their children will need guidance from people who share their ethnicity (Huh, 1997).

In identifying effective transcultural adoptions, Samuels (2010) notes several advantageous outcomes. Acculturation is the key. If the child can see herself as black and still identify with the cultural of her European American family, she will likely be more successful than if she ignored her biological heritage. The adopting family should also examine their prejudices and their understanding of privilege. These are often difficult to achieve. Rene summed this challenge well:

> I grew up [with] my parents letting me know ... I was black. Trying to do things ... dolls, books, anything to expose me to ... what their idea of my culture was. But still not really having any understanding ... culturally of what it MEANS to be African American, of mixed race ... I was just searching, seeking out ... I was looking for not just a friend, but almost like ... kinship with someone. Someone ... more like me. And ... maybe just being ... around this person I could get some sense of who I am. (Samuels, 2010, p. 32)

Rene's concern and disassociation with her two cultures is common for many bicultural individuals. They often search for ways to display their ethnic identity. Buying cultural artwork is a common process for bicultural individuals (Zolfagharian, 2010). It is often common for friends of bicultural people to make comments like, "Oh, I forgot you were black!" (Samuels, 2010).

In some cases, identifying with a single ethnicity may be difficult for people from diverse heritages. I tend to compare such a situation to a tree that has been grafted for several generations with other varieties. Earlier generations are relatively simple to identify, but the subsequent intermixing makes identification more complex. For humans—who thankfully have greater self-awareness than trees—the process of identification becomes an internal activity. We can choose to highlight the elements of our history that are most dear to us, but we should not reject any of the other elements. Each component is part of our history and our identity.

GEOGRAPHY AND BICULTURALISM

Even when people share similar ethnic heritages, their cultural identities may be linked to geographical areas. Wilson and Ferris (1989) helped edit an encyclopedia of Southern culture. The book helped familiarize readers with such cultural elements as fried chicken, mint juleps, the *Dukes of Hazzard*, *Foxfire*, the magazine *Southern Living*, the Lost Cause Myth, the Kentucky Derby, snake handlers, the Texas Rangers, Indians, the Civil War, industrialization, and country music. One of the interesting elements of the book, especially as we are discussing hidden minorities, is the authors' assertion that "Southern" culture can include people who live in northern states. The authors argue that there are Southern outposts in Midwestern and middle-Atlantic border states and even in the southern pockets of Chicago. Ultimately, being Southern has more to do with a state of mind than a geographical boundary. The same can also be said for members of other invisible minorities.

SEXUALITY AND BICULTURALISM

Multiracial ethnicity can pose unique challenges to an individual's identity, but other types of cultural blending can be even more difficult. For example, transgendered individuals spend their lives attempting to unify gender identifications within themselves. Imagine the struggles they must face to understand the cultural mores of both genders. Often, the culture of a gender is often assumed. If you ask a man or a woman to explain what seminal qualities define maleness or femaleness, they are unlikely to posit anything profound. They have been indoctrinated into those cultures from birth, and they have accepted many of the precepts without analyzing them. Transgendered individuals must learn these cultural facets as adults—without instruction from their parents.

There are also unique struggles for people who identify themselves with ethnic and sexual minority groups. Gays and lesbians who are members of ethnic minority groups often struggle with identity issues because they can never be sure if they are being discriminated against because of their ethnicity or their sexuality. This sense of vulnerability affects nearly every dimension of life. Even the way gays and lesbians come out to their parents is influenced by their ethnicity. Kennamer, Honnold, Bradford, and Hendricks (2000) interviewed gay and bisexual men (aged 15 to 77 years) concerning their disclosure to family members, heterosexual friends, gay friends, coworkers, health care workers, and members of their church. They found that European American men were much more likely than gay African

Americans to disclose their sexuality, to join gay organizations, and to have gay/bisexual friends. What is even more interesting and disconcerting were the moderating effects. As education increased, European American men were *more* likely and African American men were *less* likely to disclose sexuality and associate with gay groups. In a sense, African Americans realized that their biculturalism would have a more negative effect on their lives. The findings from this study have serious implications regarding how biculturalism should be addressed. However, one of the most immediate concerns is how these trends will affect research into African American gay issues. African American gay men may be less likely to participate in the fight against HIV/AIDS, and they may avoid involvement in gay issues as a means of protecting themselves from prejudice.

In addition to the groups discussed previously, there is another group of bicultural individuals who are more difficult to identify because they blend into the dominant culture. Nadya Fouad (2001), a psychologist and former president of the American Psychological Association's Division 17, recalls her confusion over how to view her ethnicity. Her mother was from Brazil and her father was Egyptian. Although she valued her Hispanic ancestry, most of her colleagues thought of her as white. She had an Arab surname, she looked white, but there was more to her identity than she realized. When she was elected president of Division 17, she was introduced as the "second woman of color" elected to the position. The announcement surprised many of her friends and colleagues, who had never thought of her as a "person of color" or a member of a minority group. For Dr. Fouad, who had been raised in a small Iowa town with multicultural parents, discovering her own cultural identity seemed less important than learning how to blend into the dominant society. In a very real way, she became an invisible minority, struggling to create a cultural identity without distancing herself from the dominant culture that accepted her.

The influence of invisible minority status should not be overlooked. Bicultural individuals can include immigrants who take up residence in a country other than their birthplace. Sometimes, we think of immigrants to the United States as people of non-English-speaking backgrounds, but this classification overlooks people who immigrate from Australia or England and encounter significant cultural differences when moving to the United States. For that matter, even people moving from California to the American South must contend with significant differences in culture. Southern culture in the United States is steeped in traditions and modes of communication that are often misunderstood by outsiders.

This chapter could continue through every permutation offered in this book. Each combination will require differ interventions. However, rather than offer an infinite list of options, it is important to keep in mind how every facet of culture changes a client's needs. An African Americn living in Los Angeles will present with a different cultural worldview than an African American from Iowa. A gay male who is atheist will have different concerns than a Christian gay male. In this way, every client is bicultural, and every client has a unique perspective on cultural and the world.

Rajini's Story (A Client's Viewpoint)
(24-year-old Thai female)

I came to the United States for college. My initial goal was to attend Mahidol University International College (MUIC) in Thailand but I could not receive high enough entrance scores. It is ironic that my SAT scores were good enough to get into Texas A&M University. I choose Texas because my uncle lives in Houston. We could see each other during holidays and long weekends.

While at A&M, I met John. He is a third-generation Texan. He even dressed the part. I had to giggle when he wore his cowboy hat and boots. He looked like something from a movie.

We continued dating until he asked me to marry him. I told him I would, but only if we spent our first year after graduation in Thailand. I missed my homeland and my family. He struggled to learn the language, but he managed to find a job in Bangkok.

There were things about Thailand that surprised John. For example, younger people bow deeper when greeting older people. He could not understand this, because American culture values youth. He also found our worth ethic different. He was used to working set hours and had difficulty adjusting to the more flexible hours of Thai culture. Many shops in Bangkok work 24 hours, and this took time for him to grasp.

I had hoped he would love Thailand enough to stay, but there were several problems. Every month, he was required to register with immigration. This became annoying. Such requirements would not exist for me if we lived in the States.

Once he found a good job, we moved back to Texas.

My second time in the States was different. Being a Thai student in America was easier than being a Thai wife and married to a white male. Everyone accepted me as a student, because I was a visitor. As a more permanent resident, they were more distant.

John belonged to an elite social club, which he hoped would provide me with some close friendships. They treated me more like a pet or a mascot than a friend. They could say how open they were for inviting me to events, but no one called for a personal visit. I was their token Asian.

After a year, I started getting depressed. I missed the openness of Bangkok. I missed speaking Thai. I longed for real Thai food, rather than what they called Thai food in Texas. To compensate, I spent more time on the computer with family members, decreased the social time with my white friends, and tried to focus on my job. I realized I needed help, but I was scared to see a therapist. I was fortunate to have found John.

Bruce's Story (A Counselor's Viewpoint)

(52-year-old European American male)

When Rajini started counseling, I wondered if I could help her. She had pulled away from many of the social outlets I thought would have helped her, and I needed to learn about her before I could offer suggestions.

During the first three weeks of counseling, I told her I wanted to listen as much as possible. I knew Asian clients tend to appreciate expertness, so I started our time together with a promise: I would give her practical suggestions at the start of the fourth session. I really needed that much time to grasp her struggles.

During the first session, she spoke about the intolerance of the white women at her social club. Having been part of groups like that, I could see her point. But I also wondered if she was projecting some of her own anxiety against those individuals. Rather than comment, I kept trying to imagine what it must feel like to be a young, Thai woman integrating into a new culture. There is no way I could grasp the prejudice she would experience, but I kept trying to imagine myself as her and how people at that club would feel if I were married to a young man. I'm sure they would give me even worse looks. I tried my best to see the world from her perspective.

By the end of the third session, I had reached several conclusions. Though she was not actively Buddhist, she missed the cultural identity of her home religion. The loss of her language had affected her deeply. The bonding of women in Texas differed from those in Bangkok. Bangkok women met to create together. They would sew, knit, and create flower decorations. She missed the constructiveness of the social interaction. Together, these cultural facets left her feeling isolated and out of touch.

Realizing my own cultural limitations, I consulted with a Thai therapist in Los Angeles. Though the consultation affirmed my goals for Rajini. I had expected the intervention to end Rajini's major conflicts. But I soon learned that it could create additional problems. With this in mind, we started our four session.

In our fourth session, we discussed the action plan. She valued the social club women, but it was clear they would never become close friends. Instead, she needed a new social network—one her husband may or may not join. We discussed how religion would play an important role in these new networks. There were two Buddhist temples within driving distance. She would attend one this week. She also disliked the way white culture treated the elderly. It actually hurt her to associate with a culture where youth was esteemed over wisdom. So, she would ask the monks if they were involved in visiting nursing homes or supporting the elderly. If not, she could create one. Finally, she would spend Saturday afternoons with her uncle. Even though he lived an hour away, she needed regular time with someone who spoke her language and could relate to her.

(continues)

Bruce's Story (A Counselor's Viewpoint) *(continued)*

When she returned the next week, she looked much better. She followed each component of our treatment plan and each facet worked well. The local Buddhist temple did have a nursing home group, which was entirely run by women. Each of the women in the group shared her belief that age brings wisdom and deserves respect. Rajini's uncle was thrilled she wanted to have lunch with him every Saturday, and he introduced her to a number of Thai women in Houston.

I agreed to work with Rajini for another eight weeks. Despite her success in integrating into Texan culture, she would continue to face discrimination and prejudice. In some ways, building closer relationships with Thai woman and her uncle could create new struggles with her husband and his social groups. She will need to set boundaries, assert herself, and learn to acculturate without assimiliating.

This process reinforced for me the importance of listening to each client's unique story, employing action-oriented interventions for bicultural and Asian clients, and seeking consultation to limit my own biases and blind spots.

QUESTIONS TO CONSIDER

1. Why was there a national outcry when Fuzzy Zoeller suggested that Tiger Woods might select fried chicken and collard greens at the Masters ceremonial dinner?

2. What are some examples of social trends that will influence the ways in which we view multiculturalism in the future?

3. Why are African American gay men less likely than their European American peers to disclose their sexual orientation and associate with gay groups?

4. Why is it often difficult for members of invisible minorities to create a clear cultural identity?

5. Why can adopted children not simply become part of their adopted culture?

6. How might bicultural individuals play an important role in your school or organization?

7. Assuming gender plays a role in bicultural identity, how might you incorporate this part of identity into your current or future work? Should counselors, psychologists, social workers, and family therapists address the culture of gender and sexuality?

8. How would geography play a role in the way people integrated into your area? Given that the individual ethnically fit into your dominant culture, what original geographical area might have the hardest time acculturating?

INTERVENTION EXERCISES

Counseling and Therapy: Dobry (Polish American male, age 30) lives in a Polish section of Chicago. He recently started dating a non-Polish woman, and he is facing pressure from his family, friends, and community. How would you handle the conflict between his culture and his affection?

School Psychology: Burton (European American male, age 7) spent the last two years living in the Dominican Republic. He speaks Haitian Creole and Spanish. Though his parents primarily speak English, they did not speak English around him as to assist him with his acculturation in the Dominican Republic. Now back in the United States, they wish to assess him for an honors program. What concerns might you have about the testing process?

School Counseling: Kiden (African American female, age 17) recently tested positive for AIDS. She is concerned about telling her teachers, because she thinks they will ask her to leave the school or prevent her from participating in athletics or science experiments. What questions would you want to ask her? How would you intervene?

Social Work: Leticia (female, age 14) was adopted at birth. Her adopted parents refused to disclose her cultural heritage, though she looks different from her French mother and Argentine father. Kamal has darker skin and eyes from her parents, and she believes she was born somewhere along the equator. She believes she will never fit in until she understands who she is. Her parents, however, fear disclosing more about her past because they may lose her as their own. How would you intervene?

PART **III**

Gender and Sexuality

Why do we need to discuss gender and sexual orientation in a text on multicultural counseling? In many ways, gender and sexual orientation play a more significant role toward under-standing cultural identity than any other factor. Consider Pope's (1995) impassioned argument for the inclusion of gays and lesbians in multicultural texts. Pope offered the following points:

- Sexual minorities must face identity-formation tasks similar to those of racial and ethnic minorities.
- Multicultural skills are useful and helpful when dealing with sexual minorities.
- A lesbian and gay culture exists.
- People are oppressed because of their sexual orientation.

It would be hard to deny these points, but they create more questions than answers. There are dozens of groups that might satisfy similar criteria, and the difficulty lies not in finding groups to include but in deciding where to end the process.

One reason why gender and sexual orientation differ from other cultural entities is the universality of the experience. All people define their gender. All people define their sexual orientation. For many people, this process is developmental, socially accepted, and understandable. For others, the process throws every aspect of life into a whirlwind.

Start by considering how a person's gender culture differs from sexual orientation. For example, a man can feel perfectly content with his male identity while being physically and sexually attracted to other men. His gay orientation does not interfere with his male identity. Similarly, a male transvestite who enjoys wearing women's clothing may feel that he has a feminine or female secondary identity, but most transvestites are sexually attracted to the opposite sex. His secondary female identity does not affect male core identity or his heterosexual orientation. These issues can become extremely complex, and they also have important legal consequences. Imagine you are working with a male-to-female transsexual (MtF). She was born male but recently completed a sex change operation because she has "always been female on the inside and wanted the outside to match." From her earliest awareness, she had been attracted to women. When she lived in the body of a male, people viewed her as heterosexual, but she always viewed herself as a woman and therefore considered herself a lesbian. Some people may never accept her as female, and their perceptions will interfere with how they view her sexual orientation. If she married a woman while she lived as a man, her legal marriage would be nullified in most states. With the disillusionment of the marriage, her rights as a custodial parent are also put into jeopardy.

Why do gender and sexual orientation play such important roles in our society? In the earliest prehistorical societies, (between 4,000 to 40,000 years ago), there were nearly no differences between body structure in Neanderthals (Best, 2010). This implies the sexes did the same work. Not until 4,000 years ago, when tools and craft specializations became more common, did gender-based labor become commonplace. What does this change mean? For one, it implies that chromosomes, hormones, and genes do not determine behaviors (Best, 2010). They may predisposition us toward certain actions—maybe even make some actions more efficient for groups of people—but there are other forces at work.

Unfortunately, we lack the scientific evidence to define the causes of gender- and orientation-related behaviors. We have a number of theories, each vying for dominance. Evolutionary theorists explain gender behaviors biologically. Our sex plays a role in our survival-based experiences. Social role theorists believe the division of labor stems from presumptions of gender abilities. For example, we believe boys are better at math and girls are better at language, so we construct the world to meet these expectations. Social learning theorists view sex-typed behaviors as a product of parental behaviors. We copy our families, and the process repeats itself for generations. Cognitive theorists see gender as a series of developmental cognitive structures. Gender schema theorists focus on perceived social differences between children (Best, 2010). There is enough evidence for and against each of these to imply we still lack an understanding of how gender identity develops. All we really know is that people view their own gender and the gender of others as very important. We also know this identity (for self and discriminating others) arises around the time language skills develops, and it increases in rigidity during the school years (Best, 2010).

From this discussion of gender, it should be clear that gender identity is not equivalent with biological sex. The term *sex* usually indicates an individual's biological or chromosomal sex, and the term *gender* denotes the individual's perception, interpretation, or expressed identification of his or her sex. By age three, most children have a firmly established gender identity. By age five, most children are remarkably adept at identifying the genders of other children (Feinbloom, 1976). For most individuals, their sex and gender are congruent, but for some, conflicts arise from an early age. This leads to the rather confusing issue of defining male and female issues in counseling. For example, is an intersexual (someone born with physiological characteristics of both sexes) a real woman? Is a lesbian (a female who is primarily attracted to members of her sex) a real woman? Is a male-to-female transsexual (someone who is born with XY chromosomes, who takes female hormones to grow breasts, and has his penis surgically reconstructed into a vagina) a real woman?

As a young therapist beginning a job at a college counseling center, I remember looking forward to working with my first client. I sat in my office and imagined what he or she would be like. When he arrived, I was surprised at how closely he fit my ideal image. He was an honor student, student body president, and looking forward to a promising career. He presented with his head high, made excellent eye contact, and displayed remarkable confidence.

After briefly reciting his accomplishments, he added, "Oh, and I'm gay." Without pausing, he continued, "How do you feel about this?"

A little surprised by his approach, I replied with some incoherent psychobabble such as "I think we're here to talk about you." I was ready to work with him as a client, but I was not prepared to answer questions about my own beliefs. As the session progressed, he began to explain his goals for counseling. For the past six months, he had dated a fellow college student. They had recently drifted apart and seemed to have lost interest in one another. He wanted to end the relationship, and he was seeking counseling to deal with his fear of saying the "wrong thing." It was a common story. I had heard it many times before from men conflicted about their relationships. The only difference in this case was that the client was dating another man.

To some degree, social bias against gays and lesbians is understandable. Our family members, friends, coworkers, and the media drop both subtle and blunt statements about why some people are not acceptable. Some of these images are bound to stay with us.

In saying this, I am not implying that counselors, social workers, and psychologists should refrain from holding moral convictions. Instead, we should learn to recognize when our moral convictions preclude us from working within a client's framework. If you do not feel comfortable helping a client with his presenting problem of "accepting his homosexuality," you should not attempt to do so. Know your limitations, and refer the client to another counselor. However, as you read through the following chapters, please try to do so with one intention: Try with all your might to imagine yourself as gay, transgendered, male, or female. For a day or week, try to imagine how your world would change if the person you are reading about is you. Effective counseling always starts from this viewpoint.

CHAPTER 10

People with Gender Variations

INSIGHT EXERCISE

In Tom's diversity awareness class, the discussion eventually turned to the topic of gender issues. Alicia, a female classmate, leaned over to him and whispered, "Can you imagine how messed up someone must be to think he's a girl on the inside?" Tom shook his head but said nothing. He was still wondering if he really was "messed up" for having the feelings his classmate condemned.

After class, Tom caught up with Alicia and continued chatting with her at the student lounge. They talked about children, relationships, feminism, fashion, abortion, Christmas traditions, weight loss, and moisturizers.

"I wish more people understood the continued oppression of women in this country." Alicia waved a potato chip in her hand as she gestured into the air. "Just last week, I was shopping for a car. The salesman undressed me with his eyes, bounded over to me, and said, 'I'll bet you're looking for something sleek and beautiful.' I mean, what happened to just asking if he could help me?"

"If only it was just car salesmen." Tom pulled a piece of celery from his pink lunch bag. "Yesterday, I was shopping with some friends at Macy's. The salesman, who must have been a day past high school graduation, walked up to us—literally pushed himself past two of the women— and asked Jim Biesal (do you know him?) if he wanted any help. I guess the biggest, manliest person in the group was the only one deserving attention."

"Tell me about it." Alicia shook her head. "I mean it's not like we …"

(continues)

She stopped herself. Her smile faded. She blinked twice.

"I mean, it's not like *women* ..." Recognition flashed on her face, as if she suddenly saw through Tom's façade. She realized a woman chatted with her. But *his* body did not match *her* presentation. She lacked a category for Tom.

"... *Women* get that type of treatment all the time." Alicia paused, her eyes narrowing as if angry at Tom for shaking her once steady view of the world. "But *you* wouldn't understand the depth of it—being a man and all."

Questions to Consider:

1. How can Tom find satisfaction?

2. Should he simply learn to enjoy talking about football and hunting?

3. Should he strive to realize his dream and accept his feminine nature?

4. Is there a way to choose between these options?

Of all the topics in this book, gender identity is probably the hardest to convey. Gender defines all people. It is the first category we place on an individual, and this process starts from birth. The moment an infant receives a pink or blue blanket, an identity begins. Gender influences an individual from the earliest phases of life. How a child is dressed, praised, and punished and plays is largely defined by gender (Best, 2010).

Clothing designates how others see us. Simply from a person's clothes, an observer may guess at the individual's sex, occupation (e.g., uniforms), rank (e.g., military or medical), socioeconomic status, destination (e.g., party or office clothes), activity (yard work or playing sports), or even prison status (Feinbloom, 1976). For **transgendered** people (i.e., those whose gender identities do not conform to their anatomy), the frequently unconscious nature of these symbols becomes conscious, and the images associated with attire become a passageway to another aspect of the self.

Although few mental health practitioners regularly counsel transgendered clients, nearly everyone will see at least one such client. As such, there are some basic ideas to address. This topic is too complex to tackle in detail, but some key components must be grasped.

UNIQUE CHALLENGES

Three unique challenges confront people with gender variations. First, any confusion as to identity changes the way people approach life. If you believe you are strong, a good speaker, wise, fast, creative, or some other attribute, you face the world from this perspective. What happens when you lack a clear conception of your gender? Without a clear gender identity, all other identities lose their direction.

Second, gender variation is so complex that it defies definition. Some people think people with gender dysphoria are gay. Sexual orientation (who you are attracted to) is not the same as gender identity (if you think of yourself as male or female). This is often confused by the acronym GLBT. Gay, lesbian, bisexual, and transgendered people often fight for the same basic civil rights, but they are conceptually different groups.

The third obstacle facing people with gender variations is a lack of understanding. A common conceptualization of a male-to-female transsexual is that *he* is a woman trapped in a man's body. There are multiple problems with this viewpoint. Is this person male or female? Should this person be called he or she? Is this a transwoman or a transman? Typically, when people make conscious efforts to cross gender lines, the proper etiquette is to use terms to match their perceived identity. This means a female-to-male transsexual is a transman. *He* is a man even if he still has a vagina. The scientific literature on the topic—even through the last decade—would discuss male-to-female transsexuals as *male transsexuals*. This is highly offensive and invalidates the individual's journey. *She* is no longer male as she transitions. She is a transwoman. Her journey should be recognized through pronouns and titles.

HISTORICAL CONTEXT

The idea of changing presenting genders exists in many cultures and in many different forms. In Greek and Roman culture, Hermaphroditus was the god of multiple sexed individuals and of feminine men. He is displayed as a winged youth with a penis, feminine thighs, breasts, and long flowing hair (Charles, 1860). The 18th dynasty pharaoh Hatshepsut ruled Egypt for two decades (from 1479 to 1458 B.C.). By definition, pharaohs were male, so she invented a hybrid gender to identify herself. In ancient Rome, Galli (who were eunuchs) were viewed as insane. Legend has it that they castrated themselves in fits of madness after drinking from the river Gallus. King Henry III of France frequently cross-dressed and was referred to as "her majesty" while dressed as a woman. A group of 17th century Illini Native American men were known to have dressed and acted out the social role of women. Abbe Francois Timoleon de Choisy attended a Papal inaugural ball in female dress. His memoirs (published in the 17th century) offered the first written testimony of cross-dressing. In the 18th century, female-to-male transvestites joined Nelson's Navy.

Despite this long history, when mental health professionals previously discussed gender identity, variations were not viewed favorably. In 1913, the British Mental Deficiency Act defined four categories of mental deficiency: idiot, imbecile, feeble-minded, and moral defectives. The latter included criminals, unmarried mothers, homosexuals, and transgender people. During the 1930s and 1940s, the Nazis abused, sterilized, and murdered transgender people.

It was not until the 1960s that society started to view gender variance as something other than a hideous perversion. In 1966, Harry Benjamin published *The Transsexual Phenomenon*. The transgender social group The

Beaumont Society was formed that same year. In 1980, the Harry Benjamin International Gender Dysphoria Association to promote standards of care was founded. Despite the increased awareness, debate persisted regarding how to regard gender-related issues.

Money and Ehrhardt (1972) asserted that gender identity was completely malleable for about 18 months after birth. This hypothesis implied that a medical team could surgically assign the gender of an infant who was born with ambiguous genitalia. Corrective genital surgeries were performed within the first year of life, and medicine was used to help correct nature's "mistake." It appears now that Money's theories were ill conceived (Creighton & Minto, 2001).

In her book *Intersex*, Harper (2007) describes sex as a continuum rather than a binary state. But this notion is still foreign to most Americans. So, why do people feel compelled to see sex as simply male and female?

ETIOLOGY AND DEVELOPMENT

Etiology

Gender identity appears to originate through a complex series of events. Older theories blamed the mother, suggesting mothers feminized their children and distant fathers permitted this (Stoller, 1985). Such stories are quite common throughout the transgendered community, and they have been recorded throughout history. However, other than anecdotal evidence, support for this theory is lacking.

More recent research focuses on genetic or hormonal evidence. As Veale, Clarke, and Lomax (2009) note, there is moderate evidence for a genetic component of gender-variant identities, given twins and sibling studies as well as the examination of specific genes. Male-to-female transsexuals also have fourth-to-second finger ratios closer to those of women than men (Schneider, Pickel & Stalla, 2006). Female-to-male transsexuals have dental structures in between those common to genetic men and women (Antoszewski, Żądzińska & Foczpański, 2009). These studies imply a genetic or prebirth hormonal component to transsexualism, as neither finger length nor dental structure would be changed by adult-onset hormonal changes.

Development

Even though it appears that gender identity forms within the womb, social and biological factors also play roles. There is some evidence that the amount and intensity of cross-sexed behavior in childhood becomes predictive of later gender incongruence (Drummond, Bradley, Peterson-Badali & Zucker, 2008). This trend may help to explain why children from long-term follow-up studies tend not to transition as adults. They usually identify as homosexuals without gender identity (Wilson, Griffin & Wren, 2002).

Even when children frequently cross-dress or identify with a sex different from the one assigned to them at birth, those who transition are likely to wait until middle age. This process is a little like living in an environment where society picks your life job for you at birth. Say you were told you would be a train conductor. As a child, you get your three-piece suit, shiny shoes, and conductor's hat. It feels like a game. You know it is not real.

After a few years, this role created confusion, frustration, and isolation. The heavy costume starts to smell. A musky, woolen, tangy, dirty scent. After a few more years, people start commenting on how you are "not acting right." Your gestures are too fluid; you smile too much; your voice is too melodic.

Although this job is not right for you, you cannot quit. Society picked your identity. Quitting is not allowed. Even voicing dissatisfaction with your job might shame your family, isolate you from friends, and affect your love life. So, you continue to plug along, feeling more depressed, drained, and isolated with each passing day. In the end, you see only two options: quit or die. This life-or-death decision point changes everything, and quitting starts to look like a viable option.

When people reach the point of transitioning, the process often looks expedited to outsiders. The transitioning person may look obsessed, selfish, too driven. But this is normal. The person may also go through a re-experience of childhood or adolescence. Some may play with dolls, watch the latest teen girl movies, or read the latest teen girl books. They must learn to be girls before they become women. This process is also expedited. What may take a girl 10–20 years to develop, the transsexual will do in 5–8. This only magnifies the difficulty to the family, who is already struggling to handle the changes. It is important for loved ones to understand that transitioning involves a physical, mental, and social second puberty.

WITHIN GROUP DIFFERENCES

Differences within the gender-variant community can look minor or immense. Sometimes, the difference depends entirely on the perspective of the person looking. For starters, there are four primary groups:

- Intersexed
- Cross-dressers
- Genderqueers/transgenderists
- Transsexuals

Intersexed

Intersexed individuals are born with ambiguous gender identities. Some have both testes and ovaries; some have testes but look feminine; others are genetically female but appear masculine (Fausto-Sterling. 2000). Although there is considerable debate about who is "intersexed" (Sax, 2002), there is also emerging agreement on how to handle such cases. In past years, the dominant medical treatment was to create female genitalia (which is simpler in design although complex in function) and raise the child as a girl. We now realize that this approach is harmful, and that it is better to wait to discern the child's core gender identity and perform "corrective" surgery to match the perceived gender. However, if the child can decide prior to puberty (especially if the child has a testes), actions should be taken prior to this developmental stage.

Emphasizing the child's perceived sex is more productive than trying to assess the individual's "true" sex (Hird, 2008). Gender identity comes when the client is ready to discuss it. Sometimes, the individual may remain between genders. Feder (2009) argues that the whole notion of focusing on erasing all signs of ambiguous sex is counterproductive. Instead of trying to erase questions regarding a child's gender of assignment, Feder advocates changing the focus from appearance to emphasizing quality of life, including sexual functioning and fertility.

One of my clients was born with a penis but XX chromosomes. She was raised a boy until she turned 12, when she started menstruating. It took years for her to accept herself as a girl, but she "always knew" something was different about her and was glad she could finally have a "normal" life.

Social justice issues are extremely important for intersexed individuals. A "girl" who grows a beard, a "boy" who grows breasts at puberty, or a girl who discovers she has XY chromosomes when puberty fails to start. In all these cases, being an indeterminate gender means lacking a clear gender culture. Families often react to such discoveries by trying to hide. Some families move, force children to change schools, or otherwise try to fit their child into the binary gender world. This helps some families start over in new roles. For others, it just drags the problem to a new setting. In working with such kids, normalizing their sexual identity is crucial. Being intersexed does not make them "bad" or "perverted." It is simply another way of being.

Cross-Dressers

Although society can often accept individuals who are intersexed, cross-dressers are less likely to find support. These people possess a core gender identity that matches their sex. They often discuss having an alter ego that is feminine, but they usually live this part of their life in secret.

This group is not well understood by the dominant society. Maybe people consider cross-dressers to be closeted gay individuals who are mentally disturbed. This is seldom the case. Even in 1910, when Magnus Hirschfeld coined the now-outdated term *transvestite*, he was surprised to find that most cross-dressers were heterosexual and married. Some gay men do dress as women, but they do so in a mocking style or with the intent of attracting men. Such individuals are usually referred to as *drag queens* or *female impersonators*, which make up a different culture than those of cross-dressers.

When cross-dressing is associated with sexual arousal, it is synonymous with transvestic fetishism (DSM-IV-TR) or fetishistic transvestism (ICD-10) (Lawrence, 2009). Such individuals (usually male) will wear, hold, or smell objects associated with the opposite sex for sexual excitement. This activity nearly always develops prior to puberty and may begin without any sexual component (Schott, 1995). It is estimated that about 2–3% of all males engage in some erotic cross-dressing during their lives (Lawrence, 2009). But these people will rarely come to counseling. They often use their fetish as a coping mechanism.

If there is confusion regarding one's core gender identity or if the core gender identity contrasts with that of the individual's biological sex, issues of gender incongruence arise. In some cases, gender incongruence may create a desire to transform one's physical body to correspond to one's gender identity. This condition is sometimes referred to as transsexualism and may lead to sexual reassignment surgery (SRS).

Genderqueer

Genderqueer (GQ), **intergender,** and **transgenderist** apply to both men and women who believe they possess qualities of both genders (or neither gender). They distinguish themselves from binary gender definitions and refuse to be defined medically. They are self-defined. Some genetic women have their breasts removed and then wear tight shirts to display their flat chests. Men grow breasts but otherwise appear masculine. Despite applying to both genders, people assigned female at birth are more likely to identify as genderqueer (Factor & Rothblum, 2008).

Transsexuals

Like all gender issues, it is often easier to think of this group as bimodal. People are male or female. But transsexuals are broader than this. Some do not want any medical intervention but live their lives in a role contrary to their birth assignment. Others will take hormones but not have sexual reassignment surgery (Maddux and Winstead, 2008). The range of transsexuals is quite vast. However, there are similarities.

Unlike male transvestites—who have a masculine core gender identity—male-to-female transsexuals have a feminine gender identity and often grow up with cognitions similar to those of girls. Devor (1989, p. 20) provides a succinct and helpful definition: "[A] transsexual is a person whose physical sex is unambiguous, and whose gender identity is unambiguous, but whose sex and gender do not concur." It is not uncommon to hear a transsexual claim to be living in the wrong body (Feinbloom, 1976). This is not a delusion about having the sexual characteristics of the opposite sex; it is simply a statement that the individual's core gender identity differs from his or her sex. But how does this play out in real life?

Much of the literature discussing transsexuals involves males-to-females. This led Hansbury (2005) to discuss female-to-males as almost invisible. This is partly because transmen transition through hormonal treatment very well. Apart from maintaining wider hips and a rounder facial structure, most transmen appear no different from genetic men. They have muscles, balding patterns, deep voices, and beards. The ability to break free from their birth-assigned gender and live entirely as their desired gender provides the opportunity to disappear into the binary gender world. This is sometimes called going stealth or "down low." In addition to the power of testosterone in making stealth life possible, society also appears to accept trans-male identity more than it does trans-female because society still values masculinity over femininity. Many people may simply accept *why* someone would want to live as a man in a man's world. This is not meant to diminish the prejudice and suffering transmen face (as the movie *Boys Don't Cry* accurately depicted). But it may help explain the literature's fixation on male-to-females. It may also explain why there is a higher referral rate for boys seen in gender specialty offices than girls (Wilson, Griffin & Wren, 2002).

If transsexualism has more to do with identity and less to do with sexuality, it would be reasonable to assume there is a group of people who feel like women but maintain their gender-assigned role as men. There is virtually nothing available in the literature about this group. However, a recent survey (Brammer, 2010) found that 18% of transgendered people classified themselves as "invisible transsexuals." Such individuals are likely to wear androgynous clothing or alter their bodies through hormones or surgery but for social, religious, financial, or personal reasons cannot live in their desired gender identity. One invisible transsexual told me that *he* wanted to be buried as Alicia. "I want them all to see me as I really am—my body would say, 'I was this person all my life and you never got me.'"

In the past, people who started showing signs of gender dysphoria in adolescence were dubbed **secondary transsexuals**. It was assumed that primary transsexuals—who never fully identified with their birth-assigned sex—would be more successful in their transition. But primary and secondary transsexuals do appear to appear to be "distinct from each other in respect to their sex-role identification." Instead, the role of counselors in working with all transsexuals is to help them incorporate aspects of their "... former roles into their new roles and not totally rejecting them may be safer and may constitute a good predictor for successful sex reassignment" (Herman-Jeglińska, Grabowska & Dulko, 2002, p. 533).

Consider the case of Terry, an individual somewhere along the way of gender migration. Terry was born male and appeared unremarkably masculine throughout his childhood. However, just prior to puberty, he developed a fetish:

> I started dressing in women's clothing during childhood. At first, I just wore my mother's panties. When I reached adolescence, I found my desire had extended to wearing an entire outfit, and I would masturbate while dressed. By the end of high school, I was wearing makeup and venturing outside for evening drives. During college, I was no longer sexually aroused by being feminine. My mother had started progesterone and estrogen to help with menopause. I commandeered enough pills to assist with my transition. After a few months, my breasts budded. I got scared, and I tried stopping the treatment. But I couldn't handle the emotional swings. I convinced myself that I *needed* the treatment, but I didn't want to become a woman. Now I have small breasts, and I take the estrogen in very small amounts. I'm happy with myself this way, and I don't want to go any further.

Terry could be classified as secondary. Regardless of the term, she has a female identity. During adolescence, his feminine identity was sexually charged, but this changed. For whatever reason, she now identifies as male but feels it is important to maintain some bodily conformity to her desired gender. Each person goes through the process differently. Terry might remain comfortable with her invisibility or she could seek surgery and live full-time as a woman. Forcing him into a "good candidate" or "bad candidate" for surgery based on two years of high school fetishism does not explain his current situation.

CULTURAL IDENTITY

We covered some of the differences between a few transgender groups, but there are many more. One of the most obvious cultural issues involves the terms transgendered people use to identify themselves and their communities. Self-referents such as "gender variant," "gender bender," "trangenderist," "gender outlaw," "gendertrash," "genderqueer," and "trans person" each connote significant differences (Carroll & Gilroy, 2002).

In a bi-gendered world, having some type of gender variance makes daily life challenging. For example, when is it appropriate for a male-to-female (MtF) person to use the women's restroom? Has someone transitioned enough for such a cultural rite of passage after taking sexual-reassigning hormones? Does it include a chromosomally unambiguous female who has a small penis? If a person has had a sex change to female but is still legally male, should that person be required to use a male restroom?

If you find yourself confused by these questions, your reaction is common. The complexity of defining the term *transgendered* led to its removal from *DSM-IV*. The primary reason for the change was the increasing difficulty of distinguishing between relatively mild gender identity issues and a more extreme form of desire to change sex. When an individual continues to the point of sexual-reassignment surgery (SRS), a number of unique cultural elements arise. In addition to changing the legal documents (which happens via a court-ordered name change and a gender/name change on driver's license, social security card, college/employment records, and, after SRS, birth certificate and passport). These changes are so massive, they may take years to cover grade transcripts, letters of recommendation, reunions or conferences, and others. Such issues often make changing gender identities feel like starting a new life, which poses considerable cultural challenges.

Transitioning their bodies to their desired sex makes them less vulnerable to hate crimes and social ostracism (Cole et al., 2000). However, the transsexual community continues to view mental health professionals with some skepticism, and their response is quite rational.

For most transgendered people (especially those who are ethnic minorities), the goal of their cultural activities is to exist in the bi-gendered world. Some spend their early years fighting against their identity and immerse themselves into the stereotypical behavior of their chromosomal sex. For example, genetic males may join the military, play rough sports, or become involved in other masculine rituals. Usually, these efforts fail to establish a greater sense of masculinity.

For those diagnosed with gender incongruence, there is often less difficulty passing in the female world. This is especially true for transsexuals who, from early childhood, viewed themselves as different from their natal sex. From their earliest memories, they have played with feminine toys and dolls, preferred feminine clothes, drawn pictures of attractive women, played fantasy games in which they took on feminine roles, and avoided masculine activities. But the transition process is still challenging. For MtFs, estrogen changes the way people think. Emotions become more intense, the sex drive diminishes, and there is a greater sense of body congruity and trusting intuition. Such changes happen within the first year of hormones, and they often are confusing to transwomen.

For female-to-male (FtM) transmen, the process of entering male culture is often more shocking and sudden. Given how quickly and powerfully testosterone affects the body, many transmen enter masculine culture abruptly. In his witty and engaging book *Just Add Hormones*, Matt Kailey (2005) tells several stories about entering the "secret men's club." He tells stories about strangers walking up to him and making lewd comments about the women around them. Another man, a mechanic, asked Matt to hold the phone because he has to "go to the can" after eating "Chinese for lunch." Still more stories included how drivers who used to forgive *her* for driving errors now yelled, honked, and cussed at *him*. None of these incidents happened to her as a woman. They were challenging, encouraging, angering, and motivating. But they also reinforced that Matt was not entirely male. He concluded that he has "blended the female parts and the male parts of myself into a whole being" (p. 42). For many people, this is the essence of being transgendered.

What is important for transwomen and transmen is to maintain a sense of congruity with the past. For reasons not completely understood, transmen appear to maintain some of their femininity with them, but transwomen often reject all their masculinity (Herman-Jeglińska, Grabowska & Dulko, 2002). The most adjusted individuals will keep a unified sense of self throughout the process, but this is often challenging.

Regardless of where people fall along the transgendered continuum, there is enough similarity to advocate a cultural process. Most transgendered individuals will go through the stages listed in Figure 10.1.

- **Birth-assigned role:** Individuals learn about the gender role advocated by their parents and society.
- **Androgyny/invisibility:** Individuals explore gender-divergent behaviors and often feel ostracized or invisible.
- **Exploration:** Transgendered individuals learn about others "like them" and explore ways to incorporate gender alternatives into their personalities.
- **Conflictive:** Individuals begin to accept their identity, which may involve taking hormones, dressing in ways inappropriate to their birth-gender role, and telling friends/family about their identity. Disclosure is a critical aspect of this component.
- **Integration:** Individuals continue along a unique continuum of identity. Some will accept their identity without becoming transsexuals. Others will start (or restart) hormone therapy and/or seek surgery.

These phases are similar to the ones advocated by Wester, McDonough, White, Vogel, and Taylor (2010). At any phase along this process, individuals

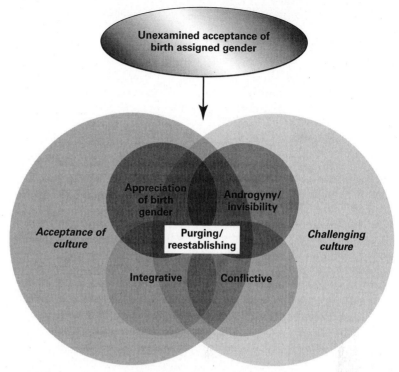

FIGURE **10.1** Cultural Identity Model: Gender Varianc

re-evaluated their path. For most, they would pause to consider if they wanted to go further. For others, they would "purge" their transition and revert back to an earlier phase. Counselors should be sensitive to the slow unfolding of gender identity for transgendered individuals. The loss of the birth role is huge. Most transsexuals will fight this many times before ultimately learning to accept it.

While sexuality plays an important role in this process, I purposely excluded it here to emphasize the independent development of gender identity. However, sexuality cannot be ignored in family dynamics.

FAMILY STRUCTURE AND DYNAMICS

Family of Origin

Common theories about family structure assume trans children are raised in enmeshed families. The mother has an intimate, unhealthy relationship with the child and the father is emotionally distant or nonexistent (Stoller, 1985). This led other theorists, such as Green (1987), to advocate for increased fatherly involvement a boy's life and for parents to enforce stricter gender boundaries on their child's behavior. However, since Stoller's anecdotal studies were published, empirical evidence has not supported his hypothesis.

Wren's (2002) qualitative analysis revealed a more typical pattern for transgendered children. She noted how parents were resistant to their children's gender identity issues. Mothers of biological girls talked about their children as tomboys who hated their bodies once they reached puberty. Children did not ask their parents for advice but merely hoped for their parents' support. Fathers discussed the importance of their roles but usually left "emotionally fraught and complex discussions" to the mothers. Nonaccepting parents viewed the gender issues as a way of covering up deeper issues, a misguided path, and unlikely to be accepted by society. They try to restore the status quo by using repetitive and inflexible tactics. Accepting parents are flexible and hopeful for their children's future. In the end, acceptance does not cause transsexuality, but it may minimize the struggles trans children face.

Even when parents accept the transition, there is a loss of the child they once knew. Transsexuals often say things like, "I'm still the same person on the inside." But this is seldom true. Transition affects every aspect of identity, and parents must get to know this changing soul. Parents also need to develop skills to talk to extended family, friends, and school officials. It is not uncommon for parents to suffer rejection from family and community members. Though uncomofortable, this rejection can sometimes help parents under some of the struggles their transgendered child is facing.

When a client is considering transition, helping him or her accept the possible loss of family is critical. Most transpeople will have a clear idea of who will accept them and who will not. They are usually wrong. A good therapeutic tool is to tell the client to 1) avoid predicting people's reactions and 2) give them space and time to work through their feelings. Both of these are very hard, as the transperson is often needing support during transition and desperately wants to connect with family and friends. But gender changes affect every dimension of relationships, and if often evokes intense feelings.

Spouses and Significant Others

No one faces a greater emotional challenge than the partner of a transperson. Jennifer Finney Boylan (2004) wrote about her relationship with her wife becoming sisterly rather than romantic. The impending end to their marital relationship was apparent to Jennifer. Throughout her book, she argued with herself, her counselor, and her family about this process. In one incredibly poignant section, she wrote about the thoughts roaming through her mind:

> I'll be goddamned if I'm going to break anyone's heart. I'll be goddamned if I'm going to let my family down. I'll be goddamned if I'm going to give up everything I've always wanted just so I can *fit*.
> To which I would respond: I know. Still.

The transitioning process is not rational. Not to the person going through it. Not to the people watching. There is simply a small, quiet, undeniable voice cancelling out all arguments against the process. Transsexuals could easily make a list of pros and cons, with hundreds of reasons not to transition only one reason to do so. They could yell and scream, passionately championing all the "cons." But no matter how much they fight and argue, the one "pro" often wins.

Such an immovable force often creates pain and rage in spouses. Consider the case of "Anne" (based on letters published on Internet support sites). She could not remember how her husband's cross-dressing began but instead recalled the fear associated with the progression.

Tim's Story

When I met Tim, I knew he loved me. He seemed "different," but I knew he was a man. He loved sports, competitions, and cars. His mannerisms were rough, bold, and assertive. I just had to accept that he enjoyed wearing a nightgown to bed. I had to transform my love into an unconditional love. I convinced myself I could handle whatever came our way.

After we were married, I approached my husband's cross-dressing with a positive attitude. I avowed, "If you can't beat 'em, join 'em." Tim joined a support group, and he learned how to dress and act feminine. It was a small part of who he was. But the more he attended the meetings, the worse things became. He obsessed over his appearance and pulled away from me. Our sex life suffered, and I sometimes felt I was with a woman. My husband was slipping away.

Every time I helped him *dress*, a piece of me was lost. Sometimes, he wanted me to play masculine roles in bed, and I fought against nausea.

Shortly before our tenth year of marriage, Tim crossed the line. He wore clear polish on his nails and traces of mascara. I begged him to hide his problem from our children. They were the one pure thing left in our marriage. Finally, he announced he was a transsexual. He couldn't fight back the tears, but I didn't have anything left for him. I had given him my very soul, but it was not enough. I felt like a failure as a woman, wife, and mother. I wallowed in self-pity for days, until I found the courage to release my anger. He had betrayed our children and me. He had allowed his self-centered fixation to ruin everything I held dear.

I'm still angry at Tim (now Tina). I want to protect my boys from this freak, but they have him (or her). I often wonder what I did wrong. Did I harbor some type of feelings that drew such a man to me? I'll probably always question myself, but I'm trying to move on. I've remarried, and I love my husband. But the pit of my stomach still shakes when I think of having an ex-wife.

Couple Counseling

Counseling should help each partner explore how their gender identity is shifting. Rules for the partnership should also be explored. One of my couples decided no cross-gender clothing would be allowed in the bedroom. Another couple made Saturdays free from all cross-gender activity. A third couple decided to allow any expression that did not expose the children. For some individuals, incorporating some cross-gender activity may be a pleasurable experience for both people (Stayton, 1996). For others, the process is disorienting for both.

Helen Boyd (2007) discussed how many of her friends asked if she planned on staying with her husband if she transitioned into womanhood. Boyd explained how this was the wrong question. Her husband would cease being her husband long before she had a vagina constructed. Estrogen changes the mind, the body, and relational styles. Boyd commented on how she wanted a partner who was different from her. She wanted him hard where she was soft, and to be otherwise would force her to question her identity too. Such issues should be explored in therapy. Some partners may be able to celebrate emerging gender identities; others may not. But women sometimes exert power in indirect ways, such as ridicule and mocking, and such patterns are likely to harm relationships and the transperson (Erhardt, 2007).

Trans Parents

When transpeople have children, everything about their relationship changes. Many partners can tolerate exploration without their relationship, but they fear exposing their children will affect the child's identity. These sentiments have led some to argue that transgendered persons are unfit to be parents. The court system is still ambivalent about such matters, alternating between affirming and denying trans parents (Elizabeth, 2007).

Children are often embarrassed by their parent's transition, and most attempt to keep it secret (White & Ettner, 2007). In White and Ettner's study, about 17% of the children felt they suffered socially because of the transition, but most (73%) maintained their grades during transition, with only two children experiencing significant academic declines. The children did not appear to have more psychopathology than the general public, and none of them had gender identity disorders.

The most significant findings White and Ettner (2007) found involved the relationship of the partners and the timing of disclosure to the children. Long-term (but not short-term) conflicts between parents led to greater problems with children's adjustments. Also, the younger the children were at the time of disclosure, the better their relationship was over time with both parents. The relationship with the child at the time of disclosure was also important. Those children who experience greater conflict during the transition tend to have greater conflict years later. Overall, most children maintained relationships with their parents as adults, with 15% of children forgoing relationship with their trans parent and 10% of children not maintaining contact with the nontrans parent.

EDUCATION

Schools provide a pivotal intervention for children. For whatever reason, transgendered families remain invisible within the school system (Ryan & Martin, 2000). Schools need to learn about transgendered families (both with transgendered parents and those with transgendered children). These families face unique social obstacles and must work against prejudice, religious biases, gender boxes, and gender assumptions.

Rands (2009) noted how schools teach children about gender. This is where girls and boys learn to socially interact within their gender. But transgender students seldom get to learn these lessons. If they present as their identified gender, they face harassment, discrimination, and physical danger. Rands advocates a social justice approach for the school system. This requires teacher education programs to prepare educators to teach gender in more complex ways. It starts by discussing how gender privilege affects every aspect of life. We often think of this as male privilege, but there are female privileges too. There are also different types of oppression given by gender expectations.

School counselors can assist transgendered students in working through issues of denial, guilt, and shame, helping them to identify ways to act on their feelings without jeopardizing their well-being. For example, if a student has a desire to cross-dress but does not want this behavior to be observed by others, the counselor can point out that cross-dressing would be difficult to conceal in a classroom or dorm but might be indulged with little risk in the privacy of one's bedroom, at a support group meeting, or at one of the many transgender conventions held across the country. If the student wishes to appear in public cross-dressed, the counselor can discuss the potential for being recognized in one's hometown or on college campuses and suggest ways the student can dress and behave in public to minimize the risk of exposure. Support groups can be especially useful in providing suggestions of this nature.

Although coping with transgendered students is important, what may prove more valuable is creating a school policy *before* trans students arrive. This forces teachers and administrators to think through the issues and identify prejudices and possible dangers. Help the school create a policy that outlines acceptable transgendered behavior (e.g., Can a genetic boy wear dresses to school? Who can use which restrooms?). Create policies to protect trans students, such as allowing the trans student to use teacher/staff restrooms and tolerating special gym clothing. Schools may also have policies to allow nicknames in their rosters, which may help if a student chooses a name matching his or her identified gender. For some children, the gender changes may be temporary. For others, they may allow for gender identity to develop more fully.

SOCIOECONOMICS

In *She's Not the Man I Married*, Boyd (2007) provides amazing insight into being the spouse of someone trans. Early in the book, she writes about how, for the transperson, "almost nothing is more important than gender: not relationships, not children, not employment, not career goals or financial stability" (p. 33). Despite the risks, transition often feels necessary, and losses do come.

When a man chooses to live as a woman, her financial prowess often suffers. Alice, a 33-year-old male-to-female transsexual, stated, "The only thing I miss about being a man is male privilege." One transsexual described her job as a manager by saying, "As a man, I would just tell employees to do X. As a woman, they bristled at commands. I had to learn to passively ask, 'It would be nice if you would do X.'"

Knowing the lower power positions women face, many male-to-female transsexuals pursue masculine careers before transitioning. They may choose masculine professions to *prove* their manhood. By the time they transition into womanhood, they may already be well-accepted in their fields. Male-to-female transsexuals are likely to be college educated, married, employed full-time in a professional occupation, and have a family income above the national average (Lombardi, 1999). This implies that for many transgendered individuals, financial hardship is not inevitable. However, clients should realize that the early transitioning phase is more likely to entail financial hardship than the latter phases.

O'Keefe and Fox (2003) provide compelling stories of transgendered individuals. The authors in their edited book discuss occupations ranging from sales to poets to broadcasters to chefs to sex workers. Part of the discussion requires an understanding of where the individual is in the process. Some transgendered individuals remain invisible in their workplace. Others may be at the start of their **real-life experience** (RLE), which is a period of one year where people live in the role of their gender identity before having corrective surgery. The RLE is where individuals experience the greatest financial hardship. This is becoming a little easier, as major companies (such as IBM, Sears, and Home Depot), major airlines, and many universities are setting policies to support transgendered people (Erhardt, 2007). But there is a long way to go.

In 2002, the state of New York passed a law protecting transgendered people from job discrimination. Despite years on the books, a control-based study exploring the hiring of transgendered people at New York retail stores found a 42% net rate of discrimination against transgender job seekers (Transgender need not apply, 2010). They matched genetic women and transwomen's qualifications and then had both apply for jobs at 24 employers. Only one transgendered tester received a job offer in the first round. In the debriefing section of the report, one of the participants said:

> If you can't get a job, that's really the worst of your problems. If you're rejected by your family and friends, that's tough, but at least you're still there for yourself. If you can support yourself, everything else follows. If you don't have a job, you don't have respect. If nobody's hiring you, well, a lot of transgender people are forced into illegal work like turning tricks. We need to work too, we're not from some other planet (p. 15).

One of the primary difficulties in the RLE is the experimental nature of the process. Many people try to keep their current job but fear reprisal from bosses or coworkers (Boylan, 2004). Even after the RLE, there are reasons to remain in one's present job. Starting somewhere new might make it difficult to get health insurance. It will also require new friendships and possibly a new city or culture. Anchoring to the familiar may also help, as hormone fluctuations affect mood. However, when people know you are transitioning, it is almost impossible to blend into one's identified gender. You are always "trans," which is enough of an identity obstacle to inspire some transsexuals to leave.

When transsexuals start fresh in a new town, counselors need to help the individual construct a new résumé. To truly have a stealth existence, transsexuals would only list the occupations and education they have had in their identified gender. Such a process definitely assists those who transition early in life. It is also important to practice interviews because this process requires significant levels of self-confidence (Pepper & Lorah, 2008). Role-playing may help with poise and correct gender expression. Individuals should also be prepared to answer difficult questions (e.g., Have you ever worked under another name? Do you have any medical conditions that could affect your work? May we contact your references?).

SPIRITUALITY AND RELIGION

In some cultures, transgendered individuals have received special regard. In more than 150 North American Indian tribes, there is evidence of "two-spirit" roles in which males dressed as females and took on women's duties or women dressed and behaved as warriors (Roscoe, 1987). Even in the annals of Western Europe, transgendered roles were frequently interwoven into religious practices prior to the dawn of Christianity (Roscoe, 1994).

For most transgendered people, religion threatens their spirituality more than it helps. Most world religions emphasize gender conformity, which makes transgendered people appear threatening. Their movement away from gender identity results in many transgender people leading from a different cultural perspective than those of nontransgender people (Kidd & Witten, 2008). Kidd and Witten's (2008) study on transgendered people and religion resulted in some helpful qualitative responses. One person wrote, "When my sister was married in my hometown church, I was only permitted to view the ceremony from the loft. I was not allowed into the church with the others" (p. 37). Others commented on how their church focused on the sexuality issues associated with their gender identity. One MtF person was welcomed into the church but only if she promised to remain celibate for the rest of her life. Still others who have moved away from families are faced with whether they are permitted to attend funerals. Their study also demonstrated the limited ability of Western religions (i.e., Judeo/Christian/Islamic) to integrate transgendered people into their fold.

It is somewhat difficult from a theological viewpoint to grasp why Judeo-Christians tend to view transgendered issues as sinful. Christians felt compelled to emphasize differences in gender clothing styles because of Biblical passages such as Deuteronomy 22:5, which reads,

[4] "You shall not see your countryman's donkey or his ox fallen down on the way, and pay no attention to them; you shall certainly help him to raise them up.
[5] "A woman shall not wear man's clothing, nor shall a man put on a woman's clothing; for whoever does these things is an abomination to the LORD your God.

[6] "If you happen to come upon a bird's nest along the way, in any tree or on the ground, with young ones or eggs, and the mother sitting on the young or on the eggs, you shall not take the mother with the young." (New American Standard Bible)

The passage is confusing, in part, because it is surrounded by instructions regarding the treatment of animals and people. The passage appears to imply that certain social duties are required by men and women. Wearing clothing associated with the opposite gender might be seen as a way to *hide* from these duties. Also of interest is the amount of attention paid to verse five. Later in the chapter, the author condemns wearing clothes made of mixed fabrics, and the chapter advocates stoning women whose honeymoon night does not indicate the traumatic tearing of the hymen. For the later, the passage concludes, "You shall purge the evil from among you."

Most Christian and Jewish sects ignore these instructions. It is also interesting to note that the contemporary condemnation against cross-dressing is unidirectional. Men are prohibited from dressing as women, but few restrictions are placed on women. In fact, during the beginning of the Christian era, women who acted like men were much admired. There are many female saints who while they were alive were thought to be men (Perkins, 1995).

PHYSICAL AND MENTAL HEALTH

The physical and mental components of transitioning continue for years. Some people imagine the process is over in days once the person has a sex change. This is never the case. Both MtF and FtM transpeople go through a series of changes that occur in stages.

Male-to-Female Reconstruction

In a very real sense, an adult male who is transitioning into a woman is going through adolescence, but unlike most adolescents, she is surrounded by men who expect her to understand adult sexual cues (Carroll & Gilroy, 2002).

MfF transsexuals often engage in estrogen and anti-androgen therapy, facial electrolysis (which takes two years), facial feminization surgery (which includes forehead reconstruction, trachea shaving, jaw and chin reshaping, nose recontouring, ear pinning, facial collagen injections, cheekbone implants, facelifts, and skin resurfacing), and sex reassignment surgery (which happens after the real-life experience). Even this is not the full story, as every aspect of the male genitals are often used in the reconstruction. This means the scrotum must undergo about 15 hours of electrolysis to be used to create the labia majora. Facial feminization surgeries may cost over $60,000. Male-to-female genital surgery is widely available for about $15,000 and is done in one or two stages. The result can be cosmetically very good, and orgasmic ability may be retained (if performed before age 30). The operation is elaborate and beyond the scope of this text, but briefly, the penis is partially flayed and pushed inside out into a newly created body cavity. Lifelong dilation is required to keep the cavity large enough to receive a penis during sex.

When a MtF decides to take estrogen (which I call hormone development therapy as opposed to hormone replacement therapy for natal women), she often looks forward to developing large breasts. Many transsexuals fail to realize that the introduction of these hormones into their bodies will cause permanent changes and have serious health consequences. For example, taking estrogen increases the risk of developing cancers of the breast, liver, and gall bladder (Ayerst Laboratories, 1988). The increased breast development actually makes the transsexual as susceptible to breast cancer as a genetic female. Estrogen also increase the risk of blood clotting in various parts of the body, leading to a higher incidence of stroke, angina (narrowing of a heart blood vessel), or pulmonary embolus (a clot that forms in the legs or pelvis and then breaks off and travels to the lungs). Even when the hormones do not produce life-threatening consequences, their use often leads to nausea, vomiting, depression, breast tenderness, and fluid retention. Estrogen may also increase or worsen existing such medical conditions as asthma, epilepsy, migraines, heart disease, or kidney disease.

In addition to all these health problems, the results of the treatment may be less dramatic than the transgendered individual anticipates. If treatment is started before age 25, breast development is usually about one size smaller than the breast size of genetic women in their family of origin, although results are difficult to accurately predict for any given individual. Some transsexuals choose to receive implants and then find their breasts continuing to grow. As many women have come to realize, large breasts can cause discomfort, backaches, and mobility problems. In addition to problems with excessive growth, some transwomen change their minds as their bodies change. Consider "Angela's" note to a transgendered newsgroup:

> After almost five months, I knew it [hormone treatment] was not what I wanted. The changes were too drastic, too all enveloping. And while my soft skin disappeared and my thighs lost their newly-found thickness, what breasts I had developed barely shrunk. They aren't so large, maybe a cup and a half, but they are there. Large nipples, my areola grew wider and is much darker. The breasts have begun to sag just a bit. I am now going to have surgery to have them removed. And even then, there will always be an extra fold of flesh there. So, everyone, until you know for sure, hold back.

Other common expectations for hormone treatment may include a reduction in facial hair, but estrogen has no impact on facial hair. The treatment may actually make electrolysis more painful by making the skin softer and more sensitive. However, beyond all these problems, there is also a loss or elimination of the masculine sex drive. As the hormones continue to affect receptor sites throughout the body, the penis can become very tender and erections may actually become painful. The penis may also atrophy, which can cause problems for sexual reassignment surgery because the penile wall is used to create the vagina. In addition to all these consequences, after a period of time (two to eight months) on hormones, permanent sterility results.

Female-to-Male

For all transsexuals, the results of hormonal treatment vary depending on how long it has been since the onset of puberty. For example, the results are considerably more dramatic in an 18-year-old than a 28-year-old, but results usually are not dramatically different between a 38-year-old and a 48-year-old (Richards, 2001).

With effective and continuous dosages of male hormones, a number of irreversible changes begin to occur. The vocal cords thicken, which deepens the voice, although not necessarily all the way down to the register of an average male. Fertility decreases as the menstrual cycle becomes irregular and then stops. The sex drive increases, and hair on the face and body begins to grow more quickly and becomes thicker. Male-pattern baldness may set in, and oil and sweat glands become more active. Muscle mass increases with light exercise. Fat is redistributed, with the face becoming more typically male in shape and fat from the hips moving upward to the waist.

Masculinizing hormones fail to change the size of the individual's breasts, although they may change in shape. Breast removal must be done surgically. There is also little change in the shape or size of bone structure, although bone density may change slightly (Richards, 2001).

If an individual continues the process to the point of seeking surgical reassignment surgery, the procedure is elaborate. For female-to-male surgery, the process is significantly more difficult. Sometimes, hormonal interventions can enlarge the clitoris, which, with surgery, may resemble a small penis. If a hysterectomy has been performed, the vaginal opening can be closed and a scrotum fashioned around prosthetic testes. Complication rates are much higher if there is an attempt to create a urinary conduit through the neophallus (Barrett, 1998). Such a procedure can eliminate orgasmic ability and create potentially serious health risks. Obtaining sufficient tissue to create a neophallus or neoscrotum may also pose problems. Some surgeons use tissue from a coincidental vulvectomy or mastectomy after previous stretching of the skin with subcutaneous tissue expanders. There are also significant costs involved. Breast reduction, hysterectomy, and genital surgery can cost from $60,000 to $100,000.

Mental Health

Valentine (2007) correctly notes that all the emphasis on transgender within the mental health community tends to come from people who are not transgendered. Adding to the problem is the inclusion of the "T" in the GLBTQ culture. Gay and lesbian groups often strive to show they are "like everyone else," which forces transgendered people to fall back into binary thinking. Such difficulties have led some people to call themselves both male and female without calling themselves transgendered. Others call themselves simply "trans" because the term "transgendered" is loaded to mean something more (or less) than they feel about themselves.

The psychological status of transgendered individuals has been misunderstood and misrepresented. This is clearly evident in the ways such individuals are depicted in film. In the movie *Sleepless in Seattle* (1992), one woman tells her friend to avoid a blind date because "The guy could be a crackhead, a psychopath, a flasher, a junkie, a transvestite, a chain-saw murderer, or someone really sick...." This perception of trans people being like drug addicts or murderers has been evidenced to a lesser degree in literature.

The psychological classification of transgendered individuals varied considerably over the 20th century. Transsexuality has been labeled a psychotic condition, a neuroendocrinopathy, a borderline syndrome, and a creative defense mechanism (Hirschauer, 1997). Clearly, the range of these nosological classifications implies the existence of a political agenda. In most cases, individuals with "gender incongruence" and "transvestic fetishism" have been perceived as maladjusted men and women who can be "treated" and made better by the medical community (Denny, 1997). Being shunned from society at nearly every level also increases the risks of suicide. Up to 45% of transgendered people may consider suicide (Grossman & D'Augelli, 2007) and up to 67% of transsexual adults (Brammer, Morgan & Albers, 2010).

If there is a general psychological issue separating transgendered individuals from nontransgendered people, it would involve an attempt to salvage a fragile sense of self. It has been well-documented that transgendered individuals often report problems with mood, anxiety, and abuse of alcohol or other drugs (Denny & Green, 1996). In older studies, these mental health concerns are supposedly related to gender identity itself, but it makes little sense. Now it appears most of the negative assessments stem from prejudices. Sánchez and Vilain (2009) found a stronger relationship among mental health and the views cross-dressers have regarding the community and their shared identities. The more positively transsexuals felt about the transsexual community, the less psychological distress they reported. Fear regarding discovery or identifying as transsexual led to greater distress. However, the process of breaking from bi-gendered norms would inevitably affect mental health to some degree. Most transgendered individuals experience some form of depression because of their gender identity (Brammer, Morgan & Albers, 2010), but very few believe transitioning was a mistake. Finding peace with self is often worth the social, relational, and occupational challenges.

INDIVIDUAL AND GROUP INTERVENTIONS

In the transgender-oriented film *Zerophilia* (2006), the fictitious sex expert tells our hero/heroine a simple line: "... one thing I learned long ago: You can't change your true nature, even if it can change you." This is the essence of transgendered identity. First, you have to realize your true nature. Then, you have to figure out how it will change you.

Most people with gender identity issues will never progress toward body transformations. They will also attempt to "purge" themselves of unacceptable gendered clothing or speech patterns. Such patterns have been consistent for decades (Buhrich, 1978; Brammer, Morgan & Albers, 2010). For cross-dressers—but less so with transsexuals—there may be a recurring cycle of buying and throwing away or destroying expensive clothing, cosmetics, and reading materials. This "binge/purge" syndrome is quite common.

Individuals who purge are likely to swear they will never cross-dress again and to divest themselves of everything that reminds them of the behavior. Material purged may include contact information that they will need when they once again begin to acknowledge and deal with their issues. In a purge phase, he or she may stop attending counseling sessions and refuse to return phone calls from the counseling center; this may be the counselor's only indication that a purge has occurred. Inevitably, the individual will once again begin to accumulate clothing—sometimes in an almost manic fashion. The inability to abide by the decision to purge can lead to additional guilt. It is important for therapists to realize that purging is usually short-lived. The gender issues will need to be integrated into the client's core personality.

These facets make the clients story and the words clients use essential to providing help. Narrative therapy, with its emphasis on language, can help address both personal and political social stories. Asking questions such as, "What would the world look like without your depression?" addresses both the individual's current functioning and the way the world is intertwined with emotion (Kamya, 2007).

Intervention for Cross-Dressers

When cross-dressers present for treatment, it is usually because they want help in salvaging their relationships (Bullough & Bullough, 1993). They usually have little or no desire to change their cross-dressing behavior, but the behavior offends the client's spouse. Honestly confronting the situation is the best place to start. Both partners need to realize that the cross-dressing is likely to continue but that the cross-dresser has the ability to curtail the compulsions.

Successful treatment will address self-acceptance and overcoming the shame associated with the cross-dressing behavior. The therapeutic process is more difficult when the individual's significant other lacks the necessary understanding. Consider the following case.

Marsha:	This is hard to talk about, but Kyle's sexual desires make me uncomfortable. *(Kyle looks down.)*
Therapist:	Can either of you tell me more?
Marsha:	He wants to dress up in women's clothing when he makes love to me. *(silence)*
Therapist:	Kyle, you have been very quiet during all this. Do you feel comfortable talking about this topic?
Kyle:	I know it sounds bad, but it's not just a sexual thing for me. I just enjoy wearing nighties.
Marsha:	When we were first married, there wasn't a problem. Then, one night, he asked if he could wear one of my nightgowns to bed. He said he was just curious what it would be like. He never told me that he had worn them for years. Slowly, he started asking more and more often—until it seemed like it was every night.

Kyle's discomfort is readily apparent, and it is clear that there are issues to work out with regard to his behavior. Kyle will need to identify what benefit he obtains from his cross-dressing and to learn to behave in a way that does not harm his relationship. The process may seem difficult for many cross-dressers. They may state that they "cannot control the impulses" and believe that their desires only get worse when abstinence is attempted.

Kyle:	I can't control it. If I try, I find myself dressing even more often. Like part of me needs to do this to survive.
Therapist:	I can sense so much tension in your replies, as if you need to defend yourself. These are really difficult issues. What's the hardest part for you?
Kyle:	My marriage. I love my wife, and it breaks me apart to hurt her.
Therapist:	So, you're pulled in two directions. You need to identify as a woman and you need to be a man for your wife. Is there a middle ground for the two of you?

Many couples can carve out this middle ground. For some, the partner will carve out a "dressing free" zone or day (like Fridays or in the bedroom). For others, dressing is only allowed at hotels or at meetings. Such boundaries help maintain the relationship, but they also create tension. Long-term counseling should address the anxiety and depression associated with such sacrifices.

Individual Interventions for Transsexuals

Research on postoperative functioning of transsexuals does not allow for unequivocal conclusions, but there is little doubt that sexual reassignment surgery (SRS) substantially alleviates the suffering of transsexuals. SRS is no panacea. Psychotherapy may be needed to help transsexuals adapt to the new situation or deal with issues that could not be addressed before treatment (Cohen-Kettenis & Gooren, 1999). How will an individual's friends, relatives, or coworkers react to his or her new gender identity? What happens if he or she comes to the conclusion that the decision was a mistake? Can he or she accept the fact that he or she will become sterile after SRS? Can he or she face the prejudice and discrimination that will inevitably follow? These are important considerations that should be explored thoroughly in therapy.

Overall satisfactory postoperative results have been reported for 87% of male-to-female transsexuals (MtFs) and for 97% of female-to-male transsexuals (FtMs) (Green and Fleming, 1990). More recent studies are even higher (Imbimbo et al., 2009), with 75% saying they had a more satisfactory sex life after SRS, and none of the participants expressed regrets (although nearly half were dissatisfied with the depth of their neovagina). However, a transsexual's quality of life appears lower than control groups. Transsexuals tend to have issues with general health, role limitation, physical limitations, and personal limitation when compared to nontranssexual controls (Kuhn et al., 2009). One transsexual summed up this difference this way, "To transition is pricey, painful, yet essential. My life sucks, yet I've never been happier. Life as a trans person is WAY better than suicide" (Brammer, Morgan & Albers, 2010).

The hormones themselves are also likely to affect the individual's emotional lability. Slabbekoorn, Van Goozen, Gooren, and Cohen-Kettenis

(2001) identified differences in the ways male-to-female and female-to-male transsexuals responded to hormonal treatments. MtFs experienced negative emotions more intensely than FtMs both before and after hormone treatment. This finding was not new. Buchanan, Eccles, and Becker (1992) concluded that adolescents' emotional swings were associated with the hormonal changes in their bodies. It is important to realize that anti-androgen and estrogen treatment will increase emotional intensity, while testosterone treatment in FtMs will likely reduce emotional intensity, with the exception of aggression and sexual excitement. These chemical changes are especially important in suicidality assessments. Unaccustomed to intense emotional fluctuations, males may find themselves at greater risk.

If clients follow the standards of care and undergo a real-life experience prior to receiving SRS, therapists should use this time to help them adjust to their internal and external changes. This waiting period provides the transsexual with an opportunity to determine whether the new gender role is congruent with his or her goals and plans. Even issues such as breast tenderness are alarming and disturbing. Clients need to feel safe talking about their bodies and going through puberty as an older girl.

Counselors should also become very familiar with the World Professional Association for Transgendered Health, Inc. (WPATH) standards of care. At the time of the sixth edition, mental health professionals were expected to have 10 tasks when working with individuals with gender identity disorders. These included diagnosis or gender identity, diagnosis of comorbid psychiatric conditions, providing individual and family counseling, ascertain readiness for hormone and surgical therapy, and to work with a team to assist with medical interventions. The **ALGBTIC** (Association for Lesbian, Gay, Bisexual & Transgender Issues in Counseling) has also issued competencies for counseling transgendered individuals.

Children with Gender Incongruence

With children, therapists and parents alike may feel a need to effectively instill a stable and sex-congruent gender identity. It is important to realize that most young children who experience gender incongruence will not seek sexual reassignment surgery as adults (Green, 1987). Among children, transgendering and sexuality may often be mixed. The process is not linear, and it is often difficult to predict how childhood behavior will evolve.

It was once believed—largely because of the case of John/Joan—that gender could be assigned at birth. In this case, John, while only eight months old, had complications during a botched circumcision. During the operation, his penis was accidentally burned through ablation. The physicians involved decided John could be raised female and convinced his parents to rename him Joan. "Joan" was given estrogen and treated as if he had always been female. The procedure was considered a success until "Joan" rejected hormonal treatment at age 12. Throughout this time, nearly everyone who knew her regarded Joan as masculine. She wore masculine clothes (against her parents' wishes), urinated standing up, and played masculine games. By age 14, she had completely rejected the feminine role thrust on her, but she had no knowledge of her male past. She simply did not feel feminine. When she refused her final feminizing surgery, her father told her about the surgery she had received as an infant. She immediately requested a mastectomy and phallus reconstruction (which was completed one month prior to his 16th birthday) and changed his name back to John (Colapinto, 1997). Sadly, John ultimately committed suicide.

Such cases have forced theorists to realize that gender is not simply a learned behavior. In all likelihood, we are not gender-neutral at birth and are strongly influenced by the prenatal environment (Diamond, 1996). If a child's gender is ambiguous, it has been argued that the individual should be allowed to make this decision because it affects every element of functioning.

By the time an individual reaches adolescence, the decision regarding surgical reassignment is no less daunting than for younger children. There is limited research in this area, but adolescents who undergo sexual reassignment surgery appear to resolve their gender incongruence (Cohen-Kettins & van Goozen, 1997). Ekins and King (2001) recommend using the gerund of transgender, namely "transgendering," to highlight the process elements. The active form of the word not only addresses an individual's process of change, but it also addresses a societal movement.

ADVOCACY AND SOCIAL JUSTICE

Willging, Salvador, and Kano (2006) found that a majority of rural mental health providers claimed that there was no difference between working with GLBT clients and non-GLBT clients. This gender-blind position is similar to the color-blind problem we discussed in the ethnic section. It ignores the unique health, relational, educational, occupational, and other issues unique to the transgendered community. It may also discourage clients from broaching sexuality and gender issues.

Counselors with limited exposure to transgendered communities sometimes exhibit a voyeuristic curiosity with transgendered clients (Ettner, 1996). The topics can be stimulating and intellectually provocative. For these reasons, counselors should establish ties with both local and national support organizations prior to beginning work with such clients (Carroll & Gilroy, 2002). Transgendered clients who belong to local support groups are significantly more likely to feel better about themselves and their gender issues (Lombardi, 1999).

Even though transgendered clients face unique challenges that require special training for therapists, another area for public advocacy is public perception. Changing the word "disorder" to "incongruence" in *DSM-IV* was a helpful step. There are clearly issues related to gender divergent identities to warrant clinical attention (e.g., depression, suicide, and relationship issues), but there is also enough evidence to suggestion gender identity (divergent or not) is a normal developmental process. Focusing on the normality of all types of gender development while simultaneously assisting people with how their particular identity will create unique joys and challenges will assist all people.

Ault and Brzuzy (2009) chronicled how transgendered people have been hospitalized for their gender issues. They are forced to fit into the bigendered society, contrary to their natural instincts. They are told there is something wrong with them because they do not fit into a biased bigendered world. It is not uncommon for transgendered folks to hear repeated comments such as, "Don't sit with your legs crossed," "You'll never attract a man like that," "Walk like a man," "Girls don't slouch," "Boys don't cry," and "Women don't talk like that." Such rules are hard enough for feminine boys and tomboys who grow up without divergent identities. They are torturous for others. Working to remove the stigma of having a "disorder" will shift the focus back on the issues deserving of attention.

In advocating for individual clients, it is also important to find a balance between encouraging and supporting. Transgendered clients need a realistic window into how the world sees them. Counselors are their eyes and ears for how they are likely to be perceived, and such feedback should be provided. At the same time, counselors must wait for clients to move before guiding them. Some clients may enter therapy ready to transition—only to change their mind a month into hormone treatment. Take each step as it comes. There is no clear pattern for gender identity. It flows, stops, turns, and moves as it will. Counselors must learn to be flexible and celebrate wherever the client is in a given week.

In terms of fighting for social justice, employment is the most important starting point. Does your agency or school have a policy specifically protecting gender identity and gender expression from discrimination? Have you advocated for the enforcement of current laws or policies on the books? Does your local school district offer training to students and staff about gender identity and discrimination? Can you conduct matched-pair studies in your area to document the discrimination taking place? These are critical steps for the survival of many transgendered folks.

Michelle's Story (A Client's Viewpoint)

Writing about my gender identity is such an exciting and shaming thing. Sometimes, I don't understand it at all. Other times, I feel so secure and complete that I want to shout it to the world. Those times are rare. I currently live as a 44-year-old male, which is the role I was assigned at birth. I've been taking estrogen for two years but at dosages to only slightly alter my body. I have small breasts (A cup on the left, AA cup on the right), have stopped the balding process, have better skin, and my brain—well, that part is hard to explain. It might take a little background info.

Some of the earliest fantasy games I played involved women's clothing and roles. I stockpiled clothing from my mother and girlfriends since I was four years old. When I played house, I tended to prefer playing child or girl roles, but most of my activities were masculine (e.g., baseball or soccer). My parents never encouraged my femininity. They simply tried to

(continues)

Michelle's Story (A Client's Viewpoint) (continued)

ignore it. When I was about eight years old, my mother asked politely if I would stop wearing her underwear. She offered to buy me my own panties, but I was too embarrassed to accept. When I was 13, my father came home early from work and caught me completely dressed as a girl. We never discussed this. At 14, I came out to my 11-year old sister. She told me that she could not accept me as a sister.

The big change happened when I was 15. I spent the night with a church youth leader, who molested me as we slept. He acted as if he was asleep, dreaming. With his huge arm draped over me, he rubbed my penis through my clothing. I broke away from his grasp and called my parents. My mother, probably trying to diffuse the situation, said, "He probably just thought you were a girl."

To this day, I'm not sure why being molested as a girl would be any better than being molested as a boy, but it was shocking that my mother saw me for who I was.

At 17, I started cross-dressing with my girlfriend. We would go to a secluded park, change clothing, and walk home. There was nothing sexual about the exchange, and I'm sure this whole process confused me.

I hoped marrying would end all this foolishness. At age 21, I married my soul mate. Unfortunately, she knew nothing about my gender issues and later said I was the "most masculine man she knew." Within a year, I was spending considerable time as a woman, and I considered transitioning. My wife seriously contemplated divorce, which scared me into purging. I went two years without dressing. Burned photos. Erased videos. Threw out hormones. But the desires came back stronger.

At 42, after growing weary about tacit suicidal thoughts, I underwent counseling for the fourth time, and I met with a physician to discuss hormone treatments. I keep telling myself this is only a phase. I will get back to where my wife needs me to be, but I'm not sure any longer. I don't know where this is heading.

Laura's Story (A Counselor's Viewpoint)

When I met Michelle, I had little exposure to the transgendered community. I had known two people who transitioned, but one of them had a coexisting mental health disorder. Michelle presented differently. She was highly educated, married, and had a good career. Together, we worked as much on managing her anxiety and fears as her gender identity. In many ways, I think she knew who she was when she entered my office. She just hadn't learned to accept it yet.

(continues)

Laura's Story (A Counselor's Viewpoint) (continued)

In the early phases of counseling, Michelle seemed trapped in the bi-gendered world. During our first meeting, I told her not to worry about making decisions. Clarity would come with time. I was also concerned about her wife's view about transsexualism being immoral and sinful. I could see Michelle would progress somewhere, but parts of her story were difficult for me to grasp.

After about a month, Michelle was frustrated. She had started estrogen, which she took "without thought." But she wanted her "male identity" back. We discussed how she seemed like she was jumping along stepping stones, and each step led to transition. She never stepped back. It became clear that she might not have a choice about her gender identity. It might choose her.

About three months into therapy, I told Michelle about a word that kept coming to mind when I thought of her. It was "binary." It was more than her attempt to fit into a binary gender world. She forced herself into multiple binary patterns. Success and failure. Accepted or rejected. It was hard for her stay in the middle.

The following session, she started by addressing how her mind was working differently. Most of her life, she had based her decisions on logic. Now she felt more intuitive, and the changed frightened her. At this point, I chuckled and said, "Welcome to womanhood." I didn't think much about the reaction, but she brought it back for the next three sessions. It was affirming and honest. She appreciated my letting down my guard—being woman to woman.

Four months into therapy, Michelle looked much more comfortable in her skin. She had a frank discussion with her wife about where things might go, and it went as well as could be expected. This lead to a quicker progression. After eight months, she doubled her hormones (under her doctor's consultation), started electrolysis, and wore more feminine clothing to work. After 11 months, people started identifying her as a "she" in public. This process scared her, and she contemplated suicide. She enjoyed being treated as a woman; but everything she had built in life occurred as a man. Her fear of hurting her family left her feeling hopeless for the future. I gave her my cell number, and she agreed to call if the ideation became any stronger.

We also discussed if she would still want to get rid of her femininity. She said, "It was the wrong question." If given two pills—one that would end her feminine identity but leave her body as is and another pill that would change her into a genetic woman—she would pick the latter. She added, "I would not even consider the options. I would take the pill, then think about it afterwards—just as I did when I took my first estrogen pill." She never stopped the estrogen therapy.

(continues)

Laura's Story (A Counselor's Viewpoint) (continued)

After a year, as her breast buds were apparent (and painful), she emailed me for help. I vaguely remembered some girls covering their nipples with Band-Aids. She seemed so relieved to have a confidant, and I realized how much of our relationship required me to educate her about womanhood (and girlhood).

Looking back on the time we shared, she really didn't change as much as I expected. She legally changed her name and gender, had surgery, and lives full-time as a woman. But she presents as the same person—only more comfortable.

I also realized that the most valuable parts of counseling were brief moments of connection between us. She hung onto small eye movements, laughs, changes in my voice. She wanted so much to receive validation about herself—whether positive or negative. In some ways, counseling simply helped her exist, even though I consciously worked to avoid pushing her one direction or another. As she became comfortable sharing all her feelings, she learned to accept those parts of herself.

Questions to Consider:

1. Michelle started hormones about the time she started counseling. Should transpeople be forced to wait until they are few months into therapy before starting hormones?
2. Michelle considered suicide after people she met considered her female. Does this imply incongruence with transsexualism?
3. Laura said the most meaningful moments of therapy came from brief moments of connection. Does this make sense? Why might this be more likely for transsexuals than others?
4. Laura mentioned gender education as being important for transsexuals. How much education should counselors provide? Should this be given in structured or unstructured ways?

INTERVENTION EXERCISES

Counseling and Therapy: Alyia is a 32-year-old male-to-female African American who is married and suicidal. She no longer feels she can live life as a man, but she cannot face the possibility of leaving her wife. "I know it would hurt my wife if I died, but sometimes, I think it would hurt less than if she had to think about having an ex-wife. How could I force such a stigma on the woman I love?" She has taken estrogen for three years, has B-cup breasts, and hair to her shoulders. She still wears men's clothes, no makeup, and presents as androgynous. How would you counsel her?

School Psychology: Gyna (Japanese American female, age 12) was caught in the eighth-grade locker room taking some type of prescription medication. When the vice principal interviewed her, she admitted that they were testosterone pills. She begged the principal not to tell her parents, saying, "I know it would crush them and embarrass the family if they found out what I was."

Before the vice principal calls home, he asks you to "find out what you can." He concludes, "I know this isn't an academic assessment *per se*, but this identity thingy is affecting her school work. We need to find out what we can before we talk to the parents." What do you do?

School Counseling: Pablo is a Mexican American ninth-grade student. Two weeks into the school year, he started wearing women's T-shirts and jeans to school. A few boys mocked him, but he continued the practice. The clothes were feminine but not markedly so. One day, he pushed the boundaries a little more. He wore a bright pink T-shirt with the word "angel" in green glittery letters. His homeroom teacher sent him to you for guidance and "breaking the dress code." The moment he sat in your office, he heaved a deep sigh and smiled. "I'm ready. I'm ready to become Pauline." He looked into your eyes and concluded, "Would you please help me tell my parents and teachers that I'm ready to become a girl full-time?" What else would you need to explore? How would you counselor Pablo?

Social Work: Mark is a 22-year-old female-to-male European American who is just starting his real-life experience. He has moved to your town and wants to know what resources are available. He has no job, a small savings, and has been disowned by his family of origin. He is hoping you will provide some help in identifying resources for housing, occupational training, and social networking.

QUESTIONS TO CONSIDER

1. What is the difference between sex and gender?
2. How would you define the difference between a preoperative transsexual and a cross-dresser?
3. Why do you believe the phrase gender identity disorder was removed from *DSM-IV*?
4. In your opinion, what are the causes of gender identity problems?
5. What advice would you give to a woman married to a male cross-dresser?
6. What is likely to pose the greatest threat to gender-dysphoric individuals in the workplace?
7. Should children with gender identity conflicts be allowed to attend school as a member of their perceived gender?
8. What are the primary effects of ingesting sex-contrary hormones?
9. The act of attempting to quit gender-dysphoric behaviors often leads to "purging." Should counselors recommend such an action?
10. How should the compulsiveness of transgendered clients be addressed?
11. What role should counselors play in "gatekeeping" the appropriateness of SRS patients?
12. What components appear most helpful for intervening with gender-dysphoric clients?

CHAPTER 11

Gays and Lesbians

INSIGHT EXERCISE

It's a little embarrassing talking about this. I mean, I'm 18 years old. I should be over this by now. *(puffs out a breath)* Okay, here it goes. I've never been attracted to a girl. I mean, I did kiss a girl. We were on a blind date when I was 16, and my friends pretty much forced me to go out with her. I guess they thought it would be funny. I kind of wanted to see what it was like too. To be honest, it was a little … bland.

But last week—I mean, wow! I was at the doctor's office, and this male nurse came to check my temperature. He put the thermometer in my mouth, but part of his finger brushed against the bottom of my lip. I don't think he meant anything by it. But it affected me instantly.

My whole body felt like it was going to explode. Tingles ran through my shoulders, and I'm sure I blushed. I had no idea what was happening, and I wasn't sure how to respond.

What does this mean? I mean, is this normal? Do other people feel like this?

Questions to Consider

1. Think about this question carefully. Picture the person in the above insight exercise. What images are running through your head? Did you realize the story does not state the person's gender? Did you assume this was a male because this chapter is about "gay" people? What does that assumption say about you?

2. How would you describe the person's personality if this were a girl? How would you see this person differently if this were a boy? Why are your views different?

3. Now the big one. In your own mind, is being gay "wrong"? Why do you believe this? How does it affect the way you interact with couples and singles?

Perhaps more than any other topic related to gender or sexuality, sexual orientation elicits strong opinions. Staunch opponents of gay and lesbian behavior view it as a "manifestation of a depraved nature and a perversion of divine standards" (Ontario Consultants on Religious Tolerance, 1998a). On the other hand, those who advocate social tolerance of gays and lesbians have likened American homophobia to the "wholesale torture and extermination of innocent people during the 'witch'-burning times" (Ontario Consultants on Religious Tolerance, 1998b). Battle lines are sharply drawn, and movement from one camp to the other seems unlikely.

GLBTQ refers to gay, lesbian, bisexual, and transgender. The letter "q" is sometimes included, although it may mean different things. It would stand for "queer" or for "questioning" (Tollerud & Slabon, 2009). Although the GLBTQ community operates with a number of unique terms and expressions, there are a few you must understand to "get" this chapter. The term *gay* usually refers to men who are attracted to other men. It is sometimes used as a general reference for all people who have a same-sex sexual orientation. Lesbians are women who are attracted to women. Bisexuals fall somewhere along the continuum of attraction—feeling attracted to men and women, although not necessarily equally. Some gay men marry women, whom they love, but do not self-identify as bisexuals. Most people explain this by saying, "If I were to leave my partner, I know I would end up with another man." From this viewpoint, "gay" fits them better than "bisexual."

The sexual orientation and gender identity aspects are split in this book because they address very different cultures and processes. Transgendered folk are often discussed with GLB issues not because of similarities in sexual orientation issues but because sexuality and gender identities share similar political struggles.

You will also read about "coming out" or being "outed." Both describe the personal and social dimensions of announcing one's sexual orientation. Some people will talk about "coming out to themselves." This means, it took them years to accept that they were gay, but they finally did. The term "straight" often refers to heterosexual couples. Homophobia—a problematic term—tends to represent any form of active resistance to gay rights. We will discuss this in great length in the culture section.

UNIQUE CHALLENGES

As gays and lesbians continue to struggle for equality, they face obstacles from a number of areas. Politically, there are still a number of challenges remaining: marriage, ordination, nondiscrimination protection, hate crime legislation, etc. These are important considerations, but they are also polarizing many countries. This struggle was highlighted clearly in Moscow. The World Health Organization removed homosexuality from its list of mental disorders on May 17, 1990. This anniversary is often remembered as a day to fight against gay injustices. In 1999, the civil protests against gay prejudice were not well-regarded. Moscow's leaders (including the mayor and his spokespeople) called gay rights marches "satanic" and that they were "destroying the moral pillars of our society." After about a minute of demonstrating, police stormed the protestors and took them off to jail. It was not a matter of squashing any protestors. In another part of the city, antigay demonstrators were tolerated (Goldberg, 2009). Such public struggles are serious, but the greatest struggles for many gays and lesbians lie elsewhere.

The biggest challenges appear less obvious. They are more likely to relate to the individual struggle rather than the global fight for equality. For many gay and lesbian clients, the biggest challenges rest in finding acceptance with family, friends, coworkers, and employers. It is still common for people to lose their jobs, churches, or parents because someone discovered they were gay. In the past year alone, I know people who faced the following:

- A lesbian received the highest performance score possible from her supervisor—only to be terminated a month later (when she was outed). The employer told her they were letting her go because she "failed to complete her pre-performance evaluation form on time."
- A gay man kept his sexual orientation hidden until he was 54 years old. He had been married twice but finally decided to live with his life partner. Even at this ripe age, his parents completely disowned him. They removed him from their will and have not had contact with him for three years.
- A 17-year-old gay male was playing guitar for his church worship band. The pastor told him he would have to be "less gay" if he wanted to keep playing for the church. They meant that he would have to control his flamboyance, colorful clothing, and expressive hand movements. The boy left the church.

These are the day-to-day struggles gays and lesbians face, and such struggles have long been part of the GLB culture.

HISTORICAL CONTEXT

The battle over the morality or appropriateness of same-sex relationships is fought in political, occupational, and religious arenas. Sometimes, the attacks leveled against gays and lesbians come from the most unpredictable sources. For example, consider the following remark:

> I can't really warm up to homosexuals.... As long as they leave me alone, I'll let them be. But if my kid ever said, "I'm gay, Daddy," I think I'd die. I still think of homosexuals as fags, queers, and fruits. (Feinbloom, 1976)

You may be surprised to learn that a male transvestite uttered the above comment. And the animosity has gone both ways. One gay professor angrily told me that transsexuals were "just playing dress up." Another gay professor accused a transsexual student of attempting to convert gay men to being transsexual. Many people wrongly connect gender expression and sexuality. If members of other "divergent" groups suggest that it is morally wrong for someone to have a same-sex sexual orientation, it is not surprising that the larger society has also conveyed animosity toward individuals who are lesbian or gay. Throughout recorded history, gays and lesbians have faced oppression from heterosexuals. Even the terminology applied to this group has a frightening origin. For example, the pejorative term *faggot* (literally, a bundle of twigs used for kindling) was originally applied to homosexuals because, in the Middle Ages, people would literally burn gays as they did kindling (Stoller, 1997). Such acts of violence are not limited to the Middle Ages. Although we would like to believe contemporary society is beyond such horrors, the past century has witnessed similar atrocities.

Many people are aware of the persecution the Jews experienced during the Nazi Holocaust, but fewer realize how gays and lesbians were treated. In Germany, gays and lesbians were forced to wear pink triangles or a patch marked "175" on their clothes. The virulent homophobia that underlay the Nazi desire to annihilate Germany's gays and lesbians led to many strategies for their degradation, imprisonment, enslavement, and extermination. During the Nazis' 12-year rule, they convicted nearly 50,000 gays and lesbians of criminal homosexuality. Most ended up in concentration camps (Kogon, 1950), where they were brutalized by both the guards and other inmates. While in the camps, they were assigned to the dirtiest jobs: They worked in the clay pits and the quarries, shoveled snow with their bare hands, and were used as living targets on the firing range. Some were told near the end of the war that they would be released if they allowed themselves to be castrated. Instead of being set free, they were shipped to the infamous Dirlwanger penal division on the Russian front (Rector, 1981). It is now known that at least 500,000 gays and lesbians died in the Holocaust (Rector, 1981). Even when liberation came, those wearing the pink triangle remained in German prisons to serve out the remainder of their sentences.

In the United States, the plight of gays, lesbians, and bisexuals followed a different path. Prior to the 1970s, psychological and psychiatric organizations considered homosexuality a "mental illness." Gay men and lesbians had to fight to preserve their civil rights. When their sexual orientation was known, they were denied jobs, housing, and even volunteer leadership positions. Unlike all other Americans, they were forced to prove their competence, reliability, and mental stability (Stoller, 1997).

With the publication of *DSM-II* in 1972, the status of homosexuality changed. The American Psychiatric Association listed it as a disorder only if it was considered "ego-dystonic." Ego-dystonic clients were those who refused to accept their sexual orientation and continued to wrestle with guilt and shame regarding sexual behaviors, while ego-syntonic clients accepted their homosexuality and viewed themselves as gay. Although this change may seem minor, its effect on the status of homosexuality was enormous. The revised perspective has been traced to Marmor's (1965) assertion that gay and lesbian people could be happy with their lives and contribute to the development of a new minority group in our society. This finding was enough to support the APA's conclusion that homosexuality did not represent an inherent disadvantage in all cultures or subcultures (American Psychological Association, 1997). Homosexuality in and of itself did not promote mental instability. Only the *belief* that one's sexual orientation was wrong made a client unstable.

By the late 1980s, the entire notion of ego-dystonic homosexuality was being questioned. Many of the arguments followed a simple line of reasoning: "Being uncomfortable with one's sexuality does not necessarily mean that a person is mentally ill." Discomfort or denial of one's sexual orientation may stem from the negative images projected by society rather than the mental health status of the gay individual. Arguments such as these led to dramatic changes in *DSM-III-R*, in which the categorization of homosexuality as pathology was removed entirely (American Psychological Association, 1997). Homosexuality could no longer be associated with mental illness because almost all people who are homosexual initially go through a phase in which their homosexuality is ego-dystonic. Whether individuals are straight or gay, they may have difficulties clarifying their sexual orientation, but this difficulty involves the anxiety of social emergence rather than sexual confusion.

In the 1990s, the American Psychological Association strengthened its position. Douglas Haldeman (chair of the APA's Committee on Lesbian, Gay, and Bisexual Issues) stated, "Gay men and lesbians do not differ from other populations in such areas as decision-making, intimate relationships, self-esteem and vocational adjustment" (Sleek, 1996). Statements like these have affected society's views about gays and lesbians, but new dangers have emerged to hinder the integration of gays and lesbians into the larger society.

Polls show more acceptance of gays and lesbians in the United States today than in the past, but there has been a concurrent rise in antigay bias. A recent Pew Research poll (Direction from Americans, 2010) demonstrates that more people than ever before consider homosexuality acceptable, with 61% supporting openly gay men serving in the military. Americans are more likely to support gays and lesbians' rights to teach, speak publicly, reside in traditional neighborhoods, and have their books in public libraries (Schafer & Shaw, 2009).

Despite this support, the majority (57%) of Americans oppose gay marriage (Jones, 2009). The ideological struggle has historically left gays and lesbians vulnerable to assault. Hunter (2008) notes that gay and lesbians are significantly overrepresented among victims of violence. Herek, Gillis, Cogan & Glunt (1997) interviewed 74 bisexual females and 73 bisexual males living in Sacramento and found that 41% of them reported having been criminally victimized at least once since the age of 16. The assaults were perceived as bias-related and were generally perpetrated by European American males. The victims of such crimes were more likely to experience depression, anxiety, anger, and posttraumatic stress syndrome than were their peers who had not been assaulted.

To counter such attacks, legislation has been introduced to increase the penalties for acts of violence and other forms of discrimination based on a person's membership in a group. In 1996, the state of Washington adopted Initiative Measure No. 669 (Munro, 1996). The act promoted equal rights for gays and lesbians without providing them special status. The difference between equal treatment and special rights was clearly delineated: "The people find that equal protection of the law, not special rights, is a fundamental principle of constitutional government and is essential to the well-being and perpetuation of a free society." The rights extended to gays, lesbians, bisexuals, transsexuals, or transvestites encompassed matters related to status, preference, orientation, conduct, act, practice, or relationships. This act also sought to protect the rights of those who opposed such lifestyles, and it prohibited teachers from acting against sincerely held views of parents on the subject. It also prohibited state organizations from promoting or approving of same-sex sexual orientation as positive, healthy, or appropriate.

There is also a movement to make such protections international. Louise Arbour, former UN high commissioner for human rights, is fighting to protect GLB people from violations to their lives, security, and privacy. She believes criminalizing harmless private relations between consenting adults fosters fear, silence, and denial of identity in GLB persons (Goldberg, 2009). But there is still a ways to go before these protections are everywhere.

DEVELOPMENT

The increased acceptance of homosexuality is due in part to a broader understanding of its origins. Homosexuality exists in virtually every culture on Earth, and in some, it is a highly respected lifestyle (Herdt, 1982). The question theorists have tried to answer is, "Why are some persons attracted to members of the same sex?" Freud (1905) traced homosexuality to an unresolved Oedipus complex, in which a young boy who failed to identify with his father was more likely to adopt the sexual orientation of his mother. Freud believed that all people were born bisexual with latent homosexual impulses. Over the course of childhood, according to Freud, a person's sexual orientation was "determined" through early interaction with his or her parents.

Stoller's (1968) early work re-established the psychoanalytic components of homosexuality. He admitted that boys raised with domineering mothers and distant fathers were more likely to demonstrate some form of sexual confusion, but he also noted that it was difficult to predict the form such an orientation would take. He believed that the same processes are at work for the transsexual and homosexual child. However, in the transsexual child, the mother completely overwhelms her son and motivates him to believe in the superiority of womanhood. The homosexual child merely adopts the mother's sexual attraction toward males.

Despite Stoller's continued arguments in favor of his position, later researchers have focused more on genetic and biological etiologies. Günter Dörner et al. (1980, 1982) offered the strongest argument in this vein, stating that homosexuality results from abnormal levels of testosterone exposure during a critical stage of prenatal brain development. Gay males, he argued, had been exposed in utero to lower than normal levels of testosterone, while lesbians had been exposed to higher than normal levels.

Dörner et al. (1980) hypothesized that lower levels of maternal testosterone might be caused by environmental stress. To test his theory, Dörner located 794 German gay males born shortly before, during, and after World War II. Based on research linking stress with decreased levels of testosterone during pregnancy. Dörner, Götz & Docke (1982) hypothesized that the stress of wartime or postwar experiences would have depleted the mother's testosterone levels. The results showed that significantly higher numbers of gay

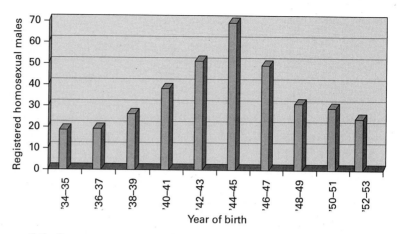

FIGURE **11.1** Relative Frequency of Homosexual Males Born in Germany (or GDR) Before, During, and After WWII (*n* = 794)

males had been born between 1942 and 1947 than in the years before and after this period (Figure 11.1).

More recent research has sought to explain the genetics of sexuality. Attempts to find an individual chromosome or gene have been unsuccessful, but others have taken a more general evolutionary approach. Schwartz et al. (2010) argue that family and twin studies demonstrate the contribution of hereditary factors to sexual orientation in men (e.g., Mustanski, Chivers & Bailey, 2002). They also found that the closer the genetic ties a gay male had to another relative increased the likelihood of the other person being gay. Brothers were significantly more likely to be gay together than cousins. First cousins more likely than second cousins. Similar findings were also found for women. Sisters with gay brothers were much more likely to be lesbians than if their brothers were straight (7.1% vs. 0.7%). These findings could be products of learning observation, but that argument seems less likely based on the ripple effect extending to cousins.

With a continued emphasis on genetic and environmental components that shape sexual orientation, it is becoming increasingly unlikely that sexuality exists in a purely dichotomous form. Rather than classifying people as either homosexual or heterosexual, it may be more realistic to acknowledge that sexual orientation has several variations based on the relative strength of attraction a person feels toward members of the same sex and the opposite sex (see Table 11.1).

From this perspective, some people have a greater predisposition toward a heterosexual orientation, while others are more likely to be homosexual, bisexual, or asexual. Unlike the dichotomous model, this model suggests that some people would find it easier than others to change their orientation. Individuals who have strong sexual attraction for members of the same sex but weak attraction for members of the opposite sex (or vice versa) are unlikely

TABLE **11.1**
Variations in Sexual Orientation

		Attraction to Same Sex	
		Low	High
Attraction to Opposite Sex	High	Heterosexual	Bisexual
	Low	Asexual	Gay or Lesbian

to change their dominant orientation under any circumstances. Others—born with more neutral predispositions—can change but are less likely to do so after they immerse themselves in a particular lifestyle. It should be noted that lasting changes in sexual orientation are rare. A Gallup poll (Born gay, 2009) showed a significant change in the way people view orientation. In 1977, the people who thought environmental factors created sexual orientation (56%) outnumbered the number of those who believed in genetic causes (13%) by more than threefold. Thirty years later, the situation is reversed, with more people supporting genetic causes than environmental (42% to 35%). This trend is important because 78% of the "born with" respondents believe the gay lifestyle is acceptable, where as 68% of the "environmental" respondents believe it is unacceptable. This tension is important for counselors too.

Let us find some agreement between the two perspectives. Think of orientation as a continuum. Imagine we had a test for sexual orientation that resembled a mood dot (i.e., a small piece of material that when placed on your body turns colors to indicate your present mood). When this imaginary dot is placed on heterosexuals, it turns white. When it is placed on a person who is gay or lesbian, it turns blue. The process seems simple enough until we start viewing the results. In real life, few people would have purely white or purely blue dots. Most would have some shade of blue, ranging from faint to dark. However, the closer the color is to blue or white the less likely an individual would be to identify with the opposite end of the continuum.

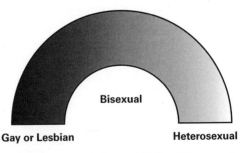

FIGURE **11.2** The Continuum of Sexual Orientation as Indicated Through the Sexual Orientation Dot

In all likelihood, this line of research will eventually demonstrate how people on either the blue or white sides of the graph have genetic predispositions or in utero hormonal influences guiding them. People toward the middle have poorer predictions for genetic/hormonal causes and more environmental influences. However, we may be decades away from such findings. Even when they arrive, it is unclear how they will influence behavior. If a group is influenced solely by environmental influences, sexual orientation will still become fixed around or before puberty.

WITHIN GROUP DIFFERENCES

Gay males and lesbians are often classified as a single unit, but these two groups are quite distinct from each other. From the dawn of the gay rights movement, the two genders sought different results. During the early years of lesbian feminism, lesbians sought to define themselves apart from men and reject male definitions of how they should feel, act, look, and live (Bunch, 1972). To be a lesbian, Bunch argued, was to love oneself as a woman. This definition views lesbianism not simply as a sexual act but as a woman's attempt to define her sense of self and energies, including sexual energies, around women. Women are important to her. She is important to herself. Lesbians must become feminists and fight against oppression of women, just as feminists must become lesbians if they hope to end male supremacy (Bunch, 1972).

Today, the feminist lesbian movement focuses primarily on achieving social acceptance rather than bringing about sweeping changes in society. Lesbians struggle to receive the recognition, validation, and support that are commonly given to heterosexual relationships (Kitzinger, 2001). They may even find validation of relationships to be lacking within their own community. It is also becoming clear that internalized heterosexism (i.e., the unexamined acceptance that heterosexual relationships are superior to lesbian relationships) is a primary cause of depression and body dissatisfaction (Haines et al., 2008).

Often, lesbians will view other lesbians as available, even when in a relationship. This makes sustaining long-lasting partnerships even more difficult (Siegel, 1985). When relationships are sustained, they face additional cultural threats. Lesbians also face a great deal of difficulty with setting boundaries and individuation within the relationship because both partners have been socialized to put the needs of others before their own (Scrivner & Eldridge, 1995). Another difficulty is potentially having dual PMS symptoms, which could result in mutual irritation, anger, or depression (Perz & Ussher, 2009). On the plus side, women in these relationships also benefit from increased connectedness, egalitarianism, and positive communication. These are powerful coping features.

Gay men face different struggles. Intimacy can present special difficulties for gay males. In European American culture, men are not socialized to foster intimate relationships (Harrison, 1987). They are expected to seek sexual gratification rather than emotional closeness, which may lead to additional difficulties with the risk of HIV infection. This risk is especially high among African Americans, who have new infection rates nearly twice as high as European Americans and three times higher than Latinos. Middle-aged men also face the highest risk, and two-thirds of those diagnosed will not live to be 45 years old (HIV and AIDS statistics by race/ethnicity, 2009).

Early in counseling, gay couples may need help with communication, courting skills, and safe sex practices. This may entail more of a psychoeducational approach than is commonly employed, but later sessions can help the couple use these skills during the session. Role-plays of courting practices, expressing feelings, and discussing dating boundaries can help the partners better understand each other.

Bisexuals of either gender face an entirely different set of problems. Although it may be possible, as Freud (1905) theorized, to consider that this orientation is common to all people, such a position is untenable to most heterosexuals or gays. Many gay and lesbian organizations consider bisexuals "closet homosexuals" and believe they are attempting to hide their sexual orientation under the guise of also being attracted to members of the opposite sex. Still others argue that bisexuals are simply going through a phase and have yet to realize their "true" sexuality (McDonald & Steinhorn, 1990). They posit that bisexuals are close to achieving a healthy "straight" relationship but are trapped within the ideology of the gay world.

Even the concept of bisexuality is sometimes difficult to define. Typically, bisexuality refers to people who are "attracted emotionally and sexually to people of either gender" (McDonald & Steinhorn, 1990, p. 30), but this is not always the case. There are many self-identified bisexual women who have not had sex with men, while some self-identified lesbians have had sexual relationships with men (Highleyman, 1993). The true definition belongs to the individual. A woman who believes herself to be a lesbian but is married to a man is stating that she is primarily attracted to women. From the viewpoint of those around her, she is likely to be described as bisexual or straight, but sexual orientation is inherently internal. It requires self-attribution. It will also depend on how the individual's various cultural groups view the relationship.

It should also be noted that sexual identity for GLB individuals parallels what would be common for the opposite sex (i.e., gay men tend to have sexual preferences similar to those reported by heterosexual women and lesbians tend to resemble the sexual preferences of heterosexual males). Bisexual men and women were their own unique cluster—at least in one study (Worthington & Reynolds, 2009).

CULTURAL IDENTITY

Just because GLB clients may have sexual interests similar to people of the opposite sex does not mean that they act like or identify with the opposite sex. Gay culture is unique, and it should be witnessed to be understood.

Before jumping into the different perceptions of ethnic differences, it is essential to grasp some of the terms associated with GLB culture. During the early part of the 20th century, repressive antisodomy laws were passed in New York and other areas with substantial proportions of homosexual residents. Police crackdowns ensued, raids were made on homosexual bars, and homosexuals were subject to arrest and imprisonment. In order to survive, homosexual men and women had to find code words to avoid entrapment by police. One such word was the term _gay,_ which probably derives from London slang. In the 17th century, the term _gay_ was expanded from its earlier meaning of cheerful and came also to refer to men with a reputation for being playboys. Its expansion to include male homosexual activity seemed a natural extension. The term _lesbian_ stems from the ancient Greek poet Sappho, who lived on the island of Lesbos. As Sappho became known for her poems celebrating love between women, the term _lesbian_ changed its primary meaning from "one who lives on Lesbos" to "a woman like Sappho and her followers."

Back in the 1960s and 1970s, the terms _gay_ and _lesbian_ were too well-known to be used safely. Other terms and expressions were developed to throw off the police. One such term was "a friend of Dorothy." This expression referred to _The Wizard of Oz_ heroine played by Judy Garland, whose musical ability and tragic life story were popular with gay audiences. Saying you were a friend of Dorothy meant you were gay. In some gay circles, myths are told how police would enter bars and begin their inquisitions with "Where is Dorothy?" The stories are told to indicate the cleverness of the gay community and the stubborn ignorance of the police.

Like other subgroups within society, gays and lesbians also use slang that is not shared by other groups. This slang may vary regionally and among different ethnic and socioeconomic subgroups. For example, "bears" are hairy, husky gay men, and many proudly self-identify as bears. There is even a Spring Thaw celebration in Seattle where the bears come out of "hibernation." A "fag hag" is a woman who prefers the company of gay men. There are also derogatory terms for other homosexuals and for outsiders. A "bull dyke" is a strong, masculine lesbian. "Campy" refers to flamboyant gay behavior. A "chicken" or "twink" is a young, boyish gay man. A "femme" can refer to either a feminine lesbian or a gay man who behaves effeminately. "Gaydar" is one's ability to readily detect a gay man or lesbian—although with gay men and lesbians living more and more openly as who they are, gaydar seems gradually to be becoming obsolete.

Learning the codes associated with the culture of sexual orientation takes place over a long process. Substantial research has been conducted over the years regarding the development of gay and lesbian identities, with possibly the clearest model being advanced by McCarn & Fassinger (1996). See Table 11.2.

Langdridge (2008) points out that models like this miss the real point of sexual development because they assume that contentment in binary sexual orientations is the ultimate goal. He feels this is boring and too conservative. Instead, he advocates the anger toward an unjust and **heterosexist** (i.e., believing heterosexual relationships are superior or preferred) society might make more sense. Leaving people to remain hostile against gays is unwise for all

TABLE **11.2**
Sexual Minority Identity Formation

	Internal Affect	Feelings About Minority Group
Stage 1: Awareness	The individual feels "different" or "odd" but is not willing to acknowledge anything else.	The individual knows very little about different sexual orientations.
Stage 2: Exploration	Strong, erotic feelings emerge for members of the same sex.	There is a growing awareness of the existence of "gay culture" but little exploration into this group.
Stage 3: Deepening/ Commitment	The individual begins to gain a sense of self-knowledge and self-fulfillment. Choices about how to act out on sexual orientation begin to crystallize.	A commitment begins to form with gay and lesbian groups. There is the awareness of oppression and the consequences of group choices.
Stage 4: Internalization/ Synthesis	The love for a same-sex partner spills over into an overall identity for self.	Across a variety of contexts, there is openness about being a member of the gay/lesbian community.

parties, and it will also harm future generations. Figure 11.3 provides a more flexible identity model.

The cultural identity model parallels McCarn and Fassinger's ideas, but the process has more to do with blending social acceptability with sexual desires. The same would hold true for heterosexual attraction. The initial impulses must blend with peer, parent, church, and socially acceptable avenues. The primary difference rests with the greater intensity of the social criticism and the sense of being "wrong" rather than just having bad taste. Most gay individuals will try "straight" dating not because they feel sexually attracted to the other sex but because it is so much easier to date in socially approved ways. This seldom lasts, as sexual impulses force reconsideration. There is often a process of a deepening commitment (i.e., I am gay) and attempts to socially integrate a gay identity within the dominant society. Sometimes, integration means hiding gay relationships; sometimes, it results in fighting for respect.

The social acceptance component is a primary element of GLB identity. Anger against heterosexist culture helps explain how the word **homophobia** came into prominence. The term is generally used to describe an irrational hate or fear of lesbians and gay men (Goldberg, 2010). Unfortunately, it is also used to connote any disagreement with gay lifestyles. At one of my workshops, a man explained how he believed homosexuality was a sin. He added that he had many gay friends but could not support their lifestyle. A woman stood, red-faced, and told him that his homophobic ideology had no place at a public university.

In attempting to settle the matter, I explained how sexuality touches on many aspects of our lives. Someone in an unloving heterosexual marriage may take comfort that she at least entered the "right" type of marriage. She

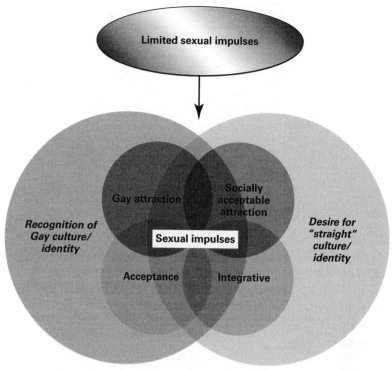

FIGURE **11.3** Cultural Identity Model:

loses this security if gay relationships are also "right." Is this position phobic or fearful? Not really. I find the term *homophobia* unfortunate. It is polarizing and inaccurate. Heterosexism is a better term (meaning the belief that heterosexual relationships are inherently superior). If we used this term as the "general" expression, then we could use homophobia in more extreme cases. Some people really do fear GLB individuals and groups.

Whether we are discussing a preference for heterosexism or a fear of gay issues, it is clear that much of the GLB experience is defined by the effects of living within a frequently unaccepting society. It is also clear that ethnic groups view gay relationships differently.

Take something as simple as unprotected sex practices. These are associated with AIDS and other sexually transmitted diseases, so you might expect their practice to be associated with something like intelligence, education, or medical knowledge. Why else would someone put themselves in harm's way through risky activities? Warren et al. (2008) found that gay and bisexual African American youths were less likely to use protection if they had been kicked out of the home for having sex with men, started sex at a young age, or were in a long-term relationship. Hispanic youth avoided safe sex practices if they were highly identified with their ethnic heritage or started sex at an older age. (No mention was made of their predominately Catholic religious beliefs, but this may have also had contributed to their avoiding birth control). On the other hand, European American youth had no predictors regarding unprotected sex. Why did African Americans and Latinos have ethnic-based predictions but not European Americans? There is no clear answer, but it may be that self protection can be deteriorated by social pressures. Being gay and suffering social abuse is hard. Being an ethnic minority and gay becomes doubly hard.

In a very real sense, gays and lesbians of color are a double minority, facing challenges from both ethnic and gender prejudices. In some ways, this dual existence forces them to choose between cultural identities; for example, are they gay or Native American? European Americans are less likely to face this dilemma. As we have already discussed, many European Americans never consider their ethnicity to be a primary component of their cultural makeup. This means that for many European American lesbians, gay men, and bisexuals, sexual orientation becomes the primary basis for identity, while for members of minority ethnic groups, the primary basis for identity may remain ethnicity (Cabaj, 1996).

The idea of a double minority might also explain why GLB clients maintain more diffuse ethnic and gender boundaries. Galupo (2009) noted that GLB individuals are more likely to maintain cross-orientation and cross-race friendships than their heterosexual peers do. Sexual orientation, sex, and race form a complex interaction in relationships, which may also explain some of the conflicts in families when individuals "come out."

FAMILY STRUCTURE AND DYNAMICS

At the turn of the millennium, the number of same-sex couples increased by nearly 30% over a five-year period (Peplau & Fingerhut, 2007). This increase is likely due to greater acceptance (as opposed to something in the water making more people gay). However, legal barriers for these families continue to exist, leading to increasing SES disparities for GLB persons and families. For example, few companies offer health care benefits to same-sex couples or unmarried heterosexual couples—despite the fact that at least 5.5 million American households are headed by unmarried couples and 13% of these are of the same sex (Factsheet 2009).

What makes the limited benefits even more frustrating are the obstacles to gays and lesbians marrying. When gays and lesbians are part of legally recognized relationships, they experience less internalized homophobia, depressive symptoms, and stress than those in unrecognized relationships. Regardless of legal recognition, simply being part of a committed relationship was associated with a sense of personal meaning when compared with their single peers (Riggle, Rostosky & Horne, 2010).

Statistics recognizing the value of marriage civil relationships has led several states to permit gay marriages. Vermont, Massachusetts, Connecticut, Iowa, and New Hampshire also sanction these marriages. The Netherlands, Belgium, Spain, Norway, Sweden, France, Denmark, and Portugal already recognize same-sex marriages. In the years to come, we are likely to see statistics justifying how marriage decreased sexually transmitted diseases, led to higher commitment rates, and provided more stability to the relationships—just as it does for heterosexual marriages. But this whole process is still new. When working with marrying clients who lack family support, it is important to involve as many people as possible. Inviting clergy members to attend sessions may be helpful, as would be inviting close friends or extended relatives (Brammer, 2009).

But critics will remain. The Pope recently said we need heterosexual marriages to "help to respond to some of today's most insidious and dangerous threats to the common good" (Donadio, 2010). The implication? Gay marriages are bad for society. What makes gay families so bad? Maybe they hurt children?

The 1990s witnessed a movement that questioned the effect families have on children. What role do parents play in the formation of their children's personalities? In regard to sexuality, it appears that biology may play a more important role than environment. Children raised in gay or lesbian households are *not* more likely to become homosexual than are children raised by heterosexual parents (Golombok & Tasker, 1996). In fact, the children of gays or lesbians do not differ from other groups of children with respect to intelligence, psychological adjustment, social adjustment, popularity with friends, development of social sex role identity, or development of sexual orientation (American Psychological Association, 1997). Although those from lesbian families were somewhat more likely to explore same-sex relationships, particularly if their childhood family environment was characterized by an openness and acceptance of lesbian and gay relationships (Golombok & Tasker, 1996).

Another stereotype is the notion that gay men have a tendency to molest children. In 1977, when Anita Bryant successfully campaigned to repeal a Dade County (Florida) ordinance prohibiting antigay discrimination, she called her organization Save Our Children. In a campaign fueled by fear, she warned, "A particularly deviant-minded [gay] teacher could sexually molest children" (Bryant, 1977, p. 114). There are some statistics showing a greater percentage of gay pedophiles than straight pedophiles, but these statistics fail to account for how pedophilia arrests "out" people, increasing the chances of being identified as gay (Clark, 2006).

Societal stereotypes depicting gay men as child abusers may be one of the reasons gay men are less likely to raise children. In 1993, a survey was conducted by the Voters News Service comparing the composition of heterosexual households to that of households headed by gays or lesbians. Lesbian and heterosexual couples were equally likely to have children living in their homes. However, gay men were half as likely as heterosexual men to have minors living with them (Goldberg, 2010). A gay man in his 20s provided some support for the latter finding:

> At this point of my life, I don't want kids. I see my friends struggling to adopt, and that's okay, but society already has a hard time with me as I am. I don't think I want to raise a child in this environment.

There are so many family and relationship issues to consider regarding sexuality. We are living in a heterosexist society, which is evident by some of the questions heterosexuals never have to ask themselves. As Smith and Shin (2008) note, most heterosexuals do not have to worry about offending their peers when talking about their partner. They do not fear harassment or abuse for holding their partner's hand in public. No one questions a heterosexual couple's right to raise children. No one assumes they do not have a right to marry. No one defines them on the basis of their sexuality alone. These are all serious issues, and they complicate the coming-out process.

These are serious considerations, and no one should enter into the coming-out process without considering the possible consequences. Most people know the advantages of living an authentic life. Sometimes, the advantages blind people of the risks. These are especially important for teens. All people considering coming out should ask themselves the following questions:

- How comfortable am I with gay sexuality?
- Am I familiar with and active in the local GLB support groups in my area?
- Am I knowledgeable enough about my sexuality to explain my feelings to others?
- Why come out *now*? Are there advantages to waiting?
- Can I handle the possible loss of my relationship with parents, siblings, and friends?
- Am I financially dependent on my parents?
- Do I have a place to live if I am thrown out of my home?
- What would I do if you lost my job or were suspended/expelled from school?
- Are you ready for possible harassment, discrimination, or physical abuse?
- Who can I depend on for support?

The answers to these questions reflect the maturity and empathy of the client. If the client is still wrestling with guilt or periods of depression, announcing a homosexual orientation will simply drain him or her of any remaining strength. In working with these clients, role-plays should include highly negative scenarios. Even liberal or open parents may react with extreme hostility. They may banish the client from the family or attack the child's character or soul. In preparing for these unwanted possibilities, every client should have a friend, relative, or group to turn to for support. This support is valuable even when parents simply require time to process the information. If the information comes as a surprise, parents may need several months or years to process it.

The likelihood of a positive resolution will also depend on the client's motive for coming out. Clients who desire to tear down the wall of secrecy between themselves and their parents are in the best position. If animosity has already developed and the client hopes to hurt his or her parents, this revelation could cause irreparable damage. The client should honestly examine the reason for discussing this topic with his or her parents. The client must acknowledge the risks involved and carefully consider each step.

Some parents go through shock, denial, and guilt. Others will find it difficult to express their feelings. Still others will reach a stage of blind acceptance (i.e., they will accept their child as long as anything "gay" remains hidden). Only a minority of parents reach full acceptance. Parental rejection presents a serious threat to the mental health of gay children, who—like all children—desire their parents' love and support.

With acceptance from nongay family and friends hard to find, gay and lesbian couples face unique challenges. When gay or lesbian couples learn to accept their orientation and build a life together, they must attempt to work through a number of social difficulties. Not the least of these involves what term to use in referring to the person with whom they have chosen to spend their life. "Hi. I'd like you to meet my partner—no, that sounds like we own a business together. Really, this is my lover—but sex is only a small part of our relationship." What other options are there? "Spouse" sounds as if the other person has no gender. The terms "husband" and "wife" may seem forced and contrived. "Life partner" has a pretentious tone. The phrase "long-time companion" and such words as "friend" or "roommate" often do not fully explain the relationship. "Mate" is often misunderstood. Some couples use the term "co-husband" or "co-wife" to stress the equality of their relationship. There is no perfect solution to this dilemma because straight couples have difficulty understanding the meaning of the relationship and there are no titles in the heterosexual world that apply to same-sex intimate relationships. The word "partner," which is often used in reference to nonmarried heterosexual relationships, is the most commonly used term. However, it should be clear that the American culture does not yet have a place for gay and lesbian relationships in mainstream society.

When gay or lesbian partnerships end, the couple is also likely to face unique challenges. Morton (1998) argued that divorcing lesbians share many experiences with their heterosexual counterparts, but unlike heterosexual women, lesbians often feel that society devalued their relationship, which makes it difficult for them to find emotional support and understanding. Even their family members may be thinking, "I'm glad *that* is finally over," leaving the woman feeling isolated and alone. Therapists who are equivocal about their feelings regarding gays and lesbians may share this ambivalence. Such an approach is unlikely to produce positive results.

Another rarely explored but equally distressing component of some gay and lesbian relationships is the possibility of domestic violence. Rates of domestic violence in gay and lesbian households are slightly higher than in heterosexual families (Burke & Follingstad, 1999), but there is little guidance concerning how to effectively intervene with violence in these relationships (Miller, Bobner & Zarski, 2000). For gay men, violence in relationships may be especially difficult to address because men are trained to be independent, strong, and autonomous. They may underreport abuse or feel intense shame regarding their inability to prevent the violence.

EDUCATION

Even when GLB individuals can avoid violence in the home, they are likely to face it at school. GLB youth face substantial risk of being involved in a fight in school (McCabe & Rubinson, 2008). The risk is so great that one study found over 90% of GLB students reporting verbal or physical assaults (compared to 62% of non-GLB teens) (Harris Interactive & Gay, Lesbian, and Straight Education Network [GLSEN], 2005).

Gay prejudice has become interwoven into the vernacular of children today. School-aged children use the term *gay* as a catchphrase for "stupid," "crazy," or "foolish." The term is used so frequently teachers often fail to reprimand students for using it (McCabe & Rubinson, 2008).

Gay and lesbian youths are regarded as being an invisible minority; a small group actively discriminates against them, but most of their friends are unaware of their struggles. Young people who are confused about their gender and sexual orientation are reported to compose 10% of our youth population (Little, 2001). If this statistic is correct, there is a huge body of students facing unique challenges who are often overlooked by teachers and school personnel. In many ways, the struggles of gay children are unparalleled. When other minority groups are harmed, there are usually advocates fighting for their equality. When gay youths are assaulted, most teachers are unaware of the reasons. They may assume the children had an innocuous argument that escalated out of control. They might even believe one boy stole something from another but was unwilling to confess. Myriad possibilities are likely to be explored before the child's sexual orientation is addressed. This puts gay and lesbian children at particular risk for physical, emotional, and social problems in the school setting (Thomas & Larrabee, 2002). When examining a sample of 3,054 students in grades 9–12, Faulkner & Cranston (1998) found that students who had reported having a gay or lesbian experience were more likely to report fighting and victimization, frequent use of alcohol or drugs, and recent suicidal behaviors. The frequency of these behaviors seems to be related to social taboos associated with this topic.

The tendency to assume that all children are heterosexual is often regarded as heterosexism. Herr (1997) notes that heterosexism and homophobia contribute to the likelihood of school "failure" among gays and lesbians. At a time when adolescents are struggling to understand themselves, homosexual students face the added challenges posed by hate crimes, risk of disease, poor self-esteem, isolation, and deciding whether to come out to their friends. Attitudes of teachers may create additional problems. Half the students surveyed by Telljohann & Price (1993) claimed that homosexuality had been discussed in their classes. However, 50% of the females and 37% of the males claimed it was handled negatively. These added pressures have led many gay and lesbian teenagers to develop poor coping mechanisms. Administrators are not helping either. In one study, 90% of principals reported having heard antigay slurs in their school, but only 21% initiated changes to their school's policy (Gay, Lesbian, and Straight Education Network [GLSEN] & Harris Interactive, 2008).

Teachers and administrators are not the only ones exhibiting heterosexist behaviors. Many clients even have difficulty discussing their sexuality with professional counselors. Telljohann & Price (1993) investigated the support gays and lesbians received from others and found that only about one-fourth of students felt comfortable talking with their school counselor about the issue. In fact, less than 20% of those surveyed could identify a supportive person in their life. This is not surprising, as nearly 75% of students in the United States have no state legal protections in schools from harassment and discrimination based on their sexual orientation (McCabe & Rubinson, 2008).

Despite the lack of support gays and lesbians receive from school counselors, most professionals in this setting regularly deal with sexual orientation issues. Fontaine (1998) investigated the extent to which school counselors work with adolescents who are questioning their sexual identity or who clearly identify themselves as gay or lesbian. At the middle school (junior high) level, 93% of the counselors surveyed by Fontaine reported working with students who were dealing with sexual identity issues. To some degree, puberty can explain part of this number, but it is important to note that sexual identity surfaces before sexual activity has taken place. Try to think back to your 10th birthday. Puberty had not yet begun to cause changes in your body, but you had vague and unexplainable reactions to certain people. When they involve members of the same sex, such thoughts can be disconcerting and frightening, which explains why 21% of elementary school counselors in Fontaine's study had seen students with these concerns. These younger students presented with issues related to identity and a growing understanding of self. Even prior to age 12, gay and lesbian students are often riddled with self-doubt, depression, poor self-esteem, social isolation, and fear of negative reactions from family and friends (Fontaine, 1998). These problems often mount until the child feels there is no escape.

Mark, who experienced his academic problems well after elementary school, provided a "typical" story regarding society's treatment of gay and lesbian children:

> People kept coming up to me and calling me horrible names. I think they enjoyed watching me cry, which I did often. Some people put letters in my locker saying how I was going to hell and how my parents probably hate me. Kids from the football team would follow me home and throw things at me along the way.
> After a while, I just didn't feel like living anymore. I thought it would probably be better to drop out of school than kill myself.

Mark's solution to the harassment is not uncommon. About 28% of gay and lesbian high school students fail to graduate from high school. They usually report that their decision was predominantly influenced by ongoing verbal and physical harassment related to their sexual orientation (Snider, 1998). Snider argued that the risk was so great that special measures should be taken to protect lesbian and gay students, but there is no clear way to accomplish this goal. The Toronto Board of Education designed a "Triangle Program" that targeted lesbian and gay youth who were at risk of dropping out of high school. Snider argued that the program backfired because it further marginalized and isolated lesbian and gay students by removing them from mainstream education. If homophobia remains unchallenged, workable solutions may be slow in coming.

When gays and lesbians enter college, their struggles continue. Rey & Gibson (1997) studied the abuse of gays and lesbians perpetrated by college students. The most likely perpetrators were found to be males with antihomosexual attitudes and low grade point averages. These were the only predictable variables found for abuse against gays and lesbians. Neither age, membership on an intercollegiate athletic team, political ideology, religiosity, nor even the number of interactions an individual had with gays and lesbians had a predictable impact on the likelihood of abuse. Abuse against gays and lesbians crosses all these dimensions. Of the 226 college students Rey and Gibson surveyed, 94.9% had perpetrated some form of discriminatory act against gays and lesbians. Even more alarming, nearly a third of those surveyed (32.7%) had committed an act that was rated as "moderately harmful or higher." For these reasons, it is not surprising that many GLB students stay in the closet during their university experience, although there are a growing number of students seeking leadership and belonging with the GLB community (Renn & Ozaki, 2010).

SOCIOECONOMICS

Just as there are two tracks for college leaders (secret gay identity and public gay identity), so are there for most professions. In jobs where traditional masculinity is emphasized (such as working-class, physical labor jobs), heterosexuality will be monitored and prescribed. In such cases, gay men may lack the freedom of their middle-class peers (Goldberg, 2010). Situations like this are even true in educated environments. One lesbian told me how she could not live with her lover of 10 years because she would be fired if anyone suspected she was gay. When I sounded incredulous, doubting such discrimination from her educated, research-based employers, she sighed and said, "It already happened at my last two jobs."

Financial threats start early for many GLB individuals. When coming out to their parents, many GLB youths are forced to leave their homes, live in transitional housing, or in the streets (Factsheet, 2009). Somewhere between 20% to 40% of all homeless youth identify as lesbian, gay, bisexual or transgender, and 26% of GLB individuals report being kicked out of their homes (Factsheet, 2009). These are staggering and disproportionate figures. Complicating matters, churches and faith-based organizations run many of the homeless youth programs, and their disapproval of homosexuality can create additional stress for the youths.

While GLB persons tend to have more education on average than the general population, evidence suggests that they make less money than their heterosexual counterparts (Egan, Edelman & Sherrill, 2008). GLB may earn as little as 68% of the wages for similarly qualified heterosexual men. Rates for poverty (below $10,000) are nearly triple for this group, and 31 states still lack any protection against termination of GLB employees (Factsheet, 2009).

Back in the 1980s, Draper & Gordon (1984) investigated how people viewed male child care workers. Not only did the participants in this study view the workers as "homosexual," but they also viewed them as "lazy." It is possible that gay workers may be regarded negatively simply because they are males and gay.

With so much prejudice against GLB workers, the struggle to find a professional identity remains difficult. For many, work is a place to explore skills, build friendships, and feel productive. For GLB employees, they struggle against heterosexism and fear of discrimination, prejudice, and even physical attacks (Bergan-Gander & von Kürthy, 2006). Because of these complications, many GLB employees take time to build trust and identify peers who they could "come out" to. They may have to become selective about their occupation, avoiding jobs that require too much personal exposure. Such pressures may lead to increased anxiety, depression, alienation, and limited social support mechanisms (Bergan-Gander & von Kürthy, 2006).

When occupational difficulties arise, there are also probable mental health effects. Ross (1990) found that changes in employment or income were strongly related to clinical depression and anxiety. Such changes were also associated with the development of AIDS in HIV-infected patients. According to Ross, the impact of work and economic-related variables was amplified when the individual was stigmatized as gay or psychologically unsound. One of my clients summed this up perfectly when he said, "I don't work for the money—I work for respect. But it pisses me off that no one at work *can* respect ME because they don't know the real ME."

SPIRITUALITY AND RELIGION

If coming out at work is difficult, imagine what it must be like at church. Unfortunately, the mental health community has done a horrible job identifying this facet of GLB life.

The American Psychological Association published a nice fact sheet on Guidelines for Psychotherapy with Lesbian, Gay, and Bisexual Clients (n.d.). In this otherwise helpful document, they recommend psychologists know most of the general material from this chapter (e.g., knowledge of family, causes, economics, ethnicity, etc.). What is conspicuously missing is an understanding of religion. This is shocking and sad. Of all the topics in this chapter, religion and spirituality are probably the most important. People from highly conservative religions are the most likely to believe that people choose their sexual orientation, which means it is also the primary reason why gays and lesbians are likely to blame themselves (and have their family blame them) for being this way (Whitehead, 2010). They are also more likely to experience more shame, guilt, and internalized homophobia.

Trying to help GLB clients without addressing religion is like using a wheelbarrow without a wheel. You can use it, but it is not going to work very well. Why have a nice piece of equipment and not add the most useful part? Some clients ask their therapists for advice on the morality of their sexual orientation. In most cases, even if someone is well-acquainted with the literature, it is best to refer the client to a pastor, rabbi, or other religious leader. Still, therapists should become familiar with the religious teachings regarding homosexuality and understand how these teachings may affect their clients' well-being.

Just about every religion has something to say about GLB issues, but they do not all spend equal time on the topic. For example, modern Hinduism tends to view gays and lesbians negatively, and transgendered individuals are part of a pariah class. The Five Precepts of Buddhism denounce all sexual misconduct, which has sometimes included homosexuality. Jainism views homosexuality as inviting negative karma. Confucianism has allowed bisexualism but not pure homosexuality (Religion & homosexuality, 2007). But the two religions that require the most attention are Islam and Christianity. The majority of clients coming for therapy to work on GLB issues are likely to come because they belong to one of these religions.

All major Islamic sects disapprove of homosexuality, with Afghanistan, Iran, Mauritania, Nigeria, Pakistan, Saudi Arabia, Sudan, the United Arab Emirates, and Yemen sentencing gays to death (Watch ILGA's spot against homophobia, 2006). There is also concern that the GLB movement is a Western threat, much like feminism was for the past generation. Some Muslim leaders view GLB leaders as missionaries seeking to infiltrate their culture and contaminate Islam (Goldberg, 2009).

Possibly even more difficult—and certainly more common in the United States—are clients coming from Judeo-Christian backgrounds. Given the frequency of this situation, it is important for all counselors, psychologists, and social workers to have some insight into the depth of the problem. In the Christian Bible, four texts address homosexuality.

These passages are subject to many different interpretations, and the difficulty is compounded by the arbitrary nature with which Biblical instructions are accepted and followed today. For example, Leviticus 23 commands followers to adhere to "complete rest" on the Sabbath day and demands that animal sacrifices be carried out according to exact instructions. Leviticus 18:19 forbids a husband from having sex with his wife during or soon after her menstrual period. Leviticus 19:19 forbids the mixed breeding of various kinds of cattle, sowing various kinds of seeds in your field, or wearing a garment made from two kinds of material mixed together. Leviticus 19:27 demands that "you shall not round off the side-growth of your heads, nor harm the edges of your beard." The next verse forbids placing "tattoo marks on yourself." Leviticus 11:1–12 forbids eating unclean animals as food, including rabbits, pigs, and shellfish. Near the end of Leviticus, a condemnation is rendered for those failing any of the laws (Brammer, 2009).

TABLE **11.3**
Varying Interpretations of Biblical Passages on GLB Activities

	Conservative Interpretation	Liberal Interpretation
Leviticus 18:21: You shall not give any of your children to sacrifice to Molech; neither shall you profane the name of your God: I am Yahweh.[18:22] *You shall not lie with a man, as with a woman. That is detestable.*	Homosexuality is specifically mentioned as a sinful lifestyle.	Verse 19 claims that a couple cannot have sex when a woman is menstruating. Few religious groups today would consider such a thing a sin. The next few verses (concerning adultery, child sacrifice, and bestiality) seem clear enough, but they appear to be confronting specific practices within the community at large. Why discuss these unless people had been engaging in these acts? Verse 21 does not condemn all child sacrifice, just those to Molech. What if the condemnation of gay and lesbianism is also related to pagan rituals? It might be better to interpret this line as, "do not engage in temple sexual practices" rather than "avoid loving gay relationships."
Leviticus 20:13: If a man lies with a male as those who lie with a woman, both of them have committed an abomination and they shall surely be put to death.[20:14] *If a man lies with a woman having her monthly period, and uncovers her nakedness; he has made naked her fountain, and she has uncovered the fountain of her blood: and both of them shall be cut off from among their people.*[20:25] *You shall therefore make a distinction between the clean animal and the unclean, and between the unclean fowl and the clean: and you shall not make yourselves abominable by animal, or by bird, or by anything with which the ground teems, which I have separated from you as unclean for you.*[20:26] *You shall be holy to me: for I, Yahweh, am holy, and have set you apart from the peoples, that you should be mine.*	Gay relationships should never be condoned and were once viewed as grounds for capital punishment.	Both of these passages are a part of the Levitical holiness code, which is not kept by any Christian and few Jewish groups. If it was enforced, almost every Christian would be excommunicated or executed. This verse refers to those taking part in the Ba'al fertility rituals (e.g., child sacrifices). The word "abomination" in Leviticus was used for anything that was considered to be religiously unclean or associated with idol worship. This is another reference to temple sex practices, not a condemnation against being gay. They had no understanding of "clean" or "pure" gay relationships. It is also interesting that we ignore many verses in this chapter. We do not kill children who curse their parents or people who have affairs. We do not make a distinction between clean and unclean animals. We only pay attention to the gay references.

(continues)

TABLE **11.3**
Varying Interpretations of Biblical Passages on GLB Activities (*continued*)

	Conservative Interpretation	Liberal Interpretation
I Corinthians 6:9: Or don't you know that the unrighteous will not inherit the Kingdom of God? Don't be deceived. Neither the sexually immoral, nor idolaters, nor adulterers, nor male prostitutes, nor homosexuals, 6:10nor thieves, nor covetous, nor drunkards, nor slanderers, nor extortioners, will inherit the Kingdom of God.	Homosexuality is listed with some of the most vile and dangerous sins. People practicing these behaviors will be kept out of Heaven.	The Greek word *arsenokoites*, translated as homosexual, was formed from two words meaning "male" and "bed." This word is not found anywhere else in the Bible and has not been found anywhere in the contemporary Greek of Paul's time. By placing *arsenokoites* between sexual sins and economic/injustice sins implies that it is a term referring to sexual injustice. For example, when *arsenokoites* is placed just before slave trader, this seems particularly appropriate because homosexual slaves were normative in both Greek and Roman societies.
Romans 1:26–27: For this reason God gave them over to degrading passions: for their women exchanged the natural use for that which is against nature. And in the same way also the men abandoned the natural use of the woman and burned in their desire toward one another, men with men committing indecent acts and receiving in their own persons the due penalty for their error.	Homosexuality is a sexual perversion that is as vile as idolatry.	This passage refers to idolatrous religious practices that were common in the time of Paul. Verse 25 is clearly a denunciation of idol worship, "For they exchanged the truth of God for a lie and worshiped and served the creature and not the Creator, who is blessed forever. Amen." This passage stands in contrast to loving homosexual couples who are acting on their "natural" gay desires and attempting to grow close to the God of the Bible.

Pastors and religious scholars will need to help the client understand which—if any—of these verses apply to the client's religious worldview and identity. It may be helpful for clients to realize that interpretation of the Bible is more complicated than it seems. Faith and discernment appear to play a considerable role in how a specific passage is understood (Brammer, 2009).

In attempting to find a place within traditional religions, gays and lesbians have redefined the essential components of religion. One lesbian pastor summed up the matter this way: "A lot of people come to me who are gay and lesbian who are alienated from the church.... Do I tell them I'm lesbian? Do they want a pastor? Or do they want a bridge back to the church? There is a difference" (Lebacqz & Barton, 1991, p. 206).

Many churches also encourage **conversion, restorative,** or **reorientation** counseling. While it is true that some individuals can shift from predominantly homosexual to predominantly heterosexual (Wakefield, 2006), success is unpredictable. Even when reorientation appears "successful," clients tend to revert back when faced with stressful events. Such reversions tend to have catastrophic results (Borowich, 2008).

Additionally, the primary motivation for seeing reorientation is not a personal or ethnical perspective; it is based on family rejection, religious fundamentalism, or spiritual beliefs (Maccio, 2010). These are all important components to identity, but as Haldeman argued, it is often easier to "change" a person's religious affiliation than change or repress sexual orientation (Brooke, 2005).

There is nothing more painful than to throw yourself before your God, beg for change with all your heart, and find your attraction unaltered. This is why most mental health organizations consider the process harmful to clients (e.g., the American Medical Association, the American Psychiatric Association, the American Psychological Association, the National Association of Social Workers, and the American Counseling Association) (Hein & Matthews, 2010).

Unfortunately, like many aspects of diversity, proponents and opponents overlook the blending of all cultures in this topic. Sexual orientation is highly resistant to change. But religious orientation is very consistent too. Sometimes, the two clash. I have worked with religious bisexuals who choose to live heterosexual lives. I believe this is possible and often fulfilling for them. However, we lack any coherent mechanism to identify who would be a good candidate for conversion therapy, and we know it is substantially more likely to fail than succeed.

I worked with a gay couple where one man was very religious and the other was not. The religious client (Thomas) said he could not move in with his lover and was considering a life of abstinence. His lover (Angelo) thought Thomas's "fixation on religion" was harmful and fooling. "You know you love me," Angelo would add.

It was quickly apparent that Angelo and Thomas would not remain together. It also seemed clear that Thomas's sexual orientation was well-established and unlikely to change. He was debating between living a life of abstinence or leaving his faith. Both were profoundly difficult decisions for him. We will return to this general topic in the "Individual Interventions" section. For now, think about what it would be like to feel trapped between your spirit and your heart. Both are essential to culture, as are our bodies and minds.

When working with clients seeking to change their orientations, I emphasize two points: 1) Very few clients seeking to change their sexual orientation are successful—as a profession, we are currently unable to identify which clients are best suited to begin such therapy; 2) Given the high rate of suicidality, raising someone's hopes under a therapy unlikely to result in change is unwise and possibly unethical. I explain both of these facts to clients, and add other details that may contribute to a poor conversation therapy fit, e.g., number of gay partners, level of gay intimacy, period of time in which some-one identified as gay, level of passion for the same sex, and reasons for want-ing to change. To date, everyone I have worked through with this approach has decided to work on peripheral issues (such as depression and anxiety).

PHYSICAL AND MENTAL HEALTH

In addition to religious pressure, there are hosts of social pressures encourag-ing gays and lesbians to change their behaviors. With little protection from harassment, gays and lesbians face physical danger throughout much of their lives. Many attempt to "go straight," but achieving a permanent change of sexual orientation may be impossible for most of those who try. As they begin to accept the permanent nature of their sexual orientation, they often enter a period of despair. The most intense difficulty is not from the orienta-tion itself but from the social pressure gay children face. It is likely that harassment and maltreatment explain some of the increased risk of suicide attempts seen during childhood or adolescence (Corliss, Cochran, Mays, Greenland & Seeman 2009). Specifically, the response from parents plays the most important role (Ryan, Huebner, Diaz & Sanchez, 2009). This affects both physical and mental health.

Physical Health

Often, most attention about physical health goes to gay males. Lesbian health is significantly overlooked, just as women's health was overlooked until the 1960s. Lesbians have more masculine patterns of sex hormones than their heterosexual peers. This is evidenced by such physical features as masculine finger-length ratio, cerebral functioning, and male-pattern inner ear problems (Fish, 2009). Lesbians also have higher risks of cervical cancer (Brown et al., 2003) and may not even realize they are at risk (Fish & Anthony, 2005). Even when diagnoses are made correctly, lesbians often find their physicians uncomfortable around them and have difficulty building rapport (Hinchliff, Gott & Galena, 2005).

All these problems are overshadowed by the threat posed by HIV and AIDS. In 1985, AIDS was still relatively rare. But by 2008, more than 25 mil-lion people had died from the disease (with 10% to 20% of these deaths being children) (Global HIV/AIDS estimates, 2009). The disease is the leading cause of death in sub-Saharan Africa (World Health Organization, 2009).

Early in the fight against AIDS, lesbians were identified as a high-risk group. Their input was generally disregarded or never requested (Fish, 2009). Instead, bisexuals received the stigma of being viewed as the prime spreaders of AIDS (Highleyman, 1993). They were believed to be responsible for turning what was once a "homosexual problem" into a "national problem" (Highleyman, 1993), but bisexuals have probably played a smaller role than the combination of unsafe sex with intravenous drug use. Sharing hypoder-mic needles is a very efficient way of spreading HIV, making prevention programs among injecting drug user populations another top priority.

Upward of 50% of injecting drug users have acquired the virus (World Health Organization, 2010).

While we know that HIV exposure is associated with some risky behaviors, there is also some evidence that people who are exposed to physical and sexual abuse are more at risk than others. Friedman et al. (2008) found that the age at which gay men become aware of their sexual orientation affects their later health risks. The earlier they come out, the more likely they were to experience "memorable harassment" and to be exposed to sexual abuse during adolescence. They ware also more likely to struggle with depression and be victimized and to experience gay-related assaults. Most significantly, people who came out earlier in life were more likely to be HIV positive as adults. This could simply be the result of having more sexual partners over the period of their lives, but it could also mean that their early abuse affected how they selected partners. Maybe they were more desperate for affection and took risks. Maybe they frequented more gay clubs, with higher numbers of HIV patrons. Whatever the case, abuse affected their later health. It did not affect their sexual orientation.

When people are diagnosed with AIDS, they often seek ways to understand meaning in their lives. Why did this happen to them? Are they condemned by God? Do their lives still have meaning? The diagnosis itself is a wakeup call to begin dealing with spiritual and religious issues once too painful to consider. Ironson's (2006) longitudinal study examined the relationship between changes in spirituality/religiosity from before and after the diagnosis of HIV. Of the 100 people they surveyed, 45 of them showed an increase in religiosity/spirituality after receiving an HIV diagnosis. Those who reported an increase in spirituality/religiosity had significantly better control of viral load (VL). These results were robust, even after controlling for church attendance, initial disease status (CD4/VL), medication, age, gender, race, education, health behaviors (adherence, risky sex, alcohol, cocaine), depression, hopelessness, optimism, coping (avoidant, proactive), and social support. If this finding generalizes to the larger population, nearly half the HIV clients coming to therapy will have experienced an increase in spirituality/religiosity, and this increase will predict slower disease progression.

One of my HIV-infected clients referred to his body as a "cell killer." He hated his body and wanted to focus on his spirit as the only spiritual aspect of his being. This one-sided focus was ineffective (Brammer, 2009). Without some appreciation of the body—even if only as a shell we are forced to exist within—spiritual growth will be limited. Such exercises as yoga or diaphragmatic breathing can help with this. Clients can learn to control their breathing, increase strength and flexibility, and view their bodies as temples (or the embodiment) of their spiritual essence.

AIDS can devastate the spiritual growth of clients. It can also encourage clients to find new ways to connect to whatever divine presence they perceive around them. Therapists can assist in this process by encouraging clients to ask questions they may not have felt safe enough to explore alone. This is an important ingredient in the physical and mental health of HIV-infected clients. Spirituality may strengthen the immune system, provide a mechanism for positive thoughts, and, in some cases, increase the life expectancy of clients. All these potentialities make it a vital facet of effective therapy.

Mental Health

In 1957, Evelyn Hooker offered the first concrete evidence that sexual orientation does not appear to cause psychopathology. She found 30 gay men who were not in therapy, matched them with 30 heterosexual men by age, education, and IQ, and gave each of the men a battery of psychological tests. She also obtained a life history of each man and provided the results of the testing and the survey to several clinical colleagues. Her colleagues were unable to identify which of the tests and surveys were from the gay men. This implies that there are no *essential* differences between the psychological adjustment of gay and heterosexual males, and there does not appear to be a "homosexual" profile apart from sexual orientation issues.

Even if being gay is not the *result* of a psychological impairment, GLB clients have common mental health presentations. We lack enough data to make definitive statements about GLB mental health. But even when individuals are concerned about their sexuality, they usually present with concomitant concerns. The most frequent presenting problems are depression, anxiety, and relationship issues. Common secondary mental health concerns include past abuses, substance abuse, finance and employment concerns, recent loss (bereavement), and family issues (Berg, Mimiaga & Safren, 2008). Of all these concerns, it is important to realize sexuality is nearly always less troubling than society's response to their sexual orientation. Gay oppression damages people and plays a substantial role in other mental health concerns (Aguinaldo, (2008).

Clients should realize that approximately 30% of all youth suicides are committed by gays and lesbians who realize that they cannot change their sexual orientation (Remafedi, 1999). Rates rise above 60% when such teens are homeless (Van Leeuwen et al., 2006). Similar statistics are true for lesbians, who are also at high risk of suicidal ideation, substance dependence, and generalized anxiety disorder (King et al., 2007). Lesbians who disclose self-harm are more likely than heterosexual women who disclose self-harm to cite their sexual identity as a reason (King et al., 2003).

Young lesbian and bisexual women are more likely than young heterosexual women to have used alcohol in the past month and more likely to have had episodes of binge drinking in the past year (Ziyadeh et al., 2007). Among adult lesbian and bisexual women, abstention rates from alcohol were found to be lower, and they were more likely than heterosexual women to report alcohol-related social consequences, alcohol dependence, and to have sought help in the past for an alcohol problem (Fish, 2009).

In reading these statistics, some religious leaders may feel more convinced of the dangers of GLB lifestyles. Some therapists may use such statistics to motivate clients to reject their intolerant religions. Both interpretations are dangerous. Failing to work from the client's worldview may increase the problem, leaving the clients more confused (Brammer, 2009)

Although gays and heterosexuals do not differ on psychological profiles, there are unique psychological elements for homosexuals. Gay men especially are at risk for certain mental health problems (Meyer, 1995) and emotional distress (Ross, 1990). Meyer proposed that these problems arise from the stress placed on gay men from discrimination and negative experiences in society. This is often referred to as the "minority stress hypothesis." At present, there is not enough information to know whether the same pattern exists for women, but there is evidence to suggest that lesbian and bisexual women may be coping with stressors resulting from their multiple minority status in maladaptive and unhealthy ways (DiPlacido, 1998).

It may be difficult to tell which comes first. Are certain mental health problems associated with being gay or lesbian or does the experience of living a gay or lesbian lifestyle create stress that becomes a type of mental fatigue? If the former were true, then there should be some evidence of problems with psychological well-being or self-esteem. A variety of studies indicate that such pathologies do not exist (Coyle, 1993; Fox, 1996; Herek, 1991). So, how can social stressors create certain mental problems?

Consider Alice and Mary. While the two women were having breakfast together, Mary began to evidence symptoms of a cardiac arrest. Alice rushed her partner to the hospital and tightly held her hand as the two rushed into the emergency room of the local hospital. As Mary struggled to survive, the hospital administrators informed Alice that she was not allowed into the ER, which was reserved for "family members" only. A few hours later, Mary died. There should be no doubt that such an incident would be associated with feelings of helplessness, depression, and disruption of normative grief processes (Berger & Kelly, 1996; Slater, 1995).

Let us try a more complicated illustration of how difficult diagnosis can be with a gay or lesbian client. For example, take the case of a 16-year-old male who presented with depression and suicidality. His physician started him on paroxetine, and he attended outpatient group psychotherapy to help cope with his depression. Six months later, his family physician sent him to a psychologist to rule out bipolar disorder. During this session, the client revealed that he was struggling with his sexual orientation and having difficulty coping. When these areas were addressed directly, his complaints of mood disturbances disappeared (Hussain & Roberts, 1998).

It may seem odd that clients would be more willing to discuss suicidality and depression than their sexual orientation, but sexuality is an extremely sensitive topic. Clients fear rejection or exposure and seek only resolution to their immediate concerns. They expect practitioners to help them with traditional mental health topics, such as depression or anxiety. In a study of depression among gay youth, researchers found that depression strikes homosexual youth four to five times more severely than their nongay peers (Hammelman, 1993).

When issues of homosexuality are addressed, other complications may arise. For example, gay male partners frequently struggle with issues of competition and hierarchy because both partners have been socialized to confirm their self-worth in this way (Scrivner & Eldridge, 1995). They may also struggle with methods of overcoming conflict. Domestic violence, or battering, within the lesbian and gay communities is thought to be underreported. When such behaviors occur in gay and lesbian couples, a "conspiracy of silence" results. These couples neither wish to discuss the violence nor expose their relationship. As difficult as it is for heterosexual couples to merge their divergent sexual identities, gay couples often experience extreme difficulty merging *matched* sexual identities. This struggle is made all the more problematic when the gay relationship is not sanctioned by society as a whole. Gay couples require a sensitive assessment, permitting disclosure in a safe, nonjudgmental setting (Cullen et al., 2010).

INDIVIDUAL AND GROUP INTERVENTIONS

Although learning about gay culture can help counselors understand their clients, such understanding is useless if the counselor harbors feelings of disgust or discomfort. Counselors who believe homosexuality is sinful or wrong should not work with gay clients unless the client wishes to change his or her orientation, which we will discuss in more detail later. Therapists who cannot comfortably interact with their clients should be honest and disqualify themselves from therapy. For example, do you find yourself asking questions that would not be appropriate to ask a heterosexual client? Can you ask sexual questions without passing judgment? Your answers to these questions may reveal limitations to your ability to counsel such clients.

Male counselors who find themselves hostile to homosexuality face additional difficulties in therapy. A University of Georgia study found that men who scored high on homophobia measures appeared more aroused by homoerotic stimuli than those with lower homophobia scores (Adams, Wright & Lohr, 1998). The arousal was measured using penile plethysmography, which measures penile engorgement. Both homophobic and nonhomophobic men were equally aroused when watching a video depicting either a man or a woman having sex or a tape showing lesbian sex scenes. Homophobic men showed a significant increase (54%) in penile circumference when viewing the male-male video compared to the nonhomophobic men (24%), but they were also more likely to underreport their arousal. If this arousal can be interpreted as sexual attraction, homophobic counselors may find themselves both attracted to and resentful of their clients. This condition is not conducive to effective therapy.

Individual Interventions

When counselors have adequately examined themselves and feel comfortable with gay clients, they should then prepare for their interventions. Sometimes, counselors focus on issues related to the origin of the client's sexual orientation. For example, it is not uncommon for counselors to ask, "How long have you known you were gay?" Even worse, counselors could ask, "How do you and your partner have sex?" In general, it is better to address only those questions you would ask heterosexual clients. Questions concerning sexuality could be discussed from a more neutral viewpoint. For example, the counselor could inquire, "How did you adapt to your early sexual feelings?" As we discussed, many gay clients are uncomfortable discussing their sexual orientation. Asking inappropriate questions only decreases the likelihood of an effective intervention.

In addition to the danger of inappropriate counselor questions, a number of other challenges involve the openness of gay clients regarding their sexuality. Hollander & Shidlo (Sleek, 1996) found that some homosexuals may have "internalized homophobia." These clients are less likely to reveal anything about their sexuality. An example of such feelings is illustrated by the following quote:

> I was very unhappy. I was drinking far too much and really hating my life. I was not being honest about who I was. I came to realize how internalized my homophobia was, how much I felt inferior because I was gay.... I would second-guess myself when the partners would ask me what I thought about a case. I would never say what I was thinking. I would think, "What does he want me to think?" Admittedly, that concern is there for everyone, but it is an extra burden for closeted gays and lesbians because we spend all our time dealing with that pressure.... Hiding takes energy on a constant basis. It's stressful—there's always the fear of discovery or slipping up, substituting pronouns, using "my friend"-type language, "sanitizing" the nature of events. (Shime, 1992)

In the past, homosexuals who had difficulty accepting their orientation were referred to as ego-dystonic, which means they could not accept themselves because of their sexual orientation. Their sexuality clashes with the other ways they conceptualize themselves. People who are more open about their homosexuality include the following:

- Those who have discussed their sexuality with friends and acquaintances, particularly with heterosexuals
- Women who have told their parents about their sexual orientation
- People who have strong support both within and outside the gay or lesbian community
- Gay and bisexual men who have told their mothers about their sexual orientation

When homosexual clients appear unwilling to discuss their sexuality or believe their sexuality is wrong, counselors must proceed with care. As we discussed, young homosexual clients are most vulnerable to suicidal ideation when they believe their sexuality is wrong but cannot be changed. When counselors encourage their clients to "overcome" or "cure" themselves of their sexual orientation, the counselor may unwittingly increase the client's feelings of despair.

Probably the most important consideration when working with clients who wish to change their sexual orientation is answering the question "Why am I gay?" It is not uncommon for clients to use the Bible to support their contention that they are wicked and evil. This dimension often rests outside a counselor's range of expertise. Instead of turning a session into a theological debate, counselors should focus on the shame and guilt associated with such positions. Consider the following discussion:

Client:	I was at church this week, and the sermon was on homosexuality. The pastor spoke with such anger and fear. He read passages from the Old and New Testaments that referred to homosexuals as "depraved." He also said that homosexuals could never enter the kingdom of Heaven. I left feeling so dirty and sad. I feel really bad right now.
Therapist:	Must be hard to go back when you leave church feeling dirty.
Client:	Maybe I am dirty.
Therapist:	It must be very painful to feel like you were made one way only to be rejected.
Client:	Yes, it is. I'm not sure I can take it anymore.
Therapist:	*(pause)*
Client:	I'm not sure I can live like this.
Therapist:	You almost sound like you're ready to give up.
Client:	I just can't live like this.
Therapist:	*(softly)* Are you considering suicide?
Client:	Well … *(laughs)* It's entered my mind! *(laughs again)*
Therapist:	*(sigh)*I don't want you to die. You have no idea how much you can contribute to this world.

This session could have deteriorated into a theological debate, which would have served little purpose. At the moment, saving the client's life was of utmost importance. Most clinicians have moral views regarding homosexual celibacy or religious conversion. By advocating celibacy, an assumption is made that monogamous homosexual relationships are inferior to heterosexual relationships. This presumption can increase the client's shame and lead to future complications. By advocating a change in religion, the clients may lose a critical component of their identity and feel isolated, depressed, and alone. However, therapists can help clients work through these issues if the client continues to work with them. Considering both options provided this client with a sense of hope, which is invaluable to someone who feels completely hopeless.

For religious clients, the start to hope is likely a restoration of their faith. Regardless of the belief structure, any religious framework can guide people to improved mental health. However, what are necessary are insight skills, compassion for self/world, and a belief that one's actions have purpose (Zohar & Marshall, 2004). From here, only a few doctrinal elements must be addressed. These are not discussed in the current literature, but they flow from the idea that people seek religion for the purpose of guidance, direction, and healing. These elements include (Brammer, 2009):

- **Power:** How much control does the divine have over the universe? Does this power influence human actions? Do individuals have free will?

- **Knowledge:** Can knowledge and wisdom come from praying? Will contact with the divine help you gain insight into your life?
- **Love:** Do you believe the divine loves you? What metaphor best represents this type of love (e.g., a mother, father, or something else)? Can anything cause the divine to stop loving you?

This latter element—love—is especially important. If individuals can accept the love of their God, they are more likely to offer prayers and attend church. Spirituality may also lead to forgiveness, which is a helpful psychological tool (Hargrave, Froeschle & Castillo, 2009).

When clients desire spiritual healing but experience difficulty reaching their goals, exercises such as a spiritual coming-out ritual can be restorative. Sometimes performed as an empty chair activity (or "addressing the sky"), clients learn to share their stories with the divine. Coming out with family members is often difficult. It may be even harder with a god. When debriefing, it is important to discuss how the client believes the divine would respond. Would this entity understand? Would there be acceptance or condemnation? (Brammer, 2009).

Not all gays and lesbians who seek therapy want to change their sexual orientation. Gays and lesbians may seek counseling for much more mundane reasons. For example, they may seek psychological help to "come out" or to deal with prejudice, discrimination, and violence. When therapy focuses on these or other clinical issues, the client's sexual orientation may still play a role in the therapeutic process, but the secondary issues are usually more important. For example, consider a young gay male who harbors beliefs about hierarchy in relationships, how men express vulnerability or tenderness, and how to use work as a means of achieving identity. If others have identified him as gay during his childhood, he may hold these masculine ideals to an extreme. His counselor may need to challenge his assumptions or beliefs about gender roles.

In addition to complex cultural issues, homosexual couples face several other difficult life issues requiring special attention from their counselors. Many counselors do not feel prepared to deal with clients who are currently married to members of the opposite sex or seeking help in disclosing their sexuality to their children. However, such cases are quite common (McDonald & Steinhorn, 1990). They are also some of the most challenging cases a therapist can face.

Group and Family Counseling

Counselors are often surprised when they discover that one of their married clients is gay. Even when clients make this announcement, counselors should not presume to know what they expect out of therapy. Some people will decide to keep their lifestyle secret, which often leads to increased shame and hardship, but it is a decision that the client should make. Others may wish to use therapy as a means of telling their spouses. When a spouse does not suspect the client's sexual orientation, such sessions can be painful for all involved. Sometimes the unsuspecting spouse will become angry at the therapist, who is seen as a co-conspirator. Others may direct their anger toward the client, becoming violent. Caught in the middle, therapists often feel trapped. Consider the following interaction:

Therapist:	Kathy, I'm glad you could join us here today. Mark had some things he wanted to discuss with you and thought this might be the best way to do it. This must be a little scary for you. Do you have any idea what this is about?
Kathy:	*(Later in the session)* I have an idea. I think—well, I think he's having an affair with his secretary.
Mark:	Kathy, I really love you but I feel like I'm living a lie. I can't keep this up. Honey, I'm gay.
Kathy:	Can't keep what up? Your marriage? Your commitment to love and honor until death? I can't believe you're doing this! Why didn't you tell me before we had children! You f--king jerk!
Mark:	Hell, I wasn't sure. I do love you. I …
Kathy:	Don't you dare talk to me about love.
Therapist:	*(deep sigh) (softly)* There's so much pain in this room. *(pause)* Kathy clearly feels betrayed, hurt, and scared. Mark wants to make everything better but wants to pursue his heart.
Kathy:	*(to the therapist)* How can you pretend to care about me? You probably put this idea in his mind anyway.
Mark:	*(to his wife)* Hey, this is me. Nobody made me like this.
Kathy:	*(sobbing and quiet)*
Therapist:	You both have some very difficult decisions to make. After today, your relationship has changed. Mark, I think you want a quick resolution, but as we discussed before, it will take time to heal these wounds.

Throughout a session of this type, counselors should help their clients express their feelings and discuss their plans. If the counselor has seen one client individually, his or her partner may view the therapist as a co-conspirator, which is what happened in this example. Even when such blaming occurs, the counselor can help direct the flow of the discussion by helping the couple work through their pain and anger. If these issues are avoided, the couple will attempt to solve their problems on their own, which may lead them to lash out at each other through their pain. The gay client's shame and guilt could lead to suicide, while the spouse's anger could lead to physical, financial, or emotional harm.

Parents seeking to announce their sexuality to their children face similar conflicts. Children desire the love and respect of their parents, but they also expect their parents to stay together. Disillusionment with a relationship is difficult for children to understand. Similarly, gay and lesbian parents fear their children's rejection when they are told about their parent's sexual orientation. They may attempt to hide their relationships from their children even if they are "out" with everyone else. It may help your client to learn that children are relatively indifferent to the sexual orientation of their parents (Stacey & Biblarz, 2007). Instead, they are more concerned about the quality of the relationship they have with their parents (Miller, 1979).

In addition to dreading their children's reaction, many gays and lesbians fear rejection from employers, spouses, friends, and others. These fears are often justified. In order to gain a better understanding of the potential benefits and complications related to coming out, all homosexual clients should contact a local gay or lesbian organization. These groups often hold monthly meetings or regular activities that can help clients increase their self-acceptance. Some examples of regional organizations include the Hetrick Martin Institute in New York; the Sexual Minority Youth Assistance League in Washington, D.C.; Horizons in Chicago; and the Gay and Lesbian Community Service Center in Hollywood. These organizations are usually well-prepared to help clients address their sexuality and explore it in a safe and positive fashion.

Heterosexual therapists can also benefit by participating in these organizations. In order to understand lesbian and gay culture, it is necessary to interact with and enjoy the environment you may recommend to your clients. It may also help you to better understand the struggles and pressures homosexuals face. In addition to attending such groups, reading narratives about gay and lesbian life can benefit therapists and clients alike.

Exposure is one of the most important facets to helping. Therapists should have enough contact with GLB people to be able to offer warm and supportive care (Green, Murphy, Blumer & Palmanteer, 2009). This is especially true for counselors working with children. Many school counselors avoid group work with GLB people because of concerns with awareness, knowledge, or skills. The professional literature for school counseling rarely devotes special attention to GLB issues; school counselors often work with adults when doing their training school counseling, and they feel they lack the necessary skills to help (Goodrich & Luke, 2010). When they do help, they often realize that students will let anyone into their world who listens to them without judgment.

ADVOCACY AND SOCIAL JUSTICE

There are three primary ways to advocate for the GLB community: support, politics, and nonjudgmental counseling.

One of the most disconcerting aspects about society's response to GLB clients is that prejudice against them is okay. One graduate student announced in my class, "My church and the Bible say being gay is a sin, so I don't think I could counsel these people." This is frightening on multiple levels. I have counseled serial killers, serial child rapists, attempted suicide victims without faces, drug addicts, vets who wanted to kill people for their ignorance, and many other difficult clients. Are graduate students saying they cannot counsel anyone whose lifestyle differs from their beliefs? I am not a vegetarian, but I can counsel them. I prefer one religion, but I can counsel people from any. I am sometimes uncomfortable around homeless people, but that only inspired me to live with a homeless woman for a day. In the end, counseling is about trusting each client to find his or her own way. It is not about us. But if our belief in "right and wrong" is so great that we cannot encourage and support someone through legally acceptable pathways of love and affection, then we are the ones with the problem.

In fact, graduate students admitted in one study that they would admonish students in a classroom for antigay harassment but only for using hurtful words or teasing. They would not punish the student for his/her heterosexism. This is tacit approval of the problem (McCabe & Rubinson, 2008). It is the equivalent of saying, "Make sure you are nicer when you rip apart that gay student next time." We cannot allow this.

In combating GLB harassment, we need more studies on what it is like to be gay. We should include things such as SES in our research, practice, and educational endeavors. The American Psychological Association (Factsheet, 2009) recommends including socioeconomic status in your explored variables. How do education and income affect people in your study? Is this finding different for gays and lesbians? Incomes and educations are just one important variable. Others would include health concerns, responses to oppression, and development.

Research should also include stages of development. Brown (2009) points out how older GLB people have been ignored from theories about sexual orientation development. This results in the silencing of such people, hiding their experiences from others, and leaving many without adequate social or material supports. For example, many gays and lesbians frequent gay bars or other such settings. Older folks may not feel comfortable in those settings, removing them from another layer of social networking. One client, Bill, told me he could not talk to anyone at his nursing home about his past. He was afraid his peers might shun him if they discovered that his lover of 34 years died from AIDS.

The threat from oppression has also changed the perspective of research and politics. In many ways, the true psychological threat comes from the oppression GLB clients face rather than their sexuality (Aguinaldo, 2008). In combating prejudice and discrimination and against the GLB community, shifts in politics must also occur.

Sometimes, we get stuck on the most controversial elements (such as gay marriage, open gays serving in the military, etc.), but those topics should come after the more obvious ones, such as protecting gays and lesbians from being fired, harassed, assaulted, and unable to care for their loved ones. These elements are essential to the mental health of gay and lesbian clients, and they should receive more attention. No hospital should be allowed to forbid a gay lover from holding his hand as he dies (because they are "not family"). No secretary should lose her job because she had the audacity to ask her boss if her lover could attend the company Christmas party. But these stories happen all too often, and the victims are often unable to fight back.

Another component counselors should advocate for is the normalization of the relationships. Gay relationships often lack normative relationship patterns. Apart from online chat rooms, gay bars, and limited clubs and socials, gay couples lack the social mechanisms for establishing lasting social networks (Green, 2007). Advocating for healthy social networks would foster healthier relationships and potentially decrease the risk for AIDS and other diseases.

In counseling, the most important advocacy issue is to convey acceptance. The very first client I ever saw walked into my office, sat down, and said, "I'm gay. How do you feel about that?" It was a test, but I could tell that he also was desperate for someone to respond favorably to him. He did not need me to say "Congratulations" (although I am sure he would have appreciated it). He only needed me to look him in the eye, smile, and say, "I'm glad you could share that with me. I can imagine you've had some incredible reactions when you tell other people." This is the essence to work with the GLB clients. Reach out to their humanity. Help them feel valued, and find the reason they are in your office.

Bill's Story (A Client's Viewpoint)

(17-year-old European American male)

I'm so tired of all this shit. I'm a senior, okay? I have a 3.8 grade point average. I was class president last year, starred in the school drama, lettered in tennis, and dated a cheerleader. Then, it all goes to hell. One girl. One person caught me kissing a guy at a club. We were 30 miles from the school, and she just happens to be there and just happened to spot me in a crowd of hundreds. Then, everything fell apart.

Someone stuffed a hate letter in my locker. Kids started whispering things about me as they passed. Mrs. Martone, my English teacher, even looked uncomfortable handing back my essay. Like I was going to contaminate her or something if our skin touched.

Someone pained "fag" on my car door. That pissed my dad off. It cost $400 to buff it out. Dad's always one for money. I think the money bothered him more than the assault.

Then, it got worse. Much worse. Jake Lassore, captain of the football team, decided he was going to teach me a lesson. He bumped into me as we crossed in the fall, deliberately knocking my books out of my hand. He chuckled at his accomplishment, but I just glared back. As he walked away, I mumbled, "Jock strap for a brain."

The next thing I knew, I was in the air, lifted by the front of my shirt.

"You think is funny?" Jake was red with anger. "You think I want to share the hall with some goddamned faggot?"

By this time, a crowd had gathered. I struggled to get free. Twisting and pulling against him with all my might.

Some of Jake's friends nodded at him, and he threw me to the ground. Literally.

I don't want to go on like this. I mean, really, could death be any worse?

(continues)

Bill's Story (A Client's Viewpoint) (continued)

My parents try to help, but I think they secretly think I'm some reprobate too. The teachers don't know what to do. The principal said he would "do everything in this power to prevent harassment." Apparently, that meant sit in his office and hope I went away.

Oh, and my church. The pastor said he didn't want me to get "thrown under the bus." He promised to make sure people were sensitive. But you know, that ended up being worse. No one talks to me at church. They just ignore me. I'd rather have them yelling. This way, I don't get run over by the bus, but the bus drove somewhere else without me.

I just don't get the point of all this.

Andrea's Story (A Counselor's Viewpoint)

(57-year-old European American female)

When I met Bill, I sensed very quickly how serious his suicidality was. He never expressed *how* he planned on killing himself, but he lacked hope.

Rather than address the suicidality directly, I went another direction. I followed up with the other things he didn't discuss.

About 30 minutes into our first session, I asked, "You spoke a lot about how the boys at school, your church, and even your parents misunderstand you and have treated you badly. I kept waiting to hear you talk about how *you* feel about your sexuality."

Bill puffed out a breath and looked down. After a moment of silence, he stared into my eyes. He stared so intently, I could tell he was looking for something. He must have found it because he finally spoke.

"I don't want to go to hell." His voice took on an air of conviction blended with fear.

"Why would you?"

He looked around the room. He neck tightening. "I don't think I'll go to hell for being gay, but suicide …"

"I see." I realized instantly that this was over my head. I didn't have a religious background, and I couldn't simply tell him he was not going to hell. Without thinking through my next line of thought, I tried to describe his world from my viewpoint. "I'm not sure I believe in hell, but when you said that, I tried imagine you there. Fire, anger, demons. It looked frightening."

"Yeah." Bill looked resigned, as if hell would come for him no matter what. "I'm not sure I believe in hell either, but I don't think it's worth the risk."

"And God?" I met his face, relaxing my face as much as possible. "Do you think God wants you in hell?"

(continues)

Andrea's Story (A Counselor's Viewpoint) (continued)

"No!" He looked shocked.

"Then, why would you go? Isn't God in charge of that?"

He thought about that for a minute and then didn't answer.

"Look." I leaned closer. "You're going to figure out that religious stuff on your own, and I'll help however I can, but I got to tell you something else. I've know you for, what, 40 minutes? And I already like you. You're tough, confident, see the world plain and accurately, know who you, and you're sensitive. Being gay doesn't rob you of these things. You're just living in a hick town where people don't get you yet. If you check out now, you'll miss the great stuff coming, and I promise you, it's coming. Your death would also devastate me."

His eyebrows rose in surprise and then narrowed in skepticism.

"I see what you can bring to the world. If you don't—if I can't convince you in time—I'll beat myself up for the rest of my life. Seriously."

From here, our relationship improved. He stayed in counseling for 12 weeks, and we kept in contact for the next decade. In later sessions, we discussed his dating (which he hid from his parents), his goals, college, friends, and how to live in society as a gay male. He proved me right. He did make a great contribution to the world as a scholar himself, and I was honored to play a role in helping him reach that point.

QUESTIONS TO CONSIDER

1. Does heterosexism exist? If so, what steps should be taken in schools and businesses to help gays and lesbians feel more comfortable in these environments?

2. Is homosexuality learned, biological, or some combination?

3. Families often have difficulty accepting the nontraditional sexual orientation of their children. How should they be equipped to handle such news? When is the best time to tell them?

4. Many lesbians have great difficulty with economic issues. Should these issues be addressed in a counseling setting? How should it be done?

5. What responsibilities or ethical obligations does a therapist have when working with a client who has AIDS?

6. How would you begin a conjoint (marital) therapy session with a man attempting to tell his wife that he is gay?

7. Jim is a 16-year-old male who seems to be doing well in life. He is a captain of the football team, earns As and Bs, and has a host of friends. He comes to counseling because he is "scared" that he is bisexual. His first sexual experience happened earlier this year. He just earned his driver's license and had intercourse with a cheerleader. Since that time, he has been fantasizing about a fellow football player. He still finds women attractive but feels "consumed" by his passion for this boy. How would you counsel Jim? Would you discourage the exploration of his homoerotic feelings?

8. Alice, a 17-year-old female, was raised Baptist and believes that the Bible is the inspired Word of God. She is troubled by a repeated dream in which she caresses the naked body of another woman. The woman in the dream is a friend of hers, and she fears she will act on these impulses. "How can I do that?" she asks. "Fondling another woman is a sin." In working with Alice, how would you address these theological issues?

9. Tom is a middle-aged man with three children (ages seven, five, and two). He has been married for 20 years and considers his wife the "most important person" in his life. Still, he believes that he has lied to her for their entire marriage because he is not attracted to her. He loves her as the mother of his children but has only been attracted to men. Last month, he had his first extramarital affair. It was with a man at his office, and he is contemplating moving in with him. "I don't want to hurt my wife," he said, "but I want to have just one passionate relationship during my lifetime." How would you respond to Tom? Would your bias in this situation come across?

10. Sam and Sue have brought their 12-year-old son Scott in for therapy. During the intake session, Sam states that they believe Scott is "gay," and they want you to help Scott become "normal" again. They are willing to have therapy continue for "as long as it takes" because they realize how much pain he will experience if he "chooses" a gay lifestyle. Would you continue to work with this family? Would you work with the parents and child separately?

INTERVENTION EXERCISES

Counseling and Therapy: Ava (age 19) has dated men for most of her teenage life. During this time, she often believed that her lack of interest was simply due to the boys' inexperience as sexual partners. When she entered college, she found herself attracted to her roommate. They had their first sexual encounter last week, and Eva is scared that it will affect her living situation. She now believes that she is a lesbian, but she does not think that her roommate is. So, now she has the awkward job of trying to rebuild a friendship with her roommate. She is debating dropping out of school and avoiding the confrontation. How would you help her?

School Psychology: Jacob's (age 12) grades have fallen dramatically this quarter. On the recommendation of his teacher, you have started testing him. Despite earning high grades in all his classes until this quarter, Jacobs scored in the below average range for his verbal and quantitative IQ. During your assessment of Jacob, he confessed that he has found it difficult to concentrate on anything, including tests in your assessment. He finds himself focusing on a boy in his seventh-grade math class. He said he has become distracted and depressed because he doesn't believe this boy will want him. How would you intervene, and what information which you communicate with the school where his parents?

School Counseling: Latoya (age 16) was sent to the principal's office for fighting during lunch. Another girl called her a "dyke," and a fight ensued. The principal told her not to worry about what other girls say. But the principal sent her to you when she realized that that Latoya was still angry. During your first three minutes with Latoya, she confessed that she could not allow anyone to disclose her sexuality to her peers. She concluded with, "If anyone ever says that to me again, I will do worse next time." How would you help her, and how would you involve a teacher and principal?

Social Work: DaJon (age 16) is homeless and has been on the street for the past two years. He left after his mother discovered him reading pornographic gay magazines. He has had no contact with family members. He sleeps in an abandoned barn on the outskirts of town but has been able to attend school by lying about his current address. How would you intervene with him, and would you make his sexual orientation an issue?

CHAPTER 12

Women and Feminism

INSIGHT EXERCISE

(Story compiled from several African American clients and friends)

I tried to imagine what it would be like if all the men in the world suddenly disappeared. How would things change? My first impression was that the change would be marvelous. No more wars, spousal abuse, or social denigration of women. The image was peaceful and refreshing, but it was not real. I started to think about the sensitive men and aggressive women I know. I began to wonder if women would fill the voided roles once occupied by men. They might; it's hard to say.

I turned to my daughter and wondered how her life might change without men in the world. She would never have to question her competence in so-called masculine occupations. She would never have to fear walking to a park alone or wonder if her outfit was too provocative. The world—even if just for her—would probably seem safer and possibly more caring.

Is this assessment fair? I'm not really sure, but it is interesting that the first thought that came to my mind regarding "living as a woman" involved "men." Maybe this is the deeper issue at hand. Can we define womanhood without contrasting it with manhood?

(continues)

INSIGHT EXERCISE *(continued)*

Questions to Consider

1. How do men contribute positively and negatively to the culture of women? Why is womanhood somehow requiring this question to be asked?

2. Are there fundamental differences between men and women or are the differences contrived and nonessential?

3. What makes you a man or woman? Could you function in the other gender? How does gender play a role in your identity of self?

Women's roles, identities, and occupations changed dramatically during the 20th century. Within a hundred years, American women won the right to vote, challenged men in traditionally masculine jobs, were elected to office at the national level, and sought to become "superwomen" who could work outside the home, manage a household, and raise children—doing all these things well. These changing roles have led to new understanding of the sexes and new psychotherapeutic approaches for women.

During the 1960s and 1970s, at the apex of the feminist movement, biological differences between the sexes were downplayed. This trend reversed a previous overemphasis on the supposed gentleness and meekness of the "fairer sex," but it may have swung the pendulum too far in the other direction. Sociobiologists and evolutionary psychologists noted that differences between the sexes had an evolutionary origin, but few considered how—or even if—those differences continued to affect contemporary behavior (Ehrenreich, 1999).

In addition to the obvious physical differences between the sexes, there are more subtle distinctions that are generally accepted by researchers. For example, women are more likely to be right-handed and less likely to be color-blind than men. Their brains are smaller, as befits their smaller body size, but more densely packed with neurons. Women have more immunoglobulins in their blood, while men have more hemoglobin. Men are more tuned in to their internal aches and pains, while more regions of women's brains are devoted to sadness. These are just a few of the proven differences between the sexes, and these differences affect many aspects of life. Nevertheless, similarities are more numerous than the differences. An anonymous joke spreading across the Internet advises: "Men are from Earth. Women are from Earth. Deal with it." The fact that women and men are more similar than they are different is often considered unworthy of media attention or even the attention of researchers (Unger, 1990).

Although women and men share similar strengths and weaknesses, today's women are more independent, self-sufficient, and economically stable than ever before. But they must still contend with discrimination and prejudice. Their newfound freedoms and responsibilities have also created a series of new challenges that are likely to remain for some time.

UNIQUE CHALLENGES

Women have faced considerable oppression regarding their sexuality. Pornography, rape, involuntary prostitution, physical abuse, and sexual harassment all stem from men's attempts to control female sexuality (Tong, 2009). These direct sexual references are relatively easy to identify as problematic. Other issues are harder to connect to sex. Such social/cultural customs as foot binding, female circumcision, purdah, clitoridectomy, body piercings, jewelry, and makeup are also sexualized behaviors and have been imposed on women for eons.

Sexualized customs and practices are rooted in many cultures, and they affect the way women see themselves. It is often difficult for men to understand. But understanding does emerge in certain situations.

I was walking down a hallway with a woman on my right and a man to my left. Coming the other way were three young men. The man closest to us locked his eyes on the woman next to me. His eyes never wavered, and he greeted her with an artificially low-pitched "Hi."

After we passed, the man in our group looked nauseous. He explained how he was in the woods the year before and saw a wolf staring at him through the darkness. The predator's eyes looked just like those of the would-be romancer. He wondered if we should report the man for harassment.

It took a few days (literally) to convince him that women experience those looks on a daily basis. He simply refused to believe us; instead, he asked every woman he knew if they had experienced such harassment. They all had, even his mother, and this revelation had a profound impact on him.

Women operate in a sexualized culture where they are viewed as objects. This affects clothing, education, work, family, and every relationship we have.

HISTORICAL CONTEXT

Women have played important roles in every culture and every ethnicity throughout history, but they have also been oppressed in most of these groups. One helpful introduction to this topic comes from evolutionary psychologists Daly & Wilson (1990). They researched the economic arrangements surrounding marriage rituals in more than 1,000 cross-cultural settings and found that women were devalued in many of these societies. In 580 societies, the groom or his family pays the bride's family. The woman is viewed as a commodity to be sold. Marriage arrangements in many other cultures are not much better. In 27 societies, women are exchanged between family groups (e.g., daughter for daughter). In 53 societies, bride prices are set, and in 27 societies, dowries are offered to lure wealthy husbands. More equitable arrangements are significantly less common: In 205 societies, there is no formal exchange of goods, and in 53 societies, both parties exchange gifts.

Treating brides like chattel stems from a systematic, multicultural mistreatment of women, but there have been cultures that have exalted femininity.

Prior to the rise of Judaism, goddess-based religions and cults thrived in Europe and Asia. Many of these religions were based on matriarchal power structures in which women were revered as spiritual beings who could create new life. Women have been valued in Egyptian dynasties and preclassical Greece matriarchies as well as some Native Indian Navajo tribes. As the male role in procreation became more apparent, patriarchies began to arise. Reverence for the womb gave way to phallus worship.

As social power structures became predominantly masculine, mistreatment of women became more prevalent. Consider the historical role of women in China. For millennia, the feudal patriarchal system restricted the political, economic, cultural, social, and familial power of women. During most of China's history, women had no political power, economically depended on their husbands or families, had no inheritance rights, and possessed no independent source of income. They were banned from formal education, could not participate in most social activities, and were completely subservient to their husbands. Women's lives were so restricted that they were even forbidden to remarry if their spouse died. Given these circumstances, it should not be surprising to learn that infant girls' feet were routinely broken and bound, and many women were subjected to other forms of physical and mental torture. In 1898, a small group of dissidents started the Reform Movement, whose advocates urged the government to ban foot binding and establish schools for women. Little else changed for women until the People's Republic of China was formed in the latter half of the 20th century.

Eastern countries were not the only mistreating women. Throughout the ages, women in many different societies have faced considerable tyranny at the hands of men. During the Middle Ages in Europe, Friar Cherubino (Martin, 1987, p. 23) wrote a book entitled *Rules of Marriage*, in which he stated that if a husband's verbal correction of his wife was ineffective, then he was "obligated to beat her with a stick." The purpose of the beating was to "strike his wife out of concern for her soul." Beating was viewed as the only way to restore her to spiritual health. Another "marriage enrichment" manual of the time stated that the control of women should extend not only to wives but also to daughters. Women were viewed as "an empty thing, easily swayed," and at great risk when away from their husbands or fathers (O'Faolain & Martines, 1973, p. 169). A good father and husband was one who ruled his household the same way a king would rule over his subjects. Fathers were instructed to keep their daughters busy with domestic chores, such as cooking and sewing. Reading and other intellectual pursuits were considered appropriate only for women who intended to become nuns.

Without access to gainful employment or education, most women were expected to marry a man and raise his children. Augustine argued that marriage served three purposes: to procreate the race, as a metaphor of fidelity, and as a sacrament before God (Cole, 1877). From this viewpoint, sex was viewed only as a means to an end: procreation. Augustine described sexuality in the following way: "A man can direct the wild horse of lust into the bridle path of domesticity if he will exert all of his strength and allow it to run only when intent upon the carnal generation of children" (Cole, 1877, p. 52). The issue of women's sexual enjoyment was not even addressed. Women were simply required to perform their wifely duties.

The view of woman as the ruin of man reached its apogee in the medieval theory of witchcraft. The alleged malevolent magic of women was said to emanate from a compact with the devil. Women toppled men from their devotion to God by using their powers to engage men's passions.

These feminine powers came to be associated with demonic forces and spawned a legacy of genocide that has often been overlooked. The practice of identifying and convicting women as witches began in the 1400s and spread through much of Europe and the Americas. The most recently recorded conviction and execution for witchcraft took place in 1792 in Poland, although it is possible that the Jesuits were burning heretics as late as the 1830s in South America. The organized practice of burning witches lasted for more than 300 years, constituting a female Holocaust during which 487 "witches" per year were tortured and murdered (Ontario Consultants on Religious Tolerance, 1998b). Nearly 150,000 women died in this fashion.

During the Romantic Era of the late 18th century, a subtle shift occurred concerning the objectification of women. The Romantics turned away from the debasing objectification of women and replaced it with a diametrically opposite image. Women were now depicted as goddesses rather than sinners. A woman was seen as virtuous, pure, and innocent. By raising the Western white female to a goddess-like status, European men effectively removed the stigma imposed on women during the Middle Ages.

During the so-called Age of Reason, women were viewed as porcelain dolls requiring men to nourish and sustain them. Physicians of the 19th century focused on the physiology of menstruation to explain why women were inferior and weaker than their male counterparts. They asserted the importance of menstruation in defining a woman's overall health (Owen, 1993) and recommended that women rest during this time of the month. They also argued that women's regular loss of blood was associated with their weakened condition and fainting spells. In reality, both problems were most likely caused by tightly laced corsets.

The development of the silk industry in Italy and Spain created fabrics that needed a more severe treatment to reveal the body's form. Italy is credited with the first artificial support to the body, called the coche, later accepted by Europe as the busk. It gave a smooth, straight line when the garment was laced. The earliest known corset was made of iron in 1556. Between the 16th and 20th centuries, women's undergarments compressed their bodies so tightly that they could literally faint from lack of oxygen. They even ran the risk of having their lungs punctured by their rib cages, which would change shape as a result of constant pressure during adolescence. As to their weakened condition, the corset eventually caused the muscles around the spine to atrophy, leaving women physically weak and less mobile. Meals had to be much smaller and more frequent because the corset compressed the intestines, leading to severe pain from once "normal" meals. Some corset designs, such as the wasp-waist or S-curve corset, put significant pressure on the spine and bent it at severe angles. To properly wear a wasp-waist corset, women had to begin training in adolescence to prevent the rib cage from growing normally. The corset literally raised the position of the waist on the torso.

Women's traditional social roles were almost as restrictive as their undergarments, contributing to an image of female frailty. Many women allow their life choices to be made for them by others. Pleasing their fathers, lovers, or husbands or defining themselves through their families become ways of achieving justification at different stages of women's lives (Haaken, 1990). In many contemporary cultures, femininity is still undervalued or misused. Philpot, Brooks, Lusterman & Nutt (1997) recount a story in which a Greek grandmother threw her newborn granddaughter out of a two-story window because she was not a boy. They argue that such stories help to explain why more girls express a desire to be male than boys express a wish to be female. Girls internalize their society's devaluation of femininity and come to believe that domination by males is natural and acceptable.

Psychological theory has also contributed to the oppression of women by objectifying them and encouraging conformity to socially assigned roles. Worell & Remer (1992) argued that traditional theories of psychology have typically advanced the following misogynistic ideas:

- **Androcentrism:** Conclusions about human nature are based on the experiences of men.
- **Gendercentric theories:** When ideas involving women are discussed, they are seen as separate paths from those of men.
- **Ethnocentricity:** Little or no understanding of cultural diversity has been incorporated into psychological theories.
- **Heterosexism:** Same-sex relationships are often devalued.
- **Intrapsychic orientation:** All problems are thought to originate from the individual's mental process, without regard to social environment, sexism, or racism.
- **Determinism:** Personalities are fixed early in life and must simply be accepted.

Psychological techniques have been devised to assist female clients more effectively. These new approaches will be discussed in the section on psychology.

DEVELOPMENT

Despite a greater sensitivity to women's issues and feminine culture, a rift between the sexes still exists. From early childhood, girls are treated differently from boys. Mothers expect their daughters to help more around the house; fathers play with their sons more on weekends (Beets et al., 2007). Fathers will throw their young boys into the air, while mothers will hug and coo at young girls. Even the way adults communicate with boys and girls differ. When examining the speech patterns of mothers and fathers, Leaper, Anderson & Sanders (1998) found that mothers tended to talk more, use more supportive speech, and provide fewer directives than fathers. This tendency held true for both sons and daughters, but even though mothers were more likely than fathers to engage in such dialogue, they still talked more and used more supportive speech when talking to their infant daughters than their sons.

The early treatment of girls creates some difficult paradoxes. A girl who adopts stereotypically feminine mannerisms is punished by society (e.g., girls who cry too often are mocked for their effusiveness). Girls who avoid crying are criticized for their lack of femininity. This double bind appears to stem from changing views of womanhood and a misunderstanding of feminine culture. Some strides are being made to appreciate and celebrate feminine culture, but these are still in their nascence.

When girls reach puberty, their "difference" from the dominant masculine culture becomes more obvious. This is something girls are supposed to hide, as if becoming a woman is somehow bad. Gloria Steinem (1978, p. 110) once wrote that if men could menstruate, "Street guys would brag 'I'm a three-pad man' or answer praise from a buddy ('Man, you lookin' good!') by giving high-fives and saying, 'Yeah, man, I'm on the rag!'" Okay, so maybe that would not happen. It is interesting that milestones of normal male development, such as voice changes, increased muscle tone and body mass, and even ejaculation, are accepted as positive stages of development, but menstruation is mentioned only in private.

Owen (1993) wrote a fascinating book about her experiences with menstruation. Like most women, she grew up thinking of her period as a "nuisance." It was just a messy intrusion that caused unpleasant symptoms, forced her to do her laundry more often, interfered with her sex life, and drained her energy. Still, even from adolescence, there was always a part of her that was relieved. She simultaneously felt a sense of achievement, excitement, curiosity, and embarrassment. Her first menses signaled something new—the beginning of womanhood—but everyone around her treated the event as commonplace.

As time progressed, her early pride and excitement were replaced with shame. She could not discuss the topic with her brothers or father, and the monthly event was never discussed in school, except in biology class. She kept trying to understand why she felt differently from the women in tampon advertisements, who were shown running gleefully toward the ocean and wearing tight white pants while jumping onto horses. She felt inadequate and weak.

As an adult, she began to study the way other cultures viewed menstruation. She studied goddess religious practices and found that ritual practices were connected to the monthly bleeding of women, and menstrual blood itself was highly valued as possessing magical power. She also found that many Native Indian tribes honored women during menstruation. Women would traditionally go to a menstrual hut or "moon lodge" to pass the time of their bleeding. During this time, they reached the zenith of their spiritual power. They concentrated all their energies toward meditation and the accumulation of spiritual energy.

Owen notes that many women might have trouble taking a positive view of menstruation, and she adds that she had the same difficulty accepting this perspective. When attending a workshop on Native Indian menstruation views, she encountered Harley Swiftdeer Reagan. At the time, Owen suffered from cervical dysplasia and severe cramps. She asked Swiftdeer what she could do to heal herself. His advice was to dig a hole in her garden and release her negative thoughts about her womanhood into the hole. Unsurprisingly, she felt silly talking into a hole, but she was amazed at how many thoughts sprang to mind. When she finished, she covered the hole and felt more connected to herself and the earth. Her youthful resentment about being female vanished and was replaced with a growing sense of wonder at the intricacies and depths and possibilities offered by the monthly cycle. Her depression lifted, she had more energy, and she seemed to understand her anger better. Owen's positive views of menstruation are not unique. Angier (Ehrenreich, 1999) claims that premenstrual symptoms are experienced by many as a state of heightened activity, intellectual clarity, and feelings of well-being.

Although views of menstruation can become more positive, they should not overshadow the potential difficulties caused by monthly hormonal fluctuations. Premenstrual syndrome (PMS) is a cluster of physical and emotional symptoms that appear on a regular basis before the onset of menstrual bleeding. Common symptoms include water retention, breast pain, ankle swelling, increased body weight, irritability, aggressiveness, depression, lethargy, and food cravings (Deuster, Tilahun & South-Paul, 1999). Barnhart, Freeman & Sondheimer (1995) argue that approximately 75% of women complain of some PMS symptoms, but only 3% to 8% suffer from a more severe condition known as premenstrual dysphoric disorder (PMDD).

To be diagnosed with PMDD, a woman must experience symptoms during most menstrual cycles over the course of a year. The symptoms must begin to remit within a few days after the end of menstrual discharge. Common symptoms include depression, anxiety, mood swings, anger or irritability, decreased interest in usual activities, difficulty concentrating, lethargy, change in appetite, hypersomnia or insomnia, sense of being overwhelmed, and such physical symptoms as breast tenderness or swelling, headaches, joint or muscle pain, and a sensation of "bloating."

Even if all these symptoms are present, the diagnosis cannot be made unless the disturbance markedly interferes with work, school, or relationships. These problems create a vicious cycle in the disorder because women reporting significant life stresses are universally more likely to rate premenstrual symptoms as severe. Deuster, Tilahun & South-Paul (1999) found that after controlling for a variety of biological, social, and behavioral factors, perceived stress was still the strongest predictor of PMDD. So, as women experience difficulties with work, school, or relationships, they are likely to experience anxiety, which is likely to increase their premenstrual symptoms.

For many years, the symptoms of PMDD appeared untreatable. The assumption was that providing estrogen and other female hormones would eliminate the hormonally related symptoms. However, there is now sufficient evidence to suggest that estrogen may actually increase premenstrual problems (Mortola, 1998), and diuretics, progesterone, mineral or herbal mixtures, and vitamins also seem to have little effect. Mood conditions such as PMDD respond well to selective serotonin reuptake inhibitors (SSRIs), but does this response make the condition an illness? Despite the obvious physical issues associated with hormonal fluctuations, there is no way to rule out how much of the "disorder" is cultural (Ussher, 2010). Feminists have argued that these changes are only positioned as a "disorder" because our culture emphasizes the negative and debilitating features of the premenstrual phase. In cultures where menstruation is seen as a natural part of female life, women are less likely to view the menstrual phase as pathological (Ussher, 2010).

Although the physical components of puberty shape a girl's development, the social components of adolescence may be even greater. In addition to starting high school, dating, becoming sexually active, and defining their independence, girls also develop unique social relationships. Technology is creating new twists to these old patterns too. Adolescent girls are now the largest demographic of bloggers in the United States (Davis, 2010). They use their blogging for self-expression and for peer interaction. This has become a way girls develop. Unlike the diaries of the past, which were largely private, these are public forums reflecting key changes in self-development and peer relationships. These have become visible signs of the transition from adolescence to adulthood (Davis, 2010).

Blogging is only one way girls and boys differ socially. Frequently, man's sense of creativity involves making things work. Masculine professions emphasize tools; masculine philosophy emphasizes structure. On the other hand, women as real or potential mothers possess a sense of relatedness by which they let something grow, nurture it, and allow it to follow the mysterious law of becoming. This relatedness has inspired the notion of sisterhood, which has been used to rally women to work together to fight for equality. This ideal is seldom met, and the culture of womanhood has historically been one of the obstacles in the fight for women's equality.

WITHIN GROUP DIFFERENCES

Ethnic differences among women also contribute to feminine identity. Kenneth Stampp (Tong, 2009) once said that black people were only white people with black skin. This is like saying women are like men only without a penis. Why is white maleness the norm? Why do we not think of men as women without vaginas or white people as just black people with white skin? Tong (2009) argues that assumptions like these have led people to reject feminist thought because not celebrating our differences ignores our strengths and beauty. Multicultural feminists also recognize the unique position of minority women. A European American woman traveling through Los Angeles might stop for a Day of the Dead festival. If she finds it distasteful, she can drive home, continue her daily routine, and forget the whole thing. A Mexican American woman could not do the same. She will be inundated with European American culture no matter where she goes. It will affect her identity.

As discussed in the section on African Americans, women of minority groups struggle to define themselves both as women and as members of a cultural minority. In a racist and misogynistic society, a European American woman may be considered inferior because of her sex but also superior because of her race. Sadly, early feminism did little to address this situation. As women attempted to fight for liberation, they failed to realize that minority women would require additional support. Feminists tended to evoke an image of women as a collective group, and they were compared with blacks as two distinct groups. This constant comparison between women and blacks deflected attention away from the fact that black women were victimized by both racism and sexism—a fact which, had it been emphasized, might have diverted public attention away from the complaints of middle- and upper-class white feminists (Hooks, 1991).

The plight of minority women has made it difficult for mental health professionals to effectively intervene with some groups. Sanders-Phillips (1996), a psychologist at the King/Drew Medical Center in South Central Los Angeles, studied African Americans, recent Mexican-immigrants and Mexican American women over a 10-year period. She found that ethnic-minority women have little trust in the health care system and often believe they will encounter racism if they seek treatment. These perceptions also decrease the chances that the women will comply with a medical regimen, whether it is visiting with a psychologist, taking prescribed medications, or avoiding drugs and alcohol.

In some ways, differences between ethnic minority women are easier to understand than differences between lesbian and heterosexual women. The early feminist movement often promoted lesbianism (Brown, 1994), viewing oppression against lesbians as a sign of misogyny. The emphasis on sexuality created some distance between women who were comfortable with their roles as wives and mothers and those who sought political and economic changes (Williams & Wittig, 1997). In many ways, contemporary heterosexual women view lesbianism the way the Ancient Greeks did. In ancient texts, *Lesbiazein* connoted female lasciviousness and especially fellatio. It basically included any kind of promiscuity. The Romans later added the homoerotic connotation (Rabinowitz, 2002). Although most Americans view lesbianism as a valid alternative lifestyle, a large minority still equates the practice with perversion (Newport, 2001). These social perceptions make it difficult for lesbian women to find acceptance from heterosexual women and men.

Women with triple minority status also evidence unique strengths and coping skills. The most striking of these are Muslim women who attempt to maintain their traditional Islamic appearance while residing in Western countries. In order to better understand this population, I met with a group of European American women who had spent a month in Iran. They had all experienced intense frustration from the moment their plane had landed. It had been their intention to live among the native women and adopt their standards. Although they had thought they were well-prepared, they found that they did not understand the culture well. They were expected to keep their hair, ankles, and wrists covered at all times, avoid any public eye contact with men, avoid addressing a man before being addressed, and never walk in front of a man, sit in front of a man, or walk across a man's path in public.

From the outside, it may appear that the treatment of Iranian women is harsh, but the women within that environment view it otherwise. They reported a type of sisterhood and stated that they felt extremely safe. Some of the women discussed how they were able to roam the streets at night without any fear of attack. They also reported fewer crimes against women in general because Islamic codes strongly condemn any such crimes. Are these benefits worth the costs? Some women clearly believe they are. When such women immigrate to the West, they often find that their clothing offers a weaker protection against masculine crimes. But there are few alternatives available. One of the women from the tourism group mentioned here decided to continue wearing the *burka* after returning from her pilgrimage. She reported that she lost her job within a week. "It's okay," she said, "I found something more important."

Although ethnic culture clearly plays a role in the way gender culture is formed, there are unique feminine cultures. Singh-Manoux (2000) conducted a study to explore the effect of gender on the emotional processes of social sharing and mental rumination. She created a questionnaire and administered it to Indian, immigrant Indian, and English adolescents. As predicted, she found that females were more likely to initiate sharing, to share feelings, and to realize the relational benefits of sharing. The surveyed girls were also more likely to report being affected by their emotions, and they had more mental ruminations. Interestingly, the cultures that were examined viewed male and female roles differently. Singh-Manoux concluded that gender and cultural differences cannot be explained by the same psychological dimensions.

CULTURAL IDENTITY

Judy Mann (1994) tells the story of watching a mother learn how to braid her daughter's hair. The little girl remained relatively motionless but was admonished when she made any movement. Mann noted that such a lesson in forced femininity included many different elements. The girl appeared exhausted and pained from the experience, but she was still coaxed into thanking the hairdresser for the treatment. Such experiences help to create "good little girls" who are grateful, polite, still, calm, and obedient.

These subordinating elements of feminine social conditioning are apparent in much of Western culture. Even the language used tends to view men as the representative humans, but over the past few decades, this has changed. The pronoun "he" is no longer considered a universal referent. Instead, we often use "he or she" when referring to an unidentified or hypothetical individual. *Chairman* has changed to chairperson, chair, or moderator; *foreman* has become supervisor; *mankind* has become humanity; *manmade* is handcrafted, synthetic, handmade, or artificial; *newsmen* are reporters; *firemen* are firefighters; *mailmen* are mail carriers; *manpower* is labor, staffing, or workforce; *forefathers* are ancestors or forebears. All these changes encourage or reflect the growing equality of women.

Although society is moving toward greater equality for women, a paradox remains. Women are different, and these differences should be nourished.

The interpersonal dimension of womanhood has been wonderfully depicted in *Women's Ways of Knowing* by Field-Belenky et al. (1986). Here, the authors describe women's epistemological foundations (methods of learning) as differing from those of men. Rather than view knowledge as external facts, the women in their studies learned to interact with knowledge relationally. Furthermore, they argued, women appear to follow a different process of acquiring knowledge. The process described by Field-Belenky et al. is summarized here:

- First, women learn through silence. Their families, husbands, and others typically undervalue them, which leaves them feeling voiceless and unable to think.
- Second, in this quiet state, they learn to listen to the voices of others. Women at this stage had no respect for their own opinions and regarded other people and books as the source of all knowledge.
- Third, as their knowledge coalesces with their experiences, they begin to identify an inner voice—a form of subjective knowledge. At this point, some women may reject the masculine world as being alien and qualitatively different from their own experience of knowing.
- At this point, there are two options that some women take. We will call the first option stage 4a, and it is a type of doubting game. Only knowledge capable of standing up to the increased scrutiny is accepted.
- The alternative fourth stage, 4b, is a type of believing game. There is an attempt to get inside an idea—in a sense, to play with the possibilities and explore it experientially. Often, this is accomplished through interaction with others who are also seeking truth through this means. The process resembles gossip more than debate. Fellow participants are viewed as colleagues seeking precious ways of knowing.
- Finally, the fifth stage is one of constructing knowledge by integrating the voices. Objectivity and subjectivity are blended together, but both must also be transcended to reach knowledge. In a sense, this is a trained subjectivity with its own heuristics and guidelines.

Women who reach the final stage can solve complex problems with this reasoned subjectivity. One example involves the process of buying cereal from a grocery story. Women were monitored and asked why they were buying a particular size, brand, or quantity of the products. Some women with very little education were able to deduce which product was the most economical by using simple heuristics and subjective measurements. Others were able to envision the space in their pantry and purchase the size of box that would fit into the available space. In other cases, women solved applied problems, which—from an objective viewpoint—would require complex calculus or trigonometry and take several minutes to solve. However, these experienced women could accurately solve the problems within seconds.

The foundations for feminine culture appear to stem from human evolution. Joseph (2000) argued that evolutionary neurology explains human sex differences in language, sexuality, and visual-spatial skills. Trends in the division of labor were established early in human development and became amplified with the emergence of the "big-brained" *Homo erectus*. Exaggerated sex differences in the division of labor derived from "innate" sex differences in visual-spatial versus language skills. "Women's work"—such as child-rearing, food gathering, and domestic tool construction and manipulation—contributed to the functional evolution of the angular gyrus. These activities therefore gave rise to a female superiority in grammatical vocabulary-rich language. Hunting as a way of life does not require speech but relies on excellent visual-spatial skills and, thus, contributed to a male visual-spatial superiority and sex differences in the brain.

Whatever the reason for women's superior language skills, the sex difference plays a significant role in the culture of women. There is an identifiable "woman's language." This includes a special vocabulary for "woman's work." Magenta, shirr, dress dart, etc. These words mean little to men. Women also use such exaggerated adjectives as divine, cute, or delicious. They use hedging phrases, such as "kinda," "y'know," or "do you think?" They ask questions when making statements (e.g., "That's a cute car, isn't it?"). Women are more likely to use hypercorrect grammar and avoid vulgarities and jokes (Lakoff, 2004). All these language elements stem from a lower power position (as opposed to men) and a larger social network. Women's language is more facilitative and less directive. All these components also address a highly social culture.

Although women's language may be less directive than men's, feminine culture has strict rules. Dress codes may be the most obvious, especially for young women. In one study, young women were critical of the dress code for their school. They would resist the notion of people telling them what was appropriate, but they would also scorn girls for wearing "too revealing" clothing (Raby, 2010). This is a common facet to girlhood (and womanhood). There is a fine line between self-expression and social regulation, and feminine culture plays a substantial role in maintaining this structure.

With girls placing so much importance on social groups, their identity development is often complicated by conflicting social messages. The process of recognizing and dealing with sexist assumptions led Helms (1990) to create the womanist identity model (WIM). Although it is sometimes associated with women of color (Crawford & Unger, 2000), it is also considered a general model of female identity development. Like the models for the development of ethnic and racial identity, this model consists of four stages, which are listed in Table 12.1.

As with the ethnicity models, this process is too linear to be useful. But the stages give an idea of a common process for some women. The earliest stage involves a lack of awareness about the differences between male and female cultures. In the pre-encounter stage, a young woman fails to realize that she lives in a sexist world. She may simply believe that women must resign themselves to the roles assigned to them because things have always worked this way or she will not acknowledge that her culture may limit her goals to feminine pursuits.

In the encounter stage, which is sometimes accompanied by anger, there is an awareness of sexism—often emerging from sexual harassment or

TABLE **12.1**
Womanist Identity Model (WIM)

	Process
Stage 1: Pre-Encounter	The individual accepts the limited roles prescribed for women and fails to recognize or accept institutional sexism.
Stage 2: Encounter	Sexual harassment, discrimination, or some other incident shocks the woman into accepting the fact that sexism exists.
Stage 3: Immersion/Emersion	There is an involvement in feminist or woman-oriented groups, and there is a clear effort to help women work toward their full potential.
Stage 4: Internalization	Femininity is accepted, but there is also a willingness to participate in the positive elements of the dominant culture. Sexism is still viewed as an enemy, but masculine culture is not necessarily harmful.

discrimination. This awareness triggers the immersion/emersion stage, in which she may become involved in feminist groups and begin to identify with women who seek to realize their potential. Finally, for some, there is a period of internalization. Here, a woman realizes she is free to make her own choices and follow the path of her heart, but she moves beyond the anger present from the encounter stage. She understands the value of femininity and still seeks to defeat sexism but also learns to appreciate the positive elements of the dominant culture.

African American and European American women have different patterns of responses to both feminist and mental health scales. For European American women, immersion/emersion and, to a lesser extent, encounter and pre-encounter attitudes have been found to be related to common psychological symptomatology. For African American women, no such relationship between womanist attitudes and mental health was found (Carter & Parks, 1996).

In this context, the term *womanist* is differentiated from feminist because the latter became associated with too many things, while the former was associated with African American women. Other movements include socialist feminism (emphasizing discrimination based on social structures), radical feminism (emphasizing the elimination of male domination of women), liberal feminism (striving for political equality), care-focused feminism (emphasizing caring as a measurement of feminine ethics), ecofeminism (emphasizing women's connection to Mother Earth), and cultural feminism (celebrating the differences between women and men) (Tong, 2009). Although each of these is important and deserves attention, there are other cultural issues that must also be examined. For example, such psychological variables as fear of racism, anger, and stress often affect the health of ethnic minority women more than that of ethnic minority men and white women.

This cultural identity model differs from the womanist model in that it starts with a notion of training in girlhood. Girls learn to see their world in a separate-but-equal framework. Girls are polite, kind, pretty, and cooperative.

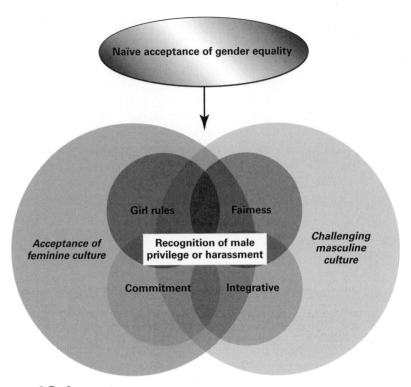

FIGURE **12.1** Cultural Identity Model: Women

Boys are rough, independent, and forceful. For young children, the dichotomy is often accepted without question. But toward the end of elementary school or into middle school, issues of fairness arise. Boys receive special privileges for sporting events, can stay out later, are chaperoned less, are punished less often, etc. These issues are confronted—either in peer groups or directly toward authorizes. As girls develop, they become more committed to their gender roles and identities, but harassment and privilege continue to affect the way they see themselves. Some women experience abuse and go back to girl rules (of being subservient and quiet). Others challenge the situation and integrate fairness within their sense of self.

This model contradicts the precepts of radical feminism. Radical feminism considers gender identity a social construction (i.e., there is no inherent male or female ways of being). They believe all social ways of interacting (e.g., religious, family, political, educational, etc.) must be re-examined from the perspective of containing gender biases (Kahn, 2009). The problem with this viewpoint is that it ignores the research on how hormones affect gender identity. While we do not understand *how* or *why* estrogen and testosterone affect the brain and behavior, we do know that they do (Sherwin, 2008). The social construction of gender also exists, and the two probably feed off each other. The problem stems from how social and biological constructions lead to prejudices. Women may be biologically and socially best at child-rearing. Does that mean they are less skilled at other jobs or that fathers—in some settings—may not make the optimal parent? The problem with basing social mores on biological features (such as giving birth) is that it necessarily overemphasizes the scope of those biological features—usually in order to control or dominate a group of people.

Biological explanations of gender can only explain a small component of who we are. And society makes several assumptions about feminine culture being the "nice" culture. Chesler's (2001) thought-provoking text *Woman's Inhumanity to Woman* challenges popular notions about women's lack of aggressiveness. She admits that women's violence is usually less direct than men's tactics, but the results can be extremely damaging. Women and girls judge each other harshly—in life and on juries—hold grudges, gossip, exclude, envy, and compete against each other. These harmful behaviors, Chesler argues, stem from a feminine culture advocating emotional and physical intimacy with other women. The desire to bond with other females leads to the formation of cliques and "in groups." Such elitism creates a power structure that enforces female conformity and discourages female independence.

FAMILY STRUCTURE AND DYNAMICS

The feminist movement of the 1970s targeted the traditional family structure as one of the most important barriers to equal rights for women. Hare-Mustin (1978) asserted that the family was the principal arena for the exploitation of women. In relation to men, married women are more likely to be depressed, perform unpaid caring services, and feel financial pressure to remain married (Ussher, 2010). Even during the 1970s, when feminism made significant inroads in traditional ways of thinking, researchers found that the majority of women continued to take responsibility for maintaining their intimate relationships and to view divorce as a personal failure (Chodorow, 1978). As more people studied women's familial roles, there was a growing understanding that—regardless of ethnicity—women undergo significant strain. Married women begin to question what it means to be a woman (e.g., must one be a mother?), they suffer with problems such as depression, and they often feel they have limited social support when traumas occur (Levant & Philpot, 2002).

Why is family life often difficult for women? There is no clear answer to this question, and some of the answers in the literature contradict each other. Brooks (2000) argues that women tend to experience discomfort in marriage when they conform to stereotypically female behaviors and personality styles (e.g., meekness, unassertiveness, and deference to their husbands). To improve marital quality, Brooks posited, women and men should enter marriage with similar perspectives, skills, and insights. Schell & Weisfeld (1999) offered a completely different perspective. They found that marital satisfaction for both sexes was correlated with male leadership in decision making. If the couples said that the husband made more decisions or if dominance was reflected in his nonverbal signaling, the couple tended to be happier. Their actual behavior was unrelated to marital satisfaction.

As women gain more independence and social power, a logical outcome would be a change in the way they select partners. O'Reilly, Knox & Zusman (2009) surveyed college students at a large southeastern university. They wanted to find what women wanted from prospective marital partners. Unlike the men in their study, women were more likely to identify such expressive characteristics as "considerate," "dependable," and "intelligent." Although this still emphasizes leadership, in some ways, it is also moving away from wanting a "provider." Today's women are looking more for a supportive partner than a source of financial protection. This finding is even holding true for women who marry older men. If the partners are similar in ethnicity, social class, occupational status, and education, marrying an older man does not lead to male dominance. It may even lead to more androgyny from the new husband, as gender identity shifts with age. But the more cultural differences there are between the couple, the more likely older men will dominate (Pyke & Adams, 2010).

So, who is right? What helps women feel empowered and happy in their relationships? The answer is complex. Over the long term, women report the greatest marital satisfaction when their partner sees them more positively than they see themselves and when they see their partner as someone beyond what they deserve. This is different for the prediction variables of husbands, who had the strongest life marriages when they lacked neuroticism and were openness to new experiences, agreeable, and conscientiousness (O'Rourke, Neufeld, Claxton & Smith, 2010). For lesbian couples, stress and conflict are reduced by the destabilizing of traditional gender scripts and splitting household labor jobs (Rawsthorne & Costello, 2010), and lesbian women tend to be happier than women married to men (Ussher, 2010).

The levels of violence and aggression in a family also affect supportiveness and satisfaction, especially in transitional periods, such as pregnancy. Between 3% and 17% of pregnant women are beaten by their partners. Violence against women increases during pregnancy, with at least 1% of all women with no history of abuse facing it for the first time during pregnancy. Pregnant women are physically vulnerable during this time: The woman's body changes, there are increased economic pressures, and there is less frequent sex (Jeanjot, Barlow & Rozenberg, 2008).

In an attempt to find ways to reduce the threat of domestic violence to pregnant women, McFarlane & Wiist (1997) studied a program involving mentor mothers. The mentors were provided to pregnant women who had been identified as abused through routine screening of new prenatal patients at three public health clinics. Mentoring activities consisted of weekly social support visits, education about pregnancy and violence, and referrals when intervention was needed. Pregnant women who participated in the program believed that the mentors' intervention was helpful across all the areas studied. Mentor involvement was not proven to decrease abuse, but it prevented the women from becoming isolated.

Geography also plays a role in spousal abuse. Alhabib, Nur & Jones (2010) did an international meta-analysis to explore the prevalence of violence against women. Most of the studies were conducted in North America (41%), followed by Europe (20%). Lifetime domestic violence rates varied from 1.9% in Washington State to 70% in southeast U.S. Latinas. The highest rates were found for women who attended psychiatric and obstetric/gynecology clinics.

When violence happens against mothers, another level of concern arises. Children who witness parent abuse are more likely to externalize problems (Jouriles et al., 1996). Once these processes have occurred, the family is often unable to correct the behavioral outbursts. Children are likely to act out in school, engage in inappropriate and violent behaviors with other children, and appear withdrawn and depressed. Although we used to think the violence itself triggered these problems, it now appears that the violence causes maternal depression, which is then directly associated with children's internalizing and externalizing problems (Dehon & Weems, 2010). This implies the need for counseling interventions whenever violence occurs but especially when the couple has children.

However, not all women want children or are ready to become mothers. Yagley (2010) has argued that for many women, unplanned-pregnancy decisions are made rashly to escape a situation as quickly as possible and are often made under coercion from the woman's parents or partner. It is important to note that when a woman terminates a pregnancy for the sake of a relationship, the relationships end most of the time. However, as women gain wealth and education, they are choosing to become single mothers more often. Either from adoption, artificial insemination, or conception from a nonpartner, a new American family is emerging (Kefalas, 2008).

Some women feel unfulfilled until they become mothers. DePaulo (2011) laments that many women still feel they need a husband and family to be complete. Women are bombarded with messages such as, "If you don't have a mate, you'd better sacrifice everything you have to get one." These messages are difficult to ignore, even if a woman enjoys success in a career. Some women elevate work and career aspirations above creating a family, but they may find themselves questioning their decision later in life. Hewlett (2002) found that 42% of women in corporate America are childless at age 40 (compared to 25% of men), but only 14% had planned not to have children. The more a woman succeeds in her career, the less likely it is that she will have a partner or a baby. For men, the opposite is true: The more successful a man is professionally, the more likely he is to be married with children. This double standard can leave career women feeling cheated. The growing number of women who have postponed pregnancy until their mid-30s or older has also led to a booming infertility treatment market.

When women have difficulty bearing children (either with problems conceiving or delivering), they face a profound identity shift. So much of womanhood is connected to bearing children. The monthly cycle is supposed to "serve a purpose." When that purpose is no longer possible, the disorientation can become profound. One client described her body as a "baby killer." After her second miscarriage, she hated her body. She viewed herself as a murderer, and her body had "no purpose."

In counseling, we worked on forgiving her body and reconciling with it. She had dissociated from her womb, talking about her body as "it." We started with safe body images. She would picture her heart beating and sustaining her. Then, we focused on her arms. She would caress them, as if caring for another person. Eventually, we made it to her womb. Instead of addressing the "murdering" nature of her body, we addressed the grieving process. This part of her could not fulfill its most basic mission, and we imagined the sadness "it" would feel. "It" lost the one thing it wanted most and may not be given another chance. Reintegrating her sense of self with her body helped her take ownership of her feelings. After two months, she learned to forgive herself and grieve her loss.

Infertility is just one of the familial struggles women can face. When women reach midlife, they may be taking care of elderly parents as well as growing children. Some women cope with these demands more successfully than others—often for attitudinal reasons. Atienza, Stephens & Townsend (2002) explored the effects of dispositional optimism (DO) on the well-being of women caring for elderly parents. These 296 women simultaneously occupied multiple roles as mother, wife, and employee while also acting as the primary caregiver to a parent (aged 50 to 94 years). The researchers found that optimism—regardless of the level of stress experienced by the caregiver—reduced depressive symptoms and increased life satisfaction. The effects remained even after controlling for household income and physical health.

However, optimism is sometimes insufficient to help women bear the burden of caring for aging parents. If their parents' condition degrades to include dementia, daughters are unlikely to be prepared for the resulting role reversal, which could undermine their sense of identity. Role reversal tends to be difficult for both parties, with both mother and daughter feeling disempowered. Cecchin (2001) advocates discussing mother/daughter roles while both persons are healthy. Regarding dependency as a predictable aspect of aging can normalize changes in the mother-daughter relationship and increase opportunities for reciprocity. For example, an elderly mother who needs help bathing can still demonstrate support for the family by cleaning or performing other household chores. What must be avoided is the notion that cognitive decline equals worthlessness.

EDUCATION

For decades, we have known that boys and girls do not differ in basic mathematical abilities (Orenstein, 2000). Despite similar achievement skills, boys like math better (Else-Quest, Hyde & Linn, 2010). Throughout elementary school and middle school, girls tend to outperform their male peers and express interest in math. In high school, girls continue to earn better grades in math classes than boys, but they appear to lose their competitive advantage on standardized tests (Eccles, 1989).

Jones and Jacka (1995) argue that the attention given to girls' lower math and science test scores has wrongly overshadowed the success of girls' academic performance. It gives the impression that girls lack intelligence. This perception, they argue—while attempting to provide increased resources to girls—paradoxically leads to a societal impression that girls need more help and are somehow less capable than boys. Girls tend to underestimate their ability to succeed in math and science and to view these fields as masculine.

However, efforts to encourage positive attributions are offset by many social ills. Elementary school teachers—who themselves were socialized to emphasize the success of men—may actively resist efforts to promote gender-inclusive science education. There is also evidence that the white male world of science is taught in ways that diverge from feminine and minority education styles (Hanson, 2009). Such views have permeated education for decades, as evidenced by the following quote:

> I have a teacher who calls me "airhead" and "ditz." I used to think I was smart, but now I don't know. Maybe I'm not. What if he's right? The more he treats me like an airhead, the more I think maybe I am. (Sadker & Sadker, 1994, p. 135)

This young woman is likely to doubt her own abilities because of her teacher's dismissive attitude. Some might argue that girls' lack of confidence stems from a decreased ability to succeed, but the self-devaluation appears to start during junior high school, when girls are still outperforming boys in math ability (Crawford & Unger, 2000). A more reasonable hypothesis would be that their lack of confidence seriously limits their continued achievement.

Boys and girls also have similar confidence levels about their reading, but girls value reading more than boys (Marinak & Gambrell, 2010). With girls reading and writing more than boys, their greater Internet usage also makes sense. Girls spend more time online than boys, but they use the Internet differently. Girls are more likely to search for information, chat, and socialize online. Boys are mostly likely to use the Internet to play games (where only a quarter of girls do). Because of the differences in activities, boys' parents were more likely to monitor computer activity and time usage, which causes them to use Internet cafes. These differences in Internet activities also affect their educational activities. The more time both genders spend online, the lower they scored on high school entrance exams. Parents can help their children's scores by monitoring the amount of time they spend online.

There are a variety of legal and social reforms designed to promote equal rights in school settings. Without a doubt, Title IX of the Education Amendments of 1972 (Title 20 U.S.C. Sections 1681–1688) had the greatest impact on sex equity in education. This led to a 600% increase in girls' sports participation between 1972 and 1978 (Kaestner & Xu, 2010). The law mandated equality in all educational activities, including sports. It required schools to allocate finances based on the total number of male and female athletes, with equal amounts going to male and female athletes. The regulation is so specific that it examines the number of athletes; quality, suitability, quantity, availability, and maintenance of equipment and supplies; number of competitive events per sport; modes of transportation; opportunities to receive academic tutoring; opportunities to receive coaching, assignment, and compensation; quality of locker rooms and facilities; medical and training facilities and services; expenses for publicity; support services for each sporting discipline; and recruitment of student-athletes. These changes have dramatically increased the number of female athletes, but there have also been costs. Gavora (2002) believes Title IX was well-intentioned but misguided. She notes that some of the most prestigious men's sports programs have been eliminated in the name of "gender equity." Providence College's baseball team, Princeton's wrestling squad, Boston University's football team, and the UCLA men's swimming program are among the hundreds of men's sports teams eliminated. Given the recent negative attention Title IX has received, the program's future may be in jeopardy.

There is no doubt that Title IX and other programs have helped women, even though they may have harmed men. Adult women who were affected by Title IX participated in more athletic programs, had a lower body mass index (BMI), and reported feeling more physically active than women who went to school before Title IX (Kaestner & Xu, 2010).

Despite positive strides, women continue to face prejudice in academic settings. The desensitization of university students to women's issues is apparent in the following quote by an anonymous student teacher:

> I really do not feel like there needs to be changes in education for females. This may sound harsh, but if females truly want to be treated like males, then they should learn to work and function in the system that exists. Having said that, I really do not believe that education is differentiated between the sexes. I have yet to discriminate or see discrimination aimed at a girl solely based on gender. Seems like many people just look for things to gripe about.

This male student believed that women wish to be treated "like males" instead of being treated like human beings. He failed to realize that the prejudices women face within school settings are subtle and covert. Boys do not block the doors to prevent girls from entering the classrooms. Teachers do not force girls to sit in the back of the class and remain quiet. However, the discrimination that this student teacher did not see is just as real as these examples and in some ways can be even more detrimental. Teachers can convey prejudice in tones of voice, minimal eye contact, or decreased expectations.

SOCIOECONOMICS

Title IX has also affected women's occupations. Women who enjoy working in higher-paying, male-dominated fields are more likely to have played competitive sports during childhood and to have had more male playmates and fewer female playmates than women employed in typically feminine professions (Coats & Overman, 1992). However, many people continue to view women in nontraditional fields negatively. Even though women have successfully found employment in even the most stereotypically masculine jobs, they are still likely to face intense discrimination. To combat such psychological obstacles, women who feel that they are underappreciated or mistreated may benefit from joining a support group or a stress-management program to help them cope with pressures at home and at the workplace.

Despite the increased career options available to women today, social pressure continues to nudge girls toward traditionally feminine occupations. Yoder & Schleicher (1996) found that women who excelled in currently female-incongruent fields were rated by undergraduates as having personal problems and being unfeminine. These sentiments appear to stem from the continued media campaign directed toward girls and women. More women are employed today than ever before, but income disparity continues. Over the past 40 years, job growth for women has been unprecedented. The U.S. Department of Labor, Women's Bureau (2010) reported that nearly 60% of females 16 or older were in the labor force. This is 46.8% of the total work-force, and women are projected to take the majority of jobs by 2018. Despite this growth, women continue to remain in "feminine" jobs. The three most common occupations for women in 2009 were secretaries, nurses, and tea-chers. The women who earned the most money (as a group) were pharma-cists, lawyers, or computer executives or managers. Overall, women still earn less than men, despite cutting the gap substantially over the past 40 years.

In addition to gender differences, there is a growing gap in wages *among* women (Blau & Kahn, 2007). This is largely education-related, as college graduate earn more than those who have not completed high school. When using high school graduates as a baseline, women who only completed one year of high school will earn comparatively less today than then they would have in 1974, whereas women with a college degree will earn comparatively more today than they would have in 2003 (Blau & Kahn, 2007).

Regardless of their income or social status, women also find themselves struggling with how work affects their roles as partners and mothers. When women feel their partners are better caregivers to their young children, they often wrestle with lower self-competence. Men do not face such issues. The competency of their female partners' caregiving is unrelated to their own sense of competence. Women still feel caring for children is associated with their personal competence and often struggle to balance work and family roles (Sasaki, Hazen & Swann, 2010).

From a global perspective, limiting women's economic potential due to gender bias has the effect of increasing population growth rates. Women in many parts of the world view childbearing as their only form of economic security. In fact, rising female literacy rates have been linked to declining birth rates. But girls are less likely to attend school than boys. Murray & Marks (2010) argue that ending hunger, malnutrition, illness, and loss of economic productivity requires the elimination of gender biases. When women receive better access to education, opportunities for business owner-ship, and supplies, the global population will stabilize and third-world coun-tries will increase their economic strength. In subsistence economies, which include more than half the world's population, women are often the primary economic providers, but even in these economies they face legal barriers to owning land, the threat of violence by men, difficulty obtaining child care, and educational barriers. Such biases not only limit women's ability to succeed but also force many third-world nations to remain in poverty (Unicef, 2009).

As society continues to devalue women and attempts to confine them within rigid gender roles, it is not surprising that female workers face frequent and consistent gender harassment. More than half of all women, regardless of ethnicity, face gender harassment in their respective occupations (Ilies, Hauserman, Schwochau & Stibal, 2003). Furthermore, although many women do not see themselves as victims of harassment, they are likely to experience negative psychological and job-related outcomes. Sexual harassment can affect relationships with teachers or supervisors, academic achievement, work environments, morale, illness, injuries depression, anxiety, and PTSD symptoms (Woods, Buchanan & Settles, 2009). Many of these components relate to power and control issues, and dominance over women has been common in most social settings. We already looked at family, education, and occupations. But religion and spirituality have also been areas of empowerment and control.

SPIRITUALITY AND RELIGION

Although most religions are patriarchal, spirituality and religion also focus on freedom and liberation. These components have long been associated with women's empowerment (Comas-Diaz, 2007). Feminist culture has also been responsible for a shift in the way some women view their spirituality. During the 1980s, a movement arose that attempted to explore feminine elements of the divine (Merchant, 1983). Feminist theology affirmed the necessity of feminine energy in spirituality. Nature (including the body) is seen as something that is born of God. It is not alien to God but flows out of God as if being formed through a process of gestation (McFague, 1988). This spirituality is nature-based, earth-grounded, and cosmically conscious. It does not look for an external God who transcends the world, but attempts to find a union with God in the creation process of the life cycle (Weber, 1987). This panentheistic theology embodies a rebellion against the transcendence of patriarchical religions. The entire cosmos is seen as a passageway in which the ineffable Mystery of Being (sometimes called God) flows in and through us.

Walker (2010) wrote about helping women develop a cultural sense of their religion and spirituality. She argues for the existence of three counseling stages:

1. **Discernment:** What has pulled this person from God or their spirituality and how does this relate to her social experiences? During this stage, as the therapeutic relationship develops, empathy, acceptance, and understanding are important.
2. **Interpretation:** This is where the client explores meaning and value in her life. Where does she feel helpless or powerless? How can she let go of feeling self-destructive to feeling self-empathy? How have these feelings led to feeling alone, frustrated, or dependent?
3. **Reconnection:** Faith and social reconnection start to grow again. Here, new spiritual images and narratives arise. The client feels empowered, hopeful, and has a clear sense of value and meaning.

Religion appears to play an important and valuable role in women's health. However, the emotional benefits are sometimes linked with other burdens or chores. Women attending conservative Christian churches do more hours of housework than their more liberal peers, although their husbands do not. They also tend to have lower educational achievement, marry earlier, have children earlier, and work at home (Nicholson, Rose & Bobak, 2010). These are traditional feminist arguments against traditional religions. They reinforce the status quo, relegate women to subservient positions, and encourage male dominance over women. It is disappointing to find the lack of housework conservative religious men do, as the principles of their religion emphasize the importance of family and men placing the family's well-being above work achievement or personal gain.

Although there is an apparent power imbalance in gendered religion, women still find the process valuable. Depending on the country women come from, their regular religious attendance ranges from 4% to 62%. Their daily prayer ranges from 8% to 82%. In nearly every country examined, women report greater religious attendance, prayer, and beliefs (Nicholson, Rose & Bobak, 2010). One of the most interesting conclusions from this study was a connection between decreased religious service frequency and self-rated health. Men and women who attended religious services but reported no private prayer reported the best health. Those who prayed daily but never attended services reported the worst health. It did not matter how religious the person felt; their health only improved with attendance.

What makes religious attendance so important, and why is it associated with physical health? We have already discussed how women's language is more social than men's. It would make sense to also extend this to other issues. Religion provides a social mechanism for sharing stories, grooming, volunteering, focusing on others, greeting new people, interacting with children, etc. But there may be something more esoteric too. Women find it easier to ask for help and to find comfort, even in powerlessness. This may also explain why women may also ask for help when experiencing physical symptoms.

But religion is not a panacea. Religion does not change behaviors as much as attitudes. This might best illustrated in the case of HIV and AIDS. In a study of African women, religion had no effect on HIV infection or condom. What did impact HIV use was living close to family (either her husband's or her own) (Muula, 2010). These social facets explain much about women—even the way they handle physical and mental health.

PHYSICAL AND MENTAL HEALTH

In general, women are more likely than men to seek out health care, and they visit a physician almost three times as often as men. Even though women realize the importance of annual physicals, healthy diets, and exercise, other health issues remain. Women must wrestle with immune problems that do not seem to affect men's bodies. The reason for this vulnerability is unclear. Women's immune systems attack invaders more aggressively than do men's, but the response is dampened during pregnancy. Perhaps owing to this on-off intensity, women are more prone to develop autoimmune disorders, such as lupus, rheumatoid arthritis, and multiple sclerosis—conditions in which the immune system attacks healthy tissue. Women also deal with health concerns related to such potentially embarrassing topics as menstruation and breast exams.

Physical Health

Although medical and mental health professionals have only recently championed the legitimacy of PMS symptoms, other female health issues have long been taken seriously. Breast cancer takes a severe toll on the lives of many women. For many, it is a mysterious enemy that relentlessly stalks its prey. That was the view Susan Ballard took. While she was in her 20s, she nursed her mother through the agonizing process of breast cancer until she died an excruciating death. The process inspired her to completely change her lifestyle. She switched to a vegetarian diet, eating only whole grains, fruits, vegetables, and soy products. She took up yoga and exercise and followed a variety of other health-promoting practices. Still, at age 56, she was diagnosed with breast cancer.

Breast Cancer

Susan's story is not uncommon. Judith Hirshfield-Bartek, a nurse manager for the breast care center at Beth Israel Deaconess Medical Center, said, "All I see is women with breast cancer, and so often they say, 'I ate a healthy diet, I don't smoke, I did all the right things, and I still got breast cancer'" (Saltus, 1997). Environmental factors, such as diet, do affect the likelihood of cancer, but genetic influences are equally important—if not more so. If a woman inherits a mutant form of BRCA1 or BRCA2, she is likely to develop breast or ovarian cancer during the course of her lifetime (Ader, Susswein, Callanan & Evans, 2009). Overall, breast cancer is the number one killer of women ages 40–79 (Hurdle, 2007).

There also seem to be cultural factors involved in breast cancer development. Mexican Americans, Japanese and Filipino women living in Hawaii, American Indians, Seventh-Day Adventists, and Mormons are less likely to contract the disease, while Jewish women have a higher than average risk. The reasons for these differences are still unclear. However, breast feeding may play a role. The longer women breast-feed, the lower their risk for breast cancer (Jernström, 2004).

Hormones also play a role. A huge study (16,608 women) by the Women's Health Initiative found that hormone replacement therapy increased a woman's risk for breast cancer, heart disease, and stroke (Chlebowski et al., 2010). But while significant, the risks are low. Teaching such behavioral skills as healthy eating, regular exercise, stress management skills, and avoiding black tea (Larsson, Bergkvist & Wolk, 2009) are better interventions for offsetting cancer and cardiovascular threats.

To combat breast cancer, breast self-examinations (BSE) should be practiced beginning in early adulthood. Breast changes such as lumps, thickening, swelling, dimpling, skin irritation, distortion, retraction, scaliness and tenderness or unusual discharge should be immediately reported to a physician

(Hurdle, 2007). However, finding breast abnormalities is only half of the battle. When Marsha found a lump in her breast at age 57, she ignored it. She considered something benign and told herself it would go away. Over the next three months, the lump did not appear to grow, but when she finally had it examined, it was nearly an inch in diameter. Eventually, she underwent a lumpectomy (surgical removal of the lump) to remove the cancer. Later, Marsha commented, "I simply didn't want to believe it could happen to me—It was a devastating blow to face my own mortality." Losing a breast can have a powerful effect on a woman's sense of self. Discussing their loss with others who have successfully adapted can speed the healing process.

Infertility

Just as losing a breast may affect how women view themselves, infertility may make women question their womanhood. If she focuses on the anger, she may find herself admonished to "get over it." If she begins to envy women who have children, she may retreat from social contact and become isolated and withdrawn. Of all the emotional reactions to infertility, the most painful is anxiety. Most women realize their anxiety may increase the difficulty of becoming pregnant (Domar, 1997), but their inability to release their fears and anxiety creates guilt and additional stress. One infertile woman summed up her feelings in this way:

> I knew things were getting bad when I couldn't attend Mother's Day ceremonies at church any more. It was just too painful. Person after person came up to me with flowers and, while smiling, asked, "Are you a mother?" Once I just said "Yes" so no one else would offer me one. The following year, the first happy volunteer who discovered that I wasn't a mother gave me a flower anyway. She just smiled knowingly and said, "Well, you'll be a mother someday." That was the last Mother's Day service I attended—I couldn't take the stress.

How do we help ease the emotions enveloping infertile women? We should start by realizing the seriousness of the crisis. Women facing infertility are substantially more likely to suffer from anxiety or depression (Noorbala, Ramezanzadeh, Abedinia, & Naghizadeh, 2009). When these mental health issues become significant, they can decrease the success of in vitro fertilization and embryo transfer (IVF-ET) treatments (Li, Xu & Gao, 2009).

Rape

Breast cancer has women fearing their bodies; infertility leaves some women questioning their body's worth or value. Rape makes the body unclean and weak. Rape can include all the following definitions:

- Having sex with a minor
- Forcing someone to have sex or continuing with a sex act after the individual has requested an end to the act
- Having sex with someone who is unable to consent to the act (e.g., people who are drugged or mentally ill)
- Having sex with someone who has not verbal given consent (*Note:* Lack of verbal or physical resistance by the victim, resulting from the use of force or threat by the accused, *does not* constitute consent.)

When rape occurs, women are likely to feel an overpowering sense of shame. They may try to "cleanse" themselves from the assault by showering, throwing away clothes, or washing bed sheets, but these actions will only hinder prosecution of the offender. The best action to follow is to call the police as well as write down anything that can be remembered about the assailant (e.g., height in reference to something at the scene, hair and eye color, scars, tattoos, physical defects, what the offender sounded like, or what he smelled like). However, most women will debate reporting the crime. Whether the rape was violent or not, a woman may enter a type of emotional shock. She may experience self-blame, vulnerability, a loss of power and control, and fear/anger toward all men (Resnick, 2001). The idea of reporting the crime and reliving the event is not appealing to any victim.

With the aftermath of rape so severe, rape prevention programs in high schools are common. However, most of these programs treat males as the problem rather than finding ways to cooperate with men. Program appears more effective when training programs regard men as allies in the solution. This reduces male defensiveness, which may promote more lasting change (Hillenbrand-Gunn, Heppner, Mauch & Park, 2010).

Therapists can help their clients realize that a host of emotional reactions are common and, to some degree, expected. Problems arise not with the manifestation of symptoms per se but with minimizing or denying the event. Sometimes, clients will compare their trauma to someone else's and conclude that their ordeal "wasn't as bad." When this happens, therapists must ensure support the client's right to feel traumatized.

I ran a rape survivors group where one woman told the story about being raped by her uncle and father over the course of five years. Their treatment of her was horrific, including bondage, videos, and emotional shaming. After she finished, the woman next to her just hung her head.

"I don't deserve to be here," the woman said with an air of rejection. "My father only raped me once."

In some ways, the second woman's story was harder for me to hear. Her rape had permeated everything she was. I asked all the women in the group to make a fist and put it over their hearts. Then, I asked them to cup their other hand over their fist so both hands were between their breasts.

"Imagine what it would feel like if someone reached in through your chest and pulled out your heart." I let the idea sink in as they continued holding their hands against their bodies. "Would it really matter how many times they pulled? Wouldn't one yank still kill you? We've all had our hearts hurt, and we're all here to help each other heal."

Abuse

When clients are known to be in abusive relationships, Walker (1985) suggests working with them to devise an escape plan. The plan should include all the following:

- Developing cognitive recognition of signs of an impending battering incident (e.g., face turning red, eyes looking menacing, fingers twitching, etc.)
- Method of and timing for leaving the house safely
- Items she would need to bring with her (car keys, spare cash, etc.)

- Provisions for children
- Location of nearest public telephone or neighbor to whom she can run for help

When all these components are included, the client should rehearse the plan with the therapist in much the same manner as a fire drill. Ask the client to review every possible scenario. What might happen if the abuser returned when you were moving toward the door? How should you get the children out of the house? What would you do if your abuser found out where you were going? Many clients may view these provisions as unnecessary, but therapists should explain that even the possibility of violence is life-threatening.

After establishing an escape plan, therapy with women clients should address the role they play in the family. Survivors of spousal abuse often come to view themselves as peacemakers. They view themselves as being responsible for violence in the family, and they feel that they must exude forgiveness, patience, love, and support at all times.

Given the overlap between women's physical and mental health, therapists should work with psychiatrists and physicians in findings way to assist with medical treatments.

Mental Health

When addressing the psychology of women, it is important to point out that research biases have long pathologized women for acting the way society wanted them to act (Collier, 1982). Even traditional psychotherapies have an obvious androcentric orientation. Freud (1932) argued that women secretly rebelled against their femininity and desired to possess a penis to experience manhood. According to Freud's theory, girls realized that boys had something that they lacked, which led them to develop penis envy. A girl would blame her mother for this physical inadequacy and turn to the father for love. In this process, she underwent a loss of the mother's support and attempted to identify with her to retain the mother's support. The girl's lack of castration anxiety meant that she had no reason to resolve the Oedipal complex. As a result, Freud argued, girls had weaker superegos and were likely to wish to have a baby boy of their own to finally possess a penis.

These impulses, Freud argued, made women prone to hysterical reactions because they could not express their sexuality freely. From his viewpoint, women would not even allow themselves to contemplate the sexual side of their nature. Decades later, while politely admitting that sexual repression might have caused hysterical reactions in the past, Betty Friedan (1963) noted that such complications had become much less common for liberated women. She suggested that Freud's entire notion of developmental psychology as a sexual process no longer seemed accurate.

Adding to the difficulties of understanding women is confusion regarding how to define positive mental health traits. Bem (1974) conducted a study to discover the most-used adjectives to describe the typical male or female. Feminine adjectives included gentle, yielding, understanding, naïve, childlike, and sensitive to the needs of others. Masculine adjectives included ambitious, athletic, self-reliant, independent, dominant, and competitive. When comparing these qualities with what is considered "mentally healthy" for all people, the masculine adjectives, in general, are typically more positive. This poses a dilemma for women. They can either become more masculine and "healthy" or more feminine and needy (Collier, 1982). Bem's stereotypical adjectives used to describe women and men are still accurate today (Choi, Fuqua & Newman, 2008).

With today's increased emphasis on biochemical roots of behavior, there is more and more evidence of hormonal and genetic differences that may explain some of the differences between the sexes. For example, high oxytocin and low testosterone are associated with parental bonding, nurturance, and intimacy. High testosterone assists with dominance and competition (Eagly, 2009). At the same time, the socially created differences between the sexes are important and likely to explain more than we realize. Sociological causes can be difficult to discover because of the notorious complexities inherent in the study of people. For these reasons, our discussion of psychological issues will be dedicated more to biological causes than social ones, although we should always keep in mind that biology and environment do not operate independently.

Depression

Ussher (2010) addressed how the biomedical, psychological, and sociocultural models each offer competing explanations for why depression hits women harder. Social constructionism may dismiss women's legitimate distress, and biomedical arguments may pathologize any form of social pressure. Ussher argues for a critical-realist epistemology. This will examine the various intrapsychic experiences constructed as depression. Such an approach will provide mechanisms for treating with medication, but it also goes deeper. For example, Atwood (2001) found that girls coming from abusive or otherwise sexist households were more likely to have problems with gender role socialization, depression in adulthood, involvement in demeaning intimate relationships, self-doubt, and a tendency to sacrifice their own personal and relational development for the sake of others. Even when medication is prescribed, it should be tailored to women's special needs. Evidence is mounting that the brains of females may respond differently to hormones and brain chemicals than those of males. Women produce less serotonin, a mood-regulating chemical, than men, and they are more sensitive to changes in serotonin levels, which are in turn regulated by estrogen (DeSoto, 2007). Examining these issues in conjunction with the sociocultural and psychological features of depression will likely yield the best result.

Eating Disorders

Like depression, eating disorders have biomedical and sociocultural influences. After studying nearly 2,000 identical and fraternal twins, Bulik, Sullivan, Wade & Kendler (2000) concluded that genes account for 83% of female susceptibility to bulimia. However, they noted that these genetic influences interact with known environmental factors in unpredictable ways. Henss (2000) examined how men viewed the attractiveness of women based on waist-to-hip ratio. In accordance with evolutionary psychological expectations (i.e., that men select the partner who is most likely to be fertile), a lower ratio was more attractive than a higher one. In addition to body shape, there is evidence that facial attractiveness plays an important role in the treatment of women. Women are encouraged to become "objects of desire" instead of agents of their own pleasures and desires. Weight and body size are important factors in these perceptions and roles.

From a counseling viewpoint, the intervention for eating disorders tends to focus on identifying and expressing negative feelings. Young women with eating disorders tend to believe that expressing emotions is a sign of weakness (Meyer et al., 2010). When working with girls with anorexia, I tell them to wait three weeks before expecting growth. I will even warn the girls that their weight might even get worse, as they are learning to express their feelings. But all my clients end that month experiencing catharsis. Once they accept their anxiety and depression, we can address their dietary concerns. However, reaching the point where people seek counseling is becoming more complicated. Few women with bulimia (bingeing and purging) admit to needing help until signs of physical damage appear. A number of physical concerns are present with bulimia. If vomiting is the primary mechanism of expulsion, the esophagus can degrade and eventually rupture, the stomach lining can tear, and tooth enamel can be eroded by stomach acids. For anorexia nervosa (less than 85% of expected weight through self-starvation), the denial may be even greater. "Anna" was 19 when she wrote the following:

> Sometimes, when I get really down, I just go for days without eating. Once, I went three weeks and no one seemed to notice. I would just chew gum or drink water. Sometimes, people would ask if that was all I was planning to eat. I would just tell them I wasn't hungry.

Even after treatment, Anna confessed that she had to "force" herself to eat. As her disorder progressed, she felt disgusted with herself and the way she ate. She found it virtually impossible to eat in the presence of other people, especially strangers. Pro-eating-disorder websites are also glorifying self-starvation and purging. Girls will swap tips on how to hide their anorexia or speed the weight loss process (Day & Keys, 2008).

Regardless of the etiology of the disorder, one of the most important interventions involves a direct attack on the client's sense of self-inadequacy and shame. Burney and Irwin (2000) explored the relationship between the guilt women feel regarding their eating behaviors and an underlying sense of shame. Guilt—which is defined as feelings of culpability especially for imagined offenses—was an effective predictor of developing an eating disorder when the feelings were associated with eating behavior. Shame—which is defined as a condition of humiliating disgrace or disrepute—was the strongest predictor of the severity of eating-disorder symptomatology. High standards may also be problematic when they combined with anxiety (Davis, Claridge & Fox, 2000). It is a paradox. Clients feel intense shame, which they believe is directly related to their physical appearance, but it probably stems from an inability to cope with the pressures of their past—a limitation that eventually interferes with their ability to function socially, occupationally, or academically. This progression is depicted in the case of 21-year-old Sissy:

> I don't know how to describe it. I just feel "bad" when I eat. I feel the fat inside of me, and it hurts. It, like, attacks me and makes me feel like I'm going to explode. Then, I look at myself, and it's like I can see the fat I just ate building on my hips. I can't take it anymore. I have to get rid of it.
>
> I'm starting to pull away from everyone in my life because they are always telling me to just "get over it" and start eating. Even my dad tells me that. He can't understand why it's taken me this long to get over the stuff he did to me. Even now, when I walk by a closet, I feel uncomfortable. He would take me in there and put sex toys into me. I know I should have stopped him; I was just too weak. And now, it seems that I'm too weak to get better, but I'm trying. I really am.

Sissy was unaware of the relationship between her body image and her sexual history. All she knew was that she hated herself. She hated herself for being sexually abused as a girl, and she hated herself for being hospitalized for anorexia (bingeing/purging type). Together, these forces combined to obstruct her recovery. If she started to eat, she felt shame from her past. If she worked on the past, she found her eating disorders worsened. The intervention that finally proved successful kept both components ever-present. She needed to be able to focus on her pain without focusing on her diet.

INDIVIDUAL AND GROUP INTERVENTIONS

At the beginning of this chapter, it was argued that the differences—and sometimes the similarities—between men and women have been exaggerated. Sadly, both errors appear necessary to provide a realistic perspective on the cultural issues involved in therapy. It is important to realize that women and men are capable of the same emotions, thoughts, and behaviors. Nevertheless, there are cultural, social, and biological differences between the sexes that cannot be overlooked, and these influence the way thoughts, feelings, and behaviors are processed.

Although medical interventions are usually outside the scope of a therapist's practice, a brief comment about gender differences in medicine may shed some light on the uniqueness of women's bodies. Women have a slower metabolism than men do, which causes them to metabolize drugs differently. Even if a man and a woman eat the same thing, it may take the woman much longer to digest it. This difference leaves women three times as vulnerable to chronic constipation as men and twice as likely to develop intestinal disorders. They also feel the effects of alcohol more quickly, and aspirin stays in their systems longer.

Other biochemical differences allow women to respond better to drugs affecting serotonin production (such as Prozac), while men tend to respond better to drugs that also affect norepinephrine—a neurotransmitter secreted by the adrenal glands and by nerve endings during stress (see Van, Schoevers & Dekker, 2008). Other drugs, including beta blockers and tricyclics, also affect women and men differently (Ingram & Trenary-Smith Park, 2008). Drugs such as Inderal—prescribed to reduce blood pressure and migraine pain—take longer to metabolize in women than in men, and the dosage must be more carefully monitored to avoid side effects. More recent research has even targeted specific serotonin transporter genes, demonstrating that women respond differently to such antidepressants (Gressier et al., 2009).

In light of the differences between women's and men's bodies, therapeutic interventions for women should also be unique. Awareness of differences between the sexes led to the development of feminist psychology, but the term frightened away many women (Buschman & Lenart, 1996) Something about the word *feminist* causes people to react negatively. Feminists were viewed as man-hating, masculine extremists, and a vocal minority may have fit this description.

Despite the fear of feminism (sometimes referred to as "the f-word"), feminist interventions have long been helpful to women. Smith and Siegel (1985) outlined three fundamental stages for feminist therapy. Two decades later, these basic stages still seem applicable to helping women understand the social politics that create pathology.

Stage One: The woman comes to recognize the social etiology of her so-called pathology (i.e., she understands that there are political and social influences in all personal problems). For example, a female is told she is more fragile and less capable than a male. By affirming a social context of the woman's feelings, we enable the woman to recognize her fears of leaving the familiar world of dependent females to risk the judgments of the establishment—both female and male—as she enters the world of achievement.

The central dilemma of women's lives, as Simone de Beauvoir viewed it, is that women do not shape their own experience but allow their life choices to be made for them by others. Pleasing their fathers, lovers, and husbands and defining themselves through them and through their children become ways of achieving justification at different stages of women's lives (Plaskow, 2001). Because marriage and motherhood have depended (and in great measure still depend) on a profound male-female inequality of power, status, and economic reward, any critique is bound to be opposed by powerful elements within our society.

Stage Two: This stage focuses on those aspects of female development that become distorted (e.g., power, dependency, or responsibility). In this stage, the woman learns to recognize the conflict between autonomy and dependency as evidenced in her particular family dynamics and, in general, as she grew up. The idea of victim is shifted to one of survivor, and definitions of "mental illness" are reformulated. In this stage, there is no "disease model" of mental illness. Instead, psychological distress is viewed as a means of coping with harsh conditions. Depression may simply be an expression of an unjust system. Resistance may be a way for the woman to remain alive and powerful in the face of oppression (Brown, 1994). One way to think about this topic may be to consider the possibility that psychological pitfalls may be different for women and men. For men, the greatest sin may be pride, but for women—who are often belittled, raped, controlled, or abused—it may be a greater sin to succumb to oppression and fail to realize one's freedom.

Stage Three: This final stage involves liberating oneself from gender stereotypes. At this stage, a woman is increasingly able to recognize the legitimacy of her needs and to establish her personal power in a healthy manner. She is able to accept her feelings as valid, find ways of pleasing herself, identify personal strengths, and accept her personal imperfections. The following techniques may be helpful in reaching this stage:

- Countering negative self-statements
- Identifying perfectionism in self
- Defining social and cultural sources of the devaluation of women
- Modeling exercises (women receive admiration from each member of the group)
- Self-appreciation and compliments exercise: Share positive thoughts about the strengths of others in the group
- Celebrating women's experience: Patriarchal, objective truth must give way to a feminist consciousness that encourages women to express their emotions and intuition
- Boasting (three minutes of boasting before the group)

With women today often feeling more empowered than they had in the 1970s, today's culture is often called "postfeminist," and feminist goals in counseling have changed a little in the last two decades. One therapist described her adaptation as becoming less structured and more narrative. She viewed her practice as a "relaxed way of bringing the expressive arts," which includes having the women journal, blog, bring avatars, draw, share music, and use textiles. All these are integrated into the one-on-one experience (Wright, 2009).

Often, the best way to begin assisting a client who is mired in dependency is by helping her feel more aware of her environment and her desires. In a basic assertiveness training model, there is a progression from accepting feelings toward working on weaknesses. For example:

Week 1: Acceptance of feelings as being valid. Anger, frustration, fear, and other "negative" emotions are part of interacting with the world. If we turn these off, we take away some of our power.

Week 2: Finding ways of pleasing self. What would we like to see changed in the world? How would things be different if we had what we wanted?

Week 3: Identifying personal strengths. These may include typically feminine tasks, such as raising children, cooking, or cleaning, but it could also include anything else. The point is to expand the possibilities for each individual—unlimited by sex-typed roles.

Week 4: Recognize and accept personal imperfections. Once talents are identified, their application must be realistic. If someone is direct and assertive, using these skills to confront an abusive husband is unlikely to be productive. Similarly, attempting to fulfill all the demands placed on wife, mother, and employee can often require re-adjusting priorities and learning how to say "No."

When creating an intervention, the counselor must be careful to avoid fostering passivity and dependence by taking too dominant a role. The client may feel that she cannot find health on her own and requires the assistance of the counselor. In extreme cases, the woman may feel paralyzed and completely incapable of helping herself. This should be evident in the following scenario. Maria came to counseling because she "could not deal with the stress of college," and she was suffering from bulimia. During the early stages of counseling, she was introduced to biofeedback. During her first biofeedback experience, we reviewed the various controls and sensors. She watched the screen as it depicted her heart rate, skin temperature, pulse, etc. As the calming music started and she noticed her heart rate decrease, she burst into tears.

"What's the matter?" I asked.

Maria looked up, smiling proudly but still crying. "I didn't know I could do that!"

It was the first time she realized she had control over her body, and it was her first step toward becoming a self-sufficient woman.

Maria's lack of self-efficacy is commonly observed in women with eating disorders. Self-doubt and shame can cripple the individual and lead to social isolation. They may withdraw from social contact, hide their behavior, and deny their eating patterns. For these reasons, changing thoughts and behaviors is not enough. Achieving lasting improvement requires an exploration into the issues underlying the eating disorder. Psychotherapy often focuses on improving the individual's personal relationships, using medication, and learning new techniques for coping with anxiety and depression.

Sharf (2000) examined many of the disorders predominantly diagnosed in women. In addition to eating disorders, common *DSM-IV* diagnoses include depression, posttraumatic stress disorder, borderline personality disorder, and generalized anxiety disorder. Why are these more common among women? Perhaps because women have been taught to be dependent, submissive, and self-sacrificing. Even as women become more empowered, feminine culture remains passive. Herlihy and Corey (2001) suggest that the main goal of feminist therapy is empowerment, which often stems from promoting self-acceptance, self-confidence, joy, and self-actualization. In order to become empowered, clients must understand their anxiety and defenses. They must gain an understanding of power issues and examine the external forces that influence their behaviors.

In order to reach self-awareness and conceptualize how gender biases have helped create the "pathology" women experience, therapists can help their clients undergo *gender role analysis*. In this process, the therapist helps the client explore the gender messages that have been communicated. Without judgment, counselors simply explore some of the comments that have been offered during the session and then seek to reinterpret them. In the case of Elizabeth, a 32-year-old woman who has been working as a waitress, gender role analysis might proceed as follows:

Matthew: Do you want to tell me more about that conversation with your father?

Elizabeth: Not really. *(pause)* It's not really important. *(pause)* Well, if you really want me to tell you.

Matthew: *(smiles)* It's okay not to talk about it if you are uncomfortable. This is your time. *(pause)*

Elizabeth: *(sighs)* Well, okay, but it really wasn't a big deal. It happened about two months after I started my period. I ran up to my father, who was sitting in his chair watching TV, and I flung myself onto his lap. I had done it countless times before, and he would usually embrace me with a bear hug. This time, he stiffened up, looked around me to the game, and tried not to notice me. I was a little stunned. I didn't say anything. I didn't move. Finally, he started talking about the cheerleaders on the screen and blurted out that I had better watch my weight if I wanted to be on a team like that.

Matthew: That's not the message a 12-year-old wants to hear.

Elizabeth: No! *(pause)* It's not.

Matthew: How did that conversation affect what happened next in your life?

Elizabeth: Oddly enough, I stayed with cheerleading. I liked dancing, and cheerleading was a good way to increase my dancing skills. But I think this was a mistake. When I started college, I started thinking of myself as fat, and I felt like I just didn't care about anything anymore.

Matthew: I wonder how your life would be different if he had just loved you when you ran to him.

Elizabeth: I wouldn't have become a cheerleader—that's for sure.

Matthew: What about the dancing?

Elizabeth: It was too much work—emotional work. It left me feeling like I was just a *thing* who supported others. I did like the dancing, but I hated the ever-present requirement for happiness.

Matthew: Is that what society expects of cheerleaders—for them to become vapid, eternally happy things?

Elizabeth: Well, yeah. *(laughs)*

Matthew: It seems like the thing you enjoy most—dancing—became just another feminine entrapment. It's as if society said, "Feel free to dance but only in the prison we designed for you."

Elizabeth: Well, maybe it wasn't a prison.

Matthew: There were some positive elements?

Elizabeth: *(tosses her hair)* I ... I liked the attention and being in front of the crowds.

Matthew: You seem to feel guilty saying that.

Elizabeth: I am—I don't want to be thought of as a cheerleader.

Matthew: Maybe what we have to do is redefine what the experience meant to you. You don't like being thought of as vapid because you are creative and dynamic. You enjoy feeling happy but want—as we all do—moments to process pain. Let's explore what society missed in you and what you hope to become.

As this session ends, Matthew has directed Elizabeth to reframe her gender-prescribed experiences. She learns to accept her past and focus on breaking away from the prescribed roles that followed her throughout adolescence. Although the session was positive, there were serious problems. For example, Matthew's gender may have contributed to Elizabeth's growth and simultaneously hindered it. Elizabeth deferred to his authority at the beginning of the session and discussed the topic he initiated. This should have been explored in more detail, and eventually, Elizabeth should have been encouraged to take control of the session. However, despite this weakness, Elizabeth was also able to define her gender role with a sympathetic and generally empowering man.

ADVOCACY AND SOCIAL JUSTICE

The various groups advocating for women often take contradictory stances. Racial-libertarian feminists argue that the differences between the sexes are socially created. They argue that such "feminine" characteristics as gentleness, appreciation for children, and compassion are human qualities and should not belong to women alone. But radical-cultural feminists believe there are unique feminine characteristics and argue that society should become more accepting of femininity (Tong, 2009).

Regardless of the perspective, all feminists believe men and would deserve equal treatment. This may be the easiest place to begin. Liberal feminism exists to create equality between men and women. The National Organization of Women (NOW) believes women should have equal membership in all aspects of leadership. Until this happens, they believe discrimination and prejudice are the cause (Tong, 2009). Although women may be less likely to seek leadership positions for reasons other than prejudice, striving for equal access to leadership is necessary. As long as barriers exist, prejudice will remain.

Even the definition of womanhood requires redefinition. Increased acceptance of lesbianism and transsexualism has affected feminist issues and policies. Which group falls under the umbrella of women: lesbians, transgenderists, female-to-male transsexuals, or male-to-female transsexuals? Unfortunately, the issue has become difficult to solve because the various groups interact infrequently. Feminists, in particular, have focused more on political issues rather than political identities (Johnson, 2007).

Even though we live in a postfeminist age where the initial demands of feminism no longer consume the nation's attention, women's issues continue to require attention. Worldwide, women continue to suffer abuses, and the United States has not played an active role in changing this. On July 17, 1980, then-president Jimmy Carter signed the international Convention on the Elimination of All Forms of Discrimination Against Women (CEDAW). The treaty was never brought before the Senate. The treaty focuses on protecting women from domestic and sexual violence, education, employment, and health care. Only seven countries have yet to ratify it: Iran, Sudan, Somalia, Palau, Nauru, Tonga, and the United States (US: Ratify Women's Rights Treaty, 2010). When we lag behind 186 countries on a basic issue such as this, it is difficult to take the United States seriously in its pledge to end injustice against women.

From a more immediate perspective, advocating for women requires similar steps in liberation. In counseling (especially when men counsel women), it is important to help female clients define themselves. This means not rushing to rescue them, encouraging them to find their own voice, giving them time to process their pain, allowing them to grieve being victims, and learning to appreciate their femininity and femaleness. Feminine culture values intimacy, which requires significant levels of trust. This must be nurtured over time, as depicted in the following case.

Hope's Story (A Client's Viewpoint)
(22-year-old European American female)

People often asked me how I ended up with Bart. I suppose, to them, any rational woman would have seen the abuse coming, but I don't think it is ever that easy. I was a little concerned about how controlling he was. He would prevent me from spending my own money on things, saying we didn't need them or they were too expensive. But he would also devote all his attention to me, made me feel protected, and encouraged me to follow my dreams.

In many ways, Bart was the first man to care about me. Granted, his "care" often led to trying to improve me. He would comment on my weight, clothing, friends, and interests. But I could have lived with those things. I could have lived with all of it until he hit me.

We started arguing about the rent, and I told him we needed to start a budget. He spent too much money on his motorcycle, and we could no longer afford the racing and extras and our rent. I told him, "I won't let you ruin our credit," and he struck me—hard across the cheek. I remember standing there, unable to feel the pain. Numb. In shock. After what seemed like an eternity, I fell to the ground, curled into a ball, and just cried.

After that, the events felt choppy. He carried me to bed—all the while apologizing, saying he would never hurt me. Blah blah blah.

The next morning, I awoke to a room full of flowers, breakfast in bed, and a five-page letter. He explained how sorry he was. How he would never hurt me again. How he would start counseling. All the right words to get me to stay.

But over the coming months, he started correcting my behavior more. I wasn't cleaning the kitchen "right"; I wasn't respectful enough to him in public; I complained too much about all sorts of things. Still, he continued buying me gifts, writing notes, and encouraging me. Building me up while tearing me down.

That's when it happened again.

(continues)

Hope's Story (A Client's Viewpoint) (continued)

Our daughter Samantha spit up on him as he was leaving for work. He dropped her onto the couch hard enough to make her cry. When I rushed to care for Samantha, Bart started yelling, "Get a cloth and wipe this up! I have a meeting in 20 minutes!"

I just held Samantha, cradling her, stroking her seven-month-old hair. "*You* can clean yourself up; she needs me right now."

Something changed in his eyes. He looked like an animal.

He cleaned himself off, and I just watched in quiet horror. After a few seconds, I put Samantha down and stood silently. As he headed off to work, I simply said, "Hope your day goes well."

Bart spun on his heels, marched over to me, and grabbed my hair. He lifted me off the ground, growling "Don't mock me!" Then, with his elbow, he struck the back of my head, and I blacked out.

He told me he didn't hit me—that I fell and hit the coffee table after he grabbed my hair. And I believed him. I also worked on perfecting myself. Never saying the "wrong" things. Being the woman who could keep him calm. I feared making any mistake, which made me the problem, not him. If I was perfect, he was fine. If said or did something to set him off, our lives fell apart.

I might have stayed with him, but when Samantha was five, he slapped her across the face. She had refused to eat her broccoli, and he "corrected" her. I called my mom, who begged me to leave home and start counseling. She even gave me Melissa's number.

Melissa's Story (A Client's Viewpoint)

(36-year-old Iranian female [adopted by European Americans at birth])

Hope definitely challenged me. The systematic abuse she suffered affected everything she thought about herself and the world. Even when reading her story, it looks like she faced two assaults and watched Samantha get slapped once. Throughout our sessions, she kept introducing other "lesser" abuses. Slaps to the face, grabbing her arm, one episode of rape, and even a choking incident.

I started just helping Hope feel safe. I broke away from my usual intake style because it seemed to shut her down. When she discussed Bart—even the mention of his name—she would cast her gaze down and speak softer. I just followed up by asking soft questions, such as, "Did you ever tell anyone?" or "What does it feel like to say that?"

(continues)

Melissa's Story (A Client's Viewpoint) (continued)

But at the end of the first session, I did drop a bombshell. I went back to the blackout abuse, and I asked her, "Why do you think Bart used his elbow to strike the back of your head?"

At first, she tried repeating Bart's version—that she feel and hit her head. I tried to let her stay with what she thought was true, but her memory of the event was very clear. She remembers the attack.

She started by saying he was enraged and couldn't control himself, which just made me repeat, "Why the *back* of the head?" It took a few minutes for her to realize that striking her head with his elbow would leave no noticeable marks. Nothing the police would report. Nothing that her mother would ask about.

Once she realized this one fact, she just cried. She cried for 10 minutes, and I let her go over her session.

The next week, I talked about me. Adopted at six months. Never knew my birth family. People keep asking if I'm from Mexico, even though I speak seven languages and look Iranian. I often feel lost in America, even though I know nothing else. But I know my value. I know I can contribute. And I speak my mind.

We spent the first half of the session just chatting about life, as if we were having lunch together. During the second half, I asked her about how America treats women—if she understood how her personal lack of confidence stems not just from Bart but from a culture that undervalues us.

I saw a spark in her eye. Something hopeful, as if she no longer felt alone.

During the third week, we discussed soothing activities. I wanted to know what she did for fun and how she took care of herself. She literally had no activities she did for herself, other than take 20-minute showers, which made her feel guilty. We brainstormed some activities, and the best she could do was to take a 30-minute bubble bath instead of a shower.

I did something I had never done before. I invited her to the yoga class I attended, and she came. The instructor did a wonderful job helping her accept her beginning-level skills. Yoga is about self-acceptance, not simply physical skill, and she enjoyed the time. We continue to attend together two years later.

In the third session, we started off more clinically. We jumped into her goals, and she sounded like a new person. She wanted to go back to college, find her own apartment (she was living with her mother at the time), divorce Bart, and start attending a Christian church. I tried to get her to pick one activity, but she said she wanted to make steps toward all these during the week.

In the fourth session, she started by looking sheepish. She had enrolled at a college, put a deposit on an apartment, and visited a church she liked. But she had not contacted a lawyer and wasn't sure if she was ready for

(continues)

Melissa's Story (A Client's Viewpoint) *(continued)*

divorce. She made incredible strides but could not forgive herself for not wanting to let go.

We knew each other well by this point, and we practiced some breathing together. I told her this is what I did doing the yoga routine. With each breath in, I would tell myself, "I accept myself strengths and my limitations—as if the air I breathe has both helpful and harmful particles." With each exhale, I think, "I release my guilt and inadequacies." We just breathed for a minute, which helped me too. Because, frankly, I was feeling inadequate as her counselor.

Over the course of the next four months, Hope filed for legal separation (she never divorced her husband, who still hopes to reconcile). She has a 3.6 GPA toward her psychology degree, and she is working as a supervisor at a customer service company. During each week we shared, she gained a little more strength and let go of her perfectionism and fear. I told her it took years for abuse to steal her soul; it would take months to build herself back up. She could accept this timeline, and she worked hard to redesign herself. I'm so proud of who she is, and I feel honored to have walked this journey alongside her.

QUESTIONS TO CONSIDER

1. Women were once described as "a necessary evil." Do you believe that sentiment still exists today? Why or why not?
2. Hare-Mustin (1978) wrote that the family has been the principle arena for the exploitation of women. Do you think this opinion is accurate?
3. How common is child sexual abuse against girls, and what are the probable consequences of such acts?
4. Are women likely to earn as much as men? Traditionally, what were the reasons for women earning less?
5. Even though girls are more interested in careers than ever before, women still find themselves torn between their responsibilities to their families and occupations. What advice would you give to a young woman wrestling with such conflicts?
6. Girls often devalue their ability to succeed in math and science, and they tend to view professions related to these subjects as masculine. With this being the case, how would you explain their great success in college?
7. Why are girls uncomfortable talking about menstruation, and what might be done to help them become more comfortable with the topic?
8. Should premenstrual dysphoric disorder be considered a psychiatric disorder?
9. What are the chief health risks for women? What can be done to prevent these health problems?
10. How is evolutionary psychology used to explain the relationship between low body weight and women's self-perceptions of body image?

11. Do women still undergo the stages outlined by the womanist identity model (WIM)?
12. Why are women more likely than men to experience clinical levels of depression?
13. What is wrong with the phrase "women and minorities"?
14. Iranian women reported belonging to a type of sisterhood and stated that they felt extremely safe. Are these benefits worth the costs of clearly defined gender roles?
15. Women tend to do better on certain psychiatric medications than others. Why is this the case?
16. What is feminism, and why is it viewed so negatively by many people?
17. What are the stages of feminist therapy? Are these more likely to be useful with women having certain diagnoses or social problems?
18. What should be done after determining the potential for violence in an abusive family?
19. When is conjoint therapy recommended for women in domestic violence situations?

INTERVENTION EXERCISES

Counseling and Therapy: Ta-Lisa (African American) is a 30-year-old mother of two (girls, ages four and eight). She and her husband wanted a third child because her husband "really wanted a son." After three miscarriages, her doctor has recommended not to try again. She feels inadequate as a wife and mother, and she has started feeling depressed. She is not sleeping well, she has lost 10 pounds, and she feels she can no longer take care of her girls. How would you intervene?

School Psychology: Chiyoko (9-year-old Japanese American) is having difficulty working in groups. However, when given individual assignments, she does fine. Her fear of groups is so intense that she asks to see the nurse or will miss school on days when group projects are planned. Her greatest fear is working with boys. She will not explain why, and she will remain completely silent (only nodding to answer questions) when in group discussions with a boy present. What intervention would you recommend?

School Counseling: Hannah (a 10-year-old Jewish American) has been wearing baggy sweaters to school, even though the temperature has been warm. Her face looks gaunt, and she complains that she has no energy. After chatting with her, she admits to eating only an apple and gum for lunch and rarely eats more than a stalk of celery for dinner. She adds, "I just want to be beautiful like the other girls." Her weight is within the normal range (possibly on the low side), but she hopes to lose another 15 pounds. How would you intervene? Would you involve her family?

Social Work: Olivia is a 19-year-old European American. She was abducted at age 12, raped, and kept hostage for three days. Her abuser is up for parole, and she is expected to testify. She is terrified and feeling like a 12-year-old again. How would you help?

CHAPTER 13

Men and the Men's Movement

INSIGHT EXERCISE

(Story compiled from several African American clients and friends)

What does it mean to be male? Beats me—I'm still trying to figure out what it means to be human. Maybe it means being human with a penis. Wait, that didn't come across the way I had intended. Gender issues never really seemed very important to me, but now that I think about it, maybe they should be. I had always been expected to be the "responsible one" in our family. My wife stayed home with our children, and I was expected to work harder to make this possible. When our marriage was in trouble, I was told to "get help" because *I* needed to learn how to communicate better. When our beloved cat died, *I* was expected to take the carcass to the vet for disposal. I guess these are all gender issues, but I never thought of them as such. I don't really mind being responsible for solving problems because, I think, with that responsibility comes the freedom to set priorities, goals, and direction—at least in part.

What does it mean to be male? For now, I think it means being a savior and villain. I bear the responsibility for failures and the glory of successes, even if, in either case, I had little to do with the process. It does make me wonder, though, are men the ones responsible for the world's

(continues)

INSIGHT EXERCISE *(continued)*

problems and economic successes? I don't think so. I know men tend to take charge and be "leaders," but we are all part of the same world.

Last week, I was listening to women at work talk about how "men" never understand them and were basically ignorant, stupid, angry, and cruel. I didn't like hearing any of that, and I don't think those things describe me. I want to be helpful, considerate, encouraging, and efficient. Sure, sometimes I'll watch football, drink some beers, and enjoy my male friends. But male time and leadership don't make me a bad person. At least, I don't think they do.

Questions to Consider

1. How have perceptions about men changed over the years?
2. Do you believe males are regarded at saviors and villains? Why?
3. If malehood could be defined in one sentence, how would you define the culture?

One of the problems with referring to men and women as "opposite sexes" is the implied assumption that there are more differences than similarities. As we covered in the section on women, there are more similarities than differences in the genders (Hyde, 2005). Many of the differences between the genders are rooted in cultural norms. Men involve themselves in different activities, have different traits, and possess different values from women.

In a society where sexist assumptions are accepted by many people, an overemphasis on differences could be construed as an argument for the superiority of men. Such a position would be ill-founded. Physical and mental differences between the genders have been researched for more than a hundred years. No one has ever discovered psychological traits or cognitive abilities on which men and women differ completely (Crawford & Unger, 2000). There may be slight but statistically significant differences in given abilities or traits, but these differences are usually less than 5%, which implies that men and women are more alike than they are different.

With this said, no one who has actually watched men and women interact would believe they are the same. There are differences between the sexes. Gender is a significant culture. In many ways, the culture of women is easier to explain because it was carved out from within the dominant masculine culture. To address the culture of men, we have to also address how it is changing over time.

UNIQUE CHALLENGES

Men's issues are difficult to address because of men's changing roles in society. Fifty years ago, the roles men played (at least, European American men) were clearly defined, generally accepted, and, in some circles, considered divinely sanctioned. With the rise of civil rights and feminism and the birth of the men's movement, men's roles are no longer as clear-cut as they once were. Today's men are more likely to act as primary caregivers for their children, to enter traditionally feminine occupations, and to express their feelings. However, men's changing roles may create a new set of prejudices that could evolve in unpredictable ways.

The comic Dave Barry is attributed to saying, "If a woman has to choose between catching a fly ball and saving an infant's life, she will choose to save the infant's life without even considering if there are men on base." When I told this joke to some men, they looked speculative for a minute, as if they wondered if they would check the bases. Of course, they would also save the child's life, but men tend to operate with a general interest in things or events, while women emphasize people and relationships (Su, Rounds & Armstrong, 2009). These are subtle differences, but they create challenges for men and women. They also provide a basis for the definition of male culture.

Another key consideration when thinking about gender is the variability within men. Decades of studies have demonstrated that men have a wider range of intelligence scores than women. There are more men at the extremes of both ends (i.e., more with intellectual disabilities and intellectually gifted). Lehre, Lehre, Laake & Danbolt (2009) also found that there is more variability is many facets of male functioning. They looked at birth weights, adult weight, height, body mass index, blood parameters, physical performance, and psychological performance and found males had more diverse scores. They conclude that variability is greater in males than in females. This makes the "culture" of men even harder to define.

HISTORICAL CONTEXT

During one of my multicultural classes, a student walked up and asked what the lecture was about that day. Her reply really struck me. She said, "I was hoping we were going to discuss something boring today—like men. I have to study for a test." After overcoming the stunned reaction to her audacity (Note to students: Do not tell your professor you want to ignore her lecture to study for another class), I learned something very important that day. Male culture is not valued in our society. This has not always been the case.

There is no need to document the privilege men received throughout history and in most cultures. Men have captured most leadership positions, run the biggest businesses, and made the most money. When considering how long men remained in power, there has to be some consideration as to what it cost to maintain such dominance. After all, leadership and dominance are cultures too, and men had to learn how to work from within this culture.

Nelson Mandela (1995, pp. 30–36) described the process of learning to be a "man" in his autobiography. In the Xhosa tradition, becoming a man (at age 16) meant undergoing ritual circumcision. He discussed feeling "scared" of the procedure but "happy" he was making the transition into manhood. "We were clad only in our blankets and as the ceremony began, with drums pounding, we were ordered to sit on a blanket on the ground with our legs spread out in front of us. I was tense and anxious, uncertain of how I would react when the critical moment came. Flinching or crying out was a sign of weakness and stigmatized one's manhood. I was determined not to disgrace myself, the group or my guardian. Circumcision is a trial of bravery and stoicism; no anaesthetic is used; a man must suffer in silence.... Without a word, he took my foreskin, pulled it forward, and then, in a single motion, brought down his assegai. I felt as if fire was shooting through my veins; the pain was so intense that I buried my chin in my chest. Many seconds seemed to pass before I remembered the cry, and then I recovered and called out, 'Ndiyindoda!' [I am a man!]"

What struck me the most about the story was how he described his guilt. He felt ashamed for being overcome with pain. In those few seconds it took him to scream out his cry, he shamed himself. "A boy may cry; a man conceals his pain."

Although we can argue what it means for men to have functioned in power roles for millennia, there is little doubt that the culture of manhood played a role. When emotions of vulnerability are taboo, men can fight, push, pull, and climb quickly. This mentality creates a type of strength that lends itself to hunger-gathering cultures and to capitalism.

IMMIGRATION AND DEVELOPMENT

Although babies and young children show no gender differences in crying frequency, girls start to cry more than boys beginning at about age 11 to 13 (prior to menarche), and the gap between the sexes widens through adulthood. Older boys cry less often than younger boys, while older girls cry more often than their younger cohorts (Van Tilburg, Unterberg & Vingerhoets, 2002). Avoiding crying is so critical to manhood that Truijers and Vingerhoets (1999) found that adolescent boys scored higher than girls on only one item of their shame inventory: "I feel shame when I cry."

This notion of self-presentation and shutting down vulnerable emotions are part of what Pollack (1998) called the "boy code." From early childhood, boys are trained to be adventurous, take risks, state their desires, be dominant (in sports and other activities), avoid vulnerable feelings, and leave other boys to fend for themselves. Violating the boy code can result in intense taunting or even physical abuse.

This code stays with boys as they move into adulthood. David Wexler (2009) writes about a trip with his family in Paris. During a meal when the family moved to another eating area, his wife asked him to grab her purse, as her hands were full of shopping bags. He could not do it. He is an expert in gender culture, and he could not convince himself to carry her purse for 15 seconds. As with many cultural traditions, there are benefits and losses to such a mentality. Avoiding the shaming behaviors of femininity allows men to remain dominant, but it comes at the cost of limited intimacy.

The socialization of gender development becomes very clear at birth. In the United States, more than half of all infant boys (56%) are subjected to a painful, invasive procedure called circumcision. This is down from 63% in 2001 (The Circumcision Reference Library, 2008). Circumcision of male infants for nonreligious reasons is rare in most countries, including such technologically advanced nations as Japan and Sweden. While most medical organizations discourage the procedure, there are medical benefits. The American Medical Association (1999) reported that the procedure reduces urinary tract infection in infant males, diminishes penile cancer in adult males, and decreases the susceptibility to some sexually transmissible diseases. The latter has resulted in a greater acceptance of the practice, with the Centers for Disease Control and Prevention (2009) recommending circumcision as a method of reducing HIV infection for male-to-female sexual behavior. The recommendation is also for infant circumcision because it costs 10 times less than when the procedure occurs after infancy.

By the time men reach midlife, they often re-evaluate the path of their life. This process can take them in any number of directions. Although this may not result in a stereotypical "midlife crisis," there are often significant life transitions that require evaluation. As they find themselves no longer able to climb higher socially, they may experience economic concerns, health problems, marital or relationship difficulties, concern over their children's futures, age discrimination, pressures of caring for elderly parents, and fears about whether their life has meaning (Javors, 2008). These concerns make midlife men an "at risk" population and a group that has been trained not to ask for help.

CULTURAL IDENTITY

While masculine culture contains many unique facets, the foundation of its examination begins with feminism (Kahn, 2009). Much of the men's movement arose in a reaction to women's liberation (Brooks, 2010), but both movements share some common themes.

The feminist model allows for an examination of gender as a political endeavor. It also explores how marginalization affects individuals and social groups. Both of these issues apply to men and women. For example, one of the primary issues in defining masculinity involves the assumption that male privilege erases the possibility of hardship. Such a supposition is untrue. American males are subject to forms of oppression that often go unrecognized and unaddressed. Masculinity is also described in terms of differences with femininity. In Italy, men often greet each other with a kiss. Such a practice would be considered too feminine for many American men. Regardless of its social value or purpose, the appearance of femininity often drives men in another direction.

For much of Western history, men avoided feminine life. This led to the masculine ideals appearing superior, but that perspective is changing. In the past two decades, the status of being male has fallen. To be a man was once admired—perhaps even envied—but not any longer. Bettina Arndt (1993) illustrates this point by describing the plot from a *Roseanne* episode. The 1990s American sitcom had Roseanne's husband Dan making an insensitive remark to one of their daughters, which caused the girl to flee in tears. Roseanne exclaims, "Oh, Dan, you're such a ... a *man*" as she leaves to comfort her daughter. D.J. (Dan Junior), who witnessed the incident, asks his father about what happened. "Dad," he inquires, "why did Mom call you a *man*?" Dan sighs and replies, "Because she's mad at me." Still curious, the boy continues, "I thought it was good to be a man." The father quips, "Oh, no, son, not since the late '60s."

Most any magazine or newspaper is filled with evidence that masculinity is no longer respected. Men are portrayed as incompetent lovers, inept family members, emotionally bankrupt, and sometimes as violent and dangerous. Oddly enough, men seem reluctant to offer a contrary image. Some men are reluctant to comment on the changing gender roles because they wish to avoid the appearance of sexism. Any male promoting the role of fathers is seen as criticizing single mothers, while a husband who supports his wife's role as a full-time homemaker is suspected of thwarting her career ambitions.

So, what does it mean to be a man in contemporary culture? One of the problems with defining the culture of manhood stems from diffuse ways of thinking about gender. Kahn (2009) summarizes the dominate theories by starting with Jungian psychology. Here, masculine energy is presented through archetypical energies. Balanced masculinity is represented through Kings, warriors, magicians, and lovers. Unbalanced masculinity is either selfish (e.g., weakling prince, masochist, impotent) or oppressive (tyrant, sadist, manipulator, addict). One of the problems with this perspective is the assumption that all aspects of masculinity are power-related. Similar problems exist with viewing gender as two distinct ways of being (the two-factor model). From this perspective, the overlap between gendered ways of acting are marginal. A three-factor model includes androgyny as a separate construct. But these approaches are still working from a binary assumption of differences. There is still a male and female way of being, with a new construct in between.

Other common approaches include the evolutionary psychology model, where masculinity is associated with procreation. Men act the way they do to attract women. Female's primary roles involve nursing and raising children. Males provide food and protection. They fight predators and create power systems. In the social constructivist model, gender is a form of discourse. As such, hermeneutics provides insight into gender roles (Kahn, 2009).

Theory aside, men are still trying to figure out the meaning of male culture from more personal levels. When I asked a group of Texas men to define "manhood," I received answers like:

- Men take care of their families and do what is right.
- They satisfy and protect their women.

- They work hard, follow God, and do not take anything from anybody.
- They make their mark on the world. Head high. No regrets.

Years later, I followed up with these men and learned that none of them had lived up to their definitions. One could no longer physically function sexually; another had an affair and left his church; still another felt helpless as his daughter engaged in drugs. Their views of masculinity involved other people, and they could not control their social interactions. This may partly explain the midlife crises.

Combining these ideas with the notion of self-responsibility implies that men tend to work within a culture where they are responsible for themselves, but they are also responsible for the protection and welfare of others. Given that they view themselves as in control of their environment, this makes them feel safer in the world. On average, men are more likely to regard their daily routine and the future of the world as safe (Slovic, 1999). Slovic's study revealed that men feel confident refraining from seat belt use, believe the world is safe from nuclear power accidents, and are more likely to view the world as fair. What is interesting about this finding is that the gender difference was generated by only a small subset of men. European American men lacked fear in almost every area, while most men of color expressed concerns that paralleled those of the women surveyed. The European American men were typically the ones who were more likely to take risks and tended to feel more in control of their lives. Minority men and most women viewed themselves as more vulnerable and to see the world as being more risky.

We have already discussed how the boy code defines much of boys' identities. However, it is also important to realize how accepting boyness also includes rejecting girls and women. Boys are socialized to avoid feminine activities, games, clothes, makeup, perfumes, mannerisms, social cues, and environments. For example, female-to-male author Matt Kailey (2005) wrote how *he* approached a young mother and cooed at the woman's infant. The woman looked terrified and may have become violent had Matt not realized the danger. What would have been encouraged for *her* as a woman was taboo for a man.

Cultural differences in the ways males and females form relationships can be seen from the earliest formation of social networks. During the early school years, girls are better able to build relationships based on nonexclusive intimacy. They can have friendship groups and multiple close friends. They also form nonreciprocal triads. Boys are more likely to have one close friend, and their relationships are likely to be reciprocal. This means their communication is filled with statements such as, "I'll be your best friend if you'll be mine" (Rose & Asher, 2000). Men also categorize their relationships. Greif (2009) hypothesizes that men have four types of friends: must friends (always in the loop of earthshaking news), trust friends (there for advice and regular interaction), lust friends (casual acquaintances/sport buddies), and rust friends (long-shared histories and drift in and out of each other's lives). These relationships are action-oriented and often involve sports, hobbies, or work.

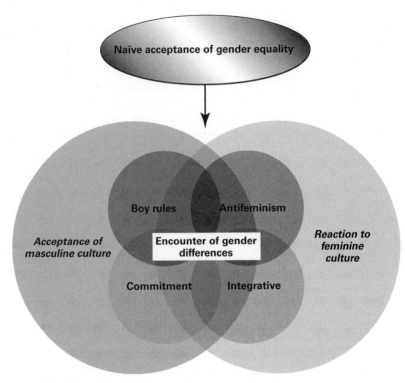

FIGURE **13.1** Cultural Identity Model: Men

Men ultimately commitment to their male identities, and they often synthesize feminine facets into their identities. However, the boy code remains a significant part of who they are. The active component of male relationships permeates much of masculine culture. For example, in counseling, men often respond well to metaphors involving the military (to fight through pain; to overcome a battle), sports (run to the finish line; step up to the plate), and other forms of competitive innuendo (beat those who oppose you; reach your dreams). I once used a baseball metaphor with a man who feared job interviews. Although I had never played or followed the sport, he was an avid fan. The metaphor was intergrated into much of his life. We discussed his fear of interviewing with "stepping up to the plate." Even great baseball players strike out. They prepare as best they can, watch for curve balls, and mentally prepare themselves for success. We broke down the specifics of preparing to hit and connected it with interviewing; e.g., swinging the bat ahead of time might be practicing some possible interview questions in the car; watching the picture might be evaluating the interviewer's body language and change of pitch; sprinting to base might be staying with a topic that appears productive and strong for him. Although such metaphors may not work with all male clients, this baseball-oriented client found it motivational.

WITHIN GROUP DIFFERENCES

Defining ethnic differences to masculinity may seem out of place here. Why not cover them in cultural issues? It is important to realize that there is a masculine cultural identity, and this sometimes transcends ethnic lines. For example, regardless of ethnicity, masculinity appears to be associated with dismissing negative emotions and exercising one's independence. Fernandez et al. (2000) surveyed 4,784 people living in 21 countries. A variety of data were collected, including information on sociodemographics as well as information about verbal and nonverbal behavior. The primary focus of study was how people expressed three prototypical emotions (i.e., anger, sadness, and joy). They found that Asians have the strongest set of restrictions governing emotional displays, but their system also expects similar emotional expressions for men and woman. As they investigated this topic further, they found that societies that encouraged verbal and nonverbal emotional expression were most likely to also have a strong cultural concept of masculinity. When men are allowed to show anger or contentment but few negative emotions (e.g., crying, sadness, fear, etc.), the gender differences are more acute. The differences are so apparent that many have considered emotions to be the language of the genders, and these features are reinforced and encouraged.

One difficulty with men being able to display fewer emotions has been evidenced in the way inner-city African American teenage boys deal with violence. Wilson (2001) studied 200 inner-city teens and observed that African American boys who regularly witness neighborhood violence are at higher risk of elevated blood pressure and possibly heart disease and stroke. These results may be expected, but the surprising element of the study involves the observed gender differences. Girls with the same degree of exposure to violence did not evidence the same pattern of nondipping blood pressure. The implication is that girls may have better coping skills than boys. Girls may find it easier to walk away from violence, while boys are more likely to get involved, which appears, in part, to be based on hormonal influences (Sanchez-Martin et al., 2000). Coping with violence may also play a role in why men of color—and especially African American men—have higher levels of mental disorders, unemployment, limited educational attainment, substance abuse, and health impairments (Brooks, 2010).

Unlike African American men, Asian men often experience confusion over how to fit into American masculine culture. They are stereotyped as being good at math, poor at sports, and passively polite. Such negative assumptions may limit their goals and desires. It may also force them to unnecessarily question themselves and their skills.

Many men struggle to determine what their masculinity means. Most girls know what is expected of them (which presents problems as well as benefits), but the definition of manhood is often less clear. Table 13.1 depicts some of the ethnic definitions of manhood. Although there are some similarities, the differences demonstrate the lack of uniformity in defining a universal form of masculinity.

TABLE **13.1**
Ethnic Components of Manhood

Group	Elements of Manhood
African Americans	Macho: African American males often view manhood in terms of strength, physical ability, or sexual prowess (Parker, Howard-Hamilton & Parham, 1998). This viewpoint may be fostered by the media's portrayal of African American males.
Latinos	Machismo: This prevalent cultural ideal is intimately connected to family leadership. The closest European concept may be the idea of chivalry. Men are expected to care for and protect their families, especially women, while stoically defining selfhood through hard work, avoiding shame, and acting in a dignified manner.
Asian Americans	Structure over function: There are expectations that an Asian male is expected to fulfill, but the actual performance of the job may fall to someone else. For example, a man is expected to care for his ailing parents, but the actual job of caregiving may fall to his wife or children.
European Americans	Puritan: Successful males are those who financially provide for their immediate families and succeed in their occupations.
Native Americans	Interrelational: Man's identity and sense of worth come from immersion with nature, providing for one's tribe/relatives, and gaining wisdom by communing with the spirits.

FAMILY STRUCTURE AND DYNAMICS

One area where men often felt comfortable defining their masculinity was in their role as husband and father. Today, a man's position in family life is filled with paradoxes. On the one hand, men have long benefitted from the family structure, and they are usually happier and healthier when they are married. They are also less likely to benefit from ending an unhappy marriage than women are (Waite, Luo & Lewin, 2009).

Men may state that their family is their top priority, but they may invest very little time at home. Still, fatherhood is very important. Close paternal bonds are associated with cognitive development, educational attainment and interests, capacity for empathy, social skills, emotional well-being, higher self-esteem, and life satisfaction. Despite these parental strengths, the more educated or significantly employed fathers are, the less time they spend with their children (Halme, Åstedt-Kurki & Tarkka, 2009).

Men also have different views on their romantic relationships. Despite an emphasis on individualism and mutual respect, European American families are less egalitarian than some other ethnic groups. For example, African American couples are more egalitarian in their performance of household tasks. European American men tend to offer little domestic support and instead strive to increase the family's income (Vespa, 2009). In many ways, the lack of egalitarian duties stems from an interpretation of the boy code. Men are trained to value cooperating with household duties, but if they are labeled feminine, they must be avoided. In some ways and for some men, this elevates the boy code above the relationship itself. This creates additional problems when communication problems and frustrations lead to violence.

Consider the way we view domestic violence. Men are often assumed to be the perpetrators in all (or at least most) cases of domestic abuse. Most of the treatments tend to focus on ways to help men act more relationally with women and to control their anger, but the programs are generally ineffective (Campbell, Neil, Jaffe & Kelly, 2010). In Campbell et al.'s study of male abusers, about two-thirds of the participants said they had sought help regarding the intimate relationship violence (usually from physicians, lawyers, teachers, or other social acknowledged experts), but only half of them received help for violence. Of that half, only one-quarter found the help to be useful or effective. Why such weak statistics?

It all goes back to the boy code. Men are trained from young ages to take charge, not ask for help, and not be vulnerable. When they need help, they must first become willing to ask for help and then they must find out where to seek help (because they lack the life experiences of help-seeking behaviors). One participant from the Campbell et al. study summed this up well:

> I was embarrassed, too damn proud. You know, this is something I thought all these years I can handle, I can get a hold of, just like I got over my drinking and that didn't work out either.... I never discussed it with anyone. (p. 417)

If self-reliance and closing off vulnerable feelings are hard for abusers, imagine the process for male victims of domestic violence. Violence directed at men is more prevalent than people realize. Even back in 1988, 2 million men reported being assaulted by a wife or girlfriend (Straus & Gelles, 1988). More recent studies maintain this research, demonstrating that women initiate physical aggression at least as often (possible more) than men. They do not act in self-defense, and they usually act out to express frustration, control their partner, or to retaliate (Muller, Desmarais & Hamel, 2009). Despite this consistent trend, men are arrested for domestic violence 80% of the time, and they are mandated for treatment 90% of the time (Price & Rosenbaum, 2007).

Abused husbands are even the butt of many American jokes. Half a decade ago, Saenger (1963) reported that in newspaper comic strips, wives were the perpetrators in 73% of the domestic violence scenes depicted. Apparently, it was acceptable—and even humorous—for a woman to hit a man. The comic strips depict men who are never hurt or unable to defend themselves and who are, in some ways, deserving of the abuse. These social messages add to the humiliation often felt by abused men. Even in films, such as Disney's *The Parent Trap*, abuse against men has been presented in a humorous light. In the 1961 version of the movie, the hot-tempered Irish wife punches her husband in the eye when their conversation becomes heated. After the assault, the husband simply puts his hand over his eye and says, "Why did you have to do something like that?"

Although we do not know how men respond to chronic violence, we have several good theories depicting how women respond to male violence. Walker's (1979) classic text on battered women depicts three stages that commonly occur in male-to-female domestic violence. Early in the relationship, the couple enters phase one: the tension-building phase. During this time, minor verbal abuse or physical beatings occur. The survivor attempts to defuse the violence by trying to please her partner, by denying her own anger, and by attempting to pacify his anger. When she realizes the futility of her actions and withdraws from the abuser, the abuser reacts and oppresses her more openly. The couple enters phase two: the acute battering incident. The abuser discharges tensions in an apparently uncontrollable manner. He realizes he is out of control, but both members continue to look for external causes, such as work-related stress or alcohol use. Only the abuser can end this phase. The survivor simply has to find a safe place to hide. Survivors tend to downplay the extent of the violence and attempt to minimize the risks (e.g., "It's not like he used a knife. He didn't even break the skin."). Such denial can be enormous, as in the case of Felicity.

Felicity: He really can't control it. He just gets so angry that he lets go.

Counselor: *(sigh)* So, he hit you on your head so hard that he left a soft spot on your skull and left you unconscious on the floor.

Felicity: Yeah.

Counselor: Why do you think he hit you on the back of the head?

Felicity: I don't know.

Counselor: You were probably facing him when you argued with him, right?

Felicity: Yeah.

Counselor: So, it seems like he had to think about where he was going to hit you.

Felicity: *(long pause)* Well, I suppose. *(Tears form.)*

Counselor: *(sigh)* I'm really concerned that if you go back that he's going to kill you.

Felicity: *(weeping)* I can't leave him!

Many couples presenting for therapy want the therapist to preserve the marriage (Leeder, 1994). This places the therapist in a difficult bind. Do you work on building the couple's relationship skills while placing the survivor at great risk or do you assist the couple in accepting the permanence of abuse and help them to end the relationship? Such questions are especially difficult if the abuser has ended phase two and started to take some responsibility for his actions. In phase three, kindness and contrite loving behavior typify the relationship. During this "honeymoon" period, little energy is exerted toward solving significant problems in the relationship. The abuser acts like a little boy who is sorry for his actions and begs for forgiveness. The abuser may believe he will never attack his partner again and may convince others by giving up drinking, visiting his mother, spending more time with his partner, buying expensive gifts, or any other temporary remedy. If his partner has left him, he may even volunteer for psychotherapy as a way of getting her back. Walker (1979) noted that this phase appears to last longer than phase two.

During the extended calm following the violence, the abuser may appear kinder and more willing to grow. These factors—combined with the desperation of the abuser—often compel the survivor to continue with the relationship. However, without any distinct end to either the violence or the relationship, the couple finds itself back in phase one. When the aggressor begins to feel his control slip away, the likelihood of a violent episode increases. Violence becomes the primary method of maintaining control (Pence & Paymar, 1990).

The delicate balance between the abuser's sense of control and his insecurity is easily upset. Franchina, Eisler & Moore (2001) investigated whether men who experienced gender-related stress would more likely abuse their partners. When the men in their study viewed their female partners' behavior as a threat to their masculinity, they were more likely to react with depression and verbal aggression. The greater the gender-related stress, the greater the potential for abuse. The most threatening topics to men—and the ones most likely to result in violence—are those involving the management of children or finances (Martin, 1987). Women are likely to control the management of children and the family expenses. In a violent household, a woman may acquiesce to her husband's demands in an attempt to pacify him. However, when issues are important to both parties, it is unlikely that the woman will comply indefinitely. A confrontation is inevitable.

Increased attention to men's issues and the role they play in the family structure has led to renewed efforts to understand how to intervene with male victims of abuse. Abuse against men occurs with great frequency and requires targeted intervention. From my clinical experience with female spousal abusers, some common themes have arisen. The women speak about feeling "out of control" and distant from their spouses. Their hostility often stems from frustration rather than the rage reported by male abusers. These components are depicted well by "Maria's" remarks below:

> I don't really know why it happens. My mother used to hit me, and I guess it rubbed off. When I argue with my husband, I sometimes feel like he's mocking me. He doesn't say anything, but it seems like he isn't listening—or he doesn't care. Sometimes, I just lose control. I get so angry, I'll throw something at him. Maybe I just want to get his attention. I don't mean to hurt him, but I know it does.

These statements are different from those of men who tend to abuse their spouses. As indicated from Maria's comments, she accepts responsibility for her actions and views the cycle as her fault. The guilt improves the prognosis for successful intervention. However, for male abusers, a different cycle exists, and ultimately, the woman often blames herself for the crisis. Given that Maria is willing to take responsibility for the critical incident, the prognosis for therapy is improved. However, such cases are unlikely to reach a therapist's doors because neither party is likely to report the violence.

The initial victim is not the only casualty in abuse. Regardless of their gender, children who witness violence between their parents are more likely to have behavioral problems. Smith, Berthelsen & O'Connor (1997) found that 42% of children aged three to six who have witnessed parental violence exhibited behavioral problems that warranted clinical intervention. The amount of violence that the child witnessed, the child's responses when the violence occurred, and whether the child copied the violent partner's behavior were associated with the child's behavioral adjustment scores. Once these processes have occurred, the family is often unable to correct the behavioral outbursts. Children are likely to act out in school, engage in inappropriate and violent behaviors with other children, or may appear withdrawn and depressed. Unfortunately, if one partner is abusive, the other parent cannot offset the effects through nurturing and compassion (Smith, Berthelsen & O'Connor, 1997). The only clearly effective intervention is to prevent the abuse from occurring.

One reason conflicts may arise stems from the shifting identity and roles couples face when having children. Regardless of ethnicity, parenthood reinforces traditional gender roles, as mothers become primary caregivers (Vespa, 2009). Although men have been increasing as primary caregivers, they still only number about 150,000. However, older research showed staying home increased gender role confusions. More recent studies have shown these men to be happy and well-adjusted. They are also glad to have the opportunity to develop deeper relationships with their children (Heppner & Heppner, 2009).

However, with so few stay-at-home dads, there are few social networks available to them. One man entered a women's chat room and wrote, "I come into these [online] chat rooms because I find that I don't really have anyone to talk to. It's kinda isolating, at times, being a stay-at-home dad. I hope it's okay for me to be here."

Stories about stay-at-home-dads have redefined the notion of the American Dream. The mythological idea about working hard and having a nice house, a nice car, and a loving family of 2.5 children is fading from popular culture. Instead, men are realizing the emotional costs of working all the time and viewing financial support as the only way to provide for spouses and children. Such re-evaluations have led to changes in more areas than occupations. Men are redefining themselves existentially and spiritually. Many of these changes are also associated with how boys and men view their training (Magnuson, 2008).

EDUCATION

Changes in family structure may be driven, in part, based on changes in educational demographics. At the beginning of the last century, women were a rare minority in college. Today, being male may be one of the best predictors of college self-withdrawal (Kahn, 2009). When compared to women, men tend to have lower reading, writing, and speaking skills throughout their education (Kahn, 2009).

The educational "gender gap" appears to be growing. Girls are more likely to attend college, receive higher grades, and aspire to higher status occupations. The gap exists in rural and urban locations as well as in rich and poor settings. These findings have led some to hypothesize that the gender gap stems from the boy code, self-sufficiency, and an attempt to define themselves independently of others (Morris, 2008).

The differences in college and academic achievement come despite no apparent difference in ability. Several meta-analyses found no differences between genders in math, science, verbal skills, assertiveness, or many other facets (Lott, 2010). So, what is causing the shift?

Boys and girls are treated differently from infancy onward. Even prior to beginning school, parents have different expectations for their sons and daughters. Morrongiello & Dawber (1999) examined the treatment of preschool-aged boys and girls (between two and four years old) in 48 families. They found that both mothers and fathers provided their sons with more directives, offered fewer explanations, and asked them more questions about their actions than they did their daughters. The boys were also expected to complete tasks without parental support, while the parents were more likely to intervene and help their daughters. These expectations were present despite the fact that the sons and daughters in the study possessed equivalent skills. The parents simply encouraged the boys to be independent risk-takers.

During the preschool years, boys also spend more time in rough-and-tumble play and girls spend more time drawing or playing with stuffed animals (Lindsey & Mize, 2001; Maccoby, 1990). These differences perpetuate the stereotype that boys are less capable of fine motor skills and girls are physically weaker. In some ways, these early behaviors create societal stereotypes. The more the sexes engage in sex-matched behaviors, the more likely they are to continue these practices through adolescence. Even friendships are based on these factors. School-aged boys base friendships on similar physical abilities, while girls emphasize similarity of attractiveness of personality and social network size (Hartup & Stevens, 1997).

Boys are also more likely to base friendships on traditionally masculine traits, such as physical aggressiveness and shared activities (Underwood, 2007). Rodkin et al. (2000) studied the behavioral patterns of 452 fourth-through sixth-grade boys and found, as expected, that the popular but socially compliant boys were rated by teachers as cool, athletic, leaders, cooperative, studious, not shy, and nonaggressive. However, the boys their peers perceived as cool were tough, athletic, and antisocial. Teachers described the same boys as argumentative, disruptive, frequently in trouble, and often involved in fighting. Such findings suggest that highly aggressive boys can be among the most popular and socially connected children in elementary classrooms.

In addition to aggressiveness, concentration difficulties and hyperactivity affect boys' educational experiences. There is some evidence to suggest that attention deficit hyperactivity disorder (ADHD) is frequently comorbid with oppositional defiant disorder, conduct disorder, and behavioral disturbances, especially for boys. Boys may not be more likely to have ADHD, but they are more likely to have ADHD with a co-occurring mood disorder. They are also more likely to have their attention problem or other behavioral concerns result in suspension (Bauermeister et al., 2007).

Conduct disorder is more prevalent in boys than girls and often wreaks havoc with their academic performance. Lahey et al. (1999) studied 347 seventh-grade boys over a period of six years. Their primary intent was to determine what factors were most closely associated with entering a gang. They concluded that an individual's first gang entry was predicted by both baseline conduct disorder (CD) behaviors and increasing levels of CD behaviors prior to gang entry. This suggests that the boys who enter aggressive gangs are furthering the development of their existing antisocial behavior. They found a critical window in this trend. Having friends prior to gang entry who engaged in aggressive delinquency increased the risk of gang entry further but only during early adolescence. As the children aged, they were better able to fend off threats of gang involvement. Given the likelihood of aggression and behavioral problems, school counselors and social workers are likely to work with these children (Olsson, 2009).

Gang involvement and antisocial behaviors may also be partly responsible for obstacles to academic success. Girls now make up 57% of straight-A students, while boys make up 57% of high school dropouts. Girls are also more likely to take upper-level courses in algebra, chemistry, and biology. Only physics is still dominated by males during high school (Young, 2001), and this may be simply because the topic is not interesting to girls (Baram-Tsabari & Yarden, 2008). These trends carry over to college, where women now make up 56% of college enrollment in America, and female college freshmen are more likely than men to earn a degree within four years. The gender gap in higher education also has differences among various cultural groups. African American men are earning significantly more bachelor's degrees than they did in 1977, but they are far outpaced by the increase among African American women (36% of African American men graduate versus 47% of African American women) (Black Student College Graduation Rates, 2007). This gap—and the lower rates in overall—led the Urban League to express "concern" for black males (Young, 2001).

Gurian (2005) noted that the disappearance of men attending college should evoke significant concerns. Boys with limited educations are significantly more likely to end up in prison. To save this generation of boys, we need to adapt the classroom to male ways of learning. We need to incorporate more activities, more group interactions, more competitions, and more practical assignments. Just as the last 100 years helped women integrate into the classroom, now we have to start doing the same for men.

SOCIOECONOMICS

Despite the decrease in education, men continue to link their occupation with their identity (Hockey, 2009). This trend was hypothesized by Levinson (1978), who found that men undergo three distinct stages in their occupational lives. In the first phase—the novice phase—the young adult explores various life choices. This phase often involves the formation of an adult dream (e.g., becoming a successful novelist, being promoted to vice president of a company, etc.), forming of mentor relationships, selecting an occupation, and finding a "special woman" who is lover, friend, and helper. The partner plays an important role because she assists in the acquisition of the dream.

As mentioned earlier, this developmental process is different from that of women, who are less likely to find a "special man" to assist with their dreams.

Even when men find that "special woman" to help with their career dreams, the men may find the stress of their employment overwhelming. Nordstrom et al. (2001) explored whether there was a connection between the existence of carotid lesions and intima-media thickness (both associated with artery hardening), with scores obtained from a state-anxiety test. Eighteen months after giving the questionnaires, the researchers performed B-mode ultrasounds on their subjects. After adjusting for differences in age, they found that the prevalence of carotid lesions among men scoring in the highest stress quintile was 36%, compared with 21% among men in the lowest quintile. These findings suggest that men with greater work-related stress are at an increased risk for atherosclerotic disease. The interesting part of the study came when they also looked at women's scores. At the 18-month follow-up exam, they found no relationship between stress and lesions or intima-media thickness. For some reason, women were protected from the effects of work-related stress, whereas the environment was literally making men sick.

For many men, work provides a mechanism to prove one's worth and, in some ways, one's manhood (Brooks, 2010). The problem with the notion of being a "good provider," though, is the inherent difficulty of defining how much is enough. I once asked the son of a very wealthy businessman if he wanted to grow up to own a big house like his parents. The boy looked confused, turned back to look at the 10,000-square-foot mansion with the Ferrari in front, and said, "Oh, no. When I grow up, I want a *big* house."

Times are changing though. Men are no longer able to find "lifetime jobs," and this has shifted some of their goals (Hockey, 2009). Men are also starting to explore professions that have been traditionally considered feminine. Women have long suffered through the process of breaking into "men's" work and have met with considerable success. However, men are still struggling with obtaining the same vocational freedom. If a man's profession follows traditionally feminine paths, he may even question his identity. We used to think these differences would disappear as equal gender access arose. However, this did not happen. Lippa (2010) looked at over 200,000 individuals from 53 nations. Using regression analysis, he examined whether sex-based power, gender equality, or sex itself predicted personality issues. Only sex predicted means for all four traits, and sex explained extraversion, agreeableness, neuroticism, and male-versus-female-typical occupational preferences.

Given the remaining gender lines for some occupations, individuals who break gender lines to pursue nontraditional jobs may feel out of place. Consider Tom's vocational experiences, as described below. Although he had successfully created an occupational identity, he continued to question his future and even his perception of himself:

> When I announced my decision, everyone gave me a strange look. "Why do you want to teach elementary school?" my mother asked. They didn't understand that

I enjoyed being with children or that money wasn't very important to me. My mother thought I should become a doctor; my father thought I was nuts and should just go into the family business. I don't know if I can explain how I made the decision. Maybe it was partly to show them that I could do what I wanted to do.

At the time, I thought telling my parents was the worst part of my decision. I was wrong. I will never forget applying to my first job. At my interview, my potential supervisor said, "It's so nice to have a man here." I didn't really know how to take that, but at least it sounded positive. After they offered me the job, I noticed that I was viewed as an outsider. Other than the principal, there were no men. Some of the children's parents even seemed uncomfortable with me—at least at first. Once, a woman came in asking for the teacher. The receptionist pointed me out to her, and she replied, "No, I need the teacher, not her husband."

At my next school, I was literally the only male employed at the school. During my interview, I remarked that I thought I could contribute something to the office because I was involved with men's issues. The principal responded, "I would have hired you even if you weren't male."

There is just something odd about being a man in a female-dominated profession that used to be male-dominated. I don't think it would be so odd being a male psychologist or nurse. I could be wrong, but it seems like the women in those professions expect their male colleagues to be "different" from other men. In education, I think the women expected me to make some great contribution or to become power hungry. I became a symbol of the male-dominated aspect of profession and seemed to personify the positive and negative aspects of this. Maybe my parents were right. It seems hard, struggling to forge an identity through a profession that is less likely to accept men than women. But I guess that's what women have put up with for centuries. If nothing else, these experiences should help me understand what women in many professions still face daily.

Despite some of the challenges associated with working in "feminine" occupations, exploring alternatives has changed the nature of men's work. Men are redefining the American Dream. Rather than view themselves as work machines, they are recognizing the damage a work-oriented mindset can have on their spouses, children, and others in their lives. As a result, more men are deprioritizing work and economic success in favor of emotional values and spiritual well-being (Magnuson, 2008). This does not mean men are suddenly defining themselves through family and friendships. They are simply creating more balance.

As Su, Rounds & Armstrong (2009) observed, men are still focused on thing-oriented jobs, while women emphasize people. They determined this by look at interest inventories from Holland's (1959, 1997) categories (realistic, investigative, artistic, social, enterprising, and conventional). They looked at 503,188 respondents and found men preferred working in realistic and investigative jobs, while women emphasized artistic, social, and conventional interests. The effect size for this study was quite large on the things versus people dimension ($d = 0.93$).

The notion of men emphasizing things over people has long been part of masculine culture. It helps explain the preference for math, science, philosophy, and even the way we focus on religion. The latter has become an interesting twist, as women are now more likely to attend religious services than men, but men are still more likely to maintain leadership positions.

SPIRITUALITY AND RELIGION

Hintikka, Koskela, Kontula & Viinamaeki (2000) investigated how men and women benefit from attending church. They surveyed 869 women and 773 men and gathered information about sociodemographic variables, frequency of religious attendance, social contacts, and perceived social and family support. They found that women not only attended religious events more often than men, but they were also more likely to attend regularly. Women who chose not to attend religious events were significantly more likely to suffer from "minor mental disorders" (such as adjustment disorders or mild depression) than those who attended regularly. However, among men, no such finding was present. The researchers' multivariate analysis revealed that women experienced increased social contacts through church attendance and that men gained a happier family life.

The way religion enhances family life is tricky to understand. Civettini & Glass (2008) wanted to see if conservative Christianity was more likely to affect family issues than more liberal church attendance. They found that women in conservative settings were taught to submit to their husbands and put family ahead of career. Men were responsible for the well-being of their families and leading the wife and family in a kind and loving way. They assumed men in these environments would marry early (because they were expected to satisfy their sexual desires through marriage), become fathers earlier in life, spend fewer hours in paid employment per week, earn lower hourly wages (because work would be secondary to family), spend more hours engaged in housework, and spend more time caring for their children. Most of these were not supported by their research. Conservative Christian men earned lower wages, but their religious beliefs had no impact on sharing household duties or even spending time with family or child care. They concluded that conservative women follow the message of putting family first but that religiously conservative men do not.

Although religious men may not change their family patterns, their religious activity is associated with decreased mortality. It appears this improved lifespan has more to do with the social facets of religion than the private practice of spirituality. In fact, praying without adding a social/religious component may actually increase rumination and decrease self-reported health (Nicholson, Rose & Bobak, 2010). The major benefit of religious activity for men appears to be the adoption of a healthier lifestyle (e.g., engaging in fewer dangerous activities or avoiding illicit drugs). It is also important to note that men appear to benefit most from religious beliefs where God is powerful enough to guide events around them. Women experience a sense of hopelessness when they view God as controlling, but men feel less hopeless when their perception of God is controlling (Steenwyk, Atkins, Bedics & Whitley, 2010).

In counseling, spiritual and religious beliefs may be useful in guiding certain behaviors. Suicidal men may fear being sent to hell if they act on their desires. Men considering divorce, an affair, violence, a legal activity, or any other form of destructive action may benefit from prayer, meditating, or interacting with other Christian men. The downside of this support is that such a man may feel overwhelmed with responsibilities. They may also feel ashamed and unforgivable. An intervention must balance the wellness properties of spirituality with the damaging effects of some religious beliefs. It should also realize that religion and spirituality may play a smaller part in the narrative of one's life than they do for women (Ganzevoort, 2001).

In working with one suicidal man, we used religion as a way to create a foundation of hope. Note how the counselor never endorses a religious belief but works from the client's orientation and builds a shared metaphor for both religion and mental health:

Client:	I've reached the end of my rope. I can't go on like this.
Counselor:	Does that mean you are considering hurting yourself?
Client:	*(sigh) (pause)* I can't kill myself. I can't go to hell.
Counselor:	You mentioned that before. God would send you to hell for taking your life. But it hardly seems fair. So, your God would condemn you without providing a path for healing?
Client:	I hadn't thought about it like that. You mean that whole "closing a door, opening a window" thing?
Counselor:	Maybe. I just keep picturing you at the end of your rope. I can't picture a God dangling a pair of scissors above you with an evil grin. But I can picture a God encouraging you. Maybe saying something like, "Come on, Dave. I made you with enough strength to climb that rope.

PHYSICAL AND MENTAL HEALTH

Although religion may mitigate some negative health risks, others remain. Men are significantly more likely to engage in risk-taking behaviors than women, with upward of 75% of men's health problems related to these activities (Kahn, 2009). Men are more likely to smoke, drink, engage in unsafe sexual behaviors, work in dangerous occupations, and engage in stressful activities.

Physical Health

Benrud & Reddy (1998) conducted an interesting test regarding gender and physical health. They asked 433 people (301 women and 132 men) to read a description of a gender difference in acute and chronic conditions that placed either women or men at a health disadvantage. As the authors expected, when the woman was perceived to have the greater health disadvantage, the participants attributed it primarily to relatively uncontrollable, constitutional factors (e.g., biology). When the man was perceived as having the same physical illness, participants attributed it primarily to relatively controllable, nonconstitutional factors (e.g., behavior). Interestingly, both women and men demonstrated the same bias and held men more responsible for their physical health.

Infrequent contact with health care professionals also leaves men vulnerable to unexpected problems. For example, just as women often view heart attacks as a "male" problem, so men view cancer and especially breast cancer afflictions as only affecting women. Even back in 1995, 1,400 American men discovered they had breast cancer. During the same year, 240 American men died of breast cancer, accounting for 0.5% of total breast cancer deaths and 0.08% of cancer deaths among men. Although the mortality risk for this disease in males is low, the incidence of breast cancer in men—like that in women—increases with age. Most men do not realize that they are even susceptible to the disease. Because of this, men often fail to seek medical assistance until they are in the advanced stages of breast cancer (Male breast cancer, 2010).

Even when men are aware of the risks, they may still lack the motivation to seek treatment. Prostate cancer is the fifth-leading cause of death by cancer. In the year 2010, approximately 27,360 men died of the disease (Cancer trends progress report, 2010). This makes prostate cancer the number two killer of men. Despite this problem, men are unlikely to go for yearly physicals and may not catch the disease before it advances. Even when the problem is found, the treatment can pose significant identity threats. Most patients receive hormonal therapy, which can sometimes produce breast growth. Radiation therapy and radical prostatectomy may have detrimental effects on urinary, bowel, and sexual functions, which can create feelings of helplessness, loss of control, and disturbances in self-concept. Stanford et al. (2000) found that even after 18 months or more had passed since their surgery, at least 8.4% of the patients were incontinent (lacked urinary control) and at least 59.9% were impotent (unable to achieve an erection sufficient for sexual intercourse). At 24 months after surgery, 8.7% of men were bothered by lack of urinary control, and 41.9% reported that sexual function was a moderate-to-major problem. Therapists should address these topics directly. No one likes to talk about impotence. Having an uncomfortable therapist just makes the subject all the more difficult to address.

Prostate cancer also appears to affect various cultural groups differently. The lowest incidence rates are found in Native Americans, and all other groups have lower rates than whites and blacks. In contrast, African Americans are 60% more likely than European Americans to contract the disease. The reasons for these differences are not yet understood. Another confusing element is that Native Americans appear to have the poorest survival rates of all racial/ethnic groups when the cancer is localized within the prostate, while African Americans and Latinos have the lowest five-year relative survival rates among patients with distant metastatic prostate cancer (Centers for Disease Control and Prevention, 2010).

Skin cancer is also a significant threat to men's health. According to the Centers for Disease Prevention and Control, 5,000 men die annually from skin cancers (U.S. Cancer Statistics Working Group, 2009). An older report in the *Journal of the National Cancer Institute* (Autier et al., 1999) found that skin cancer rates had increased by 191% in males and 84% in females from 1950 to 1994, with more Americans seeking to tan themselves. The reason for the higher rates among men is unclear but probably involves the increased likelihood of men working outside. Many men tend to dismiss skin problems (or ignore them), which significantly increases mortality rates. Survival rates can be as low as 20% for people with advanced melanoma.

The tendency for men to ignore early symptoms of cancer is a small component of a much larger problem. Some men believe there is no reason to seek medical assistance because their longevity is determined by their genes, but this is hardly the case. A study using the Danish twin registry (Bortz, 2001)—one of the most comprehensive registries in the world—found that fewer than 10% of monozygotic twins died within a year of each other, and dizygotic twins were even less likely to die during the same year. Choosing nutritious foods and forming social connections could significantly extend men's longevity regardless of their genetic history.

Men appear to have internalized the notion that sickness is something they should be able to control. This erroneous belief has made men reluctant to seek medical help. Women see a doctor almost three times as often as men and live about seven years longer. It appears that women may become more involved with the health care system because they are typically the ones who care for their children's health. On the other hand, men are afraid of being considered weak and will ignore minor symptoms. This is more than men being afraid to ask for directions. It can affect their mortality.

Men are also experiencing physical difficulties because of stress. Let us start with a basic physiological problem, such as heart disorders. Men are more likely than women to suffer from most cardiac problems. One theory for this addresses how people who avoid conflicts put greater strain on their hearts. The more people avoid initiating discussions about conflicts, the more likely they are to experience cardiac stress (Denton, Burleson & Brubaker, 2009). Comparisons between the sexes also reveal gender differences in psychosocial and behavioral coronary risk factors, including excessive alcohol consumption and smoking, favoring women. Overall, it appears that men's coping with stressful events may be less adaptive physiologically, behaviorally, and emotionally, contributing to their increased risk for coronary heart disease.

Other physical concerns arise early in the lives of men. From early in life, boys are taught to value their physical prowess and to be strong (Silverman, 1990). If the desire to reach perfect masculinity continues unchecked, some men may start using anabolic steroids to improve muscle tone and build strength. Others may diet to improve sports performance or they may have gender-identity conflicts. In the end, the comorbid conditions common to females with eating disorders are present for males. Men are also attempting to obtain the impossible bodies of magazines and TVs by losing weight and bulking up (Tager, Good & Morrison, 2006).

Although the ratio of women to men being diagnosed with anorexia and bulimia is close to 10 to 1, there are certain groups of males with elevated risk. For example, male wrestlers often diet to make certain weight levels. Some boys will lose 10 or more pounds in an attempt to reach their desired weight category. These repeated weight loss attempts can translate into a clinical eating disorder in which the client sees himself as "fat" (Andersen, 1995). By focusing on the parts of his body that tend to be overweight, his cognitive pattern shifts to believing that he *should* lose weight. Gay men are also more likely to experience body shame and are more likely to have image concerns resembling heterosexual women (Wiseman & Moradi, 2010).

Mental Health

Gay issues may affect components of health associated with traditionally feminine concerns, such as dieting, but traditional heterosexual masculinity evokes other problems. Smith, Tran & Thompson (2008) used structural equation modeling to show how traditional masculinity and failure to ask for help are not the whole story. There is a mediating variable: attitudes toward help seeking. When traditional men believe help seeking is a sign of weakness, they are less likely to seek help. Not a terribly controversial notion, but it provides additional intervention ideas. To help men overcome this notion, we can either attempt to alter their traditional masculinity, their attitudes toward therapy, or the very nature of therapy. The latter idea has received some attention, as men are more likely to prefer such alternative therapy formats as workshops, seminars, and weekend self-help groups.

The tendency for men to focus on ideas and women to address relationships explains some of the differences in mental health. As mentioned in the previous chapter, women are more likely to have problems with social/physical issues, such as eating disorders, as well as concerns with depression or affective lability (mood swings). Men tend to struggle with problems involving control, perception, or nonrelational excitement, such as drugs or harmful sexual practices (Tomori, Zalar & Plesnicar, 2000). This is not to say that men deal with categorically different problems from women. Instead, the difference seems to stem from the way males cope with frustration, depression, and anxiety.

It all goes back to the boy code, which includes so many constricting assumptions, models, and rules about boys that it limits who men can be (Pollack, 1999). Young males are still told they should be "strong" and not show fear or sadness. When emotional pain arises, boys are expected to push it down so no one can see it. Although such behaviors may help men to appear functional, they also encourage boys to externalize their problems. This tendency means that males will often handle psychological issues differently from females, even when they are facing the same behavioral symptoms.

Back in 1694, Richard Morton, a London physician, announced the first case of anorexia nervosa in a 16-year-old male. After the initial treatment failed, Morgan admonished the patient to "abandon his studies, to go into the country air, and to use riding, and a milk diet … for a long time." Such advice would no longer be given, but the sentiment from Morton's comment still lingers. Eating disorders among women are taken seriously, while similar problems among men are given less significance.

When the media addresses "men's health" or "social concerns," there is inevitably a discussion of physical violence, sexual assault, and substance abuse (Brooks, 2010). All of these are action-oriented problems, and the intervention for men is likely to look different than it does for women.

For example, dealing with substance abuse typically involves overcoming denial. If they admit to struggling with alcohol, alcoholics often deny any personal problems besides alcohol addiction. Both motivational interviewing and more confrontational approaches to therapy focus on ways to overcome denial, minimizing, blaming, excusing, generalizing, dodging, attacking, and repression of anger (Polcin, 2006). However, overcoming denial in men may look different than it does for women, especially in specific cultural circles.

I once witnessed a group counseling session at an inpatient treatment center for drug abusers who were military veterans. The therapist politely asked the relatively large group (more than 30 clients) how they were feeling. A few apathetically responded with "Fine." With this, the therapist's face changed, turning red with anger. His eyes open widely and pointed toward one of the group members who responded. Suddenly, he screamed out, "*FINE?* You're not *fine*. You're in a goddamn treatment center!" After startling the members of the group, he continued. "Your lives are all full of shit, and you are fucked up." The onslaught continued for about a minute—until the therapist quickly and unexpectedly changed gears. "I would imagine," he yelled, "some of you are here because your childhoods were so screwed up that you never learned that you could amount to anything." Without pausing, he asked, "How many of you were sexually abused?"

Remarkably, three people raised their hands. He pointed to one of them and said, "You! Tell us your story." The veteran pulled up his sleeve and revealed the cigarette burns his father had given him as a child.

"Yeah," the speaker said. His voice calm now.

One by one, others share. One spoke about being sexually molested by his uncle. During the story, the therapist's manner relaxed even more.

His voice softened, and he compassionately responded, "Yeah, that must have been hard."

What appears necessary when confronting men with substance abuse is to stay focused on the problem behavior while finding a way to approach negative feelings. The therapist from the Veterans Administration did this by taking clients off guard by using client-oriented language and showing compassion. The mechanism that is used may be less important than reaching a balance between confrontation and compassion.

INDIVIDUAL AND GROUP INTERVENTIONS

Confrontation and compassion are both important features of male culture. Men want to know what people think, but they also want to know they will be treated fairly. Given this tendency, is unlikely that they will present for counseling to deal with affective or emotional concerns. Instead, men often seek help for such relationship issues as infidelity, infertility, boundary issues, pornography, spousal abuse, and so on. It is important to realize that all these issues involve relationships with others. As a result, therapists who counsel men frequently also find themselves working with the person responsible for his coming to therapy.

Marsha's Story

I have been through a lot this year. My husband, Mark, revealed to me that he was unhappy with our marriage, and I was four months pregnant with our second child. I was devastated. When I thought he was telling me this because he was leaving me, I told him that it would be easier to take if he could at least tell me that there was someone else. Well, he admitted to being "passionately in love" with a coworker with whom he had an affair four years ago. They supposedly stopped their affair, but, of course, his feelings for her never went away. I prayed to God for a miracle to keep our marriage together. My husband was willing to go to counseling. I figured that if he wasn't happy with our marriage, it was something he had to figure out. He finally came around and began working with me on what he really wanted in our relationship.

Marsha was the reason for her husband coming to therapy. During the intake, Marsha repeatedly explained how Mark "agreed" to enter therapy. Mark demonstrated little desire to be there and almost appeared as if he were being dragged along. As Marsha continued to describe the condition of their marriage, Mark's face grew pale, and he became very quiet. He had been "caught" and wanted to be anywhere other than where he was. For many men, this position of shame and embarrassment is equivalent to an alcoholic "hitting bottom." They will work to end this negative feeling, which is usually untenable and painful. It is the goal of ending this discomfort that often motivates them to work in therapy.

Shame is a key component in men's mental health. Some men are willing to address their feelings directly, but most men are only aware of anger and shame. Discussing shame becomes a way to help them understand other emotions that they have refused to examine. When shame begins to overwhelm men, they begin to feel a greater need for affection. Shame is often common in response to chronic relationship guilt, and it is especially true for younger gay men (Bybee, Sullivan, Zielonka & Moes, 2009). This is sometimes sublimated into a compulsive need to work, but it may also take such highly dysfunctional shapes as voyeurism and child sexual abuse, which only increase the problem and create vicious circles. When a man feels inadequate, he may open himself up to negative behaviors he might not entertain otherwise. If a desire for having sex with children arises, shame is likely to compound his sense of inadequacy. He starts thinking, "Now I know why I'm a failure—I'm attracted to children." If he acts on his impulses, his shame and inadequacy increase, and he starts to feel "out of control." The cycle increases his shame, which leaves him vulnerable to more negative behaviors.

Paul's Story

I think my whole problem started when I was in college. I was dating this girl, Jennifer, and we had a thing. It was all going really well, and we were together for four years. Then, out of the blue, she just said that she was ready to move on. I couldn't believe it, but I told her that I understood. I'm not really sure that I've had a girlfriend since that time. Instead, I find myself addicted to pornography, and I can't seem to break the habit. I know it's wrong and a sin, but I can't stop. I find myself driving by the liquor store, and I know full well that if I go in, I will buy a magazine, but I convince myself that I just need some milk. I will only get milk. Once I'm inside, I convince myself that I could just walk down the magazine aisle—just to see if there is anything different and new. Inevitably, I will buy pornography and then I will go into my room and masturbate.

Paul was troubled by his lack of intimacy, and he felt unworthy of love. His method of dealing with loneliness was to create a fantasy. On the surface, the compulsion to view pornography appears to be about creating the illusion of being with beauty. For Paul, pornography was not a method of viewing himself with beautiful women; it was a means of creating a fantasy in which beautiful women were infatuated with him. He would view himself meeting the women in the pictures and rescuing them from their tawdry lives. The method of healing such pain is to address the shame.

Above all else, Paul wanted to stop his obsession, which he viewed as his sole downfall. He blamed his poor social skills, inability to date, problems at work, and inability to save money on his need to attend strip shows and buy dirty magazines and videos. He never once stopped to consider whether the pornography was actually a means of coping with his problems—whether, by submerging himself in these fantasies, he was able to accomplish two very important things.

The first coping skill Paul gained through pornography was an ability to protect himself from failure. Although he was failing in nearly every aspect of his life, he attributed these failures to a cause outside of himself. It was the pornography that led his boss to view him as passive, obedient, and uncreative. It was the vileness of pornography beneath his clean-cut persona that kept him from dating. No one could see the real Paul, and as such, no one could blame him for failure. Others may believe they see him, but they see only the illusion—the tainted exterior.

The other benefit Paul gained through his addiction to pornography was an ability to view himself as more than he was. In his fantasies, he played the pure knight who rescued seductresses from themselves. In many ways, this fantasy was the only positive image he had of himself, even though he realized that it was illusory. Still, it allowed him to escape the drudgery of his daily life and enter into a world of excitement, strength, prowess, and honor. These are all noble dreams, but his method of achieving them would never reach fruition.

When working with someone like Paul, our primary task should not be to fight against the specific behavior—in this case, his use of pornography. Instead, we should focus on the goals behind the behaviors (i.e., find a way for the client to overcome his shame and begin to behave in ways that are proud, brave, strong, exciting, and honorable). For Paul, such a path began with the admission that women might find him attractive. We created lists of his positive qualities, delved into the strengths he lost when pornography took over his life, and discussed the things he would like to do with his life. Next, we attempted to find new ways in which he could protect himself from failure and open himself to taking risks. When he no longer felt "addicted" to pornography (whether or not he continued to use it), how would he defend himself against the pain of rejection, being passed over for a promotion, or feeling alone and isolated?

For some men, finding the answers to the existential questions around them rests in stereotypical masculine metaphors. For example, one client stated that he felt the world was constantly shooting arrows at him. He needed all the shields he could find to defend himself. We started to discuss what happens when an arrow enters the body. It is something every guy should be familiar with because it is an important scene in any action film depicting pre-20th century events. The injured party does not rip the arrow out the moment it enters because the arrow may have nicked a vital organ and removing it could spell death. Instead, the wounded hero must lay still and wait for his body to heal the damaged area. The same is true for all wounds—whether physical or psychological. Even when an assault causes our heart to break, if we can rest quietly for a moment and not panic, the pain will usually subside and someone else will be along to help us recover.

Brooks (2010) recommends a three-facet approach to therapy with men: Bond with the client, formulate goals, and identify tasks. This is a practical approach for counseling, and it will inevitably require an encouraging, conversational style with psychoeducational features.

Group Interventions

The same basic rules apply to group counseling, and it starts with creating a shared bond. An important starting point is to identify the value of masculinity. Men are sometimes blamed for causing wars, bankrupting companies, and creating social problems with infidelity. Wexler (2009) points out how any culture will have strengths and weaknesses, but the strengths should not be ignored because of the problems. The ability to suspend one's feelings to perform heroic tasks (like pulling a friend from a burning building, performing in competition, or defending the country) are valuable. Classic gender roles have served men well for millennia. They led to hunting, positive social interactions, family togetherness, and others. If men can take pride in their masculine culture, they can use these skills to move into a change.

Wexler also provides some specific guidelines for working with men. First, it is often advisable to have a men's group run by a male therapist. When women are leading such a group, it is important to encourage the men to take ownership of the group and share with each other. Men tend to depend on women for emotional expressiveness. Having a group where men share among themselves is more likely to be generalized into other settings.

As the group gets started, spend some time sharing how the group is likely to help each individual member. The what's-in-it-for-me mentality is common among men. It is also important to build trust quickly and to create environment where nothing is forbidden. As shame plays an important role in men's lives, they may be resistant to share about sexuality, depression, or views on their relationships. The group must become nonjudgmental and willing to let each person share safely. Some men's groups employ a conch or talking stick to ensure each member has a chance to speak without interruption. Conflicts from avoiding conflict (i.e., the I've-got-your-back mentality) may be just as dangerous as direct confrontations or judgments. Both can shut down more meaningful self-revelations.

To help men overcome the desire to skirt emotional issues, it may be useful to implement standard responses to issues. For example, if someone says, "It's really nothing," they could be required to talk about what happened in their childhood to make serious matters feel like "nothing." If someone shares about a stressful event from the day, have him start by identifying the physical location of the emotion in his body. Doing this before articulating the emotion may help clarify the feelings, make them safer to discuss, and help the other men in the group identify with the emotion.

ADVOCACY AND SOCIAL JUSTICE

Learning to work with men is challenging, as much of therapy is built around feminine ways of expression. This is an odd notion, as most theories and therapeutic approaches were created by men. But this is why advocacy for men remains important.

When discussing "dominant" groups, such as men, it is sometimes difficult to think about how we should advocate for them. However, each group—no matter how powerful—is disempowered in some settings. For men, they are often disempowered in any matter related to the family (Brooks, 2010). Men are at an automatic disadvantage in child custody cases. They are often viewed as the cause of divorce. In domestic violence, they are considered the perpetrator before all the facts are known.

One of my clients was a male domestic violence survivor. When his wife became angry, she would throw objects at him; hair dryers, plates, a camera, hairbrushes, shoes, etc. Once, she loaded up with a number of items. He blocked the first two (which cut his arm) and then struck her hand, knocking away the third item. She called the police, and he was arrested. That happened years before I worked with him. When he came to therapy, he said he could never call the police because she would say he had hurt her again.

If abuse is one end of the continuum, the other would be fatherhood. The role of father has taken a beating over the past four decades. During the 1960s and 1970s, fathers were assumed to lack relevance. More recently, the protection value of fathers has become more apparent, but even more interesting is the role of fatherhood to the father himself. Being a good father is an important role for men, providing stability and purpose (Englar-Carlson, 2009).

Other areas for advocacy include finding ways to engage and retain boys in school, helping men and boys create a sense of gender identity, and changing the structure of therapy. The latter may be one of the most immediate ways to reach out. We already know men seek out help less than women. Most psychotherapy models emphasize vulnerability and insight development (Brooks, 2010). These features are foreign to many men. They are used to learning about practical skills through activity and competition. Try to imagine pitching this to a man about coming to therapy: "I'd like you to talk about your emotions in an intimate, vulnerable setting that may leave you feeling a little out of control or helpless. This state is only temporary; it will probably end after you experience a flood of emotions (catharsis) and see yourself in a new way."

Instead of advocating for men through traditional paths, we need to create alternatives. We need to get out of the office and play basketball with clients. Engage them in competitive games (even if they receive huge handicaps). Set up wilderness therapy trips or adventure therapy as a way of creating preventative skills. Create a current library of bibliotherapy texts and encourage men to complete homework. Create a future-oriented therapy, where goals for career, finances, relationships, and education are quantified. These areas are all important ways to build rapport and foster a masculine therapeutic relationship.

Carlos's Story (A Client's Viewpoint)
(32-year-old Latino and former Army sergeant)

The Veterans Administration required me to attend counseling. They said it was part of the condition for my PTSD disability payments. I did not want to go. I dreaded going so much that I considered giving back the money.

At first, counseling was as bad as I thought it would be. My counselor would ask questions like, "What was it was like to fight in Iraq?"

I remember responding with, "Do you really want to know the answer to that question?"

He said he did, but I didn't trust them. This guy had no war experience. Hell, he had never even served in the military. I had known men like

(continues)

Carlos's Story (A Client's Viewpoint) *(continued)*

him. College educated. Life given to them on a platter. He could never understand my world.

You should have seen his face when I told him the story of my best friend's death. We're running from snipers, and a bomb went off maybe 10 feet from us. I kept holding on to my friend as we raced along the street, and his head literally ripped apart from his body and stayed in my hand. I kept going for another few feet before I even realized what had happened. Horror doesn't even begin to describe it. It was worse than a nightmare. It was worse than I thought hell would have been like.

When I talked about stories like this, Matthew would keep digging deeper. One week, I told him that coming to counseling was like standing with my arms wide open and being cut into pieces. I felt like I bled onto the floor every week I attended. We took things a little slower after that.

.What shocked the hell out of me was the fact that he really did understand *me*. Since starting therapy over six months ago, I have a better relationship with my wife, I am doing better at work, I have more friends, and I am sleeping. I've also learned how to accept myself and my limitations. I realize I will never be the person I was before the war, but I can still be an acceptable person. I'm not to the point where I think I deserve to be alive, but it is at least a possibility. I would not have thought that six months ago.

Matthew's Story (A Counselor's Viewpoint)

(48-year-old Israli American Male)

When I started working with Carlos, I had only worked with two other war veterans. Neither of them had seen the things are Carlos had seen. He mentioned that I could not understand what this must have been like for them. That is an understatement. The night after he told me about his friend's death, I had nightmares. I pictured myself in that event, holding my friend's head. I doubt I would have handled it as well as Carlos.

Despite my ignorance and lack of experience, I was able to help Carlos with one meaningful piece of information. It is a fairly simple notion, but it has helped many other veterans too. The Army had trained Carlos to work as a machine. This is not unique to soldiers. Most men grow up thinking of themselves as machines. We are not allowed to feel. We are trained to believe that feelings get in the way of our dreams and successes. However, in civilian life, men are still permitted to feel things like anger, love, jealousy, passion, and commitment. A soldier is denied all of these. He must

(continues)

Matthew's Story (A Counselor's Viewpoint) (continued)

only process commands. No emotional responses are tolerated. To survive, he must obey without question and act without fear.

It takes some time for these men to realize that becoming human again is not like flipping a switch. When your very life was given to you by turning off your emotions, you can't just turn them back on again. You have to take the process slowly. Work on some small emotions, like enjoying a sunset. Smiling as children play. Feeling affection when your wife touches you. Allow the machine to thaw over time.

I get the sense that recovering from war is, in many ways, recovering from hyper masculinity too. In a way, war is the epitome of masculine pursuits. To get past it, many men need to expand their views of themselves. I never tell these men to explore their feminine side. Such a request would turn them off. But we can discuss how the women in their lives need to see them show emotions, like fear, sadness, and vulnerability. They get it from that viewpoint, and they tend to make good progress over time.

Questions to Consider

1. Carlos spoke about being "cut" in therapy. How should this confrontation be addressed? Does it mean the therapist should pull back or just be more sensitive?
2. The military trains people to become machines. What techniques would you employ to help them reorient to becoming "people" again? Where you would you start?
3. How did shame play a unique role in Carlos's life? How is this similar to the issues for other men?
4. What types of outside-therapy exercises or experiences might be helpful for clients such as Carlos? What about with other boys/men?

INTERVENTION EXERCISES

Counseling and Therapy: Tavor is a 24-year-old Jewish American who starts therapy by confessing a secret: "I have been having an affair for two years, and my wife does not yet know." He continues to explain that he has fathered a child with his mistress and would like you to help break the news to his wife. He added that he hopes you can explain that this is simply something many men do. How do you proceed?

School Psychology: Bahari is a developmentally appropriate third-grader who has been referred for testing. When in the waiting room, he becomes belligerent, saying, "I ain't lett'n some shrink tell me I'm stupid!" He knocked over a plant before calming down and fighting tears. How would you intervene?

School Counseling: Ghaith recently moved here from Iraq. He is 10 years old and is having nightmares about bombs and gunfire. Although he has been in the States for two years now, he still must sleep with the light on and is terrified of any loud noise at school (including chairs moving, books falling, etc.). His parents are considering homeschooling but wanted to talk to you first. How would you intervene?

Social Work: Kenji is a 44-year-old Japanese American who lost his job six months ago. He was too ashamed to tell his partner and instead pretended to go to work each day. He is now afraid that he will lose his house and his partner (Jiro, a 38-year-old man) if an intervention cannot be found quickly. He hopes you can help him find community resources and assist with counseling his lover.

QUESTIONS TO CONSIDER

1. Do you believe male victims of domestic violence receive adequate psychological support? If not, what might need to change before this occurs?
2. Why do women stay with abusive husbands?
3. What is the value of fatherhood?
4. What needs to happen for men to feel more comfortable in traditionally feminine occupations?
5. What factors contribute to the disparity between the skills of European Americans and African Americans who are homeless?
6. How does sexual harassment affect men?
7. Girls now make up the majority of straight-A students, and boys make up the majority of high school dropouts. If this trend continues, how might it affect gender roles in the future?
8. Men tend to ignore health problems. What are the consequences of this tendency?
9. Men tend to believe their world is completely safe. What might be the possible advantages and consequences of such a belief?
10. Are there differences between masculine and feminine morality?
11. How would you counsel a man wrestling with "feminine" psychopathology, such as anorexia?
12. Why are men more likely than women to display feelings of grandiosity?
13. How do various cultures dictate how men display emotions?
14. Shame is a key component in men's mental health. How would you use this concept in your therapeutic intervention?
15. Why are alcoholism and spousal abuse different from most other pathologies experienced by men?

CHAPTER 14

Culture of Appearance

Throughout this book, the effect of gender and ethnicity play critical roles in defining identity. This also affects the relationship between client and counselor. Minority clients are likely to be more guarded with a European American therapist. Years of prejudice and discrimination have forced these clients to reveal themselves cautiously. Some counselors do not understand this. They wonder why anyone would distrust them when they have not discriminated against anyone.

Imagine you are working with a client (Becky) who is taunted by her coworkers. "None of them seem to understand me, and I think Kathy has it in for me."

Before moving forward, picture this client in your mind. Was Kathy masculine/feminine, gay/straight, white/not white, slender/heavy, short/tall, young/old, etc. Gender and ethnicity only define part of the cultural experience we have with clients. But other cultural experiences must also be considered.

In this case, Becky was a 42-year-old European-American woman who was morbidly obese. Early in our counseling sessions, she expressed her doubt in my being able to understand her (I am a size 4 woman). Sadly, she was at least partially correct. I was indeed wondering whether she was paranoid, but I did not want her to see my concern, so I remained silent.

When she commented on the expression in my eyes, my initial reaction was one of defensiveness and denial. What a horrid thing to view a client so negatively. After thinking about the situation for a second or two, I realized that I needed to take a different route.

I sighed and nodded. "You seem to have some special gifts. Yes, I was thinking that you were seeing problems that didn't really exist, but now that you have read me so perfectly, I'm starting to think that Kathy might really have it in for you!"

The client smiled, and our relationship improved. Rather than feel threatened by my negative view, she felt comfortable with my trustworthiness.

To reach this point of competence, we must continually return to our prejudices, realize we will never completely overcome them, and be willing to learn from our clients as they learn from us. These issues are most important with the "invisible" or "marginalized" cultures. Some of these have nothing to do with ethnicity, social class, or even gender. They are best clustered into cultures of appearance, and they play a substantial role in our society.

PEOPLE WITH DISABILITIES

Although they are certainly not invisible, there are other minority groups that society often refuses to identity or accept. One of the most overlooked groups includes people with physical or mental disabilities. Even the term *disabled* seems to imply an inability to function in the world, which understandably leaves many people with disabilities resentful of the impersonal terms used to describe them. Physical complications may limit some activities, but in reality, we are all "differently abled." A rocket scientist is unlikely to be a professional athlete. An artist is unlikely to excel in politics. The important component when dealing with any individual is learning to emphasize the strengths of an individual rather than that person's limitations. For these reasons, the expression "people with disabilities" is preferred to such terms as *disabled*, *handicapped*, or *disabled people* because the former expression emphasizes the humanity of the individual and views the disability as a single characteristic of a person. Even better would be to use a term that refer to individuals wrestling with a specific disability (e.g., we could refer to "people with epilepsy" or "people who are hearing impaired" rather than "epileptics" or "the deaf").

If you find the use of the term *differently abled* confusing, keep in mind that it is just the tip of the iceberg. There are subtle differences between the terms *disadvantage*, *impairment*, and *disability*. If we are discussing someone with a spinal cord injury, all three of these terms can be used. If the spinal cord damage has created paraplegia, the paraplegia is an impairment. If that person had worked in a job requiring physical mobility (e.g., a firefighter), the effect of the impairment on the person's ability to walk is a disability. If the person lives in an area that lacks wheelchair accessibility or he or she is discriminated against because of the impairment, then he or she suffers a disadvantage.

Esses & Beaufoy (1994) argued that for individuals with physical disabilities, the negative attitudes of society often represent a more formidable barrier than the disability itself. Individuals who are dealing with mental illnesses face even greater stigma. In 1986, the National Institute of Mental Health (NIMH) reported that social stigma was the most debilitating handicap faced by former mental health patients. More recent reports confirm the ongoing negative effects of stigma on the quality of life for individuals with mental illnesses. Several researchers have claimed that the debilitating effects of stigma for current and former mental patients are as difficult to overcome as the illness itself (Granello & Wheaton, 2001). Consequently, for individuals with physical disabilities or mental illnesses, research has demonstrated that negative stereotypes have led to discrimination in housing, employment, schooling, and social interactions—even when their disability has had no bearing on the job or situation before them (Corrigan et al., 2000).

The discrimination leveled against differently abled individuals comes in many different forms, and it is not applied to all people equally. There is much evidence that rather than stigmatizing all persons with disabilities equally, the public makes distinctions between types of disabilities and reacts differently to people with different disabilities (Corrigan et al., 2000), but the way people stigmatize and discriminate against people with disabilities is often very subtle. The more "different" a person appears, the more likely they are to face prejudice. Imagine you are walking into a mall, and you observe a person in a wheelchair. For many people, the first reaction would be to quickly avert their eyes in order to keep the person from feeling uncomfortable. Now switch places with that person, and imagine that you are walking through the store and everyone you pass quickly looks away as you approach. You would probably begin to wonder if there was something seriously wrong with your appearance. You might even rush into the restroom to examine yourself in the mirror.

Physical appearance is only one element people consider when viewing differently abled individuals. The other key component is the person's apparent ability to change. If the disability is viewed as something beyond the person's control, the public appears more willing to accept and interact with this individual. If the person could have avoided or controlled the disability, there is less sympathy. For example, back in the early days of AIDS, participants in a study by Esses & Beaufoy (1994) were more accepting of persons who were amputees than those who were diagnosed with AIDS. They reasoned that individuals with AIDS were more responsible for their disability. Similar studies have been done comparing mental disabilities with physical disabilities. Until recently, mental disabilities were viewed more negatively—apparently because they were considered to be more controllable (Granello & Wheaton, 2001), and there are still problems with the way our society addresses mental disabilities. Stefan (2002) examined the failure of the Americans with Disabilities Act to help people with mental disabilities fight discrimination. People with mental disabilities still struggle to find employment, to get time off from work to attend therapy sessions, and to obtain fair treatment. Many times, discrimination is veiled behind the stipulation that employees must be "qualified individuals." The assumption behind this statement is that individuals who are experiencing intense anxiety are unable to perform their duties. This may be true in some instances, but people with anxiety disorders can often focus their energy on their work. There have been positive strides with the Americans with Disabilities Act, as individuals are winning cases against employers even if they have family members with disabilities (Robertson, 2009). Employers must learn to evaluate an individual's competencies based on the nature of the work rather than the person's diagnosis, and they need to understand the effects of caring for family members with disabilities.

Working with differently abled individuals requires wide-ranging skills, ingenuity, and adaptability. Many of the issues confronted are multifaceted and will require diverse interventions. Consider the challenges faced by an individual recovering from a stroke. The brain trauma may have diminished the individual's mobility or cognitive functioning, which may require physical therapy or medical interventions. The individual may also be afraid of the physical, emotional, and financial consequences of trauma, which would require psychotherapeutic interventions. Clinicians expecting to work with such individuals would be wise to establish a clear multidisciplinary referral list.

Building a referral list of multidisciplinary professionals can be difficult when working with differently abled individuals. The most important difficulty to overcome is the problem of failing to recognize or value the culture of the differently abled. Cooke & Standen (2002) found that differently abled children who were screened for child abuse were less likely to be placed on a child protection register than a control group of nondisabled children. She noted that there was a tendency for professionals "not to see" the abuse of differently abled children. Despite this oversight, European American children with disabilities are more likely than nondisabled children to be physically abused by their parents (Randall, Sobsey & Parrila, 2001).

Education can play an important role in increasing acceptance of people with disabilities. School counselors and therapists working with children can use techniques such as theatrical interventions to help shape the way children view differently abled persons. D'Amico et al. (2001) examined the attitudes of 84 children (aged 9 to 13 years) toward actors with disabilities. They exposed the children to a musical that incorporated a variety of differently abled individuals in positive situations. After viewing the musical, the researchers explored how the children viewed the actors. The play significantly influenced the way the children viewed differently abled individuals, and after the play, the children reported that differently abled people were capable of singing, acting, working cooperatively, and establishing friendships.

School counselors and school psychologists will play an important role intervening with differently abled students. The Individuals with Disabilities Education Act (IDEA) was introduced in 1975, passed in 1990, and reauthorized in 1997. It requires schools to provide education in the "least restrictive environment" (LRE). It also requires free and appropriate public education to all students, regardless of ability, and requires postsecondary planning. School counselors play an important role in identifying students who may need changes to their Individual Education Plan (IEP), and school psychologists provide the assessments to determine what modifications may be necessary. Under the law, in rare instances, school counselors may even advocate for student assessments without parental consent (Baumberger & Harper, 2007). I have only seen this happen once, when a single parent believed his daughter "didn't deserve testing" because she was "too stupid to benefit from school." He was unable to homeschool her, used public education as a free babysitter, and refused to play any role in her educational development. She was diagnosed with pervasive developmental disorder NOS (not otherwise specified). The school provided her with special modifications including individualized homework, sitting closer to the teacher, and daily tutoring. At the end of the year, her reading skills improved three grade levels.

Baumberger & Harper (2007) recommend school counselors follow the SMART model when working with differently abled kids. This includes creating *S*pecific and *M*easureable goals that are *A*ction-oriented (rather than simply avoiding negative settings). They should also be *R*ealistic and accomplishable within a set period of *T*ime.

Steward (2002) argues that confronting and eliminating prejudices against differently abled children is an important and necessary role for all school employees. At-risk children should never be overlooked, no matter how confident they may appear. Anything that makes adolescents appear different can interfere with the developmental process. Disabilities can increase the stress of this phase of life (Trevatt, 2001). Part of the challenge of functioning in an able-bodied culture involves maintaining a positive view of one's body. People with physical disabilities often struggle to maintain a positive view of their bodies, but there is evidence that having a disability does not preclude positive physical and global self-perceptions (Guthrie & Castelnuovo, 2001). There is often a grieving process if some of their physical beauty is lost, but therapists can help clients find parts of their bodies that had been underexplored. Some clients have never really considered the beauty of their eyes or the softness of their skin. They may not appreciate the texture of their hair or the strength of their muscles. The trick is learning to value the positive aspects of one's body in order to build a new concept of self.

One of the most egregious forms of discrimination involves finding a job. Differently abled people often face a significant struggle with this, which is where counselors can play an important role. More than a quarter of differently abled people live in poverty (which is about $11,000 for one person and $14,000 for two people). Roughly 75% of differently abled people make less than $20,000 a year (Kundu, Dutta & Chan, 2010). This inability to support one's self creates added stress and compounds mental health issues. This is where advocacy becomes critical. In addition to using listening skills to support clients as the express frustration, Kundu, Dutta, & Chan (2010) also recommend selective counseling to provide guidance. Some people will need direct interventions to find employment (e.g., job-skills training, contacts at agencies, or guidance in becoming self-employed).

WEALTH AND CLASSISM

It may seem odd to think of income levels creating a culture, but it may be one of the more rigid cultures we have. In psychology, we tend to think of culture in terms of power. The least powerful groups are the ones requiring the most attention. Classism, the notion that one's socioeconomic status influences a person's social role, is just as significant as racism, sexism, heterosexism, and ableism (Smith, 2008). We have already discussed most of these. Ableism is discriminating against someone's worth based on physical abilities (e.g., someone in a wheelchair maybe viewed as well socially valuable as someone who can walk). Classism looks at the poor and regards them as less socially significant. But this is more than just downgrading the value of the poorest citizens. Poverty addresses those who cannot meet their basic needs, but there are also categories for the working class (i.e., lower income and education levels but can meet their basic needs), the middle class (i.e., people who work for their livelihood but enjoy more economic security than those in the working class), and the owning class (i.e., people who possess enough wealth that they no longer need to work). Discrimination may come between any of these levels.

Most of the theories in counseling and psychology are based on middle-class values and philosophies (Smith, 2008). This means they may not work well for impoverished or wealthy individuals. Much of our behavior is guided by our income and the culture built around it. For example, how much money we have affects the way we view the future. For many years, we thought giving impoverished people money would lead to savings. This does not appear to be the case. One study even found a negative relationship between increased income and savings among poor families. The higher their income rose, the *less* likely they were to save (Ozawa, Kim & Joo, 2006). Some people would pay off expenses or loans. But others simply wanted to buy things. Families who have lived with wealth were more likely to value the future need of their income, which creates a different cultural belief.

This tendency to spend what we have fits into the Western philosophical tenant of individualism. If we have plenty of money, we can do what feels good and still plan for the future. If we lack the resources to satisfy our daily wants, we may sacrifice the future to meet these immediate goals. What confounds this problem is the difficulty addressing poverty. Western values offer little mechanisms to help (Caldwell, 2009). We expect every individual (or at least every family) to meet their own needs and prepare for their own futures. This makes it difficult to change neighborhoods and cultures with substandard education, violence, limited recreational options, and economic struggles.

With wages and housing equity at their lowest levels since the Great Depression, there are more poor American families than ever before (Goodman et al., 2010). This is also changing the world culture. Homelessness can stem from multiple issues. Common causes include stressful life conditions, traumatic events (like violence and sexual abuse), physical health problems, substance abuse, and social isolation. Gender also plays a role in homelessness. Homeless men and women face similar struggles, such as mental illness, addiction, and poverty (Gordon et al., 2010), but women are more likely to also contend with child-rearing issues. DeWard & Moe (2010) argue that women are more likely to receive governmental-based social services, including the use of shelters. Shelters have played an important role in providing immediate shelter to women and children, but there are also concerns. There is often an adversarial relationship between shelter employees and their clientele. This means the homeless need advocates, including case management and aid in securing employment and stable housing. This may sound like social work and not counseling, but anyone working with the homeless will need to build interdisciplinary coalitions (Caldwell, 2009)

It is also important to give homeless individuals time to normalize their experiences and share their stories. This process can empower individuals, help them identify injustices, and work on overcoming marginalization. Such an intervention also provides a place to feel comfortable and safe, which facilitates growth (Brubaker et al., 2010).

AGEISM AND THE ELDERLY

Occupational issues also affect the elderly. Those living on Social Security pensions make $12,500 a year, and nearly a third of Americans over 65 years of age found retirement to be "stressful" (Glicken, 2009). For many, no other form of income is possible. As a society, we tend to overlook the financial struggles of elderly adults, investing more time with others. For example, in regards to disabilities, the elderly composes the largest single demographic of differently abled people. The percentage of children with physical disabilities ranges from 16.6% for Asian Americans to 24.4% for African Americans and Native Americans. For people over 65 years of age, the numbers jump to a low of 40.4% for European Americans and a high of 52.8% for African Americans (Balcazar et al., 2010). This means that nearly half of all Americans over the age of 65 will face some type of mental or physical disability.

In 1968, Robert Butler (1993) coined the term *ageism*. He came up with the concept when he heard about a group of middle-aged citizens protesting the construction of a luxury apartment building for the elderly poor. The protesters were not fighting for the right to rent the proposed apartments. They simply wanted the structure to be built somewhere else. In many respects, ageism stems from society's struggle to find a balance between providing for the needs of vulnerable elders and maintaining "entitlement" programs, such as Medicare and Medicaid, at the expense of other groups, but it also reflects a limited understanding of the aging process and the special needs of the elderly. In addition to benefitting from perceived privileges, the elderly are more likely to face ambivalence or negativity because—unlike gender, ethnicity, or sexual orientation—aging involves physical decline (Warren, 1998).

Despite significant challenges facing them, geriatric clients are less likely to seek counseling than younger people. People over 65 make up 13% of the U.S. population, but they only account for 6% of community mental health services and 9% of psychiatric services (Pesky, n.d.). Despite not seeking services, there is considerable evidence showing that any counseling (but especially cognitive and behavioral approaches) can mitigate depression and help elderly clients. There is also evidence that simply changing diet and exercise can significantly help physical and mental functioning (Glicken, 2009).

There are challenges to the therapist too. Therapists may have countertransference issues, as the client may remind them of a parent or grandparent. Therapists may have difficulty thinking about elderly clients as sexually active, even though this is an important component to life at any age.

When working with elderly clients, therapists must ensure their assessment remains complete. Some practitioners and physicians anchor on a particular point, missing something else critical in the process. We focus on readily available information rather than gathering everything pertinent (Groopman, 2007). For example, say you were concerned about retirement stress. Vaillant, DiRago, & Mukamal's (2006) decades-long longitudinal study found that retirement satisfaction was not linked to physical health, income, or even depression. Instead, such risk factors as low IQ, limited education, family conflicts, and poor mental health were better determinants, but even these could be counteracted. People who had a good marriage, limited neuroticism, enjoyed vacations, and played regularly could make retirement a new adventure. All these factors make a complete assessment vital to effective interventions, but assessment is more than identifying problems. Diagnoses are clusters of symptoms. They cannot describe the essence of the individual. To reach cultural competence, the individual must receive attention. This will include looking at goals, possibilities, and what is already working (Glicken, 2009).

Even with comprehensive assessments, it is often difficult to identify the cause of affective disturbances in the elderly. Powell et al. (2001) found no observable predictors for geriatric depression (other than education). Despite not finding any "cause," they were able to identify solutions. Support groups provided important social resources and helped a significant number of clients improve. They also found that people stopped attending the groups as they started feeling better. They only wanted a jumpstart to feeling better.

Other cultural issues can also affect the aging process. Aging European American women have few positive role models because white culture devalues the aging process, especially for women (Dorsey, 2010). African American elderly are more likely to be physically ill or disabled, and they experience higher mortality rates. They are also more likely to be abused, which is yet another underexplored component of geriatric life. Whether elder abuse is defined in terms of physical maltreatment, financial exploitation, neglect, misuse of medication, violation of rights, or psychological abuse, elderly African Americans are more likely to experience abuse than are their European American peers (Baruth & Manning, 1999), although 4% to 10% of all elderly citizens will face abuse in America (Wolf, 1998). Latino elderly are more likely than other groups to be confined to bed because of an illness (AARP, 1995). Traditional screening tools are unlikely to detect depression in Asian Americans, especially Korean Americans (Pang, 1995). Native American elders have the highest mortality rate, in part because of their distrust of European healing interventions (Baruth & Manning, 1999). The estimated 3.5 million gays and lesbians over 60 often feel the need to create their own support groups in order to have their needs met (Slusher, Mayer & Dunkle, 1996). All these unique elements make geriatric issues difficult to address, but it is important to realize that geriatric issues are cultural issues, and cultural sensitivity is just as important in this arena as in any other.

Bicultural issues for geriatrics are complex, but there are a number of issues common to the geriatric minority that warrant attention. Table 14.1 depicts some of the common themes in geriatric psychotherapy. As with all developmental groups, there are physical, social, affective, and cognitive issues unique to this age group. The table provides introductory descriptions of common problems and some basic foundations or techniques to employ when dealing with each area.

In addition to intervention for specific issues, other treatment considerations may be wise. For example, religion and spirituality can play a powerful role. Emery and Pargament (2004) believe religion helps older adults by offering routines/traditions, a social network, a sense of support/understanding, a sense of meaning, and a feeling of empowerment. But the benefit of private spirituality implies that there is some value in believing in a higher power (George et al., 2000). McCullough et al. (2000) conducted a meta-analysis of data from 42 independent samples examining the association of a measure of religious involvement and all-cause mortality. Religious involvement was significantly associated with lower mortality rates (odds ratio = 1.29; 95% confidence interval: 1.20–1.39). People who are religious are more likely to live longer than those who are not. An interesting aspect of the study was the fact that it explored both public and private religiosity. In the past, similar findings were attributed to the idea that people who attended church, synagogue, or mosque were conditioned to pursue more healthy lifestyles. This is why they are less likely to be obese, lonely, or immobile. They were more likely to have better social support networks, regular activities, and long-term friendships, which helped them remain physically healthy and mentally alert (Burgess, Schmeeckle & Bengtson, 1998).

Working on practical considerations may also benefit aging clients. Practitioners help their elderly clients by raising such topics as relationships with their children, estate planning, and mental issues (especially depression). Even when working with depressed and anxious clients, psychotherapy is as effective as pharmacological interventions (Lebowitz et al., 1997). It is important

TABLE **14.1**
Geriatric Counseling Issues

	Symptoms	Interventions
Physical Issues	Changes in appearance; feeling like you are not the same person	The most important element when counseling someone who is feeling self-alienated is finding the cause of the feeling. Sometimes, subtle changes in voice or dexterity may be more significant than balding or wrinkles. Physical exercise and better nutrition can rejuvenate the skin and improve health, but ultimately, the client needs to shift to defining the self through being rather than doing. When clients base their identity on their level of activity, they will likely experience depression as their physical condition declines. Transpersonal/spiritual growth will assist clients in coping with physical changes. Effective therapy may incorporate personal myths and stories to explore the client's definition of self and the meaning of life.
	Diminished sensory functioning; loss of hearing or poor eyesight	Sensory perception changes can be significant for a number of reasons. They tend to isolate people from friends whose hearing and vision are not impaired, and the disability can lead to feelings of incompetence, shame, or inadequacy. Helping to find assistive technology (e.g., hearing aids) is often an important first step. Support groups may also help to provide an avenue in which people can share their concerns with others in similar situations. The key is finding a way to optimize existing physical abilities while compensating for deficits.
Social Issues	Loss of a spouse or close friend	The grieving process is different for every individual, but for an elderly spouse, losing one's partner creates a significant shift in identity. It is also important to realize that friendships provide helpful transitions into widowhood, and clients should be encouraged to spend more time with their friends and relatives. Therapists are strongly advised to incorporate the entire family when helping geriatric clients cope with bereavement because the loss of a parent or grandparent may interfere with the family dynamic, which may leave the widow feeling more isolated or lonely. Individually, therapists can help clients continue to explore how they will address their sexual desires (which may remain strong well into their 80s).
	Limited mobility, decreasing social outlets	Therapists must ascertain whether the client's limited social contact stems from shame or a lack of knowledge. Clients may simply be unaware of the things they can do without the use of their legs or arms. Occupational therapists may also be helpful in training elderly clients to explore new activities and daily routines.
Affective Issues	Possible changes in personality	Older adults show markedly consistent personality scores over time, and age appears to explain only about 4% of financial circumstances, career transitions and retirement, the effects of physical changes, and affective personality variance (Costa, Yang & McCrae, 1998). When changes are observed, medical reasons should be explored before being ruled out. Clients

(continues)

TABLE **14.1**
Geriatric Counseling Issues (*Continued*)

	Symptoms	Interventions
		should realize that personality changes are not a natural part of aging, and they are often able to continue developing positive traits.
	Depression	Depression in the elderly often remains undetected. Although older adults are less susceptible to depression and other mental health disorders (except dementia) than younger people, depression can have a powerful influence on their lives. Most will get better after their first episode, but half of those will become depressed again (Glicken, 2009). Diagnostic difficulties stem from the multiple causes of depression. Sometimes, changes in estrogen levels or neurotransmitter functioning may create the need for pharmacological interventions. Functional depression may arise from changes in ability, performance, or relationships. The key intervention appears to be helping the client maintain ego integrity over despair. If they have a reason to hope, they can fight against depression, but they need something to hang on to. For example, depression often emerges as chronic illnesses develop. Providing hope may take the form of helping the client to connect with family members or to write out a positive narrative of his or her life. Short-term interventions reducing shame and normalizing the experience are often the most helpful.
Cognitive Issues	Memory loss	When memory loss occurs, it is usually a loss of recent memory rather than remote memory. In these cases, reminiscent therapy can be extremely beneficial. Clients can be encouraged to reflect on their past relationships, accomplishments, and acquisition of wisdom as a means of feeling integrated and whole.
	Difficulty learning	When learning new skills becomes increasingly difficult, maintaining the development of already-acquired skills may be a helpful substitution. If a client has previously mastered quilting, piano playing, or cards, he or she can be encouraged to spend more time maintaining and perfecting this skill.
	Dementia	Families often treat dementia and cognitive malfunction as taboo topics. The family assumes nothing can be done and regards the problem as something best left alone. Avoidance of this topic tends to create divisions within the family, with the impaired client correctly assuming that his or her family is keeping secrets. The situation becomes even more complicated if the impaired individual is considered to be the head of the household. Although discussing the topic openly may produce considerable strife, it is the best way to help the family create a new homeostasis. The family can also help their loved one cope with changes in memory and affect (e.g., anger, frustration, and fear).

to realize that therapy with geriatric clients must take an approach that differs from therapy with younger people. Instead of focusing on a linear goal, the intervention requires a cyclical perspective (Nordhus, Nielsen & Kvale, 1998). Within this perspective, there is no immediate focus on reaching a certain level of insight or achieving a specific behavioral change. Instead, there is a mutual understanding that the cycle has no beginning or end. The client's condition may retrace the same path several times or start an entirely different cycle without warning. The client's ability to regulate the therapeutic process is encouraged, therapy is conducted through shorter and more frequent sessions, and the interactional style between client and counselor is often more relaxed and informal than with other clients.

WEIGHT, HEIGHT, AND BEAUTY

One of the emerging notions of culture involves attractiveness. Beautiful people are viewed as nicer, kinder, more altruistic, better volunteers, more sociable, more enthusiastic, have better sex, get better jobs, and are more committed (Lemay, Clark & Greenberg, 2010). Think about how such issues as height, weight, and physical appearance can show up in microaggressions and unexamined prejudices. Tall people hear comments such as, "Did you play basketball?" Short people hear, "It might be nice for people to think of you as young." Heavy people hear, "You may as well eat two; it's not like you're watching your weight." Thin people hear, "You're going to melt away to nothing if you keep working out like that." These comments are often made jokingly. The speaker may not even realize how prejudiced he or she is toward the victim.

Of all the appearance cultures, weight is becoming especially important. Recently, the number of Americans with obesity started outnumbering merely overweight (Cotugna & Mallick, 2010). People with obesity are more likely to miss work (13 times higher among the heaviest employees), they experience prejudice and discrimination in their private and public lives, they often become distressed when weight loss attempts fail, and weight has a synergistic effect on disability status and mental health (Gariepy et al., 2010). When someone wrestles with a disability, depression and anxiety tend to follow. Add obesity to this, and the depression and anxiety are magnified many times over. This is an especially sinister pattern, as childhood junk food consumption is associated with happiness (Chang & Nayga, 2010). Like many addictions, early consumption of unhealthy foods fights off depression, but adolescent and adult obesity results in more depression.

In counseling, therapists sometimes try to "advocate" for people with weight issues by working directly on the weight issues. This has met with mixed results. Given the shame associated with weight in our society, making weight the primary issue may only serve to increate the shame, paradoxically making the situation worse. Such interventions are also avenues for prejudice. People who have not lived on restrictive calorie intakes should not be recommending them (Cotugna & Mallick, 2010).

CONCLUSIONS

It should be clear how all counseling is multicultural counseling. This is especially true when the client feels marginalized and insignificant. In all multicultural contexts, flexibility, tolerance, and open-mindedness are essential components for working with clients. The cultural dimensions of counseling make the therapeutic process dynamic and ever-changing. In medical interventions, the physician's job involves examining the patient and narrowing down the possible diagnoses until only one remains. In multicultural therapy, the therapist must continue to expand the realm of possibility. Basically, we must realize that the assessment skills taught in general assessment classes may not always apply to multicultural clients. A depressed African American man may have a chemical imbalance, but he may also feel unable to cope with the pressures imposed by a racist society. A woman who is starving herself may be genetically predisposed to do so, but she may also have fallen prey to a cultural overemphasis on physical beauty.

In a sense, medical and general psychological training can provide helpful starting points when dealing with clients, but ongoing multicultural training allows therapists to transcend medical and general issues. Therapy becomes a sociological process in which the individual can only be understood within the culture and environments from which he or she has emerged. Ideally, you will continue to develop your multicultural skills throughout your career. To do so, you should spend as much time as possible with members of diverse cultures, become familiar with the myths and stories of different groups, and continue to examine the ways in which your cultural worldview has shaped your perspective on diverse individuals. By doing such things, you will foster your growth as a therapist and as a person.

Anabelle's Story (A Client's Viewpoint)
(18-year-old European American female)

I'm not really sure how it all started. It's not like I wanted to hurt myself or, really, even diet. Sometime in high school, around my freshmen year, I weighed about 105 pounds and ran track. That was the heaviest I had ever been in my life. Just the year before, I weighed only 92 pounds, but I was okay with my body. At least, I was until spring break. I got back from spending time with my grandparents, and I felt a little bloated. My grandparents always had tons of food: ice cream, chips, and sodas.

Anyway, the week after I got back, my coach commented on my stomach. He actually patted my belly and said, "Looks like someone got a food baby over break."

That was it. I wasn't going to have people commenting on my weight. I had only gained one pound, but I could see my belly growth too.

(continues)

Anabelle's Story (A Client's Viewpoint) *(continued)*

The first week, I didn't eat anything. I just had gum, water, and breath mints. After a couple of weeks of eating virtually nothing, my stomach looked a little better. But my body didn't look the way it used to. It seemed like any time I ate real food, I could see the pudginess come back.

I started working out harder, running for about two hours a day. It felt good to be in control of my life. And that was the key. Eating and exercise gave me a sense of control. My body was the one aspect of my life I could manage. My parents, boyfriend, classes, friends, job, and social life were a struggle. But weight was something I could manage.

After a few years, I got to the point where I couldn't imagine eating a normal meal. My diet was my life. I weighed 82 pounds, my period stopped, and I had to wear baggy shirts to avoid getting stares in public. That's when my mom made me go to counseling.

Julie's Story (A Client's Viewpoint)

(41-year-old European American female)

When I started working with Anabelle, I realized the first month would be the most difficult. She had just been released from the hospital, where she gained a few pounds after being on an IV for a week. But she had already resumed her anorexic diet within days of her release. We had to change her perspective quickly.

Session 1

Julie:	When you said you couldn't live if you didn't lose weight, what did you mean?
Anabelle:	*(sighs)* I'm not going to kill myself, if that's what you mean. But I don't see the point of living like this.
Julie:	So, unless you lose weight, you can't accept yourself or have any value in society?
Anabelle:	*(hangs her head) (pauses)* Yeah.
Julie:	If you were black or homeless or gay but thin, would you still be worthless?
Anabelle:	*(scoffs)* No! I'm not prejudiced or anything.
Julie:	But you think your weight marginalizes you, just like society marginalizes all those people.
Anabelle:	I haven't thought about it like that.

(continues)

Julie's Story (A Client's Viewpoint) (continued)

Julie:	For me, weight loss is like building something. You have lay a good foundation because the exercise and dieting it takes are stressful and hard.
Anabelle:	You're saying I can't lose weight because I don't like myself?
Julie:	Not exactly. I'm sure there are many causes for your weight: genetics, diet, exercise, stress, metabolism. But if you're going to put yourself through a lifestyle change, you need to be ready for the stress. Getting rid of your self-hatred and fears will make it easier to succeed.
Anabelle:	*(sighs)* Okay, this is going to sound funny, but I'm not sure I'm ready to like myself.

Session 2

Anabelle:	I tried not think about my weight this week.
Julie:	How did it go?
Anabelle:	It was … weird.
Julie:	Yeah? What happened?
Anabelle:	Well, Tuesday, I really didn't eat much. I thought my problems were over, and I would lose weight without any difficulties.
Julie:	I take it one of the other days was harder?
Anabelle:	Yeah. Thursday, I ordered three meals for lunch and I ATE THEM ALL.
Julie:	How did you feel afterward? Did it make you feel worthless?
Anabelle:	That was the weird thing. I *wanted* to feel worthless. I know that sounds crazy. But I actually had to *make* myself feel bad.
Julie:	Sounds like an important first step. You realize you're a valuable person, no matter what you weigh.
Anabelle:	I guess I do. Does this mean we can work on a weight loss plan now?
Julie:	You're getting close! But you were saying earlier that food was also your way of relieving stress. Let's find some new ways to get yourself calm and then you'll have something to do when your life gets hard. I just don't want to see you get derailed once we get started. Okay?

It took six weeks before she started gaining weight, but when she did, she made a full recovery. She graduated high school, started college, and maintained a healthy weight for the next five years.

QUESTIONS TO CONSIDER

1. Why are European American children with disabilities more likely to be physically abused than disabled children from other ethnic groups?
2. How can school counselors help to reduce stigma toward people with disabilities?
3. How should therapists advocate for the housing, employment, schooling, and social interactions of people with disabilities?
4. When would school counselors or school psychologists advocate for student assessments without parental consent?
5. How might disabilities increase phase of life stress?
6. What is ageism, and why does it exist?
7. Why do savings sometimes decrease with added wealth?
8. How do Western values contribute to substandard education, violence, limited recreational options, and economic struggles?
9. What interdisciplinary coalitions could you create to help work with the poor?
10. In what ways can religious involvement help elderly individuals?
11. How do older individuals tend to cope with depression and personality changes? Are these common facets of the aging process?
12. How does age play a role in the care of those with physical disabilities?
13. Obesity may become the single-biggest health crisis in America. How should therapists help fight the problem?
14. Why would obesity have a synergistic (i.e., more than additive) effect on depression for people who also have physical disabilities?

INTERVENTION EXERCISES

Counseling and Therapy: Axel (age 20) was referred to counseling after inciting "aggressive behavior" at his Virginian college. He attended a meeting where a leader from the ACLU was giving a talk on first amendment rights. When the speaker discussed a recent case involving defending the rights of homeless people to voice their concerns at the state capital, Axel hacked into the microphone system and started chanting, "Gritters gotta go." His parents, who have made substantial donations to the university, asked that the incident be kept out of the university discipline system and negotiated 10 counseling sessions. How would you help? What would your priorities be?

School Psychology: Isabella's (age 9) grades have fluctuated over the course of the year. Her grades in math and science tend to be As; she is struggling with language and social sciences. When giving her an intelligence test, she scored significantly higher on the perceptual reasoning subtests versus the VCI and full-scale scores. It also became clear she was having difficulty following verbal instructions but excelled when reading directions. What additional testing would you recommend? What behavioral modifications might you suggest?

School Counseling: Ren (age 13) currently weighs 210 pounds. He is having difficulty with his physical education class and is regularly taunted at school for his obesity. His parents have asked for assistance regarding both of these issues. They would like a modified physical education program and stricter punishments for the children who taunt him. How would you intervene? What are the ramifications for helping and not helping?

Social Work: Ahmed (age 67) is at the early stages of Alzheimer's and having difficulty remembering the names of significant others and even his address. Last week, he walked to the grocery store and was unable to find his way home. He walked for four hours before a police officer helped him find his way. His family has asked for assistance. What would you recommend to the family?

REFERENCES

A guide to African-Americans and religion. (2007). Religion Link. Retrieved from http://www.religionlink.com/tip_070108.php.

Aberle, D. (1966). *The peyote religion among the Navaho*. Chicago: Aldine.

Abu-Baker, K. (2006). Arab/Muslim families in the United States. In M. Dwairy (Ed.), *Counseling and psychotherapy with Arabs and Muslims: A culturally sensitive approach* (pp. 29–46). New York: Teacher's College Press.

Abudabbeh, N. (2005). Arab families: An overview. In M. McGoldrick, J. Giordano & J. K. Pearce (Eds.), *Ethnicity and family therapy* (2nd ed., pp. 423–436). New York: The Guilford Press.

Adams, H. E., Wright, L. W., Lohr, B. A. (1998). Is homophobia associated with homosexual arousal? *Journal of Abnormal Psychology*, 105(3), 440–445.

Adelabu, D.H. (2008). Future time perspective, hope, and ethnic identity among African American adolescents. *Urban Education*, 43(3), 347–360.

Ader, T., Susswein, L., Callanan, N. & Evans, J. (2009). Attitudes and practice of genetic counselors regarding anonymous testing for BRCA1/2. *Journal of Genetic Counseling*, 18(6), 606–617.

African Americans show solid gains at all academic degree levels. (2009). *Journal of Blacks in High Education*. Retrieved on October 21, 2010, from http://www.jbhe.com/features/64_degreelevels.html.

Aguinaldo, J. (2008). The social construction of gay oppression as a determinant of gay men's health: "Homophobia is killing us." *Critical Public Health*, 18(1), 87–96.

Ailinger, R. L. & Dear, Margaret R. (1997). Latino immigrants' explanatory models of tuberculosis infection. *Qualitative Health Research*, 7(4), 521–531.

Aizenman, N. C. (2008). Study finds America is again becoming a land of immigrants. *The Providence Journal*, p. A1.

Alcántara, C. & Gone, J. (2007). Reviewing suicide in Native American communities: Situating risk and protective factors within a transactional-ecological framework. *Death Studies*, 31(5), 457–477.

Alegría, M. & Woo, M. (2009). Conceptual issues in Latino mental health. In F. A. Villarruel, G. Carlo, J. M. Grau, M. Azmitia, N. J. Cabrera & T. J. Chahin (Eds.), *Handbook of U.S. Latino psychology: Developmental and community-based perspectives* (pp. 15–30). Los Angeles, CA: Sage Publications.

Alexander, F. G. & Selesnick, S. T. (1966). *The history of psychiatry: An evaluation of psychiatric thought and practice from prehistoric times to the present*. New York: Harper & Row, Publishers.

Alhabib, S., Nur, U. & Jones, R. (2010). Domestic violence against women: Systematic review of prevalence studies. *Journal of Family Violence*, 25, 369–382.

Ali, H., Baynouna, L. & Bernsen, R. (2010). Barriers and facilitators of weight management: Perspectives of Arab women at risk for type 2 diabetes. *Health & Social Care in the Community*, 18(2), 219–228.

Ali, R. S., Mahmood, A., Moel, J., Hudson, C. & Leathers, L. (2008). A qualitative investigation of Muslim and Christian women's views of religion and feminism in their lives. *Cultural Diversity & Ethnic Minority Psychology*, 14, 38–46.

Al-Krenawi, A., Graham, J., Dean, Y. & Eltaiba, N. (2004). Cross-national study of attitudes towards seeking professional help: Jordan, United Arab Emirates (UAE) and Arabs in Israel. *International Journal of Social Psychiatry*, 50(2), 102–114.

Allen, P. G. (1998). Angry women are building: Issues and struggles facing American Indian women today. In M. L. Anderson & P. H. Collins (Eds.), *Race, class, and gender: An anthology* (3rd ed., pp. 43–47). Belmont, CA: Wadsworth Publishing Company.

Altman, A., Inman, A., Fine, S., Ritter, H. & Howard, E. (2010). Exploration of Jewish ethnic identity. *Journal of Counseling & Development*, 88(2), 163–173.

Alvarez, L. (2007). Derecho u obligación?: Parents' and youths' understanding of parental legitimacy in a Mexican origin familial context. *Hispanic Journal of Behavioral Sciences*, 29(2), 192–208.

American Medical Association. (1999). *Summaries and recommendations of council on scientific affairs reports: 1999 AMA interim meeting.* Retrieved on October 25, 2010, from http://www.ama-assn.org/ama1/pub/upload/mm/443/csai-99.pdf.

American Psychological Association (2009). See: Factsheet: Lesbian, gay, bisexual, and transgender persons and socioeconomic status. (2009). American Psychological Association. Retrieved on May 12, 2010, from http://www.apa.org/pi/ses/resources/publications/factsheet- lgbt.aspx.

American School Counselor Association. (1997). *Position statements of the American school counselor association.* Alexandria, VA: American School Counselor Association.

Andersen, A. E. (1995). Eating Disorders in males. In K. Brownell & C. G. Fairburn, *Eating disorders and obesity: A comprehensive handbook* (pp. 177–182). Guilford: New York.

Anderson, M. J. & Ellis, R. (1995). On the reservation. In N. A. Vacc, S. B. DeVaney & J. Wittmer (Eds.), *Experiencing and counseling multicultural and diverse populations* (3rd ed., pp. 179–198). Bristol, PA: Accelerated Development.

Annie E. Casey Foundation (2001). Using the new racial categories in the 2000 census. Retrieved on June 15, 2001, from http://www.aecf.org/upload/publicationfiles/using%20new%20racial%20categories.pdf.

Antoszewski, B., Ządzińska, E. & Foczpański, J. (2009). The metric features of teeth in female-to-male transsexuals. *Archives of Sexual Behavior*, 38(3), 351–358.

APA Task Force on Diversity Issues at the Precollege and Undergraduate Levels of Education in Psychology. (1998, March). Enriching the focus on ethnicity and race. *APA Monitor*, 29(3), 43.

Aponte, J. F. & Crouch, R. T. (1995). The changing ethnic profile of the United States. In J. F. Aponte, R. Y. Rivers & J. Wohl (Eds.), *Psychological interventions and cultural diversity* (pp. 1–18). Boston: Allyn & Bacon.

Aponte, J. F. & Morrow, C. A. (1995). Community approaches with ethnic groups. In J. F. Aponte, R. Y. Rivers & J. Wohl (Eds.), *Psychological interventions and cultural diversity* (pp. 128–144). Boston: Allyn & Bacon.

Armour, S. (July 5, 2005). Post-9/11 workplace discrimination continues. *USA Today.* Retrieved on June 12, 2010, from http://www.usatoday.com/money/workplace/2005-07-05-anti-arab-workplace_x.htm.

Arndt, B. (1993). Men under siege. *The Weekend Australia.* 22/5 Retrieved on October 27, 2000, from http://www.wellsphere.com/relationships-sex-article/men-under-siege-1312/1296425

Arredondo, P., Toporek, M. S., Brown, S., Jones, J., Locke, D. C., Sanchez, J. & Stadler, H. (1996). *Operationalization of the multicultural counseling competencies.* AMCD: Alexandria, VA.

Asakawa, K. (2010). Flow experience, culture, and well-being: How do autotelic Japanese college students feel, behave, and think in their daily lives? *Journal of Happiness Studies*, 11(2), 205–223.

Asakawa, K., & Csikszentmihalyi, M. (1998). The quality of experience of Asian American adolescents in academic activities: An exploration of educational achievement. *Journal of Research on Adolescence*, 8(2), 241–262.

Asian/Pacific American Heritage Month (2008). U.S. Census Bureau. Retrieved on June 5, 2010, from http://www.imdiversity.com/villages/asian/reference/census_asian_pacific_american_heritage_2008.asp.

Assessment Resources.

Atienza, A., Stephens, M. & Townsend, A. (2002). Dispositional optimism, role-specific stress, and the well-being of adult daughter caregivers. *Research on Aging*, 24(2), 193–217.

Atkinson, D. R., Morton, G. & Sue, D. W. (1998). *Counseling American minorities: A cross-cultural perspective* (5th ed.). Boston: McGraw-Hill.

Atwood, N. C. (2001). Gender bias in families and its clinical implications for women. *Social Work, 46*(1), 23–36.

Ault, A. & Brzuzy, S. (2009). Removing gender identity disorder from the *Diagnostic and statistical manual of mental disorders*: A call for action. *Social Work, 54*(2), 187–189.

Autier, P., Doré, J-F., Négrier, S., Liénard, D., Panizzon, R., Lejeune, F. J., Guggisberg, D. & Eggermont, A. M. M (1999). Sunscreen use and duration of sun exposure: A double-blind, randomized trial. *Journal of the National Cancer Institute, 91*(15), 1304–1309.

Axelson, J. A. (1999). *Counseling and development in a multicultural society* (3rd ed.). Pacific Grove, CA: Brooks/Cole Publishing Company.

Ayerst Laboratories. (1988). Hormones: Dream goal or time bomb? Retrieved on June 2000 from http://www.tgguide.com/Library/bbs/hormoneb.txt.

Baharudin, R. & Luster, T. (1998, July). Factors related to the quality of the home environment and children's achievement. *Journal of Family Issues, 19*(4), 375–403.

Baier, C. J. & Wright, B. R. E. (2001). "If you love me, keep my commandments": A meta-analysis of the effect of religion on crime. *Journal of Research in Crime and Delinquency, 38*(1), 3–21.

Balagopal, S. S. (1999). The case of the brown memsahib: Issues that confront working South Asian wives and mothers. In S. R. Gupta (Ed.), *Emerging voices: South Asian American women redefine self, family, and community* (pp. 146–168). Walnut Creek, CA: Altamira Press.

Balcazar, F., Suarez-Balcazar, Y., Willis, C., Alvarado, F. (2010). Cultural competence: A review of conceptual frameworks. In F. E. Balcazar , Y. Suarez-Balcazar, T. Taylor-Ritzler & C. B. Keys (Eds.), *Race, culture and disability: Rehabilitation science and practice* (pp. 281–305). Boston, MA: Jones and Bartlett Publishers.

Banks-Wallace, J. & Parks, L. (2004). It's all sacred: African American women's perspectives on spirituality. *Issues in Mental Health Nursing, 25*(1), 25–45.

Baram-Tsabari, A. & Yarden, A. (2008). Girls' biology, boys' physics: Evidence from free-choice science learning settings. *Research in Science Technological Education, 26*(1), 75–92.

Barnhart, K. T., Freeman E. W. & Sondheimer, S. J. (1995). A clinician's guide to the premenstrual syndrome. *Medical Clinics of North America, 79*, 1457–1472.

Barrett, J. (1998). Psychological and social function before and after phalloplasty. *The International Journal of Transgenderism*. Retrieved on January 10, 2001, from http://www.iiav.nl/ezines/web/IJT/97-03/numbers/symposion/ijtc0301.htm.

Baruth, L. G. & Manning, M. L. (1991). Multicultural counseling and psychotherapy: A lifespan perspective. Englewood Cliffs, NJ: Prentice Hall/Merrill.

Baruth, L. G. & Manning, M. L. (1999). Multicultural counseling and psychotherapy: A lifespan perspective (2nd ed.). Upper Saddle River, NJ: Prentice Hall/Merrill.

Bauermeister, J., Shrout, P., Chávez, L., Rubio-Stipec, M., Ramírez, R., Padilla, L., et al. (2007). ADHD and gender: Are risks and sequela of ADHD the same for boys and girls? *Journal of Child Psychology and Psychiatry, 48*(8), 831–839.

Baumberger, J. P. & Harper, R. E. (2007). *Assisting students with disabilities: A handbook for school counselors* (2nd ed.). Thousand Oaks, CA: Corwin Press.

Beals, J., Belcourt-Dittloff, A., Freedenthal, S., Kaufman, C., Mitchell, C., Whitesell, N., et al. (2009). Reflections on a proposed theory of reservation-dwelling American Indian alcohol use: Comment on Spillane and Smith (2007). *Psychological Bulletin, 135*(2), 339–343.

Beaver, B. & Tuck, B. (1998). The adjustment of overseas students at a tertiary institution in New Zealand. *New Zealand Journal of Educational Studies, 33*(2), 167–179.

Beech, H. (1999). Don't you dare list them as "other": Multiracial Americans seek full recognition. *U.S. News & World Report*. Retrieved on June 11, 2001, from http://www.usnews.com/usnews/issue/birace.htm.

Beets, M., Vogel, R., Chapman, S., Pitetti, K. & Cardinal, B. (2007). Parent's social support for children's outdoor physical activity: Do weekdays and weekends matter? *Sex Roles, 56*(1–2), 125–131.

Bem, S. L. (1974). The measurement of psychological androgyny. *Journal of Consulting and Clinical Psychology, 42*, 155–162.

Bemak, F. & Chung, R. (2008). New professional roles and advocacy strategies for school counselors: A multicultural/social justice perspective to move beyond the nice counselor syndrome. *Journal of Counseling & Development, 86*(3), 372–381.

Benrud, L. M. & Reddy, D. M. (1998). Differential explanations of illness in women and men. *Sex Roles, 38*, 375–386.

Berg, A. (2003). Ancestor reverence and mental health in South Africa. *Transcultural Psychiatry, 40*(2), 194.

Berg, I. K. & Jaya, A. (1993). Different and same: Family therapy with Asian-American families. *Journal of Marital & Family Therapy, 19*(1), 31–38.

Berg, M., Mimiaga, M. & Safren, S. (2008). Mental health concerns of gay and bisexual men seeking mental health services. *Journal of Homosexuality, 54*(3), 293–306.

Bergan-Gander, R. & von Kürthy, H. (2006). Sexual orientation and occupation: Gay men and women's lived experiences of occupational participation. *British Journal of Occupational Therapy, 69*(9), 402–408.

Berger, G. & Aibel, J. (1997). *Westie Side Story.* In B. Sheesley (director), *King of the Hill.* Hollywood, CA: Fox Broadcasting Company.

Berger, R. & Kelly, J. (1996). Gay men and lesbians grown older. In R. Cabaj & T. Stein (Eds.), *Textbook of homosexuality and mental health* (pp. 305–316). Washington, DC: American Psychiatric Press.

Bergman, M. (2005). College degree nearly doubles annual earnings. Washington, DC: U.S. Census Bureau.

Bergman, R. L. (1973). A school for medicine men. *American Journal of Psychiatry, 130,* 663–666.

Bernal, G. & Flores-Ortiz, Y. (1982). Latino families in therapy: Engagement and evaluation. *Journal of Marital & Family Therapy, 8*(3), 357–365.

Berry, H. L., Butler, J. R. A, Burgess, C. P., King, U. G., et al. (2010). Mind, body, spirit: Co-benefits for mental health from climate change adaptation and caring for country in remote aboriginal Australian communities. *New South Wales Public Health Bulletin, 21*(6), 139–145.

Best, D. L. (2010). Gender. In M. H. Bornstein (Ed.), *Handbook of cultural developmental science* (pp. 209–222). New York: Psychology Press.

Bhattacharjee, A. (1999). The habit of ex-nomination: Nation, woman, and the Indian immigrant bourgeoisie. In S. R. Gupta (Ed), *Emerging voices: South Asian American women redefine self, family, and community* (pp. 229–252). Walnut Creek, CA: Altamira Press.

Bierhorst, J. (2009). *Latin American folktales: Stories from Hispanic and Indian traditions.* New York: Pantheon.

Bierman, A. (2006). Does religion buffer the effects of discrimination on mental health? Differing effects by race. *Journal for the Scientific Study of Religion, 45*(4), 551–565.

Black student college graduation rates inch higher but a large racial gap persists (2007). *Journal of Blacks in Higher Education.* Retrieved on May 25, 2010, from http://www .jbhe.com/preview/winter07 preview.html.

Blank, S. (1998). Hearth and home: The living arrangements of Mexican immigrants and U.S.-born Mexican Americans. *Sociological Forum, 13*(1), 35–57.

Blau, F. D. & Kahn, L. M. (2007). The U.S. gender pay gap in the 1990s: Slowing convergence. *Industrial & Labor Relations Review, 60*(1). Retrieved from http://digitalcommons.ilr.cor nell.edu/ilrreview/vol60/iss1/3.

Blumberg, R. L. (1991). Afterword: Racial ethnic women's labor: Factoring in gender stratification. In R. L. Blumberg (Ed.), *Gender, family, and economy: The triple overlap* (pp. 201–208). Newbury Park, CA: Sage Publications.

Borges, A. & Nakamura, E. (2009). Social norms of sexual initiation among adolescents and gender relations. *Revista*

Latino-Americana de Enfermagem, 17(1), 94–100.

Born gay. (2009). Gallup Poll. Retrieved from http://borngay .procon.org/view.source.php? sourceID=004313.

Bornstein, M. H. & Lansford, J. E. (2010). Parenting. In M. H. Bornstein (Ed.), *Handbook of cultural developmental science* (pp. 259–277). New York: Psychology Press.

Borowich, A. (2008). Failed reparative therapy of orthodox Jewish homosexuals. *Journal of Gay & Lesbian Mental Health, 12*(3), 167–177.

Bortz II, W. M. (2001). *Living longer for dummies.* New York: Hungry Minds.

Boutte, G. (1999). *Multicultural education: Raising consciousness.* Belmont: CA: Wadsworth.

Boyd, H. (2007). *She's not the man I married: My life with a transgendered husband.* Emeryville, CA: Seal Press.

Boylan, J. F. (2004). *She's not there: A life in two genders.* New York, NY: Broadway Books.

Brammer, R. (1997). Case conceptualization strategies: The relationship between psychologists' experience levels, academic training, and mode of clinical inquiry. *Journal of Educational Research, 9*(4), 333–352.

Brammer, R. (2009). AIDS, sexuality, and spirituality. *Journal of GLBT family studies, 5*(3), 203–214.

Brammer, R. (2010). African immigrant families. In A. Zagelbaum & J. Carlson (Eds.), *Working with immigrant families: A practical guide for counselors* (pp. 103–120). New York: Routledge.

Brammer, R., Morgan, S. & Albers, A. (March 2010). *Invisible gender identity: How to counsel people living in two gender worlds.* Poster presented at the 2010

Convention of the American Counseling Association. Pittsburgh, PA.

Britt, D. (1994, March 15). Lights, camera, sad reaction. *Washington Post*. P. B01.

Brooke, H. (2005). "Gays, ex-gays, ex-ex-gays: Examining key religious, ethical, and diversity issues": A follow-up interview with Douglas Haldeman, Ariel Shidlo, Warren Throckmorton, and Mark Yarhouse. *Journal of Psychology and Christianity*, 24(4), 343–351.

Brooke, J. (1998, April 9). Indians strive to save their languages. *The New York Times*, A1.

Brookeman C. (1990). *The Native American peoples of the United States*. Liverpool: American Studies Resources Centre.

Brooks, G. (2000). The role of gender in marital dysfunction. *Handbook of gender, culture, and health* (pp. 449–470). Mahwah, NJ: Lawrence Erlbaum Associates.

Brooks, G. R. (2010). *Beyond the crisis of masculinity: A transtheoretical model for male-friendly therapy*. Washington, DC: American Psychological Association.

Brown v. Board of Education, 347 U.S. 483 (1954).

Brown, A., Hassard, J., Fernbach, M., Szabo, E. & Wakefield, M. (2003). Lesbians' experiences of cervical screening. *Health Promotion Journal of Australia*, 14(2), 128–132.

Brown, D. (1979). *Bury my heart at Wounded Knee: An Indian history of the American West*. New York: Henry Holt & Company.

Brown, J. W. & Curland, M. (2005). *Zerophilia* [motion picture]. United States: Microangelo Entertainment.

Brown, L. W. (1994). *Subversive dialogues: Theory in feminist theory*. New York: Basic Books.

Brown, M. (2009). LGBT aging and rhetorical silence. *Sexuality Research & Social Policy: A Journal of the NSRC*, 6(4), 65–78.

Brown, R. K. & Adamczyk, A. (2009). Racial/ethnic difference in the provision of health-related programs among American religious congregations. *Journal of Sociology and Social Welfare*, 36(2), 105–123.

Brown, S. (2006). A match made in heaven: A marginalized methodology for studying the marginalized. *Quality & Quantity: International Journal of Methodology*, 40(3), 361–382.

Brown, S. L. & May, K. M. (2009). Counseling with women. In C. M. Ellis & J. Carlson (Eds.), *Cross cultural awareness and social justice in counseling* (pp. 61–87). New York: Routledge.

Brown, T. L., Linver, M. R., Evans, M. & DeGennaro, D. (2009). African- American parents' racial and ethnic socialization and adolescent academic grades: Teasing out the role of gender. *Journal of Youth and Adolescence*, 38(2), 214–227.

Brubaker, M., Garrett, M., Rivera, E. & Tate, K. (2010). Justice making in groups for homeless adults: The emancipatory communitarian way. *Journal for Specialists in Group Work*, 35(2), 124–133.

Bryant, A. (1977). *The Anita Bryant story: The survival of our nation's families and the threat of militant homosexuality*. Old Tappan, NJ: Fleming H. Revell.

Buchanan, C. M., Eccles, J. S. & Becker, J. B. (1992). Are adolescents the victims of raging hormones?: Evidence for activational effects of hormones on moods and behavior at adolescence. *Psychological Bulletin*, 111, 62–107.

Bucks, B. K., Kennickell, A. B., Mach, T. L. & Moore, K. B. (2009). *Changes in U.S. Family Finances from 2004 to 2007: Evidence from the Survey of Consumer Finances*.

Washington, DC: The Federal Reserve Board's Survey of Consumer Finances for 2007.

Buhrich, N. (1978). Motivation for cross-dressing in heterosexual transvestism. *Acta Psychiatrica Scandinavica*, 57(2), 145–152.

Bui, H. N. & Thongniramol, O. (2005). Immigration and self-reported delinquency: The interplay of immigration generations, gender, race and ethnicity. *Journal of Crime and Justice*, 28(2), 71–99.

Bulik, C. M., Sullivan, P. F., Wade, T. D. & Kendler, K. S. (2000). Twin studies of eating disorders: A review. *International Journal of Eating Disorders*, 27(1), 2–20.

Bullough, V. L. & Bullough, B. (1993). *Cross dressing, sex, and gender*. Philadelphia: University of Pennsylvania Press.

Bunch, C. (1972). Lesbians in revolt: Male supremacy quakes and quivers. *The Furies: Lesbian/ Feminist Monthly*, 1, 8–9.

Burgess, E. O., Schmeeckle, M. & Bengtson, V. L. (1998). Aging individuals and societal contexts. In I. H. Nordhus, G. R. VandenBos, S. Berg & P. Fromholt (Eds.), *Clinical Geropsychology*, pp. 15–32. Washington, DC: American Psychological Association.

Buriel, R. & De Ment, T. (1997). Immigration and sociocultural change in Mexican, Chinese, and Vietnamese American families. In A. Booth & A. C. Crouter (Eds.), *Immigration and the family: Research and policy on U.S. immigrants* (pp. 165–200). Mahwah, NJ: Lawrence Erlbaum Associates.

Burke, L. K. & Follingstad, D. R. (1999). Violence in lesbian and gay relationships: Theory, prevalence, and correlational factors. *Clinical Psychology Review*, 19(5), 487–512.

Burnes, T. & Ross, K. (2010). Applying social justice to oppression and marginalization in group process: Interventions and strategies for group counselors. *Journal for Specialists in Group Work*, 35(2), 169–176.

Burney, J. & Irwin, H. J. (2000). Shame and guilt in women with eating-disorder symptomatology. *Journal of Clinical Psychology*, 56(1), 51–61.

Buschman, J. K. & Lenart, S. (1996). I am not a feminist, but ...: College women, feminism, and negative experiences. *Political Psychology*, 17, 59–75.

Bush, G. W. Address before a joint session of the Congress on the state of the union, January 29, 2002. *White House news releases*. Retrieved on March 4, 2010, from http://archives.cnn .com/2002/ALLPOLITICS/01/ 29/bush.speech.txt.

Butler, R. N. (1993). Dispelling ageism: The cross-cutting intervention. *Generations*, 17(2), 75–78.

Bybee, J., Sullivan, E., Zielonka, E. & Moes, E. (2009). Are gay men in worse mental health than heterosexual men? The role of age, shame and guilt, and coming-out. *Journal of Adult Development*, 16(3), 144–154.

Cabaj, R. P. (1996). Native two-spirit people. In R. P. Cabaj & T. S. Stein (Eds.), *Textbook of homosexuality and mental health* (pp. 103–620). Washington, DC: American Psychiatric Press.

Caldwell, H. L. (1996). *African-American music: A chronology, 1619–1995*. Los Angeles, CA: Ikoro Communications.

Caldwell, L. D. & White, J. L. (2005). African-centered therapeutic and counseling interventions for African American males. In G. E. Good & G. R. Brooks (Eds.), *The new handbook of psychotherapy and counseling with men: A comprehensive guide to settings, problems, and treatment approaches* (pp. 323–336).

San Francisco, CA: Jossey-Bass Publishers.

Caldwell, L. D. (2009). Counseling with the poor, underserved, and underrepresented. In C. M. Ellis and J. Carlson (Eds.), *Cross cultural awareness and social justice in counseling* (pp. 283–299). New York: Routledge.

Cameron, A. (1996). *Daughters of copper women*. Vancouver: Press Gang Publishers

Campbell, C., Gibbs, A., Maimane, S., Nair, Y. & Sibiya, Z. (2009). Youth participation in the fight against AIDS in South Africa: From policy to practice. *Journal of Youth Studies*, 12(1), 93–109.

Campbell, M., Neil, J., Jaffe, P. & Kelly, T. (2010). Engaging abusive men in seeking community intervention: A critical research & practice priority. *Journal of Family Violence*, 25(4), 413–422.

Camus, A. (2002). *The plague*. New York: Modern Library Edition.

Cancer trends progress report. (2010). National Cancer Institute. Retrieved on May 30, 2010, from http://progressre port.cancer.gov.

Capps, R., Castañeda, R. M., Chaudry, A. & Santos, R. (2007). *Paying the price: The impact of immigration raids on America's children*. Washington, DC: Urban Institute.

Carolan, M. T., Bagherinia, G. T., Juhari, R., Himelright, J. & Mouton, M. (2000). Contemporary Muslim families: Research and practice. *Contemporary Family Therapy*, 22, 67–79.

Carroll, L. & Gilroy, P. (2002). Transgender issues in counselor preparation. *Counselor Education and Supervision*, 41(3), 233–242.

Carson, L. R. (2009). "I am because we are": Collectivism as a foundational characteristic of African American college

student identity and academic achievement. *Social Psychology of Education*, 12(3), 327–344.

Carter again cites racism as factor in Obama's treatment (September 17, 2009). Cable News Network. Retrieved on October 18, 2009, from http://www.cnn.com/2009/ POLITICS/09/15/carter .obama/index.html.

Carter, D. L. (2010). Mr. Seneca's smokes: Where tobacco, taxes and treaties converge. The Ithaca Journal. Retrieved from http://www.tobacco.org/news/ 301407.html.

Carter, R. T. & Parks, E. E. (1996). Womanist identity and mental health. *Journal of Counseling & Development*, 74(5), 484–489.

Cattelino, J. R. (2008). *High stakes: Seminole gaming and sovereignty*. Durham, NC: Duke University Press.

Cecchin, M. (2001). Reconsidering the role of being a daughter of a mother with dementia. *Journal of Family Studies*, 7(1), 101–107.

Center for Mental Health Services (2000). Alternative approaches to mental health care. Retrieved on September 10, 2000, from http://counsellin gresource.com/types/alterna tive.html

Centers for Disease Control and Prevention (2010). Prostate cancer rates by race and ethnicity. Retrieved from http:// www.cdc.gov/cancer/prostate/ statistics/race.htm.

Centers for Disease Control and Prevention. National Center for HIV, STD and TB Prevention. Divisions of HIV/AIDS Prevention. (2008). Male circumcision and risk for HIV transmission and other health conditions: Implications for the United States. CDC HIV/AIDS Science Facts. Retrieved from http://www.cdc.gov/hiv/ resources/factsheets/PDF/ circumcision.pdf.

Cerel, J., Jordan, J. R. & Duberstein, P. R. (2008). The impact of suicide on the family. *Crisis*, 29, 38–44.

Chadiha, L. A., Veroff, J. & Leber, D. (1998). Newlywed's narrative themes: Meaning in the first year of marriage for African American and white couples. *Journal of Comparative Family Studies*, 29(1), 115–130.

Chan, S. (1991). Asian Americans: An interpretive history. Boston: Twayne Publishers.

Chang, H. & Nayga, R. (2010). Childhood obesity and unhappiness: The influence of soft drinks and fast food consumption. *Journal of Happiness Studies*, 11(3), 261–275.

Charles, A. (1860). A new classical dictionary of Greek and Roman biography, mythology and geography. Partly based upon the *Dictionary of Greek and Roman Biography and Mythology* by William Smith. New York, NY: Harper & Brothers, Publishers.

Chen, X., Cen, G., Li, D. & He, Y. (2005). Social functioning and adjustment in Chinese children: The Imprint of historical time. *Child Development*, 76(1), 182–195.

Chesler, P. (2001). *Woman's inhumanity to woman*. New York: Avalon.

Chlebowski, R. T., Anderson, G. L., Gass, M., Lane, D. S., et al. (2010). Estrogen plus progestin and breast cancer incidence and mortality in postmenopausal women. *The Journal of the American Medical Association*, 304(15), 1684–1692.

Chodorow, N. (1978). *The reproduction of mothering*. Berkeley, CA: University of California Press.

Choi, N., Fuqua, D. & Newman, J. (2008). The Bem sex-role inventory: Continuing theoretical problems. *Educational and Psychological Measurement*, 68(5), 881–900.

Christie-Mizell, C. A., Pryor, E. M. & Grossman, E. R. B. (2008). Child depressive symptoms, spanking, and emotional support: Differences between African American and European American youth. *Family Relations*, 57(3), 335–350.

Chu, L. & Kao, H. (2005). The moderation of meditation experience and emotional intelligence on the relationship between perceived stress and negative mental health. *Chinese Journal of Psychology*, 47(2), 178–194.

Churchill, W. & LaDuke, W. (1992). Native North America: The political economy of radioactive colonialism. In M. A. Jaimes (Ed.), *The state of Native America: Genocide, colonization, and resistance* (pp. 241–266) Boston: South End Press.

Cimmarusti, R. A. (1999). Exploring aspects of Filipino American families. In K. S. Ng (Ed.), *Counseling Asian families from a systems perspective* (pp. 63–81). Alexandria, VA: American Counseling Association.

Circumcision Reference Library. (2008). United States circumcision incidence. Retrieved on May 22, 2010, from http://www.cirp.org/library/statistics/USA.

Civettini, N. & Glass, J. (2008). The impact of religious conservatism on men's work and family involvement. *Gender & Society*, 22(2), 172–193.

Clark, K. B. & Clark, M. K. (1947). Racial identification and preference in Negro children. In T. M. Newcomb & E. L. Hartley (Eds.), *Readings in social psychology* (pp. 169–178). New York: Holt Rinehart, and Winston.

Clark, S. (2006). Gay priests and other bogeymen. *Journal of Homosexuality*, 51(4), 1–13.

Cline, W. R. (2007). Global warming and agriculture: Impact estimates by country.

Washington DC: Peterson Institute for International Economics.

Coats, P. B. & Overman, S. J. (1992). Childhood play experiences of women in traditional and nontraditional professions. *Sex Roles*, 26(7–8), 261–271.

Cohen, A., Malka, A., Hill, E., Thoemmes, F., Hill, P. & Sundie, J. (2009). Race as a moderator of the relationship between religiosity and political alignment. *Personality and Social Psychology Bulletin*, 35(3), 271–282.

Cohen-Kettenis, P. T. & Gooren, L. J. G. (1999). Transsexualism: A review of etiology, diagnosis, and treatment. *Journal of Psychosomatic Research*, 46, 315–333.

Cohen-Kettenis, P. T. & van Goozen, S. H. M. (1997). Sex reassignment of adolescent transsexuals: A follow-up study. *Journal of the American Academy of Child and Adolescent Psychiatry*. 36(2), 263–271.

Coker, A. D. & Bryant, R. (2003). Counseling African Americans: Understanding racial tasks and cultural values. *The AABSS [American Association of Behavioral and Social Sciences] Journal*, 7–18.

Colapinto, J. (1997). The true story of John/Joan. *Rolling Stone*, 775, 54–97.

Cole, H. W. (1877), Saint Augustine: A poem in eight books. Edinburgh: T. & T. Clark.

Cole, S., Denny, D., Eyler, A. & Samons, S. (2000). Issues of transgender. *Psychological perspectives on human sexuality* (pp. 149–195). Hoboken, NJ: John Wiley & Sons.

Coleman, H. L. K., Wampold, B. E. & Casali, S. L. (1995). Ethnic minorities' rating of ethnically similar and European American counselors: A meta-analysis. *Journal of Counseling Psychology*, 42, 55–64.

Collier, H. V. (1982). *Counseling women: A guide for therapists.* New York: Free Press.

Comas-Diaz, L. (2007). Ethnopolitical psychology: Healing and transformation. In E. Aldarondo (Ed.), *Advancing social justice through clinical practice* (pp. 91–118). Mahwah, NJ: Lawrence Erlbaum Associates.

Comas-Díaza, L. & Jacobsen, F. M. (1991). Ethnocultural transference and countertransference in the therapeutic dyad. *American Journal of Orthopsychiatry, 61,* 392–402.

Constantine, M. G. (2007). Racial microaggressions against African American clients in cross-racial counseling relationships. *Journal of Counseling Psychology, 54,* 1–15.

Constantine, M. G., Hage, S. M., Kindaichi, M. M. & Bryant, R. M. (2007). Social justice and multicultural issues: Implications for the practice and training of counselors and counseling psychologists. *Journal of Counseling and Development, 85*(1), 24–29.

Constantino, G. & Rivera, C. (1994). Culturally sensitive treatment modalities for Puerto Rican children. *Journal of Consulting and Clinical Psychology, 54*(5), 639–645.

Contreras, F. (2005). Access, achievement, and social capital: Standardized exams and the Latino college-bound population. *Journal of Hispanic Higher Education, 4*(3), 197–214.

Cook, A. & Jordan, M. (1997). Explaining variation in income between Hispanic and white female-headed households in Washington. *Hispanic Journal of Behavioral Sciences, 19*(4), 433–445.

Cook, N. D. (1998). *Born to die: Disease and New World conquest, 1492–1650 (New Approaches to the Americas).* Cambridge, England: Cambridge University Press.

Cooke, P. & Standen, P. (2002). Abuse and disabled children: Hidden needs...? *Child Abuse Review, 11*(1), 1–18.

Corliss, H., Cochran, S., Mays, V., Greenland, S. & Seeman, T. (2009). Age of minority sexual orientation development and risk of childhood maltreatment and suicide attempts in women. *American Journal of Orthopsychiatry, 79*(4), 511–521.

Cornwell, J. (1998). Do GPs prescribe antidepressants differently for South Asian patients? *Family Practice, 15*(Suppl. 1), S16–S18.

Corrigan, P. W., River, L. P., Lundin, R. K., Wasowski, K. U., Campion, J., Mathisen, J., Goldstein, H., Bergman, M., Gagnon C. & Kubiak, M. A. (2000). Stigmatizing attributions about mental illness. *Journal of Community Psychology, 28,* 91–102.

Costa Jr., P. T., Yang, J. & McCrae, R. R. (1998). Aging and personality traits: Generalizations and clinical implications. In I. H. Nordhus, G. R. VandenBos, S. Berg & P. Fromholt (Eds.), *Clinical geropsychology* (pp. 33–48). Washington, DC: American Psychological Association.

Cotugna, N. & Mallick, A. (2010). Following a calorie-restricted diet may help in reducing healthcare students' fat-phobia . *Journal of Community Health: The Publication for Health Promotion and Disease Prevention, 35*(3), 321–324.

Council for Accreditation of Counseling and Related Educational Programs (CACREP). (2009). 2009 Standards. Retrieved from http://www. cacrep.org/doc/2009%20Standards%20with%20cover.pdf.

Council on American-Islamic Relations (CAIR). (2005). The status of Muslim civil rights in the United States: Unequal protection. *CAIR Report.*

Retrieved on June 10, 2010, from http://www.cair.com/PDF/2005CivilRightsReport.pdf.

Council on Social Work Education (CSWE). (2008). Educational policy and accreditation standards. Retrieved on October 21, 2010, from http://www.cswe.org/File.aspx?id=13780.

Coyhis, D. & Simonelli, R. (2008). The Native American healing experience. *Substance Use & Misuse, 43*(12–13), 1927–1949.

Coyle, A. (1993). A study of psychological well-being among gay men using the GHQ-30. *British Journal of Clinical Psychology, 32*(2), 218–220.

Crawford, M. & Unger, R. (2000). *Women and gender* (3rd ed.). Boston: McGraw-Hill.

Creighton, S. & Minto, C. (2001). Managing intersex. *BMJ: British Medical Journal, 323*(7324), 1264–1265.

Crethar, H., Rivera, E. & Nash, S. (2008). In search of common threads: Linking multicultural, feminist, and social justice counseling paradigms. *Journal of Counseling & Development, 86*(3), 269–278.

Croghan, I., Hurt, R., Ebbert, J., Croghan, G., Polk, O., Stella, P., et al. (2010). Racial differences in smoking abstinence rates in a multicenter, randomized, open-label trial in the United States. *Journal of Public Health, 18*(1), 59–68.

Cross, W. E. (1971). The Negro-to-black conversion experience: Towards a psychology of black liberation. *Black World, 20,* 13–27.

Cross, W. E. (1991). *Shades of black: Diversity in African American identity.* Philadelphia: Temple University Press.

Cross, W. E. (1995). The psychology of nigrescence: Revising the Cross model. In J. G. Ponterotto, J. M. Casas, L. A. Suzuki & C. M. Alexander (Eds.), *Handbook of*

Multicultural Counseling (pp. 93–122). Thousand Oaks, CA: Sage.

Cross, W. E. (2001). Encountering nigrescence. In J. G. Ponterotto, J. M. Casas, L. A. Suzuki & C. M. Alexander (Eds.), *Handbook of multicultural counseling* (2nd ed., pp. 30–44). Thousand Oaks, CA: Sage Publications.

Cruz, M. & Taylor, D. (2009). Inner-city violence in the United States: What pediatricians can do to make a difference. *International Journal of Child and Adolescent Health*, 2(1), 3–12.

Cullen, J., Courbasson, C., Quintero, D., Myslik, J., & Guimond, T. (2010). Comparing mental health and addiction characteristics of lesbian/gay/bisexual/transgender/transsexual/queer and non–lesbian/gay/bisexual/transgender/transsexual/queer clients in a residential treatment setting. *Journal of Substance Abuse Treatment*, doi:10.1016/j.jsat.2010.09.005

Cultural competency in health services and care: A guide for health care providers (2010). Washington State Department of Health. Retrieved from http://www.doh.wa.gov/hsqa/professions/Publications/documents/CulturalComp.pdf.

D'Amico, M., Barrafato, A., Peterson, L., Snow, S. & Tanguay, D. (2001). Using theatre to examine children's attitudes toward individuals with disabilities. *Developmental Disabilities Bulletin*, 29(1), p. 23–38.

D'Andrea, M. & Daniels, J. (2001). RESPECTFUL counseling: An integrative multidimensional model for counselors. In D. B. Pope-Davis & H. L. K. Coleman (Eds.), *The intersection of race, class, and gender in multicultural counseling* (pp. 417–466). Thousand Oaks, CA: Sage Publications.

Dalla, R., Jacobs-Hagen, S., Jareske, B. & Sukup, J. (2009). Examining the lives of Navajo Native American teenage mothers in context: A 12- to 15-year follow-up. *Family Relations*, 58(2), 148–161.

Daly, M. & Wilson, M. (1990). *Homicide: Foundations of human behavior*. New York: Aldine de Gruyter.

Dandy, J. & Nettelbeck, T. (2002). The relationship between IQ, homework, aspirations and academic achievement for Chinese, Vietnamese and Anglo-Celtic Australian school children. *Educational Psychology*, 22(3), 267–276.

Daoud, N., Shtarkshall, R., Laufer, N., Verbov, G., Bar-el, H., Abu-Gosh, N., et al. (2010). What do women gain from volunteering? The experience of lay Arab and Jewish women volunteers in the Women for Women's Health programme in Israel. *Health & Social Care in the Community*, 18(2), 208–218.

Das, S. A. (2001). *What is yoga*. Retrieved on December 13, 2001, from http://www.vedicacademy.com/articles/vedanta/what_is_yoga.htm.

Davis, C., Claridge, G., Fox, J. (2000). Not just a pretty face: Physical attractiveness and perfectionism in the risk for eating disorders. *International Journal of Eating Disorders*, 27(1), 67–73.

Davis, K. (2010). Coming of age online: The developmental underpinnings of girls' blogs. *Journal of Adolescent Research*, 25(1), 145–171.

Davis, M. P. (1990). *Mexican voices, American dreams: An oral history of Mexican immigration to the United States*. New York: Holt.

Davison-Aviles, R. M. & Spokane, A. R. (1999). The vocational interests of Hispanic, African American, and white middle school students. *Measurement*

& Evaluation in Counseling & Development, 32(3), 138–148.

Day, K. & Keys, T. (2008). Starving in cyberspace: A discourse analysis of pro-eating-disorder websites. *Journal of Gender Studies*, 17(1), 1–15.

Deater-Deckard, K., Dodge, K. A., Bates, J. E. & Pettit, G. S. (1998). Physical discipline among African American and European American mothers: Links to children's externalizing behaviors. *Developmental Psychology*, 32(6), 1–8.

Dehon, C. & Weems, C. (2010). Emotional development in the context of conflict: The indirect effects of interparental violence on children. *Journal of Child and Family Studies*, 19(3), 287–297.

Denny, D. (1997). Transgendered youth at risk for exploitation, HIV, hate crimes. Unpublished manuscript.

Denny, D. and Green, J. (1996). Gender identity and bisexuality. In B. Firestein (Ed.), *Bisexuality: The psychology and politics of an invisible minority* (pp. 84–102). Sage: Thousand Oaks.

Denton, W., Burleson, B. & Brubaker, P. (2009). Avoidance may be bad for the heart: A comparison of dyadic initiator tendency in cardiac rehabilitation patients and matched controls. *Behavioral Medicine*, 35(4), 133–142.

DePaulo, B. (2011). Living single: Lightening up those dark, dopey myths. In W. R. Cupach, B. H. Spitzberg, W. R. Cupach, B. H. Spitzberg (Eds.), *The dark side of close relationships II* (pp. 409–439). New York, NY: Routledge/Taylor & Francis Group.

DeSoto, M. (2007). Borderline personality disorder, gender and serotonin: Does estrogen play a role? In M. Czerbskas (Ed.), *Psychoneuroendocrinology research trends* (pp. 149–160).

Hauppauge, NY: Nova Biomedical Books.

Deuster, P. A., Tilahun A. & South-Paul, J. (1999). Biological, social, and behavioral factors associated with premenstrual syndrome. *Archives of Family Medicine, 8,* 122–128.

Devji, M. S. (1999). The paradoxes of the Kama Sutra and the veil: Asian-Indian women and marital sexuality. In S. R. Gupta (Ed.), *Emerging voices: South Asian American women redefine self, family, and community* (pp. 169–192). Walnut Creek, CA: Altamira Press.

Devor, H. (1989). *Gender bending: Confronting the limits of duality.* Bloomington, IN: Indiana University Press.

Devos, T. & Heng, L. (2009). Whites are granted the American identity more swiftly than Asians: Disentangling the role of automatic and controlled processes. *Social Psychology, 40*(4), 192–201.

DeWard, S. & Moe, A. (2010). "Like a prison!": Homeless women's narratives of surviving shelter. *Journal of Sociology and Social Welfare, 37*(1), 115–135.

Diamond, M. (1996). Prenatal predisposition and the clinical management of some pediatric conditions. *Journal of Sex & Marital Therapy, 22,* 139–147.

DiPlacido, J. (1998). Minority stress among lesbians, gay men and bisexuals: A consequence of heterosexism, homophobia, and stigmatization. In G. Herek (Ed.), *Psychological perspectives on lesbian and gay issues: Vol. 4. Stigma and sexual orientation: Understanding prejudice against lesbians, gay men, and bisexuals* (pp. 138–159). Thousand Oaks, CA: Sage Publications.

Direction from Americans: Update. (2010). Gallup. Retrieved on May 10, 2010, http://polling matters.gallup.com/2010/02/

policy-direction-from-ameri cans-update.html.

Dixon, P. (2009). Marriage among African Americans: What does the research reveal? *Journal of African American Studies, 13*(1), 29–46.

Domar, A. D. (1997). Stress and infertility in women. In Sandra Risa Leiblum (Ed.), *Infertility: Psychological issues and counseling strategies* (Wiley series in couples and family dynamics and treatment) (pp. 67–82). New York: John Wiley & Sons.

Donadio, R. (May 13, 2010). Pope decries gay marriage in Portugal visit. *New York Times.* Retrieved on May 19, 2010, from http://www.nytimes.com/ 2010/05/14/world/europe/ 14pope.html.

Dörner, G., Geier, T. H., Athrens, L., Krell, L, Münx, G. Sieler, H., Kittner, E. & Müller, H. (1980). Prenatal stress as possible aetiogentic factor of homosexuality in human males. *Endokrinologie, 75,* 205–212.

Dörner, G., Götz, F. & Docke, W. D. (1982). Prevention of demasculinization and the feminization of the brain in prenatally stressed male rats by perinatal androgen treatment. *Experimental Clinical Endocrinology, 81,* 88–90.

Dorsey, L. W. (2010). Gyn/ecology: Woman as symbol of carrier, protector, and nourisher of life. In J. Stevenson-Moessner & T. Snorton (Eds.), *Women out of order* (pp. 78–92). Minneapolis: Fortress Press.

Draguns, J. G. (1989). Dilemmas and choices in cross-cultural counseling. In P. B. Pedersen, J. G. Draguns, W. J. Lonner & J. E. Trimble (Eds.), *Counseling across cultures*, (2nd ed., pp. 3–22). Honolulu: University of Hawaii Press.

Draper, T. W. & Gordon, T. (1984). Ichabod Crane, in day care: Prospective child care professionals' concerns about male caregivers. *Academic*

Psychology Bulletin, 6(3), 301–308.

Drummond, K., Bradley, S., Peterson-Badali, M. & Zucker, K. (2008). A follow-up study of girls with gender identity disorder. *Developmental Psychology, 44*(1), 34–45.

Durodoye, B. A. & Coker, A. D. (2008). Crossing cultures in marriage: Implications for counseling African American/African couples. *International Journal for the Advancement of Counseling, 30*(1), 25–37.

Dutton, S. E., Singer, J. A. & Devlin, A. S. (1998). Racial identity of children in integrated, predominantly white, and black schools. *Journal of Social Psychology, 138*(1), 41–53.

Dwairy, M. (2006). *Counseling and psychotherapy with Arabs and Muslims: A culturally sensitive approach.* New York: Teacher's College Press.

Eagly, A. (2009). The his and hers of prosocial behavior: An examination of the social psychology of gender. *American Psychologist, 64*(8), 644–658.

Eccles, J. S. (1989). Bringing young women to math and science. In M. Crawford and M. Gentry (Eds.), *Gender and thought: Psychological perspectives* (pp. 36–58). New York: Spinger-Verlag.

Edmo, E. (Shoshone-Bannock). (1989, December 26). Finding the best of two worlds: Teaching children about prejudices. *Lakota Times.*

Education of the Handicapped Act (1975). 20 U.S.C., 1400–1485.

Edwards, L. M. & Romero, A. J. (2008). Coping with discrimination among Mexican descent adolescents. *Hispanic Journal of Behavioral Sciences, 30*(1), 24–39.

Edwards, S. D. (2008). Breath psychology: Fundamentals and applications. *Psychology and Developing Societies, 20,* 131–164.

Egan, P. J., Edelman, M. S. & Sherrill, K. (2008). *Findings from the Hunter College poll of lesbians, gays and bisexuals: New discoveries about identity, political attitudes, and civil engagement.* Hunter College, City University of New York. Retrieved on May 19, 2010, from http://www.hrc .org/documents/Hunter_ College_Report.pdf.

Ehrenreich, B. (March 8, 1999). The real truth about the female body. *Time, 153*(9). Retrieved on August 15, 2000, from http://www.time.com/time/maga zine/article/0,9171,20616,00 .html

Ekins, R. & King, D. (2001). Transgendering, migrating and love of oneself as a woman: A contribution to a sociology of autogynephilia. *The International Journal of Transgenderism, 5*(3), http://www.iiav.nl/ ezines/web/IJT/97-03/ numbers/ symposion/ijtvo05no03_01.htm.

Elizabeth, M. (2007). *Legal aspects of transsexualism.* Retrieved on December 24, 2009, from http://www.transgendercare. com/guidance/resources/legal_ aspects_ts.htm.

Ellickson, P. L., Collins, R. L. & Bell, R. M. (1999). Adolescent use of illicit drugs other than marijuana: How important is social bonding and for which ethic groups? *Substance Use & Misuse, 34*(3), 317–346.

Elman, C. & O'Rand, A. M. (2004). The race is to the swift: Socioeconomic origins, adult education, and wage attainment. *American Journal of Sociology, 110*(1), 123–160.

Else-Quest, N., Hyde, J. & Linn, M. (2010). Cross-national patterns of gender differences in mathematics: A meta-analysis. *Psychological Bulletin, 136*(1), 103–127.

Emery, E. E. & Pargament, K. I. (2004). The many faces of religious coping in late life: Conceptualization, measurement, and links to well-being.

Aging International, 29(1), 3–27.

Englar-Carlson, M. (2009). Counseling with men. In C. M. Ellis & J. Carlson (Eds.), *Cross cultural awareness and social justice in counseling* (pp. 89–120). New York: Routledge.

Ennis Jr., W., Ennis, W. III, Durodoye, B., Ennis-Cole, D. & Bolden, V. (2004). Counseling African American clients: Professional counselors and religious institutions. *Journal of Humanistic Counseling, Education, and Development, 43*, 197–210.

Ephron, N. (Director) & Arch, J. (Writer). (2002). *Sleepless in Seattle* [motion picture]. United States: TriStar Pictures.

Erhardt, V. (2007). *Head over heels: Wives who stay with cross dressers and transsexuals.* New York: The Hawthorn Press.

Erikson, E. (1950). *Childhood and society.* New York: W. W. Norton.

Esses, V. M. & Beaufoy, S. L. (1994). Determinants of attitudes toward people with disabilities. *Journal of Social Behavior and Personality, 9*(5), 43–64.

Estiritu, Y. L. (1999). Gender and labor in Asian immigrant families. *American Behavioral Scientist, 42*(4), 628–647.

Ettner, R. (1996). *Confessions of a gender defender: A psychologist's reflections on life among the transgendered.* Evanston, IL: Chicago Spectrum Press.

Evans-Campbell, T. (2008). Historical trauma in American Indian/Native Alaska communities: A multilevel framework for exploring impacts on individuals, families, and communities. *Journal of Interpersonal Violence, 23*(3), 316–338.

Evanzz, K. (1999). *The messenger: The rise and fall of Elijah Muhammad.* New York: Pantheon Books.

Factor, R. & Rothblum, E. (2008). Exploring gender identity and

community among three groups of transgender individuals in the United States: MTFs, FTMs, and genderqueers. *Health Sociology Review, 17*(3), 235–253.

Factsheet: Lesbian, gay, bisexual, and transgender persons and socioeconomic status. (2009). American Psychological Association. Retrieved on May 12, 2010, from http://www.apa.org/ pi/ses/resources/publications/ factsheet-lgbt.aspx.

Fagan, J. & Holland, C. (2007). Racial equality in intelligence: Predictions from a theory of intelligence as processing. *Intelligence, 35*(4), 319–334.

Falicov, C. J. (1998). *Latino families in therapy: A guide to multicultural practice.* New York: Guilford Press.

Falicov, C. J. (2006). Family organization: The safety net of close and extended kin. In R. L. Smith & R. E. Montilla (Eds.), *Counseling and family therapy with Latino populations: Strategies that work* (pp. 41–62). New York: Routledge.

Faulkner, A. H. & Cranston, K. (1998). Correlates of same-sex sexual behavior in a random sample of Massachusetts high school students. *American Journal of Public Health, 88*(2), Feb 1998, 262–266.

Fausto-Sterling, A. (2000). Sexing the body. New York: Basic Books.

Feder, E. (2009). Normalizing medicine: Between "intersexuals" and individuals with "'disorders of sex development." *Health Care Analysis, 17*(2), 134–143.

Feinbloom, D. H. (1976). *Transvestites & transsexuals: Mixed views.* New York: Delacorte Press/Seymour Lawrence.

Felix-Ortiz, M. & Newcomb, M. D. (1995). Cultural identity and drug use among Latino adolescents. In G. Botvin, S. Schinke & M. Orlandi (Eds.), *Drug abuse prevention with multiethnic youth* (pp. 147–165). Newbury Park, CA: Sage.

Fernandez, I., Carrera, P., Sanchez, F., Paez, D. & Candia, L. (2000). Differences between cultures in emotional verbal and nonverbal reactions. *Psicothema*, 12, 83–92.

Fetini, A (2009). Understanding the Sunni-Shi'ite divide. Time.com. Retrieved on June 19, 2010, from http://www .time.com/time/world/article/ 0,8599,1924116,00.html.

Field-Belenky, M., McVicker-Clinchy, B., Rule-Goldberger, N. & Mattuck-Tarule, J. (1986). *Women's ways of knowing*. New York: Basic Books.

Finkler, K. (1985). Symptomatic differences between the sexes in rural Mexico. *Culture, Medicine and Psychiatry*, 9(1), 27–57.

Fish, J. (2009). Our health, our say: Towards a feminist perspective of lesbian health psychology. *Feminism & Psychology*, 19(4), 437–453.

Fish, J. and Anthony, D. (2005). "UK National Lesbians and Health Care Survey," *Women and Health* 41(3), 27–45.

Fisher, M. A. (April 14, 1999). The color chasm. *The Columbus Dispatch*, 1A–5A.

Fitzgibbon, M. L., Spring, B., Avellone, M. E., Blackman, L. R., Pingitore, R. & Stolley, M. R. (1998). Correlates of binge eating in Hispanic, black, and white women. *International Journal of Eating Disorders*, 24(1), 43–52.

Flaskerud, J. H. & Liu, P. Y. (1991). Effects of an Asian client-therapist language, ethnicity and gender match on utilization and outcome of therapy. *Community Mental Health Journal*, 27(1), 31–42.

Flexner, S. B. (Ed.). (1987). Random House dictionary of the English language (2nd ed.). New York: Random House.

Fontaine, J. H. (1998). Evidencing a need: School counselors'

experiences with gay and lesbian students. *Professional School Counseling*, 11(3), 8–14.

Foster, E. (2002). How economists think about family resources and child development. *Child Development*, 73(6), 1904–1914.

Fouad, N. A. (2001). Reflections of a nonvisible racial/ethnic minority. In J. G. Ponterotto, J. M. Casas, L. A. Suzuki & C. M. Alexander (Eds.), *Handbook of multicultural counseling* (2nd ed., pp. 55–63). Thousand Oaks, CA: Sage Publications.

Fox, R. (1996). Bisexuality in perspective: A review of theory and research. In B. Firestein (Ed.), Bisexuality: The psychology and politics of an invisible minority (pp. 3–50). Newbury Park, CA: Sage Publications.

Frabutt, J. M., Walker, A. M. & MacKinnon-Lewis, C. (2002). Racial socialization messages and the quality of mother/ child interactions in African American families. *The Journal of Early Adolescence*, 22(2), 200–217.

Franchina, J. J., Eisler, R. M., Moore, T. M. (2001). Masculine gender role stress and intimate abuse: Effects of masculine gender relevance of dating situations and female threat on men's attributions and affective responses. *Psychology of Men & Masculinity*, 2(1), 34–41.

Franklin, A. (1998). Treating anger in African American men. *New psychotherapy for men* (pp. 239–258). Hoboken, NJ: John Wiley & Sons.

Freud, S. (1905). Three essays in the theory of sexuality. In James Strachey (Ed.), *The standard edition of the complete works of Sigmund Freud*, Vol. 7. London: Hogarth Press.

Freud, S. (1932). Lecture XXXV: A philosophy of life. Retrieved on May 11, 2001, from http://

www.marxists.org/reference/ subject/philosophy/works/at/ freud.htm

Freundlich, M. (2000). *Adoption and ethics: The market forces in adoption*. Washington, DC: Child Welfare League of America.

Friedan, B. (1963). The Sexual Solipsism of Sigmund Freud. *The Feminine Mystique*. Retrieved from http://www .marxists.org/reference/ subject/philosophy/works/us/ friedan.htm.

Friedman, C., Leaper, C. & Bigler, R. (2007). Do mothers' gender-related attitudes or comments predict young children's gender beliefs? *Parenting: Science and Practice*, 7(4), 357–366.

Friedman, M., Marshal, M., Stall, R., Cheong, J. & Wright, E. (2008). Gay-related development, early abuse and adult health outcomes among gay males. *AIDS and Behavior*, 12(6), 891–902.

Fuentes, M., Hart-Johnson, T. & Green, C. (2007). The association among neighborhood socioeconomic status, race and chronic pain in black and white older adults. *Journal of the National Medical Association*, 99(10), 1160–1169.

Fuligni, A. J. & Fuligni, A. S. (2007). Immigrant families and the educational development of their children. In J. Lansford, K. Deater Deckard & M. Bornstein (Eds.), *Immigrant families in America* (pp. 231–249). New York: Guilford Press.

Fuligni, A., Witkow, M. & Garcia, C. (2005). Ethnic identity and the academic adjustment of adolescents from Mexican, Chinese, and European backgrounds. *Developmental Psychology*, 41(5), 799–811.

Fuller, J. O. (1995). Getting in touch with your heritage. In N. Vacc, S. DeVaney & J. Wittmer (Eds.), *Experiencing and counseling multicultural* and diverse populations (3rd ed., pp. 9–27). Bristol, PA: Accelerated Development.

Gabriel, K. (1998). Gambling and spirituality: A new anthropological perspective. Retrieved on September 11, 2000, from http://nmweddingphotos.com/articles/professional/myths.html

Galupo, M. (2009). Cross-category friendship patterns: Comparison of heterosexual and sexual minority adults. *Journal of Social and Personal Relationships*, 26(6-7), 811–831.

Ganzevoort, R. (2001). Religion in rewriting the story: Case study of a sexually abused man. *International Journal for the Psychology of Religion*, 11(1), 45–62.

Garibaldi, A. M. (2007). The educational status of African American males in the 21st century. *Journal of Negro Education*, 76(3), 324–333.

Gariepy, G., Wang, J., Lesage, A. & Schmitz, N. (2010). The interaction of obesity and psychological distress on disability. *Social Psychiatry and Psychiatric Epidemiology*, 45(5), 531–540.

Garrett, M., Brubaker, M., Torres-Rivera, E., West-Olatunji, C. & Conwill, W. (2008). The medicine of coming to center: Use of the Native American centering technique—Ayeli—to promote wellness and healing in group work. *Journal for Specialists in Group Work*, 33(2), 179–198.

Garriott, P., Love, K., Tyler, K., Thomas, D., Roan-Belle, C. & Brown, C. (2010). Testing an attachment model of Latina/o college students' psychological adjustment. *Hispanic Journal of Behavioral Sciences*, 32(1), 104–117.

Gavin, A., Walton, E., Chae, D., Alegria, M., Jackson, J. & Takeuchi, D. (2010). The associations between socioeconomic status and major

depressive disorder among blacks, Latinos, Asians and non-Hispanic whites: Findings from the Collaborative Psychiatric Epidemiology Studies. *Psychological Medicine: A Journal of Research in Psychiatry and the Allied Sciences*, 40(1), 51–61.

Gavora, J. (2002). The inequity of gender equity. *Chronicle of Higher Education*, 48(34), B11.

Gay, Lesbian, and Straight Education Network & Harris Interactive. (2008). *The principal's perspective: School safety, bullying and harassment, a survey of public school principals*. New York: Gay, Lesbian, and Straight Education Network.

Gaylord-Harden, N. K. & Cunningham, J. A. (2009). The impact of racial discrimination and coping strategies on internalizing symptoms in African American youth. *Journal of Youth and Adolescence*, 38(4), 532–543.

George, C. (1996). A representational perspective of child abuse and prevention: Internal working models of attachment and caregiving. *Child Abuse & Neglect*, 20, 411–424.

George, L., Larson, D., Koenig, H. & McCullough, M. (2000). Spirituality and health: What we know, what we need to know. *Journal of Social and Clinical Psychology*, 19(1), 102–116.

Gerber, L. A. (2007). Social justice concerns and clinical practice. In E. Aldarondo (Ed.), *Advancing social justice through clinical practice* (pp. 43–61). Mahwah, NJ: Lawrence Erlbaum Associates.

Germán, M., Gonzales, N. & Dumka, L. (2009). Familism values as a protective factor for Mexican-origin adolescents exposed to deviant peers. *The Journal of Early Adolescence*, 29(1), 16–42.

Gibson, R. L. & Mitchell, M. H. (2002). *Introduction to*

Counseling and Guidance (6th ed.). New York: Prentice Hall.

Gil, A. G., Vega, W. A. & Biafora, F. (1998). Temporal influences of family structure and family risk factors on drug use initiation in a multiethnic sample of adolescent boys. *Journal of Youth & Adolescence*. 27(3), 373–393.

Gil, A. G., Wagner, E. F. & Vega, W. A. (2000). Acculturation, familism, and alcohol use among Latino adolescent males: Longitudinal relations. *Journal of Community Psychology*, 28(4), 443–458.

Givens, J. L., Houston, T. K., Van Voorhees, B. W., Ford, D. E., & Cooper, L. A. (2007). Ethnicity and preferences for depression treatment. *General Hospital Psychiatry*, 29(3), 182–191.

Glazer, N. & Moynihan, D. P. (1970). Beyond the melting pot: Negroes, Puerto Ricans, Jews, Italians, and Irish of New York City. Cambridge: MIT Press.

Glick, J. & White, M. (2004). Postsecondary school participation of immigrant and native youth: The role of familial resources and educational expectations. *Social Science Research*, 33(2), 272–299.

Glicken, M. D. (2009). *Evidence-based counseling and psychotherapy for an aging population*. Amsterdam: Academic Press.

Global HIV/AIDS estimates, end of 2008. (2009). AVERT. Retrieved on May 16, 2010, from http://www.avert.org/worldstats.htm.

Goldberg, A. (2010). Partners but not parents: Intimate relationships of lesbians and gay men. *Lesbian and gay parents and their children: Research on the family life cycle* (pp. 15–48). Washington, DC: American Psychological Association.

Goldberg, M. (May 19, 2009). Is homophobia the new

anti-Semitism? *The American Prospect*. Retrieved on May 12, 2010, from http://www .prospect.org/cs/articles?arti cle=is_homophobia_the_ new_anti_semitism.

Goldenberg, C. H. (1998). Methods, early literacy, and home-school compatibilities: A response to Sledge et al. *Anthropology and Education Quarterly*, 19(4), 425–432.

Golombok, S. & Tasker, F. (1996). Do parents influence the sexual orientation of their children? Findings from a longitudinal study of lesbian families. *Developmental Psychology*, 32(1), 3–11.

Gong, L. (2007). Ethnic identity and identification with the majority group: Relations with national identity and self-esteem. *International Journal of Intercultural Relations*, 31(4), 503–523.

Gonzales, N. A., German, M., Kim, S. Y., George, P., Fabrett, F. C., Millsap, R., et al. (2008). Mexican American adolescents' cultural orientation, externalizing behavior and academic engagement: The role of traditional cultural values. *American Journal of Community Psychology*, 41, 151–164.

González de Alba, L. (January 17, 1994). *Todos somos blancos. La Jornade*, 28–29.

Gonzalez-Ramos, G., Zayas, L. H. & Cohen, E. V. (1998). Child-rearing values of low-income, urban Puerto Rican mothers of preschool children. *Professional Psychology - Research & Practice*, 29(4), 377–382.

Goodman, L. A., Litwin, A., Bohlig, A., Weintraub, S. R., et al., (2010). Applying feminist theory to community practice: A multilevel empowerment intervention for low-income women with depression. In E. Aldarondo (Ed.), *Advancing social justice through clinical practice* (pp. 265–290).

Mahwah, NJ: Lawrence Erlbaum Associates.

Goodnow, J. J. (2010). Culture. In M.H. Bornstein (Ed.), *Handbook of cultural developmental science* (pp. 3–19). New York: Psychology Press.

Goodrich, K. & Luke, M. (2010). The experiences of school counselors-in-training in group work with LGBTQ adolescents. *Journal for Specialists in Group Work*, 35(2), 143–159.

Gordon, A., Haas, G., Luther, J., Hilton, M. & Goldstein, G. (2010). Personal, medical, and healthcare utilization among homeless veterans served by metropolitan and nonmetropolitan veteran facilities. *Psychological Services*, 7(2), 65–74.

Graham, S., Bellmore, A., Nishina, A. & Juvonen, J. (2009). "It must be me": Ethnic diversity and attributions for peer victimization in middle school. *Journal of Youth and Adolescence*, 38, 487–499.

Granello, D. H. & Wheaton, J. E. (2001). Attitudes of undergraduate students towards persons with physical disabilities and mental illness. *Journal of Applied Rehabilitation Counseling*, 32(3), 9–21.

Graves Jr., S. L., & Wright, L. B. (2009). Historically black colleges and university students' and faculties' views of school psychology: Implications for increasing diversity in higher education. *Psychology in the Schools*, 46(7), 616–626.

Green, M., Murphy, M., Blumer, M. & Palmanteer, D. (2009). Marriage and family therapists' comfort level working with gay and lesbian individuals, couples, and families. *American Journal of Family Therapy*, 37(2), 159–168.

Green, R. & Fleming, D. (1990). Transsexual surgery follow-up: Status in the 1990s. *Annual Review of Sex Research*, 7, 351–369.

Green, R. (1987). *The 'sissy boy syndrome' and the development of homosexuality*. New Haven, CT: Yale University Press.

Green, R. (2008). Gay and lesbian couples: Successful coping with minority stress. In M. McGoldrick & K. V. Hardy (Eds.), *Re-visioning family therapy: Race, culture, and gender in clinical practice* (2nd ed., pp. 300–310).

Green, R. J. (2007). Gay and lesbian couples in therapy: A social justice perspective. In E. Aldarondo (Ed.), *Advancing social justice through clinical practice* (pp. 119–149). Mahwah, NJ: Lawrence Erlbaum Associates.

Greene, R., Watkins, M., McNutt, J. & Lopez, L. (1998). Diversity defined. In R. R. Greene & M. Watkins (Eds.), *Serving diverse constituencies* (pp. 29–57). New York, NY: Aldine de Gruyter.

Greenslade, L., Pearson, M. & Madden, M. (1995). A good man's fault: Alcohol and Irish people at home and abroad. *Alcohol & Alcoholism*, 30(4), 407–417.

Greif, G. (2009). *Buddy system: Understanding male friendships*. New York, NY: Oxford University Press.

Gressier, F., Bouaziz, E., Verstuyft, C., Hardy, P., Becquemont, L. & Corruble, E. (2009). 5-HTTLPR modulates antidepressant efficacy in depressed women. *Psychiatric Genetics*, 19(4), 195–200.

Grieco, E. (2004). *The African foreign born in the United States*. Washington, DC: Immigration Information Source. Retrieved on November 23, 2009, from http://www .migrationinformation .org/usfocus/display.cfm? id=250.

Griesler, P. C. & Kandel, D. B. (1998). Ethnic differences in correlates of adolescent cigarette smoking. *Journal of Adolescent Health*, 23(3), 167–180.

Griesler, P., Kandel, D. & Davies, M. (2002). Ethnic differences in predictors of initiation and persistence of adolescent cigarette smoking in the National Longitudinal Survey of Youth. *Nicotine & Tobacco Research*, 4(1), 79–93.

Gritz, E. R., Prokhorov, A. V., Hudmon, K. S., Chamberlain, R. M., Taylor, W. C., DiClemente, C. C., Johnston, D. A., Hu, S., Jones, L. A., Jones, M. M., Rosenblum, C. K., Ayars, C. L. & Amos, C. I. (1998). Cigarette smoking in a multiethnic population of youth: Methods and baseline findings. *Preventive Medicine: An International Devoted to Practice & Theory*, 27(3), 365–384.

Groopman, J. (2007). *How doctors think*. Boston, MA: Houghton Mifflin.

Grossman, A. & D'Augelli, A. (2007). Transgender youth and life-threatening behaviors. *Suicide & Life-Threatening Behavior*, 37(5), 527–537.

Guerra, N. S. (2004). *LIBRE problem solving handbook*. Academy of Teacher Excellence. San Antonio, TX: University of Texas at San Antonio.

Guidelines for Psychotherapy with Lesbian, Gay, and Bisexual Clients (n.d). American Psychological Association. Retrieved on October 21, 2010, from http://www.apa.org/practice/guidelines/glbt.pdf.

Guild, P. (1994). The culture/learning style connection. *Educational Leadership*, 51(8), 16–21.

Guinote, A., Willis, G. & Martellotta, C. (2010). Social power increases implicit prejudice. *Journal of Experimental Social Psychology*, 46(2), 299–307.

Gupta, S. R. (1999). Walking on the edge: Indian-American women speak out on dating and marriage. In S. R. Gupta (Ed.), *Emerging voices: South Asian American women redefine self, family, and community* (pp. 120–145). Walnut Creek, CA: Altamira Press.

Gurian, M. (December 4, 2005). Disappearing act: Where have the men gone? No place good. *Washington Post*. Retrieved on May 27, 2010, from http://www.washingtonpost.com/wp-dyn/content/article/2005/12/02/AR2005120201334.html.

Guthrie, S. R. & Castelnuovo, S. (2001). Disability management among women with physical impairments: The contribution of physical activity. *Sociology of Sport Journal*, 18(1), 5–20.

Gutierres, S. F. & Todd, M. (1997). The impact of childhood abuse on treatment outcomes. *Professional Psychology: Research and Practice*, 28, 348–654.

Haaken, J. (1990). A critical analysis of the co-dependence construct. *Psychiatry*, 53(4), 396–406.

Haines, M., Erchull, M., Liss, M., Turner, D., Nelson, J., Ramsey, L., et al. (2008). Predictors and effects of self-objectification in lesbians. *Psychology of Women Quarterly*, 32(2), 181–187.

Haley, Alex. (1976). *Roots*. Garden City, NY: Doubleday.

Hallinan, M. T. & Williams, R. A. (1989). Interracial friendship choices in secondary schools. *American Sociological Review*, 54(1), 67–78.

Halme, N., Åstedt-Kurki, P. & Tarkka, M. (2009). Fathers' involvement with their preschool-age children: How fathers spend time with their children in different family structures. *Child & Youth Care Forum*, 38(3), 103–119.

Hammelman, T. (1993). Gay and lesbian youth contributing factors to serious attempts or considerations of suicide. *Journal of Gay and Lesbian Psychotherapy*, 2(1), 77–89.

Hanna, F. J., Bemak, F. & Chi-Ying Chung, R. (1999). Toward a new paradigm for multicultural counseling. *Journal of Counseling and Development*, 77, 125–134.

Hansbury, G. (2005). The middle men: Introduction to the transmasculine identities. *Studies in Gender and Sexuality*, 6(3), 241–264.

Hanson, S. L. (2009). *Swimming against the tide: African American girls and science education*. Philadelphia, PA: Temple University Press.

Hardaway, C. R. & McLoyd, V. C. (2009). Escaping poverty and securing middle class status: How race and socioeconomic status shape mobility prospects for African Americans during the transition to adulthood. *Journal of Youth and Adolescence*, 38(2), 242–256.

Hare-Mustin, R. T. (1978). A feminist approach to family therapy. *Family Process*, 17, 181–194.

Hargrave, T. D., Froeschle, J. & Castillo, Y. (2009). Forgiveness and spirituality: Elements of healing in relationships. In F. Walsh (Ed.), *Spiritual resources in family therapy* (2nd ed., pp. 301–322). New York, NY: Guilford Press.

Harju, B. L., Long, T. E. & Allred, L. J. (1998). Cross cultural reactions of international students to US health care. *College Student Journal*, 32(1), 112–120.

Harper, C. (2007). *Intersex*. Oxford, UK: Berg Publishers.

Harris Interactive & Gay, Lesbian, and Straight Education Network. (2005). *From teasing to torment: School climate in America, a survey of students and teachers*. New York: Gay, Lesbian, and Straight Education Network.

Harrison, J. (1987). Counseling gay men. In M. Scher, M. Stevens, G. Good & G. A. Eichenfield's (Eds.), *Handbook of counseling*

& psychotherapy with men (pp. 220–231). Newbury Park: Sage Publications.

Hart, J. D. (1978). *A Companion to California*. New York: Oxford University Press,

Hartup, W. W. & Stevens, N. (1997). Friendships and adaptation in the life course. *Psychological Bulletin, 121*(3), 355–370.

Harwood, R. L., Schoelmerich, A., Schulze, P. A. & Gonzalez, Z. (1999). Cultural differences in maternal beliefs and behaviors: A study of middle-class Anglo and Puerto Rican mother-infant pairs in four everyday situations. *Child Development, 70*(4), 1005–1016.

Hatcher, S. S., Maschi, T., Morgen, K. & Toldson, I. A. (2009). Exploring the impact of racial and ethnic differences in the emotional and behavioral responses of maltreated youth: Implications for culturally competent services. *Children and Youth Services Review, 31*(9), 1042–1048.

Havenaar, J., Geerlings, M., Vivian, L., Collinson, M. & Robertson, B. (2008). Common mental health problems in historically disadvantaged urban and rural communities in South Africa: Prevalence and risk factors. *Social Psychiatry & Psychiatric Epidemiology, 43*(3), 209–215.

Headden, S. (1997). The Hispanic dropout mystery. *U.S. News & World Report, 123*, 64–65.

Heflin, C. M. & Pattillo, M. (2006). Poverty in the family: Race, siblings, and socioeconomic heterogeneity. *Social Science Research, 35*(4), 804–822.

Hein, L. & Matthews, A. (2010). Reparative therapy: The adolescent, the psych nurse, and the issues. *Journal of Child and Adolescent Psychiatric Nursing, 23*(1), 29–35.

Helms, J. E. (1984). Toward a theoretical explanation for the effects of race on counseling: A black and white model. *Counseling Psychologist, 12*, 153–165.

Helms, J. E. (1990). Introduction: Review of racial identity terminology. In J. E. Helms (Ed.), *Black and white racial identity: Theory, research, and practice* (pp. 3–8). New York: Greenwood Press.

Helms, J. E. (1995). An update of Helm's white and people of color racial identity models. In J. Ponterotto, M. Casas, L. Suzuki & C. Alexander (Eds.). *Handbook of multicultural counseling* (pp. 181–198). Thousand Oaks, CA; Sage.

Henss, R. (2000). Waist-to-hip ratio and female attractiveness. Evidence from photographic stimuli and methodological considerations. *Personality & Individual Differences, 28*(3), 501–513.

Heppner, M. & Heppner, P. (2009). On men and work: Taking the road less traveled. *Journal of Career Development, 36*(1), 49–67.

Herdt, G. H. (Ed.). (1982). *Rituals of manhood: Male initiation in Papua, New Guinea*. Berkeley: University of California Press.

Herek, G. (1991). Stigma, prejudice and violence against lesbians and gay men. In J. Gonsiorek & J. Weinrich (Eds.), *Homosexuality: Research implications for public policy* (pp. 60–80). Newbury Park, CA: Sage Publications.

Herek, G. M., Gillis, J. R., Cogan, J. C. & Glunt, E. K . (1997). Hate crime victimization among lesbian, gay, and bisexual adults. *Journal of Interpersonal Violence, 12*(2), 195–215.

Herhandez, H. (1989). Multicultural education: A teachers' guide to content and practice. Upper Saddle River, NJ: Merrill/Prentice Hall.

Herlihy, B. & Corey, G. (2001). Feminist therapy. In G. Corey (Ed.), *Theory and practice of counseling and psychotherapy* (6th ed., pp. 341–381). Belmont, CA: Wadsworth/ Thomson Learning.

Herman-Jeglińska, A., Grabowska, A. & Dulko, S. (2002). Masculinity, femininity, and transsexualism. *Archives of Sexual Behavior, 31*(6), 527–534.

Herr, K. (1997). Learning lessons from school: Homophobia, heterosexism, and the construction of failure. In M. B. Harris et al. (Eds.), *School experiences of gay and lesbian youth: The invisible minority* (pp. 51–64). New York: Harrington Park Press/ The Haworth Press.

Herring, R. (1999). Helping Native American Indian and Alaska Native male youth. *Handbook of counseling boys and adolescent males: A practitioner's guide* (pp. 117–136). Thousand Oaks, CA: Sage Publications.

Herrnstein, R. J. & Murray, C. A. (1996). The bell curve: Intelligence and class structure in American life (2nd ed.) New York: First Free Press.

Herskovits, M. J. (1948). *Man and his works*. New York: Knopf.

Hertz, T. (2005). Rags, riches, and race: The intergenerational economic mobility of black and white families in the United States. In S. Bowles, H. Gintis & M. Osbourne (Eds.), *Unequal chances: Family background and economic success* (pp. 165–191). Princeton, NJ: Princeton University Press.

Hess, D. (1994). Samba in the might: Spiritism in Brazil. New York: Columbia University Press.

Hewlett, S. A. (2002). Creating a life: Professional women and the quest for children. New York: Miramax Books.

Highleyman, L. A. (1993). A brief history of the bisexual

movement. Retrieved on May 11, 2001, from http://www.ncf.carleton.ca/freenet/rootdir/menus/sigs/life/gay/bi/bi.

Hillenbrand-Gunn, T., Heppner, M., Mauch, P. & Park, H. (2010). Men as allies: The efficacy of a high school rape prevention intervention. *Journal of Counseling & Development*, 88(1), 43–51.

Hinchliff, S., Gott, M. & Galena, E. (2005). "I daresay I might find it embarrassing": General practitioners' perspectives on discussing sexual health issues with lesbian and gay patients. *Health and Social Care in the Community*, 13(4), 345–353.

Hintikka, J., Koskela, K., Kontula, O. & Viinamaeki, H. (2000). Gender differences in associations between religious attendance and mental health in Finland. *Journal of Nervous & Mental Disease*, 188, 772–776.

Hird, M. (2008). Queer(y)ing intersex: Reflections on counselling people with intersex conditions. In L. Moon (Ed.), *Feeling queer or queer feelings? Radical approaches to counselling sex, sexualities and genders* (pp. 54–71). New York, NY: Routledge/Taylor & Francis Group.

Hirschauer, S. (1997). The medicalization of gender migration. *The International Journal of Transgenderism*, 2. Retrieved on December 8, 2000, from http://www.iiav.nl/ezines/web/IJT/97-03/numbers/symposion/ijtc0104.htm.

Hirschfeld M. (1910). Die transvestiten. Eine untersuchung uber den erotischen verkleidungstrieb mit umfangreichem casuistischem und historischem Material. Alfred Pulvermacher & Co, Berlin, Vol I–II.

Hirschfelder, A. (2000). *Native Americans*. London: Dorling Kindersley.

HIV and AIDS statistics by race/ethnicity. (2009). AVERT. Retrieved on May 25, 2010, from http://www.avert.org/usa-race-age.htm.

Ho, C. (1990). An analysis of domestic violence in Asian Americans communities: A multicultural approach to counseling. In L. Brown & M. Root (Eds.), *Diversity and complexity in feminist therapy* (pp. 129–149). New York: Harrington Park.

Hockey, J. (2009). The life course anticipated: Gender and chronologisation among young people. *Journal of Youth Studies*, 12(2), 227–241.

Holcomb-McCoy, C. (2004). Assessing the multicultural competence of school counselors: A checklist. *Professional School Counseling*. Retrieved on September 1, 2009, from http://findarticles.com/p/articles/mi_m0KOC/is_3_7/ai_114784733.

Holland, J. L. (1959). A theory of occupational choice. *Journal of Counseling*, 6(1), 35–45.

Holland, J. L. (1997). *Making vocational choices: A theory of vocational personalities and work environments* (3rd ed.). Odessa, FL US: Psychological Assessment Resources.

Hong, H. (2010). Bicultural competence and its impact on team effectiveness. *International Journal of Cross Cultural Management*, 10(1), 93–120.

Hooker, E. (1957). The adjustment of the male overt homosexual. *Journal of Projective Techniques*, 21, 18–31.

Hooks, B. (1991). *Ain't I a woman: Black women and feminism* (2nd ed.). Boston, MA: South End Press.

Horwedel, D. M. (2006). For illegal college students, an uncertain future. *Diverse: Issues in Higher Education*, 23, 22–26.

Hoste, R. & le Grange, D. (2008). Expressed emotion among white and ethnic minority families of adolescents with bulimia nervosa. *European Eating Disorders Review*, 16(5), 395–400.

Hoste, R., Hewell, K. & le Grange, D. (2007). Family interaction among white and ethnic minority adolescents with bulimia nervosa and their parents. *European Eating Disorders Review*, 15(2), 152–158.

Huang, A. & Oei, T. (1996). Behind the myth. *Teaching Tolerance*, 5(2), 56–57.

Huh, N. S. (1997). Korean children's ethnic identity formation and understanding of adoption. *Dissertation Abstracts International*, 58(02), 586.

Hunter, E. (2008). What's good for the gays is good for the gander: Making homeless youth housing safer for lesbian, gay, bisexual, and transgender youth. *Family Court Review*, 46(3), 543–557.

Hurdle, D. (2007). Breast cancer prevention with older women: A gender-focused intervention study. *Health Care for Women International*, 28(10), 872–887.

Hurtado, M. T. & Gauvain, M. (1997). Acculturation and planning for college among youth of Mexican descent. *Hispanic Journal of Behavioral Sciences*, 19(4), 506–516.

Hussain, S. & Roberts, N. (1998). Psychiatric presentation of adolescent homosexuality. *Canadian Journal of Psychiatry*, 43(4), 420–421.

Hyde, J. (2005). The gender similarities hypothesis. *American Psychologist*, 60(6), 581–592.

Ibrahim, F. A. (1985). Effective cross-cultural counseling and psychotherapy: A framework. *The Counseling Psychologist*, 13, 625–638.

Ihara, E. (2009). Ethnicity matters: The socioeconomic gradient in health among Asian American. *Journal of Sociology and Social Welfare*, 36(2), 125–144.

Ilies, R., Hauserman, N., Schwochau, S. & Stibal, J. (2003). Reported incidence rates of work-related sexual harassment in the United States: Using meta-analysis to explain reported rate disparities. *Personnel Psychology, 56,* 607–631.

Imbimbo, C., Verze, P., Palmieri, A., Longo, N., Fusco, F., Arcaniolo, D., et al. (2009). A report from a single institute's 14-year experience in treatment of male-to-female transsexuals. *Journal of Sexual Medicine,* 6(10), 2736–2745.

In R. Satow & G. Vastola (Eds.), *Gender and social life: A workbook* (pp. 149–152). Boston: Allyn & Bacon.

Ingram, R., Trenary-Smith, L. (2008). Mood disorders. In J.E. Maddux, & B.A. Winstead, *Psychopathology: foundations for a contemporary understanding* (2nd ed.), pp, 171–199. NewYork: Routledge.

Ip, P. (2009). Is Confucianism good for business ethics in China? *Journal of Business Ethics,* 88(3), 463–476.

Iritani, F. & Iritani, J. (1995). *Ten visits.* San Mateo, CA: Asian American Curriculum Project.

Ironson, G. (2006). An increase in religiousness/spirituality occurs after HIV diagnosis and predicts slower disease progression over 4 years in people with HIV. *Journal of General Internal Medicine,* 21(5), S62–S68.

Ishii-Kuntz, M. (1997). Intergenerational relationships among Chinese, Japanese, and Korean Americans. *Family Relations: Interdisciplinary Journal of Applied Family Studies,* 46(1), 23–32.

Jackson, M. L. (2001). Multicultural counseling: Historical perspectives. In J. G. Ponterotto, C. M. Alexander, L. A. Suzuki & J. M. Casas (Eds.), *Handbook of multicultural counseling* (pp. 3–16). Newbury Park, CA: Sage Publications.

Jackson-Newsom, J., Buchanan, C. & McDonald, R. (2008). Parenting and perceived maternal warmth in European American and African American adolescents. *Journal of Marriage and Family,* 70(1), 62–75.

Jacobs, E. A., Rolle, I., Ferrans, C. E., Whitaker, E. E., Warnecke, R. B. (2006). Understanding African Americans' views of the trustworthiness of physicians. *Journal of General Internal Medicine,* 21(6), 642–647.

Jacobs, S. (November 1, 2010). *Briefing on international adoption issues.* U.S. State Department, Bureau of Public Affairs. Retrieved from http://www .state.gov/r/pa/prs/ps/2010/11/ 150255.htm.

Jain, A. K. & Joy, A. (1997). Money matters: An exploratory study of the socio-cultural context of consumption, saving, and investment patterns. *Journal of Economic Psychology,* 18(6), 649–675.

Jamil, H., Templin, T., Fakhouri, M., Rice, V., Khouri, R., Fakhouri, H., et al. (2009). Comparison of personal characteristics, tobacco use, and health status in Chaldean, Arab American, and non-Middle Eastern White adults. *Journal of Immigrant and Minority Health,* 11(4), 310–317.

Jang, M., Lee, E. & Woo, K. (1998). Income, language, and citizenship status: Factors affecting the health care access and utilization of Chinese Americans. *Health & Social Work,* 23(2), 136–145.

Jaret, C. & Reitzes, D. (2009). Currents in a stream: College student identities and ethnic identities and their relationship with self-esteem, efficacy, and grade point average in an urban university. *Social Science Quarterly,* 90(2), 345–367.

Javors, I. (2008). Is middle age an age of anxiety? *Annals of the American Psychotherapy Association,* 11(2), 48.

Jeanjot, I., Barlow, P. & Rozenberg, S. (2008). Domestic violence during pregnancy: Survey of patients and healthcare providers. *Journal of Women's Health,* 17(4), 557–567.

Jenkins, C. N. H., McPhee, S. J., Bird, J. A., Pham, G. Q., Nguyen, B. H., Nguyen, T., Lai, K. Q., Wong, C. & Davis, T. B. (1999). Effect of a media-led education campaign on breast and cervical cancer screening among Vietnamese-American women. *Preventive Medicine: An International Devoted to Practice & Theory,* 28(4), 395–406.

Jenkins, O. B. (2007). Dealing with cultural differences: *Contrasting the African and European worldviews.* Limuru, Kenya: Communication Press

Jensen, Arthur R. (1968). Social class, race and genetics: Implications for education. *American Educational Research Journal,* 5(1), 1–42.

Jernström, H., Lubinski J., Lynch, H. T., Ghadirian, P., Neuhausen, S., Isaacs, C., Weber, B. L., Horsman, D., Rosen, B., Foulkes, W. D., Friedman, E., Gershoni-Baruch, R., Ainsworth, P., Daly, M., Garber, J., Olsson, H., Sun, P. & Narod, S. A. (2004). Breast-feeding and the risk of breast cancer in BRCA1 and BRCA2 mutation carriers. *Journal of the National Cancer Institute,* 96(14). 1094–1098.

Jing, H. (2007). What Confucianism can contribute to psychological counseling. *Acta Psychologica Sinica,* 39(2), 371–380.

Johnson, B. (May 8, 2010). Curator of T.O. museum works to better lives, understanding. *Ventura County Star.* Retrieved on May 8, 2010, from http://www.vcstar .com/news/2010/may/08/pro tector-of-his-people.

Johnson, D. (1994). Stress, depression, substance abuse, and racism. *American Indian &*

Alaska Native Mental Health Research, 6(1), 29–33.

Johnson, K. (2007). Fragmented identities, frustrated politics: Transsexuals, lesbians and "queer." *Journal of Lesbian Studies*, 11(1–2), 107–125.

Jones, A. & Jacka, S. (1995). Discourse of disadvantage: Girls' school achievement. *New Zealand Journal of Educational Studies*, 30(2), 165–175.

Jones, J. M. (2009). Majority of Americans continue to oppose gay marriage. Gallup. Retrieved on May 14, 2010, from http://www.gallup.com/poll/118378/majority-americans-continue-oppose-gay-marriage.aspx.

Jordan, P. & Hernandez-Reif, M. (2009). Reexamination of young children's racial attitudes and skin tone preferences. *Journal of Black Psychology*, 35(3), 388–403.

Joseph, R. (2000). The evolution of sex differences in language, sexuality, and visual-spatial skills. *Archives of Sexual Behavior*, 29(1), 35–66.

Josephy, A. (1973). *Indian heritage of America*. New York: Knopf Publisher.

Jou, Y. H. & Fukada, H. (1997). Stress and social support in mental and physical health of Chinese students in Japan. *Psychological Reports*, 81(3, Pt. 2), 1303–1312.

Jouriles, E. N., Norwood, W. D., McDonald, R., Vincent, J. P., et al. (1996). Physical violence and other forms of marital aggression: Links with children's behavior problems. *Journal of Family Psychology*, 10(2), 223–234.

Jun, H. (2010). *Social justice, multicultural counseling, and practice: Beyond a conventional approach*. Los Angeles: Sage Publications.

Jung, M. (1998). Chinese American family therapy. *Treatment Today*, 10(1), 12–13.

Kaestner, R. & Xu, X. (2010). Title IX, girls' sports participation, and adult female physical activity and weight. *Evaluation Review*, 34(1), 52–78.

Kagan, J. K. (2010). Emotions and temperament. In M. H. Bornstein (Ed.), *Handbook of cultural developmental science* (pp. 175–194). New York: Psychology Press.

Kahn, J. S. (2009). An introduction to masculinities. Chichester, UK: Wiley-Blackwell.

Kailey, M. (2005). *Just add hormones: An insider's guide to the transsexual experience*. Boston: Beacon Press.

Kakar, S. (1978). *The inner world: A psychoanalytic study of childhood and society in India*. Delhi: Oxford University Press.

Kamya, H. (2007). Narrative practice and culture. In E. Aldarondo (Ed.), *Advancing social justice through clinical practice* (pp. 207–220). Mahwah, NJ: Lawrence Erlbaum Associates.

Kanellos, N. (1994). The Hispanic almanac: From Columbus to corporate America. Mt. Kisco, NY: Visible Ink Press.

Kao, G. & Tienda, M. (1998). Educational aspirations of minority youth. *American Journal of Education*, 106(3), 349–384.

Kaplan, C. P., Erickson, P. I., Stewart, S. L. & Crane, L. A. (2001). Young Latinas and abortion: The role of cultural factors, reproductive behavior, and alternative roles to motherhood. *Health Care for Women International*, 22, 667–689.

Kastèn, W. C. (1992). Bridging the horizon: American Indian beliefs and whole language learning. *Anthropology & Education Quarterly*, 23(2), 108–119.

Kaufman, A. S. & McLean, J. E. (1996). Profiles of Hispanic adolescents and adults on the

Holland themes and basic interest scales of the strong interest inventory. *Psychological Reports*, 79, 1279–1288.

Kauh, Tae-Ock. (1997). Intergenerational relations: Older Korean-Americans' experiences. *Journal of Cross-Cultural Gerontology*, 12(3), 245–271.

Kaushal, N. (2009). Wealth, race/ethnicity, and children's educational outcomes. *Children and Youth Services Review*, 31(9), 963–971.

Kay, A. (1998). Generativity in the shadow of genocide: The Holocaust experience and generativity. In D. P. McAdams and E. de St. Aubin (Eds.), *Generativity and adult development: How and why we care for the next generation* (pp. 335–359). Washington, DC: American Psychological Association.

Keane, E. M., Dick, R. W., Bechtold, D. W. & Manson, S. M. (1996). Predictive and concurrent validity of the Suicide Ideation Questionnaire among American Indian adolescents. *Journal of Abnormal Child Psychology*, 24, 735–747.

Kefalas, M. (2008). Review of *Single by chance, mothers by choice: How women are choosing parenthood without marriage and creating the new American family*. *Gender & Society*, 22(4), 518–520.

Kennamer, J. D., Honnold, J., Bradford, J. & Hendricks, M. (2000). Differences in disclosure of sexuality among African American and white gay/bisexual men: Implications for HIV/AIDS prevention. *AIDS Education & Prevention*, 12(6), 519–531.

Kennedy, B., Mathis, C. & Woods, A. (2007). African Americans and their distrust of the health care system: healthcare for diverse populations. *Journal of Cultural Diversity*, 14(2), 56–60.

Khalsa, S., Shorter, S., Cope, S., Wyshak, G. & Sklar, E. (2009). Yoga ameliorates performance anxiety and mood disturbance in young professional musicians. *Applied Psychophysiology and Biofeedback*, 34(4), 279–289.

Khoury-Kassabri, M. (2010). Attitudes of Arab and Jewish mothers towards punitive and non-punitive discipline methods. *Child & Family Social Work*, 15(2), 135–144.

Kidd, J. & Witten, T. (2008). Understanding spirituality and religiosity in the transgender community: Implications for aging. *Journal of Religion, Spirituality & Aging*, 20(1), 29–62.

Kim, B., Soliz, A., Orellana, B. & Alamilla, S. (2009). Latino/a values scale: Development, reliablility, and validity. *Measurement and Evaluation in Counseling and Development*, 42(2), 71–91.

Kim, H., Rendon, L. & Valadez, J. (1998). Student characteristics, school characteristics, and educational aspirations of six Asian American ethnic groups. *Journal of Multicultural Counseling & Development*, 26(3), 166–176.

Kim, S. C. (1985). Family therapy for Asian Americans: A strategic-structural framework. *Psychotherapy*, 22(2), 342–348.

Kim, W. J. & Shin, Yee-Jin. Carey, M. P. (1999). Comparison of Korean-American adoptees and biological children of their adoptive parents: A pilot study. *Child Psychiatry & Human Development*, 29(3), 221–228.

Kim, W., Zrull, J., Davenport, C. & Weaver, M. (1992). Characteristics of adopted juvenile delinquents. *Journal of the American Academy of Child & Adolescent Psychiatry*, 31(3), 525–532.

King Jr., M. L. (1963). *I have a dream*. Speech delivered August 28, 1963, at the Lincoln Memorial, Washington DC. Retrieved on October 14, 2009, from http://www .americanrhetoric.com/speeches/ mlkihaveadream.htm.

King, M. L. (2010). *Where do we go from here: Chaos or community?* Boston, MA: Beacon Press.

King, M., McKeown, E., Warner, J., Ramsay, A., Johnson, K., Cort, C., Wright, L., Blizard, R. & Davidson, O. (2003). Mental health and quality of life of gay men and lesbians in England and Wales: Controlled, cross-sectional study. *British Journal of Psychiatry*, 183(6), 552–558.

King, M., Semelyn, J., Tai, S. S., Killaspy, H., Osborn, D., Popelyuk, D. & Nazareth, I. (2007). *Mental disorders, suicide, and deliberate self harm in lesbian, gay and bisexual people: A systematic review of the literature*. London: National Institute for Mental Health England.

Kirschner Cook, A. & Welsh Jordan, M. (1997). Explaining variation in income between Hispanic and White female-headed households in Washington. *Hispanic Journal of Behavioral Sciences*, 19(4), 433–445.

Kiselica, M. S. (2004). When duty calls: The implications of social justice work for policy, research, education, and practice in the mental health professions. *The Counseling Psychologist*, 32, 838–854.

Kitchener, K.S. (1984). Intuition, critical evaluation and ethical principles: The foundation for ethical decision in counseling psychology. *The Counseling Psychologist*, 12(3), 43–55.

Kitzinger, C. (2001). Sexualities. In R. K. Unger (Ed.), *Handbook of the psychology of women and gender* (pp. 272–285). Hoboken, NJ: John Wiley & Sons.

Kniffen, F. B., Gregory, H. F. & Stokes, G. A. (1987). The historic tribes of Louisiana. Baton Rouge: Louisiana State University Press.

Koenig, L. B. & Vaillant, G. E. (2009). A prospective study of church attendance and health over the lifespan. *Health Psychology*, 28, 117–124.

Kogon, E. (1950). *The theory and practice of hell*. New York: Farrar, Straus and Giroux.

Komarraju, M. & Cokley, K. (2008). Horizontal and vertical dimensions of individualism-collectivism: A comparison of African Americans and European Americans. *Cultural Diversity and Ethnic Minority Psychology*, 14(4), 336–343.

Koss-Chiono, J. (1995). Traditional and folk approaches among ethnic minorities. In J. F. Aponte, R. Y. Rivers & J. Wohl (Eds.), *Psychological interventions and cultural diversity* (pp. 145–163). Boston: Allyn & Bacon.

Kridli, S. & Libbus, K. (2001). Contraception in Jordan: A cultural and religious perspective. *International Nursing Review*, 48(3), 144–151.

Krishnan, A. & Sweeney, C. J. (1997). Asian vs. non-Asian differences in achievement-related background variables of medical students. *Psychology & Developing Societies*, 9(2), 189–224.

Kubrin, C. & Wadsworth, T. (2009). Explaining suicide among blacks and whites: How socioeconomic factors and gun availability affect race-specific suicide rates. *Social Science Quarterly*, 90(5), 1203–1227.

Kuhn, A., Bodmer, C., Stadlmayr, W., Kuhn, P., Mueller, M. & Birkhäuser, M. (2009). Quality of life 15 years after sex reassignment surgery for transsexualism. *Fertility And Sterility*, 92(5), 1685–1689.

Kundu, M. M., Dutta & A., Chan, F. (2010). A systems approach to placement: A culturally sensitive model for people with disabilities. In F. E. Balcazar, Y. Suarez-Balcazar, T. Taylor-Ritzler & C. B. Keys (Eds.), *Race, culture and disability: Rehabilitation science and practice* (pp. 325–344). Boston, MA: Jones and Bartlett Publishers.

Kung, H. C. & Liu, X. & Juon, H. S. (1998). Risk factors for suicide in Caucasians and in African-Americans: A matched case-control study. *Social Psychiatry, 33*(4), 155–161.

LaDuke, W. (1999). *All our relations: Native struggles for land and life*. Cambridge: South End Press.

LaFromboise, T., Coleman, H. & Gerton, J. (1993). Psychological impact of biculturalism: Evidence and theory. *Psychological Bulletin, 114*(3), 395–412.

Lahey, B. B., Gordon, R. A. Loeber, R., Stouthamer-Loeber, M. & Farrington, D. P. (1999). Boys who join gangs: A prospective study of predictors of first gang entry. *Journal of Abnormal Child Psychology, 27*(4), 261–276.

Lai, T (1998). Asian American women: Not for sale. In M. L. Anderson & P. H. Collins (Eds.), *Race, class, and gender: An anthology* (3rd ed., pp. 209–216). Belmont, CA: Wadsworth Publishing Company.

Lakoff, R. T. (2004). *Language and woman's place*. Oxford: Oxford University Press.

Lambert, M., Smart, D., Campbell, M., Hawkins, E., Harmon, C. & Slade, K. (2006). Psychotherapy outcome, as measured by the OQ-45, in African American, Asian/Pacific Islander, Latino/a, and Native American clients compared with matched Caucasian clients. *Journal of College Student Psychotherapy, 20*(4), 17–29.

Lang, P. & Torres, M. I. (1997–1998). Vietnamese perceptions of community and health: Implications for the practice of community health education. *International Quarterly of Community Health Education, 17*(4), 389–404.

Langdridge, D. (2008). Are you angry or are you heterosexual? A queer critique of lesbian and gay models of identity development. In L. Moon (Ed.), *Feeling queer or queer feelings?: Radical approaches to counselling sex, sexualities and genders* (pp. 23–35). New York, NY: Routledge/Taylor & Francis Group.

Lange, G. (2003). Smallpox epidemic ravages Native Americans on the northwest coast of North America in the 1770s. *The Free Online Encyclopedia of Washington State History*. Retrieved from http://www.historylink.org/index.cfm?DisplayPage=output.cfm&File_Id=5100.

Langman, P. F. (1997). *White culture, Jewish culture, and the origins of psychotherapy. Psychotherapy, 34*(2), 207–218.

Larry P. v. Riles. (1979, 1984, 1986, 1992). 343 F. Supp. 1306 (N. D. Cal. 1972) (preliminary injunction). Add 502 F. 2d 963 (9th cir. 1974); 495 F. Supp. 926 (N. D. Cal. 1979) (decision) on merits add (9th cir. No. 80-427 Jan. 23, 1984). Order modifying judgment, C-71-2270 RFP, September 25, 1986.

Larsson, S., Bergkvist, L. & Wolk, A. (2009). Coffee and black tea consumption and risk of breast cancer by estrogen and progesterone receptor status in a Swedish cohort. *Cancer Causes & Control, 20*(10), 2039–2044.

Larzelere, R. E. (2000). Child outcomes of nonabusive and customary physical punishment by parents: An updated literature review. *Clinical Child & Family Psychology Review, 3*(4), 199–221.

Latz, S., Wolf, A. W. & Lozoff, B. (1999). Sleep practices and problems in young children in Japan and the United States. *Archives of Pediatric Adolescent Medicine, 153*, 339–346.

Law, C. & Schneiderman, L. (1992). Policy implications of factors associated with economic self-sufficiency of Southeast Asian refugees. In D. Chung & K. Murase (Eds.), *Social work practice with Asian Americans* (pp. 167–183). Thousand Oaks, CA: Sage Publications.

Lawrence, A. (2009). Erotic target location errors: An underappreciated paraphilic dimension. *Journal of Sex Research, 46*(2), 194–215.

Leaper, C., Anderson, K. J. Sanders, P. (1998). Moderators of gender effects on parents' talk to their children: A meta-analysis. *Developmental Psychology, 34*(1), 3–27.

Lear, J. G. (2005, February 25). Children in immigrant families. *In Focus*, 1–4.

Lebacqz & Barton (1991). *Sex in the parish*. Louisville: Westminster John Knox Press.

Lebowitz, B., Pearson, J., Schneider, L., Reynolds, C., Alexopoulos, G., Bruce, M., et al. (1997). Diagnosis and treatment of depression in late life: Consensus statement update. *JAMA: Journal of the American Medical Association, 278*(14), 1186–1190.

Lee, E. (1997a). Overview: Assessment and treatment. In, E. Lee (Ed.), *Working with Asian Americans*, pp. 3–35. New York: Guilford Press.

Lee, E. (1997b). Chinese Americans Families. In, E. Lee (Ed.), *Working with Asian Americans*, pp. 47–77. New York: Guilford Press.

Lee, S. M. & Fernandez, M. (1998). Trends in Asian American racial/ethnic intermarriage: A comparison of 1980 and 1990 census data. *Sociological Perspectives, 41*(2), 323–342.

Leeder, E. (1994). Treating abuse in families: A feminist and community approach. New York: Springer Publishing Company.

Lehre, A., Lehre, K., Laake, P. & Danbolt, N. (2009). Greater intrasex phenotype variability in males than in females is a fundamental aspect of the gender differences in humans. *Developmental Psychobiology*, *51*(2), 198–206.

Leland, S. (1992). Coming of age. Retrieved on September 23, 2000, from http://www.earth circle.org/sadiemoon.html.

Lemay, E., Clark, M. & Greenberg, A. (2010). What is beautiful is good because what is beautiful is desired: Physical attractiveness stereotyping as projection of interpersonal goals. *Personality and Social Psychology Bulletin*, *36*(3), 339–353.

Lester, D. (1994). Suicide rates in Native Americans by state and size of population. *Perceptual & Motor Skills*, *78*, 954.

Lester, D. (1996). American Indian suicide and homicide rates and unemployment. *Perceptual & Motor Skills*, *83*, 1170.

Lester, D. (1997). Note on a Mohave theory of suicide. *Cross-Cultural Research: the Journal of Comparative Social Science*, *31*(3), 268–272.

Levant, R. & Philpot, C. (2002). Conceptualizing gender in marital and family therapy research: The gender role strain paradigm. In H. A. Liddle, D. A Santisteban, & R. F. Levant (Eds.), *Family psychology: Science-based interventions* (pp. 301–329). Washington DC: American Psychological Association.

Levin, J., Chatters, L. M. & Taylor, R. J. (2005). Religion, health and medicine in African Americans: Implications for physicians. *Journal of the National Medical Association*, *97*(2), 237–249.

Levinson, D. J. (1978). *The seasons of a man's life.* New York: Knopf.

Lewis, E. W., Duran, E. & Woodis, W. (1999). *Psychotherapy in the American Indian population. Psychiatric Annals*, *29*(8), 477–479.

Lewis, M., Takai-Kawakami, K., Kawakami, K. & Sullivan, M. (2010). Cultural differences in emotional responses to success and failure. *International Journal of Behavioral Development*, *34*(1), 53–61.

Li, Y., Xu, H. & Gao, S. (2009). Mental health status of infertile women undergoing in vitro fertilization and embryo transfer. *Chinese Journal of Clinical Psychology*, *17*(6), 770–772.

Lindsey, E. & Mize, J. (2001). Contextual differences in parent-child play: Implications for children's gender role development. *Sex Roles*, *44*(3–4), 155–176.

Lippa, R. (2010). Sex differences in personality traits and gender-related occupational preferences across 53 nations: Testing evolutionary and social-environmental theories. *Archives of Sexual Behavior*, *39*(3), 619–636.

Little, J. (2001). Embracing gay, lesbian, bisexual, and transgendered youth in school-based settings. *Child & Youth Care Forum*, *30*(2), 99–110.

Lomawaima, K. T. (1995). Educating Native Americans. In J. A. Banks and C. A. M. Banks (Eds.), *Handbook of research on multicultural education*. New York: Macmillian.

Lombardi, E. L. (1999). Integration within a transgender social network and its effect upon members' social and political activity. *Journal of Homosexuality*, *37*, 109–126.

Lonegren, S. (1996). Spiritual dowsing. Glastonbury: Gothic Image.

Losoya, S. H., Knight, G. P., Chassin, L., Little, M., Vargas-Chanes, D., Mauricio, A., et al. (2008). Trajectories of acculturation and enculturation in relation to heavy episodic drinking and marijuana use in a sample of Mexican American serious juvenile offenders. *Journal of Drug Issues*, *38*(1), 171–198.

Lott, B. (2010). *Multiculturalism and diversity: A social psychological perspective.* Chichester, West Sussex: John Wiley & Sons.

Lovinger, R. J. (1996). *Religion and the clinical practice of psychology.* Washington, DC: American Psychological Association Books.

Lowe, E. (2003). Identity, activity, and the well-being of adolescents and youths: Lessons from young people in a Micronesian society. *Culture*, Medicine and Psychiatry, *27*(2), 187–219.

Lubchansky, I., Egri, G. & Stokes, J. (1970). Puerto Rican spiritualists view mental illness: the faith healer as a paraprofessional. *American Journal of Psychiatry*, *127*, 312–321.

Maccio, E. (2010). Influence of family, religion, and social conformity on client participation in sexual reorientation therapy. *Journal of Homosexuality*, *57*(3), 441–458.

Maccoby, E. E. (1990). Gender and relationships: A developmental account. *American Psychologist*, *45*, 513–520.

MacPhee, D., Fritz, J. & Miller-Heyl, J. (1996). Ethnic variations in personal social networks and parenting. *Child Development*, *67*(6), 3278–3295.

Macpherson, C. (1995). Samoan medicine. In C. D. F. Parsons (Ed.), *Healing practices in the South Pacific* (pp. 1–15). Honolulu, HI: University of Hawaii Press.

Madden, B. (2005). Navajo phones could ring on Sacred Wind's plan. *New Mexico Business Weekly*. Retrieved on May 9, 2010, from http://albuquerque .bizjournals.com/albuquerque/

stories/2005/01/10/story5 .html.

Maddux, J. & Winstead, B. (Eds.). (2008). *Psychopathology: Foundations for a contemporary understanding* (2nd ed.). London: Routledge.

Magnuson, E. (2008). Rejecting the American dream: Men creating alternative life goals. *Journal of Contemporary Ethnography, 37*(3), 255–290.

Major, B., Gramzow, R. H., McCoy, S., Levin, S., Schmader, T., Sidanius, J., et al. (2002). Perceiving personal discrimination: The role of group status and legitimizing ideology. *Journal of Personality and Social Psychology, 82,* 269–282.

Male breast cancer (2010). Mayo Clinic. Retrieved on May 29, 2010, from http://www.mayo clinic.com/health/male-breast-cancer/DS00661.

Manaster, G. J., Rhodes, C., Marcus, M. B. & Chan, J. C. (1998). The role of birth order in the acculturation of Japanese Americans. *Psychologia: An International Journal of Psychology in the Orient, 41*(3), 155–170.

Mandela, N. (1995). Long walk to freedom: The autobiography of Nelson Mandela. New York: Back Bay Books.

Manis, A. A., Brown, S. L. & Paylo, M. J. (2009). The helping professional as an advocate. In C. M. Ellis & J. Carlson (Eds.), *Cross cultural awareness and social justice in counseling* (pp. 23–43). New York: Routledge.

Mann, J. (1994). *The difference: Growing up female in America*. New York: Warner Books.

Mansbach-Kleinfeld, I., Palti, H., Farbstein, I., Geraisy, N., Levinson, D., Brent, D., et al. (2010). Service use for mental disorders and unmet need: Results from the Israel survey on mental health among adolescents. *Psychiatric Services, 61*(3), 241–249.

Maquinna, Chief of Nootka (2003). To the editor. In Petrone, P. (Ed.), *First people, first voices* (pp. 69–71). Toronto: University of Toronto Press.

Marinak, B. & Gambrell, L. (2010). Reading motivation: Exploring the elementary gender gap. *Literacy Research and Instruction, 49*(2), 129–141.

Marmor, J. (1965). Sexual inversion: The multiple roots of homosexuality. New York: Basic Books.

Martin, G. L. (1987). *Counseling for family violence and abuse*. Waco, Texas: Word Books.

Martin, J., McCaughtry, N. & Shen, B. (2008). Predicting physical activity in Arab American school children. *Journal of Teaching in Physical Education, 27*(2), 205–219.

Martínez-Taboas, A. (2005). Psychogenic seizures in an espiritismo context: The role of culturally sensitive psychotherapy. *Psychotherapy: Theory, Research, Practice, Training, 42*(1), 6–13.

Martini, M. (1996). "What's new?" at the dinner table: Family dynamics during mealtimes in two cultural groups in Hawaii. *Early Development & Parenting, 5*(1), 23–34.

Maslim, A. & Bjorck, J. (2009). Reasons for conversion to Islam among women in the United States. *Psychology of Religion and Spirituality, 1*(2), 97–111.

Massey, D. S. & Denton, N. A. (1993). *American apartheid: Segregation and the making of the underclass*. Cambridge, MA: Harvard University Press.

Maton, K. I., Hrabowski, F. A. & Greif, G. L. (1998). Preparing the way: A qualitative study of high-achieving African American males and the role of the family. *American Journal of Community Psychology, 26*(4), 639–668.

Matsuoka, J. K., Breaux, C., Ryujin, D. H. (1997). National utilization of mental health services by Asian Americans/ Pacific Islanders. *Journal of Community Psychology, 25*(2), 141–145.

McBrier, D. B. & Wilson, G. (2004). Going down? Race and downward occupational mobility for white-collar workers in the 1990s. *Work and Occupations, 31*(3), 283–322.

McCabe, P. & Rubinson, F. (2008). Committing to social justice: The behavioral intention of school psychology and education trainees to advocate for lesbian, gay, bisexual, and transgendered youth. *School Psychology Review, 37*(4), 469–486.

McCarn, S. R. & Fassinger, R. E. (1996). Revisioning sexual minority identity formation: A new model of lesbian identity and its implications for counseling and research. *Counseling Psychologist, 24*(3), 508–534.

McCullough, M. E., Hoyt, W. T., Larson, D. B., Koenig, H. G. & Thoresen, C. (2000). Religious involvement and mortality: A meta-analytic review. *Health Psychology, 19*(3), 211–222.

McCunn, R. L. (1981). *Thousand pieces of gold: A biographical novel*. San Francisco: Design Enterprises of San Francisco.

McDonald, H. B. & Steinhorn, A. I. (1990). *Homosexuality: A practical guide to counseling lesbians, gay men, and their families*. New York: The Continuum Publishing Company.

McFadden, John (1999). *Transcultural counseling*. Alexandia, VA: American Counseling Association.

McFague, S. (1988). Models of God for an ecological, evolutionary era: God as mother of the universe. In R. J. Russell, W. R. Stoeger & G. V. Coyne (Eds.), *Physics, philosophy, and theology: A common quest for understanding*. Vatican City State: Vatican Observatory.

McFarlane, J. & Wiist, W. (1997). Preventing abuse to pregnant women: Implementation of a "mentor mother" advocacy model. *Journal of Community Health Nursing,14*(4),237–249.

McQueen, A., Getz, J. G. & Bray, J. H. (2003). Acculturation, substance use, and deviant behavior: Examining separation and family conflict as mediators. *Child Development, 74*(6), 1737–1750.

McRoy, R. G. (1994). Attachment and racial identity issues: Implications for child placement decision making. *Journal of Multicultural Social Work, 3*(3), 59–74.

Meet the Press (April 13, 1997). Farrakhan meets the press. National Broadcast Company. Retrieved on October 11, 2009, from http://www .finalcall.com.

Merchant, C. (1983). Mining the Earth's womb. In J. Rothschild (Ed.), *Machina ex dea: Feminist perspectives on technology,* New York: Pergamon Press.

Meyer, C., Leung, N., Barry, L. & De Feo, D. (2010). Emotion and eating psychopathology: Links with attitudes toward emotional expression among young women. *International Journal of Eating Disorders, 43*(2), 187–189.

Meyer, I. (1995). Minority stress and mental health in gay men. *Journal of Health and Social Behavior, 7,* 9–25.

Mignone, J. & O'Neil, J. (2005). Social capital and youth suicide risk factors in First Nations communities. *Canadian Journal of Public Health, 96,* S51–S54.

Mikulas, W. L. (2002). The integrative helper: Convergence of Eastern and Western traditions. Pacific Grove, CA: Brooks/Cole.

Miller, A. & Josephs, L. (2009). Whiteness as pathological narcissism. *Contemporary Psychoanalysis, 45*(1), 93–119.

Miller, A. J., Bobner, R. F. & Zarski, J. J. (2000). Sexual identity development: A base for work with same-sex couple partner abuse. *Contemporary Family Therapy, 22*(2), 189–200.

Miller, B. (1979). Unpromised paternity: Lifestyles of gay fathers, In N. M. Levine (Ed.), *Gay men: Sociological of male homosexuality* (pp. 239–252). New York: Harper & Row.

Miller, G. V. F. & Travers, C. J. (2005). The relationship between ethnicity and work stress. In A. G. Alexander-Stamatios & C. L. Cooper (Eds.), *Research companion to organizational health psychology* (pp. 87–101). Northampton, MA: Edward Elgar Publishing.

Mintz, B. & Krymkowski, D. (2010). The ethnic, race, and gender gaps in workplace authority: Changes over time in the United States. *The Sociological Quarterly, 51*(1), 20–45.

Miranda, A. O. & Matheny, K. B. (2000). Socio-psychological predictors of acculturative stress among Latino adults. *Journal of Mental Health Counseling, 22,* 306–317.

Mitchell, B. & Javed, N. (June 16, 2010). "I killed my daughter ... with my hands": Domineering father and son plead guilty to strangling rebellious teenager. *The Toronto Star.* Retrieved on June 17, 2010, from http://www.thestar.com/ news/gta/crime/article/824133– i-killed-my-daughter-with-my-hands.

Moisan, P. A., Sanders-Phillips, K. & Moisan, P. M. (1997). Ethnic differences in circumstances of abuse and symptoms of depression and anger among sexually abused black and Latino boys. *Child Abuse & Neglect, 21*(5), 473–488.

Money, J. & Ehrhardt, A. (1972). *Man and woman/boy and girl: Differentiation and dimorphism of gender identity from conception to maturity.* Baltimore: Johns Hopkins Press.

Montilla, R. E. & Smith, R. L. (2006). Working with Latino populations: Background and historical perspectives. In R. L. Smith & R. E. Montilla (Eds.), *Counseling and family therapy with Latino populations: Strategies that work* (pp. 27–40). New York: Routledge.

Moon, A. (1999). Elder abuse and neglect among the Korean elderly in the United States. In Toshio Tatara (Ed.), *Understanding elder abuse in minority populations* (pp. 109–118). Philadelphia: Brunner/Mazel.

Morain, D. (September 10, 2000). State baffled by casinos' check for $34 million gaming: Tribes send in the payment without a breakdown of what it's for. Critics say problem shows ambiguities in the law regulating gambling. *Los Angeles Times.* Retrieved on September 11, 2000, from http://articles .latimes.com/2000/sep/10/ news/mn-18709

Morales, M. C. (2009). Ethnic-controlled economy or segregation? Exploring inequality in Latina/o co-ethnic jobsites. *Sociological Forum, 24*(3), 589–610.

Morris, E. (2008). "Rednecks," "rutters," and 'rithmetic: Social class, masculinity, and schooling in a rural context. *Gender & Society, 22*(6), 728–751.

Morrongiello, B. A. & Dawber, T. (1999). Parental influences on toddlers' injury-risk behaviors: Are sons and daughters socialized differently? *Journal of Applied Developmental Psychology, 20,* 227–251.

Mortola, J. F. (1998). Premenstrual syndrome: Pathophysiologic considerations. *The New England Journal of Medicine, 338*(4), 256.

Morton, S. B. (1998). Lesbian divorce. *American Journal of Orthopsychiatry, 68*(3), 410–419.

Mott, F. L. (2004). The utility of the HOME Scale for child development research in large national longitudinal survey: The National Longitudinal Survey of Youth, 1979 cohort. *Parenting: Science and Practice, 4*, 261–273.

Mourad, M. & Carolan, M. (2010). An ecological approach to culturally sensitive intervention for Arab American women and their families. *The Family Journal, 18*(2), 178–183.

Moyers, B. (2004). *End times*. CommonDreams.org. Retrieved on May 7, 2010, from http://www.nativeamericanchurch.com/Signs/End Times.html.

Mrug, S. & Windle, M. (2009a). Bidirectional influences of violence exposure and adjustment in early adolescence: Externalizing behaviors and school connectedness. *Journal of Abnormal Child Psychology: An Official Publication of the International Society for Research in Child and Adolescent Psychopathology, 37*(5), 611–623.

Mrug, S. & Windle, M., (2009b). Moderators of negative peer influence on early adolescent externalizing behaviors: Individual behavior, parenting, and school connectedness. *The Journal of Early Adolescence, 29*(4), 518–540.

Muhammad, E. (1997). *The supreme wisdom* (vol. 1). Atlanta: MEMPS Publications.

Muhammad, E. (2009). *Time is at hand*. Retrieved from http://www.finalcall.com/artman/publish/Columns_4/Time_is_at_hand.shtml. Reprinted from Muhammad, E. (1997). *Message to the Blackman in America* Phoenix, AZ: Secretarius Memps Publications.

Muller, H., Desmarais, S. & Hamel, J. (2009). Do judicial responses to restraining order requests discriminate against male victims of domestic violence? *Journal of Family Violence, 24*(8), 625–637.

Muller, L. E. (2002). Group counseling for African American males: When all you have are European American counselors. *Journal for Specialists in Group Work, 27*(3), 299–313.

Munro, R. (March 14, 1996). State of Washington Initiative 669. Retrieved from www.secstate.wa.gov/elections/initiatives/text/i669.pdf

Murray, B. (1996). Self-esteem varies among ethnic-minority girls. *APA Monitor*, p. 42.

Murray, J., Batalova, J. & Fix, M. (2007). Educating the children of immigrants. In M. Fix (Ed.), *Securing the future: US immigrant integration policy, a reader*. Washington, DC: Migration Policy Institute.

Murray, M., & Marks, D. F. (2010). Health psychology, poverty and poverty reduction. *Journal of Health Psychology, 15*(7), doi:10.1177/1359105310378386

Museus, S. (2008). The role of ethnic student organizations in fostering African American and Asian American students' cultural adjustment and membership at predominantly White institutions. *Journal of College Student Development, 49*(6), 568–586.

Mustanski, B. S., Chivers, M. L. & Bailey, J. M. (2002). A critical review of recent biological research on human sexual orientation. *Annual Review of Sex Research, 13*, 89–140.

Muula, A. (2010). Marriage, not religion, is associated with HIV infection among women in rural Malawi. *AIDS and Behavior, 14*(1), 125–131.

Myerson, J., Rank, M. R., Raines, F. Q. & Schnitzler, M. A. (1998). Race and general

cognitive ability: The myth of diminishing returns to education. *Psychological Science, 9*(2), 139–142.

Mzimkulu, K. G. & Simbayi, L. C. (2006). Perspectives and practices of Xhosa-speaking African traditional healers when managing psychosis. *Human Research Council, South Africa International Journal of Disability, Development and Education, 53*, 417–431.

National Association of School Psychologists (2010). Standards for graduate preparation of school psychologists. Retrieved from http://www.nasponline.org/standards/2010standards/1_Graduate_Preparation.pdf.

Native Americans. (2009). U.S. Diplomatic Mission to Germany. Retrieved on May 8, 2010, from http://usa.usembassy.de/society-natives.htm.

Naylor, G. (1993). The myth of matriarch. In J. Madden and S. M. Blake (1992). *Emerging voices: Readings in the American experience* (2nd, ed., pp. 13–15). Fort Worth: Harcourt Brace College Publishers.

Newport, F. (June 4, 2001). American attitudes toward homosexuality continue to become more tolerant. Princeton, NJ: Gallup News Service.

Ngai, P. (2006). Grassroots suggestions for linking Native-language learning, Native American studies, and mainstream education in reservation schools with mixed Indian and white student populations. *Language, Culture and Curriculum, 19*(2), 220–236.

Nguyen, H. (2006). Acculturation in the United States. In David Sam and John Berry (Eds.), *Cambridge Handbook of Acculturation Psychology*. UK: Cambridge University Press.

Nicholson, A., Rose, R. & Bobak, M. (2010). Associations between different dimensions of religious involvement and self-rated health in diverse European populations. *Health Psychology, 29*(2), 227–235.

Nicholson, B. L. (1997). The influence of pre-emigration and postemigration stressors on mental health: A study of Southeast Asian refugees. *Social Work Research, 21*(1), 19–31.

Nobles, A. Y. & Sciarra, D. T. (2000). Cultural determinants in the treatment of Arab Americans: A primer for mainstream therapists. *American Journal of Orthopsychiatry, 70*, 182–191.

Nobles, W. (2006). *Seeking the Sakhu: Foundational writings for an African psychology.* Chicago: Third World Press.

Noorbala, A., Ramezanzadeh, F., Abedinia, N. & Naghizadeh, M. (2009). Psychiatric disorders among infertile and fertile women. *Social Psychiatry and Psychiatric Epidemiology, 44*(7), 587–591.

Nordhus, I. H., Nielsen, G. J. & Kvale, G. (1998). Psychotherapy with older adults. In I. H. Nordhus, G. R. VandenBos, S. Berg & P. Fromholt (Eds.), *Clinical geropsychology*, pp. 289–311. Washington, DC: American Psychological Association.

Nordstrom, C. K., Dwyer, K. M., Merz, C. N., Shircore, A. & Dwyer, J. H. (2001). Work-related stress and early atherosclerosis. *Epidemiology, 12*(2), 180–185.

Novas, H. (1994). *Everything you need to know about Latino history* (2nd ed.). New York: Penguin Press.

Nwoye, A. (2006). A narrative approach to child and family therapy in Africa. *Contemporary Family Therapy: An International Journal, 28*(1), 1–23.

O'Connor, S. & Vandenberg, B. (2005). Psychosis or faith? Clinicians' assessment of religious beliefs. *Journal of Consulting and Clinical Psychology, 73*(4), 610–616.

O'Faolain, J. & Martines, L. (Eds.). (1973). *Not in God's image.* New York: Thomas T. Crowell Co.

O'Keefe, T. & Fox, K. (2003). *Finding the real me: True tales of sex and gender diversity.* San Francisco, CA: Jossey-Bass.

O'Reilly, S., Knox, D. & Zusman, M. (2009). What college women want in a marriage partner. *College Student Journal, 43*(2), 503–506.

O'Rourke, N., Neufeld, E., Claxton, A. & Smith, J. (2010). Knowing me—knowing you: Reported personality and trait discrepancies as predictors of marital idealization between long-wed spouses. *Psychology and Aging, 25*(2), 412–421.

Obama, B. (1995). Dreams from my father: A story of race and inheritance. New York, NY: Three Rivers Press.

Obasi, E. & Leong, F. (2009). Psychological distress, acculturation, and mental health-seeking attitudes among people of African descent in the United States: A preliminary investigation. *Journal of Counseling Psychology, 56*(2), 227–238.

Obeng, C. S. (2007). Immigrants families and childcare preferences: Do immigrants' cultures influence their childcare decisions? *Early Childhood Education Journal, 34*(4), 259–264.

Obiakor, F. & Afoláyan, M. (2007). African immigrant families in the United States: Surviving the sociocultural tide. *The Family Journal, 15*(3), 265–270.

Obisesan, T., Livingston, I. Trulear, H.D. & Gillum, F. (2006). Frequency of attendance at religious services, cardiovascular disease, metabolic risk factors and dietary intake in Americans: An age-stratified exploratory analysis. *International Journal of Psychiatry in Medicine, 36*(4), 435–448.

Office of Minority Health & Health Disparities (2005). Highlights in minority health. Atlanta: Centers for Disease Control and Prevention. Retrieved on October 11, 2009, from http://www.cdc.gov/omhd.

Okakok, L. (1989). Serving the purpose of education. *Harvard Educational Review, 59*(4), 405–422.

Old Dog Cross, P. (1982). Sexual abuse, a new threat to the Native American woman: An overview. *Listening post: A periodical of the mental health programs of Indian health services, 6*(2), 18.

Olsson, M. (2009). DSM diagnosis of conduct disorder (CD)—A review. *Nordic Journal of Psychiatry, 63*(2), 102–112.

Ong, A. D., Fuller-Rowell, T., Burrow, A. L. (2009). Racial discrimination and the stress process. *Journal of Personality and Social Psychology, 96*(6), 1259–1271.

Ontario Consultants on Religious Tolerance (1998b). Genocide of gay and lesbian youth Retrieved on January 15, 2000, from http://www.religioustolerance .org/hom_suic.htm.

Ontario Consultants on Religious Tolerance. (1998a). Southern Baptist Convention and Homosexuality. Retrieved August 2000 from http://www.religious tolerance.org/hom_sbc.htm.

Orenstein, P. (2000). Unbalanced equations: Girls, math, and the confidence gap.

Orlando, L. (April 5, 2006). African-American spirituality plays an important role in healing. Buzzle.com. Retrieved on October 11, 2009, from http://www.buzzle.com.

Osborne, J. W. (1998). Race and academic disidentification. *Journal of Educational Psychology, 89*(4), 1–8.

Oseguera, L., Locks, A. M. & Vega, I. (2009). Increasing Latina/o students' baccalaureate attainment: A focus on retention. *Journal of Hispanic Higher Education, 8*(1), 23–53.

Otsuki, M., Tinsley, B., Chao, R. & Unger, J. (2008). An ecological perspective on smoking among Asian American college students: The roles of social smoking and smoking motives. *Psychology of Addictive Behaviors, 22*(4), 514–523.

Owen, Lara. (1993). *Her blood is gold: Celebrating the power of menstruation.* San Francisco, CA: Harper & Row, Publishers.

Owen, R. & Pamuk, S. (1999). *A history of Middle East economies of the twentieth century.* Cambridge, MA: Harvard University Press.

Ozawa, M., Kim, J. & Joo, M. (2006). Income class and the accumulation of net worth in the United States. *Social Work Research, 30*(4), 211–222.

Pachter, L. M. & Coll, C. G. (2009). Racism and child health: A review of the literature and future directions. *Journal of Developmental and Behavioral Pediatrics, 30*(3), 255–263.

Padilla, Yolanda C. (1997). Determinants of Hispanic poverty in the course of the transition to adulthood. *Hispanic Journal of Behavioral Sciences, 19,* 416–432.

Pakman, M. G. (2007). Risk reduction and the micropolitics of social justice in mental health care. In E. Aldarondo (Ed.), *Advancing social justice through clinical practice* (pp. 151–173). Mahwah, NJ: Lawrence Erlbaum Associates.

Pang, K. U. (1995). A cross-cultural understanding of depression among elderly Korean immigrants: Prevalence symptoms, and diagnosis. *Clinical Gerontologists, 15,* 3–20.

Parker, W. & Schwartz, R. (2002). On the experience of shame in multicultural counselling: Implications for white counsellors-in-training. *British Journal of Guidance & Counselling, 30*(3), 311–318.

Parker, W. M., Howard-Hamilton, M. & Parham, G. (1998). Counseling interventions with African American males. In W. M. Parker (Ed.), *Consciousness-raising: A primer for multicultural counseling* (2nd ed.), pp. 147–175. Springfield, IL: Charles C Thomas Publisher, LTD.

Paschall, M. J. & Hubbard, M. L. (1998). Effects of neighborhood and family stressors on African American male adolescents' self-worth and propensity for violent behavior. *Journal of Consulting & Clinical Psychology, 66*(5), 825–831

Passano, P. (1995). Taking care of one's own: A conversation with Shamita Das Dasgupta. *Manushi Magazine, 89,* 17–26.

Pearlin, L. I., Schieman, S., Fazio, E. M. & Meersman, S. C. (2005). Stress, health, and the life course: Some conceptual perspectives. *Journal of Health and Social Behavior, 46,* 205–219.

Pedersen, P. (2000). *A handbook for developing multicultural awareness* (3rd ed.). Alexandria, VA: American Counseling Association.

Pence, E. & Paymar, M. (1990). *Power and control, tactics of men who batter: An educational curriculum.* Duluth, MN: Minnesota Program Development.

Peplau, L. & Fingerhut, A. (2007). The close relationships of lesbian and gay men. *Annual Review of Psychology, 58,* 405–424.

Pepper, S. & Lorah, P. (2008). Career issues and workplace considerations for the transsexual community: Bridging a gap of knowledge for career counselors and mental health care providers. *The Career Development Quarterly, 56*(4), 330–343.

Perkins, R. (1995). The golden age of female trannies in medieval Europe. *Polare, 6.* Retrieved on December 12, 2009, from http://www.gendercentre.org.au/6article2.htm.

Perreira, K., Harris, K. M. & Lee, D. (2006). Making it in America: High school completion among immigrant youth. *Demography, 43,* 511–536.

Perz, J. & Ussher, J. (2009). Connectedness, communication, and reciprocity in lesbian relationships: Implications for women's construction and experience of PMS. *The story of sexual identity: Narrative perspectives on the gay and lesbian life course* (pp. 223–250). New York, NY: Oxford University Press.

Pesky, T. (n.d.). Overlooked and underserved: Elders in need of mental health care. *Mental health and aging: Getting information.* Retrieved on June 25, 2010, from http://mhaging.org/info/olus.html.

Peterson, J. V. & Nisenholz, B. (1987). *Orientation to counseling.* Boston: Allyn & Bacon.

Philpot, C. L., Brooks, G. R., Lusterman, D. D., Nutt, R. L. (1997). *Bridging separate gender worlds: Why men and women clash and how therapists can bring them together.* Washington, DC: American Psychological Association.

Phinney, J. S., DuPont, S., Espinosa, C., Revill, J. & Sanders, K. (1994). Ethnic identity and American identification among ethnic minority youths. In A. Bouvy, F. J. R. van de Vijer, P. Boski & P. Schmitz (Eds.), *Journeys into cross-cultural psychology* (pp. 167–183). Berwyn, PA: Swets & Zeitlinger.

Phinney, J. S., Ferguson, D. L. & Tate, J. D. (1997). Intergroup attitudes among ethnic minority adolescents: A causal model. *Child Development, 68*(5), 955–969.

Phipps, E., Cohen, M. H., Sorn, R. & Braitman, L. E. (1999). A pilot study of cancer knowledge and screening behaviors of Vietnamese and Cambodian women. *Health Care for Women International, 20*(2), 195–207.

Plaskow, J. (2001). Setting the problem, laying the ground. In R. Satow, (Ed.), *Gender and social life* (pp. 239–244). Boston: Allyn & Bacon.

Polcin, D. (2006). Reexamining confrontation and motivational interviewing. *Addictive Disorders & Their Treatment, 5*(4), 201–209.

Polednak, Anthony P. (1997). Gender and acculturation in relation to alcohol use among Hispanic (Latino) adults in two areas of the northeastern United States. *Substance Use & Misuse, 32*(11), 1513–1524.

Pollack, W. S. (1998). Real boys: rescuing our sons from the myths of boyhood. New York: Random House.

Pollack, W. S. (1999). Real boys: Rescuing our sons from the myths of boyhood. New York: Henry Holt & Company.

Ponterotto, J. G. (1988). Racial consciousness development among white counselor trainees: a stage model. *Journal of Multicultural Counseling and Development, 16*, 146–156.

Pope, M. (1995). The "salad bowl" is big enough for us all: An argument for the inclusion of lesbians and gay men in any definition of multiculturalism. *Journal of Counseling & Development, 73*(3), 301–304.

Portes, A. & Rumbaut, R. G. (2001). *Legacies: The story of the second generation.* Berkeley: University of California Press.

Powell, T. J., Yeaton, W., Hill, E. M. & Silk, K. R. (2001). Predictors of psychosocial outcomes for patients with mood disorders: The effects of self-help group participation.

Psychiatric Rehabilitation Journal, 25(1), 3–12.

Powell-Hopson, D. & Hopson D. S. (1988). Implications of doll color preferences among black preschool children and white preschool children. *Journal of Black Psychology, 14*(2), 57–63.

Prathikanti, S. (1997). East Indian American families. In, E. Lee (Ed.), *Working with Asian Americans*, pp. 79–99. New York: Guidford Press.

Price, B. & Rosenbaum, A. (2007). National survey of batterer intervention programs. Paper presented at the International Family Violence and Child Victimization Research Conference, Portsmouth, NH.

Prilleltensky, I., Dokecki, P., Frieden, G. & Ota Wang, V. (2007). Counseling for wellness and justice: Foundations and ethical dilemmas. In E. Aldarondo (Ed.), *Advancing social justice through clinical practice* (pp. 19–42). Mahwah, NJ: Lawrence Erlbaum Associates.

Pyke, K. & Adams, M. (2010). What's age got to do with it? A case study analysis of power and gender in husband-older marriages. *Journal of Family Issues, 31*(6), 748–777.

Rabinowitz, N. S. (2002). Excavating female homoeroticism in ancient Greece: The evidence from attic vase painting. In N. S. Rabinowitz & L. Auanger. (Eds.), *Among women: From the homosocial to the homoerotic in the ancient world* (pp. 106–166). Austin: Texas University Press.

Raby, R. (2010). "Tank tops are ok but I don't want to see her thong": Girls' engagements with secondary school dress codes. *Youth & Society, 41*(3), 333–356.

Randall, W., Sobsey, D. & Parrila, R. (2001). Ethnicity, disability, and risk for abuse. *Developmental Disabilities Bulletin, 29*(1), 60–80.

Rands, K. E. (2009). Considering transgender people in education: A gender-complex approach. *Journal of Teacher Education, 60*, 419–431.

Rawsthorne, M. & Costello, M. (2010). Cleaning the sink: Exploring the experiences of Australian lesbian parents reconciling work/family responsibilities. *Community, Work & Family, 13*(2), 189–204.

Reay, D. (2008). Psychosocial aspects of white middle-class identities: Desiring and defending against the class and ethnic "other" in urban multi-ethnic schooling. *Sociology, 42*(6), 1072–1088.

Rector, F. (1981). *The Nazi extermination of homosexuals.* New York: Stein and Day.

Reed, M. K., McLeod, S., Randall, Y. & Walker, B. (1996). Depressive symptoms in African American women. *Journal of Multicultural Counseling and Development, 24*, 6–14.

Religion and homosexuality (2007). Wikimedia Foundation. Retrieved on April 18, 2009, from http://en.wikipe dia.org/wiki/ Homosexuality_and_religion.

Remafedi, G. (1999). Sexual orientation and youth suicide. *Journal of the American Medical Association, 282*(13), 1291–1292.

Renn, K. & Ozaki, C. (2010). Psychosocial and leadership identities among leaders of identity-based campus organizations. *Journal of Diversity in Higher Education, 3*(1), 14–26.

Renshon, S. A., (2005). The 50% American: Immigration and national identity in an age of terror. Washington, DC: Georgetown University Press.

Resnick, J. (2001). From hate to healing: Sexual assault recovery. *Journal of College Student Psychotherapy, 16*(1–2), 43–63.

Rey, A. M. & Gibson, P. R. (1997). Beyond high school: Heterosexuals' self-reported anti-gay/lesbian behaviors and attitudes. In Mary Bierman Harris et al. (Eds.), *School experiences of gay and lesbian youth: The invisible minority* (pp. 65–84). New York: Harrington Park Press/ The Haworth Press.

Richards, A. (2001). Breast development (in male-to-female transsexuals). Retrieved December 2010 from http://www.secondtype.info/breastdev.htm.

Richardson, V (05/04/2010). U.N. treaty to give American land back to Indians. *Human Events*. Retrieved on May 12, 2010, from http://www.humanevents.com/article.php?id=36809.

Ridley, C. R. (1989). Racism in counseling as an adversive behavior process. In P. B. Pedersen, J. G. Draguns, W. J. Lonner & J. E. Trimble (Eds.), *Counseling across cultures*, (2nd ed., pp. 55–78). Honolulu: University of Hawaii Press.

Riggle, E., Rostosky, S. & Horne, S. (2010). Psychological distress, well-being, and legal recognition in same-sex couple relationships. *Journal of Family Psychology, 24*(1), 82–86.

Rivas-Drake, D. & Mooney, M. (2009). Neither colorblind nor oppositional: Perceived minority status and trajectories of academic adjustment among Latinos in elite higher education. *Developmental Psychology, 45*(3), 642–651.

Rivers, R. Y. (1995). Clinical issues and intervention with ethnic minority women. In J. F. Aponte, R. Y. Rivers & J. Wohl (Eds.), *Psychological interventions and cultural diversity* (pp. 181–198). Boston: Allyn & Bacon.

Ro, M. & Yee, A. (2010). Out of the shadows: Asian Americans, Native Hawaiians, and Pacific Islanders. *American Journal of Public Health, 100*(5), 776–778.

Robertson, P. (2009). In sickness and in health: Recent judicial developments in Americans with Disabilities Act association discrimination cases. *Employee Responsibilities and Rights Journal, 21*(3), 171–193.

Roby, J. & Shaw, S. (2006). The African orphan crisis and international adoption. *Social Work, 51*(3), 199–210.

Rodkin, P. C, Farmer, T. W., Pearl, R. & Van Acker, R. (2000). Heterogeneity of popular boys: Antisocial and prosocial configurations. *Developmental Psychology, 36*(1), 14–24.

Rodriguez, N., Myers, H. F., Mira, C. B., Flores, T. & Garcia-Hernandez, L. (2002). Development of the multidimensional acculturative stress inventory for adults of Mexican origin. *Psychological Assessment, 14*, 451–461.

Rogers, R. G., Hummer, R. A., Nam, C. B. & Peters, K. (1996). Demographic, socioeconomic, and behavioral factors affecting ethnic mortality by cause. *Social Forces, 74*(4), 1419–1438.

Rolph, A., (2008). Minority students' dropout rates at crisis levels. *Seattlepi.com.* Retrieved on May 9, 2010, from http://www.seattlepi.com/local/365309_dropout12.html.

Roscoe, W. (1987). Bibliography of berdache and alternative gender roles among American Indians. *Journal of Homosexuality, 14*, 81–171.

Roscoe, W. (1994). Priests of the goddess: Gender transgression in the ancient world. Presented at the 109th Annual Meeting of the American Historical Association, San Francisco, CA.

Rose, A. J. & Asher, S. R. (2000). Children's friendships. In C. Hendrick, S. S. Hendrick et al. (Eds.), *Close relationships: A sourcebook* (pp. 47–57). Thousand Oaks, CA: Sage Publications.

Ross, M. W. (1990). The relationship between life events and mental health in homosexual men. *Journal of Clinical Psychology, 46*(4), 402–411.

Rowe, W. (2006). White racial identity: Science, faith, and pseudoscience. *Journal of Multicultural Counseling and Development, 34*, 235–243.

Rowe, W., Bennett, S. K. & Atkinson, D. R. (1994). White racial identity models: A critique and alternative proposal. *The Counseling Psychologist, 22*, 129–146.

Rowley, S. J., Burchinal, M. R., Roberts, J. E. & Zeisel, S. A. (2008). Racial identity, social context, and race-related social cognition in African Americans during middle childhood. *Developmental Psychology, 44*(6), 1537–1546.

Roy, B. (2007). Racial psychiatry: An approach to personal and political change. In E. Aldarondo (Ed.), *Advancing social justice through clinical practice* (pp. 43–61). Mahwah, NJ: Lawrence Erlbaum Associates.

Roysircar, G. (2008). A response to "social privilege, social justice, and group counseling: An inquiry": Social privilege: Counselors' competence with systemically determined inequalities. *The Journal for Specialists in Group Work, 33*, 377–384.

Rubin, K. H., Cheah, C. & Menzer, M. M. (2010). Peers. In M. H. Bornstein (Ed.), *Handbook of cultural developmental science* (pp. 223–237). New York: Psychology Press.

Ruiz, A. S. (1990). Ethnic identity: Crisis and resolution. *Journal of Multicultural Counseling and Development, 18*, 29–40.

Rushton, A. & Minnis, H. (1997). Annotation: Transracial family placements. *Journal of Child Psychology and Psychiatry, 38*, 147–159.

Ryan, C., Huebner, D., Diaz, R. M. & Sanchez, J. (2009). Family rejection as a predictor of negative health outcomes in white and Latino lesbian, gay, and bisexual young adults. *Pediatrics, 123,* 346–352.

Ryan, D. & Martin, A. (2000). Lesbian, gay, bisexual, and transgender parents in the school systems. *School Psychology Review, 29*(2), 207–216.

Ryder, A. G., Alden, L. E. & Paulhus, D. L. (2000). Is acculturation unidimensional or bidimensional? A head-to-head comparison in the prediction of personality, self-identity, and adjustment. *Journal of Personality and Social Psychology, 79,* 49–65.

Sable, M., Campbell, J., Schwarz, L., Brandt, J. & Dannerbeck, A. (2006). Male Hispanic immigrants talk about family planning. *Journal of Health Care for the Poor and Underserved, 17*(2), 386–399.

Sadker, M. & Sadker, D. (1994). Failing at fairness: How America's schools cheat girls (2nd ed.). New York: Scribner.

Saenger, G. (1963). Male and female relation in the American comic strips. In M. White & R. H. Abel (Eds.), *The funnies: An American idiom,* pp. 219–223. Glencoe, IL: The Free Press.

Saez, P., Casado, A. & Wade, J. (2009). Factors influencing masculinity ideology among Latino men. *The Journal of Men's Studies, 17*(2), 116–128.

Saltus, R. A. (January 13, 1997). Breast cancer: The risk factors. *The Boston Globe.* Retrieved on September 9, 2000, from http://www.boston.com.

Samuels, G. (2010). Building kinship and community: Relational processes of bicultural identity among adult multiracial adoptees. *Family Process, 49*(1), 26–42.

Sánchez, F. & Vilain, E. (2009). Collective self-esteem as a coping resource for male-to-female transsexuals. *Journal of Counseling Psychology, 56*(1), 202–209.

Sánchez, P. & Machado-Casas, M. (2009). At the intersection of transnationalism, Latina/o immigrants, and education. *The High School Journal, 92*(4), 3–15.

Sánchez-Martín, J., Fano, E., Ahedo, L., Cardas, J., Brain, P. & Azpíroz, A. (2000). Relating testosterone levels and free play social behavior in male and female preschool children. *Psychoneuroendocrinology, 25*(8), 773–783.

Sandels, A. (June 19, 2010). Business flourishes at sex shops abiding by Islamic standards. *Los Angeles Times.* Retrieved on June 22, 2010, from http://latimesblogs.latimes.com/babylonbeyond/2010/06/arab-world-muslim-sex-shops.html.

Sanders-Phillips, K. (1996). The ecology of urban violence: Its relationship to health promotion behaviors in low-income black and Latino communities. *American Journal of Health Promotion, 10*(4), 308–317.

Sarker. A. (2004). *Understand my Muslim people.* Newburg: Barclay Press.

Sasaki, T., Hazen, N. & Swann, W. (2010). The supermom trap: Do involved dads erode moms' self-competence? *Personal Relationships, 17*(1), 71–79.

Sax, L. (2002). How common is intersex? A response to Anne Fausto-Sterling. *Journal of Sex Research, 39,* 174–179.

Sayegh, M., Castrucci, B., Lewis, K. & Hobbs-Lopez, A. (2010). Teen pregnancy in Texas: 2005 to 2015. *Maternal and Child Health Journal, 14*(1), 94–101.

Schafer, C. & Shaw, G. (2009). The polls—trends: Tolerance in the United States. *Public Opinion Quarterly, 73*(2), 404–431.

Schell, N. & Weisfeld, C. (1999). Marital power dynamics: A Darwinian perspective. *The Darwinian heritage and sociobiology* (pp. 253–259). Westport, CT: Praeger Publishers/Greenwood Publishing Group.

Schlosser, L. (2006). Affirmative psychotherapy for American Jews. *Psychotherapy: Theory, Research, Practice, Training, 43*(4), 424–435.

Schmader, T., Johns, M. & Barquissau, M. (2004). The costs of accepting gender differences: The role of stereotype endorsement in women's experience in the math domain. *Sex Roles, 50,* 835–850.

Schmader, T., Major, B., Eccleston, C. P. & McCoy, S. K. (2001). Devaluing domains in response to threatening intergroup comparisons: Perceived legitimacy and the status value asymmetry. *Journal of Personality and Social Psychology, 80,* 782–796.

Schmitt, E. (April 4, 2001). Analysis of census finds segregation along with diversity. *New York Times.* Retrieved on June 2, 2001, from http://www.nytimes.com/2001/04/04/national/04CENS.html.

Schnauzer, M. (2006). Qigong: The art of self-healing. *Perspectives in Psychiatric Care, 42*(1), 53–54.

Schneider, H., Pickel, J. & Stalla, G. (2006). Typical female 2nd-4th finger length (2D:4D) ratios in male-to-female transsexuals—possible implications for prenatal androgen exposure. *Psychoneuroendocrinology, 31*(2), 265–269.

Schon, I. (1978). *A bicultural heritage: Themes for the exploration of Mexican and Mexican-American culture in books for children and adolescents.* Metuchen, NJ: The Scarecrow Press.

Schott, R. L. (1995). The childhood and family dynamics of transvestites. *Archives of Sexual Behavior, 24,* 309–327.

Schwartz, G., Kim, R., Kolundzija, A., Rieger, G. & Sanders, A.

(2010). Biodemographic and physical correlates of sexual orientation in men. *Archives of Sexual Behavior, 39*(1), 93–109.

Schweizer, T., Schnegg, M. & Berzborn, S. (1998). Personal networks and social support in a multiethnic community of southern California. *Social Networks, 20*(1), 1–21.

Sciarra, D. T. (1999). Multiculturalism in Counseling. Itasca, IL: F. E. Peacock Publishers.

Sciolino, E. & Mekhennet, S. (2008). In Europe, debate over Islam and virginity. New York Times. Retrieved on June 20, 2010, from http://www .nytimes.com/2008/06/11/ world/europe/11virgin.html.

Scrivner, R. & Eldridge, N (1995). Lesbian and gay family psychology. In R. Mikesell, D. D. Lusterman & S. McDaniel (Eds.), *Integrating family therapy: Handbook of family psychology and systems theory* (pp. 327–346). Washington, DC: American Psychological Association.

Semmler, P. & Williams, C. (2000). Narrative therapy: A storied context for multicultural counseling. *Journal of Multicultural Counseling and Development, 28*(1), 51–62.

Seo, S. (2006). A study of Korean working mothers with infants: Implications for research and social policy. *Early Child Development and Care, 176*(5), 479–492.

Seppa, N. (May 1996). A multicultural guide to less spanking and yelling. *APA Monitor*, 37.

Serbin, L. (1997). Research on international adoption: Implications for developmental theory and social policy. *International Journal of Behavioral Development, 20*(1), 83–92.

Sharf, R. S. (2000). *Theories of psychotherapy and counseling: Concepts and cases* (2nd ed.). Pacific Grove, CA: Brooks-Cole Wadsworth.

Sharma, R. (2010). *Folk tales from Latin America*. New York: Amazon Digital Services.

Sherwin, B. (2008). Hormones, the brain, and me. *Canadian Psychology/Psychologie canadienne, 49*(1), 42–48.

Shiang, J. (1998). Does culture make a difference? Racial/ethnic patterns of completed suicide in San Francisco, CA, 1987–1996 and clinical applications. *Suicide & Life-Threatening Behavior, 28*(4), 338–354.

Shime, P. (1992). *Homophobia in the law: The experiences of lesbians and gay men in the legal profession.* Unpublished manuscript, p. 18.

Shin, S., Chow, C., Camacho-Gonsalves, T., Levy, R., Allen, I. & Leff, H. (2005). A meta-analytic review of racial-ethnic matching for African American and Caucasian American clients and clinicians. *Journal of Counseling Psychology, 52*(1), 45–56.

Shorris, E. (1992). *Latinos: A biography of the people*. New York: Norton.

Siegel, R. J. (1985). Beyond homophobia: Learning to work with lesbian clients. In L. B. Rosewater and L. E. A. Walker (Eds.), *Handbook of feminist therapy: Women's issues in psychotherapy* (pp. 183–190). New York: Springer Publishing Company.

Silverman, J. A. (1990). Anorexia mervosa in males. In A. Anderson & A. E. Brunner (Eds.), *Males with eating disorders* (pp. 3–8). Mazel: New York.

Simmons, R., Levy, S., Riley, E., Madra, N. & Mattson, S. (2009). Central and peripheral timing variability in children with heavy prenatal alcohol exposure. *Alcoholism: Clinical and Experimental Research, 33*(3), 400–407.

Simms, W. F. (1999). The Native American Indian client: A tale of two cultures. In Y. M. Jenkins (Ed.), *Diversity in college settings: New directions for college mental health* (pp. 21–35). New York: Routledge.

Simon, R. & Schaler, J. (2007). Anti-Semitism the world over in the twenty-first century. *Current Psychology, 26*(3–4), 152–182.

Sinacore, A., Mikhail, A., Kassan, A. & Lerner, A. (2009). Cultural transitioning of Jewish immigrants: Education, employment and integration. *International Journal for Educational and Vocational Guidance, 9*(3), 157–176.

Singer, M., Fisher, C. B., Hodge, G. D., Saleheen, H. N. & Mahadevan, M. (2009). Ethical issues in conducting research with Latino drug users. In F. A. Villarruel, G. Carlo, J. M. Grau, M. Azmitia, N. J. Cabrera & T. J. Chahin (Eds.), *Handbook of U.S. Latino psychology: Developmental and community-based perspectives* (pp. 63–80). Los Angeles, CA: Sage Publications.

Singh, A., Hays, D., Chung, Y. & Watson, L. (2010). South Asian immigrant women who have survived child sexual abuse: Resilience and healing. *Violence Against Women, 16*(4), 444–458.

Singh, A., Urbano, A., Haston, M. & McMahon, E. (2010). School counselors' strategies for social justice change: A grounded theory of what works in the real world. *Professional School Counseling, 13*(3), 135–145.

Singh, A. A. (2009). Counseling with Asian Americans. In C. M. Ellis & J. Carlson (Eds.), Cross cultural awareness and social justice in counseling (pp. 147–168). New York: Routledge.

Singh-Manoux, A. (2000). Culture and gender issues in adolescence: Evidence from studies on emotion. *Psicothema, 12* (Suppl.), 93–100.

Slabbekoorn, D., Van Goozen, S., Gooren, L. & Cohen-Kettenis, P. (2001). Effects of cross-sex hormone treatment on emotionality in transsexuals. *International Journal of Transgenderism, 5*(3). Retrieved from http://www.iiav.nl/ezines/web/IJT/97-03/numbers/symposion/ijtvo05no03_02.htm

Slater, S. (1995). *The lesbian family life cycle.* New York: Free Press.

Sleek, S. (October 1996). Research identifies causes of internal homophobia: Gay men, lesbians and bisexuals not only face bigotry from society, but sometimes from their own psyches. *APA Monitor, 57.*

Sloan, F., Ayyagari, P., Salm, M. & Grossman, D. (2010). The longevity gap between black and white men in the United States at the beginning and end of the 20th century. *American Journal of Public Health, 100*(2), 357–363.

Slovic, P. (1999). Trust, emotion, sex, politics, and science: Surveying the risk-assessment battlefield. *Risk Analysis, 19*(4), 689–701.

Slusher, M. P., Mayer, C. J. & Dunkle, R. E. (1996). Gays and lesbians older and wiser (GLOW): A support group for older gay people. *Gerontologist, 36*, 118–123.

Smith, A. J. & Siegel, R. F. (1985). Feminist therapy: Redefining power for the powerless. In L. B. Rosewater and L. E. A. Walker (Eds.), *Handbook of feminist therapy: Women's issues in psychotherapy* (pp. 13–22). New York: Springer Publishing Company.

Smith, J., Berthelsen, D. & O'Connor, I. (1997). Child adjustment in high conflict families. *Child: Care, Health & Development, 23*(2), 113–133.

Smith, J., Tran, G. & Thompson, R. (2008). Can the theory of planned behavior help explain men's psychological help-seeking? Evidence for a mediation effect and clinical implications. *Psychology of Men & Masculinity, 9*(3), 179–192.

Smith, L. & Shin, R. (2008). Social privilege, social justice, and group counseling: An inquiry. *Journal for Specialists in Group Work, 33*(4), 351–366.

Smith, L. (2008). Positioning classism within counseling psychology's social justice agenda. *The Counseling Psychologist, 36*(6), 895–924.

Smith, R. L., Bakir, N. & Montilla, R. E. (2006). Counseling and therapy with Latino families. In R. L. Smith & R. E. Montilla (Eds.), *Counseling and family therapy with Latino populations: Strategies that work* (pp. 3–26) New York: Routledge.

Snider, K. (1998). Race and sexual orientation: The (im)possibility of these intersections in educational policy: Reply. *Harvard Educational Review, 68*(1), 103–105.

Society for the Psychological Study of Ethical Minority Issues (2002). Guidelines for multicultural counseling proficiency for psychologists: Implications for education and training, research and clinical practice. American Psychological Association. Retrieved from http://www.apa.org/pi/oema/resources/policy/multicultural-guidelines.aspx

Sommers, I., Fagan, J. & Baskin, D. (1993). Sociocultural influences on the explanation of delinquency for Puerto Rican youths. *Hispanic Journal of Behavioral Sciences, 15*(1), 36–62.

South, S. & Crowder, K. (1997). Escaping distressed neighborhoods: Individual, community, and metropolitan influences. *American Journal of Sociology, 102*(4), 1040–1084.

Southern, S. (2006). Sexual counseling with Latino couples. In R. L. Smith & R. E. Montilla (Eds.), *Counseling and family therapy with Latino populations: Strategies that work* (pp. 177–196). New York: Routledge.

Sow, A. I. (1980). *Anthropological structures of madness in black Africa.* New York: International Universities Press.

Stacey, J., & Biblarz, T. J. (2007). (How) does the sexual orientation of parents matter?. In S. J. Ferguson, S. J. Ferguson (Eds.), *Shifting the center: Understanding contemporary families (3rd ed.)* (pp. 299–323). New York, NY US: McGraw-Hill.

Stacks, A. M., Oshio, T., Gerard, J. & Roe, J. (2009). The moderating effect of parental warmth on the association between spanking and child aggression: A longitudinal approach. *Infant and Child Development, 18*(2), 178–194.

Stanford, J. L. & Ziding F., Hamilton, A.S., et al. (2000). Urinary and sexual function after radical prostatectomy for clinically localized prostate cancer. *Journal of the American Medical Association, 283*, 354–360.

Stansbury, K. L., Harley, D. A. & Stansbury, K. L. (2009). Rural African American clergy: Are they literate on late-life depression? *Aging & Mental Health, 13*(1), 9–16.

Stayton, W. (1996). Sexual and gender identity disorders in a relational perspective. In F. W. Kaslow (Ed.), *Handbook of relational diagnosis and dysfunctional family patterns* (pp. 357–370). New York: John Wiley & Sons.

Steele, C. M. & Aronson, J. (2000). Stereotype threat and the intellectual test performance of African Americans. In C. Stangor (Ed.), *Stereotypes and prejudice: Essential readings. Key readings in social psychology* (pp. 369–389).

Philadelphia, PA: Psychology Press/Taylor & Francis.

Steenwyk, S., Atkins, D., Bedics, J. & Whitley, B. (2010). Images of God as they relate to life satisfaction and hopelessness. *International Journal for the Psychology of Religion*, 20(2), 85–96.

Stefan, S. (2002). Hollow promises: Employment discrimination against people with mental disabilities. American Psychological Association Press.

Steinem, G. (October, 1978). If men could menstruate. *Ms.*, 8, 100.

Sterrett, E. M, Jones, D. J. & Kincaid, C. (2009). Psychosocial adjustment of low-income African American youth from single mother homes: The role of the youth-coparent relationship. *Journal of Clinical Child and Adolescent Psychology*, 38(3), 427–438.

Steward, M. S. (2002). Illness: A crisis for children. In J. Sandoval (Ed.), *Handbook of crisis counseling, intervention, and prevention in the schools* (2nd ed., pp. 183–211). Mahwah, NJ: Lawrence Erlbaum Associates.

Stoller, R. (1968). *Sex and gender (Vol. I): The development of masculinity and femininity.* New York: Jason Aronson.

Stoller, R. (1985). *Presentations of gender.* New Haven: Yale University Press.

Stoller, R. (1997). *Splitting: A case of female masculinity.* New Haven: Yale University Press.

Straus, M. A. & Gelles, R. J. (1988). How violent are American families? Estimates from the National Family Violence Resurvey and other studies. In G. T. Horaling, D. Finkelhor, J. T. Kirkpatrick & M. A. Straus (Eds.), *Family abuse and its consequences: New directions in research* (pp. 14–36). Beverly Hills, CA; Sage.

Stroink, M. & Lalonde, R. (2009). Bicultural identity conflict in second-generation Asian Canadians. *The Journal of Social Psychology*, 149(1), 44–65.

Strong, S. R. (1969). Counseling: An interpersonal influence process. *Journal of Counseling Psychology*, 15, 31–35.

Su, R., Rounds, J. & Armstrong, P. (2009). Men and things, women and people: A meta-analysis of sex differences in interests. *Psychological Bulletin*, 135(6), 859–884.

Subrahmanyan, L. (1999). A generation in transition: Gender ideology of graduate students from India at an American university. In S. R. Gupta, (Ed), *Emerging voices: South Asian American women redefine self, family, and community* (pp. 58–78). Walnut Creek, CA: Altamira Press.

Suchet, M. (2010). Face to face. *Psychoanalytic Dialogues*, 20(2), 158–171.

Sue, D. & Sundberg, N. D. (1996). Research and research hypotheses about effectiveness in intercultural counseling. In P. B. Pedersen, J. G. Draguns, W. J. Lonner & J. E. Trimble (Eds.), *Counseling across cultures* (4th ed., pp. 323–352). Thousand Oaks, CA: Sage Publications.

Sue, D. W. & Sue, D. (1999). *Counseling the culturally different: Theory and practice* (3rd ed.). New York: John Wiley & Sons.

Sue, D. W. & Sue, D. (2008). *Counseling the culturally different: Theory and practice* (5th ed.). New York: John Wiley & Sons.

Sue, D. W. (2009). Racial microaggressions and worldviews. *American Psychologist*, 64(3), 220–221.

Sue, D. W., Capodilupo, C. M., Holder, A. (2008). Racial microaggressions in the life experience of black Americans. *Professional Psychology: Research and Practice*, 39(3), 329–336.

Sue, S., Chun, C-A. & Gee, K. (1995). Ethnic minority intervention and treatment research. In J. F. Aponte, R. Y. Rivers & J. Wohl (Eds.), *Psychological interventions and cultural diversity* (pp. 266–282). Boston: Allyn & Bacon.

Suinn, R. M. (1999). Scaling the summit: Valuing ethnicity. *APA Monitor*, 30, 2.

Sun, Y. (1998). The academic success of East-Asian-American students: An investment model. *Social Science Research*, 27(4), 432–456.

Sweezy, C. (1967). *The Arapaho way: A memoir of an Indian boyhood* (edited by A. Bass). New York: C. N. Potter.

Tafur, M., Crowe, T. & Torres, E. (2009). A review of curanderismo and healing practices among Mexicans and Mexican Americans. *Occupational Therapy International*, 16(1), 82–88.

Tager, D., Good, G. & Morrison, J. (2006). Our bodies, ourselves revisited: Male body image and psychological well-being. *International Journal of Men's Health*, 5(3), 228–237.

Tamaki, J. (August 17, 2000). Indians find that money buys a. *Los Angeles Times*. Special Section, 1.

Tang, C. (2008). Gendered economic, social, and cultural challenges to HIV/AIDS prevention and intervention for Chinese women. *Journal of Human Behavior in the Social Environment*, 17(3–4), 339–360.

Telljohann, S. K. & Price, J. H. (1993). A qualitative examination of adolescent homosexuals' life experiences: Ramifications for secondary school personnel. *Journal of Homosexuality*, 26(1), 41–56.

Thandeka. (1999). White racial induction and Christian shame theology: A primer. *Gender & Psychoanalysis*, 4(4), 455–495.

Thier, J. (1999). *Vision quest: A journey of empowerment.* Missoula, MT: Montana Free Press.

Thomas, A. & Sillen, S. (1972). *Racism and psychiatry.* Secaucus, NJ: Citadel Press.

Thomas, D. C., Elron, E., Stahl, G., Ekelund, B. Z., et al. (2008). Cultural intelligence: Domain and assessment. *International Journal of Cross Cultural Management, 8*(123), 124–143.

Thomas, H. (1999). *The slave trade: The story of the Atlantic slave trade: 1440–1870.* New York: Simon & Schuster.

Thomas, S. & Larrabee, T. (2002). Gay, lesbian, bisexual, and questioning youth. *Handbook of crisis counseling*, intervention, and prevention in the schools (2nd ed., pp. 301–322). Mahwah, NJ: Lawrence Erlbaum Associates.

Thompson, R. F. (1983). *Flash of the spirit: African & Afro-American art & philosophy.* New York: Random House.

Thurman, P. J., Swaim, R. & Plested, B. (1995). Intervention and treatment of ethnic minority substance abusers. In J. F. Aponte, R. Y. Rivers & J. Wohl (Eds.), *Psychological interventions and cultural diversity* (pp. 215–233). Boston: Allyn & Bacon.

Ting-Toomey, S., Yee-Jung, K. K., Shapiro, R. B., Garcia, W., Wright, T. J. & Oetzel, J. G. (2000). Ethnic/cultural identity salience and conflict styles in four US ethnic groups. *International Journal of Intercultural Relations, 24*(1), 47–81.

Tollerud, T. R. & Slabon, L. S. (2009). Counseling with gay, lesbian, bisexual, and transgender people. In C. M. Ellis & J. Carlson (Eds.), *Cross cultural awareness and social justice in counseling* (pp. 211–242). New York: Routledge.

Tomita, S. K. (1999). Exploration of elder mistreatment among the Japanese. In Toshio Tatara (Ed.), *Understanding elder abuse in minority populations* (pp. 119–139). Philadelphia: Brunner/Mazel.

Tomori, M., Zalar, B. & Plesnicar, B. K. (2000). Gender differences in psychosocial risk factors among Slovenian adolescents. *Adolescence, 35,* 431–443.

Tong, R. (2009). *Feminist thought: A more comprehensive introduction.* Philadelphia: Westview Press.

Transgender need not apply: A report on gender identity job discrimination (2010). New York: Make the Road. Retrieved from http://www.maketheroad.org/pix_reports/TransNeedNotApplyReport_05.10.pdf.

Trevatt, D. (2001). Working in a school for severely physically disabled children. In G. Baruch (Ed.), *Community-based psychotherapy with young people: Evidence and innovation in practice,* pp. 89–102. Philadelphia: Brunner-Routledge.

Trimble, J. & Lafromboise, T. (1987). American Indians and the counseling process: Culture, adaptation, and style. In P. Pederson (Ed.), Handbook of cross-cultural counseling and therapy. Wesport, CN: Greenwood Press.

Trimble, J. (2010). The virtues of cultural resonance, competence, and relational collaboration with Native American Indian communities: A synthesis of the counseling and psychotherapy literature. *The Counseling Psychologist, 38*(2), 243–256.

Truijers, A. & Vingerhoets, A. J. J. M. (1999). Shame, embarrassment, personality and well-being. Poster presented at the 2nd International Conference on the (Non) Expressions of Emotions in Health and Disease, Tilburg, The Netherlands.

Tucker, T. & Makgoba, M. (2008). Public-private partnerships and scientific imperialism. *Science, 320*(5879), 1016–1017.

U.S. Bureau of the Census. (1991). *Statistical abstract.* Washington, DC: U.S. Government Printing Office.

U.S. Cancer Statistics Working Group (2009). *United States cancer statistics: 1999–2005. Incidence and mortality web-based report.* Atlanta: Department of Health and Human Services, Centers for Disease Control and Prevention, and National Cancer. Retrieved on May 31, 2010, from http://www.cdc.gov/uscs.

U.S. Department of Health and Human Services, Indian Health Service (1997). *Trends in Indian health.* United States Government: Office of Planning, Evaluation, and Legislation, Division of Program Statistics.

U.S. Department of State (2009). Total adoptions to the United States. Retrieved from http://www.adoption.state.gov/news/total_chart.html.

U.S. Environmental Protection Agency. (1999). *Understanding Native Americans.* United States Government: EPA.

Underwood, M. (2007). Gender and children's friendships: Do girls' and boys' friendships constitute different peer cultures, and what are the trade-offs for development? *Merrill-Palmer Quarterly: Journal of Developmental Psychology, 53*(3), 319–324.

Unger, R. K. (1990). Imperfect reflections of reality: Psychology and the construction of gender. In R. Hare-Mustin & J. Marecek (Eds.), *Making a difference: Representations of gender in psychology* (pp. 102–149). New Haven: Yale University Press.

Unicef (2009). *2009 State of women and children report.* New York: United Nations Children's Fund

US: Ratify women's rights treaty: 30 years on, Obama administration, senate leaders should press for action. (July 15, 2010). Human Rights Watch. Retrieved on July 15, 2010, from http://www.hrw.org/en/news/2010/07/15/us-ratify-women-s-rights-treaty.

Ussher, J. (2010). Are we medicalizing women's misery? A critical review of women's higher rates of reported depression. *Feminism & Psychology*, 20(1), 9–35.

Vaillant, G., DiRago, A. & Mukamal, K. (2006). Natural history of male psychological health, XV: Retirement satisfaction. *The American Journal of Psychiatry*, 163(4), 682–688.

Valentine, D. (2007). *Whose imagination? Complicating attempts in locating the transgender community imagining transgender: An ethnography of a category.* Durham, NC: Duke University Press.

van Dyk, A. (2001). Traditional African beliefs and customs: Implications for AIDS education and prevention in Africa. *South African Journal of Psychology*, 31(2), 60–66.

Van Hout, M. (2009). An illustrative picture of Irish youth substance use: Letter to the editor. *Journal of Alcohol and Drug Education*, 53(1), 7–15.

Van Leeuwen, J. M., Boyle, S., Salomonsen-Sautel, S., Baker, D. N., Garcia, J. T., Hoffman, A., et al. (2006). Lesbian, gay, and bisexual homeless youth: An eight-city public health perspective. *Child Welfare Journal*, 85(2), 151–170.

Van Ryzin, M., Gravely, A. & Roseth, C. (2009). Autonomy, belongingness, and engagement in school as contributors to adolescent psychological well-being. *Journal of Youth and Adolescence*, 38(1), 1–12.

Van Tilburg, M., Unterberg, M. & Vingerhoets, A. (2002). Crying during adolescence: The role of gender, menarche, and empathy. *British Journal of Developmental Psychology*, 20(1), 77–87.

Van, H., Schoevers, R. & Dekker, J. (2008). Predicting the outcome of antidepressants and psychotherapy for depression: A qualitative, systematic review. *Harvard Review of Psychiatry*, 16(4), 225–234.

Veale, J., Clarke, D. & Lomax, T. (2009). Reply to Lawrence and Bailey (2008). *Archives of Sexual Behavior*, 38(2), 176–177.

Vega, W. A., Gil, A. G., Warheit, G. J., Zimmerman, R. S. & Apospori, E. (1993). Acculturation and delinquent behavior among Cuban American adolescents: Toward an empirical model. *American Journal of Community Psychology*, 21(1), 113–125.

Vega, W. A., Kolody, B., Aguilar-Gaxiola, S., Alderte, E., Catalano, R. & Caraveo-Anduaga, H. (1998). Lifetime prevalence of DSM-III-R psychiatric disorders among urban and rural Mexican Americans in California. *Archives of General Psychiatry*, 55, 771–778.

Verdi, B. (May 6, 1997). In Tiger Woods' case, perhaps we should remember the human race. *Chicago Tribune*. Retrieved on June 11, 2001, from http://www.texnews.com/tiger/verdi050697.html.

Vespa, J. (2009). Gender ideology construction: A life course and intersectional approach. *Gender & Society*, 23(3), 363–387.

Villanueva, M., Tonigan, J. & Miller, W. (2007). Response of Native American clients to three treatment methods for alcohol dependence. *Journal of Ethnicity in Substance Abuse*, 6(2), 41–48.

Vonk, M. (2001). Cultural competence for transracial adoptive parents. *Social Work*, 46(3), 246–255.

Vontress, C. (1991). Traditional healing in Africa: Implications for cross-cultural counseling. *Journal of Counseling & Development*, 70(1), 242–249.

Wagner, P., Viegi, G., Luna, C., Fukuchi, Y., Kvale, P. & El Sony, A. (2006). "Major causes of death among men and women in China": Comment. *The New England Journal of Medicine*, 354(8), 874.

Waite, L., Luo, Y. & Lewin, A. (2009). Marital happiness and marital stability: Consequences for psychological well-being. *Social Science Research*, 38(1), 201–212.

Wakefield, J. (2006). *Sexual reorientation therapy: Is it ever ethical? Can it ever change sexual orientation?* Binghamton, NY: Harrington Park Press/The Haworth Press.

Walker, E. J. (2010). Counseling grace: A pastoral theology. In J. Stevenson-Moessner & T. Snorton (Eds.), *Women out of order* (pp. 243–254). Minneapolis: Fortress Press.

Walker, L. E. (1979). *The battered woman*. New York: Harper and Row,

Walker, L. E. (1985). Psychological impact of the criminalization of domestic violence on victims. *Victimology: An International Journal*, 10, 281–300.

Walton, G. M. & Cohen, G. L. (2007). A question of belonging: Race, social fit, and achievement. *Journal of Personality and Social Psychology*, 92, 82–96

Wamwara-Mbugua, L., Cornwell, T. & Boller, G. (2008). Triple acculturation: The role of African Americans in the consumer acculturation of Kenyan immigrants. *Journal of Business Research*, 61(2), 83–90.

Ward, N. & Al Bayyari, Y. (2010). American and Arab perceptions of an Arabic turn-taking cue. *Journal of Cross-Cultural Psychology*, 41(2), 270–275.

Warren, C. A. B. (1998). Aging and identity in premodern times. *Research on Aging*, 20(1), 11–35.

Warren, J., Fernández, M., Harper, G., Hidalgo, M., Jamil, O. & Torres, R. (2008). Predictors of unprotected sex among young sexually active African American, Hispanic, and white MSM: The importance of ethnicity and culture. *AIDS and Behavior*, 12(3), 459–468.

Warriner, D. S. (2008). Language learning and the politics of belonging: Sudanese women refugees becoming and being "American." *Anthropology & Education Quarterly*, 38(4), 342–359.

Waters, M. (1998). Optional ethnicities: For whites only? In M. L. Anderson & P. H. Collins (Eds.), *Race*, class, and gender: An anthology (3rd ed., pp. 403–412). Belmont, CA: Wadsworth Publishing Company.

Waylen, A. & Stewart-Brown, S. (2010). Factors influencing parenting in early childhood: A prospective longitudinal study focusing on change. *Child Care, Health & Development*, 36(2), 198–207.

Weber, C. L. (1987). *Womanchrist: A new vision of feminist spirituality*. San Francisco: Harper & Row, Publishers.

Wei, M., Liao, K., Chao, R., Mallinckrodt, B., Tsai, P. & Botello-Zamarron, R. (2010). Minority stress, perceived bicultural competence, and depressive symptoms among ethnic minority college students. *Journal of Counseling Psychology*, 57(4), 411–422.

Weiner, B. (1995). *Judgments of responsibility: A foundation for a theory of social conduct*. New York: Guilford Press.

Wester, S. R., McDonough, T. A., White, M., Vogel, D. L., and Taylor, L. (2010). Using gender role conflict theory in counseling male-to-female transgender individuals. *Journal of Counseling & Development*, 88, 214–219.

Wexler, D. B. (2009). *Men in therapy: New approaches for effective treatment*. New York: W. W. Norton & Co.

Whaley, A. (2000). Sociocultural differences in the developmental consequences of the use of physical discipline during childhood for African Americans. *Cultural Diversity & Ethnic Minority Psychology*, 6, 5–12.

Wheary, J. (2006). *The future middle class: African Americans, Latinos, and economic opportunity*. New York: Demos: A Network for Ideas and Action.

Whitaker, C. (March 1991). Do black males need special schools? Educational experiments with boys-only classes arouse hope and controversy. *Ebony*, 17–22.

Whitbeck, L., Adams, G., Hoyt, D. & Chen, X. (2004). Conceptualizing and measuring historical trauma among American Indian people. *American Journal of Community Psychology*, 33, 119–130.

White, T. & Ettner, R. (2007). Adaptation and adjustment in children of transsexual parents. *European Child & Adolescent Psychiatry*, 16(4), 215–221.

Whitehead, A. (2010). Sacred rites and civil rights: Religion's effect on attitudes toward same-sex unions and the perceived cause of homosexuality. *Social Science Quarterly*, 91(1), 63–79.

Wijn, R. & van den Bos, K. (2010). On the social-communicative function of justice: The influence of communication goals and personal involvement on the use of justice assertions. *Personality and Social Psychology Bulletin*, 36(2), 161–172.

Wilcox, H. C., Storr, C. L., Breslau, N. (2009). Posttraumatic stress disorder and suicide attempts in a community sample of urban American young adults. *Archives of General Psychiatry*, 66(3), 305–311.

Willging, C., Salvador, M. & Kano, M. (2006). Brief reports: Unequal treatment: mental health care for sexual and gender minority groups in a rural state. *Psychiatric Services (Washington, D.C.)*, 57(6), 867–870.

Williams, R. & Wittig, M.A. (1997). "I'm not a feminist but … ": Factors contributing to the discrepancy between pro-feminist orientation and feminist social identity. *Sex Roles*, 37, 885–904.

Willis, W. B. (1998). *The Adinkra dictionary: A visual primer on the language of Adinkra*. Utica, NY: Pyramid Publishing.

Wilson, C. R. & Ferris, W. (Eds.). (1989). The Encyclopedia of Southern Culture. Raleigh, NC: University of North Carolina Press.

Wilson, D. K. (2001). Violence may affect blood pressure in Black boys. Presented at the sixteenth scientific meeting and exposition of the American Society of Hypertension, San Francisco, California.

Wilson, G. & McBrier, D. (2005). Race and loss of privilege: African American/white differences in the determinants of job layoffs from upper-tier occupations. *Sociological Forum*, 20(2), 301–321.

Wilson, I., Griffin, C. & Wren, B. (2002). The validity of the diagnosis of gender identity disorder (child and adolescent criteria). *Clinical Child Psychology and Psychiatry*, 7(3), 335–351.

Wiseman, M. & Moradi, B. (2010). Body image and eating disorder symptoms in sexual minority men: A test and extension of objectification theory. *Journal of Counseling Psychology*, 57(2), 154–166.

Wolf, R. S. (1998). Domestic elder abuse and neglect. In I. H. Nordhus, G. R. VandenBos, S. Berg & P. Fromholt (Eds.), *Clinical geropsychology*, pp. 161–165. Washington, DC: American Psychological Association.

Women's Bureau (2010). Quick stats on women workers, 2009. United States Department of Labor. Retrieved on June 25, 2010, from http://www.dol.gov/wb/stats/main.htm.

Wong, P., Lai, C. F., Nagasawa, R. & Lin, T. (1998). Asian Americans as a model minority: Self-perceptions and perceptions by other racial groups. *Sociological Perspectives*, 41(1), 1998, 95–118.

Wood, P. B. & Clay, W. C. (1996). Perceived structural barriers and academic performance among American Indian high school students. *Youth and Society*, 28, 40–61.

Woods, K., Buchanan, N. & Settles, I. (2009). Sexual harassment across the color line: Experiences and outcomes of cross- versus intraracial sexual harassment among black women. *Cultural Diversity and Ethnic Minority Psychology*, 15(1), 67–76.

Worell, J. & Remer, P. (1992). *Feminist perspectives in therapy: An empowerment model for women.* New York: Wiley.

World Health Organization (2010). Human rights—a central concern for the global HIV response. Retrieved from http://www.who.int/mediacentre/news/statements/2010/AIDS_Day_20101130/en.

World Health Organization. (2009). HIV/AIDS epidemiological surveillance report for the WHO African region 2007 update. Retrieved from http://www.who.int/hiv/pub/surveillance/epi_afro2007/en/index.html.

Worrell, F. C. & Gardner-Kitt, D. L. (2006). The relationship between racial and ethnic identity in black adolescents: The cross racial identity scale and the multigroup ethnic identity measure. *Identity: An International Journal of Theory and Research*, 6(4), 293–315.

Worthington, R. L. & Reynolds, A. L. (2009). Within-group differences in sexual orientation and identity. *Journal of Counseling Psychology*, 56, 44–55.

Wren, B. (2002). "I can accept my child is transsexual but if I ever see him in a dress I'll hit him": Dilemmas in parenting a transgendered adolescent. *Clinical Child Psychology and Psychiatry*, 7(3), 377–397.

Wright, B. R. & Younts, C. (2009). Reconsidering the relationship between race and crime: Positive and negative predictors of crime among African American youth. *Journal of Research in Crime and Delinquency*, 46(3), 327–352.

Wright, J. (2009). Unfinished business with feminist thinking and counselling and guidance practice. *British Journal of Guidance & Counselling*, 37(1), 73–82.

Yagley, B. (2010) , S. (1995). State must act on 'Coerced abortion' bill. The Oakland Press. Retrieved from http://www.theoaklandpress.com/articles/2010/07/23/opinion/doc4c47bf0f405d7429037238.txt.

Yalom, I. (1995). *The theory and practice of group psychotherapy* (4th ed.). New York: Basic Books.

Yazzie-Mintz, T. (2007). From a place deep inside: Culturally appropriate curriculum as the embodiment of Navajo-ness in classroom pedagogy. *Journal of American Indian Education*, 46 (Special Issue), 72–93.

Yeh, M., Eastman, K., Cheung, M. K. (1994). Children and adolescents in community health centers: Does the ethnicity or the language of the therapist matter? *Journal of Community Psychology*, 22(2), 153–163.

Yeo, S., Meiser, B., Barlow-Stewart, K., Goldstein, D., Tucker, K. & Eisenbruch, M. (2005). Understanding community beliefs of Chinese-Australians about cancer: Initial insights using an ethnographic approach. *Psycho-Oncology*, 14(3), 174–186.

Yi, J. K. (1998). Vietnamese American college students' knowledge and attitudes toward HIV/AIDS. *Journal of American College Health*, 47(1), 37–42.

Yoder, J. D. & Schleicher, T. L. (1996). Undergraduates regard deviation from occupational gender stereotypes as costly for women. *Sex Roles*, 34(3-4), 171–188.

Yoshioka, M., DiNoia, J. & Ullah, K. (2001). Attitudes toward marital violence. *Violence Against Women*, 7(8), 900–926.

Youman, K., Drapalski, A., Stuewig, J., Bagley, K. & Tangney, J. (2010). Race differences in psychopathology and disparities in treatment seeking: Community and jail-based treatment-seeking patterns. *Psychological Services*, 7(1), 11–26.

Young, C. (2001). Where the boys are: Is America short-changing male children? *Reason*. Retrieved on January 22, 2000, from http://reason.com/archives/2001/02/01/where-the-boys-are.

Young, T. J. & French, L. A. (1996). Suicide and homicide rates among U.S. Indian health service areas: The income inequality hypothesis. *Social Behavior & Personality*, 24(4), 365–366.

Zane, N., Enomoto, K., Chun, C. A (1994). Treatment outcomes of Asian- and white-American clients in outpatient therapy. *Journal of Community Psychology*, 22(2), 177–191.

Zane, N., Norton, T., Chu, J., Lin, N. (2008). Counseling and psychotherapy with Asian American clients. In G. C. Gamst, A. Der-Karabetian & R. H. Dana (Eds.), *Readings in Multicultural Practice* (pp. 241–256). Los Angeles: Sage Publications.

Zedan, R. (2010). New dimensions in the classroom climate. *Learning Environments Research*, 13(1), 75–88.

Ziyadeh, N. J., Prokop, L. A., Fisher, L. B., Rosario, M., Field, A. E., Camargo, J., Carlos A. & Bryn Austin, S. (2007). Sexual orientation, gender, and alcohol use in a cohort study of US adolescent girls and boys. *Drug and Alcohol Dependence*, 16(87), 119–130.

Zohar, D. & Marshall, I. (2004). *Spiritual capital: Wealth we can live by*. San Francisco: Berrett-Koehler.

Zolfagharian, M. (2010). Identification, uniqueness and art consumption among bicultural consumers. *Journal of Consumer Marketing*, 27(1), 17–25.

NAME INDEX

A

Abedinia, N., 337
Aberle, D., 188
Abernathy, R., 100
Abudabbeh, N., 207
Adamczyk, A., 86
Adams, G., 176
Adams, H. E., 300
Adams, M., 328
Adelabu, D. H., 81
Ader, T., 336
Afoláyan, M., 70, 94, 98
Aguinaldo, J., 298, 306
Aibel, J., 165
Ailinger, R. L., 125
Al Bayyari, Y., 208
Alamilla, S., 117
Albers, A., 261, 263
Alcántara, C., 191
Alden, L. E., 225
Alegría, M., 126
Alexander, F. G., 25
Alhabib, S., 328
Ali, H., 218
Al-Krenawi, A., 208, 210, 211, 217, 218, 219
Allen, P. G., 173, 175, 186
Allred, L. J., 158
Altman, A., 208, 209
Alvarez, L., 118
Andersen, A. E., 374
Anderson, K. J., 317

Anderson, M. J., 182
Anthony, D., 296
Antoszewski, B., 244
Aponte, J. F., 186, 192
Apospori, E., 118
Arbour, L., 276
Armour, S., 206
Armstrong, P., 355, 370
Arndt, B., 358
Aronson, J., 21
Arredondo, P., 17, 36
Asakawa, K., 152
Asher, S. R., 359
Åstedt-Kurki, P., 362
Atienza, A., 330
Atkins, D., 371
Atkinson, D. R., 8
Atwood, N. C., 340
Augustine, Saint, 315
Ault, A., 266
Autier, P., 373
Axelson, J. A., 9, 52, 177
Ayyagari, P., 58

B

Baharudin, R., 54
Baier, C. J., 80
Bailey, J. M., 277
Bakir, N., 123, 127, 128
Ballard, S., 336
Banks-Wallace, J., 94

Barlow, P., 328
Barnhart, K. T., 319
Barquissau, M., 83
Barrett, J., 260
Barry, D., 355
Barton, R. G., 294
Baruth, L. G., 8, 11, 75, 393
Baskin, D., 118
Bates, J. E., 80
Bauermeister, J., 367
Baumberger, J. P., 389
Baynouna, L., 218
Beals, J., 190
Beaufoy, S. L., 387
Beauvoir, S. de, 343
Beaver, B., 153
Bechtold, D. W., 185
Becker, J. B., 264
Bedics, J., 371
Beech, H., 227
Beets, M., 317
Bell, R. M., 153
Bellmore, A., 72
Bem, S. L., 339
Bemak, F., 33, 35
Bengtson, V. L., 393
Benjamin, H., 243, 244
Benrud, L. M., 372
Berg, A., 89
Berg, I. K., 163
Berg, M., 298
Bergan-Gander, R., 291
Berger, G., 165

441

SUBJECT INDEX